THE
VISUAL BASIC 5
COURSEBOOK

Forest Lin

Tulsa Community College

Scott/Jones, Inc., Publishers
P. O. Box 696
El Granada, CA 94018

Voice: (415) 726-2436
Fax: (415) 726-4693
E-mail: scotjones2@aol.com
Web: http://www.scottjonespub.com

The Visual Basic 5 Coursebook

Forest Lin

ISBN 1-57676-004-9

Book Manufacturing: Data Reproduction
Cover Design: Vicki Lin and Art Central Illustration & Design

0 9 8   X Y Z

ADDITIONAL TITLES OF INTEREST FROM SCOTT/JONES

Visual Basic Programming
Visual Basic 5 Coursebook: Advanced (forthcoming)
The DOS 6 Coursebook
by Forest Lin

Visual Basic with Applications 2nd Ed
by Mark Simkin

Principles of Programming Using Visual Basic
by Gary Bronson

Short Course in Windows 95
The Windows 95 Textbook - Standard Edition
The Windows 95 Textbook - Extended Edition
The Windows NT Textbook
by Stewart Venit:

The Access Guidebook: Short Course
Access Guidebook: Full Course
by Maggie Trigg and Phyllis Dobson.

C Through Objects, by John Connely
Problem Solving with C, by Jacqueline Jones & Keith Harrow
C by Discovery, 2nd Edition, by L.S. Foster
Essential Excel for Windows 95, by Marvin Harris

Visual Basic 5 Coursebook
Table of Contents

I. Exploratory

II. Elementary

Appendix

Index   A97

 *Introduction*

This book provides a comprehensive coverage of Visual Basic 5 (VB5). It covers most of the features in the Learning (formerly Standard) Edition and some additional features available in the Professional Edition. As its predecessor (*The Visual Basic 4 Coursebook*), it attempts to be all things to all people. You can use it even if you have no experience in Basic or Windows. If you have some experience in these, you can quickly master the materials in the first few chapters and proceed to later chapters to do more sophisticated things. You should become quite proficient in Visual Basic by the time you complete the book.

The book is based on the Professional Edition and uses it for examples (some screen pictures may differ minutely from those in the Learning Edition) and covers some additional Professional features. Quite a few users of the previous edition of this book have suggested an expanded coverage of the most popular features available in the Professional Edition, particularly database and the additional custom controls. Since then VB5 Pro has included many more new features, most of which are related to the Internet. Including these features in this book will make it huge and unwieldy. So a decision was made to package them in a separate book, *The Visual Basic 5 Coursebook: Advanced*. It should be available in the near future.

VISUAL BASIC AS A RAD TOOL

Before we proceed to discuss more about this book, it may be useful for beginners to know where Visual Basic (VB) came from and where it is headed.

When Microsoft Windows 3.x began to dominate the PC world, there was a tremendous need for a rapid application development (RAD) tool so that programmers could quickly develop programs to run in the Windows environment. The traditional character-based languages like Basic or C was not suited for creating programs for Windows' graphical environment. As part of its effort to promote Windows, Microsoft released Visual Basic version 1 (VB1) as a Windows RAD tool.

VB1 and VB2, like Windows 1 and 2, gained some but not many adherents. It was VB3, like Windows 3.x, that became wildly popular. Programmers began to use VB to develop commercial applications. Businesses began to hire VB programmers to develop applications for internal use. Colleges began to offer classes to train VB programmers. This momentum continues to gain speed. While rival vendors offer some sophisticated RAD tools that attract some users, VB continues to hold the lion's share of this vast and expanding market.

Learning VB will not only increase your chances for employment, but also ensure that what you learn will not become obsolete in the foreseeable future. The language you learn here has been added to other popular applications marketed by Microsoft, such as Word, Excel, and Access. Visual Basic for Applications (VBA), the language component of Visual Basic, is now available in those applications—replacing their original macro languages. What you learn here can thus be applied to many other places. Other major software vendors are also beginning to bundle a similar and compatible language with their popular applications; many even license VBA from Microsoft to be included in their applications. If this trend continues, Basic may become the universal programming language, the only one most computer users will ever need to learn.

Visual Basic Script (VBScript), a subset (slimmed-down version) of VBA, has entered the Internet, the ubiquitous Information Superhighway. After you master Visual Basic, you should have no trouble making Internet objects come alive with some simple programming tricks.

All these points should convince you to dedicate more time and effort to mastering Visual Basic. A bright future awaits you if you become a Visual Basic master.

If you need more incentive, consider this: Visual Basic is fun to use. I can personally vow for this. In all the scores of PC programs and languages I have used, none can match the amusement value that Visual Basic can provide. Some of the Fun and Game programs at the end of each chapter in this book can serve as examples of this point. So enjoy yourself as you learn something useful.

EDITIONS OF VISUAL BASIC 5

There are now three or four editions of Visual Basic, depending on how you count them. The following three paragraphs are quoted from *Mastering Microsoft Visual Basic 5*:

Learning Edition   The Visual Basic Learning Edition enables you to create powerful applications for Microsoft Windows 95 and Windows NT. It includes all intrinsic Visual Basic controls, along with grid, tab, and data-bound controls.

Professional Edition   The Professional Edition provides a full-featured set of tools for developing solutions for others. It includes all of the features of the Learning Edition, along with additional ActiveX controls, including Internet controls and the Crystal Reports for Visual Basic.

Enterprise Edition   The Enterprise Edition enables you to create robust distributed applications in a team setting. It provides all of the features of the Professional Edition, and also includes features such as the Automation Manager, Component Manager, database management tools, and the Microsoft Visual SourceSafe project-oriented version control system.

The **Learning Edition** comes with a tutorial CD. A promotional flyer from Microsoft has this to say:

> Jump-start the learning process with a self-paced, instructional CD-ROM that includes multimedia video lessons, narrated demonstrations, and hands-on lab exercises.

Don't expect much depth from this CD. If you want more depth, try *Mastering Visual Basic 5*, a separate CD marketed by Microsoft for about $50. This CD is included in the other editions.

Of all these editions, the most widely used is the **Professional Edition**. If you are interested in owning a copy, this is the one to buy. The full version retails for about $500. The upgrade version (contains the same thing as the full version) for owners of previous VB versions or competitive products, the price is $250 (Microsoft used to charge $90 for previous upgrade versions). The Enterprise Edition costs about twice as much.

There is good news for people in academia. Microsoft is giving you a offer which you cannot refuse—if you are a full-time instructor or student. A Professional Edition marked with an "Academic Price" label sells for about $100 in a campus store. Some national mail-order retailers sell it for $80 and the Standard Edition for about half of that.

The academic package that I bought contains lots of software but few hard copies. The soft part includes four CDs: Visual Basic Professional Edition, Mastering Visual Basic 5, Microsoft Developer Network, and Windows NT 4.0 Workstation. The hard part includes three little booklets, one of which contains nothing but advertisements from numerous vendors of VB-related products. There is a coupon which you can send to Microsoft to get three books, but you have to pay

$7.50 shipping cost. If you want to order two other books that used to come with previous versions, you'll have to shell out another 65 bucks. Fortunately, most of that stuff can be found in the online help.

Finally, some Microsoft flyers list still another edition: **Control Creation Edition**. This edition is used to create **ActiveX controls**, but not standalone executables. It was first released on the Internet for anybody to download free of charge; it's still available on Microsoft's Web site. It is also integrated into the Professional and Enterprise editions.

BOOK ORGANIZATION

The book contains 12 chapters (not counting Chapter 0, which briefly covers Windows 95). They are organized in a logical and progressive manner. Elementary and common features are covered in earlier chapters and the more complex and less common ones in later chapters. You gain a basic understanding early. As you progress to later chapters, you will learn to do more complex and impressive things with Visual Basic.

Chapter 1 gives you a quick tour through the Visual Basic environment. You get the overall picture and learn to use some simple features. Besides introducing the Visual Basic environment, the chapter walks you through the steps of creating a couple of simple applications. You get a general idea of how to actually write a Visual Basic program.

Chapter 2 explains how to use the Code window where you enter and edit program code lines. It also covers some nitty-gritty chores such as printing text to the printer and creating and saving simple text files. The last two sections briefly introduce simple debugging techniques.

Chapter 3 explains the role played by forms, which turn into windows when a program runs. You learn how to set form properties at design time and run time, and to maneuver multiple forms. The last two sections explore various techniques of outputting text to a form.

Chapter 4 deals with the most commonly used controls. These are the objects you see in a window when a Windows program runs. Nearly half of the standard controls available in the Standard Edition are covered here.

Chapter 5 introduces the Basic component of Visual Basic. This language component resembles an earlier version of Basic such as QBasic or Quick Basic. Here you get familiar with elementary programming concepts and techniques.

Chapter 6 continues to cover the Basic component. You learn various commands and techniques to control program flow—away from the typical top to bottom manner.

Chapter 7 handles the numerous built-in functions that come with Visual Basic. These can do lots of work with little or no programming from you.

Chapter 8 teaches you how to create your own functions and other types of subroutines. These devices can make your programs shorter and sweeter—and run faster as well.

Chapter 9 gets into some of the most technical aspects of programming, including arrays, control arrays, user-defined types, and collections. These allow you to do fancy things, but they also require considerable programming savvy.

Chapter 10 covers a variety of controls and commands to manage permanent data, the stuff that you want to save to disk.

Chapter 11 is partly for fun and partly for serious work. You learn to use a number of controls and commands to embellish a user interface and to create entertaining graphics.

Chapter 12 contains the less commonly used features. Some of these are treated with less depth than they deserve. Should you decide to explore them further, ways are provided for you to proceed on your own.

As you can see from the above, the two components of Visual Basic—namely Visual (the graphical component) and Basic (the language component)—are blended together. First, you learn the graphical component to design screen user interfaces. Then you learn to use the language component to maneuver the screen objects. Eventually, you learn to integrate the two to create useful applications.

Some people favor covering Basic before Visual. If you belong to this group, you might want to move Chapters 5 and 6 before 3 and 4, thus following the chapters in this sequence: 1, 2, 5, 6, 3, 4, 7….

The first few chapters also shallowly cover some topics that are more fully explained in later chapters. Some reviewers argue that more features should be introduced early. These sections are marked as "a first look at an advanced topic." These can mostly be ignored without interrupting the flow of material.

The book is feature oriented. The primary objective is to help you learn and use Visual Basic's available features. The text explains many intricate points and rules. Numerous short examples help illustrate these points and rules. Some sample programs are longer and have practical use. These are available on the accompanying disk.

Some books follow the project-oriented approach. Each chapter simulates a project. You are told how to assemble various Visual Basic tools and how to put them together to accomplish the project. Although that approach is not suitable for beginners, it does mimic the way professional programmers do their work in real life. To add this aspect to this book, I initially planned to have a last chapter totally devoted to this approach. This Advanced Applications chapter would include a series of projects and you would be shown the steps of accomplishing them. The problem with that arrangement is that these projects would be detached from the Visual Basic features covered in previous chapters. A reasonable solution for this dilemma is to integrate these projects into the previous chapters. So the projects originally intended for a separate chapter have now been modified and attached to the end of appropriate chapters as chapter projects.

A few chapter projects span several chapters. They begin in small scales and expand or are modified as they reappear. These are intended to simulate real-life scenarios where programmers continue to modify and expand existing programs.

CHAPTER ACCESSORIES

Each chapter contains a number of auxiliary items intended to provide heuristic aid or convenient reference for the user, including the following:

• **Key Terms**   Each chapter starts with a glossary of the special terms that you will encounter in the chapter. These are placed at the beginning for easy reference; you can more quickly look up something at the beginning of the chapter. These items are also gathered together and put in Appendix A (Glossary). The terms in both places are arranged in alphabetic order. These terms are also bolded when they first appear in the text.

• **Drill**   Each chapter contains 30 drill (true-false, multiple-choice, matching, and fill-in) questions. A few of them are placed after a few sections in the text. As you try to answer these objective questions, you can look up pertinent information in the preceding sections in the text. If you need feedback (computer-fed) instructions, try the disk version explained later.

• **Practice**   Each chapter includes about 30 questions that require you to do something. Some ask you to write essay answers. Others require you to design user interfaces and write program code to perform tasks.

• **Chapter Project**   Each chapter contains about half a dozen chapter projects. Compared to those found in Practice, these are more involved and challenging problems. You need to utilize the knowledge accumulated from the current and previous chapters to complete such projects. Since you need considerable expertise on Visual Basic to tackle these problems, more of them are placed in later chapters than in earlier ones.

• **Fun and Game**   Included at the end of each chapter are two programs mostly for fun. All work and no play makes Bob a boring boy. With that in mind, I decided to add one short (so as not to take up too much precious book space) and entertaining program at the end of each chapter. Reviewers unanimously endorsed the idea. So I decided to double the fun by doubling the original number. (I thoroughly enjoyed writing and playing with these programs. I hope you do too. Who says programming is boring?) These programs all involve colors, graphics, and/or animation. The shorter and simpler ones are placed in earlier chapters. The techniques used in these programs may not be explained in the relevant chapter. The copious comments, however, provide some crude clues as to what's going on. When you learn more in later chapters, you can come back and dissect or tinker with these programs. In the meantime, you can run them as they are and have fun. See the next section about disk files.

INCLUDED SOFTWARE

A 3.5-inch floppy disk accompanies this book. It contains 200-300 files stored in the following directories:

Root Directory   The root directory contains the **DRILL.EXE** program and a database file named **DrillVB5.mdb**. The former is the CAI (computer-assisted instruction) engine that drives the database to provide an interactive tutorial. The database contains the same drill questions found in the text. The main difference is that if you supply a wrong answer here, the program will display a corrective instruction. See the next section for more details.

PROGRAM Directory   This directory contains files with the FRM (form) or VBP (project) extensions. They are the disk version of the relatively lengthy source code files found in the text. Code listings in the text will show the names, if available, of their disk files.

PRACTICE Directory   This directory also contains files with the FRM or VBP extensions. These are the answers for some of the practice questions. Appendix D contains the answers for all the practice questions. Sometimes you may find file names instead of explanatory text or code lines. These file names indicate the availability of disk files.

PROJECT Directory   This directory is available only on the Professor (not Student) disk. It contains the answers for all the chapter projects.

TEXTFILE Directory   Some projects require data for demonstration. If you wish, you can enter the displayed data from the keyboard. To save you the trouble, I've included an Open button in some projects. Clicking it at run time leads the program to open the specified file from the TEXTFILE directory in drive A. If the file is not found there, an error message appears. So make sure to insert the included disk before clicking this button. If the disk must be placed in drive B, then change A to B in the source code before running the program.

FUN Directory   The Fun and Game programs shown at the end of each chapter are all stored here. The beginning of each program listing in the text shows the file name for the program. Open the pertinent form or VBP file, press F5 to run, and just sit back and enjoy it; on the other hand, you may have to do something if you want to play a game.

The FRM and VBP files can be retrieved to Visual Basic to save you the trouble of having to type lengthy code lines or design complex user interfaces. These file names contain two parts, chapter number and file purpose. Each file name starts with a number. It signifies the chapter number. So a file name starting with 11 belongs in Chapter 11. A file name may also end with a number, which signifies a slight variation of another file of the same name but with a different number. Consider the following two examples. Both files are stored in the PROGRAM directory and they belong to Chapter 7. They are slightly different from each other.

        \PROGRAM\7MORT1.FRM
        \PROGRAM\7MORT2.FRM

If you cannot find a file from the accompanying disk, try another directory. Reread the preceding paragraphs to make sure you are in the right directory.

Opening a FRM file retrieves a single form file; opening a VBP file retrieves two or more associated files.

When you want to open a project, Visual Basic automatically shows all the files matching the *.VBP, *.MAK, or *.VBG patterns. If you intend to retrieve a form file, change the mask to *.FRM to show all the form files. You can also choose a screen option to show all the files, those matching the *.* pattern.

To retrieve one of the disk files to Visual Basic, insert the provided disk in drive A or B. Choose Open Project from the File menu (or click the Open Project icon). Choose drive A or B from the Look-in list. If necessary, change the file mask to *.FRM or *.* in the File-name box. When a desired file is displayed, double-click it to open. If necessary, open the Project window by clicking the Project Explorer button on the Standard toolbar. Then click the form name in this window and click View Form or View Code to load the item.

RUNNING THE CAI PROGRAM

The **DRILL.EXE** program is written in Visual Basic. It can be run like any Windows program. However, there is a major difference. This program, like any program written in Visual Basic, requires the presence of the MSVBVM50.DLL (more than 1.3MB) run-time module that comes with the Visual Basic package. If your system contains this file (in the WINDOWS\SYSTEM directory), which is the case after VB5 has been installed, then there should be no problem. If you want to run it in another system which contains no Visual Basic, then the run-time module must be supplied. If you ask Windows to run DRILL.EXE, it will try to find the run-time module first; failing to do that will result in an error.

Since the DRILL program drives a database file, it also needs another file named VB5DB.DLL (77KB). This file is also stored in the same directory as described above. Since this file is relatively short, you can store it in drive A if you intend to run the DRILL program from drive A.

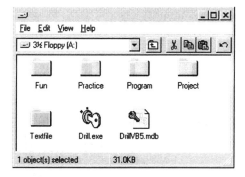

Figure 1   My Computer window showing Drive A's root directory

To run DRILL.EXE, use the numerous options explained in Chapter 0. Figure 1 shows the items in drive A displayed in the My Computer window. You can just double-click the program to start it.

The initial screen instructions tell you to click the Start button. (These instructions are also available after you've started a lesson—just press F1 and a message box will pop up.) An input box appears, showing the current directory (where the DRILL program is stored) and the name of the database. If you press Enter or click OK, a combo box appears at the top-right corner. Click the down arrow, and all the chapter titles appear. Click a chapter name, and the first question appears.

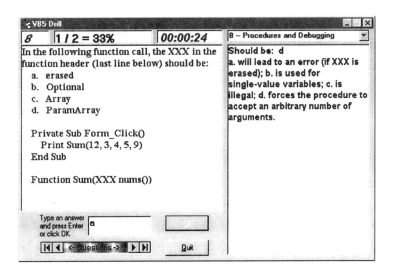

Figure 2   A sample display of the DRILL program

You can now scroll to each of the 30 available questions by pressing the PgUp or PgDn key or clicking one of the buttons on the data control (these buttons serve the same purposes as those found on your VCR). To answer a displayed question, type something in the bottom-left text box and press Enter or click OK. The right-side box shows a message in response, telling you that you're right or why you're wrong. If you scroll back to a question to which you already supplied an answer, your original answer to that question will reappear in the text box where you typed it and the original response by the program will reappear in the right-side box. So you can answer the questions in any order and go back to any question to review what you have done.

Three top-left boxes keep some scores. The first (leftmost) shows the current question's number. The second tracks the numbers of right/wrong answers and the percentage (correct number divided by total). The third box shows the elapsed time since the beginning of the current chapter.

To move on to another chapter, use the combo box to navigate to any of the 12 available chapters. If you have at least one correct answer, the program will prompt you with Yes/No to abandon the previous chapter. The same thing happens if you click X or Quit.

The most convenient way for multiple users is to copy DRILL.EXE and the database file to a hard disk directory. Then add a shortcut to the desktop. A user can then double-click the shortcut to run the program. The techniques of creating shortcuts are explained in Chapter 0.

The DRILL program will go to the directory where it is stored to open the companion database file. If the file is not there, you'll be prompted to supply a different path. This may or may not work. So try to put the two files in the same directory.

THE AUTHOR

Dr. Forest Lin is an author, professor, and programmer. He has taught at several colleges; currently he teaches at Tulsa Community College. He has published a dozen computer books, some college texts and some advanced trade books.

ACKNOWLEDGMENTS

The following professors examined parts or all of the manuscript. I'd like to express my gratitude to them for their immeasurable contributions.

Marlene Camper
Manchester Community Technical College

Stan Foster
Sacramento City College

Carol Peterson
South Plains College

Merrill Parker
Chattanooga State Technical CC

Pete Brown
Schoolcraft College

Brad Chilton
Tarleton State University

John Parker
Santa Barbara City College

Wade Graves
Grayson County College

Sid Brounstein
Montgomery College

Robert Johnson
Chemeketa Community College

Dain Smith
Lane Community College

Mark Simkin
University of Nevada

Jose Cabera
San Antonio College

Robert Fitzgerald
University of Northern Florida

Jim Murchison
Columbia State Community College

Lee Hunt
Collin County Community College

Paul Lecoq
Spokane Falls Community College

Melinda White
Santa Fe Community College

Mary Admunson-Miller
Greenville Technical College

Professor Marlene Camper deserves another mention. She developed a booklet of test items to accompany this book. In the process, she went over the chapters with a fine-toothed comb and uncovered quite a few errors and ambiguities. Thanks to her exhaustive effort, this edition is much improved over the previous.

Chapter 0
Opening Windows 95

This chapter tries to accommodate the complete novice who knows little or nothing about computers. Think of the 0 in the chapter number as a non-credit remedial course you have to take before you can enroll in a credit course. You need to know what is covered here before you can effectively learn to use Visual Basic. If you already know this stuff, you can simply ignore this chapter and move on to the next.

When you turn on your **PC** (personal computer), **DOS** (disk operating system) is booted (started). Windows then runs on top of DOS. A Windows-compliant program like Visual Basic then runs on top of Windows. As a Visual Basic user, you need to know a little about what lies underneath it. This chapter will concentrate mostly on Windows because you are likely to have more interaction with it than the layers below.

PERSONAL COMPUTER

A PC consists of the main parts shown in Figure 0.1 The **system unit** contains a **CPU** (central processing unit, the electronic brain), **RAM** (random-access memory) for temporary storage of data, a motherboard to integrate all the parts, controller cards (boards) with electronic circuitry to connect to peripherals such as modem (for sending and receiving electronic messages), printer, keyboard, and so on. Inside the system unit, there is usually a hard disk (also known as a hard drive), and one or two floppy drives, which have openings for you to insert floppy disks (diskettes) to save data. A more recently manufactured PC may also have a CD-ROM drive and a sound card connected to internal or external speakers.

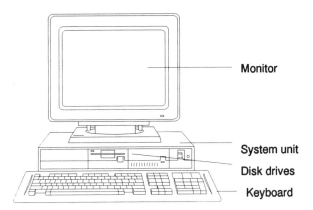

Figure 0.1   A personal computer

The **keyboard** is an input device. You type something and press Enter to give an instruction to the PC. The PC keyboard has a row of 12 function keys marked F1-F12. These keys are used by different programs for different purposes. The Caps Lock key turns on/off uppercase letters. The Num Lock key turns on/off the numeric keypad on the right side of the keyboard. When on, pressing a key here displays a number on the screen; when off, the arrow (cursor-control) keys are activated. The Shift, Ctrl, and Alt keys are combined with other keys for a variety of purposes.

The **monitor** is an output device. It displays what you have done and what the PC is doing in response. In a graphical program, the objects on the screen can be maneuvered with a **mouse**, which is another input device like a keyboard.

To store your own data, you need to be equipped with floppy disks. These come in two sizes, 5.25 inch (Figure 0.2) and 3.5 inch (Figure 0.3). These are not compatible; a 3.5-inch disk cannot be used by a 5.25-inch drive. If your PC has two different floppy drives, you can use either type of disks. If it has only one drive, you must have the exact matching type of floppy disks.

Each floppy disk has a write-protect device, shown at the top right of the two figures. On a 5.25-inch disk, you cover this hole with an adhesive tape to prevent writing data to the disk or erasing the existing data. On a 3.5-inch disk, you slide the built-in tab to the edge to show a see-through hole to write-protect the disk.

Figure 0.2   A 5.25-inch diskette

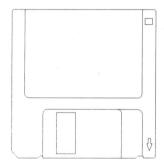

Figure 0.3   A 3.5-inch diskette

Most floppy disks for sale today come preformatted; they are ready to store data without your having to do anything. If they are not formatted, you need to use the DOS FORMAT command or a Windows menu option to format it; the latter will be explained later in this chapter.

WINDOWS' ROLE AND PARTS

Before Windows 95, turning on a PC would load DOS. Users wanting to run Windows-compliant graphical programs would then run Windows on top of DOS. Then they would run a spreadsheet or word processor on top of Windows.

In Windows 95, turning on your PC automatically starts Windows. DOS no longer exists as a separate package. It is still available for anyone who needs it to run an old program that cannot run on Windows.

DOS was commonly known as an **operating system** and Windows 3.1 (and before) as an **operating environment**. Since Windows 95 no longer depends on a separate DOS, it is now commonly called an operating system (OS).

Windows is a shell program. Like a sea shell, it wraps around your entire system and provides an **graphical user interface** (GUI) for you to use the hardware. This provides a uniform standard for hardware and software vendors to follow and makes life easier for PC users.

A uniform standard is also imposed on **applications**. These are programs performing narrower tasks such as word processing and database management. Application vendors who want their programs certified as Windows-compliant must follow the standard set by Microsoft (Windows' vendor), and provide a common user interface. Users benefit from this arrangement because most programs provide similar interfaces and follow similar menus. After you learn to use one package, you can quickly master another. Once you become familiar with Windows, all other programs will begin to look familiar to you.

This arrangement does not allow you to escape from Windows. When your PC starts, you're facing Windows. When you do something in an application, it often uses the services provided by Windows. So when you save a file from your word processor, it goes through Windows to reach the disk. When you exit your application, you're back to Windows again. In this environment, being reasonably familiar with Windows can make you a more productive PC user and solve many of your problems with your PC.

Windows is a complex package with many parts. Some of them are automatically run and visible. Others are not run but available for your use. The following list shows the major components. Later sections will provide details for most of them.

- Task launcher and switcher
- Disk and file manager
- Clipboard manager
- Hardware manager (printer, audio, video, fax, modem, monitor, etc.)
- Software accessories (word processor, painting program, calculator, games, etc.)

TIP: Mouse Jargon and Techniques

If you are new to a graphical user environment (GUI), you need to get familiar with some of the following basic terms and techniques of using a mouse, which is commonly used to control that environment.

Point	Move the mouse pointer to an object. Some (not all) objects may respond.
Click	Move the mouse pointer to a desired object, press the left mouse button and quickly release it. This may select the object, or an action may be taken.
Right-click	Click an object with the right mouse button. A shortcut (context) menu, if available, will pop up.
Double-click	Press the left button twice in rapid succession when the pointer is on a desired object. An action is taken on the object.
Drag and Drop	Move the mouse pointer to an object, hold down the left button, and roll the mouse to another location. An object will appear for you to drag. Release the button to drop the object in the target place.
Right-drag	Drag an object by holding down the right button. A number of options will appear for you to choose.

ENTERING AND EXITING

If your PC has Windows 95 installed on a hard disk, leave drive A open and turn on the PC to run Windows. The initial screen, shown in the next section, will eventually appear. If there is a disk in drive A, your PC will try to boot from there or, if that's not possible, an error message will appear. In that case, open the drive door and press a key to continue.

To exit Windows, click the Start button at the left end of the taskbar (Figure 0.5); a list of options pops up. Click Shut Down, and the Shut Down Windows dialog box (Figure 0.4) appears; a **dialog box** is a separate window for the user to communicate with the program. (In the future, we'll use a simpler expression in such a situation by telling you to choose Start | Shut Down.)

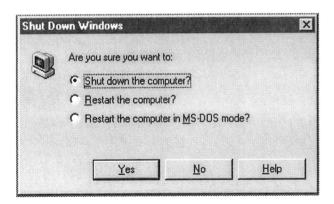

Figure 0.4   Shutting down the system

In the Shut Down Windows dialog box, the *Shut down the computer* option is selected by default and the Yes button has the focus. If this is what you want, just click Yes, press Enter, or press Alt+Y. After a while a message tells you that you can shut off the computer, which you can do by switching off the power supply. If you don't want to exit when this dialog appears, just click No. If you need help, click the Help button.

You can have a fresh start by choosing the *Restart the computer* option. This option will clear from the computer's memory (RAM) all the running programs and data you may have entered. Some programs may not manage RAM efficiently and cause problems for the entire system. Restarting your PC may fix such a problem. If you hold down Shift and click Yes, Windows is restarted but the system is not rebooted; this takes much less time.

The last option (you may have other options if you are on a network) lets you restart the PC by running DOS rather than Windows. You can then enter DOS commands or run DOS programs. If you want to run Windows from there, go to the right directory (usually WINDOWS) and enter WIN.

WINDOWS DESKTOP

The central theme of Windows is to let the user open a series of windows and switch from one to another to perform different tasks. All these begin from the **Windows desktop**. Your monitor screen is treated as a desktop and objects are displayed and arranged as you would on your own desktop.

Keep in mind that the Windows desktop is like a chameleon. It can be changed many ways. What is shown here may not resemble what your screen will show. If you wish, your screen can be made to look like this.

The Windows desktop contains a series of **objects**. Each object is a distinct unit (program) that can be manipulated in many ways by the user. The initial screen is likely to consist of the following objects shown in Figure 0.5:

- Desktop icons (left)
- Windows (right)
- Taskbar (bottom)

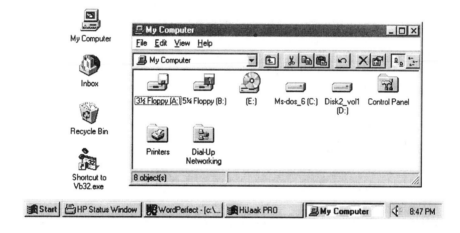

Figure 0.5   The Windows desktop

Each time you run your PC, the initial screen is the same as the one you left when you shut down your PC; the screen arrangement is automatically saved upon exit and retrieved upon startup.

Desktop Icons

A **desktop icon** is a picture symbol of a program. Figure 0.5 shows four desktop icons on the left side; your screen may show more or fewer icons. Double-clicking an icon opens a window. For example, double-clicking the My Computer icon opens the My Computer window; double-clicking Recycle Bin will open the Recycle Bin window.

Each desktop icon consists of a picture at the top and a label at the bottom. You can change the label. To do that, click it twice (don't double click). The first click highlights it and the second makes it editable. You can use any editing key to make changes. If you want to replace the whole thing, just start typing; what you type will replace the highlighted text. If you want to make changes, press an arrow key to move to the desired place and then delete or add text. When you are done, press Enter or click another area. You can enter a name as long as 255 characters. You can change any label here except the Recycle Bin label.

The desktop icons can be managed in many ways. You can drag each to any empty area. You can also select them and drag them together. To select multiple icons, hold down Ctrl and click each (click it another time if you wish to deselect it). You can also move the pointer to one corner and drag it to draw a rectangle. All the icons inside will be selected (highlighted). If you wish to select all the icons on the screen, just press Ctrl+A. When you drag one, all the selected icons will move as well. Clicking an empty area will deselect all.

Standard and Shortcut Menus

You can use menus to manage the desktop. When you want to tell Windows to do something, you need to issue an instruction called **command**. Commands are grouped into **menus**. When you open a menu, you may see a list of commands or options. Choosing one may lead to an action or another list (submenu) of options. After a command is issued, the menu will close.

There are two types of menus: **standard menus** and **shortcut menus**. Standard menus appear on the **menu bar** near the top of each window, as shown in the My Computer window in Figure 0.5. To use such a menu, just click the name, such as View. A list will drop down. You can then click one option to choose it. If an option contains a triangle (▸) on the right, you can point to it to open its list of options. If an option has a bullet (•) on the left, it marks the selected option; clicking another option will move the bullet to the new option. If a check mark (✓) appears, it turns on a particular feature; clicking it repeatedly will turn (toggle) it on or off.

You can also use menus by pressing proper keyboard keys. To activate the menu system, just press the Alt key; you can press it another time (or Esc) to deactivate the menu system. The first menu will be highlighted. You can press a left or right arrow key to highlight another menu. To open the highlighted menu, press Enter or a down arrow key. A list will drop down and the first option will be highlighted. You can then use an up or down arrow key to highlight another.

Press Enter to issue the highlighted command. The action is taken and the menu closes. You can also hold down Alt and an underlined letter to open a menu; for example, Alt+V opens the View menu. As you use menu options, read the changing messages on the status bar at the bottom of the window telling you what you are doing.

You can also use a **shortcut menu** (also known as a **context menu** or **popup menu**) for an easy access to the menu system. A shortcut menu includes the commonly used commands normally scattered in several standard menus. Using a shortcut menu to perform a common task can save you time. For an uncommon task, you'll need to use a standard menu to find the needed command.

Windows 95 and compatible programs are full of shortcut menus. Most visible objects on the screen has a shortcut menu. To see whether an object has a shortcut menu, just right-click it (or press Shift+F10). If so, a menu pops up; otherwise, nothing happens.

We can use a shortcut menu to mange the objects on the desktop. To show this menu, right-click the desktop (any blank area). Figure 0.6 (left side only) appears. When such a menu appears, you can click an option to do something. If you click another object, such as the desktop, the menu disappears and no action is taken; you can press Esc to do the same thing. You can also bring up this menu by pressing Shift+F10 when no object on the desktop is selected.

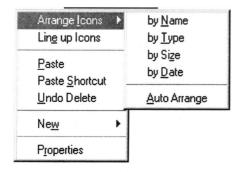

Figure 0.6   A shortcut (context) menu

Some options may be dimmed. In that case, they are not available at this time. They may become available (not dimmed) in another situation.

The first option is called **Arrange Icons**. There is also a triangle (▸) at the right of the name. Pointing to this option opens a **cascading menu** with another list of options as shown in Figure 0.6. Clicking any of these will move the icons to vertical alignment on the left margin of the screen. If you don't want that to happen, choose **Line Up Icons** after dragging them to the desired location. They will be horizontally or vertically aligned at the current location.

If you click the Properties option, the **Display Properties** dialog box appears. This dialog will show four tabs: Background, Screen Saver, Appearance, and Settings. A **tab** resembles in appearance the top of a manila folder, which lets you easily open the folder. You can click a tab to open up another list of options. A **tabbed dialog** can offer multiple tabs all of which share the same commands or menus. You can use the Display Properties dialog to change many things on the Windows desktop, including colors, wallpaper, screen saver, and so on.

Every shortcut menu has the Properties option at the bottom. This leads to the **property sheet** of the object. This sheet, such as the Display Properties dialog box discussed above, tells a great deal about an object. Whenever you want to know more about an object or change its attributes, use its property sheet. You can also use it to customize many objects. The property sheet of an object can be displayed by right-clicking an icon such as My Computer and then choosing Properties from the shortcut menu; right-clicking any blank area of the open window (My Computer) will bring up the same shortcut menu. You can also click an icon to select it and then press Alt+Enter to open its property sheet.

New Folders and Shortcuts

The **New** option from the desktop shortcut menu leads to a submenu with two parts divided by a line. The top part has two options: **Folder** and **Shortcut**. You use Folder to create a new folder; a folder is the equivalent of a DOS directory (the two terms are often interchangeably used), a device used to store and manage files. A folder icon (looks like a Manila folder) with the New Folder label will appear. The cursor also stays on the label for you to edit. The default name is highlighted. If you start typing, it will disappear. If you want to edit it, move a cursor key and make necessary changes. When you are done, press Enter or click another item on the screen.

You can place a **shortcut** on the desktop and then double-click it to run a program linked to the shortcut. You can use the **New | Shortcut** command to create a shortcut. The **Create Shortcut** dialog box appears. You can type a program name (together with a necessary directory path to specify where the program is located) or use the **Browse** button to search for it. It leads to the Browse dialog box (Figure 0.8). When you find the desired program, double-click it. Then click

Next and then Finish. If a program does not have an icon, you'll be asked to select one.

The bottom part of the New menu lists various documents which you can choose to create a shortcut; your list depends on the applications installed. When you click one, the pertinent program's icon will appear on the desktop. The bottom part of the icon also shows a label with the program's name (plus New added at the beginning) and the default document (file) name; the cursor also goes to the label for you to edit it. When you Double-click this icon in the future, the program will run and the supplied label will become the default data file name.

There is an easier way to create a shortcut. Just drag the desired object to a desired location. For example, Figure 0.5 shows *Shortcut to Printers*. To create this shortcut, just drag the Printers object from the My Computer window to the desktop. A message says that you can't move it and gives the Yes/No prompt to create a shortcut. (The same thing also happens if you choose File | Shortcut from the My Computer window.) If you right-drag the same object instead, you can then choose to cancel or create a shortcut from the popup menu.

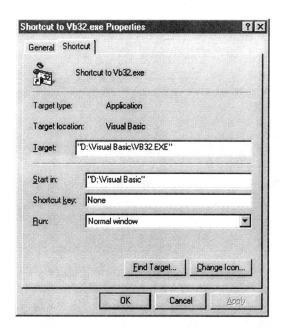

Figure 0.7   The property sheet of a shortcut file

A shortcut is a short (less than 1KB) file pointing to a program (or file or folder). It is saved to the folder (directory) where the icon appears. The file name is the label shown on the screen, plus the LNK extension. A shortcut icon has a bent arrow at the bottom left of its picture. Figure 0.5 shows two shortcut icons.

A shortcut's property sheet (right-click it and choose Properties) has two tabs. The General tab shows various file attributes, including the file's name and length. The file name shown in a property sheet uses a DOS file name with the 8.3 limitations. So a shortcut's name may be shortened to SHORTC ~ 1.LNK. When a long name is encountered, DOS displays only the first eight characters. If this result in two or more files in the same directory sharing an identical name, then only the first six characters and a ~ are shown, plus a sequential number starting from 1 to distinguish one file from another.

The Shortcut tab (Figure 0.7) shows how a shortcut is connected to its original file. The label appears in the title bar. A text box shows the name and directory path of the original program file. This and other items can be edited.

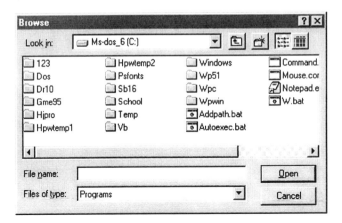

Figure 0.8   The Browse dialog box

There are some occasions when you are given the Browse button. Using the desktop shortcut menu to create a shortcut leads to it, as explained earlier; so does choosing Start | Run. Clicking this button leads to the **Browse dialog box** (Figure 0.8). This dialog lets you find a desired file to open. You can click the Look-in box or its down arrow to drop down a list of drives and folders and click one to go there. There is no menu. Instead, there four buttons on the toolbar at the top. You can move the pointer to each to show its **tooltip**, which is a label showing the command name. You can use the Up One Level button (leftmost; or the Backspace key) to move up the directory path, the Create New Folder button to create a new folder, the List icon to display the folder contents as a list (default), or the Details icon to show detailed information. You can double-click a folder to open it up. When the desired file is found, you can double-click it to open; you can also click it and then click the Open button.

Recycle Bin

If you have created shortcuts demonstrated in previous sections, you may want to delete them. As you delete shortcuts, files, or folders, they are normally sent to the **Recycle Bin**. When the bin is full, older ones are discarded. You can clean it up to free up some disk space.

To delete a shortcut created earlier, just click it to select it and press Del from the keyboard. A prompt appears asking whether you want to send it to the Recycle Bin. If you click No, no deletion is done. If you click Yes, the icon disappears. The same prompt will appear if you right-click an icon and choose Delete from the shortcut menu.

If you are sure of what you are doing and don't want to send the deleted item to the Recycle Bin, hold down Shift as you press Del or choose Delete from the shortcut menu. The resulting prompt asks you whether you want to remove the item, not send it to the Recycle Bin. The above discussion applies only to a hard disk. If you delete an item from a floppy disk, the item will be removed, not sent to the Recycle Bin.

All the deletions from a hard disk using Windows 95 will be sent to the Recycle Bin (unless you hold down Shift during deletion). Using other applications to do deletion may not send files here.

The Recycle Bin stores your discards. You can restore them if you change your mind or make a mistake. To restore a file, just select it and choose File | Restore; this option is also available from the shortcut menu. If the original folder already has a file of the same name, a dialog box will show the two files' differences and ask you for Yes or No. Deleting a folder sends only files to the Recycle Bin. If you try to restore one of these files, a new matching folder will be created.

To examine the Recycle Bin, double-click its desktop icon to open it (Figure 0.9). The display shows five columns. You can click each column heading to sort by that column. Clicking Size, for example, leads to all the items arranged according to size. You can click the same heading repeatedly to toggle between the ascending or descending sort order.

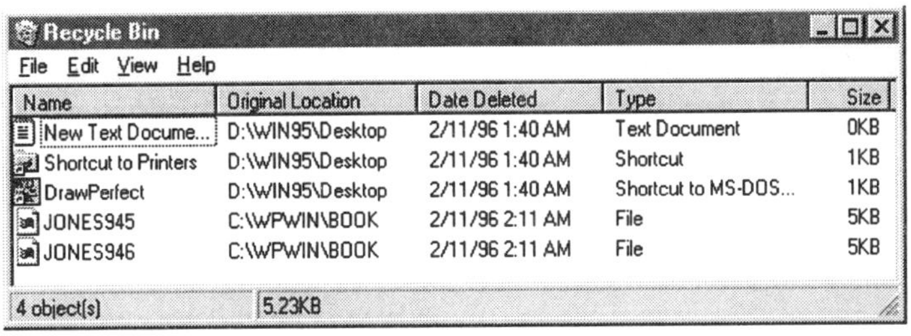

Recycle Bin				_ □ ✕
File Edit View Help				
Name	**Original Location**	**Date Deleted**	**Type**	**Size**
New Text Docume...	D:\WIN95\Desktop	2/11/96 1:40 AM	Text Document	0KB
Shortcut to Printers	D:\WIN95\Desktop	2/11/96 1:40 AM	Shortcut	1KB
DrawPerfect	D:\WIN95\Desktop	2/11/96 1:40 AM	Shortcut to MS-DOS...	1KB
JONES945	C:\WPWIN\BOOK	2/11/96 2:11 AM	File	5KB
JONES946	C:\WPWIN\BOOK	2/11/96 2:11 AM	File	5KB
4 object(s)	5.23KB			

Figure 0.9   The Recycle Bin window

When a list like Figure 0.9 appears, you can select multiple items by clicking each while holding down Ctrl. You can also click the first and hold down Shift while clicking the other end to select the entire block. You can continue to select outside the block by holding down Ctrl (or in combination with Shift) and clicking additional items. Clicking another item without holding down Ctrl and/or Shift will deselect previous selections. If you want to select all, just press Ctrl+A or choose Edit | Select All. After items are selected, you can use a command (menu option) to do something to all of them, such as deleting them (you can also press Del or choose File | Delete). The File menu has the Empty Recycle Bin option; you can use it to clear everything.

When the Recycle Bin window is open, you can drag other visible items from the desktop or another window to this window. The items will be moved from the original folder to the Recycle Bin. You can also drag items out of this window if you don't want to discard them.

You can use a shortcut menu to manage the Recycle Bin. Right-click its desktop icon and choose Empty Recycle Bin to empty the contents. Choose Properties to configure the Recycle Bin. You can use the resulting dialog box to set aside a different amount of disk space or disable the recycling altogether.

By default 10% of each hard drive you have is set aside to store deleted files. When the space is exceeded, earlier files are then thrown out. You can allocate a different amount of disk space. Just use its property sheet (right-click the trash-can icon or any blank area inside its window and then click Properties). Drag the slider to change the default value.

A WINDOW'S COMPONENTS

When you double-click a desktop icon, a window opens. This is where you do most of your work. This is also where Windows manage things by putting related items together.

Figures 0.5 and 0.9 show window examples. A typical window consists of the following major components.

Title bar   Each window has a title bar. You can drag this bar to move the entire window. This is the easiest way for you to move a displayed window.

Menu bar/Toolbar   Some windows contain a menu bar. In that case, you can choose a menu option to execute a command. Some of the frequently used commands (actually shortcuts) also appear as buttons on the toolbar, located just below the menu bar. When you point to each icon, a tooltip (an explanatory label) will appear to show the command's name.

Control/System menu   Each window has a **control menu** (also known as **system menu**) at the top-left corner. Double-clicking it closes the window. You may be prompted to save data or with a Yes/No prompt. Clicking the control-menu icon (also known as the control box) displays a menu, most of which are redundant because you can use other items to do the same things more quickly.

Minimize/Maximize/Restore/Close buttons   The top-right corner of each window shows usually three of these four buttons: ▬ ☐ ⊟ ☒. You can use these buttons to reduce a window to a button on the taskbar, expand it to fill up the entire screen, restore its previous size, or close the window. When a window is maximized, a Restore button (two overlapping squares) replaces the Maximize button (a single square); you can click it to restore the window's previous size.

Borders   Each window has border lines. When you move the pointer over a border, the pointer becomes double-headed. You can then drag it to change the window's size. When the pointer is over a corner, the double head becomes slanted. You can then drag it to resize the window both horizontally and vertically.

Scroll bars   When a window does not display all the available items, one or both scroll bars may appear. You can drag the scroll box in the middle to show more. You can also click a displayed arrow to do the same in a small increment. You can click the area between the box and an arrow to scroll by a large increment. If there are many undisplayed items, the scroll box gets proportionally smaller.

Status bar   The bottom of the window may feature a status bar showing temporary information. Different messages will appear here on different occasions. Read them carefully when you are not sure what to do.

Shortcut menus   A context menu may pop up when you right-click something in a window. In the My Computer window, for example, you can click the title bar, the control-menu icon, a drive icon, a folder icon, and an empty area to pop up different menus.

NOTE   You can double-click a window's title bar to toggle (switch) between the normal size and the maximized size. Each time you double-click, the window is switched to the opposite size.

When multiple windows are open, only one can be active. Its title bar is highlighted. It may also cover up other windows. You can make a window active by clicking any exposed area of that window. This will bring it to the top (foreground) of multiple overlapping windows. To switch to hidden windows, use the techniques discussed in the next several sections.

THE TASKBAR

The **taskbar** is the replacement for Program Manager available in previous versions. It is a long bar normally placed at the bottom of the screen. It has a Start button to let you run programs. The loaded program names appear on the bar. You can click one to open its window or bring it to the top.

The taskbar can be dragged to any screen border. To do that, just drag an empty area of the bar to any of the four sides. The bar will move and change to fit in the new location.

The Start Button

The **Start** button is located at the left (or top) end of the taskbar. This is the famous image that appeared in most Microsoft ads for Windows 95.

There are several ways to activate this button. Clicking it is the simplest. You can also press Ctrl+Esc to bring it up. Newer keyboards have a Start key to activate this button.

The Start button opens up the initial menu (Figure 0.10), which in turn can open up a series of cascading menus. When you point to an option with a triangle (▸), a submenu will appear. When you find the desired program, click it to run.

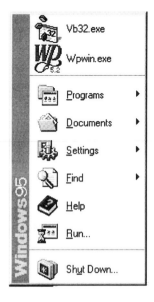

Figure 0.10   The Start menu

After a program is run, its name appears in a button on the taskbar. The active program's button also has a sunken look to distinguish it from the others. Clicking a button here makes that program active and all the others inactive.

Figure 0.10 shows the Start menu having three areas divided by two lines. The top part can be customized, which we'll discuss later. The bottom two parts include these options:

Shut Down   It leads to three options discussed at the beginning of this chapter.

Run   A dialog box will open up for you to run a program. The most recently run program's name will also be selected. If that's the one, just click OK or press Enter. If not, click the down arrow to show all the programs run by this method. Select one and then click OK. If the list doesn't show the desired program, click Browse and go to various folders to find it, and then click OK.

Help   Use this to run the online help. It will be covered in another section below.

Find   Use this to find files and folders. See another section below for details.

Settings   This opens up three options: Control Panel, Printers, and Taskbar. The last will be covered in the next section; the others will be explained later.

Documents   A list of documents will appear. These are the files you have recently used. Clicking one will open the related program and retrieve the document.

Programs   This leads to a series of cascading menus showing all the programs you can click to run. These are added during installation of Windows 95 (previous version's program groups are placed here) or another software package. Some of them can be customized, as will be explained shortly.

The top portion of the Start menu (above the dividing line) shows the shortcuts placed there by the user. You can click (single click) a shortcut here to run the program; this has the same effect as double-clicking a comparable shortcut on the desktop (or inside a folder). You can place a shortcut in one or both places.

Right-clicking the Start button shows three options: Open, Explore, and Find. The last two let you locate a program to be added the Start menu. The first opens up the **Start Menu** window (Figure 0.11). Notice the two shortcut icons; they are identical to those shown on the desktop (Figure 0.5).

Figure 0.11   The Start Menu window

You can copy or move a shortcut (or file) between the desktop (or another folder) and this folder. To move, just drag it from one location to another. To copy, hold down Ctrl as you drag. Alternatively, you can right-drag it; a popup menu will appear for you to choose Copy or Move.

The **Programs** program group in the Start Menu window was created during installation. Windows 95 also places here the previous version's program groups. Other software programs may insert items here during installation You can customize it as you wish. To add a shortcut to it, just drag a desired icon to it. You can also open the window and drag an icon to an open place inside the window. You can also remove items from this window. The items appearing in this window appear on the Programs menu when you open the Start menu and point to Programs.

The Programs folder contains a subfolder named **StartUp**, also added during installation. Shortcuts placed here will automatically start after Windows is loaded. If you want certain programs to start by themselves, just drag them here. You can also use Start | Settings | Taskbar | Start Menu Programs | Add to add programs to this window. If you don't want them to start on some occasions, hold down Ctrl during startup (when the chime begins or as soon as the Start button appears.)

Customizing the Taskbar

Besides using the taskbar to switch from one program to another, you can use it to do many other things. Right-clicking an empty area on the taskbar leads to these options:

Cascade
Tile Horizontally
Tile Vertically
Minimize All Windows
Undo Cascade/Tile/Minimize
Properties

The top five options are self-explanatory. They let you arrange the existing windows or undo the rearrangement.

The Properties option leads to the Taskbar Properties window. Figure 0.12 shows the Taskbar Options tab. There are four options in this tab. As you check and uncheck each, observe the display at the top changing to reflect your new selections. If you check **Auto Hide**, the taskbar will disappear; this gives you more screen space to do your work. When you want to show the taskbar, point to the location where you've last placed the taskbar and it will automatically reappear; it will disappear after you move the pointer away.

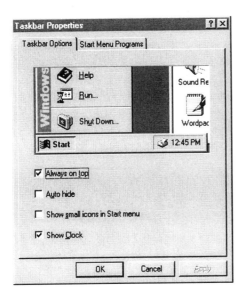

Figure 0.12   The taskbar's property sheet

The Start Menu Programs tab in the Taskbar Properties window has the Add, Remove, Advanced, and Clear buttons. The first three let you add or remove shortcuts to the Start menu; the techniques demonstrated in the previous section accomplish the same thing but are easier. Clicking Clear automatically clears all the entries in the Start | Documents menu. These documents are those that have been recently used. If you use many documents, they will all appear after you click Start and then Documents. Using the Clear command lets you start with a clean slate.

The bottom right corner of the taskbar is known as the **Notification Area**. A message may appear here when a task is being performed. Otherwise, this area shows two default items: loudspeaker and clock. Point to the first and the Volume tooltip will appear (assuming you have a multimedia system). Point to the second, the resulting tooltip shows the current date.

If you double-click the timer, The Date/Timer Properties dialog box appears (Figure 0.13). Here you can click the up or down arrow to change the year, pull down a list of months and click one to select it, or click a displayed date number to select it. To adjust time, click the desired component such as minute and then click the up or down arrow to change the number; you can also type a new number. If you wish, you can use the Time Zone tab to make a change; just drag the displayed light bar to the desired area. As you move the bar, notice how each locale is related to the GMT time.

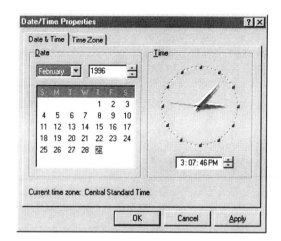

Figure 0.13   The Date/Time Properties window

You can adjust the speaker's volume. If you click the loudspeaker, a slider box appears for you to move the slider up or down. If you double-click the speaker, the Volume Control dialog box appears for you to make more adjustments.

Figure 0.14   The Media Player

If you have a MPC equipped with speakers, you can play a tune and use the Volume button to adjust the volume. To play a tune, choose Start | Programs | Accessories | Multimedia | Media Player. The Media Player dialog box (Figure

0.14) appears. Choose File | Open from the menu bar. Double-click a desired tune from the list. Click the Play (▸) button. You can now use the Volume button on the taskbar to adjust the volume.

You can use the Device menu to choose another device to play. If you choose Video for Windows, all the files with the AVI (audiovisual) extension will be displayed. If none is shown, go to the WINDOWS\HELP folder. A number of files should appear. These video clips are used by Windows online help. You can play them here as well. They feature motions but only clicking noises.

Figure 0.15   Playing a CD

If you have a music CD, you can play it and adjust the volume as explained above. The new Plug and Play (PnP) technology is supposed to let you insert a disc and Windows 95 is supposed to detect it and start playing without your doing anything. It doesn't always work that way. In that case, you can choose Start | Programs | Accessories | Multimedia | CD Play. Figure 0.15 appears. You can now click various buttons to play, pause, stop, and so on. When this window is active, these buttons have tooltips to tell you what they are supposed to do. You can also use various menus to control the playing, such as playing only selected tracks. You can continue doing other things as the disc is playing.

NOTE   As you launch more programs, each button on the taskbar shrinks in size to accommodate more buttons. Each button's caption may also be truncated, thus making it difficult to identify each launched application. You can enlarge these button by enlarging the taskbar. To do that, just drag the top border of the taskbar up (to enlarge) or down (to reduce). As you move the pointer over this border line, the pointer becomes double-headed, thus enabling you to drag.

Switching Tasks

After you have run multiple programs, their names appear on the taskbar. The active program's button appears sunken (depressed) to make it look different from the others. Clicking another program's button makes it active and its button to appear sunken.

If the taskbar is hidden (Auto-hide is checked in the Taskbar Properties dialog box), you can move the pointer to the location where you have anchored the taskbar. It will automatically appear. You can then click a program's button to make it active. The taskbar will disappear after you move the pointer away.

If the taskbar is hidden, you can also press **Ctrl+Esc** to bring it up. This key combination will also activate the Start menu regardless of whether the taskbar is hidden. Pressing Esc will clear the Start menu, but the taskbar will remain even though Auto-hide is on. Clicking any place other than the taskbar will clear it (if Auto-hide is on). After pressing Ctrl+Esc and then pressing Esc to clear the Start menu, you can press Tab repeatedly to shift the focus to three objects: the Start button, the taskbar, and the current desktop icon. When the taskbar has the focus, you can use the left or right arrow key to move the focus to one of the buttons on the taskbar. The button with the focus has a sunken look. If you want to bring it to the top, press Enter or the spacebar.

The old technique of pressing **Alt+Tab** to switch tasks is not only available but also improved. A window pops up in the middle of the screen. The next program's name appears. All the icons representing the launched programs also appear above the name. The next program's icon is also enclosed in a rectangle. If you release the keys, the targeted program will become active. You can hold down Alt and press Tab to cycle forward or Shift+Tab to cycle backward. When the desired program is shown, release the keys to move there. If you want no switch, press Esc while still holding down Alt; the window will disappear and you'll be returned to the original window.

Another way to switch tasks is to use Task Manager. Use Explorer, My Computer, or Start | Run to run the TASKMAN.EXE file located in the WINDOWS directory. All the launched programs are shown here (Figure 0.16). You can click one to quickly make it active. You can make this window appear in different ways. You can also choose an option to make it go away when not active or always stay on top.

Figure 0.16   The Task Manager window

THE ONLINE HELP

Windows 95 comes with a comprehensive online help system, which has replaced
the traditional printed manual. A similar system is also used in VB4 and other
Windows-compatible programs. Once you master this system, you can quickly
learn to use the others.

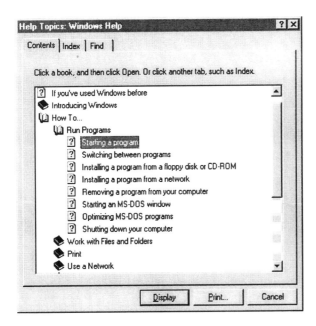

Figure 0.17   The online help's Contents tab

There are many ways to access the online help. Each open window has a Help
menu. Clicking this menu leads to two options: Help Topics and About Windows
95. The later shows copyright and license information, plus available memory.

Before you run another program, you might want to see how much memory you have left.

The Help menu's **Help Topics** leads to Figure 0.17. There are three tabs. The one previously used will appear here. So your display may be different.

The **Contents tab** shows a list of items each of which consists of an icon and a label. An icon may be one of the following three:

?	Help topic
Closed book	Closed category; double-click to open
Open book	Open category; double-click to close

You can click a question mark to show that help topic. If the desired help topic doesn't appear, double-click a closed-book icon to open it; the icon changes to an open-book icon and a list appears below. If you double-click an open-book icon, it changes to a closed-book icon and the list below is cleared.

There is also a ? button at the top right corner. This is known as the **What's This?** command. Click it and a ? follows the mouse pointer. You can then click any area of the dialog box to show a short popup help message. You can also right-click an area and the "What's This?" menu may pop up. Clicking it also shows the same help message.

When the desired topic (with the ? icon) is displayed, you can click it and then click Display to show it; you can double-click it to do the same thing. You can also click Print to print a hardcopy.

Figure 0.17   An online help topic

Figure 0.18 appears after displaying the topic highlighted in Figure 0.17; the Help Topics dialog also disappears. You can click the Help Topics button in the new window to bring it back. You can also click Back to show the preceding topic; this button is dimmed if there is no previous topic to show.

A help topic may include terms marked with a dotted underline. When you point to it, the pointer changes to a hand; you can click it to show a popup definition. The bottom of the window may also show a square icon telling you that there are related topics. Click it if you want to know more. This may lead to another topic or a dialog box showing multiple items for you to make a choice.

There is a control menu marked with a ? at the top left of the window. You can open it to do a number of things to the window. You can, however, just use the mouse to move or resize the window, or use the buttons at the top-right corner to manage the window.

You can use the Options menu to do more things. It has these options:

> Annotate
> Copy
> Print Topic
> Font
> Keep Help on Top
> Use System Colors

Annotate opens up the Annotate dialog box to let you enter or delete a message. An annotated topic has a green paper-click icon added to the left of the title. Clicking this icon opens the Annotate dialog box to show the message. After the message is deleted from this box, the paper-click icon will disappear.

Copy puts the topic in the Clipboard. You can then paste it to another application. The Clipboard will be explained more in another section below. If you want to copy only a portion, drag the pointer to highlight the desired portion before choosing Copy.

Print Topic opens up the Print dialog box. You can then change a number of settings and then choose OK to print or Cancel to abort.

You can use the last three options to customize the display: **Font** to use smaller or larger font sizes to display a topic, **Keep Help on Top** to specify its position against other windows, and **Use System Colors** to use the default color or the system color you might have set (using the Display Properties dialog box).

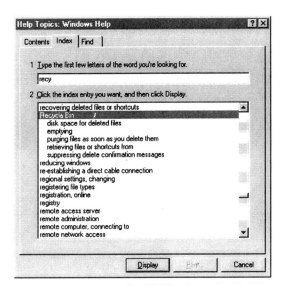

Figure 0.18   The online help's Index tab

The **Index tab** leads to Figure 0.18. The cursor stays in the top text box for you to type the beginning letters of the help topic you want. As you type, the large list box will change to reflect your search string and the matching item will be highlighted. You can also use PgDn, PgUp, or the scroll bar to scroll the list. When you find the desired one, double-click it or click it and click Display. If multiple topics are available, the Topics Found dialog box will appear for you to select one from the list. The displayed topic window may be the same as the one shown from the Contents tab. You can handle it the same as explained before.

The **Find tab** provides another way to search for desired topics. It searches relevant Help files for topics with a word that matches your search string. You type a string at the top. As you type, the bottom two boxes continue to change to show matching entries. The label at the bottom left also shows the number of matching topics. You can reduce the number of matching topics by clicking a matching word shown in the middle text box. Figure 0.19 shows the result after typing the word in the top box and clicking the highlighted item in the middle box. The matching topics are narrowed down to 6. If you double-click one here, its topic window will show up.

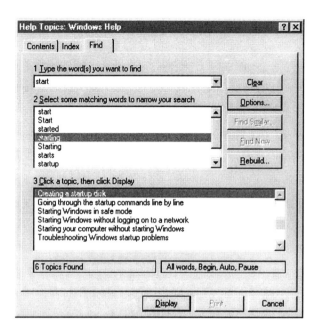

Figure 0.19   The online help's Find tab

You can use the Clear button to clear the search string in the top box, the Options button to change various settings or use another file, and the Rebuild button to do more customizing.

You can choose some topics to display video clips to have a demonstration combining some simple sounds and motions. Some may require the presence of the CD-ROM to play the clips.

From the Explorer or My Computer window (see below), you can double-click a file with the HLP (help) or AVI (audiovisual) extension to open the online help or play a video clip.

If you are still confused, you can use Help to help you. From the Contents tab, open the How To book, and then open the Use Help book. Six topics then become available; they tell you how to use this system.

WINDOWS EXPLORER

Windows **Explorer** is the replacement for File Manager available in previous versions. You can use it to manage files, disks, and folders; you can also use it to run programs.

The most straightforward way to open the Explorer window is to choose Start | Programs | Windows Explorer. The resulting display depends on the mode previously set. You can use the View menu to make a choice among: Large Icons, Small Icons, List, and Details. The last option displays most information, as shown in Figure 0.20. The other options result in less cluttered displays and may make navigation easier. These options can also be accessed by the buttons on the toolbar.

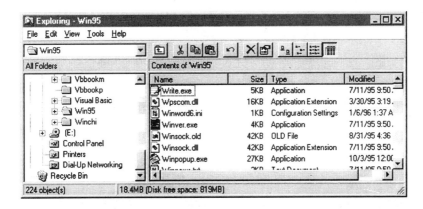

Figure 0.20   The Explorer window

If you want to explore a particular object, such as a drive, select it in the My Computer window and choose File | Explore. The Explore window opens and the title bar shows the object (drive in our example) being explored.

The Explorer window is divided into two panes. The left pane shows a directory tree, with the current directory shown as an open folder. The right pane displays the contents of the open folder. The divider line between the two panes can be changed by dragging it to the left or right to widen one side at the expense of the other. The right pane's title bar has divider lines. You can also drag these to control the width of each column.

The left pane clearly shows how many drives your system has, how many folders are in each drive, and how various units are related to one another. If there are many units, a scroll bar will automatically appear. You can scroll the items up and down to see how they are related.

If a drive or folder has subunits, it is marked on the left by a + (collapsed) or - (expanded) sign. Click the + to expand (display) its subunits; click the - to collapse (hide) them. Clicking a + does not display a folder's contents in the right pane.

When a desired drive or folder is scrolled to view in the left pane, you can click it to show its contents in the right pane. If the right pane contains a folder which you want to open, just double-click it. The folder name will appear in the left pane and its contents in the right pane.

If **View** | **Details** is chosen, the right pane appears in four columns: Name, Size, Type, and Modified. You can click a column heading to sort by that column. Clicking the same heading another time reverses the previous order. Figure 0.20 shows the names sorted in reverse order.

You can use **View** | **Status Bar** to add or remove the status bar at the bottom. The status bar shows some useful information and instructions. It also takes up extra space; removing it gives you more display room.

You can use **View** | **Toolbar** to show or hide the toolbar near the top. It includes the Look-in box on the left and 11 icons on the right. When Toolbar is checked in the View menu, these items appear; otherwise, they are not displayed. You can use the Look-in box (click inside the box or the down arrow) to make another drive or folder current. You can also use the Up One Level icon next to it to move up the directory path.

You can use **View** | **Refresh** to display the new contents after you replace a disk in a floppy drive. You can also press F5 to do the same thing.

The **File** | **New** command leads to the same options as the New command from the shortcut menu when you right-click the desktop. This was explained earlier.

The **File** | **Delete** command does the same thing as pressing Del on the keyboard; it will delete selected files or folders. The **File** | **Rename** command is not necessary. You can click a name twice (not double click) to edit it.

File | **Properties** shows an object's property sheet (you can select and object and press Alt+Enter to bring up this sheet). When the object is a drive, you can show the used and unused disk space. If the object is a file or folder, various related attributes appear. Figure 0.21 shows a file's property sheet. You can check pertinent check boxes to make this file hidden (not visible) or read-only (can't be deleted).

You can use **File | Open** to run the selected file; you can double-click the file to do the same thing. An executable file will run without opening a document. A data file, on the other hand will do both.

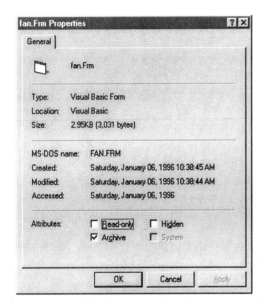

Figure 0.21   A file's property sheet

You can use **View | Options** to customize Explorer's display, including hiding certain system files, associating a data file with a program file, and enabling Quick View. More details will be available later.

You can use **File | Send To** to copy the selected file(s) to a floppy drive. You can then designate a target drive to start copying.

MY COMPUTER/CONTROL PANEL

My Computer is an icon placed on the desktop during installation. It is a special folder used to manage your system. It contains drive icons and some special folders created during installation. No shortcut or user-created folder is permitted here. This rule does not apply when you branch from the My Computer folder to another drive or folder. My Computer can be used to manage files, folders, or hardware devices.

As a file manager, My Computer shares major similarities and minor differences with Explorer. The Explorer window's title bar shows *Exploring* followed by an object such as a drive or folder name; My Computer just shows the object. Explorer has two panes; My Computer has only one (right) pane. Explorer has an additional menu named Tools with two options: Find and Go To. The latter lets you open a new folder. The former lets you search for matching files or folders. Other than these superficial differences, the two share the basic tools to manage drives, files, and folders.

By default, My Computer displays its contents as large icons, in contrast to Explorer's showing details. You can use the toolbar or the View menu to change the display. You can even make My Computer behave like Explorer. When you select a drive or folder and open the File menu, the Explore option will appear; the same thing happens when you right-click a drive or folder. If you choose Explore, an Explorer window will open up to show the contents of the drive or folder. If you want a quicker way, click the drive or folder to select it and then hold down Shift and double-click the object.

If you want to make My Computer behave like Explorer by default, follow these steps:

1. From My Computer, choose View | Options | File Types.

2. Scroll the list of types to Folder and click it.

3. Click the Edit button, and the Edit File Type dialog box appears. Two options (explore and open) are shown in the middle box and the second option is bolded.

4. Click the Set Default button and *explore* will be bolded and moved to the top of *open*.

5. Close all the open dialog boxes.

If you now right-click a drive or folder, the Explore option will be bolded and moved to the top of the list, exchanging place with Open. Explore has now replaced Open as the default-action option. If you now double-click a drive or folder, Explorer will appear. If you close My Computer and then double-click it,

Explorer will open and the window's caption becomes "Exploring - My Computer." If you want to open a window in the style of My Computer, choose Open from the File or shortcut menu. If you want to restore the default, follow the above steps and in step 4 change *explore* to *open*. If you follow the above steps when you were in Explorer to begin with, Explorer would not be affected but the future behavior of My Computer would.

One major difference between My Computer and Explorer is that My Computer tends to multiply. By default when you open a new drive or folder, a new window will open up. Having multiple windows open is useful if you want to compare drive or folder contents. You can also easily drag and drop objects.

If you want to use the same window to display another drive or folder—the way Explorer behaves, click an object to select it, then hold down Ctrl and double-click it. Clicking the Up One Level button will open that window without closing the existing one. To use the same window, hold down Ctrl and click the Up One Level button. If you want to make one window the default, choose View | Options. The Options dialog box shows these two options:

> Browse folders using a separate window for each folder.
> Browse folders by using a single window that changes as you open each folder.

The first option is checked by default. If you change it to the second option, opening another drive or folder will not open another window.

If you have multiple folder windows open, you can hold down Shift and click the last window's X (Close) button to close all of them. This trick doesn't work with multiple Explorer windows, as explained below.

Holding down Shift and double-clicking a drive or folder may open multiple Explorer windows. If you do that when the double-clicked object is not the current (selected) object, all the objects from it to the current object will be selected and all their Explorer windows will appear; this may take a long time. Holding down Shift and clicking the last window doesn't close previous Explorer windows; you'll have to close each individually.

From either My Computer or Explorer, you can use the View | Options | View tab to display or hide some system files. By default all files are displayed. When you show a file's property sheet, you can change its attributes. You can set some attributes to make a file unchangeable (read-only) or invisible (hidden).

As a folder, My Computer is the top level folder. If you click the Up One Level icon (or press the Backspace key) when the title bar shows My Computer, you'll get an error message telling you that. Keep in mind that My Computer is not the same as the root directory; it doesn't appear when you issue the DOS DIR command. By contrast, there is a DESKTOP directory which is a subdirectory of the WINDOWS directory; it stores the shortcut files appearing on the desktop.

You learned in an earlier section that you can right-click the desktop and choose Properties to display the **Display Properties** window; you can then customize the screen display. You can right-click the My Computer icon or an empty area in the My Computer window and choose Properties to show the **System Properties** window. You can use this window to show and change many hardware settings. What you see here overlaps with the information shown in the Control Panel (see below).

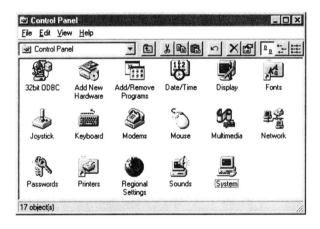

Figure 0.22   The Control Panel

The **Control Panel** icon is put in the My Computer folder during installation. You can double-click it to open the Control Panel window (Figure 0.22); you can do the same thing by choosing Start | Settings | Control Panel. Here you can change many hardware settings. For example, you can double-click the Mouse icon to open its property sheet. You can then change many default values such as switching the left and right buttons or choosing a new icon for the mouse pointer. Does your keyboard behave sluggishly? Open the Keyboard property sheet and change its repeat rate from slow to fast. Do you want to add or remove the installed accessories, or install a new application? Just use Add/Remove Programs and follow the instructions.

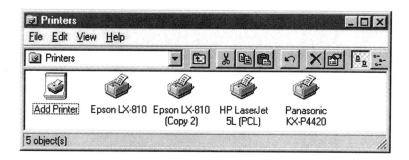

Figure 0.23   The Printers window

The My Computer window has a folder named **Printers**. A shortcut for it is also placed in the Control Panel window. Double-clicking either opens the Printers window (Figure 0.23). All the installed printers appear here. You can open a printer's property sheet to change its properties. You can also double-click each printer to open a window and do many things, such as designating one as the default printer.

If a printer doesn't work properly (its definition file may be corrupted) or if you want to install a new printer, open the Add Printer folder from the Printers window. This activates the Add Printer Wizard that guides you through a series of steps to create a new printer definition file. You can select a printer name from the internal list of the available options or supply a file provided by your printer's vendor. This process will create a file that will control how your printer should behave.

The settings in a printer window will be communicated to your application. When you print something from the application, the settings will apply. If your application doesn't print output properly, you might want to adjust the settings made in the printer's window.

If you want to print a document while doing something else, just drag the document file to the printer icon or window. If there is no problem, printing will begin. If printing is not possible, various messages will appear for you to take corrective actions.

FINDING FILES

If you vaguely remember that you have a file with a fuzzy name but you don't know its exact name and where you stored it, you can ask Windows to find it for you. You can even try to find files that contain a person's name or a specific text string.

To open the Find dialog box, try any command below:

> Start | Find | Files or Folders (taskbar)
> Tools | Find | Files or Folders (Explorer)
> File | Find (My Computer)

When you are in My Computer or Explorer, you can right-click a drive or folder. The resulting shortcut menu will include the Find option.

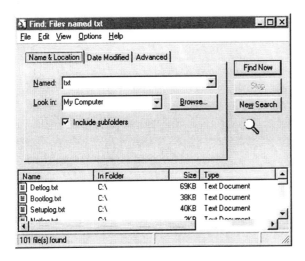

Figure 0.24   **Finding files and folders**

After the Find dialog box (Figure 0.24) opens, you can enter a partial file name and click Find Now to start. If you enter nothing or *.* in the Named box, you intend to display all files. You can specify a pattern, such as *.EXE to show only the files with the EXE extension. If you enter multiple words separated by spaces and/or commas, Windows will try to find file or folder names matching any one of the words. The strings you enter here will be stored for future use. You can click the down arrow to show them and select one to reuse it

You can keep the check mark to search all subfolders or uncheck it to limit the search to the current folder. You can use the Look-in box to go to another drive or to My Computer. If you select My Computer, the search target is the entire system. You can use the Browse button to specify a drive or a folder. You can use the New Search button to clear the previous entries and search results; you can then start a new search. If you want a search to be case sensitive, choose Options | Case Sensitive to check it; choose it another time if you want to uncheck it.

Figure 0.24 shows that we want to search all drives (and folders) for files whose names contain the TXT string. Matching files appear at the bottom box; if no match is found, this box will remain empty. The number of matching files is also shown below this box.

You can use the other two tabs to do more exotic searches. Use Date Modified to limit the search to a date range. Use Advanced to search for a specific file type (such as a spreadsheet or a database) or files containing a specified text string.

If you want to find files containing a text string, in the Name and Location tab, enter nothing in the Named box and a directory path in the Look-in box; in the Advanced tab, keep All Files and Folders in the Of-type box and a search string in the Containing-text box; and finally click Find Now.

You can save the search pattern alone or in combination with the found files. To do the former, choose File | Save Search. To do the latter, choose Options | Save Results to check it and then choose File | Save Search. A new desktop icon will appear. It may have a name like "Files named txt.fnd" If you keep saving, a sequential number will be added to each subsequent file name to distinguish one file from another. When you double-click such a file, the Find window will open and any previously entered search name and found files will appear. You can then click Find Now to update the old list.

If you want to do something with a found file, right-click it to open the shortcut menu; you can also select one or more files and choose the File menu to show a similar menu. If you double-click a file, it opens—together with any associated application when a data file is involved.

FILE ASSOCIATION AND QUICK VIEW

You can associate a data file with a program file for two purposes: editing and viewing. After a data file is associated with a program for editing, you can double-click the data file (or select the file and choose File | Open) to open both simultaneously. If a file is associated for viewing, you can view its contents from Windows without opening the file.

Many file types have by default been associated with applications for editing. For example, if you double-click a file with the XLS extension (or choose File | Open from My Computer or Explorer), Excel will open and the data file will be retrieved at the same time. When a file is already associated, the shortcut menu has the **Open** option at the top; the File menu also has the Open option. An executable file always has the Open option. (The Open option is usually bolded. That means when you double-click an object, this option will by default be executed.)

Figure 0.25   **The Open With dialog box**

If you right-click a data file and the shortcut menu shows **Open With** at the top of the options, this file has not been associated with an application. If you choose Open With, the Open With dialog box (Figure 0.25) appears for you to select an application from a list; if the list doesn't include the desired application, use the Other button to find it. If the two match, both will then open; otherwise, an error will appear. A check box near the bottom lets you determine whether you want to make this association permanent or temporary. If you make a permanent association, the file type will be registered and entered into the list in Figure 0.26. Windows uses an extension name to identify a file type for association. So a data file with no extension cannot be associated with any program file.

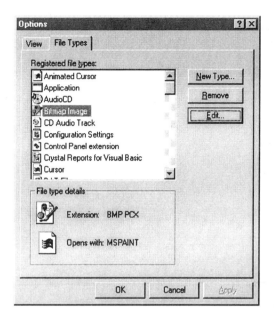

Figure 0.26   The View | Options | File Types tab

You can also use the **View | Options | File Types** tab to make or change a permanent association. There are three buttons: Edit, Remove, and New Type. Use Edit to edit an existing entry, Remove to remove an existing entry, and New to create a new entry. As you click an existing entry in the middle list box, the bottom shows the icons and file names for both data and application. Figure 0.26 shows MSPAINT associated with BMP and PCX files. So if you double-click either file type from Find, My Computer, or Explorer, Paint and the data file will open.

If you want to edit an existing entry, click it in the middle list box and then click the Edit button. A dialog box (Figure 0.27) appears. Click an item shown in the middle list box and then click Edit. Another dialog box will appear with the existing entry for you to make changes; you can use the Browse button to look for a program file. You can use Remove to remove the selected entry or Add to add a new entry. Use **Set Default** to set the selected item for the default action. The default item, usually Open, is bolded. When you double-click an object from My Computer or Explorer, the default option is executed; if you set another option here as the default, that option will be executed instead.

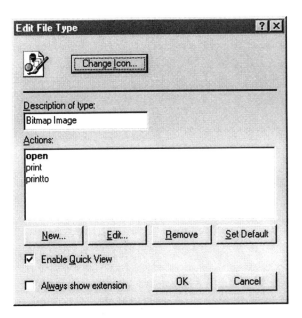

Figure 0.27   Editing file type to associate files

If you choose New Type from Figure 0.26, Figure 0.27 will appear but without any existing entry. Here you can establish a new association of your own. If you are lost, use some existing entries as examples. You can also use the ? button to tell you what each button is for.

Notice the **Enable Quick View** check mark at the bottom left in Figure 0.27. When this is checked, you can use the Quick View feature to view a file's contents. In our example, if we right-click a BMP or PCX file, the shortcut (and File) menu will include the Quick View option. If you don't see this option, it is probably not installed.

To install Quick View, follow these steps:

1. Open the Control Panel from My Computer or from Start | Settings.

2. Double-click the Add/Remove Programs icon; the Add/Remove Programs Properties window opens.

3. Choose the Windows Setup tab.

4. Select Accessories (don't uncheck it) and click the Details button; the Accessories window opens.

5. Scroll to Quick View and check it.

6. Click OK and then OK.

Quick View is now installed. If you right-click some files in the Explorer or My Computer window, Quick View should become available.

Some files are by default Quick View-enabled, but some are not. Included in the latter are Visual Basic form and project files. If you want to use Quick View to view these files, you need to enable them by using the View | Options | File Types | Edit dialog box, as shown in Figure 0.27.

NOTE   If you take the necessary steps to enable Visual Basic data files, you can use Quick View to read an enabled file from inside Visual Basic. When you use Visual Basic to open or save a file, you can right-click a file and choose Quick View to read it. If a file has not been enabled, the Quick View option is not available.

When a file is Quick View-enabled, you can right-click it and then choose Quick View to view it. If you want to open it, choose Open File for Editing from Quick View's File menu. If you've closed the Quick View window, you can double-click a file name to run the pertinent program and open the selected file for editing at the same time.

You can open two or more Quick View windows to view multiple files. This is useful if you want to compare the contents of multiple files. Each time you choose Quick View, a new window opens to show the selected file. Unless you close it, it remains open as you open more windows or do other things.

Quick View's File menu has the Open File for Editing option; this option is also available from the shortcut menu. Choosing this option closes the Quick View window and opens the associated application together with the data file.

When a Quick View window is open, you can drag a displayed file name to the window to show its contents, replacing any existing display. You can use this technique to quickly view a large number of graphics files (those with BMP or WMF extensions). If a file you drag has not been connected to any viewer program, a message appears asking whether you want to use the default viewers. If you choose Yes, the resulting display may be perfectly clear. If Quick View cannot find a matching viewer, the result may be nothing or very little.

If you want to open a data file with an application other than the associated one, select the file by clicking it and then hold down Shift and right-click it; you can also hold down Shift and click the File menu. This leads to Open and Quick View, plus the Open With option; this last option is not available if you just right-click a file. You can use Open With to use another application to open this file for this time. In the Open With dialog box, you can check the *Always use this program to open this type of file* check box; this will permanently change the previous association.

SYSTEM ISSUES

This section briefly addresses a number of system issues. They may concern you if you use your PC in an unconventional way or have installed multiple operating systems or use multiple VB versions. In the discussion below, Win 3 refers to Windows 3.x, Win 95 to Windows 95, and VB3 and VB4 to respective Visual Basic versions.

When you install Win 95, you are given an option to replace Win 3 or put Win 95 in a separate directory without replacing Win 3. If you follow the second path, you have an option of running Win 3 or Win 95.

After Win 95 is installed, running your system will automatically boot Win 95, unless you intercept. If you press F5 before Win 95 is booted, a dialog box will appear. You can choose to go to the DOS command line. When the command line appears, you can then run a batch file or go to the old Win 3 directory to run Win 3. From there you can run VB3 and other programs. If Win 95 is booted, you can run VB3 or VB4 from there.

The choices available at startup depends on the **MSDOS.SYS** file. This is an ASCII file created during installation. It determines various initial booting options. It is located in the booting drive's root directory. You can open it with Notepad (or the DOS Editor) and make changes. To open it, right-click it from My Computer or Explorer and choose Open With from the shortcut menu, and then choose Notepad from the ensuing dialog box.

To exit Win 95, click Start and then Shut Down. Choose an option from the list. You can then go to the DOS command line or a complete shutdown. If you go to the command line, you can go to the old Win 3 directory (if any) and enter WIN to run Win 3 from there. After you exit Win 3, you can go to the Win 95 directory and enter WIN to run Win 95. This technique allows you to switch between Win 3 and Win 95.

If an application locks up and won't let you do anything, you can close it without shutting down the entire system. To do that, just press **Ctrl+Alt+Del** (hold down the first two and press the last). The **Close Program** dialog box pops up. The middle box lists all the applications in memory, with the current application shown at the top and highlighted; you can select an item here and click a button to do something. There are three buttons: End Task, Shut Down, and Cancel. Use End Task to end (exit) the current task (application), Shut Down to exit Windows, and Cancel to return to the current task. If the current task is not frozen, End Task simply exits the application and closes its window. If it's frozen, another dialog box appears to tell you what's wrong and let you exit. Exiting one application doesn't affect the others still running. You may lose data in the frozen application, but the others remain alive and well; this situation would have required exiting Windows in the past.

NOTE   You can still exit Windows by using Alt+F4. This key combination will normally close the current window. When the desktop has the focus, however, it will shut down Windows by presenting the Shut Down Windows dialog box (Figure 0.4).

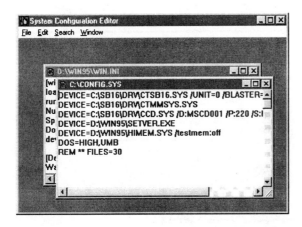

Figure 0.28   The System Configuration Editor

Besides the MSDOS.SYS file mentioned earlier, you can edit a number of other files to fine-tune your system—if you know what you are doing. If you want to edit configuration files, choose Start | Run and enter **SYSEDIT**. Figure 0.28 appears. All the system INI files, plus CONFIG.SYS and AUTOEXEC.BAT are open for you to edit. If you don't want to edit any particular file, just click its Close (X) button. If you want to edit a particular file, just go to its window and make necessary changes. When you click the X button to close, you'll be prompted to save the new file. You need considerable technical savvy before you venture to tinker with these files.

If you are technically savvy and spiritually venturesome, you can edit the registry. Choose Start | Run and enter REGEDIT. The **Registry Editor** (Figure 0.29) appears. As in the Explorer window, you can click + or - to collapse or expand a folder. When the desired folder is found, click it to show its default values in the right pane. If you want to change an item, double-click a displayed name in the right pane. A dialog box appears for you to make changes. Changes made here are saved to two database files named USER.DAT and SYSTEM.DAT; these files are routinely updated to store the current settings. They have the hidden and read-only attributes to discourage tinkering from outside. These files should not be tampered with unless you know what you are doing. If you mess up these files, Windows may not run at all.

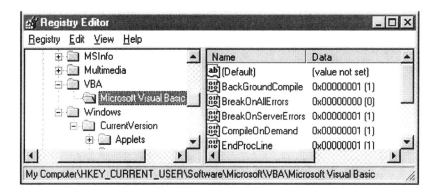

Figure 0.29   The Registry Editor

CLIPBOARD INTERACTION

Windows maintains a memory area called the **Clipboard**. You can use it to cut or copy a picture or block of text to it. Cutting means deleting the involved object and sending a copy to the Clipboard; copying sends a copy to the Clipboard without deleting it from the current document. You can then paste the Clipboard's contents to another (or the same) document as many times as you wish. Each time you send something to the Clipboard, the old one is erased.

To demonstrate how the Clipboard behaves, follow these steps:

1. Open the Clipboard Viewer by choosing Start | Programs | Accessories | Clipboard Viewer. Figure 0.30 appears.

2. Open the My Computer window if it's not already open.

3. Press **Alt+Print Screen** to capture the current window.

A picture (bitmap graphic) of the My Computer window now appears in the Clipboard Viewer window. You can maximize the Clipboard Viewer window to have a better view.

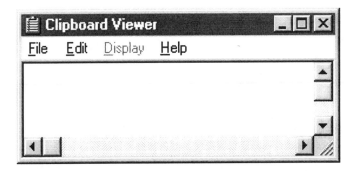

Figure 0.30   Clipboard Viewer

If you want to capture the whole screen, press **Print Screen** instead. The new screen capture will replace the old. If you want to capture a document window, maximize it to fill up the application window before pressing Alt+Print Screen.

To send a block of text to the Clipboard, select the desired text lines and choose Cut or Copy from the Edit menu. Every Windows application, including WordPad and Notepad, has these items. To paste the Clipboard contents, go to the desired application window and choose Paste from the Edit menu.

Clipboard Viewer's File menu has these three options:

Open
Save As
Exit

Open leads to the Open dialog box. All the files with the CLP extension will also be displayed. You can then select one to open. Save As is used to save the

Clipboard's contents to a file with the CLP extension. You can then open it to the Clipboard to view or paste to another application.

The Edit menu has only one option, namely Delete. It lets you clear the Clipboard. You can also press Del to do the same thing. A Yes/No prompt will appear to get your consent.

The Display menu becomes available when the Clipboard is not empty. It has Auto as its first and default (checked) option. Depending on the type of contents (text, picture, or screen capture), other options will become available to let you choose a display type.

The Clipboard can be used to transfer data to and from a DOS application. That will be covered in the next section.

WINDOWS AND DOS

Windows 95 has new capabilities to handle DOS programs. It's more nimble than its predecessor. If you don't use an old program, you have no use for the discussion in this section. But if you do, you should pay close attention here.

To go to the DOS screen, choose Start | Programs | MS-DOS Prompt. The DOS command prompt appears. Depending on what you did before, you may be placed in a window or in full screen; you can press **Alt+Enter** to toggle between the two modes. You can now enter any DOS command you wish. If you want to do something to a file with a shortened name including the ~ character, just type the names as shown on the screen. You can also go to a proper directory and run a DOS application. When you exit that application, you are returned to this DOS command prompt. To return to Windows, just type **Exit** and press Enter.

If you are an old DOS hand and want to use the familiar DOS commands, you can still find them in the WINDOWS\COMMAND directory. Most, but not all, of the old DOS commands are put here during installation. You may also find the previous version's commands stored in another directory. If you need help, the HELP command is still available; you can also use the /? parameter to show an individual help.

The EDIT command (DOS Editor) is still available. It now shows long file names. So you can open ASCII files with long names, just as in Notepad.

On the DOS command line, you can type a file name to run a program. You can also precede it with the **START** command. This new command can run both DOS and Windows programs (or folders). It can be put in a batch file to start multiple programs.

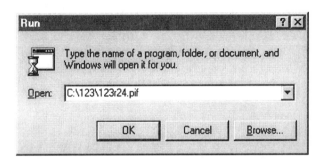

Figure 0.31   The Run dialog box

Another way to run a DOS application is to use Start | Run. The Run dialog box (Figure 0.31) appears. You can click the down arrow to show all the programs previously run this way. You can also use Browse to find the desired program. You can run a file with the EXE or **PIF** (program information file) extension. When you exit the application, you'll return to Windows rather than the DOS command prompt as in the previous situation.

Windows uses a PIF file to manage a DOS application. In previous Windows versions, a PIF editor was provided to PIF files, where you specify the conditions for running the DOS application in the Windows environment. PIF files still exist, but not the PIF editor.

To create or modify a PIF file, you use a program file's property sheet. Suppose you want to run 123.EXE (Lotus 1-2-3). When you find this file in Find, My Computer, or Explorer, right-click it to pop up the shortcut menu. Then choose Properties. You can do the same thing with a file with the PIF extension, if one exists. But this extension is usually not shown in the display box, so 123.PIF appears only as 123. Either way will lead to the same result, namely creating or changing the PIF file.

If you use a DOS application often, you might want to create a shortcut and place it on the desktop. You can do it by dragging an EXE or PIF file to the desktop. Regardless of which file you drag, a PIF file will be created, in contrast to a

normal shortcut file having the LNK extension. The icon, though, contains the
typical bent arrow pointing to the upper right.

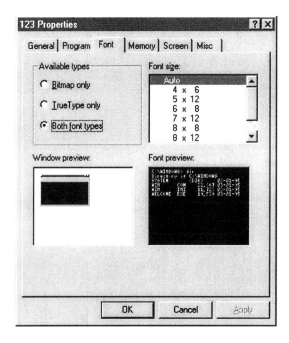

Figure 0.32   A DOS application's property sheet

As shown in Figure 0.32, a DOS application's property sheet has six tabs. The
General tab has the usual information like any other file. The Program tab lets
you specify various ways of running the application. The Font tab can be used to
specify the display; as you make changes, the bottom shows preview screens. The
Memory tab lets you specify memory amounts for various purposes; the default
Auto settings here can be changed if you know what you are doing.

You can use the Screen tab to choose between running the application in a
window or in full screen. Most large DOS applications won't run or run
sluggishly in a window, so full screen is usually the better choice.

You can use the Misc tab to, among other things, enable or disable the common
Windows keystrokes. These keystrokes are enabled by default. That means you
can still use the keystrokes discussed earlier to do task switching. You need these
keys more than ever when you run a DOS application in full screen because the
taskbar is not available. The following keys are most useful:

Alt+Tab	Pops up a window to let you switch to another application.
Ctrl+Esc	Pops up the Start menu and displays the taskbar.
Alt+Enter	Switches between window and full-screen modes.

Unless you disable the Alt+Print Screen key in the Misc tab, you can press that key combination in a DOS application to copy the screen text (not graphics) to the Clipboard. You can then paste it to another application.

If you want to do cut/copy and paste between a DOS application and a Windows application, you should switch the DOS application to the window mode (use Alt+Enter to toggle between the two). In this mode, you can click the control box (or press Alt+space bar) to pull down the control menu with additional options, including the following:

     Edit
✓ Toolbar
     Properties

You can use Edit to mark (select) text so that it can be copied. After you choose Edit | Mark, the cursor changes to a different shape. You can then move it to the desired location, hold down Shift, and move the cursor to select text; you can also drag the mouse pointer to highlight (select) text. After text is selected (marked), pull down the control menu and choose Edit | Copy. The text enters the Clipboard. If the Clipboard contains data, choosing Edit shows the Paste option; you can use it to paste data to a DOS application.

NOTE   If you want to use the mouse to do cut and paste between a DOS application and another application (DOS or Windows), click the control menu inside that application and choose Properties; you can also click the Properties button on the toolbar (Figure 0.33). The application's property sheet appears (Figure 0.32). Open the Misc tab and check **QuickEdit** in the Mouse panel (upper right). When you want to copy text, drag the pointer over the text and press Enter; the text enters the Clipboard. You can then go to another application and paste the data. In this mode, the pointer is unsuitable for normal functions such as making a menu selection.

The Toolbar option is checked by default. That means the available toolbar icons are displayed (shown at the top of Figure 0.33). You can point to each to show its tooltip. Unchecking Toolbar will clear the icons. These icons represent various options from the property sheet which you can open by choosing Properties from the control menu. Various settings discussed earlier can be altered here.

Figure 0.33   Running a DOS application in a window

If you want to use **Program Manager** or **File Manager** of **Windows 3.x,** use Start | Run and enter one of the following commands on the command line:

```
progman
winfile
```

A new window with a proper title and maybe subwindows will appear. If you are familiar with these, you already know what to do. If not, there is no need to get into those because you can do more with the new version. If you want to make it convenient to use these oldies, you can drag the file names (PROGMAN.EXE or WINFILE.EXE) from Explorer or My Computer to the desktop to create shortcuts. In the future you can just double-click an icon to open its window.

You can use DOS to manage your disks and files as before. For example, you can delete files or create directories. The new directories you create will show up as folders inside Windows. Deletions made from DOS are removed and not sent to the Recycle Bin.

TIP: Between Long and Short File Names

Old applications allow only short file names limited to 8.3 characters, but Windows 95 allows a long file name up to 255 characters. These two can coexist and you can, if you wish, travel from one world to the other.

If you want to take advantage of the long file name feature on an old application, try to create a new data file on the desktop or in a folder that allows shortcuts. Right-click the desktop or an empty area of the folder window to pop up the shortcut menu and point to **New**. The resulting list of options varies depending on your system. You may find "Microsoft Excel 5.0 Worksheet." Clicking an option like this leads to the creation of a file with a desktop icon. The cursor goes inside the label for you to edit the default label (file name). You can now enter a long file name for an Excel worksheet.

Double-clicking this icon opens Excel. The file name, displayed in the worksheet window's caption, is also shortened to conform to the 8.3 convention. If you save data, it goes to the file you've created. When you double-click this icon next time, Excel opens and the file is retrieved. If you place this file on the desktop, it is saved to the WINDOWS\DESKTOP directory. This is a data file with the XLS extension, not a shortcut file, which has the LNK extension.

When you go to the DOS command line and issue the DIR command, the old short names appear flush left as before, plus a ~ character and a number to signify shortened name and distinguish one name from another similar name. But a new column on the right will show the entire long names.

If the desired file type doesn't appear after you point to New, you can still use a long file name. From My Computer or Explorer, drag the file name to the desktop. This move creates a duplicate in the DESKTOP directory. You can now lengthen the file name by editing the label. If the file has been associated with an application, double-clicking it will open the application and retrieve the file. If not, right-click the icon and use Open With to permanently associate with an application. As explained earlier, a data file needs a unique extension name to permanently associate with an application.

WINDOWS ACCESSORIES

Windows 95 comes with lots of accessories. Most are simple utilities that can do simple jobs. Some are slimmed-down versions licensed from third-party vendors who also market their full versions. Each application (commonly known as applet) tells you who the vendor is.

Most Windows 95 applets can be accessed by choosing **Start | Programs | Accessories**. Thirteen options will pop up. We've discussed some of these options, including Clipboard Viewer and Multimedia. The following sections briefly explain the these options:

    Calculator
    Character Map
    Paint
    Notepad/WordPad
    System Tools

NOTE   Some of the accessories are placed in remote and hard to reach regions of the Windows territory. For example, you need to resort to Start | Programs | Accessories | Games | Solitaire to run this favorite game. If you play this game often, you can move its shortcut to the desktop. Right-click Start and choose Open. Open each subsequent folder (Programs, Accessories, and finally Games) until the Solitaire shortcut appear. Drag it to the desktop. In the future, just double-click this shortcut to start the game.

Calculator

Calculator simulates an electronic calculator, actually two. Figure 0.34 shows the standard calculator and Figure 0.35 the scientific calculator. You can choose either option from the View menu. You can turn on your PC's Num Lock and use the numeric keys to enter numbers into the display window; you can also click the digit buttons to do the same. You can also use the Edit menu to do copy and paste. If you are serious, use the Help menu to learn more.

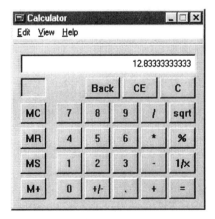

Figure 0.34   A regular calculator

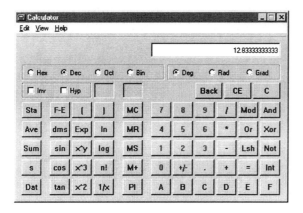

Figure 0.35 **A scientific calculator**

Character Map

You can use **Character Map** (Figure 0.36) to insert special characters into your document. Each font has its own unique set of characters; when you select a new font, a new set will appear. From the Font combo box (top left) you can pull down a list of fonts and select one to show a new set.

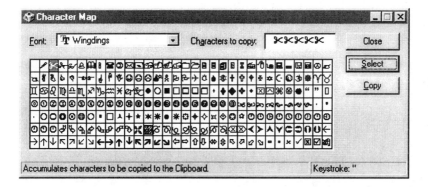

Figure 0.36 **Character Map**

After a desired font is shown, you can double-click a character to copy it to the top-right box. You can also click one and then click Select. You can select as many characters as you desire. You can even go to the top-right text box and type keyboard keys to show their corresponding characters. If you wish, you can delete characters in this box.

You can hold down the left mouse button to magnify the current character. You can hold down the left mouse button and move the pointer around to show any character in magnified state. You can also use an arrow key from the keyboard to do the same thing.

After you make selections, click Copy to send them to the Clipboard. Go to your program (a word processor, maybe). Select the same font. Then paste the characters. If you did not select the same font, the pasted characters may be different from those you have previously selected.

Each time you click a displayed character, the right side of the status bar shows the corresponding keyboard key. When you select the same font in your application, pressing this key will insert the corresponding character in your document.

Paint

Paint, formerly known as Paintbrush, is a simple painting program. It can create or modify bitmap graphics. You can use File | Open to retrieve a file with the BMP extension. You can also draw something and then save a file with that extension. The tools are shown on the left. You can point to each button and a tooltip will appear. The Help menu can provide lots of help.

You can use Paint to view bitmaps. After it's open, use My Computer or Explorer to go to the BITMAPS folder to show all the bitmap files. You can drag any of them to Paint's drawing area to copy the picture. If the default display is too small, use View | Zoom | Large Size (or Custom) to enlarge it. Figure 0.37 shows the enlarged BEANY.BMP file.

If you've enabled Quick View to view a BMP file, you can choose it from the shortcut menu to view a bitmap file. After the viewer is open, you can also drag a file to the viewing area to show the picture.

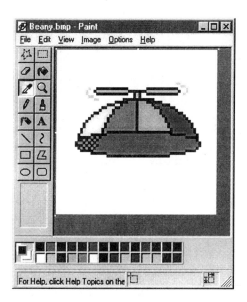

Figure 0.37   Paint

Notepad and WordPad

Notepad (Figure 0.38) is a simple text processor that can be used to edit or create ASCII (ANSI) files. If you need simple formatting features available in most word processors, use **WordPad** (Figure 0.39) instead. This program is a slimmed-down version of Microsoft Word. In either program, you can drag a file from My Computer or Explorer to the editing area to open the file. From WordPad (but not Notepad), you can also select text lines and drag them to the desktop (or another folder) to create a **scrap**, which is actually an OLE file. When you double-click such a scrap in the future, the application will open up and the text will be automatically retrieved.

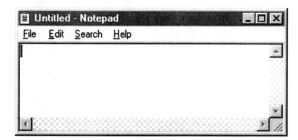

Figure 0.38   Notepad

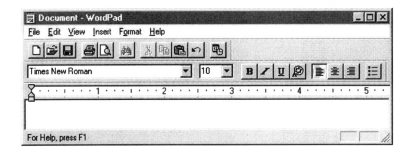

Figure 0.39   WordPad

System Tools and Disk Management

The **System Tools** option from Start | Programs | Accessories leads to a series of tools for you to monitor or fine-tune your system. These tools include:

ScanDisk
Disk Defragmenter
Resource Meter
System Monitor
DriveSpace

You can use **ScanDisk** to scan a disk to see whether its surface has been damaged or whether there are lost clusters. ScanDisk can mark sectors that are not usable so that data will not go there and get lost. It can also erase lost clusters and put them in files with the CHK extension. You might want to examine their contents and possibly salvage some lost data. If they are not readable text, you can erase them.

You can use the **Disk Defragmenter** to defrag a disk. After a disk has been used for sometime, it's likely to be fragmented, with one file scattered in various noncontiguous areas. Such a disk requires more time to read and write. The Disk Defragmenter can bring files together and store them in adjacent areas.

Defragmenting a large disk can take a long time. Fortunately, you can do something else with your computer as the tedious process is going on. A dialog box (Figure 0.40) will show you how much has been done. You can click the Show Details button to show how blocks are moved and rearranged. As your disk continues to make clicking sound, you can switch to another task. If you have a slow PC, your computer may become sluggish at times. After the defragmenting is done, the dialog box will clear away and your hard disk will stop clicking.

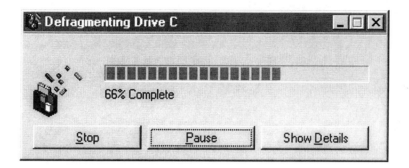

Figure 0.40   Defragmenting a disk

If you want to see how your system is performing, use **Resource Meter** and **System Monitor**. Various graphics will appear. In the case of Resource Meter, a green (safe) or red (danger) icon will be added to the Notification Area (right side of the taskbar); you can point to it to show some numbers. You can double-click it to open a dialog box to graphically show these numbers (Figure 0.41).

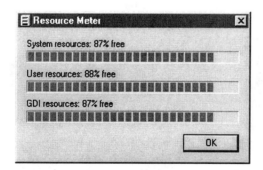

Figure 0.41   Resource Meter

If you need more disk space, use **DriveSpace** to compress files. It leads to Figure 0.42. All the compressible drives in the system appear in the bottom box. You select one and use a menu command to do something. Use the Drive menu to compress or uncompress the drive. Use Advanced to mount/unmount and change settings.

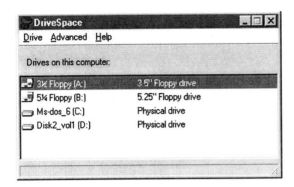

Figure 0.42   DriveSpace

DriveSpace is the successor to DoubleSpace, which was introduced with DOS 6.0. DoubleSpace caused lots of problems. So far there is no report of DriveSpace causing any problem. Depending on file types, DriveSpace could optimally double your disk capacity. The price your pay for that is slower access. If you are serious about squeezing more data into your disk space, you should consider buying Microsoft Plus (about $40), a companion to the Windows 95 package. It has more advanced and automated features to compress your drive further. On the other hand, with hard disk sizes getter ever larger and prices getting ever lower, adding a new drive may be a better alternative.

You can use a property sheet to manage a disk. When a drive is selected in My Computer or Explorer, you can press Alt+Enter or choose Properties from the shortcut menu to open this sheet. This sheet has two tabs when a drive is involved, namely General and Tools. Use the General tab to see available disk space and change the volume label. Use the Tools tab to defrag the disk, scan the disk for error, or back up the data. When you right-click a drive, the shortcut menu include the Format option; you can use it to format a disk (this will erase existing data). If you right-click a floppy drive, an additional Copy Disk option will be available; you can use it to do the equivalent of DOS DISKCOPY.

If you have files or folders you want to copy from one floppy disk to another disk in the same drive, you can select all of them (Ctrl+A or Edit | Select All) and drag them to the desktop. Insert a new disk in the same drive, select all the new items on the desktop, right-click one of the selected items to pop up the shortcut menu, and choose Cut; right-click the target drive and choose Paste. If you drag the selected items from the desktop to the target drive, you'll be copying rather than moving; you'll then have to delete the source files (press Shift+Del to remove them without entering them into the Recycle Bin). Dragging from one folder to another in the same drive will lead to moving, but doing it to another drive will lead to copying. If you right-drag, a shortcut menu will pop up for you to choose Copy, Move, Create Shortcut, or Cancel. If you change your mind in the middle of dragging, press Esc while still holding down the mouse button.

TIP: Comparing Two Floppy Disks

There are occasions when you want to compare two floppy disks of the same type to see whether they are identical. This requires special finesse if you have only one drive of the same type, such as a 3.5-inch drive. This is what you can do:

1. From My Computer, double-click drive A to open a new window. You can also select the drive and then hold down Shift and double-click it to open the drive in the Explorer style. If you wish, go to the folder which you want to compare to the next disk. Resize the window and move it to one side.

2. Insert a new disk in the same drive. Hold down Ctrl or Shift and double-click the selected drive. If you hold down Ctrl, the old window will be replaced with new contents. If you hold down Shift, another Explorer window will open to show the new disk's contents. You can now compare the two windows.

If you just double-click drive A from My Computer, only one window will open. Each time you insert a new disk and double-click the drive, the same window will be used to display the new disk's contents. This is not particularly useful for visual comparison.

If you want to redisplay the first disk, click the first window to select it, insert the first disk in drive A, and press F5 to show its contents. If you want to refresh the second window, select it, insert the second disk, and press F5.

Index for Windows 95

Chapter 1
A Quick Jour

TOPICS

KEY TERMS

Application   A complete collection of visual elements and program code, which constitute a complete program; interchangeably used with *program* or *project*.

Control   A graphical object placed on a form. A control is fetched from the Toolbox to be put on a form. When an application runs, the user can click (or take some other actions to) a control to interact with the application.

Design time   The time when you design a program interface and write program code; different from run time and break time. The Visual Basic title bar shows [design] at design time.

Designer window   A window for designing a form or an ActiveX component. A form appears inside this window. You can then add existing objects to visually design a user interface.

Dockable window   A window that can be attached (docked) to one side of the IDE window. It can also be linked to another dockable window; multiple windows can be linked to become one unit.

Event   An action which a Visual Basic object can recognize. When the user does something, such as clicking an object or pressing a key on the keyboard, the code attached to the object is executed, thus responding to the event.

Event-driven programming   The technique of writing a computer program that will await a user response and react to an event initiated by the user or the system.

Focus   The state in which an object can interact with the user. An object has the focus when it is clicked or tabbed to. It will then respond to pressing keyboard keys or clicking a mouse button. Some objects cannot receive the focus.

Form   A container that holds other objects. A form looks like a peg board at design time and is transformed into a window at run time.

Form Layout window   A window in the IDE which you can use to specify a form's position at run time. You can drag a form inside this window or right-click a form here to pop up a list of options and choose one.

IDE   Integrated Development Environment. Visual Basic's IDE provides a complete set of tools and features for you to develop an application.

Object   A graphical item appearing on the screen when a Windows program runs. An object can be a form, a control, or something concrete such as a printer. Most objects can respond to events.

Procedural programming   The technique of writing a computer program that will, when it runs, execute from top to bottom one line at a time.

Procedure   A subroutine or subprogram that performs a specific task. A procedure is usually attached to an object in order to make the object respond to an event.

Procedure template   Or empty procedure; a procedure containing only the first and last statements. Visual Basic provides a procedure template, but you are required to fill in other statements in between.

Project   A collection of elements to complete an application. At design time, you work on a project. When the project is completed, it becomes an application, which is ready to run. Multiple projects can be combined into a project group.

Project Explorer window   Also called Project window; a window that lists all the elements of the current session, including one or more projects, each of which may include one or more forms and other items.

Properties window   The window usually appearing on the right side of Visual Basic's IDE. You use this window at design time to set the properties (attributes) of objects. When no pertinent object is selected, this window is empty.

Run time   The time when your application is executed; opposite of design time. The Visual Basic title bar shows [run] at run time.

Sizing handles   The solid squares that surround a selected object. When the pointer moves to a sizing handle, it becomes a two-headed arrow. Drag this arrow to increase or decrease the object's size.

Standard EXE   A project to create a standalone executable program. VB5 lets you create several other types of projects. But a novice is most likely to use only Standard EXE projects.

Toolbar   A bar consisting of multiple buttons, each of which represents a menu option. These buttons can be used as shortcuts for menu options. VB5 includes several intrinsic toolbars. You can also create your own custom toolbars. The Standard toolbar contains the most common commands and is displayed by default.

Toolbox   A vertical window usually placed on the left side of Visual Basic's IDE. It contains all the tools available for you to add controls to the current form.

This chapter provides a quick tour of the Visual Basic environment and guides you through the steps of creating some simple applications. You get a bird's-eye view and do not see many details here; later chapters will supply those. If in later chapters you get swamped by too many details, you may want to come back and review this chapter to get a better view of how things fit together.

VISUAL BASIC'S COMPONENTS

Visual Basic contains the following four major components:

- A GUI designer
- A programming language
- A debugger
- An integrated environment

The first component consists of a series of tools which you can use to design and control a graphical user interface (GUI), just like a typical Windows program complete with command buttons, text boxes, scroll bars, and so on. This component has made it much easier to write Windows programs. A programmer no longer needs to write numerous lines of code just to draw a simple window and control its behavior.

The second component resembles any high-level programming language. If you are familiar with Microsoft's Quick Basic or QBasic, this component of Visual Basic will look very familiar to you.

The debugger comes with several windows and tools to help you catch program errors.

The above three components are welded into an integrated development environment (**IDE**) that makes it easy to create programs. You can design an interface, add program code, and debug the program all in the same setting. In this respect, Visual Basic resembles the Quick language series marketed by Microsoft and the Turbo line sold by Borland—except with a GUI designer thrown in.

Visual Basic is thus a complete tool for developing Windows applications. Before you can create an application, you need to be reasonably familiar with the development environment, which will be covered after you learn how to get in and out of Visual Basic.

ENTERING AND EXITING

You can start Visual Basic as you do any Windows program. Any of the following techniques will do:

- Double-clicking a Visual Basic shortcut on the Windows desktop
- Choosing Start | Visual Basic 5
- Choosing Start | Programs | Microsoft Visual Basic 5 | Visual Basic 5
- Choosing Start | Run, and entering a name
- Choosing Start | Documents, and clicking a displayed file name
- Using Start | Find to find Vb5.exe and double-clicking it

You can also launch Visual Basic from My Computer or Windows Explorer. See Chapter 0 for more details.

Figure 1.1   The New Project dialog box

You may see Figure 1.1 after starting Visual Basic. You can check the bottom-left check box and this dialog box will no longer appear in the future. This figure doesn't appear if you are using the **Learning Edition**. In that case, a new Standard EXE project will be created.

The **New Project dialog box** has three options: New, Existing, and Recent. The New tab appears by default, as shown in Figure 1.1. Here are the things you can do:

- Open a new project of the specified type. Double-click one of the displayed icons to start that type of project. As a beginner, you are most likely to choose **Standard EXE** to create a standalone executable program.

- Open an existing project. If you want to open a previously saved project, click the Existing tab and use the resulting dialog box to open a project.

- Open a recently saved project. Use the Recent tab to show the recent projects and then open one from there.

- Open no project. You can click Cancel if you want to open no project; you can open a project later, as explained in a section below.

- Get help. Click Help if you don't know what to do.

After Visual Basic is launched, its name appears on the **taskbar**. You can click this name to make it active—if you have switched to another application. Chapter 0 explains many other tricks which you can use to manage Windows programs.

To exit Visual Basic, choose File | Exit; you can also click the top-right X button to do the same thing. If you have unsaved data, Figure 1.2 appears. If you decide not to exit, click Cancel or X. If you want to save your work, click Yes and enter each required file name; a later section will provide details. If you don't want to save the displayed files, click No. You will then be returned to the Windows desktop.

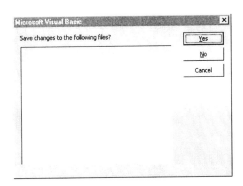

Figure 1.2   Exiting Visual Basic

THE DEVELOPMENT ENVIRONMENT

After you start Visual Basic, the window similar to Figure 1.3 appears. This is Visual Basic's integrated development environment (**IDE**), the place where you develop an application. VB5's IDE has become quite cluttered, jammed with many new features. You need to spend some time getting familiar with this place. Here familiarity will surely breed productivity.

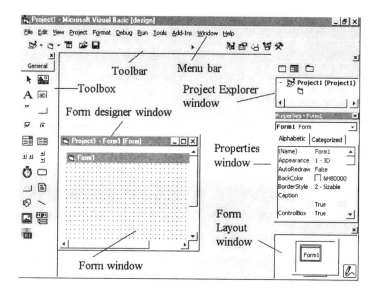

Figure 1.3   Visual Basic's IDE

Figure 1.3 may not resemble your screen. When you exit Visual Basic, the screen arrangement is saved. When you enter Visual Basic the next time, the same arrangement reappears. If your PC is used by multiple persons, as in a school lab, the initial screen you see is the one left by the previous user. If you are thoroughly familiar with the IDE, you won't get lost no matter what the previous user did.

The IDE features an outer window enveloping a series of windows. There are six distinct parts:

- Menu bar and Standard toolbar (top)
- Toolbox (left)
- Designer, form, and Code windows (middle)
- Project Explorer window (top right)

- Properties window (middle right)
- Form Layout window (bottom right)

All the parts except the menu bar are actually windows. Some appear to be attached (docked) to borders or linked to others; they can be detached or unlinked if you wish. Each window has a title bar at the top. All the windows can be moved, resized, or closed. Your screen may thus appear different from what is shown here.

Notice the title bar at the very top. The middle part of the caption shows Microsoft Visual Basic. The right side shows **[design]** at this (design) time. This will be changed to something else in other circumstances. A project name appears on the left. This is the current project's name. If you have several projects in the same session, this tells you which is active (selected).

Below this title bar appears the **menu bar** consisting of a series of menus. A number of menu-related buttons also appear below the menu bar. These are collectively known as a **toolbar**. Several toolbars may appear. The **Standard toolbar** appears by default, as shown in Figure 1.3.

The vertical window on the left is known as the **Toolbox**. It contains the tools from which you can add **controls** (graphical objects) to a form to become parts of your program.

The middle portion is where you do your work. It's occupied by a window with a form inside. This is a **designer window.** If you add another form, a new designer window with a form inside will appear. When you write code, a companion **Code window** will appear. These windows will be discussed more thoroughly in Chapter 2.

The right side of Figure 1.3 shows three windows linked together to form a seamless unit and attached to the right border of the IDE window. The top one is the **Project Explorer window** (or **Project window** for short); it is used to manage one or more projects in the current session and their different components. The **Properties window** in the middle displays the properties (attributes) of a selected object; you can use this window to change properties at design time. The **Form Layout window** at the bottom lets you specify the selected form's location at run time.

Most of the components discussed above can be customized in many ways. The sections below discuss how to do that.

THE MENU BAR

At design time, when you want to give Visual Basic a command to do something, you need to open a menu and choose an option. Visual Basic's menu system consists of the following 11 menus:

File Edit View Project Format Debug Run Tools Add-Ins Windows Help

The **File menu** lets you save files, open files, print files, create executable files, show most recent files (you can click one of these files to open it), and exit Visual Basic.

The **Edit menu** is used for editing text (code); various options become available after you have selected or deleted text. If you are familiar with any Microsoft text editor, such as the DOS Editor and Windows Notepad or WordPad, you already know how to use this menu and edit text.

The **View menu** has options for you to view/hide different components of the IDE. If your screen is cluttered, use some options here to hide the unneeded windows to make room for others. When you want to access some windows, use some options here to show them.

The **Project menu** can be used to manage the multiple projects in the current session, such as changing project properties, adding custom controls, or adding/removing forms and modules.

The **Format menu** can be used to control the appearance of a form and its controls by specifying where they will appear and locking/unlocking their specified positions.

The **Debug menu** contains a series of options to debug code. They are useful when you want to catch errors in your program code.

The **Run menu** has a few options to determine how your program will be executed.

The **Tools menu** includes some miscellaneous tools, including the **Menu Editor** and various tabs to control the IDE.

The **Add-Ins menu** can be used to access additional external programs included in various Visual Basic editions. The **Add-In Manager** included here can be used to link an add-in program to the IDE.

The **Windows menu**, like its counterparts in other Windows-compliant applications, lets you control how various windows should be displayed.

The **Help menu** supplies online help; it will be explored in another section below.

TOOLBARS

A **toolbar** is a productivity tool for the convenience of the user. It contains buttons, each of which represents a menu option. You can click a button to execute a command, instead of going into a menu to choose an option. You can live without a toolbar, but using it can save you keystrokes or mouse clicks.

VB5 comes with several intrinsic (built-in) toolbars. The **Standard toolbar** is the only one shown by default. It is also by default displayed below the menu bar. It contains 19 buttons divided into six groups. You can move the pointer to each button and a **tooltip** will appear to tell you what it's supposed to do. Depending on what you are doing, some buttons may be dimmed and are thus unavailable for the moment. If a button is available, it's also transformed into a 3-D look when the pointer is over it.

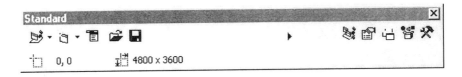

Figure 1.4   The Standard toolbar

The left end of the Standard toolbar has two vertical lines. You can drag it (or any empty area where no tooltip appears) to attach the bar to any side of the IDE window. If you double-click it or drag it to the middle of the IDE window, the toolbar becomes a window (with a new title bar) and is not attached to any side, as shown in Figure 1.4. If you now double-click the title bar of this window, the toolbar will return to its previous attached state.

TIP: Managing Windows

The last group of buttons on the Standard toolbar, from left to right, are:

Project Explorer
Properties Window
Form Layout Window
Object Browser
Toolbox

Each can bring a specific item to the top or display it if it was hidden.

The above windows can take up lots of your precious screen real estate, leaving you little room for you to do your work. So it's a good idea to close some or all of them when you are designing an interface or writing code. When you need a particular window, just click its corresponding button on the Standard toolbar to bring it up; click the window's X button to close it after you are done.

If you don't want to close these windows and if they are attached to the left and right borders as in their original arrangement, you can move their inner border to adjust the available working space. By narrowing these windows, you'll make more room for your work. When you need to access or view an available tool, temporarily widen the corresponding window.

The **Standard toolbar** can be hidden. To do so, choose the View menu to display all the options. Move the pointer to the last option called Toolbars; five options pop up (see below), with Standard showing a check mark on its left. If you now click Standard, the Standard toolbar will disappear. To bring it back, just choose View | Toolbars | Standard. A check mark will appear and the toolbar will return.

The above-mentioned five options will also appear if you right-click any empty area (where no tooltip appears) of a toolbar or the menu bar. These options are:

Debug
Edit
Form Editor
Standard
Customize...

Here you see four available toolbars which you can show or hide. These additional toolbars are useful when you do some tasks and will be discussed when appropriate.

You can also use the **Customize** option to show/hide/customize existing toolbars or create new ones. It leads to Figure 1.5. As you check/uncheck each option, the screen will respond immediately by showing or hiding the specified item. When a toolbar appears, you can also click the X button to close it; that will lead to unchecking the corresponding option in the Customize dialog box.

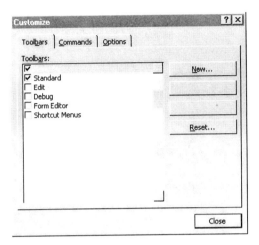

Figure 1.5   **Customizing toolbars**

You can use the **Customize dialog box** to create a custom toolbar or change the intrinsic toolbars. To create a **custom toolbar**, do the following:

1. In the Customize dialog box, click the New button; the New Toolbar dialog box appears (Figure 1.6). Supply a name (Custom 1 is the default) and click OK. A little empty toolbar pops up, ready for you to add commands.

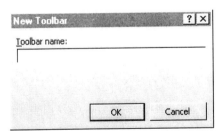

Figure 1.6   **Creating a new toolbar**

2. Go to the Commands tab and click an appropriate category to show all the related commands.

3. When the desired commands appear, drag each to the newly created toolbar.

   If you wish, you can drag a command to the menu bar or an intrinsic toolbar; it will be added to the existing items. If you want to restore the original arrangement, select the toolbar in the Customize dialog box and choose Reset.

4. Drag an icon to outside the toolbar if you want to remove it. You can use this technique to remove an additional icon you've added to an intrinsic toolbar.

5. Drag an existing item to a new position within the toolbar to rearrange the order.

6. Use the Options tab to add or remove some features.

A custom toolbar is added to the Toolbars tab in the Customize dialog box. When it's selected, the Rename and Delete buttons become available; these buttons are not available for the intrinsic toolbars.

The list of items in the Toolbars tab, including additional custom toolbars, also appears when you right-click the menu bar or any displayed toolbar, or when you choose View | Toolbars. So there are multiple ways to access a custom toolbar.

Once created, a custom toolbar can be maneuvered like any intrinsic toolbar. You can use the Options tab in the Customize dialog box to add animation and show/hide tooltips and shortcut keys. The *Show ScreenTips on toolbars* option in the Options tab is checked by default. If you uncheck it, all the toolbars will show no tooltips. Tooltips are useful and should not be turned off.

A toolbar can be attached to any border of the IDE window, just like the Windows taskbar. Dockable windows (see another section below) will make room for it. It can even be dragged above the menu bar, thus pushing the menu bar downward. The menu bar cannot be dragged, but it will yield to a toolbar.

Figure 1.7   The Shortcut Menus toolbar

The Customize dialog box shows the availability of the **Shortcut Menus toolbar**. This toolbar (Figure 1.7) includes all the shortcuts you can pop up by right-clicking different windows. This simple toolbar with only three options can branch to numerous lists of options. This toolbar is not intended for you to enter a command; it closes when the Customize dialog box closes. The numerous options can be used only to drag commands to a toolbar.

The other intrinsic toolbars shown in the Customize dialog box's Toolbars tab will be explained in later chapters when they are needed.

THE TOOLBOX

The **Toolbox** contains all the controls which you can add to a form. Figure 1.8 shows all the **standard controls**; these are also known as intrinsic or built-in controls because they are included in the program and cannot be altered by the user. There are 20 standard controls.

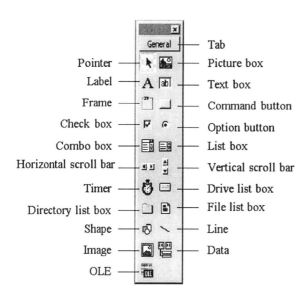

Figure 1.8   The Toolbox

The **Pointer** tool (top left) is not a control. You cannot use it to add a control to a form. Its only useful purpose is to restore the mouse pointer's default state. Normally the Pointer tool is highlighted. That means the mouse pointer is performing its regular role. When you click another tool in the Toolbox, that tool is highlighted instead and the pointer becomes a cross as it is moved to the form. If you change your mind and want to abort, just click the Pointer tool (or the form) and the pointer will return to its original state. You can also press Esc to do the same thing.

The Toolbox in your system may be slightly different from Figure 1.8. It may have additional controls appearing at the bottom. The **Learning Edition** comes with five **custom controls** (also called **ActiveX controls**). The other editions include many more. Some or all of these may have been added in your display. You can add or remove these custom controls. Chapter 8 tells you how to manage these controls.

Take advantage of the **tooltips** for the controls. Point to each button and a name will pop up. This is the official name used by Visual Basic. If you ever wonder what name to reference a control type, use the tooltip to show it.

The Toolbox appears to be glued to the left side of the IDE window. You can place it anywhere you want. Just drag the title bar. If you drag it to a border, it will attach itself there. If you drag it to the middle, it will stay there vertically as shown in Figure 1.8.

You can right-click the Toolbox to show the following options:

Components...
Add Tab...
Dockable
Hide

You use **Components** to add custom controls and insertable objects to the Toolbox. This will be covered fully in a later chapter.

You can use **Hide** to hide the Toolbox; it will disappear from the screen. You can also click the X button to close it. Use View | Toolbox to bring it back.

The **Add Tab** option lets you add a tab to the existing **General tab**. You'll be asked to enter a name. This name will then appear in the Toolbox. You can then click your tab or General to go to each tab. After you've created a tab, use the Components option to add controls. Your custom tab is useful for a quick access to a custom control.

The **Dockable** option lets you make the Toolbox dockable or undockable. When it's dockable, it can be attached (docked) to a side of the IDE window. If you then drag it to the middle, it will stay there. Double-clicking the title bar returns it to its previously docked/undocked position.

When the Toolbox is **undockable**, you can drag it anywhere inside the IDE window and it will stay there. The control menu and the three typical buttons of a window also appear (Figure 1.9). In this state, you cannot narrow the window to less than three columns (a dockable window can be narrowed to a single column or less). If you widen the window, the objects will flow horizontally to fill the enlarged window. If you double-click the title bar, the window will be maximized and attached horizontally to the top. You need then to click the Restore button near the top right to restore its previous state.

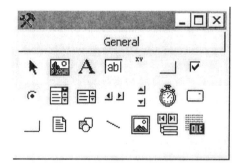

Figure 1.9   **The Toolbox undocked**

DOCKABLE WINDOWS:
Project, Properties, and Form Layout

The right side of the IDE window shows three windows melded into one seamless piece and all attached to the right border. These are known as Project Explorer window, Properties window, and Form Layout window.

The **Project Explorer[1] window** (Figure 1.10) is useful for managing multiple modules in one or more projects in the current session. VB5 allows you to work on multiple projects at one time (previous versions allow only one project). Each

---

[1]This was formerly known as the Project window and could manage only one project at a time. It can now manage multiple projects and works like Windows Explorer. So the new name reflects the combination of these two features.

project may have multiple forms and modules. The Project Explorer window simplifies the complex task of managing so many related items.

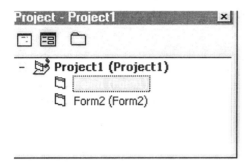

Figure 1.10   The Project Explorer window

As you add or open projects and their components, they appear in this window. You can select an item here and use one of the three command buttons to display it. You can move the pointer to these buttons to show their names as: View Code, View Object, and Toggle Folder. You use **View Code** to go to the Code window of the selected form (the Code window is where you enter code), **View Object** to view the form, and **Toggle Folders** to change the view in this window between showing all the files and in Explorer-style folders.

View Code (**F7**) and View Object (**Shift+F7**) are also the first two options in the View menu. You can use them to bring a designer window (containing a form and other items) or Code window to the top or display the respective item if it was hidden. They are helpful if the Project Explorer window is hidden.

The Project Explorer resembles Windows Explorer (see Chapter 0). Each displayed item has an icon on its left. There may also be a + or - sign. When a + sign appears, all the subitems are closed. Clicking this sign opens up the subitems. The + sign also changes to a - sign. Clicking the - sign changes it to a + sign and closes all the subitems.

The **Properties window** (Figure 1.11) is where you set an object's properties at design time. If nothing is shown in this window, no appropriate object has been selected. Selecting an object such as a form or a control on a form will lead to different contents in this window.

The Properties window lets you display the available properties in two ways: **Alphabetic** or **Categorized**. If you click the first, all the properties names, except the Name property (always at the top), will appear in alphabetic order, as shown in Figure 1.11. If you click Categorized, the names will appear in different categories. You can then click the additional + or - signs to open or close categories. If you know a property name, Alphabetic is easier to find it; if you don't know the name, Categorized may be more helpful in finding what you want.

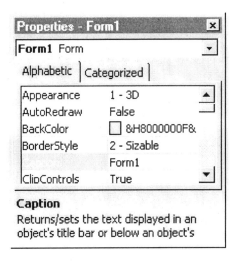

Figure 1.11   The Properties window

Right-clicking the Properties window pops up its shortcut menu, which contains the **Description** option. If you check it, selecting a property will display at the bottom a brief description, as shown in Figure 1.11.

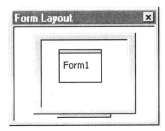

Figure 1.12   The Form Layout window

The **Form Layout window** (Figure 1.12) lets you determine at design time where the selected form will be located at run time. There is a monitor picture inside this window and a form name inside the monitor. You can drag this virtual form to various parts of the monitor. This is the position of the form against the monitor when you run this form. If you increase or decrease the actual form's size, it will be reflected inside this window. You can also pop up the shortcut menu and specify a startup position. Unlike previous editions, VB5's default setting no longer allows you to drag a real form at design time to determine its run time position.

Right-clicking each of the above three windows will pop up different shortcut menus, with all of them sharing the last two options as Dockable and Hide. Use **Dockable** to specify whether a window is dockable or not. You can use **Hide** (or the X button) to hide each window; use the View menu to bring back one or more of the three.

When a window is dockable, it can be attached to any border. You can also drag it to the middle of the IDE window (or even outside) to detach it from a border. An attached window has only one sizable border; a detached one has four.

A dockable window has only the X button on the title bar. An undockable window, on the other hand, has the three regular buttons and the usual control menu on the left. Double-clicking a dockable window's title bar toggles the window between docked and undocked states. Doing the same thing to an undockable window toggles it between maximized and normal sizes.

Two or more dockable windows can be **linked** together and treated as one unit. To link two dockable windows, drag one's title bar and drop it on the other's title bar. The new one will appear at the top. You can drag the bottom title bar to the top title bar and the two will reverse position. A new window with an extra title bar will be created to house the two. You may need to enlarge this window to display more of the windows inside.

When windows are linked, they can be maneuvered as one unit. You can drag the top title bar to move the whole thing. Dragging it to a border of the IDE will attach the whole unit to that border. In this situation, all the windows share only one outer sizable border. Changing this border will affect all the windows inside. If this group is not attached to a border, then they share three sizable borders.

Two linked windows have a border dividing them. When the pointer moves to this area, it becomes double-headed. You can then drag this symbol up or down to enlarge one and reduce the other.

Linked windows can also be arranged side by side. To do that, drag a title bar to attach that window to the right or left side of the outer window that houses the linked windows. The other windows will adjust to fit.

To unlink a window, just drag its title bar to outside the outer window. The dragged window will become a separate unit and the remaining ones will adjust to fit. You can also unlink a window by making it undockable; the window will jump out and return to where it was before linking.

When you have many windows open, use the **Window menu** to manage them. It has these options:

Split
Tile Horizontally
Tile Vertically
Cascade
Arrange Icons

Split is available only when a Code window is selected; when it's checked, the Code window is split in half horizontally. The next three options arrange the windows as they work in Windows. **Arrange Icons** lines up all the minimized windows and place them at the bottom of the IDE window.

How the windows are arranged depends on the available screen space. If a border is occupied by an attached window, then that space is not available for use by other windows.

When a window is dockable, it is not affected by the Window menu's options. A dockable window not attached to a border is always on top of the undockable windows. A dockable window can be on top of another dockable window, depending on which one has the focus.

Designer and Code windows are undockable so they can be maneuvered with the Window menu's options. It's a good idea to arrange these windows in an overlapping manner so that when a particular window is covered by another, you can quickly access it by clicking the uncovered portion to bring it to the top.

If you want to use the keyboard to bring a covered-up window to the top, hold down Ctrl and repeatedly press the Tab key. When the desired window is brought to the foreground, release the Ctrl key. **Ctrl+Tab** (or **Ctrl+F6**) cycles through all the undockable windows but skips dockable ones. This key combination is also useful when you maximize an undockable window (all the other undockable windows will also be maximized). Since the work space is completely covered by the current maximized window, use Ctrl+Tab to bring the desired one to the top.

You can also use **Tools | Options | Docking** to determine whether a window is dockable. There are nine windows here. They may be checked or unchecked, depending on what you have done from the shortcut menus. Toolbars are not included in the Docking tab. Toolbars, intrinsic or custom, are always dockable and you cannot make them undockable.

THE HELP SYSTEM

Visual Basic comes with a comprehensive help system. It is an electronic online reference providing a great deal of information. It has **hypertext** capabilities, allowing you to jump to related topics. Furthermore, it also provides **context-sensitive** help, allowing you to press the **F1** key to show help information pertinent to the task you are doing. If you have used Windows or Windows applications, you are already familiar with this system. If not, you should spend some time exploring it. Either way, you should take advantage of the vast amount of useful information stored here.

There are two ways to use the Help system: the Help menu for exploring the entire system and the F1 key for context-sensitive help.

The Help Menu

When you open the Help menu, the following options appear:

> Microsoft Visual Basic Help Topics
> Books Online...
> Obtaining Technical Support...
> Microsoft on the Web
> About Microsoft Visual Basic...

Clicking (Microsoft Visual Basic) Help Topics leads to "Help Topics: Visual Basic 5 Help" (Figure 1.13). This initial display has three tabs: Contents, Index, and Find. These are the same options that you find when you open the Help menu in Windows, as explained in Chapter 0. **Contents** leads to a series of books which you can open and close. **Index** shows a list of terms displayed in alphabetic order. **Find** lets you search for topics that contain the search word(s). You can find the same thing using any of these options.

When you open the **Index tab**, the cursor stays in the top text box. You can now type one or multiple letters to display the matching entries in the large list box. You can also scroll the list to show what you are looking for. When you find the desired one, double-click it or click it and click Display. A pertinent help topic will appear. You may see another dialog box (Topics Found) listing multiple matching entries; you select one and its help topic will appear.

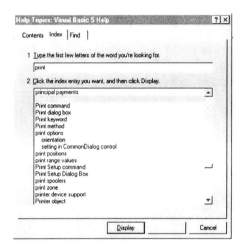

Figure 1.13   The Help dialog box's Index tab

When you open the **Find tab** the first time, you'll be asked to choose an option to build a word list. It may take some time for the computer to complete the list. Opening the tab in the future will take less time. This tab works like the Index tab. It also works the same way as illustrated in Chapter 0.

The **Contents tab** leads to a separate window with question marks (for help topics) and closed-book icons (containing other items). Double-click a question mark to show its details. Double-click a closed-book icon to open a list of contents, including question marks and perhaps closed-book icons. After it's double-clicked, a closed-book icon becomes an open-book icon. If you double-click an open-book icon, it turns into a closed-book icon and the open list is closed. This mechanism allows you to branch to any of the available topics. You can also use the Open/Close button at the bottom to open/close a book. You can also print a book or topic by clicking the Print button.

After a pertinent topic is displayed, three command buttons will be available: Help Topics, Back, and Options. These works the same as in Windows (see Chapter 0). On some occasions the Contents and Index buttons may also appear.

These two, plus Help Topics can return you to Figure 1.13. From here you can search for more topics.

If you have the Visual Basic CD, you can choose **Books Online** from the Help menu (it won't work unless you insert a proper CD in your CD-ROM drive). It contains the electronic version of the printed volumes that come with the Visual Basic package. You can find lots of useful information here.

When you use the Help menu to find a topic, a Topics Found dialog box may appear listing all the matching entries. The list may include "Jump to Visual Basic 5.0 Books Online." This also requires a CD.

Figure 1.14 shows a sample screen of Visual Basic Books Online. It works like Windows Explorer. The left side shows a series of books and documents; the right side shows the details. You can drag the middle partition line to adjust each side's display area. You can use a menu option to show both sides or only the right side. You can set book marks or print a displayed topic. There are a few audiovisual files that provide multimedia presentations. If you are serious about mastering Visual Basic, you should take full advantage of the vast resources here.[2]

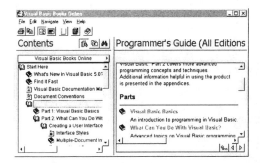

Figure 1.14   Visual Basic Books Online

If you need more help, try **Obtaining Technical Support** and **Microsoft on the Web** from the Help menu. The former leads to a series of options, most of which

---

[2]Microsoft also markets a separate CD called Mastering Visual Basic 5 for about $50. The Professional Edition includes it for no additional charge. This CD provides a lot more multimedia files than Books Online.

require additional fees. The latter supplies various Web addresses (URLs) for you to reach—if you are connected to the Internet.

Context-Sensitive Help

Instead of using the Help menu to find a help topic, you may want to try a **context-sensitive help**. The latter requires you to press the F1 key when you are doing something and want to show a pertinent help topic. Both methods will eventually lead to the same information you are looking for. But pressing F1 when you are doing something leads to the topic pertinent to the task at hand. This can save you time in getting the needed information.

For example, suppose the current form is selected, which is the case when you start out or click the form. Pressing F1 shows a topic titled "Form Window." As another example, click a tool in the Toolbox and then press F1. A different topic appears with the name of the control and related information.

If you want a summary of the Toolbox, click the **Pointer** tool at the top left and press F1. The resulting help topic shows all the standard controls. Each is shown with its button and a brief explanation.

In the Code window, you can also type a keyword (such as Print) and press F1 to show a related help topic. If a word is not recognized, the Keyword Not Found topic will appear. Correct any misspelling and try again. To find keywords used by Visual Basic, try the **Language Reference** from Help | Microsoft Visual Basic Help Topics | Contents, or Help | Books Online (a CD is required for this). A long list of alphabetic letters will appear; you can double-click one to show matching help topics.

(Previous versions of Visual Basic has the Glossary topic providing a long list of terms that have special meanings to Visual Basic. In VB5, you can still find this term in the online help, but it now contains terms and definitions relevant only to the Enterprise Edition.)

DRILL

Questions 1 - 5 are related to Visual Basic's IDE.

_____ 1.   The menu bar/ _____ toolbar is by default located at the top of the IDE window.

_____ 2.   The vertical window normally shown on the left of the IDE is known as the _____ .

_____ 3.   You use the _____ window to change object attributes.

_____ 4.   There are _____ (how many) standard (built-in) controls in the Toolbox.

_____ 5.   The Project window lets you view Object and view _____ .

_____ 6.   Double-clicking the two vertical lines at the beginning of the Standard toolbar transforms the toolbar into a window. True or false?

_____ 7.   A dockable window can be covered up by an undockable window. True or false?

Use the following to answer questions 8-12:

    a.   designer window
    b.   Project window
    c.   Properties window
    d.   Form Layout window

_____ 8.   This window lets you open a closed window or shift focus from one open window to another.

_____ 9.   This window lets you visually determine a form's size.

_____ 10.   This window lets you visually determine the run-time position of a form.

_____ 11.   This window is completely empty when a form or control is not selected.

_____ 12.   This window can show a description at the bottom.

_____ 13.   A dockable window can
    a.   be attached to an IDE border
    b.   be linked to another dockable window
    c.   float on top of an undockable window
    d.   all of the above

_____ 14.   A dockable window can be:
    a.   maximized
    b.   minimized

    c.   closed

    d.   covered up by an undockable window

_____ 15.   This key combination cycles through all the undockable windows.

    a.   Tab

    b.   Shift + Tab

    c.   Ctrl + Tab

    d.   Ctrl + F6

    e.   both c and d

_____ 16.   This is an undockable window.

    a.   a toolbar

    b.   Code window

    c.   designer window

    d.   Toolbox

    e.   Project window

PRACTICE

1. Start a new project from Visual Basic's IDE. Explain what happens after a new project is open.

2. After a new project is open, open the Code window, close the Code window and the designer window, and reopen both of them with options from the menu bar.

3. Close the Project window and reopen it. Close the Code window and the designer window, and use the Project window to open them.

4. Close the Toolbox window and then reopen it.

5. Close the Properties window and then reopen it.

6. Move and resize the Form1 window.

7. Use the Form Layout window to place Form1's run time position in the middle of the screen.

8. Explain the role of the Form Layout window.

9. How do you make a window dockable or undockable?

10. Explain the important attributes of a dockable window.

■ 11. What happens when you maximize a window in the IDE? How can you use the keyboard to bring another window to the top?

■ 12. Create a custom toolbar named My Bar, add three commands to it, and delete it.

■ 13. If you close a toolbar by clicking its X button, how can you bring it back?

■ 14. Use the F1 key to show the help topic related to the Toolbox.

■ 15. Use the Help system's Index tab to show the help topic for the text box control.

■ 16. Use the F1 key to do the above.

■ 17. Print the help topic for the text box control.

EVENT-DRIVEN PROGRAMMING

When you think of a computer program, you probably have in mind lines of program code that are executed one after another from top to bottom. Writing such a program is known as **procedural** (or **linear**) **programming**. This technique is still valid with a Windows program, except there is a new twist.

After you run a Windows program, you usually see a window with a number of objects inside the window, such as command buttons, option buttons, text boxes, and so on. The program then awaits an event. An **event** is an action usually (but not always) initiated by the user, such as moving the mouse pointer, clicking an object, or pressing Tab or Enter. After an event occurs, the program code attached to the chosen object is executed. Writing such a program is known as **event-driven programming**.

An object may have a procedure attached to it. Once an event is initiated, the procedure is executed. A **procedure** is a clearly defined subroutine (subprogram) to perform a specific task. When a procedure is executed, the traditional procedural programming kicks in.

So what you see in a Windows program is a series of subprograms (procedures) that are connected to objects. When an object is chosen by the user, the related subprogram is executed. In effect, an event-driven program adds another layer on top of the traditional procedural program.

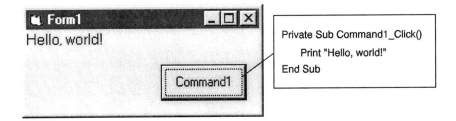

Figure 1.15   Clicking a command button

Figure 1.15 shows a simple application with a window and a command button inside. When the button is clicked, the Command1_Click procedure is executed, which in turn prints the text to the screen.

Computer programming languages have recently evolved into something called **object-oriented programming** (OOP), in which a program's components (objects) are reusable and programmable. Visual Basic has many characteristics of OOP. Screen objects can be controlled and manipulated at **design time** (when you create a program) or **run time** (when a program is executed). Since objects in Visual Basic are provided by the package and are mostly visible at design time, programmers have an easier time writing applications.

So how do you write a Visual Basic program? These are the common steps:

1. Add a new project by choosing File | New Project, and choose Standard EXE from the resulting New Project tab; this step is unnecessary if a project has been added by default. A designer window with a form inside is added to the IDE. The form serves as a container for other objects and transforms itself into a window at run time.

2. Add objects to the form so that the user can use them to interact with the program. Alter some objects' properties if necessary.

3. Attach program code to one or more objects so that the computer will do something when an object is chosen.

4. Run the program to see how it works. Improve the user interface if necessary. Edit code if it doesn't execute properly. Save the file to disk if you want to reuse it.

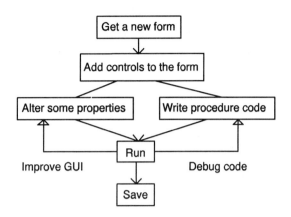

Figure 1.16   The steps of writing a Visual Basic program

Figure 1.16 shows how these steps are related. This process sounds complicated. Fortunately, Visual Basic makes it relatively easy.

The sections below guide you through the steps of creating and saving your first Visual Basic application.

DESIGNING A USER INTERFACE

The first normal step of writing a Windows application is to create a user interface. This is the window the user will see and interact with when the application runs. Creating a user interface requires you to add some controls to a form. Follow these steps to create the interface shown in Figure 1.18.

1. Start Visual Basic. If the New Project dialog box appears, choose Standard EXE in the New tab (see Figure 1.1). Form1 appears inside the designer window and is ready for you to do something. The names Project1 and Form1 also enter the Project window.

    Alternatively, you can choose File | New Project to start a new project from inside the IDE. The New Project dialog box appears. Double-click Standard EXE.

    Another way to add a new project is to click Add Standard EXE Project, the first button on the Standard toolbar. Notice that there is a down arrow next to the button. If you want another type of project, click the down arrow to show the available options. Using this technique will add a new project. If the IDE has no project, this will add Project1. If there is already a project named Project1, this will add Project2.

2. You can do a number of optional things to the designer window and the form inside (Figure 1.17). You can enlarge the designer window by dragging its borders. You can enlarge or reduce the form by using its **sizing handles** (see below). You can use the scroll bars to show different parts of the form if it's not completely shown. You can move the duo to a different location by dragging the designer's title bar. You can use the Form Layout window to specify the form's run time position.

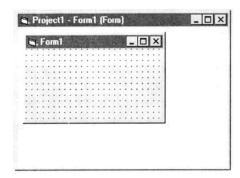

Figure 1.17   The designer window with Form1 inside

If the Toolbox does not appear on the screen, use the View menu to display it.

3. Double-click the label control tool in the Toolbox, the one with the letter A (see Figure 1.8). Label1 now appears in the middle of Form1. (If you don't want it, just click it and press Del to delete it.) Drag Label1 to the top left corner of the form.

4. Double-click the text box tool. Text1 appears in the middle of the form. Drag Text1 to just below Label1.

5. Repeat step 4 and drag Text2 to the middle of the form.

6. Double-click the command button tool. Command1 appears. Drag Command1 to the left.

7. Repeat step 6 and drag Command2 to the right.

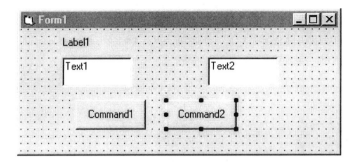

Figure 1.18 Our first user interface at design time

After the above steps, your work should look like Figure 1.18. Don't worry if the arrangement is not neat. You can always change it later.

We now need to stretch the two text boxes. Notice that Command2 in Figure 1.18 is surrounded by eight solid squares; they appear when an object is selected (clicked). These are known as **sizing handles**. To stretch the two text boxes, follow these steps:

1. Select Text1 by clicking it. The sizing handles appear.

2. Move the pointer to the middle handle on the right side of Text1. The pointer is changed to a two-headed arrow.

3. Drag the handle to the right and release the mouse button.

4. Repeat with Text2 and stretch it to the right.

The results are similar to Figure 1.20. Our crude interface is completed. Next we need to set property values.

SETTING PROPERTY VALUES

Our interface now has six objects—a form, a label, two text boxes, and two command buttons. Each object has a set of values that determine how the object will look and behave. Objects have default values set by Visual Basic. You can change them to suit your needs. We intend to change a few.

We are going to modify Label1 first. We simply want to change the Caption property, which has the default value of Label1. Follow these steps:

1. Click Label1 on the form to select it.

2. Press F4 and double-click the Caption item in the Properties window. Label1, the default caption, is now highlighted (Figure 1.19).

3. Type "Enter your first name:" As you begin to type, the original text disappears. After you finish, press Enter or click another object to register the entry. If you want to keep the original, press Esc to exit the Properties window.

In step 2, if you click the value field (where Label1 appears, to the right of Caption) in the Properties window, the original entry is not highlighted and the pointer changes to an I beam. You can then use a number of editing keys to erase or modify the original value.

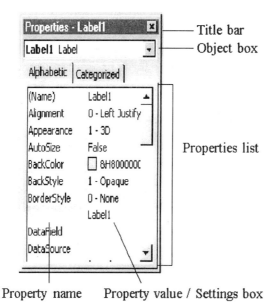

Property name   Property value / Settings box

Figure 1.19   Changing a value in the Properties window

You have now changed the Caption property of Label1. But the long new label is wrapped because there is too little room. The simple remedy is to stretch the control, the same as you stretched a text box earlier.

Next you need to change the Caption and Name properties of the two command buttons. The steps are the same as above. Follow the above steps and change the left one to Greet (Caption) and cmdGreet (Name) and the right one to Quit and cmdQuit.

The two text boxes have the default Text property of Text1 and Text2; we need to delete them. Select each object. Double-click Text in the Properties window to highlight the default value. Press Del on the keyboard to delete it. Click the next text box and do the same thing. If you wish, you can also change the two text boxes' Name properties. We will use the original names here.

Since we want the user to type something in the first text box, we also need to make sure that the cursor appears in this box when the program runs. To do that, select this object and change the **TabIndex** property to 0 in the Properties window. The original value depends on the order in which this object was created; if its value is 0, there is no need to change it. The TabIndex value also determines which object will receive the **focus** when you press the Tab key at run time. So the object with the 0 value gets the focus at the beginning of run time. When you press Tab repeatedly, the focus shifts to the object with the value 1, 2, and so on. The object with the focus is selected and can interact with the user.

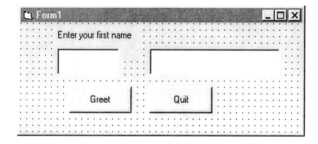

Figure 1.20   The completed user interface

Your work now appears as shown in Figure 1.20. You have completed the interface and set properties as shown below:

Object	Property	Setting
Label1	Caption	Enter your first name:
Text1	Text	(none)
	TabIndex	0
Text2	Text	(none)
Command1	Caption	Greet
	Name	cmdGreet
Command2	Caption	Quit
	Name	cmdQuit

Figure 1.19 shows the major parts of the Properties window. Selecting some properties in this window may lead to an arrow or three dots appearing in the value field on the right side. This is also known as the **Settings box**. You can click the additional arrow or three-dot button to show the available options and select one of them. Chapter 3 will discuss this topic further.

WRITING CODE

Our user interface will do nothing unless we attach code to one or more objects. When the user chooses an object, the attached code will begin to execute and something will happen.

Our interface has two command buttons. We need to attach code to each so that it will respond to a mouse click.

Follow these steps to attach code to the Greet button:

1. Double-click the Greet command button. The **Code window** appears. The Click **procedure template**, with the first and last lines, also appears. The cursor appears between the two lines, ready for you to type code lines.

2. Press Tab once and type the statement shown in Figure 1.21. As you type, a box may pop up. Just ignore it and continue typing. Chapter 2 will explain this new feature.

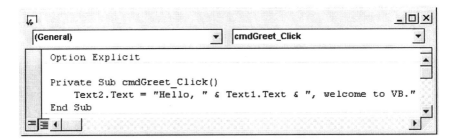

Figure 1.21   The Code window with code

3. Click the down arrow or inside the left combo box. All the object names appear. This is also known as the **Object box**; it contains the same items as the Object box in the Properties window.

4. Click the cmdQuit name. The Click procedure template for the new object appears. (If Click is not what you want, you can use the **Procedure box** on the right side to show all the available options.)

5. Press Tab and type **End**.

At this point, you can leave the Code window on while you do the next step. On the other hand, if you want to show the form window, you can click any visible portion of the form to bring it to the top (without closing the Code window) or click the X button at the top right or double-click the Code window's control box at the top left to close it.

NOTE You can type all code lines in lowercase. When you press Enter or move the cursor to another line, Visual Basic will automatically capitalize some words that have special meanings and insert extra spaces in some places to make the text more readable. Different text colors may also appear.

RUNNING A PROGRAM

You are now ready to run the program. Just press **F5**, click the **Start** button on the Standard toolbar, or choose Start from the Run menu. The user interface appears (Figure 1.22). The cursor also appears in the first text box. Type a name in the text box and click Greet. The second text box shows the name and the extra text. You can erase the name, type another, and click Greet another time to show a different result. Click Quit to end.

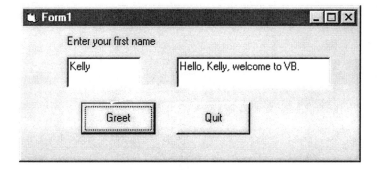

Figure 1.22   Running the application

When you click Greet, the cmdGreet_Click procedure is executed. The entry in Text1 is combined with the other words in the program and the combination is displayed in Text2. When you click Quit, the cmdQuit_Click procedure is executed. The **End** statement then ends the program. If this statement is not provided in a program, you can click the Close (X) button or double-click the control box (top left) to end the program. You can also choose End from the Run menu or click the End button on the Standard toolbar to do the same.

SAVING AND OPENING A PROJECT

If you intend to reuse a project, you must save it to disk. If you have a long program, you should periodically save it to prevent data loss due to power failure or program misbehavior. Should mishap occur, the data in RAM is lost. If you have saved a file, you can open your disk file and start from there.

The saving process can be implemented before or after you run the program. Running a complex program could freeze your computer and cause data loss; it may be a good idea then to save the file before running it.

If you want Visual Basic to do the job for you, choose Options from the Tools menu. The **Environment tab** has the following frame and three options:

When a program starts:

> Save Changes
> Prompt To Save Changes
> Don't Save Changes

The last option is the default. If you wish, you can select one of the other two.

Follow these steps to save this project.

1. Choose **Save Project** (this option becomes Save Project Group if you have added two or more projects) from the File menu (or click the diskette button on the Standard toolbar). The **Save File As** (Figure 1.23) dialog box appears. All the subfolders and form files in the current folder are displayed. You can go to another drive or folder. You are also prompted to enter a file name. The default is Form1.frm; it is also highlighted. It disappears as you type. If you want to edit the displayed text, press a cursor key and then make necessary changes.

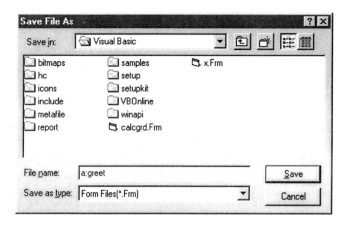

Figure 1.23   The Save File As dialog box

3. Insert a disk in drive A or B and in the File-name box type A:GREET or B:GREET (depending on where your disk is). The **FRM** extension will be added automatically. You can type something and then press Enter or click OK. You can type up to 255 characters, including spaces. If you wish, you can click the Save-in box or its down arrow to drop down a list of drives and folders. Then click A or B to make it the default. Then enter a file name in the File-name box. In that case, you can omit the drive letter before the file name. If there is an existing file, you can click it to bring it to the File-name box and then click Save. You'll be prompted with Yes/No to save over the original file. (If you are allowed to save a file to a hard disk folder, you need to follow the instructions supplied to you and save your data there.)

4. The **Save Project As** dialog box appears next. You are now prompted with the default Project1.vbp as the project file name. Enter A:GREET or B:GREET. The **VBP** extension is automatically added.

5. If you have added two or more projects, the **Save Project Group As** dialog box will eventually appear. You'll be prompted to save a file with the VBG extension. This file is useful if you want it to tie together several projects.

VB5 saves your files as ASCII text. Forms and controls are each described in a block of text marked with Begin and End. Procedures are saved as you see them in the Code window. These files can be opened by Windows Notepad or Word-Pad. Viewing these files can give you a better understanding of how Visual Basic manages them.

After you have saved a project for the first time, choosing Save Project another time leads to no prompting. If there are changes, Visual Basic simply saves the latest over the previous version. If no change has been made, choosing Save Project does nothing.

TIP: Saving Backup Files

It's a safe and sound practice to save a copy to your hard disk and another identical copy to a floppy disk. To do that, follow the above steps to save a copy to the hard disk. Then use File | Save Form As to save one or more forms (if you've added multiple forms) to the floppy disk. Finally, use File | Save Project As to save the project to the floppy disk.

In this arrangement, you can open a project file to open all the related items. If you open the hard-disk copy, the form files will be loaded from the hard disk. If you open the floppy-disk copy, the form files will come from the floppy disk. This happens because the project file remembers where the form files were saved to.

If you copy the related files from the hard disk to the floppy disk, opening the project file from the floppy disk will lead Visual Basic to open the form files from the hard disk because the project file recorded the form files as being saved to the hard disk. If the named form files don't exist on the hard disk, loading will fail.

> **NOTE**   A simpler way to save a file is to use the shortcut menu in the Project Explorer window. When a form name appears, right-click it to bring up the menu. You'll find the Save Form1 (or the name you have entered) and Save Form1 As options. This will take you to the Save File As dialog box and nowhere else, thus bypassing the Save Project As and Save Project Group As dialog boxes. If you want to save a project, right-click a project name instead.

After you have saved a project, you can open it in the future to do more work. To open a recent project, open the File menu and click one of the four displayed file names. Up to four names with the FRM, VBP, or VBG extension will be shown at the bottom. This list changes as you open and save files.

Another way is to choose **Open Project** from the File menu (or just click the Open Project button on the Standard toolbar). Since opening another project will clear the current one from memory, you will be prompted to save unsaved files. After that, the **Open Project** dialog box (similar to Figure 1.23) appears. If the file you want does not appear, you can go to another drive or folder. Click the desired file and then click Open. The file will be retrieved to memory.

After a file is open, one or more file names will appear in the Project window. If this window is not open, you need to open it by choosing View | Project Explorer, click the corresponding button on the Standard toolbar, or press Ctrl+R. You can then click the form and choose View Form (Shift+F7) or View Code (F7) to show the form designer or Code window.

TIP: Managing Files

Take advantage of the many new commands to manage your files when you open or save a file. The Open Project and Save File As dialog boxes contain some useful features. Use the available buttons and shortcut (popup) menus to do many chores. The four buttons below the title bar are (according to their tooltips):

Up One Level   Moves to a higher level folder; you can also press the **Backspace** key to do the same thing.

Create New Folder Creates a folder named New Folder in the current drive or folder; you can change the name.

List   Shows window contents as a list; default display mode.

Details   Shows contents in details; replaces List mode.

If you want to move a file to a folder, just drag the file and drop it on the folder's icon. If you want to copy instead, hold down Ctrl as you drag and drop. If the target you want to copy or move a file to is not visible, choose Copy or Cut from the shortcut menu by right-clicking the source file, go to a new folder to find the desired target, and then right-click the target and choose Paste from the new shortcut menu. You can also use the Send To option from the shortcut menu to copy a file to a floppy disk.

Since there is no menu bar, you need to right-click an object to pop up the shortcut (context) menu. Right-clicking different objects (drive, folder, data file, program file, a blank area, etc.) leads to different lists of options. If the **Quick View** option is available in the shortcut menu, you can view a file's contents before opening it or saving over it. Use the Properties option if you want to view an object's properties. If you are not familiar with these shortcut tricks, review Chapter 0.

In case you need an explanation about each part of this window, click the **?** button at the top right; a ? begins to follow the pointer. Then click any component inside to pop up a brief explanation. After you finish reading it, click the popup window to clear it.

When the Open Project or Save File As dialog box appears, you can enter a file pattern in the File-name box to display only the files matching the pattern. For example, *.FRM displays only form files and *MOTEL.FRM shows various related files in the PROJECT directory of the disk that comes with this book.

TIP: Saving/Opening Only A Form File

When you save a project, Visual Basic normally prompts you to save a form file, then a project file, and then possibly a project group file. A project file records the information found in the Project Explorer window (or part of it), plus a few other items (see Chapter 8). It is useful if a project has several forms or modules, or involves custom controls. On the other hand, if a project has only one form and no custom control, you are not required to save a project file. All you need is to save a form file.

To save only a form file, choose **Save Form1** (or another name you have entered) from the File menu. You are prompted to enter a file name for the first time. Choosing this option after that will automatically save the new data over the old and you will not be prompted to enter a file name. When you exit, you will be asked to save Project1 and maybe Group1; answer No if you don't want to save them.

If you save only a form file, how do you open it? When you choose Open Project from the File menu, the Open Project dialog box appears. The files matching the *.vbp, *.mak[3] and *.vbg patterns are displayed. You can display all the form files by typing *.FRM in the File-name box and pressing Enter. You can then double-click a displayed form file to open it. You can

---

[3]VB3 saves a project file with the MAK name extension. Such a file can also be opened by VB4/5. VB4/5 saves a project file with the VBP extension.

also click the down arrow at the bottom of the dialog box and select the All Files option. All the files, including form files, in the current folder will appear for you to select.

If the New Project dialog box appears when you start Visual Basic, go to the Recent tab to show a dialog box identical to the Open Project dialog box mentioned in the previous paragraph. You can also use the Recent tab, but it doesn't show file name extensions so you can't distinguish a form file from a project file. To open a recent file from inside the IDE, open the File menu and up to four recently opened form and project files will appear at the bottom. If the one you want to open is here, just click it to open it.

If you open a project file, all the form names, plus the project name, are displayed in the Project window. If you open only a form file, only the form name is shown (plus the default Project1). You can select the form and then click the View Object button to load the form or click View Code to load the Code window.

WARNING After you have saved a form file, you can choose **Save Form** from the File menu. The current form data is automatically saved over the disk version (this happens even though nothing has been changed). This is convenient, but it can also be hazardous on some occasions. You may open a file, tinker with it, and intend to save it to a new file. If you choose Save File in this situation, you will overwrite the older version without warning. On such an occasion, you should choose **Save Form As** and supply a new file name; if a matching file name is found, you will be prompted to overwrite it or supply another file name.

TIP: Version Variations

If you have VB4 form file, you can open it in VB5. A message at the beginning tells you that when it's resaved, it'll be saved to the VB5 format. Since a VB4 form file consists of only ASCII text, you can modify it to conform to the VB5 format. All you need to do is to open it in a text editor and change the first line from VERSION 4.0 to VERSION 5.0. After that, opening it will lead to no message.

If you open a VB5 form file in VB4, a series of error messages will appear, but the file will open and run. If you change 5.0 to 4.0 in the above line, then no error will show up.

You can use VB5 to open a VB4 project file with the VBP extension without any problem. Only when a 4.0 message is encountered in a member form file will a message appear.

MODIFYING A PROJECT

Our project can be easily modified. We intend to use a similar interface to allow the user to enter a Fahrenheit number and make the program display the equivalent Centigrade (Celsius) number. We could modify what we have done so far and save the modified version to a new file by using Save Form As. We could also start from scratch. Here we demonstrate a new project but with a similar interface.

To create this new project, choose New Project from the File menu. If you have not saved data, you will be prompted to save. When the New Project dialog box appears, choose Standard EXE. You are now ready to create the interface shown in Figure 1.25. There are seven objects added to the form. These objects have their property values changed as follows:

Object	Property	Value
Label1	Caption	Fahrenheit
Label2	Caption	Centigrade
Text1	Text	(none)
	Name	txtInput
	TabIndex	0
Text2	Text	(none)
	Name	txtOutput
Command1	Caption	Calculate
	Name	cmdCalculate
Command2	Caption	Clear
	Name	cmdClear
Command3	Caption	Quit
	Name	cmdQuit

You need to attach code for the three command buttons. These are shown in Figure 1.24. As explained in a previous section, you can double-click a command button to show its procedure template and type code inside. You can also use the two combo boxes at the top to do the same.

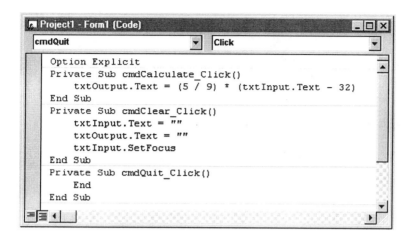

Figure 1.24   The code for the three command buttons

At design time, we change the default Text1 and Text2 Name properties to txtInput and txtOutput. We could have used the default names and produced the same results. When you use multiple controls of the same type and each has a fixed purpose, it's a good practice to give them more descriptive names because your program is easier to read.

In the code, we also add the **Text** property name after each text box's name. This is optional; you can omit it if you wish. So we could have used txtInput alone rather than txtInput.Text, and the result will be the same. Chapter 4 tells you all the property names that can be omitted.

When the Clear button is clicked, the cmdClear_Click procedure is executed. The two text boxes are assigned empty strings, thus clearing their contents.

The **SetFocus** method (a **method** is a statement directed at an object) then shifts the focus to Text1 for another entry. Without this line, the **focus** will remain with the Clear button. In that case, the user will have to press the Tab key to shift the focus to Text1. When an object has the focus, it can interact with the user. For example, you can type text in a text box when it has the focus. When a command button has the focus, it is surrounded by an outline and the user can press Enter or the spacebar to execute its Click procedure, which is the same as clicking the button.

After running the program by pressing F5, the user can enter a number in the left text box and click the Calculate button. The result appears in the second text box (Figure 1.25).

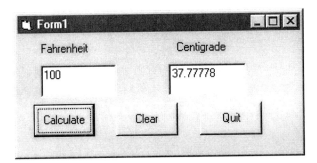

Figure 1.25   The temperature conversion program at run time

The number in the txtInput (Text1) box can be arithmetically manipulated.
Sometimes, however, Visual Basic will treat a number in a text box as a text
string. For example, if you order an addition of the two numbers in two text
boxes. The result is string concatenation, not arithmetic addition. (See Chapter 5
for more details). In this situation, you can explicitly convert one or both to
numerics by using the **Val** function. In the example below, the number in the
txtInput box is explicitly converted to a numeric:

```
txtOutput.Text = (5 / 9) * (Val(txtInput.Text) - 32)
```

You have now created a second application. If you want to save it to disk, follow
the earlier steps and save it to drive A or B as TEMPERATURE, or whatever
name you prefer, up to 255 characters. From now on, you will not be instructed
to save a file—you decide what to do. (If you are allowed to save data to a hard
disk, you can save a copy there and then save another copy to a floppy drive as a
backup.)

If you want to make a program into an executable file that can run from
Windows, choose **File | Make Project1.exe**. Provide a name, and a file with the
name plus the EXE extension will be saved to the current or specified directory.
Chapter 8 will provide more details.

Making an EXE file (compiling) creates and saves an executable file, not your
source file. An EXE file cannot be altered. If you intend to modify your project,
you must save the source file.

PRINTING FORM AND CODE

After you have designed an interface and written code, you may want to print out a hard copy. Visual Basic makes it easy for you to do that. Just choose Print from the File menu (or press Ctrl+P). The **Print dialog box** appears (Figure 1.26).

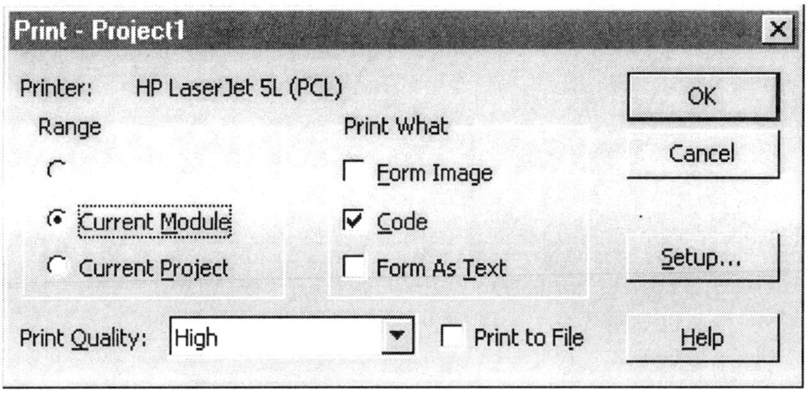

Figure 1.26   The Print dialog box to print form and code

Here you are to select one option on the left side (Range) and one or more items on the right side (Print What). **Current Module** (default) is usually the current form; Project is for an entire project, which may involve other forms and modules, if any. If you have selected text in the Code window before opening the Print dialog, then the Selection option is automatically checked; you can change to one of the other two options as well. When Selection is checked, Code is the only available option on the right side.

On the right side, you must select one, two, or three items to print. Here **Form Image** means the interface you have created; Visual Basic will print the form as you see it.

Form As Text is for printing the properties of the objects you have added to your application. Each object's name and the properties that have been changed by you will be printed. Some unchanged default properties are also printed. The result is the same text as when you save a form file. If you have many objects and changed many of their default property values, printing out Form Text lets you locate items quickly.

Code is for printing the program code you have written for the objects in the project. The printed copy resembles the one in the Code window. If your program has bugs and you have no time to debug it in the Code window, print out a copy of the code and debug it at your leisure.

Both Code and Form Text printouts are sequentially numbered and have the current form name printed as a header. These items are useful if your printout is lengthy.

The Setup button in Figure 1.26 leads to the **Print Setup** dialog, the same as when you choose Print Setup from the File menu. Here you can select another installed printer or change various properties of the selected printer, including print quality and orientation.

Figure 1.26 has the **Print to File** check box. If you check it and click OK, the selected items will be saved to a file. You'll be asked to provide a file name. This is a binary file that can be used to print the data contained in it.

If your printer does not print after you make proper selections and click OK in the Print dialog box, try the following remedies:

- Check your printer to see whether it is turned on or is online. If not, take steps to get it ready.

- If the above remedy does not work, turn off the printer and turn it on again. Use the Print dialog box to try again.

- If the above steps do not work, select another printer driver.

If you want to install a printer, you have to use Windows. Double-click the Printers folder in My Computer; the Printers window appears. Double-click the Add Printer icon and you'll be given a series of instructions. Sometimes an existing printer driver file may be corrupted and you cannot use it to print data. Installing a new driver may solve the problem in this situation.

If you want to set a default printer, open the Printers group from My Computer. Open the pertinent printer's dialog box. From the Printer menu, check Set As Default. In the future, this printer will become default and you won't have to select another. If your printer doesn't print, designating it as the default printer may get it going.

Using another program may sometimes interfere with Visual Basic's printing. If you have used your word processor to select another printer, Visual Basic may not successfully print to another printer. In that case, you may want to use the word processor to select the right printer.

DRILL

___ 17. The Code window has an Object box and a _____ box.

___ 18. To save a form file without saving a project file, you need to choose:
   a. Save Project
   b. Save Project As
   c. Save Form
   d. Save Form As
   e. both c and d

___ 19. Visual Basic can open:
   a. a MAK file
   b. a VBP file
   c. a form (FRM) file
   d. a VBG file
   e. all of the above

___ 20. The Print option in the File menu can print:
   a. form image
   b. form text
   c. program code
   d. all of the above
   e. both b and c

___ 21. A procedure template appears in this window:
   a. Code
   b. form
   c. Properties
   d. Project

Use the following to answer questions 22-26:
   a. F1, b. F4, c. F5, d. F7, e. Shift+F7

___ 22. Runs a program.

___ 23. Shows the Code window.

___ 24. Shows the form/designer window.

_____ 25. Shows the Properties window.

_____ 26. Shows context-sensitive help.

Use the following to answer questions 27-30:
  a. object,   b. event,   c. procedure,   d. control

_____ 27. An item seen in a window (including the window itself) when a Windows program runs.

_____ 28. An item fetched from the Toolbox and added to a form.

_____ 29. A subprogram consisting of statements instructing the computer what to do.

_____ 30. An action which an object can recognize and respond to.

PRACTICE

■ 18. Modify Figures 1.24 and 1.25 so that the user can enter a number representing miles in Text1 and Text2 will show the equivalent kilometers (1 mile = 1.609 kilometers).

■ 19. Modify the above so that the user can enter a kilometer number in Text1 and Text2 will show its equivalent mile number.

■ 20. Modify the above so that the user can type in Text1 an integer number representing feet and Text2 will show the equivalent number in inches.

■ 21. Print the code for the above question.

■ 22. Explain how you can save a form without saving a project.

■ 23. Explain how you can save a backup form file.

■ 24. Explain how you can open a form file without opening a project file.

■ 25. Explain how you can show a form or its Code window after opening a form file.

■ 26. What's the purpose of the TabIndex property?

■ 27. Explain what the following statements are supposed to do:

```
Text1.Setfocus
varX = Val(Text1.Text)
```

CHAPTER PROJECT

A. (1HELLO.FRM)

Write a program that will display *Hello, world* in a text box as soon as you press F5 to run it. (Hint: Write a Form_Load procedure where your code assigns a text string to a text box.)

B. (1ADD.FRM)

Write a program that will let you enter two numbers and click Add to show the sum, as shown in Figure 1.27. When Clear is clicked, the three text boxes are cleared and the focus goes to the first for more entries. (Hint: Use the Val function to convert at least one number to a numeric.)

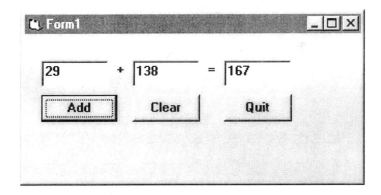

Figure 1.27   Adding two numbers

C. (1XYZCORP.FRM)

Modified from the previous project, this program displays (Figure 1.28) a new label and calculates the percentage difference in the numbers entered the first two text boxes. Use this formula:

txtChange.Text = (txtIncome2.Text - txtIncome1.Text) / txtIncome1.Text * 100

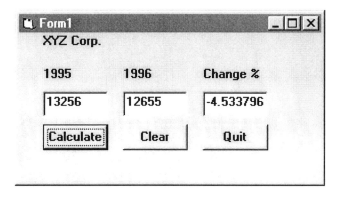

Figure 1.28   Calculating % difference

FUN AND GAME

A. (MOVE.FRM)

This program (Figure 1.29) lets you click the Move button or press Alt+M to move the button to a random location. The code has a safeguard to prevent the button from moving to an area out of sight.

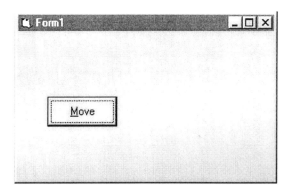

Figure 1.29   Moving a command button to a random location

```
Private Sub cmdMove_Click()
     Dim PosX As Long
     Dim PosY As Long
     Dim BH As Long
     Dim BW As Long
```

```
      Randomize               'get new random seed
      BH = cmdMove.Height  'get button height
      BW = cmdMove.Width     'get button width
      PosX = Int(Rnd * (ScaleWidth - BW))
         'from left to right minus button width
      PosY = Int(Rnd * (ScaleHeight - BH))
         'from top to bottom minus button height
   cmdMove.Move PosX, PosY
         'move button to new position
End Sub
```

B. (CLOCK.FRM)

This program simulates a moving clock hand; the first point of the hand (line) is anchored at the center and the second moves clockwise along a circle. Add a line control and a shape control to a new form at design time. The rest is controlled by code. The result is shown in Figure 1.30. To end, click the End button (or choose End from the Run menu).

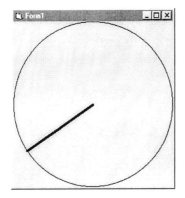

Figure 1.30   A clock hand moving inside a circle

```
Private Sub Form_Load()
    Dim I As Single
    Dim Rad As Single
    Dim Pi As Single

    Show           'show form
    Width = ScaleHeight      'make perfect square
    Width = 2 * ScaleHeight - ScaleWidth
    Line1.X1 = ScaleHeight / 2  'center 1st point
    Line1.Y1 = ScaleWidth / 2
    Line1.BorderWidth = 3     'line width
    Shape1.Top = 0            'move to top left
```

```
        Shape1.Left = 0
        Shape1.Width = ScaleWidth    'stretch to max
        Shape1.Height = ScaleHeight
        Shape1.Shape = vbShapeCircle
            'or 3; change to circle
        Scale (-1, 1)-(1, -1) 'custom scale
        Rad = 0.9                    'radius
        Pi = 4 * Atn(1)            'pi value
        Do        'continuously move 2nd point
            For I = 2 * Pi To 0 Step -0.01 'clockwise
                DoEvents      'allow break
                Line1.X2 = Rad * Cos(I)      'get x axis
                Line1.Y2 = Rad * Sin(I)      'get y axis
            Next I
        Loop                        'infinite loop
    End Sub
```

Chapter 2
Code, Output, and Debug

TOPICS

A. Form and Code Windows
B. Managing the Code Window
C. The Editing Environment
D. Editing Tools
E. Cursor Movement
F. Search and Replace
G. Some Basic Language Elements (a first look at some advanced topics)
H. Calculator Project
I. Printing Output
J. Saving and Opening Text Files (a first look at an advanced topic)
K. Preliminary Debugging (a first look at an advanced topic)
    a. Single Stepping
    b. Breakpoints
    c. The Locals Window
    d. The Immediate Window

KEY TERMS

Break mode   The state when program execution is temporarily halted. You can use many ways to make Visual Basic go into break mode. A number of debugging tools are available in break mode.

Breakpoint   The point in the Code window to pause program execution and to shift to break mode for debugging. Press F9 or click the Margin Indicator Bar to set/unset a breakpoint.

Code window   A window used to write and edit Basic code lines. You can use this window similar to the way you use Windows Notepad or the DOS Editor. The quickest way to go to this window is to press F7 or double-click an object on the form.

Comment   A remark to document program lines. Add a remark after an apostrophe ('); this is usually placed at the end of a line. You can also use Rem placed at the beginning of a separate line. Anything after ' or Rem is ignored by Visual Basic.

Data tip   Comparable to the tooltip feature available in most Windows programs. In break mode, when you move the mouse pointer over a variable name or when you select an expression, something may pop up to show the current value. This is a data tip.

Debug   To identify and eliminate program errors. This word is also recognized as an object by Visual Basic. When you use code to output to the Debug object, the result will be shown in the Immediate window.

Full Module View   All the procedures in the Code window are displayed in a continuum, normally with each separated from the next by a separator line.

Immediate window   The window where you can enter a variable or expression to get an immediate result. This was previously known as the Debug window or the Immediate pane.

IntelliSense   A feature to facilitate coding. When you type something in the Code window, a sample syntax or list box may pop up to help you complete a statement.

Locals window   A window that will show in break mode all the available variables and their current values.

Margin Indicator Bar   A gray area on the left side of the Code window where different symbols will appear to indicate different states and activities.

MDI and SDI   Multiple document interface and single document interface. The default IDE in VB5 is the MDI environment. The IDE is contained in an outer window. Forms are confined to designer windows and many individual windows can be docked to any of the four IDE borders. You can use Tools | Options | Advanced tab to check SDI Development Environment to switch to the SDI mode in the future. In SDI, the outer window is gone and forms stand by themselves.

Procedure View   Each procedure in the Code window is displayed as a separate unit. Other procedures are not visible.

Single Stepping   Executing code one statement at a time. Press F8 repeatedly to do that. Visual Basic gets into break mode. A number of tools are available for debugging your code.

Split bar   A line that splits the Code window into two halves; a little rectangle at the top of the vertical scroll bar in the Code window, just above the upward arrow. Double-clicking it adds a dividing line in the middle of the Code window; double-clicking the dividing line clears it. You can also choose Window | Split to do the same thing.

The Code window and several debugging windows are available in the Visual Basic environment. You use the former to write code and the latter to debug the code. This chapter explains how to use these vital programming tools. In addition, this chapter introduces a number of Basic language elements, supplies a project that simulates a calculator, and explains the mechanism of sending output data to the printer, screen, and disk.

FORM AND CODE WINDOWS

When you start a new project, the New Project dialog box appears. After you choose a project type (Standard EXE is the most common), a window with a form inside appears, as shown in Figure 2.1.

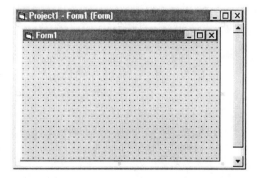

Figure 2.1   The designer window and form window

In previous versions of Visual Basic, a form is a separate entity that can be dragged at design time to any place on the screen. At run time, the form transforms itself into a window and appears in the same location. This is now changed.

In VB5, things have become a little more complicated. There is now an outside window that houses a form window (or form for short). The outer window is known as a **designer window** (or **visual designer** or **designer** for short). When you have a form inside this window, you are designing a form, so you can also call it a **form designer**. It can also be called an **Object window** because this is where you see visual objects. From the View menu (or the Project Explorer window's shortcut menu), you can choose Object to go to this window or Code to go to its companion window.

Every time you add a form, a new form designer and its companion Code window will be made available. After you already have Form1 in Project1 (see the designer's caption), you can choose Add Form from the Project menu (or click the second button on the Standard toolbar) to add a new form to the current project. The new form's default caption is Form2, and a new designer window appears with the caption Project1 - Form2 (Form). If you double-click this form, the caption becomes Project1 - Form2 (Code). To remove this form, select it and choose Remove Form2 from the Project menu. You can also display this command by right-clicking the form name in the Project window.

A form has eight **sizing handles**, but most of them are disabled. Only the three at the bottom right are enabled. You can use them to change the form's size inside the designer. You cannot use the other sizing handles to detach the form from the designer's top and left borders.

A form's title bar appears to have all the trappings of a typical window, but most of them are inactive at design time—unlike their counterparts in previous versions. The only one that will respond to you is the Maximize button which becomes the Restore button after the form is maximized. Maximizing a form at design time may make the form larger than the designer. In that case, scroll bars will appear in the designer for you to show different parts of the form. Double-clicking the title bar still works to maximize and restore the form's size.

The items on the designer window's title bar are all active at design time. If you click the Maximize button, the four buttons attach themselves to the menu bar. You'll then use these buttons to maneuver the designer window.

Both Code and designer windows are undockable. That means you cannot attach them to a border of the IDE window—unlike a toolbar, the Toolbox, the Properties window, or the Form Layout window. These windows, however, can be made undockable, as explained in Chapter 1.

When a undockable window like a Code or designer window is maximized, it will affect other undockable windows but not dockable windows. The current undockable window will fill up the available space not occupied by dockable windows attached to the borders of the IDE window. If a dockable window is not attached to a border, then its stays on top of the maximized window.

A form's design-time normal size determines its run-time size. Maximizing a form at design time does not maximize the form at run time. Running the form will restore its normal size at both design time and run time.

The run-time location of a form can be confusing. The following options are available when you right-click the form in the **Form Layout window** and choose Startup Position. The same options also appear in the **StartUpPosition** property of the form's Properties window. These two echo each other; a change in one is reflected in the other.

> Manual
> Center Owner
> Center Screen
> Windows Default

When you add a new form, the default run-time position is **Windows Default**. You can see this value in the Properties window and the Form Layout window. In this setting, the run-time position of the form changes in a cascading manner. Each time you run the form, it appears in a different location—moving rightward and downward, and then back to the top left again.

If you choose a Center option, the form will most of the time appear in the center of the screen. This position is not affected by the form's Top or Left values entered in code or set in the Properties window.

The startup position will be changed to **Manual** if you drag the form in the Form Layout window or change the Top or Left property in the Properties window.

On some occasions you may want to maximize a form window or Code window to have more working space. When a window is maximized, all the undockable windows will be maximized (and covered up) as well. On such occasions, use the following techniques to manage windows or move from one to another:

- Press Shift+F7 to open or switch to the current form/designer window.

- Press F7 to open or switch to the companion Code window.

- Press Ctrl+Tab or Ctrl+F6 to cycle through all the undockable windows.

- Use the Window menu to arrange the undockable windows.

- Double-click a form or a control on the form to move to its Code window. Use Shift+F7 to return to the form window.

- From the Code window, bring up the Project window, double-click the desired form name to go to its form window.

- Use the Project window to go to another project's form or Code window by selecting the form and then clicking View Code or View Object.

- When you need to frequently switch from one window to another, make the Project window easily accessible. You can make it dockable and attach it to one border. You can also make it dockable but let it float on top. You can then resize it and drag it to one corner so it won't interfere with your work. (You can treat the Toolbox the same way.)

- When you don't need a window, click its X button to close it. Make sure you click the second X from the top. If you click the topmost X, you'll exit the IDE, not just close a window. Some windows also have the Hide option when you pop up its shortcut menu. Choosing it has the same effect as clicking its X button. You can open a closed window by using the Project window or the Standard toolbar.

TIP: MDI and SDI

If you have used previous versions of Visual Basic, you may be surprised with VB5's IDE and the new designer window.

The IDE is enclosed in a window (see Figure 1.3 in Chapter 1), and each form is enclosed in a designer window (Figure 2.1). Both of these are new. They are controlled by the **Tools | Options | Advanced tab**. If you go to that tab, you'll find the **SDI Development Environment** unchecked by default. In this case, you are in the MDI (multiple document interface) development environment.

To be in the SDI (single document interface) environment, you check the SDI Development Environment check box and click OK. A message tells you that your change will not take effect until you restart Visual Basic. If you now restart Visual Basic, the IDE will look different. The outer window will disappear. Each form you add to a project will be by itself and not enclosed in a designer window. The IDE begins to resemble those in previous versions.

You can start Visual Basic in either mode by running the program with the /MDI or /SDI parameter on the command line. If you don't want to manually start the program, alter its shortcut's properties. Right-click the shortcut's name on the Windows desktop (or in another folder) to bring up its properties sheet. Open the Shortcut tab and add the parameter after the program name in the Target box.

In SDI, windows cannot be docked to any side because there are no borders for docking. Dockable windows can still be linked to one another. Just drag one window's title bar and drop it on another. Dockable and undockable windows can be on top of each other. In MDI, a dockable window is always on top of an undockable window.

In MDI, running a program in some situations may result in the form disappearing under the IDE. You can use the taskbar to bring the form to the top. Text written to the form may be erased. If you don't want that to happen, shrink the IDE window and drag the run-time form/window to outside the IDE-covered area.

MANAGING THE CODE WINDOW

The **Code window** serves three primary purposes, namely to:

- Manage objects and procedures
- Enter and edit code
- Debug code

You already know that the Code window (Figure 2.2) has at the top two combo boxes named **Object box** (left) and **Procedure box** (right).[1] You can pull down a list of available objects from the Object box and choose one to make it current. You can then pull down from the Procedure box a list of available events and choose one to display its procedure (or template). This arrangement lets you tie together various objects and their event procedures.

---

[1] If you move the mouse pointer over the left box, the **Object** tooltip will appear; **Procedure** will appear when the pointer goes over the right box.

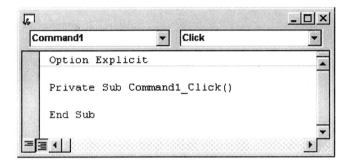

Figure 2.2   The Object and Procedure boxes in the Code window

When you want to write code for an object, you need to go to the Code window. Here are some ways to open the Code window:

- Double-click an object, such as a command button.

- Select an object and press F7.

- Select an object and then choose Code from the View menu.

- Right-click an object and choose View Code from the shortcut menu.

- Choose View | Project Explorer (Ctrl+R). The Project Explorer window opens. Select a form name in the list and click the View Code button.

- If an undockable window is maximized, press Ctrl+Tab or Ctrl+F6 to cycle through all the undockable windows.

Notice the two buttons at the bottom left corner of the Code window. These are known as **Procedure View** (left) and **Full Module View** (right). The latter is the default and appears depressed. In this view, all the procedures are shown in a continuum, each separated from another by a line. In **Procedure View**, only one procedure is shown at a time. To go to another procedure, you need to use the Procedure box or some keyboard combinations discussed in the next section. You can click either button to display your text in that view. Unless you have a good reason to do otherwise, keep the default Full Module View.

You may have written code for several procedures of an object. How do you know that? You can tell from the Procedure box's list. The bolded ones signify that they have code attached. This clue is useful when Procedure View is on.

When you finish writing code, you can leave the Code window open and run the program by pressing F5. When the program ends, this Code window reappears. This is convenient if you want to revise code. You can also close the Code window by clicking the X button. Or you can click any portion of a form to show the form without closing the Code window.

When the **Standard toolbar** is undocked and when the cursor is in the Code window, the right end of the toolbar shows two numbers, as shown in Figure 2.3. They tell you the current cursor location. The first is the line number and the second the column number. The line number is cumulative. It's the same regardless of whether you're in Procedure View or Full Module View. These numbers change when other objects have the focus. They disappear when the toolbar is docked.

Figure 2.3   The line and column numbers on the Standard toolbar

TIP: Object Browser and Procedure Switching

If you are developing a complex project, you should use the **Object Browser** to keep track of the numerous components. It has many uses that will be explained in later chapters. Here we demonstrate how you can use it to switch from one procedure to another.

To open the Object Browser, just press F2, click the Object Browser button (second from right) on the Standard toolbar, or choose Object Browser from the View menu. Figure 2.4 appears. From this dialog box, you can select a library or project (Project1 in our case) and then a class (Form1 in our example). After clicking Form1, all the available members (including procedures and properties) will be displayed.

If you click a property name in the Members list, a brief description will appear at the bottom. This is the same description at the bottom of the Properties window.

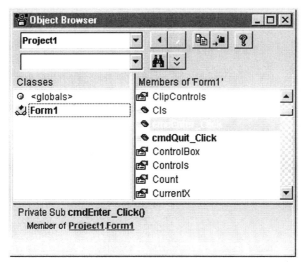

Figure 2.4   The Object Browser

Any procedures you have written also appear (and bolded) in the Members list. Figure 2.4 shows that we have written two procedures, namely cmdEnter_Click and cmdQuit_Click. If you want to view either, just click it and then click the **View Definition** button (second from the right) on the toolbar. The cursor will go to the selected procedure in the Code window. The View Definition option will also appear when you right click a procedure name.

If you have written procedures only in one form, you can easily use the Code window to find them. But if you have multiple forms and other modules, the Object Browser is faster. Just select a form or module on the left side, then select a proper procedure on the right side, and then choose View Definition to go to its Code window. Double-clicking a procedure name will take you there as well.

THE EDITING ENVIRONMENT

When you choose Options from the Tools menu, The **Options dialog box** appears. Six tabs become available: Editor, Editor Format, General, Docking, Environment, and Advanced. Editor and Editor Format are pertinent to the Code window.

The Editor tab includes several features of the new **IntelliSense technology** that first appeared in the Microsoft Office 97 suite. It can help you quickly complete a word or a statement. If you get used to it, it can save you many keystrokes while typing code.

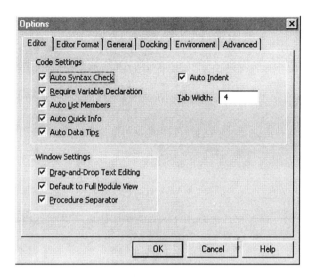

Figure 2.5   The Editor tab of the Options dialog box

Figure 2.5 shows the **Editor tab.** Notice that all the options are checked by default. If you wish, you can uncheck some or all of them; they should not be unchecked unless you have a good reason. Some of these don't have an effect until you add a new form.

Auto Syntax Check checks the syntax of your code at design time. When you enter something which Visual Basic does not understand, an error message appears to alert you. If you are developing a complex project, you may want to turn this off at the early stage. In that case, a design time error will not lead to an error message and the accompanying loud noise. An error line can still be identified because it is marked with the red color.

If **Require Variable Declaration** is checked, all the variables must be declared before use. Otherwise, an error will appear at run time. When this box is checked, adding a new Code window will automatically lead to **Option Explicit** appearing at the top of the window. Previous windows are not affected.

Auto List Members may lead to a list box popping out at the location where you are typing something. You can then scroll to the desired term, select it, and press Enter to insert the term at the cursor location. Sometimes after typing one or two letters, the desired term may be highlighted. If you press a certain key, the complete word will be inserted at the cursor location.

As an example, try typing the following in the Code window:

```
form1.
```

The moment you finish typing the period, a list pops up below where you type. At this point no word in the list is selected, and the first word of the alphabetic list appears at the top. Now type one more letter:

```
form1.c
```

This time Caption, the first word starting with C appears at the top and is highlighted. If you type a letter shown below, the consequence is described on the right:

=	Caption enters the Code window, followed by =.
spacebar	Caption and a space are entered.
Tab	Caption is entered but no additional space is added.
Enter	Caption is entered and the cursor goes down one line.
double-click	The double-clicked word in the list box is entered at the cursor location and the cursor stays after the word.

If you ignore the list and keep on typing, it will go away. You can also press Esc to shoo it away.

For this feature to work, you must supply the name of an existing object. Now try typing the following:

```
text1.
```

If a text box named Text1 has been added to the current form, a list pops up. If Text1 doesn't exist or is located in another form, nothing pops up. If Text1 is located in Form2, typing the following will pop up a list:

```
form2.text1.
```

If you want to change an existing method (procedure) or property name, you can right-click it to bring up a list of options and choose **List Properties/Methods**. A list of words will appear, with the matching one at the top of the list.

If you erase part of a word, you can bring up a list and choose one to complete the word. Just right-click the word and choose **Complete Word** from the list. If there is a match, the word is completed automatically and no list of words appears. If there is no match, the list stays and the closest match appears at the top and highlighted.

Auto Quick Info is useful when you are entering a function. The required syntax and arguments are shown so that you can correctly complete a statement. Try the following in the Code window:

```
msgbox
```

After you press the spacebar at the end of the word, a message pops up showing you how to complete this function.

Auto Data Tips will pop up a tooltip to show the value of a variable when the mouse pointer goes over the variable name. This happens only in break mode. If you want to show the value of an expression, select the expression and its value will pop up.

The default **tab width** is set at 4 and Auto Indent is on. You can change the 4 value to another value if you want a different distance when you press the Tab key. If you have long code lines, reducing the number to 2 may let you see more text at one time.

When **Auto Indent** is on, pressing Enter in the Code window keeps the cursor at the same distance from the left margin, instead of returning to flush left. This is useful for proper indentation of code lines. If you want to move the cursor to the previous tab stop on the left, press the **Backspace** key or **Shift+Tab**. Pressing the left-arrow key moves the cursor only by one character.

The Window Settings pane at the bottom has three check boxes. This is where you determine the default way of display procedures in the Code window, as explained earlier. Checking **Default to Full Module View** and **Procedure Separator** is what determines the default state of showing all the procedures, with each separated from another by a line.

With **Drag-and-Drop Text Editing** checked, you can highlight some text lines and drag them and drop them in a new location inside the same Code window, or into another Code window or the Immediate window (this will be covered at the end of this chapter). If you want to copy instead, hold down Ctrl as you drag and drop.

The **Editor Format tab** (Figure 2.6) lets you change fonts and colors. You can pull down from the Font combo box a list of all the fonts on your system and select one. You can also select a font size from the Size combo box.

The large list box on the left lets you determine colors for various text lines in the Code window. As you click each displayed line, the bottom boxes change to reflect the default or selected options. If you want to change, use one of the three combo boxes to make a selection; the result will appear in the Sample box. The default Automatic options work just fine unless you are finicky.

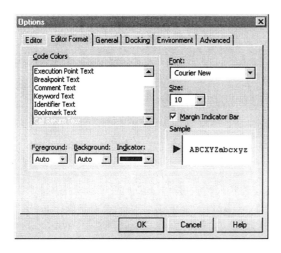

Figure 2.6   The Editor Format tab of the Options dialog box

If the **Margin Indicator Bar** is checked, clicking each item in the Code Colors list box may lead to various icons showing up in the Sample box. This is what you will see in the actual Code window. The Margin Indicator Bar is a gray vertical band on the left side of the Code window (see Figure 2.2). Various icons will appear as you try to debug your code. This bar will not appear if you uncheck Margin Indicator Bar.

Keep in mind that your alterations to the Options dialog box will be saved to disk. What you do here will affect other users of the same computer. If you are using a computer in your school's PC lab, you should not tinker with the values here.

EDITING TOOLS

When you write code, you need to know the techniques of editing text. As you need to type and edit lots of text, proficiency in editing techniques can increase your productivity. If you have used any text processor from Microsoft, such as Windows Notepad/WordPad, the DOS Editor, or the editor that comes with a

Quick language such as Quick C, you can quickly master the Code window. If not, you need to devote more time to it.

As you write and edit your code, you can use the **Edit menu** to maneuver text. The tools you find here are standard with most Windows and other Microsoft programs. If you are not familiar with this system, you should spend some time mastering it.

The first step is to get acquainted with the Edit menu. When you edit text, open this menu to show the available tools. This menu is so long that an upward and downward triangle will appear at the top or bottom for you to scroll to view some hidden options. Most options have shortcut keys. After you are familiar with this system, you can use the shortcut keys without opening this menu.

The Edit menu will have various options dimmed (unavailable) under various circumstances—depending on whether you have selected text, whether you have done something that you can undo, or whether the Clipboard contains text that can be pasted.

Cut, **Copy**, and **Paste** are commonly used tools to maneuver text. To cut text, you must select it first. To **select text**, follow these steps:

1. Move the cursor to one end of the text.

2. Hold down the Shift key.

3. Move the cursor to the other end of the text.

The portion is now highlighted. A shortcut for the above is to move the pointer (I-beam) to one end and drag the pointer to the other end.

You can do the following to selected text.

- Press Del to delete.
- Press Ctrl+X (or Shift+Del) to cut.
- Press Ctrl+C (or Ctrl+Ins) to copy.

When text is deleted, it cannot be retrieved; the only recourse is to use Undo before you do anything else. Make sure you do not confuse Del (delete) and Ctrl+X (cut).

Cut and copy are different. When text is cut, it is deleted from the screen but a copy is stored in the Clipboard. When text is copied, it remains on the screen but a copy is sent to the Clipboard.

The **Clipboard** is the Windows Clipboard. There is only one Clipboard and all Windows applications share it. You can send text or graphics from any Windows application and retrieve the contents to any Windows application. The Clipboard contents stay until something else is sent there by another application.

To **paste** the Clipboard contents, follow these steps:

1.   Move the cursor to the desired location.

2.   Press Ctrl+V (Shift+Ins), or choose Paste from the Edit menu.

If you want to cancel pasting, choose Undo from the Edit menu.

NOTE   A quick way to access most of the options in the Edit menu is to right-click the Code window. A long list of options, mostly from the Edit menu but some from other menus, will pop up. If there is selected text, the Cut and Copy options will be available.

NOTE   Some programs in compliance with the Windows 95 standards, such as WordPad, allows you to drag selected text lines to the desktop to create an OLE file called a **scrap**. You can then double-click the scrap to run the application and retrieve the text lines saved to the scrap. This feature has not been implemented in VB5.

VB5 has added many features to the bottom of the Edit menu. These options and a few others are available from the **Edit toolbar** (Figure 2.7). This toolbar can be displayed/hidden by right-clicking the menu bar or another toolbar and then checking/unchecking the Edit option in the popup menu.

     1   2   3   4   5   6   7   8   9   10   11   12   13   14

Figure 2.7   **The Edit toolbar**

The Edit toolbar's button names, from left to right, are explained below; you can move the mouse pointer to each to pop up its name.

1. **List Properties/Methods**   Shows a list of variable, property, procedure, and intrinsic constant names. Keystroke equivalent: **Ctrl+J**. See a previous section for examples.

2. **List Constants**   Displays a list of available constants. Keystroke equivalent: **Ctrl+Shift+J**. For example, if you type "Visible =", a popup will show False and True. If you want to change, place the cursor on the value after = and press Ctrl+Shift+J to pop up the options.

3. **Quick Info**   Displays a popup tip showing the syntax of an intrinsic function or an existing user-created procedure. Keystroke equivalent: **Ctrl+I**. You can cursor to a declared variable or property name and press Ctrl+I to pop up a syntax. For example, if you press Ctrl+I with the cursor on Visible, the popup will show "Visible As Boolean".

4. **Parameter Info**   Pops up a sample syntax providing parameter information how to complete a function. Keystroke equivalent: **Ctrl+Shift+I**. For example, after you type "MsgBox (", the popup appears. This is parameter info. The popup will also appear if you place the cursor inside the parentheses and press Ctrl+Shift+I.

5. **Complete Word**   Completes the word being typed. Keystroke equivalent: Ctrl+spacebar. For example, typing Msg and pressing **Ctrl+spacebar** will lead to MsgBox. If no exact match if found, the Properties/Methods list (#1 above) will appear.

6. **Indent**   Moves all the selected lines to the next tab stop. Keystroke equivalent: **Tab**.

7. **Outdent**   Moves all the selected lines to the previous tab stop. Keystroke equivalent: **Shift+Tab**.

8. **Toggle Breakpoint**   Marks/unmarks a breakpoint; from the Debug menu. Keystroke equivalent: **F9**.

9. **Comment Block**   Adds an apostrophe (') to the beginning of all the selected lines.

10. **Uncomment Block**   Removes all the leading apostrophes, if any. Comment Block and Uncomment Block are not available from any menu on the menu bar.

11. **Toggle Bookmark**   Marks/unmarks the current line; a marked line has a bookmark icon appearing on the Margin Indicator Bar.

12. **Next Bookmark**   Moves the cursor to the next bookmark.

13. **Previous Bookmark**   Moves the cursor to the previous bookmark.

14. **Clear All Bookmarks**   Removes all the bookmark icons from the Margin Indicator Bar.

CURSOR MOVEMENT

A big part of editing text has to do with moving the cursor (also known as the insertion point). You can use the mouse or keyboard to move the cursor to any place you wish.

With the mouse, you can move the I-beam (pointer) and click any visible place inside the Code window to move the cursor there. You can also use the mouse to maneuver the scroll bar to scroll text up and down. This only scrolls the display but does not move the cursor. When a new area becomes visible, clicking the editing screen moves the cursor to the new location.

To scroll text with the mouse, you can click the up (or left) or down (or right) arrow in a scroll bar to scroll by a small increment, or click the area between an arrow key and the scroll box in the middle of a scroll bar to scroll by a large increment. You can also drag a scroll box to scroll text up and down or left and right. Figure 2.2 shows all the components for scrolling text.

It is often more convenient to use the keyboard to move the cursor. Unlike using the mouse to scroll text, using a cursor key both scrolls text and moves the cursor. The following table can serve as a quick guide:

PgUp	One screen up
PgDn	One screen down
Ctrl+PgUp	One screen left
Ctrl+PgDn	One screen right
Home	Left of the current line
End	Right of the current line

Ctrl+Home	Top of the window
Ctrl+End	Bottom of the window
Ctrl+→	Right one word
Ctrl+←	Left one word
Ctrl+↑	Previous procedure
Ctrl+↓	Next procedure

When you press PgUp or PgDn, you may be moving the cursor within the current procedure. But if there is no more text to scroll, the cursor will go to the previous or next procedure—if Procedure View is on. If you want to move directly to another existing procedure, use Ctrl+↑ or Ctrl+↓ instead. This technique applies regardless of whether Procedure View or Full Module View is on.

SEARCH AND REPLACE

When you have lengthy and complex code, you can use the search and replace features to locate and/or replace text. This is easier than looking for something manually or changing text one piece at a time.

Choosing **Find** (Ctrl+F) from the Edit menu leads to a dialog box shown in Figure 2.8. If you have previously entered a search string or if there is a text string selected, it appears in the top text box. You can click Find Next or press Enter to start searching. If there is no search string or if you want to search for another item, type it here and the click Find Next.

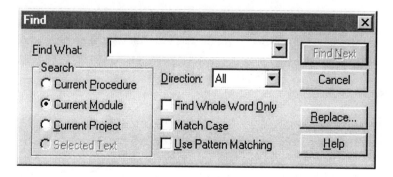

Figure 2.8   The Find dialog box to search for a text string

The three check boxes in the middle let you determine whether you want to find whole words (flanked by spaces or other delimiters), words that match the case of the search string, or a specified matching pattern. If you check **Use Pattern Matching**, then **Match Case** is not available. In that case, certain characters have special meanings. You can use the following **wildcard** characters in a search string. Keep in mind that these characters have no special meaning when Use Pattern Matching is not checked.

> ?   One single character at a fixed position
> *   0 or more characters
> #   One numeric digit (0 - 9)
> !   Excluding characters inside [ ].

Here are some search strings and their matching strings:

b?k	bok, bak, Bok, BUK
b*k	bk, book, brook, Buick
b*	from b to the end of the same line
1#3	123, 103, 193
[!123]	anything except 123

Placing the * character at the end of a search string has a sweeping implication; it means to include everything else in the same line. So if you specify *print** as the search string, it will match any text line starting from *print* to the end of the same line. Keep this in mind when you want to search and replace strings.

If you want more details about these characters, search for the ? character from the online help. Also, you can type **Like** in the Code window and press F1 to get the same result.

The default search direction is All. Each search starts from the current position forward (downward). When the end is reached, the search continues from the top. When the entire specified area has been searched, a message tells you that. You can change All to Up or Down. When the end is reached, you'll be prompted with Yes/No to continue from the other end.

When a matching string is found, it is highlighted (selected) in the Code window. You can then delete, cut, copy, or do whatever to this selected text as explained earlier. The Find dialog box remains and may cover up the found string. If you want to keep the dialog box, you can drag the Find dialog box to another spot. If the Find dialog box is still displayed, you can click Find Next (or press Alt+N) to search for the next matching string. You can close this window by pressing Esc or clicking the Cancel or Close (X) button.

When the Find dialog box is closed, you can press F3 to search for the next matching string in the direction specified in the dialog box; this does not display the Find dialog box. If you want to search in the reverse direction, press Shift+F3 instead. If you want to display the dialog box, you need to press Ctrl+F or choose Find from the Edit menu.

If you choose **Replace** (Ctrl+H) from the Edit menu, a new dialog box appears, as shown in Figure 2.9. You can also get this dialog box by clicking the Replace button from the Find dialog box. Here you need to enter a search string and a replace string; if you have previously made these entries, they'll reappear. Choose Find Next to find and highlight the next matching string. If you want to replace this string, choose Replace to replace the current string and search for the next one; if not, choose Find Next to skip the current one and search for the next matching string. If you are sure of what you are doing, choose Replace All to replace all the matching strings without pause. If the result is not what you expected, go to the Code window and press Ctrl+Z to undo.

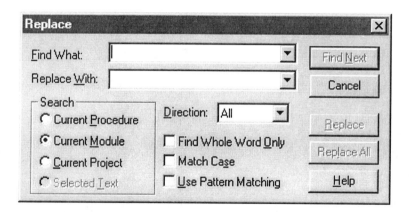

Figure 2.9   The Replace dialog box to replace text strings

While Search is case insensitive by default (when Match Case is not checked), Replace is literal—exactly the way you specify. For example, you can search for *uppercase* or *UPPERCASE* and replace it with *UpperCase*.

 WARNING   You can use Replace to erase matching strings. Just enter a search string and provide no replace string. This is dangerous when combined with wildcards and Replace All. You can wipe out many things without meaning to. If you want to reverse the action, choose Undo from the Edit menu before you do anything else.

TIP: Window Splitting

The Code window's editing area can be split into two panes, each with its own scroll bars, as shown in Figure 2.10. Splitting the window this way lets you view two separate procedures, each shown in a separate pane. If Procedure View is on, each pane can show only one procedure at a time.

To split the window into two halves, double-click the **Split bar**, a little rectangle at the top of the vertical scroll bar, just above the upward arrow. You can also choose Window | Split to do the same thing.

If you want to manually split the window, move the pointer to the Split bar. The pointer changes to another shape, with upward and downward arrows. Drag the pointer up or down to determine the dividing line.

To clear the dividing line, just double-click it; the bottom pane remains open, but the top pane is closed. To change the dividing line (after the window is split), just drag the line up or down. You can use this technique to close the top or bottom pane; drag it up to close the top pane or down to close the bottom pane.

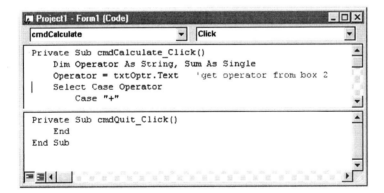

Figure 2.10   The Code window after splitting

To switch to either pane after the window is split, just click the desired side. You can also press F6 to do the switching; pressing F6 does nothing when the window is not split. As you switch up or down, notice the change in the Object and Procedure boxes; they will change to reflect the current (active) pane.

TIP: Selecting Text

Have you noticed that each line in the Code window is not aligned at the left margin? There is a little distance between the left margin and the first character of each line. This space serves a useful purpose, and you should take advantage of it.

When you move the pointer to this space, the I-beam is changed to a top-right-pointing arrow. If you left-click the mouse button once, the current line is selected (highlighted). If you right-click instead (when no text is selected), the current line is selected and a shortcut menu appears. Included in this menu are Cut, Copy, and Paste. When no text is selected, the shortcut menu that appears after right-clicking does not include Cut or Copy.

If you double-click this space, the entire current procedure is selected. You can then right-click anywhere to pop up the shortcut menu.

If you hold down Ctrl and click this space (or press Ctrl+A), everything in the current window is selected. If Full Module View is on, all the procedures are selected by this single move. If not, only the current procedure is selected.

VB5 allows you to drag and drop selected text, if the feature is not disabled in the Tools | Options | Editor tab. After selecting text, move the pointer to the selected area, hold down the left button and start dragging. An icon will appear for you to drag to the target area or another window, which must be visible. Dragging moves the selected text. If you want to copy instead, hold down Ctrl as you drag.

What is said above can mostly be applied to the Immediate window explained in another section below.

DRILL

_____ 1.   This key can be used to copy text to the Clipboard:
    a.   Del
    b.   Ctrl+X
    c.   Shift+Del
    d.   Ctrl+Ins

_____ 2.   This key is used to paste text into the Code window:

a.   Ctrl+C
b.   Ctrl+X
c.   Shift+Ins
d.   Ctrl+Ins

Choose an option below to answer questions 3-8 related to the Code window.
a. Ctrl+Home,   b. Ctrl+End,   c. Ctrl+PgUp,   d. Ctrl+PgDn
e. Ctrl+↑,   f. Ctrl+↓

_____ 3.   Moves the cursor to the top.

_____ 4.   Moves the cursor to the bottom.

_____ 5.   Moves the cursor right one screen.

_____ 6.   Moves the cursor left one screen.

_____ 7.   Shows the previous procedure.

_____ 8.   Shows the next procedure.

_____ 9.   To search for the next matching string in the Code window without opening the Find dialog box, you need to press:
a.   Ctrl+F
b.   Ctrl+R
c.   F3
d.   Shift+F3

_____ 10.   You can divide or merge the Code window by double-clicking the
_____ bar.

PRACTICE

■   1.   Explain the sizing handles of a form.

■   2.   Explain how a form behaves at run time when its default startup position is not changed.

■   3.   Explain the two additional numbers on the Standard toolbar when the toolbar is undocked and the cursor is in the Code window.

■   4.   Explain the role of the Margin Indicator Bar.

■ 5. Explain how you can use the empty area inside the left edge of the Code window to select:

   a. a single line
   b. the current procedure
   c. all the displayed code

■ 6. Write down the cursor-movement keystroke for each of the following moves in the Code window:

   One screen left
   One screen right
   Top of the current procedure
   Bottom of the current procedure
   Previous procedure
   Next procedure

■ 7. What are the names of the two buttons at the bottom left of the Code window? What do they do?

■ 8 How do you split the Code window into two panes? How do you merge them?

SOME BASIC LANGUAGE ELEMENTS
(A First Look at Some Advanced Topics)

This section introduces some simple elements of the Basic language, including For-Next, Do-Loop, Select-End Select, and arrays. Later chapters will provide more details. At this time, however, you need to have some rudimentary knowledge about them because they are needed to do other things.

The **For-Next** statement executes a block of statements a number of times until a condition is met. The following procedure will print five numbers to the screen in five separate lines. When For is first executed, variable I has the value of 1, so 1 is printed. Since I has not exceeded 5, the ending value, Next directs execution back to For. I now has the value of 2. This continues until I exceeds 5. At that point, execution continues below Next.

```
Private Sub Form_Click()
    Dim I As Integer

    For I = 1 To 5
        Print I
```

```
     Next I
End Sub
```

To write this procedure, double-click the form to go to the Code window. Pull down Click from the Procedure box on the right; the procedure template will appear. Then type the code lines as shown. Press F5 to run. Click the form to execute the procedure. When you are done, click the form's X button to close the window or the End button on the Standard toolbar to end.

A For-Next loop can include another For-Next loop. Each time the outer loop is executed, the inner loop will complete its course. In the following procedure, when I has the value of 1, J will go from 1 to 3. By the time J completes its fifth round, 15 numbers are printed to the screen, as shown in Figure 2.11.

```
Private Sub Form_Click()
    Dim I As Integer
    Dim J As Integer

    For I = 1 To 5
        For J = 1 To 3
            Print I * J,
        Next J
        Print
    Next I
End Sub
```

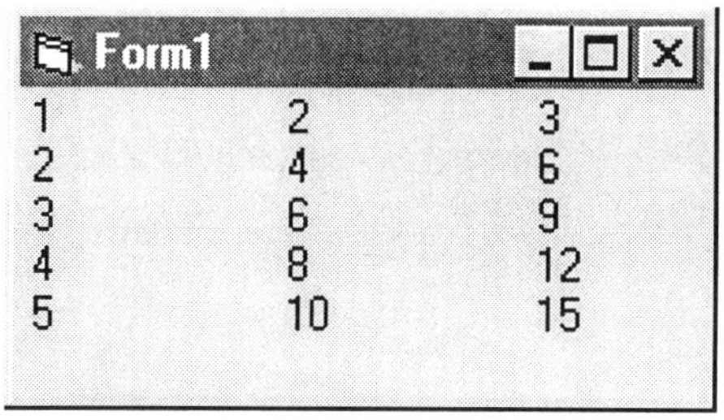

Figure 2.11   Output by two nested loops

The **Print** method by itself will print nothing and move the print head to a new line. When there is a comma (,) at the end, the print head will move to the next predetermined column position. If you want the print head to stay put, put a semicolon (;) at the end. These issues will be elaborated in Chapter 3.

The **Do-Loop** statement can do what For-Next can, except that you have to tell it how to increment a variable's value. The following procedure will print five numbers to the screen, just as our first For-Next example. Since I doesn't automatically add 1 after each loop, we have to do it in code.

```
Private Sub Form_Click()
    Dim I As Integer

    I = 1
    Do While I < 6
        Print I
        I = I + 1
    Loop
End Sub
```

The following procedure will do what our second For-Next example does and output the same as Figure 2.11.

```
Private Sub Form_Click()
    Dim I As Integer
    Dim J As Integer

    I = 1
    J = 1
    Do While I < 6
        Do While J < 4
            Print I * J,
            J = J + 1
        Loop
        Print
        J = 1
        I = I + 1
    Loop
End Sub
```

When you want your code to make a decision and choose a course of action, the simplest statement to use is **If-Then**. Here are two variations:

```
    If varX > varY Then Print "OK"

    If varX > varY Then
        Print "OK"
    Else
        Print "Not"
    End If
```

In the first example, if varX is greater than varY, OK is printed; otherwise the whole statement is ignored. In the second example, one of the two will be printed. In this multiline structure, the End If statement is necessary.

The **Select-End Select** statement is more versatile than If-Then when there are multiple options. In the following procedure, "small" will be printed to the screen because the Num value falls in that range. If Num is outside the 1-30 range, the Else Case clause will be executed. If this optional clause is absent, then nothing will be printed.

```
Private Sub Form_Click()
    Dim Num As Integer

    Num = 10
    Select Case Num
        Case 1 To 10
            Print "small"
        Case 11 To 20
            Print "medium"
        Case 21 To 30
            Print "large"
        Case Else
            Print "unknown"
    End Select
End Sub
```

Another language element you need to be aware of is an array. An **array** is a variable that contains multiple elements. They all share the same name, but are distinguished by different index numbers. It's like the Smith family all sharing the same name but identified by Smith 1, Smith 2, and so on.

In the following example, we declare Smith as a string array with five elements. By default, the first element has the 0 index value, so Smith(0) represents the first element. Then we assign a string to each element. Then we print out the names. The result is shown in Figure 2.12.

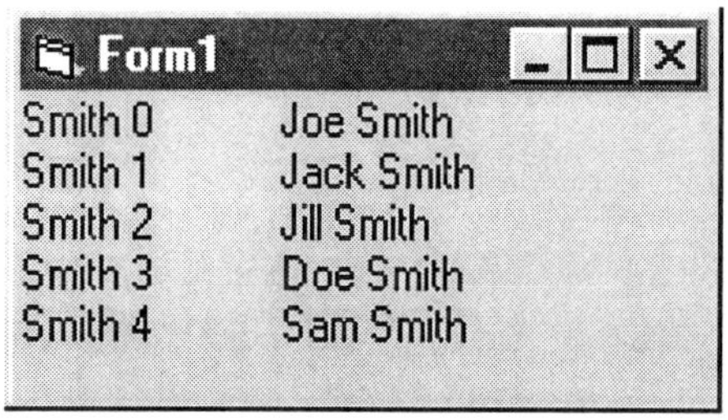

Figure 2.12   Output of array elements

```
Private Sub Form_Click()
    Dim I As Integer
    Dim Smith(4) As String

    Smith(0) = "Joe"
```

```
        Smith(1)  =  "Jack"
        Smith(2)  =  "Jill"
        Smith(3)  =  "Doe"
        Smith(4)  =  "Sam"

        For I = 0 To 4
            Print "Smith " & I,  Smith(I) & " Smith"
        Next I
End Sub
```

If you want a different value for the first element, you can specify it. In the example below, Smith has five elements, ranging from 1 to 5. Since we declare Smith as an Integer array, each element can store only an integer.

```
        Dim Smith(1 To 5) As Integer
```

CALCULATOR PROJECT

We are going to create a project that will let the user enter two numbers and an operator to calculate the result.

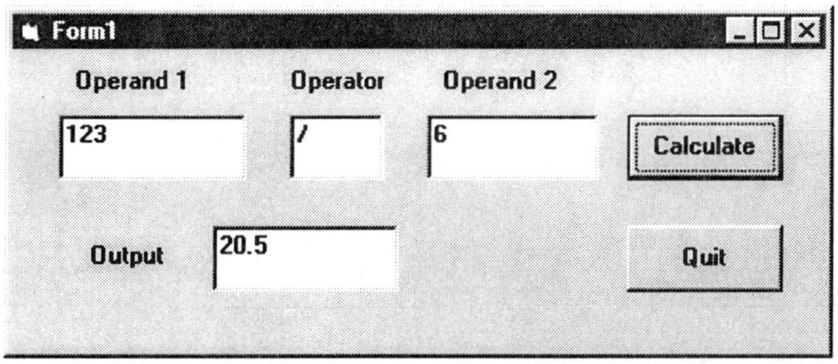

Figure 2.13   The Calculator project interface

Our project has four labels, as shown in Figure 2.13. There are also four text boxes and two command buttons. When the program runs, the user can click each of the first three text boxes and make entries. To make it convenient, at design time you can specify 0, 1, and 2 as the values for these boxes' **TabIndex** property. That way, the cursor stays in the first box when the program begins. After typing the first entry, you can then press Tab to go to the next box.

The objects have their properties changed as shown below.

Object	Property	Value
Command1	Caption	Calculate
	Name	cmdCalculate
Command1	Caption	Quit
	Name	cmdQuit
Label1	Caption	Operand1
Label2	Caption	Operator
Label3	Caption	Operand2
Label4	Caption	Output
Text1	Text	(none)
	Name	txtOp1
	TabIndex	0
Text2	Text	(none)
	Name	txtOptr
	TabIndex	1
Text3	Text	(none)
	Name	txtOp2
	TabIndex	2
Text4	Text	(none)
	Name	txtOut

The two command buttons' procedures are shown below.

(2CALC1.FRM)

```
Private Sub cmdCalculate_Click()    '--Listing 1--
    Dim Operator As String
    Dim Sum As Single

    Operator = txtOptr.Text    'get operator from box 2

    Select Case Operator
        Case "+"
            Sum = Val(txtOp1.Text) + Val(txtOp2.Text)
        Case "-"
            Sum = Val(txtOp1.Text) - Val(txtOp2.Text)
        Case "*"
            Sum = Val(txtOp1.Text) * Val(txtOp2.Text)
        Case "/"
            Sum = Val(txtOp1.Text) / Val(txtOp2.Text)
    End Select

    txtOut.Text = Sum        'show result in box 4
End Sub

Private Sub cmdQuit_Click()
    End
End Sub
```

When the Calculate button is clicked, the entry in Text2 is assigned to the variable named Operator. The Select Case structure then determines what value will be assigned to Sum. If you wish, you can use four If-Then statements instead. But that will be a less elegant approach.

The **Val** function converts a text string to a numeric, which can then be arithmetically manipulated. This function is required in an addition operation, but not in others. If this function is not used in the first If line, the two operands will be concatenated, not added.

We've also added two **comments** in our code. A comment is explanatory text placed after an apostrophe ('). Anything after the apostrophe is ignored during execution. You can also place a comment after the **Rem** statement; this statement, however, must be placed at the beginning of a line.

PRINTING OUTPUT

There are occasions when you want to output to the printer the entries you have made and the result produced by a program. To do that, you need to tell Visual Basic to print to an object named **Printer**.

Normally when you use the **Print** method[2] to print something, by default the result goes to the current form window. If you want to print to another object, you need to specify it instead. Such an object may be: Debug, Printer, or a picture box.

In the cmdPrint_Click procedure shown below, we specify the Printer object before each Print command. When this procedure is executed, all the items to be printed will go to the printer (make sure it is turned on). If we did not specify Printer, the output would go to the form window instead.

```
Sub cmdPrint_Click ()
    Printer.Print txtOp1.Text; txtOptr.Text; txtOp2.Text;
    Printer.Print "="; txtOut.Text
    Printer.EndDoc  'flush buffer
End Sub
```

---

[2]A **method**, as used in Visual Basic, means a command directed at an object. The method and the object are connected by a period, such as
`Printer.Print`.

Figure 2.14 shows a command button added to our previous interface. The Name property is also changed to cmdPrint. In this new arrangement, you handle the interface as before. If you decide to print the result, click the Print button. The four entries will then be printed in one line, exactly the way they will appear in the window if you take out all the Printer references.

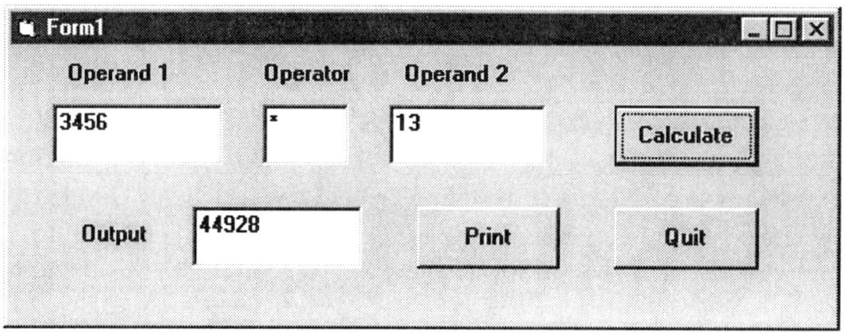

Figure 2.14   The added Print button

The **EndDoc** method applies only to the Printer object. It has the effect of emptying your printer buffer (memory). Without this statement, printing will not be done until you end the program or fill up the printer buffer. If you want to end a print job, you can use the **Printer.KillDoc** method to abruptly abort printing.

On a dot-matrix printer, the program will cause a page eject (roll the printer paper up to the beginning of the new page) even though you print just one line. There is no way to prevent this waste of paper except turning off the printer as soon as the rolling begins. You can roll back the unused portion to reuse it.

Sometimes you may want to print half a page and then continue printing at the beginning of the next page. To do that, add a **Printer.NewPage** line before printing the next item. When the NewPage method is executed, the printer rolls up the paper to the beginning of the next page. Any printing after that will be done on the new page.

The Printer object also has the **Page** property. It can be used to print a page number on a page. Here is an example:

```
Printer.Print "page # ";
Printer.Print Printer.Page
```

The first line will print the text string inside the quotes, and the second an Arabic number that is the current page number. The two lines can be combined like this:

```
Printer.Print "page # "; Printer.Page
```

We put a semicolon (;) after each item to be printed. Each item is printed on the same line with no extra space. You can also use a comma (,) instead. In that case, the item after the comma is printed in the next column. The last part of Chapter 3 fully explains various techniques of formatting screen output.

The Printer object has lots of other methods and properties. The online help on it (search for *Printer object*) will show the entire list and you can get details for each.

SAVING AND OPENING TEXT FILES
(A First Look at an Advanced Topic)

There are occasions when you want to save to disk the data you may have entered in an application or the result produced by it. You may also want to open a file to retrieve data from disk. The issues related to disk files are fairly complex, involving many considerations. They will be fully addressed in Chapter 10. In the meantime, we'll cover here some simple techniques that you can use to save and open disk files.

The command to open a file, not surprisingly, is **Open**. Here are three variations:

```
Open filename for Input As #1
Open filename for Output As #1
Open filename for Append As #1
```

Here *filename* is a text string included in code or supplied by the user from a text box. To include a fixed file name in code, you can write it as shown below. This statement will try to open the specified file in the current directory in drive A.

```
Open "a:testfile" for Input As #1
```

Input is to read data from disk and put it in memory. **Output** is to save data to disk, overriding any existing file of the same name in the specified directory. **Append** is to add to an existing file. If the file does not exist, it will be created. And #1 is the # sign followed by an integer. If you open one file, it is always 1. If you open another file without closing the previous, it will be #2.

When you want to close a file, use **Close** alone to close all the open files, or a specific number such as #1 to close that file.

As an example, we are going to create a project that will let you enter names and phone numbers. You can then save them to a disk file. You can also open the saved file to read the data, as shown in Figure 2.15.

The form's Caption property is changed at design time. There are four text boxes, the first three for entering data and the last (large one) for displaying the file's contents. This text box (Text4) has its **MultiLine** property changed at design time from False to True so that multiple text lines can be displayed.

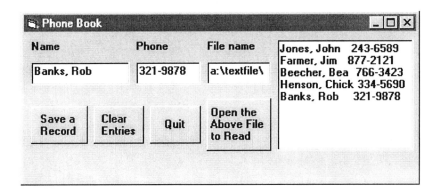

Figure 2.15   Opening and saving a file

The property values are set as follows:

Object	Property	Value
Form1	Caption	Phone Book
Label1	Caption	Name
Label2	Caption	Phone
Label3	Caption	File name
Text1	Name	txtSave
Text2	Name	txtPhone
Text3	Name	txtFile
Text4	Name	txtOut
	MultiLine	True
Command1	Name	cmdSave
Command2	Name	cmdOpen
Command3	Name	cmdClear
Command4	Name	cmdQuit

The Form_Load procedure automatically enters the full path name in the File Name (txtFile) text box. This name is required to open the specified file available on the companion disk. So as soon as you run the program, you can click the cmdOpen button to open the file to the large text box. If your disk is in another drive or you want to open another file, you need to change this entry.

In the next two procedures shown below, we set up a mechanism to reduce the chances of the program's crash. If you click Save or Open when a file name is not supplied, the program will crash and an error will appear. Our mechanism will cause a beep and exit the procedure without aborting program execution.

Still, the program can crash if you try to access a disk while the disk is not ready. So make sure you have a disk ready when you click Save. Also, click Open only after you click Save once to create a file. There are many run-time errors that can occur in this program. Chapter 8 will explain how to trap them.

```
(2FILE.FRM)
Private Sub Form_Load()
    txtFile.Text = "a:\textfile\2phone.txt"
    'this file is available on the bundled disk
End Sub

Private Sub cmdOpen_Click()
    'open the text file specified in the File Name
    'text box and show it in the large text box
    Dim Line1 As String, Lines As String

    If txtFile.Text = "" Then
        Beep          'if no file name, do nothing
        Exit Sub
    End If

    Open txtFile.Text For Input As #1
    Do While Not EOF(1)          'read all data
        Line Input #1, Line1     'assign line to x
        Lines = Lines & Line1 & vbCrLf
            'vbCrLf = carriage return & line feed
            'concatenate, can replace & with +
    Loop
    Close #1
    txtOut.Text = Lines          'output to large box
End Sub

Private Sub cmdSave_Click()
    'save three entries to file specified
    'in the File Name text box
    If txtFile.Text = "" Then
        Beep          'if no file name
        Exit Sub
    End If
```

```
        Open txtFile For Append As #1 'add to file
            Print #1, txtName.Text, txtPhone.Text
                'save 1 line
        Close #1
End Sub

Private Sub cmdClear_Click()
    txtName.Text = ""
    txtPhone.Text = ""
End Sub

Private Sub cmdQuit_Click()
    End
End Sub
```

We use **Append** and **Print #** to save data. So every time you click Save, another line is added to the specified file, 2PHONE.TXT in drive A's TEXTFILE directory in our case. When you are done with an item, click Clear to clear the first two text boxes for the next entry. When you want to see what you have stored, click Open to show all the lines in Text4.

In the cmdOpen_Click procedure, we use the **Not EOF** function to read data until the end is reached. We then store each read line in variable Line1 and add it to variable Lines. We then add two extra characters at the end so that each line will be displayed separately in the text bo. Chapter 4 provides more details.

PRELIMINARY DEBUGGING

(A First Look at an Advanced Topic)

If your program doesn't work as expected, you need to debug it.[3] This is a complex issue and Visual Basic provides many tools for this purpose. The following sections provide some simple techniques for you to get started. Chapter 8 will provide much more detail.

---

[3]The first famous bug was a moth that flew inside a huge mainframe computer and paralyzed it for many hours. (Some people claim that the term bug was used as far back as Thomas Edison's time.) After the dead bug was yanked out (debugged), the computer began to work again. Today we use the term debug mostly to free computer code of invisible pests that make a program go awry.

Single Stepping

The simplest debugging technique is **single stepping**. It involves executing code one statement at a time. To do that, you just press F8 continuously. Each time you press this key, a statement will be executed. This allows you to observe how the program is working.

As a demonstration, write the procedure shown in Figure 2.16. Press **F8** to run it in single-step mode. Click the form to execute the procedure. The first thing you should notice is the IDE window's title bar changes from [design] to [break]. You are now in **break mode**. The second thing you should notice is a yellow **margin indicator** (this color can be changed in the Tools | Options | Editor Format tab's Execution Point Text), as shown in the figure.

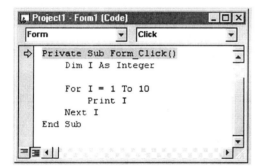

Figure 2.16   A margin indicator in break mode

You can now press F8 repeatedly to observe code execution. Each statement scheduled for execution is marked. Pressing F8 will execute it. The form window also disappears behind the IDE window if the latter is large. To see what's output to the form, you may need to move the IDE window to expose the form.

In break mode, you can move the mouse pointer to a variable name and a **data tip** will pop up. For example, you may find I=3 popping up, depending on the current value of the variable. This tip doesn't appear if you've used the Tools | Options | Editor tab to disable **Auto Data Tips**.

Breakpoints

Pressing F8 repeatedly can be tedious and slow. An alternative is to set one or more **breakpoints** and then press F5 to run the program. When execution reaches a breakpoint, break mode is entered and execution is halted. You can then press F8 to single-step or F5 to execute till the next breakpoint.

Setting a breakpoint is now very easy. Just move the pointer to the **Margin Indicator Bar** of the desired line and click to enter an indicator and a color to mark the line. Clicking the same spot clears the indicator and color. This can be done at design time or in break mode. You can also use the **F9** key to set/unset a breakpoint. To clear all breakpoints, press **Ctrl+Shift+F9**. Figure 2.17 shows the Print line set as a breakpoint.

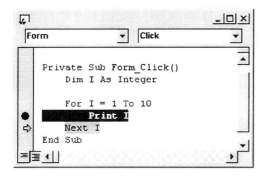

Figure 2.17   A margin indicator and a breakpoint

The Locals Window

Previous Visual Basic versions used to include a Debug window. Now it's broken up into three separate windows: Immediate, Locals, and Watch. These windows can be opened by using the View menu. The **Immediate window** lets you enter something to produce an immediate result. The **Locals window** displays variable values being processed. The **Watch window** displays variables and expressions that you want to watch. The first two are explained below; the last will be covered in Chapter 8.

To demonstrate how the **Locals window** works, follow these steps:

1. Write the procedure shown below.

2. Set the Print line as a breakpoint.

3. Press F5 to run the program and click the form to execute the procedure. Execution stops at the breakpoint.

4. If the Locals window is not open, choose View | Locals window to open it. This window can be undocked and dragged to any location.

5. Single-step through the code by pressing F8 repeatedly or press F5 to execute till the breakpoint.

```
Private Sub Form_Click()
    Dim I As Integer
    Dim J As Integer

    For I = 1 To 10
        For J = 1 To 10
            Print I * J
        Next J
    Next I
End Sub
```

Figure 2.18 shows the result after pressing F5 five times. Notice that all the variables in the procedure are shown without your doing anything. As you press F5 or F8, notice that the variables' values automatically change. This is a great way to see what your variables are doing.

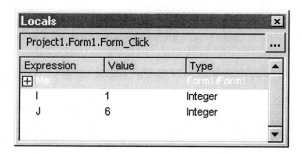

Figure 2.18   Variables in the Locals window

The Immediate Window

Another way to observe variables is to use the **Immediate window**. If it's not shown, use View | Immediate Window (Ctrl+G) to show it. Inside this window you can enter a statement to show an immediate result. Figure 2.19 shows that we try to show the product of I*J at the time when the two variables' values are as shown in Figure 2.18.

The Immediate window is still recognized as the **Debug object**. You can use the Print method to output values to this object. Suppose you change the Print line in the above procedure to the following:

```
Debug.Print I * J
```

The output will be channelled to the **Immediate window** rather than the form window—even if the Immediate window is not open.

Figure 2.19   The Immediate window showing current values

You can use the **Stop** statement to suspend code execution and get into break mode. Suppose you replace the above Print line with this:

```
If I * J > 50 Then Stop
```

Code execution stops when I reaches 6 and J reaches 9. At that point, execution is halted. A yellow arrow points to the above line. You can now do whatever you want, including opening the Immediate window and type something there.

If you don't use Stop in code, you can still switch to break mode at run time. Just press **Ctrl+Break**, click the **Break** icon (two vertical bars) on the Standard toolbar, or choose Run | Break. The cursor goes to the Code window or one of the open debugging windows.

The Immediate window lets you enter a statement at both design time and in break mode, and it will give you an immediate answer. If a statement makes no sense, you'll get an error. In Figure 2.20, the first line shows a division operation. In the second example, we assign values to two variables and show their product.

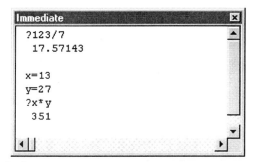

Figure 2.20   The Immediate window showing immediate results

The **Debug object** has only two methods, namely Print and Assert. **Assert** takes a True or False argument. When True, nothing happens. If False, code execution is halted and a beep is made. That's what happens when the Else clause is executed in the following example. You are now put in break mode, and you can do whatever you do in break mode.

```
If I * J < 50 Then
    Print I * J
    Debug.Assert True
Else
    Debug.Assert False
End If
```

The **Cls** method can be used to clear printing to a form or picture box, but not the Immediate window. So Debug.Cls will cause an error. To clear this window, you need to do it manually. Ctrl+A or holding down Ctrl and clicking the left side of the window will select all the text lines (the same as in the Code window); you can then press Del to delete the selected text.

Between the Code window and the Immediate window, you can do copy/cut and paste or drag and drop at design time or in break mode. The simplest way to do copying is to select the desired text in one window, hold down Ctrl and drag it to the other window.

The Immediate window lets you revise an existing statement and press Enter to produce another result. The result may be different on different occasions. A variable may have a value when a procedure is being executed. It may have no value at design time or on other occasions.

If you press Enter over a line that is not a statement, maybe an output by a statement, an error will result. If you want to create a blank line, press **Ctrl+Enter** rather than Enter alone.

The Immediate window can be opened and active at both design time and run time. The design time open/closed state of the window doesn't apply to run time, and vice versa. If you open it at design time, it'll remain open at design time. But if you close it at run time, it will remain closed at next run time—even though the window is open at design time. So if you open the window at both design time and run time, the window will always be available on both occasions.

The debugging windows—Watch, Locals, and Immediate—are all **dockable** by default. You can change that by using the Tools | Options | Docking tab. You can also right-click a window and check/uncheck Dockable to make it dockable/undockable. If there are many windows cluttering your screen, use the **Window menu** to rearrange them.

TIP: Typing Shortcuts

If you use the **Print** word often, you can save lots of time by using the question mark (**?**) as a shortcut. You don't even have to put a space after the question mark. Also, the ending quotation mark can be avoided. Here is an example:

```
?"This is a shortcut.
```

Upon pressing Enter or moving the cursor away from the typed line, Visual Basic converts it to:

```
Print "This is a shortcut."
```

You can even enter something like this:

```
debug.?"text
```

It will become this:

```
Debug.Print "text"
```

Furthermore, a space before or after an operator is most of the time not necessary; Visual Basic will automatically stretch them out. Here is an example:

```
?b+c
```

The second half of Chapter 8 covers more advanced debugging techniques which you can use to go after more tenacious bugs.

DRILL

Choose an option below to answer questions 11-15:
   a. Ctrl+Tab, b. Shift+F7, c. F7, d. F8, e. F9

_F9_ 11. To set a breakpoint.

_F7_ 12. To switch to the next dockable window.

_F8_ 13. To single-step through code lines.

_b_ 14. To show the form/designer window.

_a_ 15. To show the Code window.

_a_ 16. When program execution reaches a breakpoint,
   a. execution is halted
   b. the breakpoint is highlighted
   c. the Immediate window automatically opens
   d. all of the above
   e. both a and b

_____ 17. A comment can be placed after an apostrophe or the _REM_ command.

_b_ 18. The following statement prints

```
Debug.Print Text1.Text
```

   a. text box content to the current window
   b. text box content to the Immediate window
   c. a user entry to the text box
   d. none of the above

_e___ 19. To switch to break mode, you need to press:
a. Ctrl+Break at run time
b. Ctrl+B at run time
c. Ctrl+Break at design time
d. none of the above
e. both a and b

_a___ 20. Ctrl+G activates the Immediate window:
a. at design time
b. at run time
c. in break mode
d. all of the above
e   none of the above

_b___ 21. In the Immediate window, pressing Enter with the cursor in the middle of a line will:
a. break up the line
b. execute the line
c. cause a beep
d. do nothing

_F___ 22. You can use Cls to clear the Immediate window. True or false?

_T___ 23. An instruction can be copied from the Code window and pasted into the Immediate window. This will produce an immediate result. True or false?

Stop 24. The _____ statement halts program execution and switches to break mode.

_T___ 25. The following statement in the Code window is legal. True or false?

```
Debug.?"test
```

_T___ 26. The following line in the Immediate window is legal. True or false?

```
Debug.Print "test ";
```

EndDoc 27. The _____ method flushes your printer's memory and causes the printer to start printing the supplied data.

_F___ 28. The statement below is legal. True or false?

```
Text1.Print "xxx"
```

Input

_____ 29. To open a file to read data from disk to memory, fill in the missing word in the following statement:

```
Open "a:testfile" For _____ As #1
```

_a_ 30. To print a page number on a printout, you need to use:

    a.   Page
    b.   NewPage
    c.   PrintPage
    d.   PageNumber

PRACTICE

■ 9. Modify Listing 1 so that the user can enter ^ as the operator to calculate Operand1 to the power of Operand2.

■ 10. Add a command button to Figure 2.13. This command button should be captioned Clear and named cmdClear. When it is clicked, all the text boxes should be cleared.

■ 11. In the previous question, modify the code in such a way so that when the user clicks Clear to clear the text box contents, the focus will be moved to Text1 (txtOp1) for another entry.

■ 12. Write a Form_Click procedure that uses a For-Next loop to output to the Immediate window sequential whole numbers 1 to 10. The numbers should all appear in one line.

■ 13. What happens if you keep clicking the window after running the above program? How can you start printing each group of numbers in a new line?

■ 14. Modify the program in question 12 so that the program will pause after printing a number. How can you resume program execution?

■ 15. Modify the program in question 12 so that the numbers will be printed to the regular window as well as the Immediate window.

■ 16. Does the Cls method work in the Immediate window? How can you clear the Immediate window?

■ 17. When and how can you copy and paste between the Code window and the Immediate window?

■ 18. What does a breakpoint do?

■ 19. What does the Locals window do?

■ 20. What does the Immediate window do?

■ 21. What happens if you enter the End statement in the Immediate window in break mode?

■ 22. Explain what the following statement does.

```
Open "a:testfile" For Append As #1
```

■ 23. What does the Print method do?

■ 24. Suppose you have the following statement in the Code window. How can you pop up a data tip to show the value of I*J in break mode?

```
Print I * J
```

■ 25. What is the final value of the Num variable in the following procedure? Explain.

```
Private Sub Form_Click()
    Dim I As Integer
    Dim J As Integer
    Dim Num As Integer

    For I = 1 To 3
        For J = 1 To 3
            Num = Num + 1
        Next J
    Next I
    Print Num
End Sub
```

CHAPTER PROJECT

A. (2CALC11.FRM)

This project requires you to use an array to do the same thing as described in the Calculator project (2CALC1.FRM) discussed in the text. The array should be declared as:

```
Dim Digits(2) As Variant
```

The code should assign the three user entries (in the top text boxes) to three elements of the array. Use the array elements (instead of the Text properties) to maneuver the entries and display the results.

B. (2CALC2.FRM)

This program lets you calculate two numbers. The interface (Figure 2.21) consists of four labels, three text boxes, and five command buttons. Label1 (Operand 1), Label2 (Operand 2), and Label4 (=) have their Caption properties changed at design time. Label3 displays the caption (operator) of the command button chosen at run time.

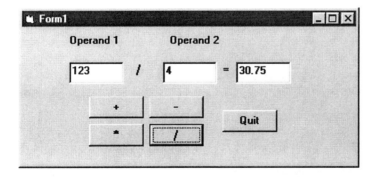

Figure 2.21   Calculating two numbers

At design time, the first four command (operator) buttons are changed to proper names and their Caption properties are also changed as shown. At run time, when the user enters numbers in Text1 and Text2 and clicks a displayed operator, the result is shown in Text3. Clicking another operator leads to another result.

C. (2REMINDR.FRM)

This program (Figure 2.22) lets you type something in a text box, save it to a disk file, print it to the printer, or open a disk file.

When the Save button is clicked, the text in the large text box (Text1) is saved to the file name specified in the small text box (Text2) above the Save button. When Open is clicked, the file name specified in Text2 is opened and displayed in Text1. When Print is clicked, Text1's contents are sent to the printer.

At design time, change Text1's MultiLine property to True (so that multiple lines can be displayed) and ScrollBars to Both (so that you can use the mouse to scroll text). Also, use the Output option of the Open command to save Text1 to a disk file, replacing any existing file of the same name in the same directory.

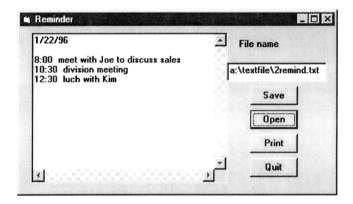

Figure 2.22   Reminder writer

D. (2MOTEL.FRM)

Mo's Model Motel charges the daily rate of $50 for a one-bed unit and $60 for a two-bed unit. This program lets you enter the numbers of days and beds and click Calculate to show the total charge.

The program should behave as follows:

1. If either text box is empty, a beep is made and nothing else happens.

2. If the number for beds is higher than 2, the same thing should happen.

3. If both numbers are acceptable, the label above the Calculate button shows the total. Figure 2.23 shows $180 for a three-day stay in a two-bed unit.

4. Save the form file with the 2MOTEL.FRM name. We will revisit it in later chapters.

(Hint: Use an If Then-Else-End If structure to determine the number of beds and calculate the total accordingly.)

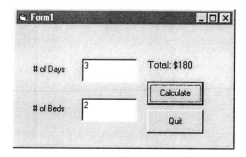

Figure 2.23   Calculating a charge

FUN AND GAME

A. (ROLLING.FRM)

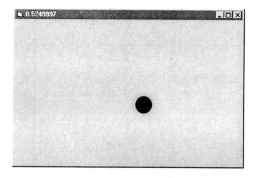

Figure 2.24   A ball rolling up and down

This program simulates a ball rolling up and down from the top left corner to the bottom right corner (Figure 2.24). The caption shows the ball's current position against both the top and left. You can double-click the form to end. You can also single-click the form to toggle between pausing and resuming the motion.

```
Private Sub Form_Click()
    Static Pause As Boolean

    Pause = Not Pause
        'toggle between pausing and resuming
    If Pause Then
        Do                      'infinite loop
            DoEvents        'allow other events
            If Not Pause Then Exit Do
        Loop
    End If
End Sub

Private Sub Form_Resize()
    Dim Pos As Single
    Dim Increment As Single

    Scale (0, 0)-(1, 1)   'top-left = 0,0; bot-right = 1,1
    Pos = 0                       'initial position
    Increment = 0.005       'increment or decrement value
    Do
        Do
            DoEvents        'allow break
            Pos = Pos + Increment
            Shape1.Top = Pos    'move top and left
            Shape1.Left = Pos
            Caption = Pos          'show current pos
        Loop Until Pos > 1 Or Pos < 0
            'reaching bot-right or top-left
        Increment = -Increment        'reverse direction
    Loop       'continue infinitely
End Sub

Private Sub Form_DblClick()
    End      'end if form double-clicked
End Sub
```

B. (WAVES.FRM)

This program draws ever widening circles starting from all four corners of the form to the opposite ends (Figure 2.25). Each circle's line has a randomly generated color. You can change the step (interval) value and the DrawWidth property (from the Properties window) to achieve different effects. Each time you resize the window, a new set of waves will begin.

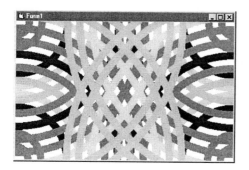

Figure 2.25   A circular pattern

```
Private Sub Form_Resize()
    Dim I As Single
    Dim SH As Long
    Dim SW As Long
    Dim Color As Long
    Dim Limit As Single
    Dim StepVal As Single
    Dim Radius As Single

    SH = ScaleHeight
    SW = ScaleWidth
    Limit = Sqr(SH ^ 2 + SW ^ 2)   'diagonal length
    StepVal = Limit / 500          'interval
    Cls                            'clear previous

    For I = StepVal To Limit Step StepVal
        DoEvents                   'allow break
        Radius = Radius + StepVal  'increment radius
        Color = RGB(Rnd * 255, Rnd * 255, Rnd * 255)
            'random color for lines
        Circle (0, 0), Radius, Color   'top left
        Circle (0, SH), Radius, Color  'bot left
        Circle (SW, 0), Radius, Color  'top right
        Circle (SW, SH), Radius, Color  'bot right
    Next I
End Sub
```

Chapter 3
Forms and Output Formatting

TOPICS

KEY TERMS

CurrentX, CurrentY   Run-time properties for form, printer, and picture box; not available at design time. You can assign a twip value to CurrentX to move the print head to a horizontal position. Use CurrentY to move the print head vertically. You can also use these to read the current position of the print head.

Ellipsis button   A button with an ellipsis (also known as a Three-dot button) appearing in the Settings box of the Properties window, in place of the usual down arrow. Clicking this button can lead to a color palette or dialog box.

Event procedure   A group of instructions placed in a procedure template (beginning with Private Sub and ending with End Sub). An Event procedure is attached to an object. When an event occurs, such as the user clicking the object, the code in the procedure is executed.

Line continuation character   It consists of a space followed by an underscore (_) placed at the end of a line in the Code window. Visual Basic will accept the line below as the continuation of the same line. This allows you to break one logical line into multiple physical lines.

Method   A statement (command) directed at one or several objects. Print, for example, is a method that can be applied to a form, printer, picture box, or the Immediate (Debug) window.

Object box   The little box under the title bar of the Properties window. It contains all the names of the objects in the current project. You can show the list by clicking the down arrow next to the box. The left combo box in the Code window is also called the same name and will show the same items.

Settings box   A little box in the Properties window; the right field in the properties list, next to a property name. The current value for the selected property appears here for you to edit. You can also click the down arrow next to it to display all the available options. If an ellipsis appears instead, click it to show a dialog box.

Twip   A unit of measurement for Visual Basic objects. A twip is 1/20 of a point, or 1/1440 of an inch.

This chapter dwells on the form object and its related attributes. You learn the role played by a form and how to maneuver its numerous events, methods, and properties. Once you know how to maneuver form-related attributes, you can use the knowledge to maneuver the attributes of other objects.

In a Windows application, a form usually serves as a container; this form role is explained in the first half of this chapter. In addition, a form can serve as an output device. In contrast to DOS, which allows only monotonous monochrome output, Windows' screen output can be more colorful and attractive. The second half of this chapter covers a form's output role.

FORM and TWIPS

A form typically serves as the base for an application. On this base you add controls. The form and the controls together constitute a complete application. When the application runs, the form becomes a window, which contains the other objects for the user to interact with the application.

In its original state, a form resembles a peg board, so it is appropriate to compare it to a peg board you may have in your home or garage. Just as you hang tools on this peg board, you can add controls to the form. Just as you reach to the peg board for a tool, you choose an object from the form window to perform a computing task.

The reason for this resemblance is the dots that appear on a form at design time. The grid dots are turned on by default. It is a good idea to keep them on at the beginning so that you will have an easier time designing a user interface.

If you are bothered by this dotty look, you can clear the dots by using the Options dialog box from the Tools menu. The **General tab** shows the following settings:

Form Grid Settings
✓ Show Grid
      Grid Units: Twips
      Width: 120
      Height: 120
✓ Align Controls to Grid

To clear the grid dots, just uncheck **Show Grid** and click the OK button.

Notice that **Align Controls to Grid** is checked by default. That means that your controls are automatically aligned to the preset grid lines. You can uncheck it if you so wish. This setting (no alignment) may give you more control if precision is important to you. If you want to align an individual control to the grid, select that control and open the Format menu. Point to **Align** (at the top) and then click **to Grid**. The selected control is then aligned to the preset grid lines—regardless of whether Show Grid or Align Controls to Grid in the General tab is checked.

Notice that both Grid Width and Grid Height are set to 120. If you change it to a lower value, the distance between dots becomes shorter. If you want precision aligning, you may want to lower this number.

The **General tab** also has the following check boxes, both are checked by default:

✓ Show ToolTips
✓ Collapse Proj. Hides Windows

If **Show ToolTips** is checked, moving the mouse pointer to the Toolbox or a toolbar will show a pertinent tooltip. This is a good idea at the beginning. If you are thoroughly familiar with all the objects and buttons, you can uncheck it to shut it off. You can also turn on/off tooltips with View | Toolbars | Customize | Options.

With **Collapse Proj. Hides Windows** checked, clicking a - sign before a project name in the Project Explorer window will not only collapse all the items related to the project but also cause them to disappear from the screen, thus making the screen less cluttered. The - sign then changes to a + sign. When you click this + sign, a - sign replaces it. The Project window is expanded and all the related windows reappear on the screen. If this check box is not checked, collapsing and expanding a project name in the Project window doesn't affect the objects on the screen.

Visual Basic uses a unique measuring unit known as a **twip** (twentieth of a point) to control object sizes and positions. By using this unit, Visual Basic can maneuver screen objects regardless of what monitor or printer you are using—thus independent of the conflicting units and standards in various hardware devices.

What is a **twip**? It is 1/20 of a **point**. What is a point? It is 1/72 of an inch. We can use an inch to compare the other units this way:

    1 inch = 72 points = 72 x 20 twips = 1440 twips

So how much is 120 twips, the number used in setting grid dots? It is 1/12 (120/1440) of an inch.

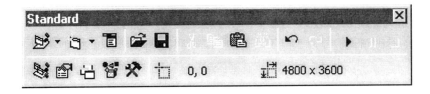

Figure 3.1   Twip numbers for the current form

As you maneuver various objects at design time, notice the numbers shown at the end of the **Standard toolbar**, shown in Figure 3.1. The two left numbers identify the top left corner of the selected object, and the two right numbers indicate the width and height of the object. These numbers appear when the Standard toolbar is undocked; they disappear when you attach the toolbar to a side of the IDE.

Figure 3.1 shows the measurements of the current form. This form is 0 twip from the left margin of the designer window and 0 twip from its top margin. Its width (from the left border to the right border of the form) is 4800 twips and its height is 3600 twips. The first two numbers (0, 0) cannot be changed for a form. But if you resize the form using the three active sizing handles, the last two numbers will change to reflect the physical dimensions.

You can add an object and maneuver it to demonstrate the changing numbers. For example, if you double-click the text box tool in the Toolbox and drag the resulting box around, you can see the two left numbers change. If you stretch or shrink the text box, notice the right numbers change.

SETTING FORM PROPERTIES

A form, like any object, has many properties. These can be set at design time or at run time. We cover the former here and address the latter in a later section in this chapter.

When you want to change the property values of an object at design time, select that object and then open the **Properties window** with one of the following techniques:

- Press F4.
- Click the Properties Window button, the fourth from the right side of the Standard toolbar.
- Choose Properties Window from the View menu.
- Right-click an object and choose Properties from the popup menu.
- If the Properties window is open and visible, click it to bring it to the top.

The Properties window has these parts:

- Title bar
- Object box
- Properties list
- Settings box
- Tabs
- Description

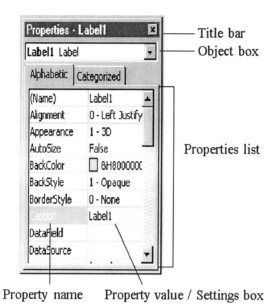

Figure 3.2   A form's Properties window

The title bar identifies this window as the properties of an object (Label1 in our example). The **Object box** just below the title bar also shows the current object, Label1 in our case. There is a down arrow on its right side. You can click this arrow to display a list of the objects on the current form. When you are done, click the arrow again to close the box.

The **Properties list** occupies most of the bottom portion of the Properties window. The left column shows property names and the right column their settings (values). If there are more items than the existing window can display, a vertical scroll bar appears. You can stretch the window up and down or left and right to show more or fewer items. You can click an item to make a selection. You can use the scroll bar or PgUp and PgDn to scroll the items. You can also press Ctrl+Home or Ctrl+End to go to the top or bottom portion.

The values shown in the Properties list reflect changes made to the selected object. It is sometimes easier to set desired values on the object than tinker with the values in the Properties window. For example, a form has Top, Left, Height, and Width properties. The values are shown in twips. They reflect the existing form's state. If you wish, you can change these numbers, and the form will actually change its size or position to reflect the changed values. On the other hand, it is easier to change the form by dragging or resizing it.

The box where a property value (setting) appears is also known as the **Settings box**. This is where you enter a property setting. This box can have the following variations:

- An edit field for you to type or edit an entry.
- A downward arrow for you to pull down a list of options.
- An ellipsis for you to open a dialog box.

An edit field requires you to type an entry or edit an existing default entry. After clicking (selecting) a property name such as Caption, you can start typing. The existing entry will disappear as you type; this happens even though the entry is not highlighted. If you click the edit field itself, the cursor goes there; you can then edit an existing entry. You can also click the property name and then press Tab. This highlights the existing entry which you can press Del to delete or other keys to edit. After you make an entry, pressing Enter or clicking another object results in the new entry being registered. If you change your mind before registering the new entry, press Esc to abort any change. The old entry will remain.

When a downward arrow appears, you are given two (True or False) or multiple options. Click the arrow and then click an available option. You can repeatedly double-click the property name or the Settings box to cycle through the available options without opening the list. You can also click the property name, press Tab, and then press an arrow key from the keyboard to cycle through the options; you can also press a letter or digit key (instead of an arrow key) that matches an available option.

When a ellipsis (...) (sometimes called an **Ellipsis button**) appears, the Font property for example, you can click it to open its dialog box; you can also double-click the property name or Settings box to do the same thing. Make necessary selections and the click OK. The new value will appear in the Settings box.

Sometimes it may be faster to set property values by using keyboard keys. This is practical in some situations. To select a control on a form, press Tab repeatedly until the desired object is selected (has the focus). Then press Ctrl+Shift+X to open the Properties window and select the property name. Here X is the first letter of the desired property's name. For example, if you press Ctrl+Shift+F, the Font property will be selected. If no name starts with the specified letter, nothing happens. If several property names start with the same letter, repeatedly press the same key combination to cycle through each.

Pressing **F4** can do different things, depending on where the focus is. If the focus not on the Properties window, pressing it once activates the Properties window (it will be opened if it was closed) and highlights the default property name. Pressing F4 at this time (after a property name has been selected) activates the Settings box by moving the cursor to the edit field (or highlighting the existing entry, if any), dropping down the list of options if there is a down arrow in this box, or opening the dialog box if there is an ellipsis. (The online help's Properties Window Shortcut Keys topic shows a long list of keystrokes that you can use to maneuver this window.)

VB5 has added two items to the Properties window, namely an additional tab and a description frame. There are now two tabs for you to choose the way the items in the window are displayed. The **Alphabetic tab** shows all the property names in alphabetic order (except Name placed at the top). All the items are displayed and you may need to scroll up or down to show what you want.

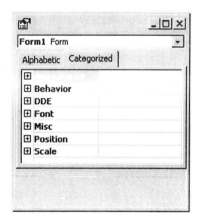

Figure 3.3   The collapsed Properties window

The **Categorized tab** lets you display some or all the properties. Each category is marked by a + or - sign. You can click the - sign to collapse it or the + sign to expand it. When all categories are collapsed, the displayed items are greatly reduced, as shown in Figure 3.3.

The **Description** frame at the bottom of the Properties window shows a brief description of the selected property. You can turn it on/off by right-clicking the window and checking/unchecking the Description check box. When it's unchecked, the extra frame will disappear.

NAME AND CAPTION

A form, like most objects, has a **Caption** property and a **Name** property. These two are distinct and should not be confused. The caption is displayed on the screen at design time and run time to identify the object for the benefit of the programmer and user—human beings, in other words. The name is not displayed. Instead, it is remembered by Visual Basic as associated with the object.

By default Visual Basic uses Form1 as the first form's Caption property as well as Name property (they can be given different values). If this value is not changed, Form1 appears in the form's title bar at both design time and run time. If you erase this Caption property (assign nothing), nothing appears in the title bar. If a new text string is assigned by code at run time, it appears in the title bar. A loaded form's caption also appears on the Windows taskbar at run time. If this form has no caption, then only its icon appears on the button.

Every object, including a form, must have a name so that Visual Basic can keep track of it and manipulate it at run time. At design time, if you assign nothing or an invalid name to an object, an error message will appear and the original name will be kept. There are limits as to what kind of name you can give to an object. The beginning of Chapter 4 discusses this issue.

The Name property appears in the Properties window's Object box. Notice the two words under the title bar in Figure 3.2. The first word, Label1, is the name; the second word, Label, identifies the type of object. Label1 will change if you assign a different value to this Name property; Label, however, does not change.

The Caption property can be maneuvered at run time. Here are some examples:

```
Caption = "My 1st Form"
Form1.Caption = "My 1st Form"
Caption = ""
```

The first two will do the same thing, namely assign a caption to the window's title bar at run time. Since no object is specified in the first example, the current form is the default. In the third example, an empty string is assigned. As a result, the window will have no caption at run time—regardless of whether you have assigned anything at design time.

The Name property cannot be altered at run time. You might consider trying the following; you will get the error shown in Figure 3.4.

```
Form1.Name = "NewName"
```

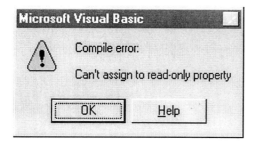

Figure 3.4   Changing a Name property at run time

On such an occasion, you can click Help to tell you what's wrong. When you click OK, the procedure's first line will be marked with yellow and a margin indicator pointing to that line. The offending item will also be highlighted (selected). After you end the program, the highlight still remains.

Some properties, such as the Name property in the above example, are **read-only** at run time. That means they cannot be changed by code at run time. Another example is the **Appearance** property available for most controls, including a form. It has two possible values, Flat (0) and 3-D (1). You can change the default 3-D setting to Flat at design time, but not at run time. You can only use code at run time to read the existing setting. Consider these examples:

```
Appearance = 1
Print Appearance
```

The first will trigger the error shown in Figure 3.4. The second will print 0 or 1 depending on the design-time setting.

WINDOW STATES

A form becomes a window at run time. Some form properties set at design time, such as changing colors or sizes, affect the form immediately; they also appear at run time. Other properties, however, manifest themselves only at run time.

The following form properties have effect only at run time in the SDI environment and in previous versions; in the default MDI environment, changing a value at design time will lead to an immediate effect. Their default values are shown on the right side:

ControlBox	True
Enabled	True
MaxButton	True
MinButton	True
BorderStyle	2 - Sizable
WindowState	0 - Normal

When you select one of the first four properties, the Settings box (after clicking the down arrow) shows two choices: True and False. If you set **ControlBox** to False, the window shows no control box at run time; all the buttons on the title bar will disappear at run time. In that case, you cannot use them to end a program. You can, however, move or resize the window; you can also double-click the title bar to maximize or restore the window—if MaxButton remains true.

When the **Enabled** property is True (default), the window responds to events at run time, such as resizing or moving the window. When it is set to False, the window no longer responds to events. You can click, double-click, or drag, but nothing will happen. Such a window may be useful for displaying a message but not allowing the user to change the window.

When **MaxButton** and **MinButton** properties are set to False, the two corresponding buttons at the upper right corner of the window disappear. You can no longer maximize or minimize the window. If only one is set to True, both remain but the False one is dimmed. (The X button is controlled by the ControlBox property and not affected by MaxButton or MinButton.)

BorderStyle offers these options:

> 0 - None
> 1 - Fixed Single
> 2 - Sizable (default)
> 3 - Fixed Dialog
> 4 - Fixed ToolWindow
> 5 - Sizable ToolWindow

In option 0, all the window trappings disappear at run time and design time (in the MDI environment). All the buttons and borders are invisible, so nothing can be changed.

When a border is Fixed, it cannot be changed, in contrast to a Sizable border which allows you to drag a border line to change it. In all the options except 0, you can drag a window to move it.

Choosing an option here may or may not automatically change MaxButton and MinButton properties. The changes in turn will affect the resulting window behavior. This can lead to confusing results. Keep this in mind if your window does not behave as you expected.

Choosing option 1 will automatically change the MinButton and MaxButton values to False. In that case, only the X button remains, and the control menu does not include the Minimize or Maximize option. You can change MaxButton and MinButton to True at design time. In that case, the window behaves as option 2, except the unchangeable fixed borders. To have sizable borders without the Minimize and Maximize buttons, choose option 2 and change MaxButton and MinButton from the default True to False.

If you choose option 3, the MaxButton and MinButton values will automatically change to False. In this case, the window behaves the same as the default option 1. If you change MaxButton and MinButton to True, additional options are added to the control menu, but no additional buttons appear next to the default X button.

In Windows 95, both options 4 and 5 supply only the X button but no control menu or other buttons. Changing MaxButton or MinButton from the default False to True does not add these extra items but does allow you to double-click the title bar to maximize or restore the window. These options may produce different results in other operating systems.

BorderStyle can affect **ShownInTaskbar**. The latter determines whether the window appears on the taskbar at run time. The default connections are shown below. When you choose the left option, the right value is set by default.

BorderStyle	ShownInTaskbar
0 - None	False
1 - Fixed Single	True
2 - Sizable (default)	True
3 - Fixed Dialog	False
4 - Fixed ToolWindow	False
5 - Sizable ToolWindow	False

These default settings can be changed. When MinButton is True, it is a good idea to set ShownInTaskbar to True. The user can minimize the window. Its button then appears on the taskbar. The button can be clicked to restore the window. ShownInTaskbar can still be set to True even when the Minimize button is not available. Even though the window cannot be minimized, it can still be covered up by another application. The user can click the button on the taskbar to bring it to the top.

If ShownInTaskbar is set to False, a minimized window does not appear on the taskbar. Instead, it appears at the bottom of the screen. It may be covered up by other full-screen applications. In that case, you can use Alt+Tab to reach it.

The **WindowState** property determines the state of the window at run time. These are the options:

> 0 - Normal (default)
> 1 - Minimized
> 2 - Maximized

In the default Normal state, the window stays the same as the original form. Changing it to 1 reduces the window to a shrunken title bar at run time. If Maximized is set, the window fills up the entire screen.

There are two new properties: **Moveable** and **StartUpPosition**. If you change the former's default True value to False (this can be changed only at design time), you cannot move the window at run time. The latter gives you four options:

> 0 - Manual
> 1 - CenterOwner
> 2 - CenterScreen
> 3 - Windows Default (default)

These are the same options on the shortcut menu of the **Form Layout window**, explained in Chapter. Changing a value in one place will be immediately reflected in the other.

NOTE   You can make a window's title bar disappear while retaining the borders. To do that, set Caption to nothing, and MaxButton, MinButton, and ControlBox to False.

NOTE   The form and most controls have the **RightToLeft** property. It's used for a language like Arabic that flows from right to left. If your Windows system is not set up for that, this property's value cannot be changed from the default False to True.

DRILL

____ 1. A form's grid dots can be cleared by using this menu:
    a.   File
    b.   Tools
    c.   Window
    d.   Edit

____ 2. A twip is
    a.   1/20 of an inch
    b.   1/20 of a point
    c.   1/1440 of an inch
    d.   both a and b
    e.   both b and c

____ 3. To align an individual control to grid lines, you need to use this menu:
    a.   Edit
    b.   File
    c.   Tools
    d.   View
    e.   Format

____ 4. Pressing Ctrl+Shift+A at design time moves the cursor to the Properties window's:
    a.   Object box
    b.   Title bar
    c.   Appearance property
    d.   nowhere

____ 5. A form's Caption property and Name property can both be changed by code at run time. True or false?

____ 6. The Properties window consists of the following items, except:
    a.   Object box
    b.   Settings box
    c.   Properties list
    d.   Menu bar

____ 7. Pressing this key leads to the display of the Properties window:
    a.   F1
    b.   F2
    c.   F3
    d.   F4

e.   F5

_____ 8.   If you want a window to be completely unresponsive to any user
action, you need to change this property:
a.   Enabled
b.   MaxButton
c.   MinButton
d.   BorderStyle
e.   WindowState

PRACTICE

■   1.   Explain the significance of the four numbers on the right side of the
Standard toolbar when the toolbar is undocked and when an object is
selected.

■   2.   What is a twip?

■   3.   What is the significance of unchecking Align to Grid?

■   4.   Set the form's ControlBox property to False. Press F5 and report the
result. How can you end such a program?

■   5.   Set the form's Enabled property to False and WindowState to 2 -
Maximized. Press F5 and report the result. How can you end the
program?

COLOR SCHEMES

At design time, there are two ways to control an object's colors:

•   From the Color Palette option of the View menu

•   From the Properties window

To use the first method, follow these steps:

1.   Click an object to select it.

2.   Choose **Color Palette** from the View menu.

3. Click one of the little color boxes (Figure 3.5) to select it.

4. Click the X button to close the Color Palette window or drag the title bar to another location.

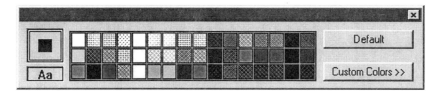

Figure 3.5   The Color Palette window

The color palette (in the middle) consists of three rows, with each row having 16 little boxes. Each of the 48 boxes appears in a distinct color. You click one of these boxes to make a color selection.

The top left box of the Color Palette window shows what the foreground (middle solid box) and background (the outer box) colors will look like. The bottom left box shows how text will appear. You can click the inner box or the outer box before you select a color. At the outset, the outer box is selected. If you now select a color other than the default gray, the selected color box will be highlighted and the two boxes on the left as well as the selected control will change to the color. If you want to change the foreground color, make sure to click the inner box first before you click one of the little color boxes. Any changes you make here will also be reflected in the Properties window. If the window is open, you can see the values change.

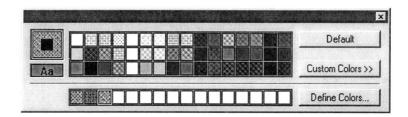

Figure 3.6   The Color Palette window with custom colors

If you want to restore the default (preset) colors for the selected object, click the Default button. When you are done, you can leave the Color Palette window there, drag it somewhere else, or click the X button to close it.

If you are not satisfied with the existing available choices, click **Custom Colors**. Another row appears at the bottom, as shown in Figure 3.6. If you have previously defined a color, click one to select it. If you want to clear this additional row, click the Custom Colors button another time.

After you click Custom Colors to open up the additional row, you can click one of the little boxes in the bottom row and then choose **Define Colors**. Figure 3.7 appears.

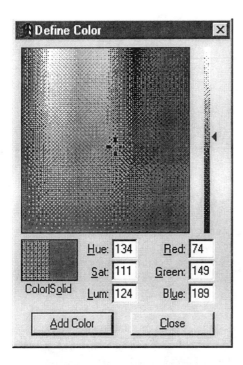

Figure 3.7   The window to let you define a custom color

You can now define a color combination for the selected box. There are two easy ways you can do that:

- Click the desired part of the color panel at the top left corner to select a color mix.

- Slide the triangle on the right side up or down to determine the darkness for the color mix.

As you click any portion of the large color panel, the middle left box displays the selected color. Keep clicking various parts until you are satisfied with the color mix. Various text boxes in the middle will change their numbers as you click different areas.

As you move the triangle down, you darken the color. Moving the triangle up has the opposite effect. You can drag this triangle to move it. You can also click an area inside the vertical color bar or to its right; the triangle moves to where you click. As you do, the middle left box will change colors, and the six text boxes will change their numbers as well. Also notice the Lum (luminance) box going up or down in value as you move the triangle up or down.

The large color panel shows a cross, which you can drag anywhere; it also moves to where you click. When you move it to the right, notice the Hue box increase in value. The Sat (saturation) box number goes up as you move the cross to the top.

When you are satisfied with your custom color combination, click Add Color to add the color to the previously selected box. If you want to abort, click Close instead. In that case, any previously defined custom color is not changed.

If you wish, you can enter numbers in various text boxes, including the amount for Red, Green, and Blue, to create your perfect combination.

The other method of setting colors involves these steps:

1. Select an object by clicking it.

2. Show the Properties window by pressing F4.

3. Select ForeColor or BackColor to set a foreground (text) or background value. The value field shows a number and a sample color. A down arrow appears on the right side of the Settings box.

4. Click the arrow (or double-click the property name). Two tabs appear. The **System tab** shows all the system colors set by Windows. The **Palette tab** shows all the available colors.

5. Click one of the little boxes from the Palette tab to select that color. The object changes color to reflect the new selection and the color palette disappears.

In step 4, the displayed color palette in the Palette tab is identical to the one shown in Figure 3.6, complete with custom colors you may have defined. If you use a different method to select a color for the same object, the second selection will negate the previous act. The Properties window does not offer a default option. If you want to restore the default (preset) color, you need to go to the Color Palette option from the View menu to do that.

Visual Basic uses a hexadecimal (base 16) number to represent a color. For example, the default BackColor value for the form is &H8000000F&. If you wish, you can use such a number to set a color. But using a palette is much easier.

SELECTING FONTS

You may want to use different font styles and sizes to make your user interface more varied or attractive. To do that, follow these steps:

1. Select an object by clicking it.

2. Press F4 to show the Properties window.

3. Click Font in the Properties window.

4. Click the ellipsis (or double-click the field) to open the Font dialog box, shown in Figure 3.8.

5. Make necessary selections and click OK to accept or Cancel to abort.

There are two font-related properties appearing in the Properties window:

Font   MS Sans Serif
FontTransparent   True

When **FontTransparent** is True, background text and graphics will show through. If this property is set to False, background text or graphics will be covered up.

The Font property opens the **Font dialog box**. Here you can select a font name from the Font list box; if the desired name does not appear, scroll it to view and then click it. Then select a style from the four options. Then select a size. The available sizes vary from one font to another. You can also enter a size value in the edit field of the Size combo box to specify a number that is different from one of the available options. If you wish, check **Strikeout** (with a horizontal line crossing in the middle) and/or Underline.

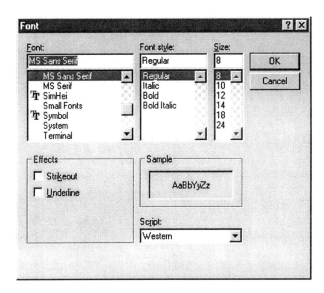

Figure 3.8   The Font dialog box

As you make a selection, examine the Sample display. It changes in response to each new selection you make. When you are satisfied, click OK. Click Cancel if you want to keep the original.

NOTE   When you change the font for a form through the Font dialog box, you change the default font for the form. When you add controls to this form in the future, the form font will be used for the controls as well. But the controls added before the form font change are not affected. If you change the font for a control, only the control itself is affected.

If you need to reference font properties in code, you need to point to the right place. Examine the difference between these two examples:

```
Form1.FontTransparent = False
Form1.Font.Bold = True
```

Both are legal. If you wish, you can omit Form1.

VB3 had the following properties available at both design time and run time:

FontBold	True
FontItalic	False
FontName	MS Sans Serif
FontSize	7.8
FontStrikethru	False
FontTransparent	True
FontUnderline	False

In VB4/5, only FontTransparent remains in the Properties window. The others can be changed only in the Font dialog box. Are these names still legal? Yes, but only at run time. So both examples below are legal:

```
Form1.Font.Bold = True
Form1.FontBold = True
```

Another section later in this chapter will have more about using fonts at run time.

TIP: Fonts, Points, and Typefaces

It is hard to imagine that there are so many ways to write (or print) the simple Roman (or Greek or other) alphabetic characters. You need to delve into desktop publishing to know some of these related arcane terms of this particular trade.

A **typeface** (type or face for short) is the overall design of a set of characters. There are many commercial typefaces. These can be divided into two major categories: **serif** and **sans serif**. The former has extra ornamental strokes (serifs) around a character, and the latter has none (sans). The most commonly used serif typeface is Times Roman (the typeface used in this book; common in American books), and the best known sans serif is Helvetica (popular in European books). Since Helvetica is the ancient name for Switzerland, Swiss is also used for this typeface's name. In Visual Basic, it is known as MS Sans Serif.

A **font** is a typeface of a particular size and attribute. A 10-point Swiss Italic is a font; a 12-point Times Roman Bold is another. Fonts and typefaces are often interchangeably used, particularly by people who are not in this Gutenberg profession.

Points are used to measure font heights. One point equals about 1/72 inch. A 36-point font is half an inch in height from the top of the letter T to the bottom of the letter y. The measurement is based on printout. Screen display, depending on the size of your monitor, may be different.

Finally, you also need to be aware of **monospaced** (fixed) and **proportional** fonts (actually typefaces). The letters in a proportional font vary in width; for example, W is wider than I. Each letter in a monospaced font (e.g., Courier) takes up the same amount of space. These fonts are measured in **pitch**: 10-pitch (pica) means 10 characters in one inch, and 12-pitch (elite) 12 characters in the same space. Measured in points, a pica letter is 12 points in width and elite is 10 points.

Visual Basic can utilize any Windows-compatible font. Your system may have more fonts than those displayed in the Font dialog box shown in Figure 3.8.

TIP: TrueType Fonts

Some fonts are marked by the **TT** symbol as **TrueType fonts**, as shown in the Font combo box (Figure 3.8). These are **scalable fonts**. If you display a large size, the characters look smooth. Those not marked as TT, including the default MS Sans Serif. These can't do the same. When they are stretched, they become dotty and ugly.

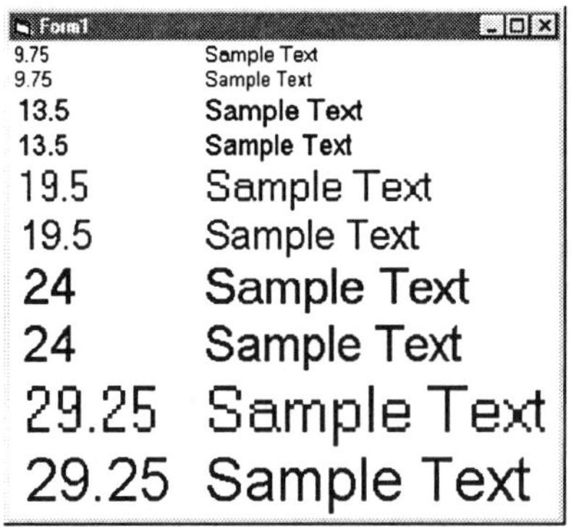

9.75	Sample Text
9.75	Sample Text
13.5	Sample Text
13.5	Sample Text
19.5	Sample Text
19.5	Sample Text
24	Sample Text
24	Sample Text
29.25	Sample Text
29.25	Sample Text

Figure 3.9   Comparing fonts

Figure 3.9 demonstrates the differences. When the default MS Sans Serif font is stretched, it becomes coarse. The Arial font, on the other hand, remains refined. The procedure below produces the display.

```
Private Sub Form_Click()
    Dim I As Integer
    Dim ST As String

    Cls
    ST = "Sample Text"
    For I = 10 To 30 Step 5
        FontSize = I
        FontName = "ms sans serif"
            'non-TrueType font
        Print FontSize;
            'print head stay on same line
        CurrentX = 2000
            'move print head to 2000 twips from left
        Print ST     'print sample text

        FontName = "arial"   'TrueType font
        Print FontSize;
        CurrentX = 2000
        Print ST
    Next I
End Sub
```

ICONS AND POINTER SHAPES

If you want to give an application some visual effects, you can use some related properties. A form has the following related properties:

Icon
MouseIcon
MousePointer

Controls, plus an object known as **Screen,** have the last two of the above three properties.

Examine the form icon at the top left corner of the form. This is the default icon for a form. Notice the **Icon** entry in the Properties window; it shows (icon). Do you know what happens if you delete this entry? The entry will be changed to (none), and the default icon on the form will immediately change to the default Windows icon.

What if you want to restore the default form icon? Just load a proper icon. Double-click Icon in the Properties window. The Load Icon dialog box (Figure 3.10) appears. Go to the GRAPHICS\ICONS\COMPUTER folder. The FORM.ICO file should be there. Double-click it, and the default form icon will reappear. If you want another icon, load it instead of FORM.ICO. VB5 comes with hundreds of icons which all have the **ICO** file name extension.

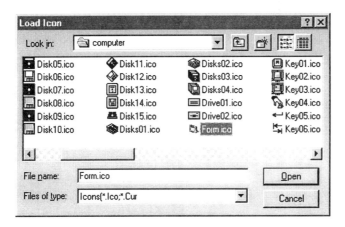

Figure 3.10   Icon files

When you save a form file, the loaded (or default) icon is attached to the file. When you open the Save As or Open Project window, the icon appears before the file name in the list of matching files. The same thing happens when you are in the My Computer or Explorer window. When you compile a project with multiple forms (see Chapter 8), you can select a particular form whose icon you want to use to identify the executable file.

At design time as well as run time, you can click the form icon to pull down the system menu (control menu) or double-click it to close the form. At run time, this icon is not available when ControlBox is False and when some BorderStyle options are selected.

The **MousePointer** property gives you 17 options (0-15, plus 99). The 0 - Default option displays at run time the typical pointer shape and occasional deviation such as an I-beam inside a text box. If you select another option, the pointer shape will change to that at run time for the specified object. You can use different shapes for different objects. Option 11 - Hourglass is commonly used to display the pointer when your application is doing something and you want the user to wait.

If you select the 99 - Custom option, the icon specified in the **MouseIcon** property is used. If this property is the default (none), then the Custom option has no effect and the Default option applies. To load a MouseIcon at design time, follow the same steps as loading a form Icon, as explained earlier.

Icons and pointer shapes can be manipulated by code at run time. Executing the following procedure changes the default pointer shape to the default form icon—if the form's Icon property is not empty.

```
Private Sub Form_Click()
    MousePointer = 99    'custom pointer shape
    MouseIcon = Icon     'use form icon for pointer shape
End Sub
```

You can load an icon at run time by using the **LoadPicture** function. This and other issues related to graphics will be explained in Chapter 11.

FORM EVENTS AND PROCEDURES

There are more than 30 different events related to a form; these appear in the Code window's Procedure box. That means a form can respond to that many events that can be triggered by the user or other procedures. You can write a procedure for each of these events, although you are likely to limit yourself to only a few.

An **event** occurs mostly because the user does something. For example, at run time, when the user clicks the form window, a Click event occurs. If you have written a Form_Click procedure, then the code in the procedure is executed. If you have not, clicking the window does nothing.

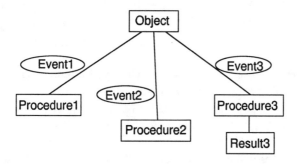

Figure 3.11   Object, events, and procedures

Figure 3.11 shows a hypothetical situation where an object (such as a form) has three event procedures attached to it. If Event3 (such as clicking the form) occurs, then Procedure3 (such as Form_Click) is executed, which in turn produces Result3.

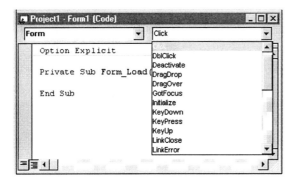

Figure 3.12   Form events

When you double-click a new form at design time, the Code window appears and the default Form_Load procedure template is automatically displayed. If you click the down arrow in the Procedure box, you can pull down a list of related events, shown in Figure 3.12. You can then scroll up and down to show other available events.

When you find the event name you want, just click it. Its procedure template appears in the editing window and the cursor stays between the beginning and the ending lines. You can then add code as you wish. If you change your mind and decide not to add code, highlight everything, including the original template and press Del to erase it. If you have not done anything to the original template, you can ignore it and go on to do something else such as closing the Code window.

To find out what each event is supposed to do, use Help | Microsoft Visual Basic Help Topics | Index, scroll to show *Form object*, and double-click it. In the ensuing help topic, click the Events jump. A Topics Found dialog box shows a long list of events. Double-click the desired one to show more details.

In the next three sections, we will demonstrate how to write procedures for some common events. Other events will be covered in later chapters. Keep in mind that many events are shared by many objects. We will explain some of those less common events and procedures when we cover other objects.

Form Events and Their Sequence

If you just press F5 to run a form and then click the X button to close it, the startup[1] form's seven events will be triggered. Each procedure that contains code will be executed in a predetermined order. The following seven procedures test the sequence of these events. A form level variable is used to keep track of the order.

```
Option Explicit
Dim Num As Integer          'form-level declaration

Private Sub Form_Load()
    Num = Num + 1
    Debug.Print Num, "Load"
End Sub

Private Sub Form_Paint()
    Num = Num + 1
    Debug.Print Num, "Paint"
End Sub

Private Sub Form_QueryUnload(Cancel As Integer, _
UnloadMode As Integer)
    Num = Num + 1
    Debug.Print Num, "QueryUnload"
End Sub

Private Sub Form_Terminate()
    Num = Num + 1
    Debug.Print Num, "Terminate"
End Sub

Private Sub Form_Unload(Cancel As Integer)
    Num = Num + 1
    Debug.Print Num, "Unload"
End Sub

Private Sub Form_Resize()
    Num = Num + 1
    Debug.Print Num, "Resize"
End Sub

Private Sub Form_Initialize()
    Num = Num + 1
```

---

[1]If you have only one form, it's automatically designated as the **startup form**. If you have multiple forms in a project and you want to change the default startup form, you can use the Project | Project Properties | General tab to select a different form in the Startup Object list box.

```
      Debug.Print Num, "Initialize"
End Sub
```

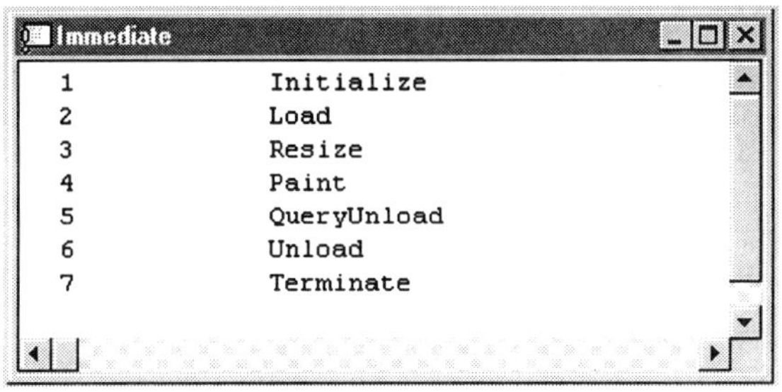

```
 Immediate                                    _ □ ×
   1              Initialize
   2              Load
   3              Resize
   4              Paint
   5              QueryUnload
   6              Unload
   7              Terminate
```

Figure 3.13   Form events and their sequence

Figure 3.13 shows the order in which the above seven events occur. Notice that the order is not affected by the position of a particular procedure in the Code window. You can rearrange these procedures in the Code window, but the result will not change. So before a form appears, these events occur in this order: **Initialize, Load, Resize,** and **Paint.** Before a form is closed, these events happen in this order: **QueryUnload, Unload,** and **Terminate.** The last three events don't happen if you choose Run | End or execute End in code.

Most of these form events normally occur only once in a form's lifetime (from creation to destruction). Some occur repeatedly, depending on what you do to the form at run time. These include **Resize** and **Paint.** If you cover and then uncover the form, you'll trigger the Paint event. If you reduce the form's size, you'll trigger the Resize event. Enlarging the form triggers Resize, followed by Paint. The Paint event can be affected by the **AutoRedraw** property discussed later in this chapter.

With all the above seven procedures in the Code window, you can test to see how Visual Basic treats them. Pressing **F7** at design time always moves the cursor to the Initialize procedure, regardless where the cursor was. Double-click the form has the same effect. If you erase the Initialize procedure, the Load procedure will get the top priority.

A form's beginning existence can go through three stages: creating, loading, and showing. In the first two stages, code is executed but the visual parts are not displayed. They are useful for performing initial chores before displaying the user interface. Different form events may trigger one or more of these stages. The same thing can happen when you reference the form's methods or properties. Some of these issues will be revisited in later chapters, particularly 11 and 12.

Form_Load and Form Properties

When you double-click an empty form, the **Form_Load** procedure template automatically appears and the cursor goes to this procedure for you to type code. The same thing happesn when you press F7 while the form has the focus.

The Form_Load procedure is useful in initializing various values in your application. You can set various property values here instead of doing it at design time. The values set at run time prevail over those set at design time. Here is an example:

```
Private Sub Form_Load ()
    Form1.Top = 0
    Form1.Left = 600
    Form1.Caption = "Form_Load Demo"
End Sub
```

The code we have put in the procedure causes the window to be displayed at the top of the screen and 600 twips from the left margin of the screen. The window's caption is also changed. The size of the window is determined at design time and not altered at run time—although you can change it at run time by code.

Most form properties can be changed at both design time and run time, but some cannot be altered at run time. If it's illegal to change a property value, the error message shown in Figure 3.4 earlier will greet you.

Among the initial chores you can do with the Form_Load procedure include: assigning a value to a public variable for access by other procedures, assigning an initial value to start a timer, creating instances (objects) of a class, and so on. These issues will be addressed in later chapters.

TIP: Showing Text with Form_Load

The startup form is displayed only after the Form_Load procedure in it completes its execution. If you use the **Print** method in that procedure to output text to the form, the text will not appear because the form was not yet available when the output was sent. To ensure that the output is displayed, put **Show** before Print in the procedure. The first procedure below will print the text string, but the second won't.

```
Private Sub Form_Load()
    Show
    Print "this is a test"
End Sub

Private Sub Form_Load()
    Print "this is a test"
    Show
End Sub
```

Click and Double Click

A **Click** or **DblClick** procedure can be attached to a form. When the form is clicked, the code in the procedure is executed. Here is an example:

```
Private Sub Form_Click ()
    FontSize = 20
    Print "The font size is: "; FontSize
    ForeColor = &H40C0&
    Print "East is red--"; ForeColor
End Sub
```

After pressing F5 to run this program, clicking the window shows the result in Figure 3.14.

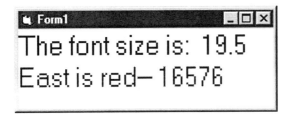

Figure 3.14   **Changing font size and text color at run time**

We specify the font size of 20, but Visual Basic gives us 19.5, the closest match available. If you specify a higher number, Visual Basic may display a larger character, but the size may be different from the specified number and the text may be distorted.

In the code, we use a hex number for red (this number is displayed when you choose a red color from the Properties window). So the second line of the window displays text in red and the equivalent decimal number.

When you double-click an object, such as a form, you actually trigger both the Click and DblClick events. If both procedures exist, they will both be executed. Suppose we add the following procedure. Double-clicking the form will show Figure 3.15.

```
Private Sub Form_DblClick ()
    Print "Double click, double trouble."
End Sub
```

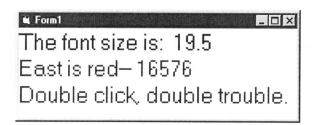

Figure 3.15   A Click event triggered by DblClick

What can you do if you just want to show the result of a double click? Add the **Cls** method to clear the previous display, such as this:

```
Private Sub Form_DblClick ()
    Cls
    Print "Double click, double trouble."
End Sub
```

When this modified program runs, double-clicking the window shows the first two lines, which will then be cleared right away. Then the third line is printed. When the DblClick procedure is executed, **Cls** clears away whatever is displayed in the window. The new line printed after that is not affected.

METHOD, PROPERTY, and PROCEDURE

We used three commands in the previous section, namely Print, Cls, and Show. In previous Microsoft Basic packages, these are known as statements or commands. In Visual Basic, they are referred to as **methods**. There are numerous methods used in Visual Basic. Most objects such as the form or command button come with multiple methods.

A **method** is a command directed at an object. (A command not directed at any object is still known as a **statement**.) So when we use Print, we tell Visual Basic to print something to a specified object. If the object is not specified, it defaults to the current form. The Print method has this syntax:

```
[object.] Print parameter
```

Here *object* is optional. If omitted, the default object is the current form. (More on this will be available later in this chapter.) The *parameter* argument supplies the text to be printed. If nothing is specified, a blank line is printed.

At this time you may be confused as to the difference between a method and a property. Consider these two examples:

```
Form1.Left = 600
Form1.Cls
```

The first is a property, but the second is a method. Although in both cases a dot (**.**) connects the two components, they are handled differently. A property is like a variable to which you can assign a value. A method, which is usually an action word, is a statement performing an act to an object.

A comparison between an event procedure and the above two items is in order. An event procedure follows this syntax:

```
Object_Event ()
```

The underscore connecting the two components distinguishes it from either a method or a property. When a recognized event, such as clicking a mouse button, is directed at an object, such as a command button, Visual Basic executes the code attached to the event procedure, which may have the first line like this:

```
Private Sub Command1_Click ()
```

If no code is attached to this procedure, Visual Basic does not attempt to execute the empty procedure.

Visual Basic internally keeps track of all the objects you have created and connects them to the events that the objects can recognize. Some objects can recognize many events, while others none or only a few. The events recognized by an object can be displayed by pulling down the Procedure list in the Code window.

The following summation may further clarify the differences:

- Properties are attributes of an object. Some objects have more properties than others. To show all the available properties of an object, select that object on the form and press F4 to show the Properties window. The resulting window shows all the properties available for the object at design time.

- An event procedure is a subprogram attached to an object. An object may recognize no event, while another may recognize many. An event is triggered when an action recognized by the related object is initiated. To show all the event procedures available to an object, double-click the object to go to the Code window and click the Procedure box's down arrow.

- A method is an action directed at an object. Each object's online help topic shows the objects' available methods. To get all the online help related to an object such as a form or control, click the object (either on the form or in the Toolbox) and press F1. You can then click the Properties, Events, or Methods jump to show more related information.

USING MULTIPLE FORMS

A simple application normally requires one form. But there may be occasions when you need two or more forms to provide more flexibility. This section explains how to use two forms. You can use the explanation to apply to as many forms as you wish.

When you need an additional form, just click the **Add Form** (second) icon on the Standard toolbar (this command is also available from the Project menu). The second icon and its tooltip may show something other than a form. In that case, click the little down arrow on the right side of the icon. A list will drop down for you to click. After you choose a form, the **Add Form dialog box** appears (Figure 3.16). The first option in the New tab is Form. If this is what you want, just double-click it. If you want to add an existing form, use the Existing tab. A dialog box like the Open Project dialog box will appear. You can go to various folder and find the desired form to add. If the new form's name conflicts with one already loaded, an error message appears and no form is added. If you still want to add that form, you'll have to change the name of the form already loaded.

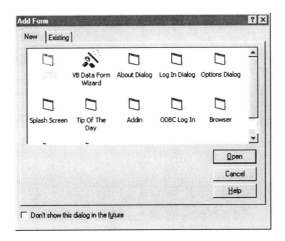

Figure 3.16   The Add Form dialog box

You may find the Add Form dialog box a bother. If you don't want it to appear in the future, just check the check box at the bottom left. After that, clicking the Add Form button or choosing Project | Add Form will no longer show this dialog box. You can do the same thing by opening Tools | Options | Environment tab and uncheck Form.

Form2, together with its own designer window, is placed on top of the original, Form1 (unless you have changed this default name). You have now two forms to play with. You can drag or resize either window. You can make either window active by clicking it. The active window's title bar has a color different from the others.

You can use the **Project window** to show all the forms (and other modules) for the current project. To do that, choose Project Explorer (Ctrl+R) from the View menu. The result is shown in Figure 3.17. The active window is highlighted. You can click one of the displayed form names to make it active. You can then choose **View Object** or **View Code** to show the selected form or its Code window. You can close the Project window by clicking the X button.

When you save a project or exit, you'll be asked to save each form if it's been changed. If you want to remove an unwanted form, select it and choose **Remove**

Form from the Project menu. A quicker way is to right-click the form name in the Project window. The Remove Form option shows up. The shortcut menu includes quite a few other options as well, including Add, Save, and Print.

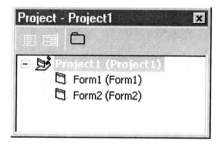

Figure 3.17   The Project window

When an application runs, only the **startup form** is shown. The startup form is by default the first form. It can be changed from the Project | Project Properties | General tab, as explained earlier. Chapter 8 will provide more details.

You can use code to handle multiple forms in the following ways:

```
FormName.ObjectName.Property
FormName.Method
```

You can use the **Show** and **Hide methods** and the **Load** and **Unload statements** to maneuver all the forms added at design time. Consider these examples:

```
Form1.Show       'method
Load Form2       'statement
```

The first shows Form1; the form name can be omitted in this situation because it's the default form. The second only puts the specified form in memory without showing it. Form2.Show, on the other hand, loads as well as shows the form. Form2.Hide hides the form without unloading it. Unload Form2, on the other hand, removes it from memory altogether.

If you want to print a graphic image of a form that will make the printout resemble the screen appearance, use the **PrintForm** method to do it, such as this:

```
Form1.PrintForm.
```

Forms and controls can be cloned and manipulated at run time. Chapter 9 will explain how to do it.

Follow these steps to show a concrete demonstration of manipulating two forms:

1. Start a new project.

2. Add Form2 to the project.

3. Use the Project window to go to Form1's Code window.

3. Write the following procedure.

4. Press F5 to run the program.

```
Private Sub Form_Load()          '--Listing 1--
    Form1.Width = Form1.Width / 2    'half the width
    Form2.Width = Form2.Width / 2
    Form1.Height = Form1.Height / 2 'half the height
    Form2.Height = Form2.Height / 2
    Form2.Top = Form1.Top    'use Form1's top for both
    Form2.Left = Form1.Left + Form1.Width
      'place Form2 on the right of Form1
    Form2.Show
End Sub
```

Figure 3.18   Maneuvering two forms by code

The result is two forms (Figure 3.18), each 1/4 (1/2 * 1/2 = 1/4) of the original size, appearing next to each other side by side.

In the code we specify Form1 and Form2 when referring to each. You can omit Form1 if you wish. When this word is absent, the default is Form1.

Form1 will be shown automatically. Form2, however, does not appear by default. So we use the Show method to make it appear.

If the **Form Layout window** is open, notice that there are two windows inside the monitor. You can drag each to a different location for run time. In our case, you can drag Form1 to a specific location, and Form2 will always appear on its right side.

If you like to see some action, try the following procedures. Start a new project and write the two procedures. The first will automatically reduce Form1 to 1/4 of its original size and keep it at the top left corner. Each time you click this form, it will move to the right, down, left, up, and continue clockwise.

```
Private Sub Form_Load()
    Width = Width / 2
    Height = Height / 2
End Sub

Private Sub Form_Click()          '--Listing 2--
    Static Num As Integer

    Num = Num + 1
    Num = Num Mod 4        'limit to 0-3
    Select Case Num
    Case 1
       Left = Left + Width
    Case 2
       Top = Top + Height
    Case 3
       Left = Left - Width
    Case 0
       Top = Top - Height
    End Select
End Sub
```

We have omitted Form1 in referring to various properties. If you wish, you can add Form1, followed by a dot, before each property name.

We use a **static variable** to retain its value and the **Mod** operator to return a remainder. We also use the **Select Case** command to control the form's position. They will be fully covered in Chapters 6.

Visual Basic uses an object named **Screen** to manipulate your monitor screen. Like a form, it has the Width and Height properties. At run time, you can use code to position objects according to these properties. The procedure below will place Form1 in the middle of the screen at run time.

```
Private Sub Form_Load()
    Form1.Left = (Screen.Width - Form1.Width) / 2
    Form1.Top = (Screen.Height - Form1.Height) / 2
End Sub
```

DRILL

____ 9.   To create a custom color, you need to use:
  a.   the Properties window
  b.   the Project window
  c.   the View menu
  d.   the Tools menu

____ 10.   After you define a color in the Define Color window and then click Close, you
  a.   assign a color to the selected box
  b.   abort color selection
  c.   clear the color palette
  d.   assign a color to the selected object

____ 11.   A custom color defined in the Define Color window can be used from the Properties window. True or false?

____ 12.   The right side of the Settings box in the Properties window may show:
  a.   a down arrow
  b.   three dots
  c.   nothing
  d.   all of the above

____ 13.   This event is triggered first at the beginning of a form's life:
  a.   Load
  b.   Initialize
  c.   Resize
  d.   Paint
  e.   Click

____ 14.   Enlarge a form at run time triggers this event:
  a.   Click
  b.   Paint
  c.   Resize
  d.   all of the above
  e.   both b and c

_____ 15. A form's FontTransparent property is by default set to True. True or false?

_____ 16. If you change a form's Font property, the controls you add to the form after the change will inherit the new font. True or false?

_____ 17. Cls is a(n):
   a. method
   b. event
   c. procedure
   d. event procedure

_____ 18. Click is a(n):
   a. method
   b. event
   c. procedure
   d. event procedure

_____ 19. Text1.FontSize is a(n):
   a. method
   b. event
   c. procedure
   d. property

_____ 20. Form_Click is a(n):
   a. method
   b. event
   c. property
   d. event procedure

PRACTICE

■ 6. Close the Form1 window at design time and then restore the window.

■ 7. Explain what happens when you double-click a property in the Properties list of the Properties window.

■ 8. How do you use the Properties window to select a new background color for the current form?

■ 9. How do you use the View menu to set a new background color for the current form?

10. How do you create a custom color?

11. Write a procedure that will change the current form's caption to *Form Demo* when the window is clicked at run time.

12. Write a procedure that will change the current form to a minimized state as soon as you press F5 to run it. How do you restore the form at run time?

13. How do events and methods differ?

14. What role does the Form_Load procedure play?

15. How do the following two code lines differ?

```
Form2.Show
Load Form2
```

16. How do the following two code lines differ?

```
Form2.Hide
Unload Form2
```

17. What does the Ctrl+F6 key combination do?

18. What does PrintForm do?

19. Create a user interface consisting of two forms, Form1 and Form2. Each form has a command button named Command1. When Form1's command button is clicked at run time, Form1 is hidden and Form2 is displayed. When Form2's command button is clicked, Form2 is hidden and Form1 is displayed.

20. Modify the above so that when Form1's command button is clicked, *Form 1 Demo* and *Form 2 Demo* appear in the respective form's caption—without altering the above-described behavior.

21. Modify the above so that as soon as the program runs, the two respective captions are assigned automatically.

22. Create a project with two forms, Form1 and Form2. Form1 contains a command button named Show2 and Form2 contains another command button named Hide2. At run time, clicking Show2 shows Form2 and clicking Hide2 hides Form2 and shows Form1.

■ 23. In Listing 1, change the code to make Form2 appear at run time diagonally at the bottom right of Form1.

■ 24. In Listing 2, change the code to make the form move counterclockwise.

PRINT FORMATTING

We have used the **Print** method to output items to a form or printer without attempting to shape their appearance. We'll remedy that here.

The Print method can output text to the following objects:

- A form (the current form is the default)
- A picture box
- A printer
- The Immediate window

With rare exceptions, we have not attempted to control the way an output item is to appear. In the following sections we are going to explore a variety of techniques to control text output.

In the examples in the following sections, you can add Printer or Picture1 before Print, such as Printer.Print or Picture1.Print to output to the specified object. If you want to output to the default printer, turn it on and get it ready before you execute a command. Before you to print to a picture box, double-click PictureBox and stretch the resulting Picture1.

Print Zones

The **Print** method follows these rules in producing a text display:

- After printing the specified text, the print head normally moves to the beginning of a new line. If no parameter (specified text) is supplied, the print head moves down one line without printing anything.

- If a **semicolon** (;) appears at the end of a parameter, the print head remains one position after printing the specified text.

- If a **comma** (,) appears at the end of a parameter, the print head moves to the next print zone, which is 14 columns from the previous zone.

- You can use **Spc, Tab, CurrentX,** and **CurrentY** to move the print head to a specific location.

- The Print keyword can be followed by multiple parameters, each separated by a proper function or punctuation mark.

The program below uses commas to move the print head to the next print zone. The result is shown in Figure 3.19.

Form1					
1	2	3	4	5	6
2	4	6	8	10	12
3	6	9	12	15	18
4	8	12	16	20	24
5	10	15	20	25	30
6	12	18	24	30	36
7	14	21	28	35	42
8	16	24	32	40	48
9	18	27	36	45	54

Figure 3.19   Output using commas

```
Private Sub Form_Click ()
    Dim I As Integer
    Dim J As Integer

    AutoRedraw = True        'turn on AutoRedraw
    For I = 1 To 9
        For J = 1 To 9
            Print I * J,     '14 columns apart
        Next J
        Print                'down 1 line
    Next I
End Sub
```

We use a For loop to nest another For loop. This arrangement produces 81 (9 x 9) iterations. The For command will be fully explained in Chapter 5

TIP: Turning On AutoRedraw

A form has an **AutoRedraw** property, which can be set to True or False (default). When AutoRedraw is not on, output to a form window appears only in the visible portion. If the output is larger than the visible portion, the remainder cannot be displayed. If the window is covered up by another object, the IDE window for example, the display in the covered portion is erased and cannot be recovered.

When AutoRedraw is turned on, Visual Basic saves a copy of the output to memory. This slows down a program, but allows you to retrieve the undisplayed or erased portion of the output. If the output is more than the existing window can show, you can enlarge the window to display more. If AutoRedraw is not on, enlarging a window does not show extra text, only more blank area.

Turning on AutoRedraw disables the form's **Paint** event. Enlarging the output window or uncovering it (after being covered up) will not trigger the Paint event as is the case when AutoRedraw is set to False.

AutoRedraw can be turned on via the Properties window at design time or via code at run time. The preceding procedure shows how to do this in code. After running this program, you can enlarge the window to show more text.

AutoRedraw can affect the **Cls** method, which can normally clear output to a form or picture box. In the following procedure, AutoRedraw is turned on and the text is written to the form. After AutoRedraw is turned off, Cls can no longer erase the text.

```
Private Sub Command1_Click ()
    AutoRedraw = True
    Print "xxx"
    AutoRedraw = False
    Cls       'disabled
End Sub
```

Using commas to control text output is practical only if the displayed items do not occupy too many columns. If you have more than a few columns, you need to use other techniques. You can use the Spc function to insert extra spaces or use the Tab function to move to a specified column.

The procedure below uses **Spc** to control screen output. The result is shown in Figure 3.20.

```
Private Sub Form_Click ()
    Dim I As Integer
    Dim J As Integer

    For I = 1 To 9
```

```
        For J = 1 To 9
            Print I * J; Spc(1);      'add 1 space
            If I * J < 10 Then Print Spc(1);
        Next J
        Print
    Next I
End Sub
```

```
┌──────────────────────────────────┐
│ ■  Form1               _ □ X      │
├──────────────────────────────────┤
│ 1   2   3   4   5   6   7   8   9 │
│ 2   4   6   8  10  12  14  16  18 │
│ 3   6   9  12  15  18  21  24  27 │
│ 4   8  12  16  20  24  28  32  36 │
│ 5  10  15  20  25  30  35  40  45 │
│ 6  12  18  24  30  36  42  48  54 │
│ 7  14  21  28  35  42  49  56  63 │
│ 8  16  24  32  40  48  56  64  72 │
│ 9  18  27  36  45  54  63  72  81 │
└──────────────────────────────────┘
```

Figure 3.20   Output using Spc

Instead of using Spc, we can use extra spaces for similar effects. The results are similar, but not identical. The distances inserted by Spc and spaces inside quotation marks can be affected by font types and sizes. In a monospaced font, each space has the same width as a character. In a proportional font, each space is about half a character in width. The distance created by Spc(1) is the average width of one character in that font. In either technique, it is difficult to precisely control the print head's location.

Print **Tab**(X) moves the print head to column X. If X is less than 1, printing is done in the first column. If X is greater than the current column position, printing is done at column X of the same line. If X is less than the current column position, printing is done at column X in the line below. Consider these two lines:

```
    Print "1234567890";
    Print Tab(15); "X"
```

In this case, X will be printed at column 15 of the same line as the number. What happens if you change 15 to 5? X will be printed at column 5 in the next line because the print head was already beyond column 5 in the first line.

If the specified column position is at least 2 higher than the current column position, printing will be done in the same line; otherwise, it will go to the next line. In our example, if we specify 12 or higher, X will be printed in the first line; otherwise, it will be done in the second line.

CurrentX and CurrentY

CurrentX and **CurrentY** are properties available at run time for three objects: form, printer, and picture box. These properties can be used to designate or return X and Y coordinate values (positions) where printing is to begin. The values are by default measured in twips (this can be changed via the ScaleMode property; see Chapter 11). By assigning different values to CurrentX (number of twips from the left margin of the form window), you can move the print head left or right; changing the value of CurrentY (number of twips from the top margin of the window) has the effect of moving the print head up or down.

You can also use CurrentX and CurrentY to tell you where the print head is at any particular time. The procedure below shows their values at various points.

```
Private Sub Form_Click ()
    Dim I As Integer
    Dim J As Integer

    FontName = "courier"
    FontSize = 10

    For I = 1 To 5
        For J = 1 To 5
            Print CurrentX; CurrentY;
        Next J
        Print        'print new line
    Next I
End Sub
```

```
Form1                                                _ □ ×
0    0   720    0   1680    0   2760    0   3840    0
0   195   960   195   2160   195   3480   195   4800
0   390   960   390   2160   390   3480   390   4800
0   585   960   585   2160   585   3480   585   4800
0   780   960   780   2160   780   3480   780   4800
```

Figure 3.21   Output by CurrentX and CurrentY

Running the program and clicking the window shows the result in Figure 3.21. The numbers in the odd-numbered columns represent the twip numbers for the X coordinate when a particular number is printed. The even-numbered columns reflect the Y coordinate values. At the top left corner of the screen, both have 0 values. As the print head moves rightward, the X value increases but the Y value remains the same. When the print head moves down to the next line, the Y value increases but the X value does not change.

In the procedure below, we move the print head 150 twips to the right after printing each number and before printing the next. At the end of each line, we move the print head to the left margin by assigning 0 to CurrentX; we also move the print head down by adding 200 twips to the existing value of CurrentY.

```
Private Sub Form_Click ()
    Dim I As Integer
    Dim J As Integer

    For I = 1 To 9
        For J = 1 To 9
            Print I * J;
            CurrentX = CurrentX + 150
                'move print head right by 150 twips
        Next J
        CurrentX = 0
                'return print head to left margin
        CurrentY = CurrentY + 200
                'move print head down by 200 twips
    Next I
End Sub
```

```
Form1                                    _ □ ✕
1  2  3   4   5   6   7   8   9
2  4  6   8   10  12  14  16  18
3  6  9   12  15  18  21  24  27
4  8  12  16  20  24  28  32  36
5  10 15  20  25  30  35  40  45
6  12 18  24  30  36  42  48  54
7  14 21  28  35  42  49  56  63
8  16 24  32  40  48  56  64  72
9  18 27  36  45  54  63  72  81
```

Figure 3.22   Output by incrementing CurrentX

The result appears in Figure 3.22. The appearance is not neatly aligned due partly to the use of a proportional font and partly to the unequal number of digits for each number. This shows that controlling text display by incrementing

CurrentX's value from the current position is comparable to adding extra spaces for the same purpose.

When you want to move the print head to an absolute position, instead of incrementing from the current position, CurrentX can do it but not Spc. In the procedure below, we set fixed positions for CurrentX, instead of adding the same value to the latest print position. The result (Figure 3.23) is comparable to using commas to control printing positions, except that with CurrentX you can determine each column position but the 14 columns that come with commas cannot be changed.

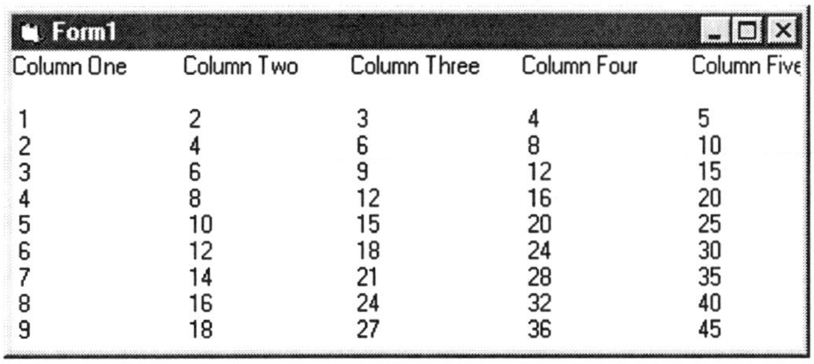

Column One	Column Two	Column Three	Column Four	Column Five
1	2	3	4	5
2	4	6	8	10
3	6	9	12	15
4	8	12	16	20
5	10	15	20	25
6	12	18	24	30
7	14	21	28	35
8	16	24	32	40
9	18	27	36	45

Figure 3.23   Aligning text with CurrentX

```
Private Sub Form_Click ()
    Dim I As Integer
    Dim J As Integer
    Dim Col(1 To 5) As String

    Col(1) = "Column One"
    Col(2) = "Column Two"
    Col(3) = "Column Three"
    Col(4) = "Column Four"
    Col(5) = "Column Five"

    For I = 0 To 4
        CurrentX = I * 1300
            'move print head by 1300 twips
        Print Col(I + 1);
            'print each string on same line
    Next I

    Print: Print             'two new lines
    For I = 1 To 9
        For J = 1 To 5
            Print I * J;     'print number first
```

```
            CurrentX = J * 1300
                              'then move print head
        Next J
        Print                    'new line
    Next I
End Sub
```

In the code we use **Dim** (you can also use **ReDim**) to define an **array**. This array is used to display the heading. An array is a group of variables sharing the same name but distinguished by index numbers. Arrays are fully covered in Chapter 9.

We play a trick in the first For loop. The counter is set from 0 to 4. But the first index number in our array is 1, not 0. By adding 1 to the first counter value of 0, we can access our first array element. You can change the counter value from 0 To 4 to 1 To 5. The other things must also be changed as shown below:

```
For I = 1 To 5
    Print Col(I);
        'print each string on same line
    CurrentX = I * 1300
        'move print head by 1300 twips
Next I
```

In this new arrangement, the first column is printed before the value of CurrentX is changed. This is the same arrangement found in the second For loop.

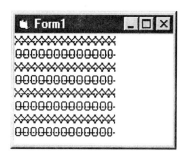

Figure 3.24   Using CurrentX to print over existing text

The techniques of using Tab, Spc, comma, or semicolon (discussed in the previous section) maneuver the print head in text mode. In contrast, CurrentX and CurrentY control the print head in graphics mode and are thus more versatile. You can use these two (but not the others) to move the print head upward or leftward over existing text. This allows you to print new text over the existing text or graphics.

Figure 3.24 shows an example of printing new text over an existing line. The procedure below shows the code to do that. The screen output is the result of using the default MS San Serif font. If another font is used, the result may be different.

```
Private Sub Form_Click ()
    Dim I As Integer

    For I = 1 To 4
        Print "XXXXXXXXXXXXXXXXX"; 'same line
        CurrentX = 0        'return to left margin
        Print "-------------------------------------"
        Print "OOOOOOOOOOOOOOOO";
        CurrentX = 0
        Print "-------------------------------------"
    Next I
End Sub
```

In all the statements in this section and the previous section, we assume Form1 to be the default output object. We could have used Form1.Print, Form1.CurrentX, and so on. Instead of using Form1, we could use Printer to output text to paper. In a form, you can use CurrentY to move the print head to previous lines to print over existing text. I have not been able to do that on a dot-matrix printer (Epson LX-810)—although CurrentX can move the print head leftward to existing text and print new text over it.

CurrentX and CurrentY are often used to control graphics output. We will revisit them in Chapter 11.

Formatting with Format

You can use the **Format function** to control the output appearance of the following items:

- Numerics
- Text strings
- Date/time numbers

The first two items are covered here; the last will be explained in Chapter 7.

Format follows this syntax:

```
Format(expression [,fmt])
```

The expression is something you want to print. The optional *fmt* argument is the way you want to control how the expression is printed. It can be one of the following:

- A format name predefined by Visual Basic
- User-defined, using one or more available characters

A format name supplied by Visual Basic can be one of those shown in Table 3.1.

Table 3.1   Predefined format names

Name	Effect
General Number	No formatting, the same as no argument
Currency	$; thousand separator; two decimal digits; parentheses for negative
Fixed	Two digits after decimal point and at least one digit before it
Standard	Thousand separator; two digits after decimal point if needed
Percent	% added; value multiplied by 100; two digits after decimal point
Scientific	Standard scientific notation
Yes/No	No for 0; Yes for nonzero
True/False	False for 0; True for nonzero
On/Off	Off for 0; On for nonzero

The procedure below demonstrates how you can use the predefined names to format numbers; the result is shown in Figure 3.25. Here we use a variable name to represent a format name. If you intend to use a format name directly, make sure to put it in quotation marks as you would any literal string.

```
Private Sub Form_Click ()
    Dim I As Integer
    Dim Num As Single
    Dim FmtName(1 To 9) As String

    FmtName(1) = "general number"
    FmtName(2) = "currency"
    FmtName(3) = "fixed"
    FmtName(4) = "standard"
    FmtName(5) = "percent"
    FmtName(6) = "scientific"
    FmtName(7) = "yes/no"
    FmtName(8) = "true/false"
```

```
      FmtName(9) = "on/off"
      Num = 22222222 / 7
      For I = 1 To 9
          Print FmtName(I);    'print format name
          CurrentX = 2000      'move print head 2000 twips
          Print Format(Num, FmtName(I))  'print number
          CurrentX = 0         'return print head to left
      Next I
End Sub
```

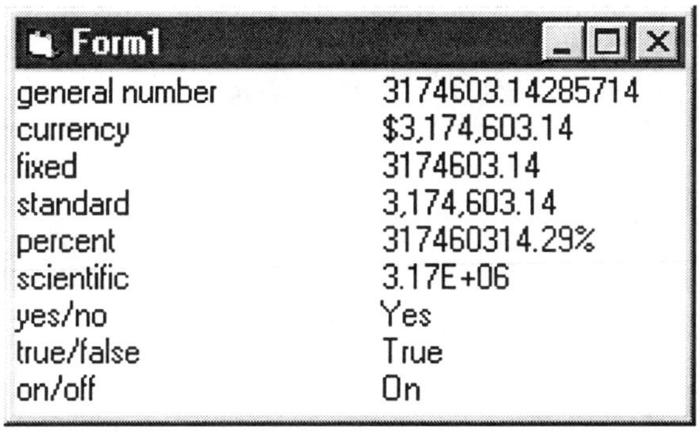

🐦 Form1	_ ▢ ✕
general number	3174603.14285714
currency	$3,174,603.14
fixed	3174603.14
standard	3,174,603.14
percent	317460314.29%
scientific	3.17E+06
yes/no	Yes
true/false	True
on/off	On

Figure 3.25   Predefined format names and results

Notice how we use CurrentX to control the position for the second column. Before each item in the second column is printed, the print head is moved to 2000 twips from the left margin. After the second column is printed, CurrentX is changed to 0, thus moving the print head back to the left margin. Actually, assigning the 0 value is redundant in this case. The previous line has no comma or semicolon. The print head returns to the beginning of the next line, which changes CurrentX's value to 0.

Format is a function (see Chapter 7). It returns a value. If you add a $ character at the end, the returned value is a string, otherwise a Variant. Part of our For-Next loop could thus be written this way:

```
      For I = 1 To 9
          N = Format(Num, FmtName(I))
          Print N
      Next I
```

You can use the characters in Table 3.2 in a user-defined format.

Table 3.2   Characters for user-defined formats

Character	Purpose
0	Digit placeholder
#	Digit placeholder
.	Decimal placeholder
,	Thousand separator
%	Percentage placeholder
e+/-, E+/-	Scientific format

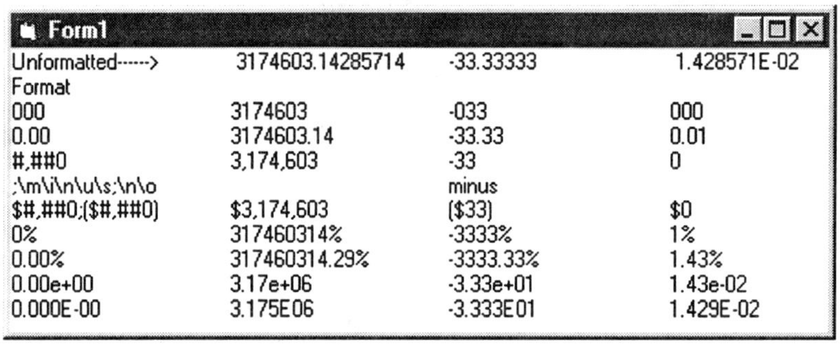

```
 Form1                                                            _ □ ×
Unformatted------>    3174603.14285714      -33.33333        1.428571E-02
Format
000                  3174603               -033             000
0.00                 3174603.14            -33.33           0.01
#,##0                3,174,603             -33              0
;\m\i\n\u\s;\n\o                            minus
$#,##0;($#,##0)      $3,174,603            ($33)            $0
0%                   317460314%            -3333%           1%
0.00%                317460314.29%         -3333.33%        1.43%
0.00e+00             3.17e+06              -3.33e+01        1.43e-02
0.000E-00            3.175E06              -3.333E01        1.429E-02
```

Figure 3.26   Results of various user-defined formats

The procedure below is modified from the preceding one. The format names shown at the top of the listing are all user-defined. Running this programs leads to the result shown in Figure 3.26.

```
Private Sub Form_click ()
    Dim I As Integer, Num1 As Single
    Dim Num2 As Single, Num3 As Single
    Dim FmtName(1 To 9) As String

    FmtName(1) = "000"
    FmtName(2) = "0.00"
    FmtName(3) = "#,##0"
    FmtName(4) = ";\m\i\n\u\s;\n\o"
    FmtName(5) = "$#,##0;($#,##0)"
    FmtName(6) = "0%"
    FmtName(7) = "0.00%"
    FmtName(8) = "0.00e+00"
    FmtName(9) = "0.000E-00"

    Num1 = 22222222 / 7
    Num2 = -100 / 3
    Num3 = 1 / 70
```

```
    Print "Unformatted----->";
    CurrentX = 1800          'print first line
    Print Num1;              'unformatted numbers
    CurrentX = 3600
    Print Num2;
    CurrentX = 5400
    Print Num3
    Print "Format"

    For I = 1 To 9
        Print FmtName(I);   'print format name
        CurrentX = 1800   'move print head 1800 twips
        Print Format(Num1, FmtName(I));   'print number
        CurrentX = 3600
        Print Format(Num2, FmtName(I));   'same line
        CurrentX = 5400
        Print Format(Num3, FmtName(I))   'new line
        CurrentX = 0        'return print head to left
    Next I
End Sub
```

The **0** and **#** signs are similar in some ways but different in others. Both are placeholders for digits. On the left side of the decimal point, if there are more digits than available placeholders, all the digits will be displayed. On the right side, however, extra digits are rounded to fit the available placeholders. If there are more placeholders than available digits, extra #'s are discarded and not displayed but extra 0's are kept and displayed; this is true on both sides of the decimal point. If you have large numbers and want to show the $ sign, thousand separator, and two decimal places, use this style: "$#,#.00".

In a user-defined format, you can supply one, two, three, or four sections, each separated by a semicolon. They have the following meanings:

One section	Applies to all values
Two sections	First for positive; second for negative
Three sections	Positive; negative; zeros
Four sections	Positive; negative; zeros; Null

If you intend to use characters to represent values, put each after the \ sign, as shown in the middle of Figure 3.26.

If you want more details of numerous other variations, type Format and, with the cursor still on the word, press F1 to show the online help topic.

If you are familiar with Basic's *Print Using* command, you already know many of the formats. Keep in mind, however, that *Using* is no longer legal in Visual Basic; Format has completely replaced it.

You can format a text string with some special characters shown below:

@   Character placeholder; right justify
&   Character placeholder; left justify
<   Convert to lowercase
>   Convert to uppercase
!   Left justify

The number of characters in a placeholder determines the number of characters for a string to be printed. If there are more placeholder characters than characters to be displayed, the extra placeholders are discarded and only the text string is displayed. If there are fewer placeholder characters, the entire string is displayed.

Each @ character reserves an unused space on the left of the text string, but the & character does not reserve space on the right. In the procedure below, we use 15 placeholder characters. The first line in Figure 3.27 shows seven empty spaces on the left and eight characters in the displayed string. The second line also reserves 15 spaces, but only the first eight are filled and the eight reserved spaces are discarded. If we concatenate the first line by putting the second portion before the first, the seven spaces will still be there. However, if we add an ! character to anywhere among the placeholder characters in the first line, the extra spaces will disappear and the text will be left-aligned.

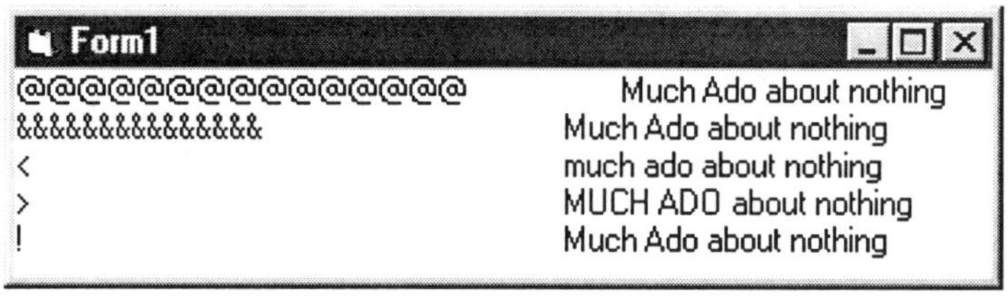

Figure 3.27   Results of various characters on strings

```
Private Sub Form_click ()
    Dim I As Integer
    Dim FmtName(1 To 5) As String
    Dim Str1 As String, Str2 As String

    FmtName(1) = "@@@@@@@@@@@@@@@"    'right justify
    FmtName(2) = "&&&&&&&&&&&&&&&"    'left justify
    FmtName(3) = "<"             'force lowercase
    FmtName(4) = ">"             'force uppercase
    FmtName(5) = "!"             'force right justify
    Str1 = "Much Ado"
```

```
    Str2 = " about nothing"

    For I = 1 To 5
        Print FmtName(I);
        CurrentX = 3000
        Print Format(Str1, FmtName(I)) & Str2
    Next I
End Sub
```

FONTS AND TEXT DISPLAY

Instead of outputting data to the form window with a monotonous typeface, as you must do in the DOS environment, you can now spice up your output displays with a variety of tools and techniques discussed here.

Fonts at Run Time

The simplest technique to improve a text display is to use different fonts and related attributes. The properties you can use include FontName, FontBold, FontItalic, FontSize, FontStrikethrough, FontUnderline, and FontTransparent. These were available in VB3 and earlier and are still legal.

Since **Font** has become an object (beginning with VB4), it's preferable to use Font.Name, Font.Bold, Font.Italic, etc. As you type Font followed by a period, a popup list box shows the available options. If the **Auto List Members** feature is turned off in the Tools | Options | Editor tab, you can still press Ctrl+J or Ctrl+spacebar to pop up this list.

Consider the following examples:

```
Font = "courier"
FontName = "courier"
Font.Name = "courier"
```

All three are legal and will do the same thing. When **Font** is used alone, it defaults to Font.Name.

The **FontCount** and **Fonts** properties are available only at run time for the **Screen** and **Printer** objects. You can use the former to count the available number of fonts and the latter to show their names.

To see how many screen and printer fonts your system has, use FontCount to tell you. Follow these steps:

1. Double-click the list box tool in the Toolbox to add a list box to an empty form; a rectangular box named List1 should appear. Enlarge it so that some text can be displayed. Position it slightly to the right of the middle as shown in Figure 3.28.

2. Add code to the Form_Load procedure, as shown below.

3. Run the program. The result is shown in Figure 3.28.

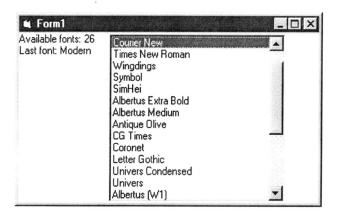

Figure 3.28   A list box showing available fonts

```
Private Sub Form_Load ()
    Dim I As Integer

    Show
    For I = 0 To Printer.FontCount - 1
            'count number of printer fonts
        List1.AddItem Printer.Fonts(I)
            'add each font name in list box
    Next I
    Print "Available fonts: " & Printer.FontCount
    Print "Last font: " & Printer.Fonts(I - 1)
End Sub
```

The list box control and the AddItem method used to add items to a list box will be explained in Chapters 4 and 10.

In our procedure, we try to count the fonts available for the **Printer** object. You can change it to **Screen**. The result may or may not be different, depending on your equipment.

When you want to use a font or size to display text, use the Font.Name or Font.Size property, such as:

```
Font.Name = "modern"
Font.Size = 12
```

In the procedure below, we specify font size 10 and output to the screen all the font names and a test line printed in each separate font. Figure 3.29 shows the result.

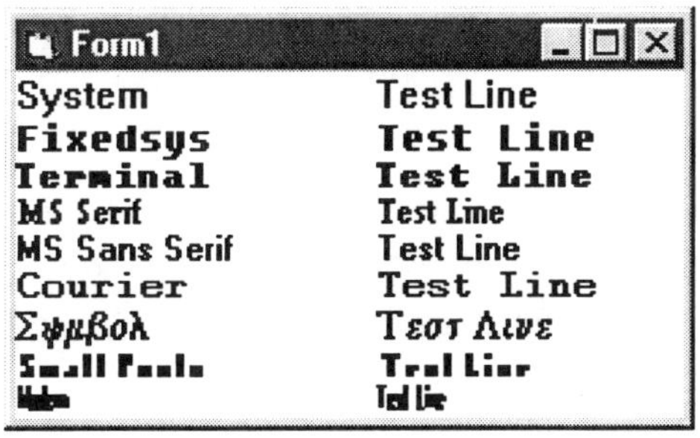

Figure 3.29   Font names and how they appear

```
Private Sub Form_Click ()
    Dim I As Integer

    FontSize = 10              'specify font size
    For I = 0 To Screen.FontCount - 1
            'count number of fonts
        Font.Name = Screen.Fonts(I)
            'use a new font
        Print Font.Name;
        CurrentX = 2000
        Print "Test Line"
    Next I
End Sub
```

NOTE   In the above procedure, using FontName (instead of Font or Font.Name) could possibly lead to the *Invalid property value* error. The reason is that FontName doesn't recognize some newer fonts.

To show the names of the fonts that are common between the screen and the printer, try this procedure:

```
Private Sub Form_Click()
    Dim I As Integer, J As Integer

    MousePointer = vbHourglass
    For I = 0 To Screen.FontCount - 1
        For J = 0 To Printer.FontCount - 1
            If Screen.Fonts(I) = Printer.Fonts(J) Then
                Print Screen.Fonts(I), Printer.Fonts(J)
                Exit For     'exit when match found
            End If
        Next J
    Next I
    MousePointer = vbDefault
End Sub
```

3-D Text

In addition to using fonts, you can give your text special effects, as shown in Figure 3.30. To give characters a 3-D look, print them twice, the second time with a different text color and a slightly different position. The procedure below shows how to do that.

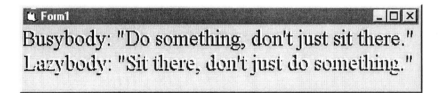

Figure 3.30   3-D text

```
Private Sub Form_Click ()
    Dim Str1 As String, Str2 As String

    Font.Name = "times new roman"
    ForeColor = QBColor(15)       'white
    FontSize = 18
    Str1 = "Busybody: " + _
    """Do something, don't just sit there."""
    Str2 = "Lazybody: " + Chr(34) + "Sit there, don't" _
    + " just do something." + Chr(34)
    Print Str1;
```

```
      ForeColor = QBColor(0)        'black
      CurrentX = -30               '30 twips to left of border
      CurrentY = CurrentY + 20     'down 20 twips
      Print Str1          'print 2nd time
      ForeColor = QBColor(0)        'black
      Print Str2;
      ForeColor = QBColor(15)       'white
      CurrentX = 30                '30 twips from left border
      CurrentY = CurrentY - 30     'up 30 twips
      Print Str2
End Sub
```

We're also demonstrating two tricks: line continuation and quotation marks. If a line is too long, you can break it up with the **line continuation character**. It consists of a space and an underscore (_) placed at the end of a line. When this character is detected, Visual Basic will treat the line below as the same line. A comment after it is illegal. Furthermore, you cannot insert this character between quotation marks. The following example is legal because the first line has an ending quote:

```
Str1 = "Busybody: ""Do something," + _
"don 't just sit there."""
```

To add a **quotation mark** to a text string, you need to insert an additional mark. Consider these examples:

```
Print ""              'empty string
Print """"            ' "
Print """"x"          ' "x
Print """"x"""        ' "x"
```

When two consecutive marks are encountered inside a pair of required marks for a string, Visual Basic will add an additional mark. If you insert an incorrect number of marks, Visual Basic may add additional ones or other punctuation marks without your consent. The result may not be what you have in mind.

Our second string (Str2) uses **Chr(34)** to insert a quotation mark. The result is the same as using two quotes to insert a single quote.

Aligning Text

There are times you when want to right-align words to make a display more attractive. How you do that? Use the **TextWidth** function to get each text string's width (measured in twips by default) and subtract the value from the right margin where you want to line up all the strings. The following procedure will do the trick; it produces the display in Figure 3.31.

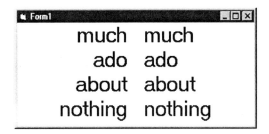

Figure 3.31   Aligning text

```
Private Sub Form_Click ()
    Dim I As Integer, Midd As Long
    Dim Txt(1 To 4) As String

    Cls
    Txt(1) = "much"        'define elements
    Txt(2) = "ado"
    Txt(3) = "about"
    Txt(4) = "nothing"
    Midd = ScaleWidth / 2   'form's horizontal midpoint
    FontSize = 25

    For I = 1 To 4          'get left pos of word
        CurrentX = (Midd - 200) - TextWidth(Txt(I))
            'end each word at 200 twips from midpoint
        Print Txt(I)       'print word
    Next I

    CurrentY = 0           'move print head to top

    For I = 1 To 4
        CurrentX = Midd + 200
                'start at 200 twips from midpoint
        Print Txt(I)        'print word
    Next I
End Sub
```

You can resize the window at run time and click it to clear the existing display and redisplay the text in the resized window. The new display will always be centered. In fact, you can change Form_Click to **Form_Resize**. Every time you resize the window, a new display will appear.

In the first For loop, the ending position of each word is 200 twips to the left of the form's horizontal midpoint. The beginning position is calculated by subtracting the width of each word. The result is that all words are right-aligned at 200 twips from the middle. In the second For loop, all words begin at 200 twips to the right of the middle, resulting in left justification.

We use the form's **ScaleWidth** property to determine a line's midpoint. It can be combined with TextWidth to center a text line. These two lines will print Text1's content horizontally centered:

```
CurrentX = (ScaleWidth - TextWidth(Text1.Text)) / 2
Print Text1.Text
```

If you want to get a form's vertical midpoint, use **ScaleHeight**. If you want to get a text line's height, use the **TextHeight** property. Using these two height properties, you can vertically center a text string. The following procedure will print the text string half way between top and bottom:

```
Private Sub Form_Click()
    Dim Strn As String

    Strn = "between top and bottom"
    CurrentY = (ScaleHeight - TextHeight(Strn)) / 2
    Print Strn
End Sub
```

DRILL

____ 21. If the print head is at column 20, Print Tab(10) will move the print head to:
   a. column 10 in the current line
   b. column 30 in the current line
   c. column 10 in the following line
   d. none of the above

____ 22. The following statement will print:

```
Print Format(12.345, "fixed")
```

   a. 12
   b. 12.34
   c. $12.34
   d. 12.35
   e. none of the above

____ 23.   This format name supplies thousand separators:
    a.   Currency
    b.   Fixed
    c.   Standard
    d.   all of the above
    e.   both a and c

____ 24.   The following statement will print _____ .

```
Print Format(12.5, "$####")
```

____ 25.   The following statement will print _____ .

```
Print Format(12.5, "$0000")
```

____ 26.   The following statement will print _____ .

```
Print Format(1234567.89, "#.#")
```

____ 27.   The following statement will print _____ .

```
Print Format(1234, "#.00")
```

____ 28.   The following statements will print the text string:

```
CurrentX = (ScaleWidth - TextWidth("xxx"))
Print "xxx"
```

    a.   right-aligned
    b.   left-aligned
    c.   horizontally centered
    d.   vertically centered

____ 29.   The following statement will:

```
Print Printer.Fonts(1)
```

    a.   show a font name
    b.   show a printer name
    c.   show an error
    d.   none of the above

____ 30.   This statement uses a new font to display text:
    a.   FontName = "courier"
    b.   Font = "courier"
    c.   FontCount = "courier"

d.   both a and b

e.   none of the above

PRACTICE

■   25. Explain the difference between a comma, a semicolon, and the absence of either in controlling the print head.

■   26. How do Tab(X) and Spc(X) differ?

■   27. How do CurrentX and CurrentY work?

■   28. Write a Form_Click procedure that will produce a display shown in Figure 3.32. Use the Tab function to control the print head.

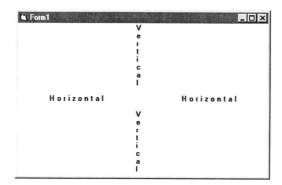

Figure 3.32   Printing lines to form a cross

■   29. Write a Form_Click procedure that will display text lines in font sizes ranging from 30 to 10 points, as shown in Figure 3.33. Use CurrentY to control the space between lines.

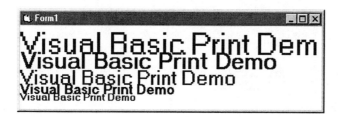

Figure 3.33   Using font sizes and CurrentY to control output

■ 30. Write a Form_Click procedure that will use the printer's font #3 and size 15 to display a text string that includes the font name and font size. Also show the second text string using font #4 and size 10.

■ 31. Write a Form_Click procedure that will print the values of CurrentX and CurrentY at 2000 twips from the left and 1500 twips from the top.

■ 32. Write a Form_Click procedure that will print four slanted lines constituting a diamond. Each line consists of 10 consecutive numbers slanting upward or downward as shown in Figure 3.34.

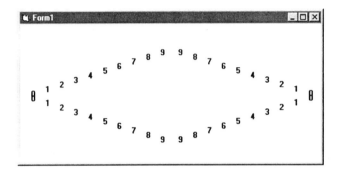

Figure 3.34   Using CurrentX and CurrentY to for a diamond

■ 33 Output the above display to the printer.

CHAPTER PROJECT

A. (3FORMS.FRM)

(Instructor: Open the disk file, follow step 1 below, and press F5 to run the program.)

This project manipulates multiple forms. Do the following at design time:

1. Use the Add Form icon (the second on the Standard toolbar) to add Form2 and Form3 to the original Form1. The three forms' default sizes and positions are not changed.

2. Add two command buttons to Form1.

3. Write procedures for the following events:

   Form1's Form_Click
   The two buttons' Click events

Clicking Form1 at run time should make the three forms appear side by side, each occupying 1/3 of the original width of Form1 and positioned next to one another. A large number is also printed to each form as shown in Figure 3.35.

When the Hide 2 button is clicked, Form2 is hidden. Form3 disappears when you click Hide 3. When Form1 is clicked, the other forms are displayed.

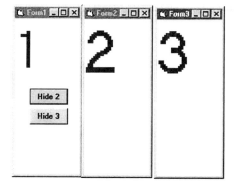

Figure 3.35   Maneuvering forms at run time

B. (3TREE.FRM)

Write a form Click procedure that will print Figure 3.36. The first line has 3 characters. Each ensuing line has 3 more than before. All lines are horizontally centered.

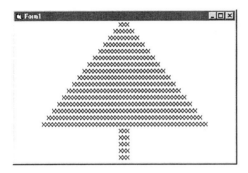

Figure 3.36   A tree with centered lines

C. (3PRFONTS.FRM)

Write a Form_Click procedure that will do the following:

1. Print the names of all the screen fonts; these names are left-justified (Figure 3.37).

2. Print the names of all the printer fonts; these are right-justified.

3. All the user to stretch the window at run time to show the undisplayed portion.

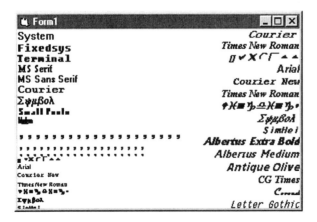

Figure 3.37   Printing with different fonts

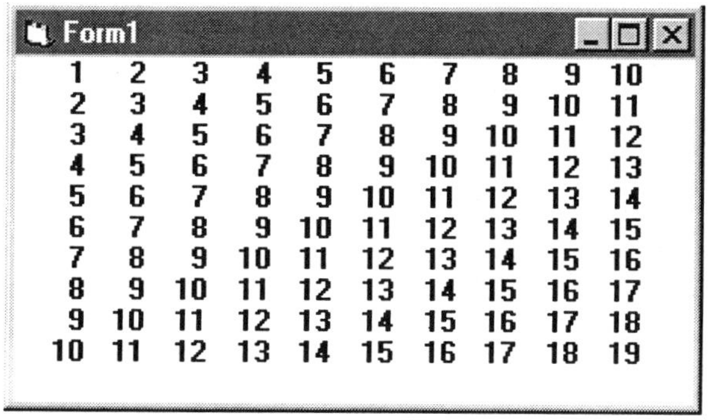

Form1
1 2 3 4 5 6 7 8 9 10
2 3 4 5 6 7 8 9 10 11
3 4 5 6 7 8 9 10 11 12
4 5 6 7 8 9 10 11 12 13
5 6 7 8 9 10 11 12 13 14
6 7 8 9 10 11 12 13 14 15
7 8 9 10 11 12 13 14 15 16
8 9 10 11 12 13 14 15 16 17
9 10 11 12 13 14 15 16 17 18
10 11 12 13 14 15 16 17 18 19

Figure 3.38 Right-justified numbers

D. (3PRNUM.FRM)

This project produces the display shown in Figure 3.38. The first row shows numbers 1-10, the second, 2-11, and so on. Each column is right aligned and 400 twips apart.

E. (3PRMIDDLE1.FRM)

Write a Form_Resize procedure that will display a text string that is centered horizontally and vertically (Figure 3.39). Set the font size at 1/100 of the form's scalable height so that it will change according to the form's size. Use a TrueType font.

Form1
Sample String

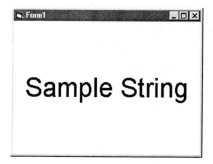

Figure 3.39 A centered output string

F. (3PRMIDDLE2.FRM)

Modify the previous procedure as follows:

1. The font size is 1/200 of the form's scalable height.
2. The sample string is printed four times, each in the middle of one of the four quadrants of the form (Figure 3.40).
3. As the form is resized, the text size and position should automatically adjust themselves.

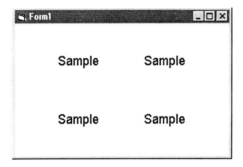

Figure 3.40   Four centered output strings

G. (3PRMIDDLE3.FRM)

This program prints Figure 3.41. Whenever the window is resized at run time, the lines reappear in the middle (horizontally and vertically). (Hints: Write a Resize event procedure; add up the text height of the four lines, subtract it from ScaleHeight, and divide the result by 2 to get the vertical midpoint.)

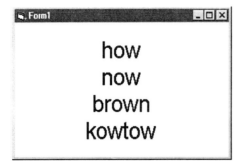

Figure 3.41   Printing text lines in the middle

H. (3MOTEL.FRM)

Jazz up the interface for Mo's Model Motel as shown in Figure 3.42 by doing the following:

1. Change the form caption as shown.

2. Add the new logo by using a label. Change the label's background color to cyan and its text to a large italic font.

3. Save the file as 3MOTEL.FRM.

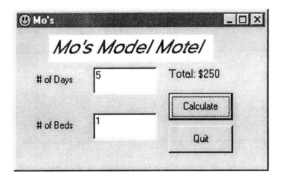

Figure 3.42   Jazzing up the interface

FUN AND GAME

A. (TITLE.FRM)

This program draws the logo shown in Figure 3.43. The BorderStyle property is set to 0 at design time. The rest is controlled by code.

Figure 3.43   Book logo

```
Private Sub Form_Load()
    Dim I As Single
    Dim J As Single
    Dim X As Single
    Dim Y As Single
    Dim Pi As Single
    Dim TopStr As Variant
    Dim BotStr As Variant

    Show
    TopStr = Array("V", "i", "s", "u", "a", _
    "l", "B", "a", "s", "i", "c")
    BotStr = Array("C", "o", "u", "r", "s", _
    "e", "b", "o", "o", "k")
        'array text strings
    FontName = "times new roman"
    FontSize = 35
    Pi = 4 * Atn(1)            'get pi
    Width = ScaleHeight        'square form
    Width = 2 * ScaleHeight - ScaleWidth

    Scale (-1, 1)-(1.2, -1)    'Cartesian scale
                    'skewed to accommodate text
    J = 0                       'top arc
    For I = Pi * 0.9 To 0 Step -Pi / 13
        'top text, clockwise motion from left to right
        X = 0.95 * Cos(I)       'get x,y on circumference
        Y = 0.95 * Sin(I)
        CurrentX = X            'position print head
        CurrentY = Y
        If J >= 11 Then Exit For
                        'avoid out of script error
```

```
        Print TopStr(J)              'print top text
        J = J + 1                'control array elements
    Next I

    Scale (-1, 1)-(1.2, -1.2)     'adjusted scale
    Circle (0.09, -0.1), 1.05    'outer circle
    FontName = "courier new"
    FontSize = 30
    J = 0                            'bottom arc
    For I = Pi * 1.07 To Pi * 2 Step Pi / 10.5
        'bottom text, counterclockwise motion
        X = 0.85 * Cos(I)    'get x,y on circumference
        Y = 0.85 * Sin(I)
        CurrentX = X
        CurrentY = Y
        If J >= 10 Then Exit For
        Print BotStr(J)              'print bottom text
        J = J + 1
    Next

    Circle (0.1, -0.2), 0.7 'inner circle
    DrawWidth = 5                'thick
    FontSize = 110
    Scale                    'restore default scale
    CurrentX = ScaleWidth / 3
    CurrentY = ScaleHeight / 4
    CurrentX = CurrentX - 280 'move right for 2nd digit
    FontName = "wingdings"
    Print Chr(176)          'print + in middle
End Sub
```

B. (CLOCKTIMER.FRM)

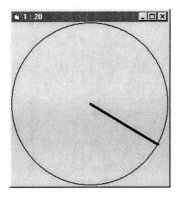

Figure 3.44   A clock with a moving second hand

This program displays a clock (Figure 3.44) with a second hand that moves at the
rate of 1/60 of the circle every second. Every time the hand moves, a new
number is shown in the caption. The caption continuously displays the elapsed
minutes and seconds.

```
Dim Radius As Single, I As Single, Pi As Single

Private Sub Form_Load()
    Show            'show form
    Width = ScaleHeight        'get perfect square
    Width = 2 * ScaleHeight - ScaleWidth
    Line1.X1 = ScaleHeight / 2  'center 1st point
    Line1.Y1 = ScaleWidth / 2
    Line1.BorderWidth = 3      'line width
    Line1.BorderColor = vbRed
    Shape1.Top = 0             'move to top left
    Shape1.Left = 0
    Shape1.BorderColor = vbBlue
    Shape1.BorderWidth = 3
    Shape1.Width = ScaleWidth   'stretch to max
    Shape1.Height = ScaleHeight
    Shape1.Shape = 3           'change to circle

    Scale (-1, 1)-(1, -1)  'Cartesian scale
    Radius = 0.9
    Pi = 4 * Atn(1)
    I = Pi / 2              'interval
        'beginning pos is 12 o'clock
    Line1.X2 = Radius * Cos(I) 'get x axis
    Line1.Y2 = Radius * Sin(I) 'get y axis
    Timer1.Interval = 1000
        'set timer interval at 1 second
End Sub

Private Sub Timer1_Timer()
    Static Min As Integer, Sec As Integer

    Sec = Sec + 1          'increment seconds
    If Sec = 60 Then
        Sec = 0
        Min = Min + 1      'increment minutes
    End If
    Caption = Min & " : " & Sec
    I = I - Pi / 30        'clockwise motion
        'interval at 1/60, or 2pi/60
    Line1.X2 = Radius * Cos(I)    'get x axis
    Line1.Y2 = Radius * Sin(I)    'get y axis
End Sub
```

 *Chapter 4*
Common Controls

TOPIC

    A. Managing Multiple Controls
        a. Controlling Multiple Controls
        b. Common Properties
        c. The Properties Window
        d. Object Naming Conventions
        e. Interface Designing Tools
    B. Classes and Modules
    C. Command Button
    D. Label
    E. Text Box
    F. List Box (a first look at an advanced topic)
    G. Scroll Bars
    H. Check Box
    I. Option Button
    J. Frame
    K. Parent and Container
    L. Input Box
    M. Message Box
    N. Customized Input Box
    O. Data Control (a first look at an advanced topic)

KEY TERMS

Access key   A letter designated in an object's Caption property to let the user press Alt and that letter key to shift the focus to that object. At design time, you add an & before a letter to designate it as an access key. The letter will be underlined.

Check box   A control that allows the user to check it to make a selection. Multiple selections can be made by the user.

Class   A program that provides the formal definition of an **object**. It determines how the included data can be manipulated by the included procedures. Users of a class (such as CommandButton or TextBox) can create copies (objects) and put them in their applications. Classes are the foundation of OOP (object-oriented programming).

Command button   A control with a unique 3-D look. A Click procedure is usually attached to a command button. When the user clicks the button, the procedure is executed.

Frame   A control to contain option buttons and other controls. Like a form, it serves as a container containing other objects.

Horizontal/Vertical scroll bar   A control that lets the user move the scroll box inside to designate a value. The designated value is the scroll box's position between the minimum value (one end of the bar) and the maximum value (the other end of the bar).

Input box   A type of window that pops up in the middle of the screen to prompt the user for an input. The user can be given quite a few options. Program execution is suspended until the user chooses an option.

Label   A control that is most often used to show a text string on the screen, usually placed next to a text box or another object to guide the user.

List box   A control that displays at run time a list of items from which the user can make one or more selections.

Message box   A small window that appears in the middle of the screen to display a message. The user can be given a limited number of options. The user must choose an option before program execution will continue.

Modal (or modeless)   A type of window that requires a user action before the focus can shift to another object; program execution is suspended until an action is taken. An input box or message box is modal. A modeless window, like a regular form window, requires no such user action. You can use argument 0 (vbModeless) or 1 (vbModal) with the Show method to make a form modeless or modal.

Module   A container of program code. Each module is saved to a separate file. There are three types of modules: form module, standard module, and class module. A **form module** can contain code and visible objects. A **standard module** contains only declarations and procedures that can be used by the entire application. A **class module** contains declarations and procedures to create a class.

Object   A program that combines code (methods) and data (properties). The code is used to maneuver the data. An object is derived from a **class** and inherits its code and data. A programmer can put together objects such as command buttons and text boxes to quickly create a useful application. This is like using prefab parts to build a house.

Option button   A control that lets the user choose only one out of the available options. Option buttons in a container are mutually exclusive; only one can be chosen. However, you can use a frame control to provide another group of options.

Text box   A control that can serve as an input or output field. You can edit an entry and use code to arithmetically maneuver entered numbers. Multiple lines can be entered or displayed, and scroll bars can also be provided to scroll the displayed text.

A Windows application, as you already know, typically has multiple objects placed inside a window. The user can choose one of the displayed objects to do something. These objects are known as **controls**. At design time, controls are fetched from the Toolbox and placed on a form. In order to respond to a user action directed at an object, you usually need to write code for one or more event procedures. When the user initiates an event, such as clicking a command button, the Click event of the button is triggered and the event procedure of the button is executed. The code you have attached to that event procedure then does something in response.

Controls thus play a crucial role. Most of the work in developing a Visual Basic program involves using these controls and attaching code to their event procedures. This chapter covers the most commonly used controls, including how to set their properties and write code for some of their event procedures. The controls we plan to cover in this chapter are shown in Figure 4.1.

In addition, this chapter also explains some common devices available in Visual Basic to deal with user interaction. These can be combined with some controls to create a responsive Visual Basic program that can intelligently interact with the user.

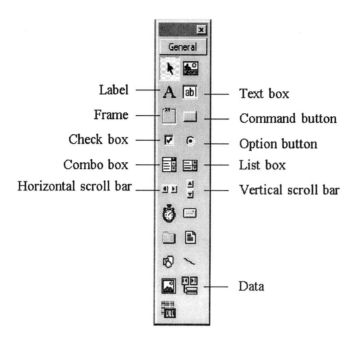

Figure 4.1   The controls covered in this chapter

MANAGING CONTROLS

This section provides a brief summation of general rules related to controls. More details about each control will be provided in separate sections later.

Controlling Multiple Controls

You can select multiple controls and do something to all of them. There are two ways to select multiple controls:

- **Hold down Shift or Ctrl and click each.**
- **Draw a box around the controls.**

In the second method, drag the pointer to draw a box to surround the objects you want to select. As you drag the pointer, a rectangular outline box appears. After you release the mouse button, all the objects inside are surrounded by gray sizing handles.

NOTE   If you want to deselect a selected object without deselecting others, hold down Shift or Ctrl and click that object.

You can do the following to selected objects:

- Press Del to delete all of them.
- Press Ctrl+X to cut them.
- Drag one to move the whole group.

When you drag an object, the whole group moves. When you reach the new location, release the mouse button. Clicking anything other than a selected object causes the sizing handles to disappear. The objects are then no longer selected.

NOTE   Right-clicking a selected object brings up a shortcut menu with the Cut, Copy, and Delete options available. You can then choose one to do something quickly.

Common Properties

Most controls have the following properties and default values:

Appearance	Flat
	3D (default)
Enabled	True (default)
	False
TabIndex	(variable)
TabStop	True (default)
	False
ToolTipText	(none)
Visible	True (default)
	False

The **Appearance** property is available for most (but not all) controls. You can change its value only at design time. It's read-only (can't be changed) at run time.

When **Visible** is set to False, mostly by code, the object becomes invisible. When **Enabled** is set to False, the object is dimmed and does not respond to an event. So, if you don't want the user to click a command button at a particular time, assign False to its Enabled property.

TabIndex determines the order for tab stops. This property value is an integer starting with 0. The first control you add to the form has 0 as its TabIndex property value. If you delete a control, later controls' numbers are automatically adjusted. You can change this value in the Properties window; all later controls will have their numbers changed.

Some controls that cannot receive the focus at run time, such as a label, cannot be reached by pressing the Tab key. Even though they retain their tab orders, they will be skipped when Tab is pressed. If you do not want others to be reached by pressing the Tab key, change the control's **TabStop** property value to False. The control, though, can still respond to events such as Click or DblClick.

Most controls have the **ToolTipText** property (new in VB5). You can assign a text string at design time or run time. When you point to the related control at run time, a tooltip appears. This can provide an additional help to a user of your program.

The Properties Window

When you have many controls on a form, you can use the Properties window to quickly alter each control's properties. When the Properties window is displayed, the selected object's name and type appear in the **Object box**, just below the title bar. Clicking its down arrow (or inside the box) pulls down all the existing objects' names and their types (Figure 4.2).

Figure 4.2   The Properties window showing object list

You can now click any of the displayed object names, and its set of properties will appear. The corresponding object on the form will also be surrounded by sizing handles just as when you click it. You can then change any values you wish. If you wish to show the top portion of the Properties window covered up by the list of objects, click the down arrow another time to clear it. By the way, you cannot select multiple objects from the this Object box.

What happens to the Properties window when you select multiple objects on the form? The Object box becomes empty. The property names and values that appear are all shared by the selected objects. If you change a property value here, you affect all the selected objects. For example, you can select all the controls and change their Appearance to 3-D or Flat. You can use this technique to quickly and precisely align objects by setting their Top, Left, Width, or Height properties. (In VB3 you could select multiple text boxes and erase their Text properties in one move. This is no longer possible in VB4/5. If you select multiple text boxes, the Text property disappears from the Properties window.)

The number of properties displayed in the Properties window may vary from those displayed in the Help system. For example, add a command button to a form, click this button, and show its Properties window by pressing F4. If you count the items shown in this window, there are 32. Next, click the command button and press F1; the CommandButton Control help topic appears. Click the Properties jump (green and with a solid underline). A separate box appears showing 36 properties. The additional 4 are available only at run time, but not at design time.

TIP: Keyboard Manipulation

You can use the keyboard to move or resize selected objects. After you have selected one or more objects, you can press the left key combination to do what's described on the right below:

Ctrl+arrow key	To move the objects
Shift+arrow key	To resize the objects

As you press Ctrl+arrow, the selected objects will all move in the direction of the arrow key.

As you press Shift+arrow, the objects will expand or shrink according to the key pressed. Use the following guide:

Shift+→	To enlarge horizontally
Shift+←	To reduce horizontally
Shift+↓	To enlarge vertically
Shift+↑	To reduce vertically

The distance involved in each move is one grid unit or one pixel (if Align
Controls to Grid is not checked in the Tools | Options | General tab).

Object Naming Conventions

Visual Basic uses lots of names to identify a project's objects, properties, and
files. Visual Basic assigns default names to these items. You can use some of
these default names and change others at your own discretion.

In writing code, you need to observe this syntax:

> *ObjectName.PropertyName*

The object name is the one you have given to an object or the default name
provided by Visual Basic, such as Text1 or Label1. This name can be changed
only at design time. If you try to change an object name by code, you will get an
error as explained in Chapter 3.

When you use code to refer to a particular property, you must use the exact name
provided by Visual Basic, such as Enabled, Visible, and so on. Some of these can
be omitted; see the "Omitting Property Names" tip in another section below.

The property name, such as Visible or Caption, cannot be changed. The object
name, however, can and should be changed in many situations. When you have
one or two controls of each kind, using the default name is expedient. On the
other hand, when you use more than a few, giving your own names may let you
more easily distinguish one from another. (This book uses the default name when
there is one object and custom names when there are multiple objects, particularly
when coding is required.)

One logical way of **naming objects**, when you have many of them, is to devise
names that combine type and purpose. For example, when you see a name like
cmdQuit, you are likely to know what it is about. There are two components in
this name, the first representing a command button and the second indicating the
purpose of this object.

Following this convention, you will start the name of a text box with *txt*, a label
with *lbl*, a form with *frm*, and so on. This arrangement gives you two advantages.
First, you can distinguish different types of controls. Second, when object names
are displayed in the **Object box** of the Code window or the Properties window, all
the related ones are listed next to one another because the names are displayed in
alphabetic order.

Table 4.1 shows in the third column all the prefixes suggested by Microsoft. The second column shows each control's class name. This will be explained in the next section.

Table 4.1   Control names and naming conventions

Object	Class	Prefix
Form	Form	frm
Check box	CheckBox	chk
Combo box	ComboBox	cbo
Command button	CommandButton	cmd
Common dialog	CommonDialog	dlg
Data	Data	dat
Directory list box	DirListBox	dir
Drive list box	DriveListBox	drv
File list box	FileListBox	fil
Frame	Frame	fra
Grid	Grid	grd
Horizontal scroll bar	HScrollBar	hsb
Image	Image	img
Label	Label	lbl
Line	Line	lin
List box	ListBox	lst
Menu	Menu	mnu
OLE container	OLE	ole
Option button	OptionButton	opt
Picture box	PictureBox	pic
Shape	Shape	shp
Text box	TextBox	txt
Timer	Timer	tmr
Vertical scroll bar	VScrollBar	vsb

Visual Basic does not care whether you type a control's name or property in uppercase or lowercase. So for convenience's sake, you can type everything in lowercase. A word that Visual Basic recognizes as having a special meaning will be automatically capitalized (or converted to mixed case) as soon as you press Enter or move the cursor away from the current line. (Sometimes this does not happen until after you run the program.)

Sometimes you may want to use mixed case for an object's name, such as cmdQuit or txtReadOutput, for increased readability. Some people also use underscores to connect a long name, such as output_textbox. As far as Visual

Basic is concerned, any legal name for a variable, up to 40 characters, is acceptable (see Chapter 5 about variable names for more details). Use your own personal style as long as you are comfortable with it.

As long as spelling is correct, Visual Basic does not care whether a name is in uppercase, lowercase, or mixed case. When you enter a name in the Properties window, Visual Basic remembers the precise name, including case. Any name you type in the Code window matching the original in spelling will be changed to conform to the original. For example, if you have used a name like Abc, Visual Basic will change abc or ABC to Abc. This is done without your consent. On some occasions, your latest version may prevail, forcing all the previous names to change to the latest one.

When you save files, Visual Basic supplies the initial default file name of Form1.frm for the form name and Project1.vbp for the project name. If you press Enter when such a name is displayed, it will be saved to the target disk. These names should definitely be changed. They provide no clue as to the purpose of a file.

TIP: Hungarian Notation

Modern computer programs can be huge and complex, involving numerous **identifiers**—names for objects, variables, procedures, etc. This situation calls for a systematic way of naming identifiers.

Today the most commonly used system is known as **Hungarian Notation**. The term comes from a Microsoft programmer named Charles Simonyi, who hails from Hungary. In a paper, he proposed, in its simplest form, the following convention:

    tagBasename

The tag, in the case of objects, is a lowercase string of 3 or 4 characters that signifies the class name. The capitalized base name is the name you give to an object. So in a name like cmdQuit, cmd denotes a command button and Quit its purpose.

In more complex situations, the system calls for adding to the above name one or more prefixes, and a qualifier at the end and, if necessary, a suffix. Such an elaborate naming convention can make names very long, but it also facilitates collaboration and code maintenance.

Interface Designing Tools

VB5 has added a series of tools to help you design a user interface. These are accessible from the Format menu and the Form Editor toolbar. These tools are useful when you have many controls on a form.

The **Format menu** has the following options:

Align	Aligns selected objects to grid or the same position (left, right, middle, and so on). The last selected object (with black sizing handles) is the guide to align other objects (with white sizing handles.)
Make Same Size	Makes all selected objects the same width, height, or both. The last selected object is the guide.
Size to Grid	Aligns selected objects to align to grid; useful when **Align Controls to Grid** is unchecked in the Tools | Options | General tab. This may expand an object's size and produce a result different from the Align option above.

Horizontal/Vertical

Spacing	Controls the distance between selected objects; can increase, decrease, remove, or equalize spaces.
Center in Form	Centers selected objects inside the form horizontally or vertically.
Order	Brings an overlapped object to the top or sends it to the back.
Lock Controls	Locks all the controls (not just selected) on the form and prevents them from being moved with the mouse.

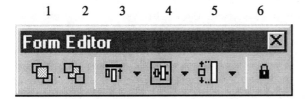

Figure 4.3   The Form Editor toolbar

The **Form Editor** toolbar (Figure 4.3) has the following buttons; they represent most of the options in the Format menu. Some buttons may be dimmed in different circumstances, such as when multiple objects are not selected or when selected objects don't overlap one another.

1. Bring to Front
2. Send to Back
3. Align . . .
4. Center . . .
5. Make . . . the Same Size
6. Lock Controls Toggle

Where you find ellipses in the above list, the options are the same as in the Format menu. As you point to each button, a tooltip appears. The same button may show slightly different tooltips on different occasions.Where you find a small down arrow, you can click it to show all the available options.

NOTE   After you finish designing an elaborate interface, you may want to lock the controls in their fixed places. To do so, just choose **Lock Controls** from the Format menu or the Form Editor toolbar. The lock icon will become depressed. Clicking a control shows white (instead of black) sizing handles. All the controls on the form can no longer be moved by using the mouse to drag them. You can, however, maneuver them by using Ctrl or Shift with an arrow key or by using the Properties window to change their values. To unlock, just choose Lock Controls again.

TIP: User Interface Design Considerations

As a novice programmer, you are faced with the issue of presenting what kind of interface to the users of your program. Like a dress, this is a subjective and personal issue. On the other hand, if you want to adhere to the mainstream, you might want to consider the following observations.

Be logical.   Place objects in a logical manner. Aligning all the command buttons vertically on the right or horizontally at the bottom is common. Place often-used buttons at the top or left, and the exiting button at the other end.

Be consistent.   If you use Quit on one occasion, Exit on another, and End on still another, you'll confuse your users.

Be moderate on decorative items. You can use fonts, colors, and icons to spice up an interface. However, refrain from overdoing it. A novice can get carried away by the fancy fonts, striking colors, and whimsical icons. The result is often a gaudy and garish appearance that cheapens the whole thing. A little spice may be refreshing, but a lot of spice can be sickening.

Learn from others. Next time you see other programs, you might want to pay attention as to what other people do. After observing many programs, you'll be able to judge what constitutes a good design or a bad design.

CLASSES AND MODULES

It's a good time to clarify a few new terms: object, class, module, and class module. These terms may not be particularly pertinent in the flow of material here. But you need to have some rudimentary understanding of them because they appear in menus and online help topics.

An **object** (also known as a programmable object) is simply a program that combines code (methods) and data (properties). An object may have a visible part. Consider a text box. The box is the visible part, but a small part. Behind the simple facade, there is a complex and invisible program that can handle text input and out and a myriad of other chores. Some objects, such as a database, have no visible part. When you use an object in your application, you are in effect using a program written by somebody else. This makes it easy for you to create an application because you are using existing components. Writing such an application can be compared to a house builder putting together prefab parts to quickly build a house.

A **class** (also known as a class object) is the definition or template of an object. Instances (copies) derived from this definition become objects and inherit the class's methods and properties. Consider the command button in the Toolbox. It's an original program that comes with Visual Basic. It has the class name of CommandButton. When you double-click this object at design time, a copy (instance) appears on the form. You've now created a control (object) with the default name of Command1. You cannot change CommandButton, but you can change Command1. A class can be compared to a rubber stamp or film negative. You cannot change them (unless you go through lots of trouble). You can make prints from them. You can make modifications only on the prints.

Each class object in Visual Basic has a class name. It's easy to find out these names. You can move the pointer to each object in the Toolbox and a tooltip will pop up; this tooltip shows the class name. The Object box in the Properties window also shows class names. There are two columns in this box. The left column shows the control names, the default names or those you have given. The right column shows the class names of the objects which you've added to the form. You can change the Name property of an object, but you cannot change the supplied class name.

A **module** is a code container. It contains program code which may or may not manifest itself in a visible object. There are three types of modules in Visual Basic:

- form module
- class module
- standard module

A form is an object which can contain other objects. You can add controls (visible) and procedures (invisible at run time). A **class module** is simply a form module minus the form. It can contain invisible code but not visible objects. After compiling, a class module becomes a class from which an object can be derived. A **standard module** (also known as a code module or simply a module) can contain only declarations and procedures; these can then be shared by other modules in the same project.

Each module is saved in a separate file with a distinct extension name. These are **FRM** for a form module, **CLS** for a class module, and **BAS** for a standard module. Module names also appear in the **Project window**.

Each module has its own Code window. All the procedures in a module are managed as a separate unit and can all be displayed in its Code window. If you want to view or edit a procedure in another module, you'll have to go to that module's Code window.

Form modules and standard modules are used to write standalone applications. They will be covered repeatedly from now on. Class modules are used to create OLE objects. This topic will be covered in Chapter 12.

COMMAND BUTTON

A **command button** is unique because when clicked it appears to be depressed. That is why it is also called a push button. When it has the focus, it is also surrounded by an outline.

A command button, as the name implies, is intended to respond to a user-initiated action such as clicking. So you need to attach code to some of the common events which a command button can respond to.

A command button can respond to about a dozen events. We have used the Click event many times; that is the most common event.

A command button has about three dozen properties. The following properties are unique:

Cancel	True	
	False	(default)
Default	True	
	False	(default)

These properties can respond to your pressing **Enter** or **Esc** from the keyboard.

When a command button's **Default** property is set to True (this can be set at both design time and run time), pressing the Enter key at run time has the effect of clicking the button. This happens when the focus is on an object that is not a command button. When the focus is on another command button, however, pressing Enter is the same as clicking that button, not the Default button. (The Default command button appears sunken at both design time and run time.)

When a command button's **Cancel** property is set to True, pressing Esc (regardless of where the focus is) has the effect of clicking the button. However, when a command button is invisible or disabled (with Visible or Enabled set to False), it is not affected by Cancel or Esc.

Only one command button can have its Cancel or Default property set to True. If you choose another command button and set one of these properties to True, a previously set True value will be changed to False.

As an example, let us bring back the TEMPERATURE project we completed at the end of Chapter 1. Open this project (Figure 4.4) if you have saved it to your disk. Run the program by pressing F5. With the cursor in the left text box, type a

number and press Enter. You hear a beep and nothing else happens. Now press
Esc. Still no action.

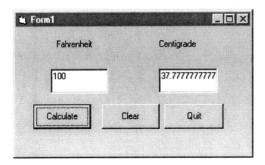

Figure 4.4   Demonstrating Default and Cancel properties

Now click Quit to end the program. Set the Calculate button's Default property to
True and the Clear button's Cancel property to True. Try again. What happens?
This time when you press Enter, you are in effect clicking Calculate. And when
you press Esc, you are clicking Clear.

If the default command button is invisible or disabled, the above pattern does not
occur. What can you do if you want to hide a default button? Use the Top or Left
properties to move it out of the visible area. The following will make the
Calculate button disappear at run time:

```
cmdCalculate.Left = -1000
```

A command button's appearance allows only limited customizing. There is no
BorderStyle property. There is no ForeColor property, so you cannot change the
caption's text color. There is the BackColor property, but it has no actual effect
on the button. There is the Appearance property, but changing the default 3-D
value to Flat has no effect on the button's 3-D appearance. Fortunately, a long
caption can now wrap to the lines below. (Version 3 and before appeared only in
one line; you could not make it appear in multiple lines.)

VB5 has added the following properties to cosmetically improve a command
button's appearance:

Style	0 - Standard (default)
	1 - Graphical
Picture	(none)

| **DisabledPicture** | (none) |
| **DownPicture** | (none) |

The **Style** property determines whether a picture can appear on the command button. In the default Standard setting, no picture appears.

After setting Style to Graphical, you need to load a picture with one of the three picture properties. To load a picture, choose the **Picture** property, click the ellipsis (...) in the Settings box, find a picture file, and open it. Figure 4.5 is the result of opening the following file:

Graphics\Bitmaps\Assorted\Happy.bmp

Figure 4.5   Loading a picture to a command button

When you load a picture to a command button, it appears above the existing caption line. If there is no caption, the picture appears in the middle of the button. If the button is too small, the picture may be clipped, thus showing only a part of it. If the button is enlarged, the picture remains fixed in size. A bitmap or icon is small and takes up little space; with a metafile, you may need to enlarge a button to show more of it. Unlike an image control (Chapter 11), a command button has no capability to stretch a picture to fit in the existing space.

Loading a picture with the Picture property makes the picture appear at design time and run time. If you wish, you can change to another picture on other occasions. Use the **DisabledPicture** property to load another picture or use the **DownPicture** property to load still another picture. In that case, the first picture appears on the button when it's disabled (when its Enabled property is False) and the second is shown when the pointer is over the command button and the left mouse button is held down.

DRILL

____ 1. To select multiple objects:
    a. Hold down Shift and click each
    b. Hold down Ctrl and click each
    c. Use the pointer to draw a rectangle around them
    d. all of the above
    e. none of the above

____ 2. When multiple objects are selected, dragging one of them moves:
    a. one object
    b. all the selected objects
    c. no object
    d. the form

____ 3. When multiple objects are selected, the Properties window shows:
    a. the title bar with the first object's name
    b. the Object box with object names
    c. property names and values
    d. nothing

____ 4. When multiple objects are selected at design time, pressing
Ctrl+arrow moves them all. True or false?

____ 5. When a command button's _default_ _____ property is set to True,
pressing Enter at run time has the same effect as clicking the button.

____ 6. When a command button's _Cancel_ _____ property is set to True,
pressing Esc has the same effect as clicking the button.

PRACTICE

■ 1. Create a user interface with two command buttons on a form, Command1
and Command2. When the program runs, only Command1 should be
visible. When you click Command1, Command1 should become
invisible, but Command2 visible. When you click Command2,
Command2 should become invisible, but Command1 visible.

■ 2. Add two command buttons to a clear form. When Command1 is clicked,
Command2 will disappear and reappear alternately. Use the Not operator
to do it.

■ 3. If you've written an event procedure for an object and then delete the object, what happens to the procedure?

■ 4. Create a user interface consisting of a text box (Text1) and a command button (Command1). Make sure the two do not overlap at design time. Everything else must be done in code. When the program runs, the following should happen:

   1. Text1 is widened to four times its original width.
   2. The cursor goes to Text1 for typing.
   3. Text1 is cleared for making an entry.

   When the user types something and presses Enter,

   1. The typed line is printed to the screen.
   2. The text box is cleared for the next entry.

■ 5. Alter the above so that before printing each new line, the screen will be cleared first.

■ 6. Create a user interface consisting of a form and a command button. The command button should be renamed CB at design time. When the program runs and the button clicked, the following should happen:

   1. The button's width should be widened to twice of the original.
   2. The button's height should be increased to twice of the original.
   3. The button should be located in the center of the window.
   4. The button's width in twips should appear as the button's caption.

LABEL

A **label** is commonly used to display instructional text for objects, such as a text box, that have no Caption property. You can also output data to a label.

You can use the following properties and their options to alter a label's appearance:

Alignment	0 - Left Justify (default)
	1 - Right Justify
	2 - Center
AutoSize	True
	False (default)
BackStyle	0 - Transparent

	1 - Opaque (default)
BorderStyle	0 - None (default)
	1 - Fixed Single
UseMnemonic	True (default)
	False
WordWrap	True
	False (default)

The UseMnemonic property will be explained in another section below.

If **BackStyle** is set to Opaque, the label's box covers up the objects underneath it; if set to Transparent, any underlying object will show through.

At design time, a label appears inside the box you have defined. If the box is too small for a long label, only a portion is shown. A lengthy line is wrapped and the excess disappears at the bottom. The display area does not automatically change. You can manually change the display area by stretching it horizontally or vertically. As you do, the text inside will change to fit in the area.

You can make the display area automatically fit the label. To do that, you need to change the **AutoSize** and **WordWrap** properties, both of which are by default set to False. If you set the first to True and second to False, a long label is fully displayed and stretched out horizontally. The display area is now stretched to fit the length of a one-line label. If both AutoSize and WordWrap are set to True, a long label is stretched vertically instead.

We can set these values via code at run time. The code listed below toggles the WordWrap property on and off. Since WordWrap is False by default, the **Not** operator negates it and makes it True. With both AutoSize and WordWrap set to True, the label is displayed vertically (Figure 4.6). When you click the label control another time, WordWrap is set to False and the label is displayed horizontally.

```
Private Sub Label1_Click()
    Label1.Caption = ""    'clear label
    Label1.AutoSize = True
    Label1.WordWrap = Not Label1.WordWrap
    Label1.Caption = "This can be stretched up or down."
End Sub
```

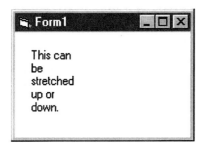

Figure 4.6   A vertical label

TIP: Omitting Property Names

Each control's property has a name. For example, Caption in
Label1.Caption is a property name. Some of them are long and tiresome to
type. Fortunately, Each control has a default property, the most commonly
used attribute, whose name can be omitted.

The tail ends of the following objects can all be omitted:

Check1.Value	Image1.Picture
CommonDialog1.Action	Label1.Caption
Combo1.Text	Line1.Visible
Command1.Value	List1.Text
Data1.Caption	Option1.Value
Dir1.Path	Picture1.Picture
Drive1.Drive	Shape1.Shape
File1.FileName	Text1.Text
Frame1.Caption	Timer1.Enabled
Grid1.Text	VScroll1.Value
HScroll1.Value	

In other words, Label1.Caption and Label1 mean the same thing to Visual
Basic. If you mean to refer to another property, you must specify it, such as
Label1.Visible.

Some of these properties are available only at run time. A good example is
the command button's Value property. This property name can be omitted.
When this value is set to True, it has the effect of the user clicking this
button. You can put one of the following equivalent statements in a
procedure:

```
Command1_Click
Command1 = True
Command1.Value = True
```

When any the above lines is executed, the Command1_Click procedure will be executed (called).

TEXT BOX

A **text box** is a versatile tool with many features built in. Also known as an edit field, it can serve as a simple text processor. It is most often used to get input data from the user or to output processed information.

A text box has 40 design-time properties. The following are unique:

Alignment	0 - Left Justify (default)
	1 - Right Justify
	2 - Center
HideSelection	True (default)
	False
Locked	True
	False (default)
MaxLength	0
MultiLine	True
	False (default)
PasswordChar	(none)
ScrollBars	0 - None (default)
	1 - Horizontal
	2 - Vertical
	3 - Both

The **MultiLine** property is crucial because it affects other properties and changes the way a text box behaves at both design time and run time. If it is False, the following patterns prevail:

- A text entry appears only in one line, regardless of the size of the text box. There is no wordwrap. Pressing Enter at run time has no effect. Pressing Ctrl+Tab (see a NOTE below) does not move the cursor.

- The Alignment property is ignored. Changing the default Left to Right or Center has no effect.

- Scroll bars don't show up no matter what value you set.

- The PasswordChar property setting is in effect.

If MultiLine is set to True, the following observations apply:

- The Alignment property's Right or Center setting begins to take effect.

- Pressing Enter at run time inserts a line break and moves the cursor to the beginning of a new line.

- Pressing Tab or Ctrl+Tab moves the cursor to the next tab stop.

- ScrollBars settings begin to take effect.

- PasswordChar has no effect.

- Wordwrap is automatic if the horizontal scroll bar does not appear. There is no wordwrap if the horizontal scroll bar exists.

NOTE If an application consists of a single text box (or contains no other object that is capable of receiving the focus) and its MultiLine property is set to True, pressing the **Tab** key at run time moves the cursor to the next tab stop inside the text box. If another object exists, then pressing Tab shifts the focus to that object. In that case, you can press **Ctrl+Tab** (or Ctrl+I) to tab inside the text box.

At design time, a text box's default **Text** property is Text1. The Settings box in the Properties window gives you a single line to edit this entry. If you change MultiLine to True, Text1 is changed to (Text). The Settings box also has an additional down arrow. Clicking this arrow pops up a rectangular box for you to make multiline entries. See a TIP below for more details.

If a text box can hold only one line of text (as is the case when MultiLine is False), excess text can be scrolled left or right at run time. If you type a long line, the left portion disappears to the left. You can use a cursor key, such as Home or End, to scroll the hidden portion to view.

If a text box contains a large amount of text, you should add one (select 1 or 2) or both (select 3) **scroll bars**. The user can then use the mouse to maneuver the scroll bars to scroll text. Keep in mind that MultiLine must also be set to True before scroll bars will appear. You can use various scrolling keys such as PgUp or PgDn regardless of whether or not there are scroll bars.

The **MaxLength** property is set to 0 by default. That means there is no maximum limit. In this case, how much text a text box can hold depends on whether the

MultiLine property is True or False. If MultiLine is False (default), a text box can hold a one-line text string whose length depends on your PC's memory. If MultiLine is True, the limit is about 32KB of text. Any excess is discarded without causing an error. You can assign to MaxLength a value of up to 65535 (64KB) without causing an error. However, that will not increase the amount of text a text box can hold.

On some occasions you may want to restrict an entry to a fixed number of characters. For example, when you want the user to enter a Social Security number, you set this property to 9. When the limit is reached, the cursor stops and no additional character will appear. An entry made at design time is not affected by this restriction.

NOTE   If the **Default** property of a command button is set to True (explained in a previous section), pressing Enter in a text box at run time does not move the cursor down one line; it invokes the Click event of the command button instead. In this situation, if you want to move the cursor down one line in the text box, press **Ctrl+Enter** instead of Enter alone.

The **PasswordChar** property can be used to hide the characters being typed in a text box. Suppose you select this property and enter an * in the Settings box. Any existing Text property is immediately changed to asterisks, with each asterisk representing an original character. If you delete the PasswordChar property, the original entry is restored. Suppose you enter a space as the PasswordChar property and delete the Text property at design time. At run time, each time you type a character, a space will appear instead.

If MultiLine is set to True, the PasswordChar property has no effect. In that case, the text box shows the Text property at design time or whatever the user types at run time.

At design time you can enter multiple characters as the PasswordChar property. But when you press Enter or do something else to register the entry, only the first will be retained and the rest discarded. You can assign multiple characters at run time; again, only the first is significant. The first statement below assigns three characters. But the second statement prints only X.

```
Text1.PasswordChar = "XYZ"
Print Text1.PasswordChar
```

The **Locked** property determines whether the user can edit the displayed text at run time. The default False setting allows editing at run time. If this is changed to

True at design time or run time, no user editing is allowed. You can select text or copy it; but deleting or pasting is not possible. You can, however, use the Text property in code to manipulate the contents. To prevent the user from changing a text box's contents at run time, change **Enabled** property to False. In that case, the text becomes dimmed and hard to read, and there is no way to change that.

HideSelection determines whether selected text remains highlighted when the text box loses the focus. The default setting is True. In that case, if you select text in the text box and then shift the focus to another object, the highlight disappears (is hidden) even though the text remains selected. If you change the True value to False, the highlight remains (not hidden) even after the text box loses the focus.

A text box, unlike other controls, has no Caption property. Instead, it has a Name property and a Text property, both with the default value of Text1 for the first text box. The Text property appears inside the box at both design time and run time.

Since a text box is used mostly for data input or to display processed output, it should not have any Text property at the outset. That means the user will be staring at an empty text box when the program runs. To provide some sort of clue, you should add a label nearby with some helpful instruction.

A text box can respond to more than 20 events, including the typical Click and DblClick. One unique event we have not explored is the **Change** event. A Change event occurs to a text box when the text is altered. This change can then be reflected somewhere else.

Figure 4.7   Converting to uppercase

Figure 4.7 shows two text boxes. The first is where you type something. The second displays each typed character in uppercase. The following procedure controls that behavior:

```
Private Sub Text1_Change ()
    Text2.Text = UCase(Text1.Text)
End Sub
```

The **UCase** function is what converts each typed character to uppercase. In the code, we added the Text extension. You can omit it if you wish, and the program's behavior will not change.

The input in one text box can be combined and output to another text box. Our next project will demonstrate that. It has a user interface shown in Figure 4.8. There are five controls placed on the form. Their properties are set as follows:

Object	Property	Value
Label1	Caption	Enter a SS #:
Text1	Text	(none)
	Name	txtInput
	MaxLength	9
	TabIndex	0
Text2	Text	(none)
	Name	txtOutput
	ScrollBars	2 - Vertical
	MultiLine	True
Command1	Caption	&Enter
	Name	cmdEnter
	Default	True
Command2	Caption	&Quit
	Name	cmdQuit
	Cancel	True

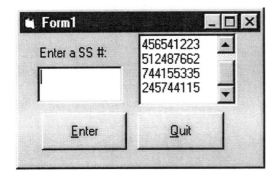

Figure 4.8   Outputting numbers vertically

The purpose of this project is to demonstrate how you can continuously enter 9-digit numbers in Text1 and show all the entries in Text2. The code shown below will concatenate all the numbers and display them vertically in Text2, as shown in Figure 4.8.

```
Private Sub cmdEnter_Click ()
    Dim NL As String

    NL = Chr(13) & Chr(10)          'new line
    txtOutput.Text = txtOutput.Text & NL & txtInput.Text
      'combine two lines
    txtInput.Text = ""
    txtInput.SetFocus
End Sub
```

A text box will receive and display text from another text box, but the incoming **line break** characters will be ignored. In order to separate one line from another, you need to use code to insert two extra characters. By adding **Chr(13)** and **Chr(10)**,[1] you instruct the program to move the cursor to the left margin (carriage return) and down one line (linefeed). These characters are assigned to a variable named NL. By putting this variable between the two Text properties, each new addition is placed at the beginning of the next line.

We have added something called **access keys** to our user interface. An access key appears with an underline. The user can hold down **Alt** and press such a key to execute its Click procedure. To add an underline character, place an **&** before the character in the Caption property, such as &Enter.

When the program runs, the user can type a number and then press Enter to send it to Text2 and clear Text1. The reason this can happen is that we have designated Command1 (the Enter button) as the **Default** button by changing this property to True. After doing that, pressing Enter (with the cursor inside a text box) is the same as clicking the Enter button or pressing Alt+E (the access key). Pressing Esc is the same as clicking Quit because we have designated it as the **Cancel** button.

The Text2 box will hold all the numbers you enter in Text1. New numbers, however, may be hidden due to the small size of the box. Since there is a scroll bar, you can use it to scroll any portion to view.

---

[1] These functions respectively return the characters for ASCII or ANSI codes 13 and 10. You can use an intrinsic constant called **vbCrLf** to replace Chr(13) & Chr(10); see Chapter 5 for more details on intrinsic constants.

A number in a text box can be maneuvered as a numeric or text string. We can also use the **Val** function to explicitly convert it to a numeric. This function is sometimes optional but mandatory on some occasions.

The code below shows the entry in Text1 being converted to a numeric, multiplied by itself, and assigned to Text2.

```
Private Sub Text1_Change ()
    Text2.Text = Val(Text1.Text) ^ 2
End Sub
```

After running the program and typing 111 in Text1, Text2 shows that number's squared value (Figure 4.9). You can erase the number and type a new one; as you type or erase a digit, a new squared value continues to change in Text2.

Figure 4.9   A number squared

In our code, we can also eliminate the Val function and the program will also work. However, if the user erases an entry or enters a text string in Text1, the *Type mismatch* error will appear. If Val is used, such an entry will be treated as 0 in value and no error will be triggered.

NOTE   Numbers in text boxes are treated as text strings. If you want to add them up, you must convert at least one to a numeric by using the **Val** function, such as Val(Text1.Text). Otherwise, string concatenation (not numeric addition) will be performed. This is not necessary when other arithmetic operators are involved. Use the **&** operator if you want to concatenate strings and/or numbers.

TIP: Access Key for a Text box

Sometimes it is convenient to provide an access key to a text box so that the user can press the key to move the focus to the text box for making an entry. How can you do that?

The answer lies in a label. As you already know, a label has the Caption property but cannot receive the focus. On the other hand, a text box can receive the focus but has no Caption property. The two objects can be combined to provide a quick access to the text box. These are the steps:

1. Place a label near a text box, as shown in Figure 4.8.

2. Arrange the label's **TabIndex** value to be one before the text box's TabIndex value.

3. Designate a letter in the label's caption as the access key.

As an example, we can place an **&** before the first S in Figure 4.8. When the program runs, pressing Alt+S moves the cursor to inside the text box. The reason for that is that the label before it in the tab order cannot receive the focus. So the object with the next tab order will get the focus instead.

A label has the **UseMnemonic** property whose default value is True. If you change it to False, the label can no longer be used as an access key. Entering an & shows the character itself and does not embed an underscore for the next character.

NOTE At run time, you can right-click a text box to pop up a shortcut menu with a few editing options. More options become available if you have selected text. You can use these to delete, cut, copy, or paste. The options become limited if you've changed the **Locked** property to True. This menu is disabled if the **Enabled** property is set to True. This feature is also available in a combo box's text (top) portion.

TIP: Entering Text at Design Time

At design time, you can enter into a text box text consisting of multiple columns and multiple lines.

After you set MultiLine property to True and click the down arrow in the Text property's Settings box, a rectangular text-entry box appears and the cursor goes inside for you to type text. This box drops down if there is enough room below; if not, the box appears above the base line (Figure 4.10). A vertical scroll box also appears.

When the cursor is inside this box, you can press Tab to move the cursor to each subsequent tab stop; this allows you to enter multicolumn text. You can press Crl+Enter if you want to move the cursor to a new line; this allows you to enter multiple lines. If you press Enter alone, the box closes and the text appears in the text box on the form. The text appears in both places the same shape.

The width of the text-entry box depends of the width of the Properties window. If you need a wider box to enter text at design time, widen the Properties window before opening the text-entry box. A wider box is useful for entering multicolumn text lines as shown in Figure 4.10.

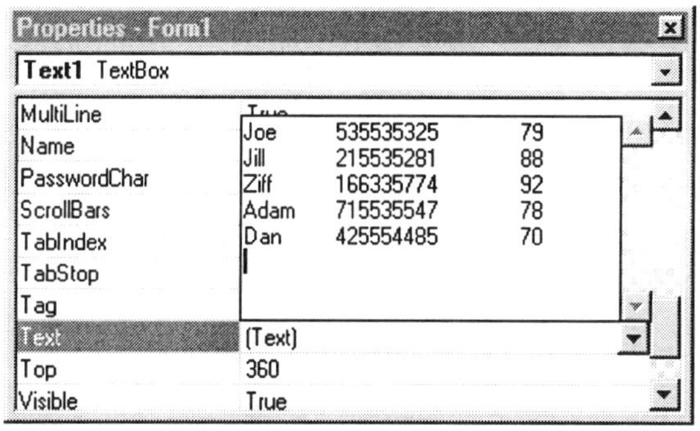

Figure 4.10   Entering text-box text in the Properties window

If you now change MultiLine to False, the text-entry box no longer appears. The existing text in the Properties window as well as in the text box is crunched into a single line. The Tab and line break characters appear as solid rectangles. If you change MultiLine back to True, the neatly aligned text will return.

When you save a form file, a **binary data file** with the same file name but the **FRX** extension may be saved to the same directory. This happens if you've entered multiline text in a text box at design time; it may also happen in other situations. Although this is a binary file, some text may be readable. In the case of a text box, every character is readable in a text processor.

Unless you know what you are doing, the paired FRM and FRX files should not be changed from outside Visual Basic. The form (FRM) file contains information about the file name, location, and size of the data file; this arrangement makes it possible for the data file to be retrieved when you open the form file. If you change the FRX file's name, location, or contents, various problems may occur. (The property sheet of an FRX file identifies it as Visual Basic Form Stash File.)

LIST BOX (A First Look at an Advanced Topic)

If you are familiar with Basic, you already know that you could store data in a program with the DATA statement. You could then use the READ command to fetch the data and other commands to maneuver them. In Visual Basic, you can use a list box (or a combo box) to store data and other commands to maneuver the stored data. This section briefly introduces this useful tool so that we can start using it. Chapter 10 will provide more details.

A **list box** is a control that displays at run time a list of items from which the user can make one or more selections by clicking them. To put an item in the box, you use the **AddItem** method. To respond to clicking, you write a Click procedure.

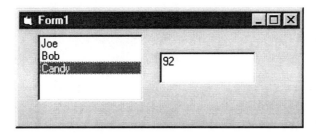

Figure 4.11   A list box at run time

Figure 4.11 shows a simple demonstration program. The list box on the left shows three names. Clicking a name displays a number in the text box. In the procedures below, the Form_Load procedure uses AddItem to put the three items in the box at run time.

When the user clicks a displayed item. The List1_Click procedure is triggered. The Select Case control structure determines which one has been selected and displays the result accordingly.

```
Private Sub Form_Load ()
    List1.AddItem "Joe"      'add items to list box
    List1.AddItem "Bob"
    List1.AddItem "Candy"
End Sub

Private Sub List1_Click ()
    Select Case List1.Text
        'determines which item selected
    Case "Joe"
        Text1.Text = 88
    Case "Bob"
        Text1.Text = 76
    Case "Candy"
        Text1.Text = 92
    End Select
End Sub
```

We can change a list box's **Sorted** property from the default False to True. In that case, all the displayed items will appear in alphabetic order. Numbers are treated as text and sorted as such, not according to their numeric values.

At design time, you can open a text-entry box by clicking the down arrow in the **List** property's Settings box. You can make multiline and multicolumn entries as you do with a text box. The entries will also be saved to the binary data file and retrieved when you open the form file next time. What was said about the text box control can be applied here as well.

What is said so far can mostly be applied to a **combo box** as well. Both of them share many other properties and methods as well. We'll explore them at the beginning of Chapter 10.

SCROLL BARS

The Toolbox contains two **scroll bar** controls. You can use these to add scroll bars to an application. Keep in mind that these are independent scroll bars, unlike those attached to a text box, discussed in a previous section.

In this section, we use horizontal scroll bars as examples. Vertical scroll bars work the same way except that they move up or down instead of left or right.

When you double-click a scroll bar tool in the Toolbox, a copy appears in the middle of the current form. You can then drag it to a new location and resize it in any way you wish.

A scroll bar has about two dozen properties. These are unique:

Max	32767
Min	0
LargeChange	1
SmallChange	1
Value	0

By default a scroll bar has the beginning (**Min**) value of 0 and ending (**Max**) value of 32767. These can be changed to suit your need. The Max value cannot go higher than the default; the Min value, however, can be as low as -32768.

LargeChange occurs when you click the scroll bar, and **SmallChange** happens when you click the arrow on either end. The default value for both is 1.

NOTE   The size of the scroll box (the middle rectangle) reflects the Large-Change property. The larger this value, the larger the box in proportion to the bar. Suppose Min is 0 and Max is 100, setting LargeChange to 100 will enlarge the box to occupy half of the bar; clicking the bar once at run time will move the box to Max or Min. If you change it to 50, you reduce box to 1/3 of the bar; clicking the bar twice will move the box from one end to the other.

The **Value** property determines the position of the scroll box against the Min and Max properties. By default, it has the value of 0, the same as Min's value. That means the scroll box will stay at the left end of the scroll bar, or the position of Min. You can change the Value property at design time or run time. For example, at design time if you set this value to half of the difference between Max and Min, the scroll box immediately jumps to the middle of the scroll bar.

A scroll bar can respond to about 10 events. The two common ones are **Change** and **Scroll**. Change is triggered after the scroll box is moved in any way. Scroll responds as you drag and move the scroll box, but not when you use other ways to move the scroll box.

Our first demonstration project has only two objects, a label and a horizontal scroll bar (Figure 4.12). The scroll bar's values are set to the following:

Max	100
Min	0
LargeChange	10
SmallChange	1

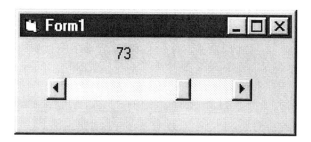

Figure 4.12   Moving the scroll bar to change the number

To respond to the scroll box movement, you can write code to show its value (position) in relation to the Max and Min values. In our case, we use a label to reflect the scroll box's location as it is moved. To write the code shown below, double-click the scroll bar. The HScroll1_Change procedure template automatically appears. Type the single line shown below and you are set.

```
Private Sub HScroll1_Change ()
    Label1.Caption = HScroll1.Value
        'show scroll value in label
End Sub
```

When the program runs, the scroll box stays at the left end (because both Min and Value properties have 0 value); it also blinks when it has the focus. When you move it left or right, the label shows the value of the box's location. The location reflects the scroll bar's Value property. As this value changes due to the changing location of the scroll box, the label's caption reflects the new value.

The two property names could be omitted in our code. We could have coded this way and the result would be the same:

```
Label1 = HScroll1
```

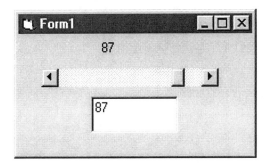

Figure 4.13   **Using a text box to move a scroll bar**

A scroll bar can also respond to changes in other objects. In Figure 4.13 we have added a text box and set its TabIndex value to 0 so that when the program runs, the cursor will go there for a user input.

The procedure below will move the scroll box in response to the user typing a number in the text box. As you type a new number (0 to 100) or erase it, the scroll box will move to reflect the value in the text box. As the scroll box moves, the label caption also changes in tandem.

```
Private Sub Text1_Change ()
    HScroll1.Value = Val(Text1.Text)
End Sub
```

Notice that we use the **Val** function to explicitly convert an entry in Text1 to a numeric. This function can be omitted in this situation. In that case, a number entry will be converted to a numeric. If the entry is not a number, the *Type mismatch* error will appear. With Val in place, a non-number entry will be converted to 0 without showing the error.

If you now move the scroll box at run time, the text box will not change. How can you make the text box reflect the scroll box's value? The simple solution is to add a second line in the HScroll1_Change procedure:

```
    Text1.Text = HScroll1.Value
```

A useful application involving a scroll bar is to let the user move the scroll box and show a temperature in Centigrade and Fahrenheit. The project you did at the end of Chapter 1 can be modified to show temperatures graphically.

Our user interface (Figure 4.14) has three objects on the form. The two labels need to be stretched horizontally so that a long label can be displayed in one line. The horizontal scroll bar retains the values set earlier.

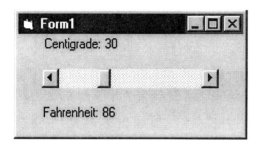

Figure 4.14   Maneuvering a scroll bar

The procedure below receives each new value from the scroll box and assigns it to the variable named Cent. A formula converts the value and assigns it to variable Fahr. We use the **&** operator to concatenate each numeric value to a text string and assign the result to a label. As the user moves the scroll box, the two labels continue to display new numbers.

```
Private Sub HScroll1_Change ()
    Dim Cent As Single
    Dim Fahr As Single

    Cent = HScroll1.Value      'get scroll value
    Fahr = (9 / 5) * Cent + 32      'change to Fahr.
    lblCent.Caption = "Centigrade: " & Cent 'show Cent.
    lblFahr.Caption = "Fahrenheit: " & Fahr 'show Fahr.
End Sub
```

NOTE   Only whole numbers are permitted in various scroll bar properties. You can, however, use simple arithmetic formulas to handle fractional values. Suppose you want the SmallChange property to change by 0.5. You can set the value to 5 at design time. At run time, you can divide the Value property by 10 to achieve the 0.5 change. So at design time you multiply everything by 10 and at run time you divide everything by 10.

There are many things you can do with scroll bars. For example, you can provide a scroll bar to let the user move the scroll box to enter a value in a limited range, thus avoiding the need to type something or preventing a wrong value. You can even use several scroll bars, which will move in tandem when the designated one is moved.

DRILL

_a_ 7.   By default a label's display is:
    a.   left justified
    b.   right justified
    c.   centered
    d.   none of the above

_a_ 8.   If a label's AutoSize is True and WordWrap is False, a long label appears:
    a.   horizontally   _P 196_
    b.   vertically

_b_ 9.   If a label's AutoSize is True and WordWrap is True, a long label appears:
    a.   horizontally
    b.   vertically

_____ 10.   Which property name below cannot be omitted in code:
    a.   Label1.Caption
    b.   Command1.Caption
    c.   Text1.Text
    d.   Hscroll1.Value

_F_ 11.   When a text box's ScrollBars property is set to Both and MultiLine set to False, scroll bars will appear. True or false?

_____ 12.   A text box's _____ property lets you hide characters being typed in the box.   _Passwordchar_

_d_ 13.   When a text box's MaxLength property is set to 0, it can hold _____ characters.
    a.   0
    b.   1
    c.   32KB
    d.   no limit

Assuming the following:
1) Text1 contains 11.
2) Text2 contains 22.

Enter a number in questions 14-17:

____ 14.   Text1.Text + Text2.Text = _____ 33 .

____ 15.   Val(Text1.Text) + Text2.Text = _____ 33 .

____ 16.   Text1.Text * 3 = _____ 33 .

____ 17.   Val(Text1.Text) & Val(Text2.Text) = __ 11,22.

____ 18.   In a vertical scroll bar, the top represents the Min property, the
            bottom the Max property, and the scroll box the ___ vertical
            property.

PRACTICE

■   7.   Create an application consisting of one label on a form. When it runs,
         the following should happen:

    1. The label shows "Click the window to change."

    2. When the window is clicked, the label becomes "This line can be
        visible or invisible."

    3. When the window is clicked again, the label alternately becomes
        visible and invisible.

■   8.   Modify the above application so that the label will be shown at 1 inch
         from the top and 2 inches from the left.

■   9.   In Figure 4.8 modify the code so that the latest number will stay on top.

■   10. In Figure 4.9, add a text box (Text3) and display in it a number that is in
         Text1 raised to the power of 3.

■   11. Create an application with two scroll bars (Figure 4.15). As the user
         moves the top scroll box, the label above it should start with 0 and go up
         to 100; the bottom scroll box should move in tandem and the label below
         it show the equivalent Fahrenheit degrees.

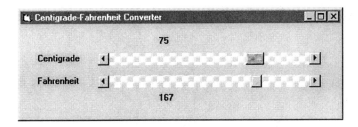

Figure 4.15   Temperature converter

■ 12. Modify the above so that the user can move the bottom scroll box (as well as the top one) and all the other elements will change accordingly.

■ 13. Suppose you invest $1000 in a 10-year certificate of deposit at 6.5% compounded annually. Create an application shown in Figure 4.16 that will let you slide the scroll bar and show each year and the value of your CD at the end of that year. Use this formula:

$$1000 * (1 + 0.065)\text{ }\hat{}\text{ year}$$

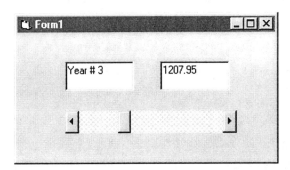

Figure 4.16   Showing interest earning

■ 14. This application (Figure 4.17) lets you calculate money exchange. Suppose $1 can be exchanged for ¥113. You enter 113 in the first text box. As you move the scroll box (0 to 100 range), the label shows the scroll value and the second text box shows the yen equivalent.

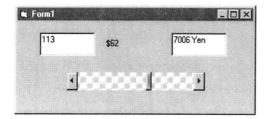

Figure 4.17   Showing money exchange

■   15. Create a project which consists of a text box and two labels, as shown in
        Figure 4.18. When the user types an hour number (hour and minute
        connected by a period) in Text1, Label2 shows the number of minutes.
        (Hint: Use the **Int** function to isolate the integer portion.)

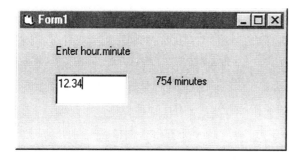

Figure 4.18   Hours converted to minutes

■   16. Modify the above project so that the user can enter *pound.ounce* to show
        the equivalent number of ounces.

■   17. What is an access key? How do you create an access key?

■   18. How can you use an access key to shift the focus to a text box?

■   19. Use a text box to enter items into a list box. After you type something in
        Text1 and press Enter, the item is added to List1 and is cleared from
        Text1; the focus also remains in Text1. The items in List1 are displayed
        in alphabetic order.

■   20. Modify the previous project so that when an item displayed in List1 is
        clicked, it appears in Text1.

CHECK BOX

You can add **check boxes** to an application to let the user check or uncheck some or all of the available choices.

A check box is similar to a text box in its properties. The Caption and Name properties both default to Check1. Its **Value** property provides these options:

    0 - Unchecked (default)
    1 - Checked
    2 - Grayed

If you change it to 1 or 2 at design time, the box responds immediately. If you want to set a default choice other than 0, make the change at design time. When 2 is set, the check box is initially grayed. This does not enable or disable it. When a check box is clicked at run time, its Value property alternates between only 0 (unchecked, blank) and 1 (checked, showing a ✓ sign).

A check box can respond to more than a dozen events, the most common being Click. You can write code to respond to such an event.

Our demonstration project shown in Figure 4.19 contains one text box and two check boxes. The property values are set as follows:

Object	Property	Value
Text1	TabIndex	0
	FontBold	False
Check1	Caption	Bold
Check2	Caption	Italic
	FontItalic	True

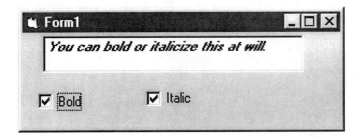

Figure 4.19   **Choosing a check box**

The code to respond to the user clicking the Bold check box is shown below. To write this code, double-click the Check1 box. The Click procedure template appears. Add lines as shown below:

```
Private Sub Check1_Click ()
    If Check1.Value = 1 Then
        'if Check1 is checked, Value can be omitted
        Text1.FontBold = True
    Else                    'if not checked
        Text1.FontBold = False
    End If
End Sub
```

To write code for Check2, pull down the object list from the Object box in the Code window and click Check2. Check2's Click procedure template appears. Add lines shown above, except changing Check1 to Check2 and FontBold to FontItalic.

After you finish the above code, press F5 to run the program. Type something in the text box. Click the Bold and Italic boxes repeatedly to show the text changing shape.

OPTION BUTTON

An **option button** resembles a check box. It responds to similar events as well, except with the addition of DblClick. Its default Name property is Option1, the same as its default Caption property.

One major difference between check boxes and option buttons is that you can check multiple boxes with check boxes, but only one option with option buttons. When another option is selected, a previously selected option is unselected.

An option button has the **Value** property of True or False (default). It can be set at design time or run time. With its Value property set to True, the circle has a solid dot inside, making it appear like a **radio button**, which is also its commonly used name. When one button's Value property is set to True, all the others in the same group will be automatically changed to False.

We are going to modify our example in the previous section to illustrate option buttons. In Figure 4.20, we took out the check boxes and added three option buttons. Their captions are changed as shown, and their Name properties are the same as their captions except with the *opt* prefix added.

Figure 4.20   Choosing an option button

We need to write three Click procedures. optBold's is shown below. The other two contain the same two lines.

```
Private Sub optBold_Click ()
    Text1.FontBold = optBold.Value   'Value can be omitted
    Text1.FontItalic = optItalic.Value
End Sub
```

When an option button is clicked (selected), its **Value** property returns True; otherwise, it evaluates to False. This in turn determines the text appearance. For example, if the Bold option is clicked, optBold.Value returns True and optItalic.Value returns False. So the text is bolded but not italicized.

When an application contains multiple option buttons, it's logical to put them in a **control array**, with all the buttons sharing one name but each referenced by a distinct index number. Chapter 9 covers this subject.

A check box or an option button has four new properties: **Picture**, **DownPicture**, **DisabledPicture**, and **Style**. These let you add pictures to these two objects. See the Command Button section discussed earlier in this chapter for details.

 TIP: Access Key Variations

Pressing an access key can do different things, depending on the object involved. If an object has the Click procedure and is capable of receiving the focus, such as a command button, pressing its access key executes its Click procedure. If these two conditions don't exist, then an access key behaves differently. A label has the Click procedure but is not capable of receiving the focus. In this case, pressing a pertinent access key only shifts the focus to the object of the next TabIndex and may or may not execute the Click procedure of the target object.

You can use two ampersands to insert an extra ampersand in a caption. For example, Up&&Down becomes Up&Down. The first & is to display the second &. What happens if you have three ampersands? The third one will be paired with the next letter. Thus Up&&&Down becomes Up&<u>D</u>own.

In each user interface, you should use a unique letter for each access key. Otherwise, the results are unpredictable. If you designate the same letter as the access key for two command buttons, such as <u>E</u>nter and <u>E</u>nd, pressing the access key (Alt+E) shifts the focus between the two buttons. Then you need to press the Enter key on the keyboard to execute the button's Click procedure. If two option buttons are involved in this situation, pressing the access key (without pressing Enter) alternately executes the two Click procedures. In the case of two check boxes, pressing the access key shifts the focus between the two. Pressing Enter does nothing. Clicking, however, does execute the Click procedure.

FRAME

If you want a new set of option buttons, you can use a frame to contain a separate group of options. This arrangement allows the user to make a choice in a separate group.

A **frame** is a container holding other objects, mostly option buttons. The options inside a frame form a group distinct from those outside the frame or inside another frame. In Figure 4.21, you can make a choice outside the frame and a choice inside the frame.

Adding a control to a frame requires unusual steps. The usual double-clicking trick does not work here. Nor can you drag an existing object to inside a frame. If you do that, you merely move the object on top of the frame, not inside (some objects, depending on their TabIndex orders, will even submerge under the frame). These are the necessary steps:

1. Create a frame first by double-clicking the frame tool in the Toolbox. Move and resize the frame as necessary.

2. Click (do not double-click) the option button tool in the Toolbox.

3. Move the pointer (now appears as a cross) to a proper position inside the frame.

4. Drag the pointer to the ending position and release the mouse button.

The option button now appears. You can move or resize it as necessary. Follow steps 2 to 4 to add more objects if necessary.

NOTE If you have existing objects you want to move to inside a frame, use cut and paste. After selecting the objects, right-click one of them to show the shortcut menu and then choose Cut. Right-click the frame and choose Paste. The objects will reappear inside the frame. You can use the same technique to move objects from a frame to a form or to another frame (or picture box). If you want to select multiple objects and pop up the shortcut menu at the same time, right-drag the mouse pointer to form an outline; the menu pops up as soon as you release the right button.

A frame has Frame1 as its default Name and Caption properties. In our application, we changed the caption to the one shown in Figure 4.21. The Name property is not changed or used.

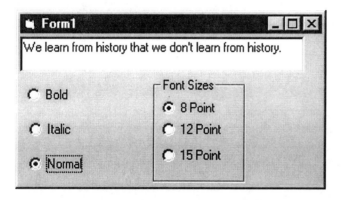

Figure 4.21   Using a frame to contain another group of options

In this modified version, we have changed the captions of the option buttons inside the frame as shown; their Name properties are the same as their captions except with the *opt* prefix added.

To respond to each new option's Click event, you need to go to the Code window and add code. The code for opt8Point is shown below. The code for the other options is the same except for different font sizes (12 and 15, instead of 8).

(4FRAME.FRM)
```
Private Sub opt8Point_Click()
    Text1.FontSize = 8
End Sub
```

After running the program, you can click one option outside the frame and another option inside the frame. In each separate group only one option can be chosen. If we had not put the last three options inside a frame, only one option out of the six could have been chosen at one time.

You can maneuver a frame to affect all the objects inside. If you want to move everything inside a frame, drag the frame and everything inside will go with it. The objects' positions will not change relative to one another. If you drag an object inside instead, only that object will move. If you select a frame and press Del, all the objects inside will be deleted as well.

NOTE   A frame can be compared to a form. A frame maintains a kind of parent-child relationship with the objects inside, just as a form does with the objects inside it. An object's Top and Left properties are determined by their positions against the parent object. Thus, if an object inside a frame has the Left property value of 0, it is aligned on the left side of the frame, not necessarily of the form.

TIP: Tabbed Dialogs

The Professional Edition of Visual Basic has a custom control for creating tabbed dialog boxes that are common in most Windows 95 applications. In the Learning Edition, you can use frame controls to create similar dialogs. Just use multiple frames and arrange them in an overlapping way so that each can be accessed. Inside each frame you place other controls and write code for them.

When a frame is partially covered up by others, you can click its exposed part to bring the frame to the top and expose the controls. Unlike a window, however, clicking a frame does not bring it to the top. One solution is to use the **ZOrder** method available for any visible object. An object's ZOrder determines whether the object should be on top or at the bottom when it and other objects overlap.

Suppose you have Frame1 and Frame2, and they overlap. To bring each to the top when it's clicked, specify 0 as the object's ZOrder in its Click procedure, such as shown below:

```
Private Sub Frame1_Click()
    Frame1.ZOrder 0      'bring Frame1 to top
End Sub

Private Sub Frame2_Click()
    Frame2.ZOrder 0      'bring Frame2 to top
End Sub
```

PARENT AND CONTAINER

All controls have the **Parent** (run time only) and **Container** properties. You can use the former to access the parent of an object to read or maneuver the parent's properties and methods. A Parent can be a form or a collection (see Chapter 9). You can use Container to set or get the container of an object. A container can be a form, frame, or picture box.

In the following procedure, Command1 can be placed on a form or inside a frame control. So Container can refer to either. On the other hand, Parent always refers to the form, not frame control.

```
Private Sub Command1_Click()
    Command1.Container.Caption = "Container"
      'change caption of Form1 or Frame1
    Command1.Parent.Left = 0   'always form
    Command1.Parent.Cls        'clear form
    Command1.Parent.Print "xyz"   'print to form
End Sub
```

To demonstrate the Container property, add Command1, Frame1, and Picture1 to an empty form. Stretch out the last two, and add the following procedure.

```
Private Sub Form_Click()
    Static Num As Integer

    Num = Num Mod 3       'rotate 0-2
    Select Case Num
    Case 0
        Set Command1.Container = Frame1
        Command1.Top = 0    'move button to frame
        Command1.Left = 0   'position at top left
    Case 1
        Set Command1.Container = Picture1
    Case 2                      'move to picture box
        Set Command1.Container = Command1.Parent
    End Select                  'back to form
    Num = Num + 1
End Sub
```

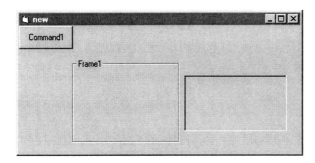

Figure 4.22   Moving an object to another container

Each time the form is clicked at run time, the Command1 button will move to one of the three containers (Figure 4.22). We use the **Mod** operator to restrict Num's value to 0 to 2. This operator will be covered in Chapter 5.

When Num has the value of 2, Command1 is moved to Form1. Here we use the Command1.Parent property as the equivalent of Form1. You can use such an expression to access the parent object. In our case, the two statements below are equivalent:

```
Command1.Parent.Caption = "New Caption"
Form1.Caption = "New Caption"
```

The Parent property refers to the form which contains Command1. This is true even though you place Command1 inside Frame1 or Picture1 at design time.

INPUT BOX

If you are familiar with some flavor of the Basic language, you should know the INPUT and LINE INPUT statements. They pause program execution and then respond to a user input. These are replaced by a function called **InputBox**. It follows this syntax:

```
Msg = InputBox(prompt [,title] [,default] [,xpos] [,ypos]
[,helpfile,context])
```

The only parameter required is a prompt message, which is a text string appearing inside the resulting input box. The title, if supplied, is a text string that appears in the title bar. The default value appears at the bottom of the box where the user is expected to enter something. If supplied, the default value appears and

is highlighted. If nothing is typed when Enter is pressed (or OK clicked), the
supplied default value is entered. If the user types something, the displayed
default value disappears.

As an example, we intend to present the user the interface shown in Figure 4.23.
We have one label, one text box, and two command buttons. The procedure for
the Start button is shown below.

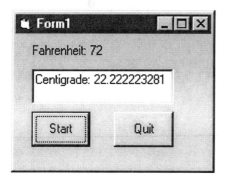

Figure 4.23   Result of converting a user input

```
Private Sub cmdStart_Click ()
    Dim Cent As Single
    Dim Fahr As Variant
    Dim Def As Single
    Dim Prompt As String
    Dim Title As String

    Prompt = "Enter a Fahrenheit number:"
    Title = "Temperature Conversion"
    Def = 0                            'default value
    Fahr = InputBox(Prompt, Title, Def, 3000, 3000)
    If Fahr = "" Then Fahr = Def       'respond to Cancel
    Cent = (5 / 9) * (Fahr - 32)       'convert to C
    Label1.Caption = "Fahrenheit: " & Fahr  'show F
    Text1.Text = "Centigrade: " & Cent      'show C
End Sub
```

After clicking the Start button, an input box appears as shown in Figure 4.24.
The prompt appears inside the box, the title in the title bar, and the default value
(0) on the input line. The box is positioned 3000 twips from both the left and top
margins of the screen, not the form window.

If the user clicks OK (or presses Enter), the default value or whatever is typed is
entered. On the other hand, if Cancel or X is clicked, an empty string is returned.

In that case, our Variant variable named Fahr is assigned the 0 value stored in the Def variable. This can prevent the *Type mismatch* error.

The value returned by InputBox is a Variant type, which can be maneuvered as a numeric or text string. On the other hand, if you expect only a string, you might want to use InputBox$ instead.

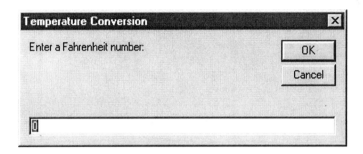

Figure 4.24   An input box prompting for an input

An input box is **modal**. That means when the box is shown, program execution is suspended and the user must do something to get rid of the box before the program will continue. The displayed input box cannot be resized. You can, however, move it by dragging the title bar. Clicking the X button is the same as clicking Cancel.

Instead of using variables as we have done so far, you can use literal strings as parameters. Here is an example:

```
Sub Form_Click ()
    Dim Msg As String

    Msg = InputBox("Do it", "Important", "Press Enter")
    Print Msg
End Sub
```

When you run this program, a clear window appears (assuming you have not added anything). Clicking the window displays an input box. If Cancel is clicked, nothing appears in the window. If OK is clicked or Enter is pressed, then the default string is printed to the window.

An input box appears in the middle of the screen, about 1/3 from the top, with a fixed size which cannot be changed. The position, however, can be shifted if you supply the *xpos* and *ypos* values in twips. You must supply both values to change the position. Supplying only one value does not cause an error, but it has no effect.

You can omit any parameter except the first. If you want to omit one in the middle, you must supply enough commas to specify the parameter to be omitted. In the following example, the title bar is empty:

```
Msg = InputBox("Do something", , "Press Enter")
```

If you did not add an extra comma, the second parameter would go to the title bar and the input line would show nothing.

An input box's prompt can be up to about 255 characters long (depending on their character width). There is automatic word wrap for a long line. If you want to control word wrap at the specified place, add **Chr(13)** (or **vbCr**) and/or **Chr(10)** (or **vbLf**) at the end of a line; unlike a text box, an input box (or a message box explained in the next section) does not require both characters. Here is an example:

```
NL = Chr(13)          'new line
A1 = "This is line 1."
A2 = "This is line 2."
Msg = InputBox(A1 & NL & NL & A2)
```

The prompt will show two text lines, separated by a blank line.

If you supply the last two arguments, a Help button will appear. The user can then click this button to show the help message you have provided. You need the Professional Edition to create a help file.

MESSAGE BOX

A **message box** is often used to display some message you want the user to see in response to some action taken, or to ask the user to make a choice from a limited list of options.

You use a message box similar to the way you use an input box. You can use it as a statement or as a function:

```
MsgBox prompt[,buttons][,title]     'statement
Msg = MsgBox(prompt[,buttons][,title][,helpfile,context])
```

Use the first example to show a message. Use the second to show a message and respond to the option chosen by the user. In either case, the only required parameter is the first. Here are two examples:

```
MsgBox "Warning!!!"

Dim Response As Integer
Response = MsgBox("Warning!!!")
```

Either statement will produce the display shown in Figure 4.25.

Figure 4.25   A message box example

If you supply a longer message, the box will expand to show it. You handle a message similar to the way you handle a prompt for an input box, except that you can put four times as much text here.

If you omit the title, the current project's name appears in the title bar, as shown in Figure 4.25.

You can supply a number or a constant to determine the buttons to appear in a message box. This number can be any one number or the sum of several numbers shown in Table 4.2; each number can be replaced with the constant shown on the right.

Table 4.2   The available values for message box types

Value	Constant
0	vbOKOnly
1	vbOKCancel
2	AbortRetryIgnore
3	vbYesNoCancel

4	vbYesNo
5	vbRetryCancel
16	vbCritical
32	vbQuestion
48	vbExclamation
64	vbInformation
0	vbDefaultButton1
256	vbDefaultButton2
512	vbDefaultButton3
768	vbDefaultButton4
0	vbApplicationModal
4096	vbSystemModal
16384	vbMsgBoxHelpButton
65536	vbMsgBoxSetForeground
524288	vbMsgBoxRight
1048576	vbMsgBoxRtlReading

If no number is supplied, 0 is the default, as shown in Figure 4.25.

If you want to customize a message box, choose a button option number from the 1-5 group, choose an icon number from the 16-64 group, choose a default button from 256 or 512, and add them up. Here is an example:

```
MsgBox "Warning!!!", 531, "Danger"
```

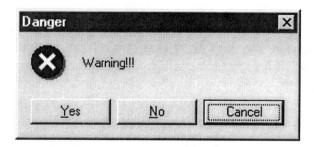

Figure 4.26   A message box with three buttons

The result is shown in Figure 4.26. The number 531 is the result of the following:

$$3 + 16 + 512 = 531$$

By default, when a message box is displayed, the current application is **modal**; it is suspended until a response is made to the message box. Other applications, however, are not suspended. If you want the entire system to be modal, which should not be done unless you have a good reason to do that, you can add the number 4096 to the total.

When you present multiple choices to the user, you should use MsgBox as a function, which returns an integer—in contrast to using it as a statement, which returns no value. After the user makes a choice, the number returned by the function can be used by your code to determine a course of action according to the choice made. The returned value can be one of those shown in Table 4.3.

Table 4.3   The values indicating a user choice of buttons

Value	Constant
1	vbOK
2	vbCancel
3	vbAbort
4	vbRetry
5	vbIgnore
6	vbYes
7	vbNo

Here is an example of showing a message box and extracting a response option from the user:

```
Response = MsgBox("Warning!!!", 3, "Danger")
```

The resulting box will show three options: Yes, No, and Cancel—with Yes as the default choice. The choice made by the user determines what value will be assigned to the variable, which could be 2 (Cancel or clicking the X button), 6 (Yes) or 7 (No). Your code then determines what course should be taken to respond to each choice.

You can also use the **constants** shown in Tables 4.2 and 4.3 to represent their equivalent numeric values. Constants are names that have built-in values. So you can use vbYesNo instead of 4 as the second argument for MsgBox. Chapter 5 explains these built-in (intrinsic) constants.

The last four options in Table 4.2 are new in VB5. vbMsgBoxHelpButton adds a Help button to the message box. You then need to supply a help file to show the message. If not, clicking the Help button does nothing.

The last two options are intended to make text flow from right to left like Hebrew or Arabic. They have no effect unless your system is set up to handle this mechanism.

TIP: List Constants

Take advantage of the **List Constants** feature, new in VB5. The Code window may pop up a list of constants for you to choose from. Sometimes you may want to pop up this list. With a pertinent list of constants at your fingertips, you no longer need to memorize or search for a required argument.

Consider the following situation:

```
msgbox "Warning!",_
```

As you type the comma after supplying the first argument, a list pops up. You can scroll to the desired one and double-click it to enter the constant in the current position.

You can use this tool to change an existing entry. If you want to change the constant for button type, right-click the second argument to pop up a shortcut menu and choose List Constants from the list. You can also move the cursor to the second argument and choose Edit | List Constants (or press Ctrl+Shift+J). If the cursor is not in the right position (after the first comma and before the second comma, if any), choosing List Constants causes your PC to make a beep and does nothing else (no list appears).

CUSTOMIZED INPUT BOX

Instead of an input box or a message box, you can use a **modal form** to let your program interact with the user. This arrangement allows you to customize an input box or a message box.

To make a form **modal** or **modeless**, add an argument 1 (**vbModal**) or 0 (**vbModeless**) after **Show**, such as the following:

```
Form2.Show 1
```

The 0 argument is redundant because it behaves the same way as no argument. The 1 argument, however, creates a modal (rather than modeless) form and

changes the form's behavior. A modal form behaves like an input box or a
message box.

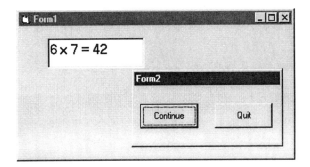

Figure 4.27   Using a custom form for user interaction

Figure 4.27 shows an interface with two forms. Form1 has a text box. Form2
contains two command buttons. To add Form2, click the Add Form (the second)
button on the Standard toolbar or choose Add Form from the Project menu.
Form2 appears, together with its designer window.

To determine the run-time appearance as shown in the figure, you need to enlarge
Form1 and reduce Form2's size. Then drag the two forms in the **Form Layout
window** to their relative startup positions.

To add objects to Form2, click it to select it. Then fetch the necessary controls
from the Toolbox. Make necessary alterations and write necessary code as you
would with Form1.

Form2's ControlBox property is also changed to False at design time; this cannot
be changed at run time. This leads to only the title bar with a caption and nothing
else at run time.

To demonstrate how a modal form behaves similar to an input box or a message
box, we need the two procedures listed below (plus End in Quit). The first is
attached to Form1 and the others to the specific objects on Form2.

```
Private Sub Form_Load ()
    Dim I As Integer
    Dim J As Integer

    Form1.Show        'show Form1, nonmodal
    Form1.Text1.FontSize = 15
```

```
    For I = 5 To 9        'multiplication table
        For J = 5 To 9
            Text1.Text = I & " x " & J & " = " & I * J
                    'show result in Form1.Text1
            Form2.Show vbModal 'show Form2, modal; pause
        Next J
    Next I
End Sub

Private Sub cmdContinue_Click ()
    Form2.Hide       'in Form2, to hide Form2
End Sub
```

The Form_Load procedure of Form1 starts out with the Form1.Show statement. Without it, the code will be executed but the result will not be shown because Form1 is not shown. Then the two For loops generate a multiplication table. After each product is displayed in Text1, the Form2.Show 1 statement displays Form2 in modal state. You must now choose one of the two command buttons before program execution will continue.

If you click the Quit button during the pause, the End statement terminates the program. If you click the Continue button instead, the Form2.Hide statement hides Form2 and thus terminates its modal state. Program execution continues with the next iteration of the For loop. This pattern continues until variable I exceeds 9.

DATA CONTROL (A First Look at an Advanced Topic)

If you have a database, you can use the **data control** to read it. This section provides a simple demonstration to read a database that comes with Visual Basic.

Add two labels, two text boxes, and a data control to a form. Stretch the last three items as shown in Figure 4.28. Then set the properties as shown below.

Object	Property	Value
Data1	DatabaseName	Biblio.mdb
	RecordSource	All Titles
Label1	Caption	Author
Label2	Caption	Title
Text1	DataSource	Data1
	DataField	Author
Text2	DataSource	Data1
	DataField	Title

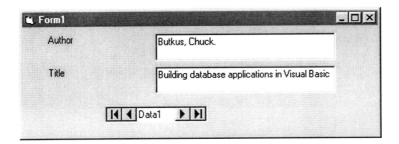

Figure 4.28   Reading a database

In setting property values, you must start with Data1 because other items depend on it. Double-clicking the **DatabaseName** property leads to a dialog box. Double-click a database name (BIBLIO.MDB in our example) and the name will go to the Properties window. This simple act establishes the necessary tie to access the database. If you now pull down the list in **RecordSource**, all the available options will be shown.

After the above steps, you can use other controls to link to the available fields in the database. After you enter Data1 as the value in Text1's **DataSource** property, the **DataField** property shows the available options; choose Author in this case. Then choose Title for Text2's DataField—after specifying its DataSource property.

You can now run the project. The first record appears in the text boxes. You can click one of the four buttons on the data control to go to the first record (first button), last record (last button), previous record (second button), or the next record (third button).

If you wish, you can pull in other fields by changing the two text boxes' DataField values. You can add more text boxes or labels to read other fields. You can also use other data-aware controls to manipulate the information. Chapter 12 will show much more.

DRILL

19. If there are multiple check boxes in an application, only one can be checked. True or false?

_____ 20. Among a group of option buttons, only one can be selected. True or false?

_____ 21. A check box is selected if its Value property is set to:
   a.   1
   b.   True
   c.   Enabled
   d.   all of the above
   e.   none of the above

_____ 22. An option button is selected if its Value property is set to:
   a.   0
   b.   True
   c.   Enabled
   d.   all of the above
   e.   none of the above

_____ 23. If you drag an object to inside the boundaries of a frame control, the object becomes part of the frame. True or false?

_____ 24. Deleting a frame deletes all the objects in it. True or false?

_____ 25. An input box's size cannot be changed, but its position can be specified by code. True or false?

_____ 26. The following statement places the input box at:

```
Msg = InputBox("", , , 0, 0)
```

   a.   the top right corner
   b.   the top left corner
   c.   the default location
   d.   nowhere because it's illegal

_____ 27. When an input box appears, it:
   a.   is modal
   b.   can be moved
   c.   can be resized
   d.   all of the above
   e.   both a and b

_____ 28. In the following two statements:

```
MsgBox "Are you OK?"
Msg = MsgBox("Are you OK?")
```

a. only the first is legal
b. only the second is legal
c. both are legal
d. both are illegal

29. In the following statement, the user will have a message box with the options of:

```
Msg = MsgBox("Your choice?", 4)
```

a. OK and Cancel
b. Yes and No
c. Yes, No, and Abort
d. Yes, No, Abort, and Cancel

30. If the user chooses Yes in the message box displayed by the following statement, Msg will have the value of:

```
Msg = MsgBox("Your choice?", 4)
```

a. 4
b. 5
c. 6
d. 7

PRACTICE

21. How can you add an object, such as an option button, inside a frame?

22. What is the relationship of a frame to the objects inside it?

23. How can you provide two separate groups of option buttons?

24. Create a user interface shown in Figure 4.29. When the user enters a number in the top text box and clicks an option button, the second text box should show the Centigrade or Fahrenheit equivalent.

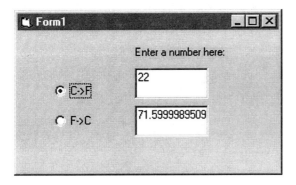

Figure 4.29   Choosing an option button to convert temperature

■ 25. Create a user interface shown in Figure 4.30. When the user types a number in the first text box and clicks an option, the second text box should show the result. (Hint: Use the Sqr function for square root.)

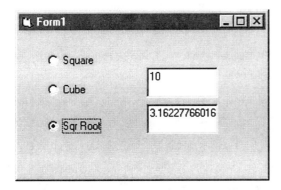

Figure 4.30   Choosing an option to calculate a number

■ 26. Add to the above another group of options as shown in Figure 4.31. When the user clicks a font size, the display in the text boxes should change to reflect the selection.

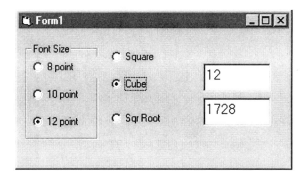

Figure 4.31   Two separate groups of option buttons

■ 27. Create a project consisting of a command button (Command1). When this button is clicked, an input box prompts the user to enter a number. This number is added to all the previously entered numbers and the sum is displayed in the title bar of the input box. If the user enters 0 or clicks Cancel, the program ends; otherwise, another input box is displayed. (Hint: Use a Static variable to store the sum of all the entered numbers; see the online help on how to use this type of variable.)

■ 28. Modify the above so that each input box's title bar shows the total and the prompt shows the average.

■ 29. Modify the above so that if the user enters 0 or clicks the Cancel button, a message box with Yes and No buttons appears. If Yes is clicked, the program ends; otherwise, the program continues.

■ 30. An input box is a function. On the other hand, a message box can be either a function or a statement. Explain.

■ 31. The following is a list of car rental rates. The car names appear in List1 at the beginning of run time (Figure 4.32). When a name is clicked, its corresponding rate appears in Text1. If Discount is checked, then the rate is discounted by 20%.

Lincoln	60
Cadillac	58
Taurus	50
Accord	44

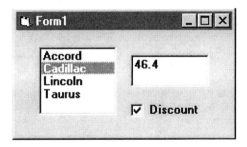

Figure 4.32 **Showing a car rental rate**

CHAPTER PROJECT

A. (4ADD.FRM)

This program simulates an adding machine. The user interface is shown in Figure 4.33. When the project runs, the following should happen:

1. The cursor goes to txtEntry (the top left text box) for an entry.

2. When a number is typed and Enter pressed, the following should happen:

   a. txtEntry is cleared.
   b. The number goes to txtList (top right), below the most recent entry.
   c. The sum of all the entries appears in txtSum (bottom right).

3. Clicking Print prints the numbers in Text2 and Text3.

4. When the Clear button is clicked, the above numbers are cleared.

5. The numbers in txtEntry and txtList are right-aligned. A vertical scroll bar is provided in txtList for the user to scroll the numbers.

6. If the user presses Esc, the program ends.

7. Three access keys are provided as shown.

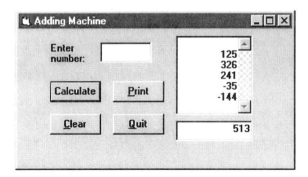

Figure 4.33   Simulating an adding machine

B.   (4TXTLEN.FRM)

This project displays the number of characters entered in a text box. The user interface consists of a text box, a vertical scroll bar, and a label (Figure 4.34). The program should behave as follows:

1.   The Max value of VScroll1 is set to 100 at run time.

2.   VScroll1's scroll box moves up and down to reflect the length of Text1. (Use the Len function to determine this value.)

3.   Label1 shows the length of the text typed in Text1.

4.   When the length of Text1 equals or exceeds the Max value of VScroll1, a beep is made and Text1 is disabled.

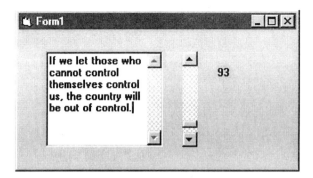

Figure 4.34   Showing the number of characters

C. (4GROWTH.FRM)

Assume the following per capita incomes and annual growth rates in 1995:

China: $500, 12%
U.S.: $25,000, 3%

Assuming the same annual growth rates in 1995-2045, you are asked to do the following:

1. Create a user interface shown in Figure 4.35.

2. When the program runs and the user moves the first scroll bar, the following should happen:

    a. The first label in the middle shows the year (1995-2045).
    b. The second label shows the number for China and the second scroll bar moves to a proper point.
    c. The third label shows the number for the U.S. and the third scroll bar moves to a proper point.

3. Will China surpass the U.S. in 50 years?

4. Change China's growth rate to 10%. Will China surpass the U.S. in 50 years?

Use the following formulas:

$$0.5 * (1 + 0.12) \char`\^ \text{yr\_num} \quad \text{'for China}$$
$$25 * (1 + 0.03) \char`\^ \text{yr\_num} \quad \text{'for US}$$

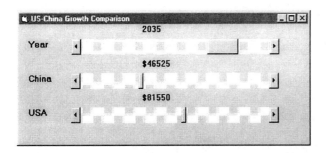

Figure 4.35   Comparing two countries' economic growth

D. (4PAY.FRM)

This program lets you quickly calculate the net pay based on the hours and rate supplied from two horizontal scroll bars.

The Hours scroll bar goes from 0 to 60, with the default value of 40. The Rate scroll bar goes from 5 to 15, with the default value of 10. It allows you to increment by 50 cents (SmallChange) or by $1 (LargeChange).

At the beginning of run time, the form's caption appears as shown in Figure 4.36. The two scroll bars' default values are also displayed on the right as shown.

When you move either scroll bar, the Gross (Hours x Rate), Deduction (15% of Gross), and Net (Gross minus Deduction) are automatically displayed.

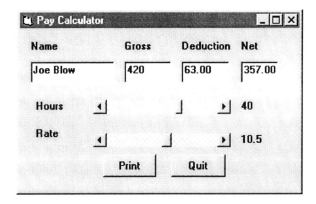

Figure 4.36   Calculating net pay

When you click Print, two lines like below are printed to the printer:

Name	Hours	Rate	Gross	Deduction	Net
Joe Blow	40	10.5	420	63.00	357.00

E. (4MATH.FRM)

This project (Figure 4.37) lets the user calculate four math numbers. The user enters a number in the top-middle text box and clicks an option in the list box to display the result in the middle-bottom text box. The following rules should be observed:

1. The four items in the list box appears as soon as the program runs.

2. The bottom-left label should change according to the selection in the list box.

3. If no acceptable entry is encountered, the program should end without crashing.

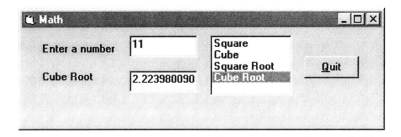

Figure 4.37   Using a list box

F. (4SALES.FRM)

This program tabulates keyboard entries. It should behave as follows:

1. At the beginning of run time, the cursor goes to Text1 (top left, Figure 4.38) for typing an entry. If Enter is pressed without typing an entry, the cursor stays and nothing else happens. If an entry is typed, pressing Enter moves the cursor to Text2 below.

2. In Text2, if no entry is made when Enter is pressed, the cursor stays and nothing else happens. If an entry has been made, then the following should happen:

   a. The total is displayed in Text3.
   b. The two user entries are combined with a Tab character between them and added to the large middle box.
   c. The two boxes are cleared and the cursor goes to the first for another entry.

3. Clicking Print sends the large box's contents to the printer.

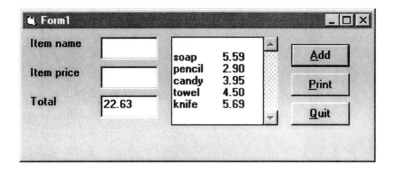

Figure 4.38   Tabulating numbers

G. (4MERGE.FRM)

This program lets you perform a mail merge operation. At run time, the list box
on the left (Figure 4.39) shows several names. Clicking a name displays a test
score in Text1 (middle). Clicking an option button displays in Text2 (the large
text box) a prepared comment. Clicking Merge combines the selected name in the
list box, the score in Text1, and insert at the beginning of Text2. Clicking Print
sends Text2's contents to the printer.

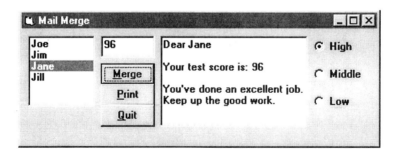

Figure 4.39   Mail merge

H. (4FONTS.FRM)

This project lets the user show on the screen all the available Screen fonts and
sizes. The user interface (Figure 4.40) consists of one text box, two labels, two
horizontal scroll bars, and a command button. The program should behave as
follows.

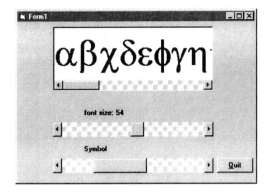

Figure 4.40   Showing fonts

1. At run time, Text1 shows the 26 alphabetic letters in the default font and size. Label1 shows the font size and Label2 the font name.

2. HScroll1's range is set at run time from 5 to 100.

3. HScroll2's range is set at run time from 0 to the number of available fonts.

4. When the user scrolls HScroll1, the font sizes in Label1 and Text1 change accordingly.

5. When the user scrolls HScroll2, the font names in Label2 and Text1 change accordingly.

FUN AND GAME

A. (MOVBALL.FRM)

This program lets you use two scroll bars to move an object (ball) on the screen (Figure 4.41). At design time, the interface as a shape control placed in the middle of the form and two scroll bars stretched out as shown. The other values are set at run time.

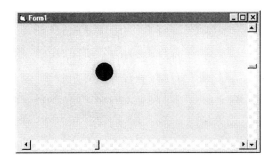

Figure 4.41   Moving a ball with scroll bars

```
Private Sub Form_Load()
    HScroll1.Max = ScaleWidth      'max left value
    VScroll1.Max = ScaleHeight     'max top value
    HScroll1.LargeChange = 100     'scroll speed
    VScroll1.LargeChange = 50
    Shape1.FillStyle = 0       'solid fill
    Shape1.Shape = 3           'circle
    Shape1.Left = HScroll1     'initial ball pos
    Shape1.Top = VScroll1      'top-left corner
End Sub

Private Sub HScroll1_Change()
    Shape1.Left = HScroll1     'control left pos of ball
End Sub

Private Sub VScroll1_Change()
    Shape1.Top = VScroll1      'control top pos of ball
End Sub
```

B.   (STAR.FRM)

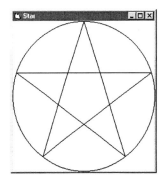

Figure 4.42   A circle and a five-pointed star

This program draws a circle and a five-pointed star inside a perfect square (Figure 4.42).

```
Private Sub Form_Load()
    Width = ScaleHeight
    Width = 2 * ScaleHeight - ScaleWidth
        'get a perfect square for drawing area
End Sub

Private Sub Form_Click()
    Dim I As Single
    Dim X As Single
    Dim Y As Single
    Dim X1 As Single
    Dim Y1 As Single
    Dim Pi As Single

    Pi = 4 * Atn(1)        'get pi value
    Scale (-1, 1)-(1, -1)      'custom scale
    Circle (0, 0), 1      'outer circle
    For I = Pi / 2 To 2 * Pi + Pi / 2 Step 2 * Pi / 5
        'counterclockwise, step 2 pi / 5
        'change 5 to 10 to get 10 angles
        X = Cos(I)         'get x axis
        Y = Sin(I)         'get y axis
            'get beginning point of each line
        X1 = Cos(I + Pi * 4 / 5)
        Y1 = Sin(I + Pi * 4 / 5)
            '2nd point for each line
        Line (X, Y)-(X1, Y1)
            'draw line from point 1 to point 2
            'along the imaginary circle
    Next I
End Sub
```

You can modify the code so that a triangle will appear at the beginning and as you click the form, more sides will appear either overlapping the previous drawing or in a clear window. You can also modify it in such a way that as you click the window, a shadowy figure will emerge. Figure 4.43 (STAR1.FRM) shows the pattern after the window is clicked 45 times. Changing a few values can produce Figure 4.44 (STAR2.FRM).

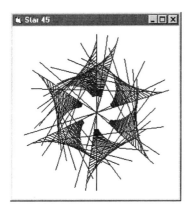

Figure 4.43   Gossamer

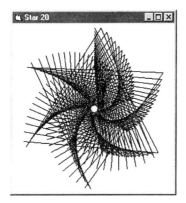

Figure 4.44   Whirlwind

Chapter 5
The Basics of Basic

TOPICS

KEY TERMS

Argument   A value, variable, or expression supplied to a command to complete a specific instruction; also known as a parameter.

Boolean expression   A conditional expression that evaluates to true or false.

Constant   A variable (symbol) with a predefined and unchanging value. Visual Basic comes with many system-defined constants known as **intrinsic constants**. So instead of using a number to assign a color, you can use vbRed, vbCyan, etc. You can use the **Const** keyword to create a user-defined constant known as a **symbolic constant**.

Declarations section   An area in the Code window where module-level variables are declared. When Full Module view is on, this is the topmost part of the Code window. When the cursor is in this area, the Object box shows (General).

Expression   A statement fragment consisting of literals, variables, and operators and returning a single value.

Module-level variable   A variable declared in the Declarations section of a module; it can be accessed by all the procedures in the module, but not outside—unless it's a public variable.

Global   The broadest variable (or procedure) scope. When a variable is declared with the **Global** or **Public** keyword in the Declarations section of a standard module, it is visible throughout the application. A public procedure is also global because it can be called by all the other procedures in the application. A private procedure can be called only from the same module.

Keyword   A word reserved for Visual Basic's use. It has a special meaning to Visual Basic and should not be used for your purpose such as a variable name.

Local   The narrowest variable scope. When a variable is local (declared or used only in a procedure), it does not exist outside the procedure.

Object Browser   A tool that allows you to browse objects. Press F2 to open its dialog box. Use Project/Library (top left combo box) to select a project or application. Use Classes (left list box) to select an object. Use Members (right list box) to select a property or method (sub or function procedure). Click a member name to show its details in the bottom pane. You can use the Object Browser to show intrinsic constants, to copy a function to the Code window, to move the focus to a procedure in another module, or to browse the objects of another application, such as Excel.

Option Explicit   A statement in the Declarations section of a module specifying that all variables must be declared before they can be used.

Scope   The extent to which a variable (or procedure) can be seen or accessed. A variable in one procedure is normally not visible to or accessible from another procedure. You can, however, broaden a variable's scope.

Standard Module   Or code module; a separate file with the BAS extension containing procedures and data declarations (but not forms or controls), which can be accessed by all the other elements in the same application.

Statement   A complete instruction to the computer to perform an act. A statement usually occupies one line. Multiple statements, however, can stay in the same line, each separated from another with a colon (:).

Static variable   A variable whose value remains (is not erased) between calls. It is visible in the area where it is declared. Declare a static variable with **Static** instead of the regular **Dim**.

Value   Anything, such as a number or a string of characters, that you assign to a variable and is stored in the specified memory area. Statements, functions, or expressions also return values.

Variable   A name specified by you to designate a memory location to store a value. A variable can be assigned different values on different occasions.

Variant   The default Visual Basic data type. If you use a variable without declaring it or specifying a data type, Visual Basic treats it as a Variant, which can hold any type of data.

This chapter covers some elementary terms and concepts about computer programming. They are tedious but necessary. They serve as building blocks, like bricks and mortar. You need a clear understanding of them before you can build something fancy. If you already have a reasonable degree of computer literacy, you can breeze through the material. If not, you need to go through these unexciting items to build a solid foundation before you can write exciting programs.

INPUT, OUTPUT, and PROCESSING

A computer is a machine. Like any machine, it processes raw material and produces an end product. More specifically, a computer is a data-processing machine. It processes raw data and produces organized and useful information. An instructor may give the computer individual test scores. The computer processes the numbers and produces results such as total, average, semester grade, and so on. One person's information may be another's raw data. The school's registrar may process the grades submitted by instructors and produce different results for use by the administration.

A computer program you write typically handles input, processes the input data, and then produces some form of output. This can be illustrated by Figure 5.1.

Input can be supplied from the following sources:

- Keyboard
- Disk file
- Scanner
- Another networked (or connected) computer

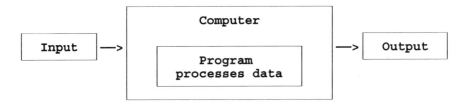

Figure 5.1   Input, processing, and output

Your program has to provide a mechanism to accept and store the input data. After inputting is done, the program then processes the data. The processed data is then sent to an output device, which can be one or more of the following:

- Monitor
- Printer
- Disk file
- Another networked (or connected) computer

Visual Basic supplies many tools for inputting data and many ways to produce output information. Chapters 3 and 4 cover most of these tools. The table below provides a summary. If you know previous versions of the Basic language, you'll know that not much has changed in the language portion since QBasic,[1] but there are many additions in visual tools. These tools are commonly used to make your programs more attractive and user friendly.

----

[1]QBasic was included in MS-DOS 5 and 6. It was derived from GW (Geewhiz) Basic, which was bundled with earlier DOS versions. For a time Microsoft also marketed a separate package called Quick Basic.

	Basic Commands	Common Visual Tools
Input	InputBox	Text box (keyboard typing)
		List box (screen selection)
		Combo box
		Check box
		Option button
		Scroll box
		Data control
Output	MsgBox	Form
	Print	Picture box
		Text box
		Label control

The rest of this chapter and the next chapter will concentrate on the *processing* aspect of computing.

A PROGRAM'S COMPONENTS

What is a program? Well, with the arrival of Visual Basic, it is getting harder to define. Instead of using this word, Visual Basic now refers to projects and applications, and sometimes uses these three terms interchangeably. We will try to compare these terms and put them in their proper places.

At design time, you work on a **project**. A project includes all the necessary components to complete your task. It may include forms, controls, and code. After you complete your project, it becomes an **application**. An application is ready for use to perform an intended task.

Visual Basic's application is what people traditionally call a **program**. A program is linear in the traditional sense because program lines are executed one line after another. A Visual Basic application, however, is **event-driven**. When an application runs, it just sits there waiting for the user to do something. When the user initiates an event, such as clicking an object, the related procedure is executed.

A Visual Basic procedure closely resembles a traditional program because both are executed linearly. A Visual Basic application typically consists of multiple procedures, each of which is comparable to a traditional program. A Visual Basic application is thus an assembly of procedures tied together by a graphical user interface.

A Visual Basic application can be compared to an essay in English. An essay may consist of multiple paragraphs. Each paragraph, in turn, contains multiple sentences. A Visual Basic application may include multiple procedures (paragraphs), each of which may contain multiple statements (sentences). As sentences can be broken down to words and phrases, statements can be divided into expressions, variables, and values. The two can be schematically compared as follows:

```
Visual Basic application        English essay
    procedure1                      paragraph1
        statements                      sentences
    procedure2                      paragraph2
        statements                      sentences
    . . .                           . . .
```

Let us now examine what constitutes a program, which is comparable to a Visual Basic procedure.

A program consists of **statements**, each of which is a complete instruction like a sentence. A statement includes **expressions**. An expression combines variables, literals (unchanging values), and operators.

A **literal** (also called **constant**) is a fixed value. It can be a **numeric literal** or a **string literal**. The former can be arithmetically maneuvered. The latter consists of one or more alphanumeric characters. A string cannot be arithmetically maneuvered, but it can be maneuvered in many other ways.

Let us use some concrete examples. A + 1 is an expression, in which A is a variable, + is an operator, and 1 is a numeric literal. On the other hand, X = A + 1 is a statement, in which the sum of A and 1 is assigned to the variable named X (stored in the memory area named X).

Statements may involve some keywords and parameters. A **keyword** is a preprogrammed command to do something. You may need to supply the necessary information to complete the job. This is known as a **parameter** or **argument**. Consider the following

```
Beep
Print "This is an order."
```

The first example is a statement that requires no argument; this command just makes a beep. In the second example, we add a parameter to tell the Print command what to print. The Print command will print a blank line if no argument is present.

Parameters are like qualifiers in English. Consider the following two sentences:

Go.
Go to Hale.

The first may provide a complete instruction and can be clearly understood under some circumstances. The second, by adding a qualifier, provides a more precise instruction different from the one without a qualifier.

As we encounter specific Visual Basic commands in later chapters, we will elaborate on their required and optional arguments.

VARIABLES AND VALUES

A **variable** is a name you give that can hold various values at various times. After you create a variable, a memory area is reserved to hold a value you may assign to it. A **value** is something, a number or a text string, that you want to put in the memory area reserved by a variable.

After you create a variable and assign a value to its memory location, you can maneuver the variable for various purposes. For example, you can create variables named A and B, and respectively assign 1 and 2 to their memory locations. If you then order A+B, your computer will add up the values in the two memory locations and produce 3. On another occasion, you may assign different values and do different things to them.

A variable name must observe these rules:

- It must be within 255 characters in length—a contrast to 40 for an object name.
- No space is permitted.
- It must start with an alphabetic letter.
- A Visual Basic keyword by itself should not be used.
- Arithmetic operators are not permitted.
- Special Visual Basic operators and data-type characters are not permitted.

A number may be included in a variable name, but not at the beginning. Thus A2B is legal, but 2End is not.

A **keyword** (or reserved word) has a special meaning to Visual Basic and is reserved for a specific purpose. You should not use a keyword alone as a variable.

However, a keyword can be embedded in a variable name. For example, For = 4 is not legal, but ForSale = 4 is.

TIP: Keywords and Variables

Keywords alone should normally not be used as variables. However, it is legal to use some of them if you declare them first. This practice should normally be avoided because it could cause confusion. Consider this example:

```
Private Sub Command1_Click()
    Dim Left As Integer

    Left = 10                'user variable
    Print Left * Left        'Print 100
    Form1.Left = 10          'move form
End Sub
```

If we did not declare it first, Left would be treated as a property of the current form. By declaring it, we tell the computer to reserve an area of memory and call it Left. After that, using Left alone refers to the memory. If you want to refer to the form property, you have to specify the form.

Now consider this scenario:

```
Private Sub Command1_Click()
    Dim Screen As Double

    Screen = 2               'user defined
    Print Screen             '2
    Print Screen.Height      '"Invalid qualifier"
End Sub
```

The last line will trigger the error shown in the comment. Visual Basic can no longer find the Screen object to show its height.

The above discussion applies only to **unrestricted keywords** but not to **restricted keywords**. You cannot use restricted keywords as variables. If you use Dim to declare them, you'll get an error right away.

You can use a restricted keyword as an object name by placing it inside a pair of square brackets. Suppose you change Command1 to Do at design time. You can reference this object like this:

```
[Do].Visible = False
```

After this line is executed, the command button will become invisible. If you didn't use brackets here, an error will appear right away.

How do you know whether a keyword is restricted? I'm unable to find it inside Visual Basic. If you use the online help's Index tab to search for *keywords*, you'll find lots of them. Some of the displayed terms are restricted, but others are not. For example, both Array and IsArray are included. But you can use IsArray as a variable but not Array. The rule seems to change too. Array was permitted in VB4, but no longer in VB5.

Visual Basic uses a number of characters for various purposes, including the following:

.	To connect an object (including form) and a property
!	Form!control delimiter in VB3; collections delimiter in VB4/5
&	To concatenate strings and numerics

These characters cannot be included in a variable name.

The underscore (_) character is used to connect an object and an event, such as Command1_Click. But it can be included in a variable name. However, such a variable name must not duplicate an existing procedure's name. For example, if you have already written code for Command1_Click, you cannot use the same name as a variable. If you did that, only one of the two will be legal.

Including arithmetic operators will lead to errors because Visual Basic expects arithmetic operations when these are encountered.

Naming variables, just like naming objects, is a matter of personal style. Some people like long names while others like them short. Each has its own advantages and disadvantages. Long names provide meaningful descriptions for variables; one can thus easily distinguish a variable from another. On the other hand, long names are laborious to type and can unnecessarily lengthen even the simplest formulas. Short names suffer from exactly opposite effects: hard to distinguish one from another but easy on typing.

In a short program involving relatively few variables, using short names is convenient. To avoid confusion among variable names, you can document each at the beginning of a procedure. If you get confused as to what variable is for what purpose, go to the beginning area to find out. In the meantime, you can save yourself lots of typing. Your complex formulas are also easy to read and debug.

In a large project involving numerous variables and multiple modules, managing variables requires more attention and forethought. To avoid confusion and duplication, you need longer (and self-explanatory) names and a systematic way of distinguishing among them. Such an approach is mandatory if several persons are collaborating on a project.

Assigning a value in Visual Basic is simple and straightforward. Here are two examples:

```
I = 0.06      'interest rate
InterestRate = 0.06
```

You can use .06, but Visual Basic will add the leading 0.

You can also use the **Let** statement as you would in Basic:

```
Let I = .06
```

If you want to assign a text string to a variable, you need to put it in double quotes (only the first is required; Visual Basic will automatically add the second— if it is located at the end of a line):

```
StuName = "Joe Blow"
```

Visual Basic objects can be maneuvered as variables. You can assign values to an object's various properties at design time or run time. Here are some code examples you can use at run time:

```
Command1.Caption = "Click here"      'change caption
Command1.Enabled = False             'disable button
Text1.Text = "Pay attention here."   'change text
```

NOTE   By default, Visual Basic treats numbers as decimal values. You can make it handle numbers as **octal** or **hexadecimal** values by preceding each number with &O or &H. For example, the following statements will produce the **decimal** numbers shown in the comments; see Appendix B for details.

```
Print &HABC      '2748
Print &O666      '438
```

TIP: Variables As Values

If you are a computer novice, you may not be aware that a variable has a value and the variable name can be used in lieu of the value. Consider the following statements:

```
Print varX
varA = varX
varX = varX + 1
varX = varX * 2
```

The variable varX is used as a value in all four statements; it is also used as a variable in the last two. In the first statement, the value of varX is printed; if it holds nothing, then nothing is printed. In the second, the value in varX is assigned to variable varA.

The last two statements often confuse beginners. In this situation, the varX on the left side of an = sign is a variable and the one on the right side is a value. Suppose varX has the original value of 10. The third statement adds 1 to it and assigns the sum to varX. varX has the value of 11 after the statement is executed. The fourth statement results in varX having the value of 22 (11 x 2).

Keep in mind that varX is just one variable. If you assign different values to it, only the last one is retained. Each time you assign a new value, it replaces the original copy.

An arithmetic operator or operation is not permitted on the left side of an = sign. Consider this statement:

```
varX + 1 = 10
```

It is permitted in math, but not in a computer program. Such a statement will be interpreted as assigning 10 to a variable named varX+1. Since no operator is permitted in a variable name, Visual Basic will throw out the + right away. If you use other operators in this situation, they will be kept at design time but generate a variety of errors at run time.

DRILL

____ 1.   An input device includes:
       a.   monitor

           b.   printer

           c.   scanner

           d.   disk drive

           e.   both c and d

____ 2.   "2Go" is a legal variable name. True or false?

____ 3.   "Num_var" is a legal variable name. True or false?

____ 4.   "Interest.rate" is a legal variable name. True or false?

Choose from the following list to answer questions 5-8:
          a. statement, b. expression, c. variable, d. value

____ 5.   A complete instruction to the computer to do something.

____ 6.   A memory area which can store different things at different times.

____ 7.   Something you put in a specified memory area.

____ 8.   An incomplete instruction combining several items and evaluating to one thing.

PRACTICE

■ 1.   What does this statement print? Explain. (Consult Appendix B.)

```
Print &HABC
```

■ 2.   What does this statement print? Explain.

```
Print &O666
```

■ 3.   What's the difference between a *restricted keyword* and an *unrestricted keyword*?

■ 4.   Explain the following three statements.

```
varX = varX + 1
varX1 = varX2
varX + 1 = varX + 2
```

■ 5.   How does Visual Basic use the following symbols?

. ! & _

■ 6. Explain how these terms differ: statement, expression, and argument.

■ 7. How do a variable and a value differ?

DATA TYPES AND DECLARATION

Since a variable is an area in memory, you can specify how large a chunk of memory you want to set aside for the value assigned or to be assigned.

Visual Basic offers numerous predefined data types. These are shown in Table 5.1.

Table 5.1 Visual Basic Data Types

Type	Prefix*/Suffix	Size (byte)	Range
Variant	vnt/none	variable	Up to Double or String
Byte	byt/none	1	0 to 255
Boolean	bln/none	2	True or False
Integer	int/%	2	-32,768 to 32,767
Long	lng/&	4	-2,147,483,648 to 2,147,483,647
Single	sng/!	4	-3402823E38 to -1401298E-45 or 1401298E-45 to 3402823E38
Double	dbl/#	8	-179769313486232E308 to -494065645841247E-324 or 494065645841247E-324 to 179769313486232E308
Currency	cur/@	8	-922,337,203,685,477.5808 to 922,337,203,685,477.5807
Date	dtm/none	8	1/1/100 to 12/31/9999
Object	obj/none	4	any object reference
String	str/$	1 per char	0 to 2 billion bytes

(*See a TIP below for prefixes.)

Before we proceed further, let us write a program to demonstrate how these data types differ. The following procedure produces the display shown in Figure 5.2. For this procedure to work, Option Explicit (explained below) must not be on. To avoid errors, you must erase it or comment it out by adding an apostrophe before it.

```
Private Sub Form_Click()
    X1 = 20 / 3
    X2% = 20 / 3
    X3& = 20 / 3
    X4! = 20 / 3
    X5# = 20 / 3
    X6@ = 20 / 3
    Print X1 & "--variant"
    Print X2% & "--integer"
    Print X3& & "--long integer"
    Print X4! & "--single-precision floating point"
    Print X5# & "--double-precision floating point"
    Print X6@ & "--currency"
End Sub
```

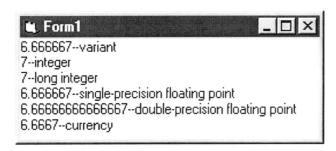

Figure 5.2   Output of various data types

Notice that different types produce different results. Notice also that Variant and Single produce the same results. When a floating number is encountered, Visual Basic converts a Variant to a Single. In different situations the conversion may result in different data types.

The **Variant** type is the default data type in Visual Basic since version 2 (Single was the default type in all previous Basic versions). This makes it easy for you to use a variable. You are not required to declare a data type before using a variable. Visual Basic automatically handles any adjustment. You can thus use a variable to hold a numeric or text string. You can even assign to such a variable different types of data on different occasions.

The code below shows the Variant variable varX being assigned an integer. The first Print statement prints 100 to the screen (Figure 5.3). Then it is given a text string. So the second Print statement produces this text. The last Print statement outputs a Double number.

```
Private Sub Form_Click ()
    Dim varX
    varX = 100
    Print "varX = "; varX
    varX = "xxx"
    Print "varX = "; varX
    varX = 100 / 1.3
    Print "varX = "; varX
End Sub
```

Figure 5.3   Showing a Variant variable

If you declare a variable as a specific type, you can no longer use the variable in such a flexible way. Suppose you change the first line in the above procedure to this:

```
Dim varX As Integer
```

Running the program again will generate the *Type mismatch* error in the line that assigns a string to the variable. The reason for that is that you restrict the variable (memory area) to only the specified type of data (integer in this case).

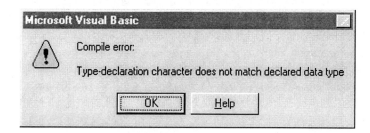

Figure 5.4   Error in using a wrong type character

If you want a variable to hold a specific data type, which in turn specifies the maximum amount of memory for a value, you can put a specific character after a variable name, as shown in the code that produces Figure 5.2. These type characters are not allowed to contradict the type previously declared with Dim or another type character. If you do, Figure 5.4 will appear.

You normally declare data types by using the **Dim** statement. This is commonly done at the beginning of a procedure. Here is an example:

```
Private Sub Command1_Click ()
    Dim varX As Integer, varY As Integer, varZ As Integer
    varX = 1
    varY = 2
    varZ = varX + varY
    Print varZ
End Sub
```

Notice that Integer is specified with every variable. What happens if you omit the first two, such as below?

```
    Dim varX, varY, varZ As Integer
```

Only the last is an integer; the others are treated as Variants.

The keywords you can use in declaring data types are shown in Table 5.1. Of course, if you want a Variant type, you need not declare it or specify a data type.

NOTE   Some languages require you to initialize a variable before its use. You must declare it and assign an initial value, such as 0; otherwise, garbage may be stored there. If you are used to this practice, you can continue to do that in Visual Basic. On the other hand, Visual Basic has taken care of such a chore. If a numeric variable such as Integer or Double is not assigned a value, it is initialized to 0, a Variant initialized to a special value called Empty, and a string (see below) initialized to an empty string (variable-length) or filled with the specified number of spaces (fixed-length). So an uninitialized variable should not have any unintended side effect.

With the **String** data type, you can specify the maximum number of characters (bytes) a variable can hold. The following declaration limits variable Str to only 15 characters:

```
    Dim Strn As String * 15
```

If you assign more than 15 characters, only the first 15 are retained. If you assign fewer, extra spaces are added at the end. Even if you assign nothing, Visual Basic considers Strn to be 15 characters in length.

When you use Dim to declare a data type, Visual Basic sets aside a specific amount of memory for the specified variable. For example, if you declare varX to be an integer, then 2 bytes are set aside for varX. The length of varX is 2 bytes regardless of whether you assign anything to it. There are two exceptions, **String** and **Variant**. If you specify no length with String, the variable's default length is 0; the same thing happens when you declare a variable to be a Variant. These variables can stretch to their limits when you assign values to them.

How can you verify the length of a variable? Use the **Len** function. For example, Len(varX) returns a number that represents the number of bytes in RAM set aside to store variable varX. Len can tell a lot about how Visual Basic handles a Variant variable; it can tell you how much memory that variable is consuming at any particular moment.

When a text string is involved, you can use the new **LenB** function to show the number of bytes in a variable; it may be different from the number of characters returned by **Len**. In the 32-bit environment, LenB is twice as large as Len. Consider the following statements and results:

```
Dim Var As Variant
Var = 123
Print Len(Var)        '3
Print LenB(Var)       '6
```

On the other hand, if we change Variant to Integer, both will return 2.

You may use numbers expressed in a scientific notation (exponential notation). Consider 1.23E+10 and 1E-10 (the number before E is the **mantissa** and the one after is the **exponent**). In the first case, where a + is used, the decimal point is 10 places to the right of the last integer. In the second case, where a - is used, the decimal point is 10 places to the left of the last integer. A Single value is returned by E. If you replace E with D, a Double value will be returned. Figure 5.5 shows Visual Basic treating a variety of expressions as equivalent.

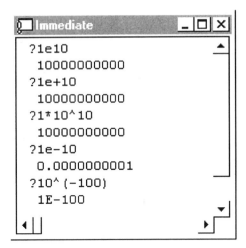

Figure 5.5   Exponential notations in the Immediate window

 ## TIP: Variable Naming Conventions

When you use numerous variables in a project, you need a systematic way of naming them. The naming convention recommended by Microsoft involves using the prefixes shown in Table 5.1. Here are some examples:

```
Dim intCounter As Integer
Dim sngAverage As Single
Dim lngScreenWidth as Long
Dim blnYesNo as Boolean
```

One advantage of this naming system is that you can easily tell what type of data each variable is holding. The disadvantage is that adding a prefix will make a variable name longer and laborious to type. Such lengthy names are unnecessary in a short project.

If you want to know more, click the Index button and search for *coding conventions* from the online help's Books Online.

Option Explicit

If you use lots of variables in a program, you might be confused by them. You may then want to ask Visual Basic to check your variables by forcing you to declare them first. You can do so by two methods:

- Enter **Option Explicit** at the top of the Code window.
- Check the **Require Variable Declaration** check box.

The first method requires you to type the specified text in the General Declarations section of the Code window. If Full Module View is on, you can move the cursor to the top of the window and type the text. If not, you need to choose (General) from the Object box and (Declarations) from the Procedure box, and then type the text, which can be above or below any existing declarations.

The second method is to ask Visual Basic to automatically enter the required text (Option Explicit). To do that, just check **Require Variable Declaration** in the Tools | Options | Editor tab. Unlike the first method, this has no effect on existing Code windows. The required text string does not appear until after you add a new module. After you do that, Option Explicit automatically appears without your doing anything else.

When Option Explicit is specified, you must declare each variable before using it. You must do so by using the Dim or Private statement, not by adding a type character at the end of a variable name. Otherwise, the error shown in Figure 5.6 will appear.

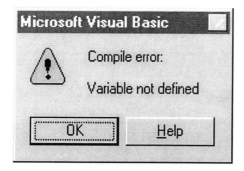

Figure 5.6   Using a variable without declaration

After you have used Dim to declare a variable as a specific type (Variant if no type is specified), you can no longer use a different type character to do it again. If the character and the previously declared type don't match, the error shown in Figure 5.4 will appear. So you may use Dim to declare varX without specifying a data type. Then you use varX! to use varX as a Single. That's when the error occurs.

If Visual Basic finds any undeclared variable, it highlights that variable and displays the message shown in Figure 5.6. This does not happen if Option Explicit is not in effect. So if you delete these two words or add an apostrophe before them, variable checking will stop.

It's a good idea to turn on Option Explicit. It imposes a strict discipline on you and forces you to manage variables carefully. In a complex program with numerous variables, errant variables can cause endless troubles and lead to mysterious bugs. These variables are less likely to stray too far when Option Explicit is on.

VarType and TypeName

Since a Variant variable may hold different data types at different times, you may want to find out what it is holding at a particular time. You can use the **VarType** function to do that. Supply a variable name as an argument, and VarType will return a value which represents a data type shown in Table 5.2.

If the variable has no assigned value, 0 is returned. If it is assigned Null (a special value indicating no valid data), then 1 is returned.

Table 5.2   The values returned by VarType

Value	Data Type (VB3)	Value	Data Type
0	Empty	New in VB4/5:	
1	Null	9	Object
2	Integer	10	Error
3	Long	11	Boolean
4	Single	12	Variant
5	Double	13	Data-access object
6	Currency	14	Decimal
7	Date/Time	17	Byte
8	String	8192	Array

Have you ever wondered how Visual Basic treats a numeric or a numeric-like string assigned to a Variant (undeclared) variable? How about a number entered in a text box? The following procedure attempts to seek some answers; it produces the display shown in Figure 5.7.

```
Private Sub Form_Click ()
    Dim Var
    Print "Value", "Type #"
```

```
      Print Var, VarType(Var)       'uninitialized
      Var = Null                    'Null value
      Print Var, VarType(Var)
      Var = "123"                   'text string
      Print Var, VarType(Var)
      Var = 456                     'numeric
      Print Var, VarType(Var)
      var = 123.456                 'numeric
      Print Var, VarType(Var)
      Var = #3/20/96#               'numeric
      Print Var, VarType(Var)
      Print Text1.Text, VarType(Text1)      'textbox entry
End Sub
```

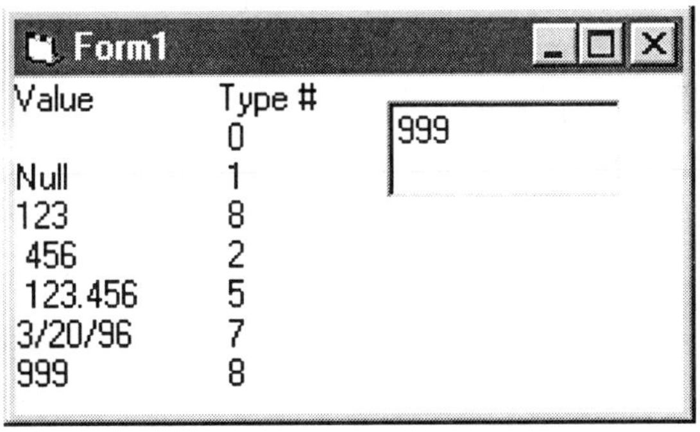

Value	Type #	
	0	999
Null	1	
123	8	
456	2	
123.456	5	
3/20/96	7	
999	8	

Figure 5.7   VarType output

Notice that a number in a text box is treated as a text string (type 8); so is a number inside quotation marks. Keep in mind, however, these are Variants and can be arithmetically maneuvered.

We use a pair of # signs to enclose a date value. This is new since VB4. If we put a pair of quotes here, the value will be treated as a text string.

VB4 also added a new function called **TypeName**. You can use it to return the type name of each variable. Figure 5.8 is the result if we change all VarType instances to TypeName in the previous procedure. The displayed names are the same as those found in Table 5.2. Notice that the last statement returns a string. If we take out the Text extension in the argument, the function will return the control name TextBox. So TypeName is able to distinguish an object from a value.

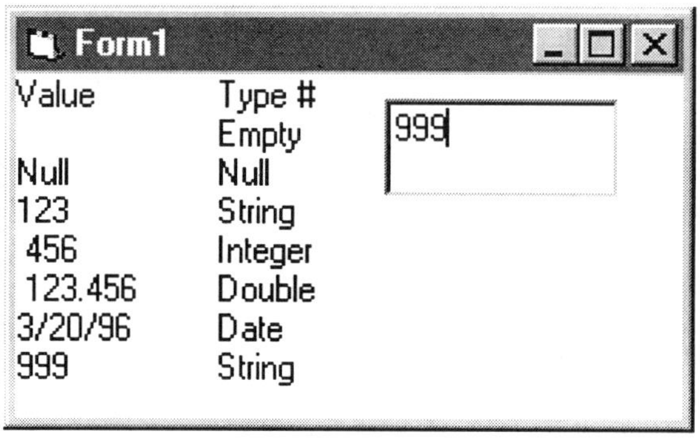

Figure 5.8   TypeName output

If you are used to older Basic versions, you can still use a **Def*Type*** (where *Type* is a data type such as Int) to declare a default data type for a range of letters, such as A-D. You must do it in the Declarations section of a module. After the declaration, all the variables starting with A, B, C, or D will by default hold the specified data type. You can, however, use Dim or a type character inside a procedure to change the default data type. In that case, the local type will prevail inside that procedure.

If Option Explicit is on, Def*Type* is not considered a valid declaration. You are still required to use Dim to declare variables. If you want to know more, search the online help for DefInt. You can also type that word in the Code window and press F1 to reach the same topic.

NOTE   According to the online help on Variant Data Type, a Variant can "contain any kind of data except fixed-length String data and user-defined types." The second part is true (see Chapter 9), but the first part isn't. Although we specify Str1as a fixed-length string in the procedure below, we have no trouble assigning its value to Variant Var1

```
Private Sub Form_Click()
    Dim Str1 As String * 2
    Dim Var1 As Variant

    Str1 = ,"abc"
    Var1 = Str1
        'assign a fixed-length string to a Variant
    Print Str1, Var1        'ab, ab
    Print TypeName(Str1), TypeName(Var1)
End Sub                'String, String
```

TIP: Overflow and Remedy

Do you know what will happen if you run the following program?

```
Private Sub Form_Click ()
    Dim num
    num = 111 * 333
    Print num
End Sub
```

It will produce the *Overflow* error; the same error will also appear even if you declare Num as a Double. You would think that Num, being a Variant, should be capable of handling a very large number. Instead, Visual Basic balks at 36963, the product of 111*333. What's the problem?

The problem is that Visual Basic, when it encounters small numbers, performs an integer multiplication by default. Since an integer is limited to 32767, the product exceeds the limit.

What's the solution? Tell Visual Basic to use another data type. Suppose you change 111 to 111.0 and run the program again. No more overflow this time. Notice that Visual Basic changes 111.0 to 111#. This suffix tells Visual Basic to use the double-precision data type. When operands of different precision levels are involved, Visual Basic goes by the highest-precision type.

An addition operation may also trigger a similar situation. Consider the following two statements:

```
    Print 1000 + 32000
    Print 1000 + 33000
```

The first will trigger an error, but not the second. In the first example, all the numbers are within an integer's limit, so Visual Basic treats the sum as an integer. When the sum exceeds the limit, the error results. In the second case, Visual Basic sees the last number as larger than the integer limit and switches to a long-integer operation.

So, when you encounter the overflow error, add a suffix such as #, &, @, and so on to go by a higher-precision data type. You can also use a type-conversion function such as CDbl to do the same thing. This will be covered in Chapter 7.

New Data Types

VB4 added four data types: **Byte**, **Boolean, Date,** and **Object**; VB5 has also added
the **Decimal** type. Byte and Boolean are discussed below. Date will be covered in
Chapter 7 when we discuss time functions; Object will be explained in Chapter 9.

Byte is the equivalent of type *char* in C; it consumes least resources. A Byte
variable may be suitable as a variable to control a For-Next loop. Consider this
procedure:

```
Private Sub Command1_Click()
    Dim I As Byte
    For I = 1 To 10
        Print I
    Next
End Sub
```

It works fine as long as the ending value does not exceed 255 and you don't go
from a higher value to a lower one. Consider this scenario:

```
    For I = 10 To 1 Step -1
        Print I
    Next
```

This will lead to the *Overflow* error because a Byte variable cannot hold a
negative value. This limits a Byte variable's usefulness.

A **Boolean** variable can be only **True** or **False**. Although there are only two
possible values, it takes up 2 bytes; it is thus not as economical as a Byte
variable. You can easily use Byte to replace Boolean on most occasions.

In the procedure below, we declare Num to be Boolean. If we assign 0 to it, it is
False. It is True if any other numeric, positive or negative, is assigned. A "0"
(in quotes) is False and a "123" is True; numbers are treated as numerics even
though they are in quotes. On the other hand, a text string in quotes will lead to
the *Type mismatch* error.

```
Private Sub Command1_Click()
    Dim Num As Boolean
    Num = 123
    Print Num      'True
End Sub
```

A Boolean True value evaluates to -1, not necessarily the number you assign to it.
The following statement, inserted at the end of the above procedure, will print

122 because Num evaluates to -1. So don't use Boolean variables to store numeric data unless you don't mind being short changed.

```
Print Num + 123                '122
```

The **Decimal** data type is new in VB5. You cannot declare it using this word. You can only convert a Variant to this type by using the **CDec** function. Since it uses 12 bytes, you get more precision in a long number.

```
Private Sub Form_Click()
    Dim Num1 As Variant
    Dim Num2 As Double
    Num1 = -1.33333333333333 / 777777
    Num2 = -1.33333333333333 / 777777
    Print "Variant", Num1
    Print "Double", Num2
    Num1 = CDec(Num1)
    Print "Decimal", Num1
End Sub
```

In the above procedure, the first Num1 holds a Variant. It produces the same result as Num2 holding a Double value. When Num1 is converted to a Decimal, however, a longer number is displayed, as shown in Figure 5.9.

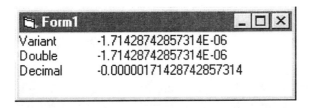

Figure 5.9   Converting a Variant to a Decimal

The Array Function

Table 5.2 shows that a Variant variable in VB4/5 can be used to store more data types than before. One useful addition is the array type. You can now use an undeclared variable (if Option Explicit is not on) or one declared as a Variant to store an array—by using the **Array** function to assign elements. This feature in effect restores the old Basic command pair of DATA...READ. Here is an example:

```
Private Sub Command1_Click()
    Dim Arr As Variant
    Dim I As Integer
    Dim Sum As Single

    Arr = Array(69, 87, 92) 'assign array elements
    For I = 0 To 2
        Sum = Sum + Arr(I)       'accumulate
    Next I
    Print "Total = "; Sum; " Average = "; Sum / I
End Sub
```

We use the Array function to assign three array elements to Variant Arr. If we did not use Array here, we would be required to do the declaration and assignment as follows:

```
Dim Arr(2)       'or ReDim
Arr(0) = 69
Arr(1) = 87
Arr(2) = 92
```

Regardless of which technique you use to declare an array, the **TypeName** and **VarType** functions can tell you it's an array. The following statements will return the output shown in the comments:

```
Print TypeName(Arr)         'Variant()
Print VarType(Arr())        '8204
```

You can optionally put an extra pair of parentheses after the array name, such as in the second example above.

According to Table 5.2, the VarType function is supposed to return 8192 for an array. Where does 8204 come from? It's from 8192 + 12. The second number signifies the data type of the array's elements as Variant. If we had used As Integer to declare our array, we would have gotten 8194 (8192 + 2). So you can use this technique to determine an array elements' data type.

If you use the Array function to create an array, the elements are all Variants and there is no way to change that. If you use the Dim or ReDim statement to declare an array, you can specify a data type, such as this:

```
ReDim Arr(2) As Byte
```

In that case, the TypeName and VarType functions will return different names and numbers.

DRILL

Choose from the following list to answer questions 9-15:
a. 0 or more bytes, b. 2 bytes, c. 4 bytes, d. 8 bytes

____ 9. Variant
____ 10. String
____ 11. Single
____ 12. Long
____ 13. Integer
____ 14. Currency
____ 15. Double

____ 16. When Option _____ is specified, all variables must be explicitly declared before they can be used.

____ 17. The _____ function returns a number to show what type of data a variable is holding.

____ 18. The last line below will print -100. True or false?

    Dim varX As Boolean
    varX = -100
    Print varX

____ 19. The last line below will lead to:

    Dim varX As Byte
    varX = -1
    Print varX

    a. 1
    b. -1
    c. 0
    d. Overflow error

PRACTICE

■ 8. What is Visual Basic's default data type? Explain.

■ 9. If you declare varX to be a Currency variable, what is the consequence?

■ 10. How can you declare variable varX to be a string that can store up to 10 characters? What happens if you assign to it a string that is more or fewer than 10 characters?

■ 11. What is the consequence of declaring varX as a String variable without specifying a length?

■ 12. What happens if you execute the following statement?

```
Print 100 * 360
```

■ 13. How do the following two statements differ?

```
Print 1000 + 32000
Print 1000& + 32000
```

■ 14. What does the following procedure output to the screen? Explain.

```
Private Sub Form_Click()
    Dim Arr, I, varX
    Arr = Array("a", "b", "c")
    For I = 0 To 2
        varX = varX & Arr(I)
    Next I
    Print varX
End Sub
```

■ 15. What items are output to the screen by the following lines?

```
Private Sub Form_Click()
    Dim varA As Variant
    varA = 123
    Print TypeName(varA)
    varA = Array(1, 2, 3)
    Print TypeName(varA)
End Sub
```

OPERATORS AND PRECEDENCE

Operators are various symbols that are used with variables and values to form expressions. Visual Basic uses several kinds of operators. We discuss each in the sections below.

Arithmetic Operators

Visual Basic's **arithmetic operators** closely resemble those found in arithmetic and other modern programming languages (or spreadsheet programs such as Excel or 1-2-3).

Operators have their order of precedence. The arithmetic operators and their precedence order are shown in Table 5.3.

Table 5.3   Arithmetic operators and their precedence

Operator	Precedence	Purpose
( )	1	Grouping
^	2	Exponentiation
-	3	Negation
* /	4	Multiplication, division
\	5	Integer division
Mod	6	Modulo arithmetic
+ -	7	Addition, subtraction

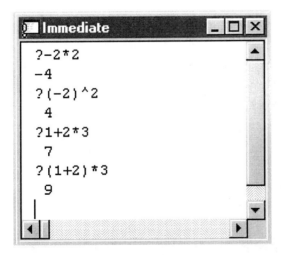

Figure 5.10   Output by various operators

When operators of equal **precedence** are encountered, evaluation goes from left to right. If they are not of equal precedence, the order in Table 5.3 applies. Figure 5.10 shows some examples. In the first example, ^ has higher precedence than -, so 2^2 is evaluated first. In the second example, since the parentheses have higher precedence, the effect is the same as (-2) * (-2). The sample principle applies to the last two examples.

The grouping operators can be used to make your code more readable without affecting an expression. In the following line, the parentheses are redundant but may make the statement easier to read:

```
If (varA > 1) Or (varB < 10) Then . . .
```

The \ and **Mod** operators can respectively extract the quotient and remainder of a division operation. Figure 5.11 shows some examples. Both operators perform whole-number operations. When floating-point operands are encountered, the numbers are rounded to whole numbers before evaluation. In our second example, 6.7 is rounded to 7 before evaluation.

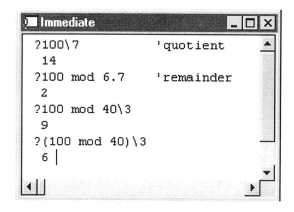

Figure 5.11   Mod and \ operators

TIP: The & and + Operators

You can use either & or + to manipulate numerics and text strings. They may produce different results and some confusion.

The & operator always concatenates two operands (regardless of their type) and returns a Variant, which, depending on the content, could be used as a numeric or text string.

The + operator can lead to a number of results. Here are some general observations:

- When both operands are text strings, such as numbers entered in text boxes or input boxes, it concatenates the strings and returns a Variant.

- When one operand is a numeric and the other a number in a text box or input box, it performs an addition and returns a numeric.

- When both operands are numerics, it performs an addition and returns a numeric, which conforms to the higher-precision data type. For example, if you add an integer to a double, the resulting number will be a double.

- If one operand is a numeric and the other a text string (not a Variant), it may trigger the *Type mismatch* error. In this situation, you can use the **Val** function to convert a text-string number to a numeric.

- If a text box number is assigned to a numeric variable, it becomes a numeric. On some rare occasions, you may get the *Type mismatch* error; in that case, use the Val function to convert the number to a numeric.

Normally, when you type code, there is no need to put a space before or after an operator such as a + or *; Visual Basic will automatically insert the additional spaces. On the other hand, you must add the necessary spaces when an **&** is involved. If not, Visual Basic will assume that you are using & to designate a long integer, not as a string-concatenation operator.

Comparison Operators

Comparison operators, shown in Table 5.4, are often used with program-flow statements such as If and While to control program flow. Here is an example:

```
If varA = varB Then
    . . .
End If
```

Here Visual Basic evaluates to see whether the conditional expression is true or false. If true, then the statements in the block (before End If) are executed; otherwise, they are ignored.

Other languages use different signs for assignment and equality testing; C, for example, uses = for assignment and = = (two equal signs) for equality testing. Since the = sign is used to test equality and make assignments, wouldn't Visual Basic be confused? Not likely. When used with If, While, or Print, Visual Basic knows it is equality testing. When = is placed between a variable and a value, with or without being preceded by **Let**, it signifies assignment, such as:

```
varA = 1
Let varA = varB
```

All the comparison operators have equal precedence. If multiple operators are used, evaluation goes from left to right.

Table 5.4   Comparison operators

Operator	Purpose
=	Equality
< >	Inequality
<	Less than
>	Greater than
< =	Less than or equal to
> =	Greater than or equal to

Logical Operators

Logical operators are often used to combine multiple expressions to form complex conditional statements. Table 5.5 shows the logical operators available in Visual Basic. The first three are commonly used in code. Here are some examples:

```
If varA > 10 And varB < 1 Then . . .
If varA < 5 Or varB >= 1 Then . . .
Command1.Enabled = Not Command1.Enabled
```

In the first example, if both expressions are true, then the statement is true. In the second, if either expression is true, then the statement is true. In the third, the property value is simply reversed, changing from True to False or False to True—depending on the original state.

You can use a single variable and the **And** operator to limit testing to a specific range. The following statement is true if A's value is in the 1-10 range:

```
If varA <= 10 And varA >= 1 Then . . .
```

Since both expressions are true, the statement as a whole is true. Do not use **Or** in this situation. If Or is used here, the statement will be true regardless of what value A has.

You can use And or Or to do **bitwise comparison**. Before we discuss further, enter in the Immediate window the following statements and see what happens:

```
?9 and 10
?9 or 10
```

The first returns 8 and the second 11.

In a bitwise comparison, And returns true (1) when both comparable bits are true; but Or returns true if either bit is true. Consider the following binary numbers (middle) and their decimal equivalents (right):

```
            varX = 1001 = 9
            varY = 1010 = 10
  varX And varY  = 1000 = 8
  varX Or varY   = 1011 = 11
```

In the And operation, only one bit is true. In the Or operation, in contrast, three bits are true.

The last three operators in Table 5.5 are used mostly for binary math. For related online help, type a specific word (such as Xor) in the Code window and press F1.

Table 5.5   Logical operators

Operator	Purpose
And	Inclusion
Not	Negation
Or	Inclusive Or
Eqv	Equivalence
Imp	Implication
Xor	Exclusive Or

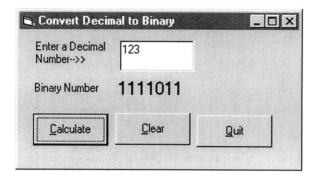

Figure 5.12   Showing the binary equivalent of a decimal number

We can use the And operator to convert a decimal number to its binary equivalent. (If you are not familiar with the binary numbering system, consult Appendix B.) Figure 5.12 shows our interface to let the user enter a decimal number in the txtDec text box and click the Calculate button to show its binary equivalent in the lblBin label control's caption.

(5DEC2BIN.FRM)
```
Private Sub cmdCalculate_Click()
    Dim DecNum As Integer
    Dim BinBit As String
    Dim BinNum As String
    Dim Pow As Integer

    If txtDec.Text = "" Then
        Beep          'if no entry
        txtDec.SetFocus
        Exit Sub      'get out
    End If

    DecNum = txtDec.Text
        'the decimal value to be converted to binary

    Do
        If DecNum And 2 ^ Pow Then
        'using And to match each bit from right to left
            BinBit = "1"
            'if both bits are 1
        Else
            BinBit = "0"
        End If

        Pow = Pow + 1    'get the next bit
        BinNum = BinBit & BinNum
        'add each bit to the beginning of binary string
```

```
        Loop While DecNum >= 2 ^ Pow
            'loop back if number >= the latest bit
        lblBin.FontSize = 15
        lblBin.Caption = BinNum
End Sub

Private Sub cmdClear_Click()
    txtDec.Text = ""       'clear display
    lblBin.Caption = ""
    txtDec.SetFocus        'for another entry
End Sub

Private Sub cmdQuit_Click()
    End
End Sub
```

In the cmdCalculate_Click procedure, we try to test each binary digit from right to left to determine whether it's 0 or 1. The following line is crucial:

```
    If DecNum And 2 ^ Pow Then
```

The Pow variable starts out with 0, so 2 ^ Pow returns 1. Then Pow becomes 1, 2, 3, and so on; so 2 ^ Pow becomes 2 (10 in binary), 4 (100), 8 (1000), and so on. Each Anding operation returns a 0 or 1, as shown below:

```
    1111011 And 1 = 1
    1111011 And 10 = 1
    1111011 And 100 = 0
    1111011 And 1000 = 1
    1111011 And 10000 = 1
    1111011 And 100000 = 1
    1111011 And 1000000 = 1
```

The left number (1111011) before And is the binary equivalent of 123 (the user-supplied decimal number). Our Anding operations simply try to find the 0's and 1's. The 0 and 1 characters are concatenated in reverse order, thus producing a string of characters that represent the way the supplied decimal number is stored internally in your computer.

Boolean Logic

Although they seem sophisticated, computers operate on simple **Boolean** logic. This term comes from George Boole, a 19th century Irish logician and mathematician. Boolean logic operates on two states: on or off, yes or no, true or false.

This forms the very foundation of binary math. A computer operates on the principle of binary math because it can handle only 1 (electricity on) or 0 (off).

Many features in Visual Basic use Boolean properties of true or false. When you set a property value, such as Visible, you can choose True or False from the Properties window. You can also use these values in code to change properties. Visual Basic is programmed to recognize these keywords, which you cannot use as variable names.

Instead of using True or False, you can use simpler numbers -1 (True) and 0 (False) in code. The two statements below are thus equivalent; both will disable a command button:

```
Command1.Enabled = False
Command1.Enabled = 0
```

You can use True or -1 to negate 0 or False. Actually, you can use any nonzero number, instead of -1, to represent True; Visual Basic will accept them all. So either statement below will reverse either statement above:

```
Command1.Enabled = True
Command1.Enabled = -1
```

In a comparison operation, the specified condition is a **Boolean expression**; Visual Basic treats such an expression as either true or false. So when combined with statements such as If or While, the returned value of True or False determines the course of action.

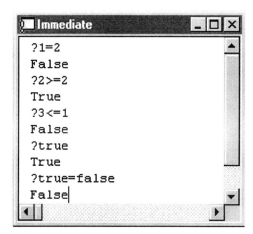

Figure 5.13   Boolean expressions

Figure 5.13 shows a variety of conditional (Boolean) expressions. In all cases, Visual Basic returns either True or False.

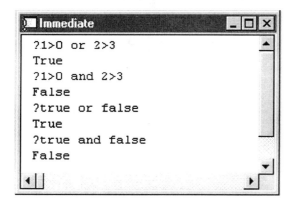

Figure 5.14   Compound Boolean expressions

Figure 5.14 shows conditional expressions involving the logical operators And and Or. Again, Visual Basic returns only two values, True or False.

TIP: True or False

True and False may represent different values depending on the data type involved. Consider this example; it will produce Figure 5.15.

```
Private Sub Form_Click()
    Dim X1 As Byte
    Call TestTF(X1)
    Dim X2 As Integer
    Call TestTF(X2)
    Dim X3 As Variant
    Call TestTF(X3)
    Dim X4 As String
    Call TestTF(X4)
End Sub

Sub TestTF(PassVal)
    PassVal = True
    Print TypeName(PassVal), PassVal
    PassVal = False
    Print TypeName(PassVal), PassVal
End Sub
```

To save space, we've put the repeatedly called routine in a separate general procedure. You don't have to understand this; Chapter 8 will explain how to do it. Here we're simply trying to show how True and False are treated due to different data types. If you want to try it, just type the lines in the Code window as shown here.

Byte X1 has the value of 255 when assigned True. But this value can be treated as -1. If we add 1 to it, the result will be 0. A numeric (Integer, Long, Single, Double, or Currency) variable treats True and False as -1 and 0.

Notice Variant X3 is changed to Boolean. When a variable is a String, Boolean, or Variant, True and False are treated as text strings. If you use Val to convert them to numeric values, 0 will show up.

Form1	
Byte	255
Byte	0
Integer	-1
Integer	0
Boolean	True
Boolean	False
String	True
String	False

Figure 5.15   True and False values

TIP: Multiple Assignments

If you've learned C, you'll know that you can make multiple assignments in a single statement. You can do the same thing in Visual Basic, but beware of the difference. Consider this procedure:

```
Private Sub Command1_Click ()
    Dim varA As Integer
    Dim varB As Integer
    Dim varC As Integer

    varA = 1: varB = 2: varC = 3
    varA = varB = varC = 10
```

```
      Print varA, varB, varC      '0  2  3
End Sub
```

varB and varC will retain their original values, but varA will be assigned 0 (for false). The expressions after the first = are treated as Boolean and each evaluated separately from right to left. First, varC = 10 evaluates to False. Then varB = False evaluates to False again. This last False is then assigned to varA.

In this situation, the variable on the left side of the first = sign will be assigned either True or False. In the following statement, varA will be assigned True:

    varA = varB = 2

Since varB = 2 evaluates to True, this value is assigned to varA.

DRILL

_____ 20. The $(1 + 2) / 3$ expression returns _____ .

_____ 21. The expression $100 \backslash 3$ returns _____ .

_____ 22. The expression 100 Mod 3 returns _____ .

_____ 23. The following statement prints _____ to the screen.

```
Print 1 + 2 = 3
```

_____ 24. If varA is greater than varB, the following statement returns _____ .

```
Print varA <= varB
```

PRACTICE

■ 16. How do the / and \ operators differ?

■ 17. How do the \ and Mod operators differ?

■ 18. What numbers are printed to the screen by these statements? Why?

```
Print 100 Mod 40 \ 3
```

```
Print (100 Mod 40) \ 3
```

19. Assuming that varA holds the value of 10 and varB that of 9, explain the following statements:

```
If varA >= varB Then . . .
If varA = 10 And varB > varA Then . . .
```

20. What does the following statement do?

```
Text1.Visible = Not Text1.Visible
```

21. What does the following statement output to the window?

```
Print 1 + 11 Mod 3
```

22. In the following program, what will the last two statements print?

```
Private Sub Form_Click ()
    Dim varA, varB, varX
    varA = 123
    varB = "123"
    varX = varA + varB
    Print varX
    Print VarType (varX)
End Sub
```

23. What happens if the first statement in the above procedure is changed to:
    varA = "123"

24. In the following statements, what values are assigned to varX and varY? Explain.

```
varX = 1 Or 2
varY = 1 And 2
```

VARIABLE SCOPE AND LIFETIME

A variable has a scope (the area where it can be visible and available) and lifetime (or longevity; how long it will last). A programmer must pay close attention to these issues.

Suppose you have two command buttons, Command1 and Command2, on a form and nothing else. You now attach the following code to these buttons:

```
Private Sub Command1_Click ()
    Dim varA As Integer
    Dim varB As Integer
    Dim varC As Integer

    varA = 10
    varB = 20
    varC = varA + varB
End Sub

Private Sub Command2_Click ()
    Dim varC As Integer
    Print varC
End Sub
```

Suppose you now run the program and click Command1 and then Command2. What do you get? Nothing. Even though we assign 30 to variable varC, the Print statement in the second procedure is not aware of its existence.

Suppose you add a new line as shown below:

```
Private Sub Command1_Click ()
    Dim varA As Integer
    Dim varB As Integer
    Dim varC As Integer

    varA = 10
    varB = 20
    varC = varA + varB
    Print varC
End Sub
```

What happens if you run the program again and click Command1 and then click Command2? The screen shows 30 for the first time, but nothing for the second time.

The above example shows that the variables in the first procedure are **local to** that procedure and not accessible to another procedure. Other procedures cannot "see" them. These variables exist only during the time when the first procedure is in execution. They are erased when execution leaves that procedure.

How can we make variables last longer and accessible to other procedures? Declare them at the form or higher level. In our example, if you want both procedures to access variable varC, go to the form's **Declarations section** and make a declaration there. Follow these steps:

1. Go to the Code window and click the **(General)** object from the Object
    box. The Procedure box should show **(Declarations)**. If Full Module
    View is on, press Ctrl+Home to go to the top of the Code window.

2. Type the line as shown in Figure 5.16. If Option Explicit is on, you can
    place your entry below or above it. If there is a separator line, you can
    type below it; the line will automatically move below your entry.

3. Delete varC in the two procedures' Dim statements.

4. Run the program and click the two buttons.

Now when you click Command2 after clicking Command1, 30 appears on the
screen. The Command2 procedure is now able to access the value of a variable
assigned in another procedure. Our variable varC is now declared at the form
level, which can be accessed by all the procedures in that form. The variable also
exists as long as the form is loaded.

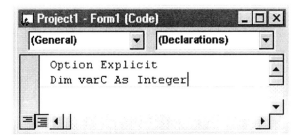

Figure 5.16   Declaring a variable in the Declarations section

In step 3 above, if you do not delete the original varC in the two procedures, you
are maintaining three different variables. The two local variables can hold two
different variables, which may be different from the module-level variable. When
execution goes to a procedure, the local variable **shadows** (prevails over) the
variable of the same name but declared at a higher level. You should normally not
declare two variables of the same name at two different levels. But if you do, you
should remember the rule of shadowing.

If you are familiar with only the original Basic, you may be a stranger to the
concept of variable scope. In Basic, a variable is accessible throughout a program
and you need not worry whether a variable exists at a particular time. Modern
programming languages have changed that.

In Visual Basic, you can declare variables at the:

- Global level
- Module level (Public or Private)
- Procedure level

A **global variable** has a global scope; it is visible and accessible throughout the entire application. A **module-level variable** can be Public (accessible from another module) or Private (limited to the current module). A procedure-level variable is **local** and has the narrowest scope. Figure 5.17 shows how these variables differ in scope.

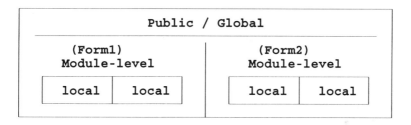

Figure 5.17   Scope of variables

Public or Private

You can use a series of keywords to declare variables. These include: **Dim**, **Public**, **Private**, and **Global** (Public and Private are available since VB4). Some are restricted to specific areas but others are allowed in several places. Keep the following rules in mind:

- A Public or Global variable declared at the module level of a **standard module** (see below) has an application-wide scope and longevity. That is, this variable exists when the application runs and it can be seen by the procedures in all modules; you can use it in any module without specifying where the variable is defined or located.

- A Public variable declared at the module level of a **form module** (or **class module**) has a module-wide scope and longevity. This variable exists when the form runs and it can be used in all the procedures in that form. From another module, you can also reference the variable by specifying the module. From Form1, you can access variable X2 in Form2 like these:

```
Print Form2.X2 + 123      'output to Form1
Form2.Print Form2.X2      'output to Form2
```

- A Private variable declared at the module level of any type of module can be accessed only from that module. In that case, the above statements are illegal because Form1 cannot see Private X2 in Form2. The resulting error message shown in Figure 5.18 shows that X2 is not visible from outside Form2. This error will not appear if X2 is a Public variable.

- The word Global is allowed only in the Declarations section of a standard module. This word was available in previous versions and is still legal in VB5.

- Use only Dim in a procedure. Public or Private is not allowed here. Dim is permitted at the module level; it is the same as Private.

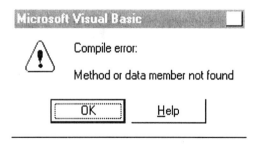

Figure 5.18   Referencing a Private variable in another module

A **standard module** is a separate file with the BAS extension name; like any Basic file, it contains only declarations and procedures, but no form or other objects. It can be created by choosing **Add Module** from the Project menu. When you exit, you will be prompted to save it as a file separate from a form file; Visual Basic will automatically supply the BAS extension. Once saved, it becomes a component of a project; it can also be incorporated into another project. A standard module typically contains procedures that can be called from other procedures. We will return to this subject in Chapter 8.

The practice of using local variables gives us some advantages:

- The same variable name can be used in several procedures. It will serve different purposes and hold different values on different occasions.

- A local variable does not create side effects. A higher-level variable may linger on longer than you want and cause trouble in unintended areas.

- Local variables make efficient use of memory. They exist (and consume memory) only when needed. They do not take up memory unnecessarily.

There are occasions when you want variables to be visible to multiple procedures. You can then declare these variables at a higher level. But you should limit those occasions whenever possible.

Static Variables

A **static variable** is another kind of variable you need to be aware of. It differs from the regular (also known as automatic) variable in a major way. A static variable's value persists (is not erased) between calls whereas a regular variable's value is erased once execution leaves the area where it is declared. When execution returns to the area where a static variable is declared, the variable becomes visible (it is not visible outside of the area) and its previous value (if any) becomes available. You have the option of using Dim to declare a regular variable or using it without declaration (when Option Explicit is not on). On the other hand, a static variable must be declared with the **Static** statement and it can be done only inside a procedure. If a variable is used without declaration, it is a Variant in type, local in scope, and transient (nonstatic) in persistence.

Figure 5.19 shows how variables behave when they are declared at different levels. There are two local variables declared as shown below. The FormVar variable is declared at the form level.

```
Dim FormVar As Integer   'form-level variable

Public Sub Form_Click()
    Dim LocalVar As Integer
    Static StaticVar As Integer

    LocalVar = LocalVar + 1
    StaticVar = StaticVar + 1
    FormVar = FormVar + 1        'module-level variable
    Print "local: " & LocalVar,
    Print "Static: " & StaticVar,
    Print "form: " & FormVar,
    Print
```

```
End Sub
```

After running the program and clicking the form five times, Figure 5.19 shows the result. Each time the form is clicked, the static and module-level variables increment their values by 1. On the other hand, the local variable starts with no value and ends with 1; when the procedure ends, the value is erased.

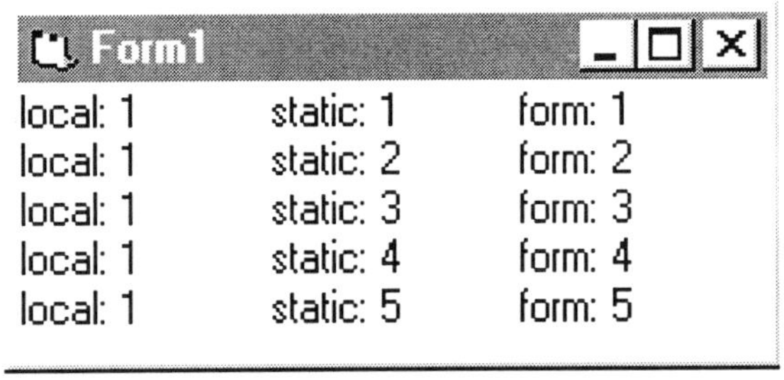

```
Form1                              _ □ X
local: 1      static: 1       form: 1
local: 1      static: 2       form: 2
local: 1      static: 3       form: 3
local: 1      static: 4       form: 4
local: 1      static: 5       form: 5
```

Figure 5.19   Showing variable behavior

In our example, both the static and module-level variables have the same value. However, keep in mind that they are quite different. Since our static variable is declared in a procedure, it is a local variable. It is visible only when the procedure is executed.; other procedures are not aware of it. Our module-level variable, on the other hand, is visible from any procedure within the form; if the variable is manipulated in other procedures, its value will change and affect other procedures.

If you wish, you can add Static before a procedure (after Private or Public) to make all the variables in that procedure static. After that, any undeclared local variables or those declared with Dim become static.

CONSTANTS

A **constant** is a name (identifier) which is assigned a permanent value. Unlike a variable whose value can change during program execution, a constant's value cannot change.

There are two kinds of constants:

- Intrinsic or system-defined
- Symbolic or user-defined

We cover these in the two separate sections below.

Intrinsic Constants

Intrinsic constants are embedded in an application. They have specific names and each has been assigned a specific value. Users can use these names where their built-in values are needed. Consider this example:

```
Text1.ForeColor = vbRed
Text1.Text = vbRed
```

The first statement will set Text1's text color to red. The second will display 255 in the text box. Here vbRed is a constant which has a built-in value of 255. This value cannot be changed. If you try (assigning a value to vbRed), you'll get the error shown in Figure 5.20.

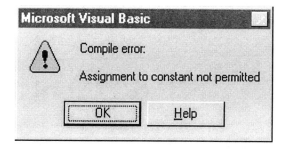

Figure 5.20   Changing a constant's value

VB5's intrinsic constants have names starting with vb in lowercase followed by meaningful names. This naming convention makes it relatively easy for you remember and use them. How do you know what names to use? Get the online help. There are two ways to do that.

First, search the online help's Index tab for *constants*. You'll see a long list of subitems, each of which contains a list of constants. Suppose you select the *color* subitem. A topic will show all the constants representing various color values. There is also a See Also jump at the top left of this topic. Clicking it shows a long list of other items which will lead to more constants. Another item to look for is *Visual Basic constants*. It will give you two choices: VB or VBA. Each will give you numerous constants.

The **Object Browser** is another possible tool to get constants. The previous version used to provide lots of constants. The current version gives you a limited number of constants in the VBA library.

Take advantage of the **IntelliSense** feature. As you type something in the Code window and don't know what constants to use, just press **Ctrl+J** or **Ctrl+spacebar**; you can also choose **View | List Properties/Methods** or click the corresponding (first) button on the **Edit toolbar**. This feature was explained in Chapter 2.

Symbolic Constants

Visual Basic allows a programmer to use a symbol to represent a constant value. A text string (variable name) that is assigned a constant value is known as a **symbolic constant** or manifest constant.

C programmers commonly use uppercase for symbolic constants. Visual Basic users were previously advised to follow that practice. However, like anything else in Visual Basic, you can use either case. VB4/5 online (and printed) examples use mixed case like other variables.

The procedure shown below demonstrates how we can use PI to represent the value 3.1416. Once defined (declared and assigned a value) with the **Const** statement, it becomes permanent and can no longer be reassigned another value during run time. If you try to assign another value, the error shown earlier in Figure 5.20 will appear as well.

```
Private Sub Form_Click ()
    Dim Area As Single, Circ As Single
    Dim Rad As Single
    Dim Msg As String
    Dim Title As String
    Const PI As Single = 3.1416   'define constant
    Msg = "Enter the radius"
    Rad = InputBox(Msg)        'get radius from user
    Circ = 2 * PI * Rad        'calc circumference.
    Area = PI * Rad ^ 2        'calc area
    Msg = "circumf   = " & Circ & vbCr
    Msg = Msg & "area       = " & Area & vbCr
    Title = "Radius = " & Rad
    MsgBox Msg, , Title        'show result
End Sub
```

In the procedure we use another intrinsic constant, namely **vbCr** (carriage return). You can replace it with **vbLf** (linefeed) or **vbCrLf** (combining both). You can

Line-feed

also use **Chr(13)** and/or **Chr(10)** to replace either. The last two were the only ones allowed in previous versions before VB4. VB5 has added still another option, namely **vbNewLine**, which is the equivalent of vbCrLf.

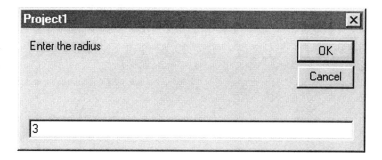

Figure 5.21   An input box prompting for an entry

After a value is supplied (Figure 5.21), a message box shows the result (Figure 5.22).

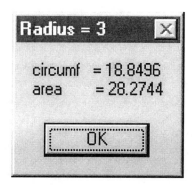

Figure 5.22   A message box showing output

Since we define PI inside a procedure, another procedure cannot access it. If you want to make it available to more areas, define it at a higher level. You can also add **Public** or **Global** before Const in the Declarations section of a standard module (not a form module) to create a **global constant**. You can also use one Const to declare multiple constants, with each separated from another by a comma, such as below:

Public const gsPI As single

```
Const Num = 123.34, FName As String = "Joe"
```

A constant value is either a numeric or string literal, or an expression that will return either. It's legal to specify a data type, but you must specify it right after a variable name and before the = sign.

WRITING READABLE CODE

When writing Basic code, you should make your code more readable by following some or all of the following rules:

- Put only one statement in a line.

- Use a blank line to separate dinstinct groups.

- Indent a related group to the same distance from the left margin.

- Add comments at proper locations.

None of these rules are mandatory; your program will work regardless of how you space or indent the code lines. These arrangements may be a bother if all you want is a simple program.

On the other hand, when you write a lengthy and complex program, these rules will serve you well. They enable you to more quickly find and correct errors. That makes you more productive.

Basic code usually consists of statements, each of which occupies a separate line. Although it is not advisable, it is legal to put several statements in one line, with a colon separating one from another. Here is an example:

```
Print "Line 1" : Print : Print "Line 2"
```

Here we cram three statements in one line. The reason why this is not a good idea is that such lines are difficult to read, debug, and document.

Blank lines and indentations are ignored when your code is executed. They will not interfere with the code's performance in any manner. You are thus free to add any of these at your own discretion.

Comments provide explanations about some complex instructions. They can help you debug your program in the future. You may know what you are doing when you write a tricky statement. But you may be puzzled when you look at it a month later. Having a comment to go by will certainly go a long way in reminding you of the original purpose.

A comment can be added after an apostrophe ('), which can be in a separate line or at the end of a code line. Anything after the apostrophe is ignored during the code's execution. If there are multiple apostrophes in one line, anything after the first one is ignored.

You can also add remarks after the **Rem** command. This must be placed at the beginning of a line. Anything after this command is also ignored.

Comments appear in green color on a color monitor. This color can be changed in the Editor Format tab after choosing Tools | Options.

You can **comment out** an instruction to debug code. Just add an apostrophe at a proper place to prevent the execution of a line or the portion after the apostrophe. This might help you isolate bugs. Try to comment out various lines and run the program to see whether it will still behave the same way.

A long logical line can be broken up with a **line continuation** character. It consists of a space and an underline (_) placed at the end of a line. When such a character is encountered, the line below will be treated as the same line. No comment is allowed after the character.

TIP: Block Indent and Comment

You can select a group of text lines and do something to all of them, including indenting/outdenting or commenting them out.

There are many ways to select text lines, as discussed in Chapter 2. Don't forget to take advantage of the blank vertical area on the left side of the Code window. You can click or double-click this area to quickly select a number of lines.

If you want to indent multiple adjacent lines, just select them and press **Tab** (indent) or **Shift+Tab** (outdent) to move the entire group to the desired position.

When text lines are selected, you can use the **Comment Block** command to add an apostrophe at the beginning of each line to comment it out. You can also use **Uncomment Block** to remove these initial apostrophes.

These commands are available only from the **Edit toolbar**. This toolbar also has Indent and Outdent. The toolbar can be shown or hidden via View | Toolbars.

DRILL

_____ 25.   You can put a comment after:
  a.   Rem
  b.   '
  c.   :
  d.   all of the above
  (e.) both a and b

_____ 26.   Suppose you declare varX at the form level and assign to it the value of 100 in the Command1_Click procedure. Then you declare varX in the Command2_Click procedure and assign 200. The value of varX is _____ when you click Command2.

_____ 27.   A variable that has the broadest scope is known as a _global_ variable.

_____ 28.   A file containing only declarations and procedures, but no form or object, is known as a _standard_ module.

_____ 29.   A local variable that retains its value between calls is known as a _static_ variable.

_____ 30.   You use the ____ PublicConst ____ statement to define a symbolic constant that is visible throughout an application.

PRACTICE

■ 25.   Explain the two ways of adding comments to a program.

■ 26.   Is it legal to put two or more statements in one line? Explain.

■ 27.   What is a standard module?   _page 252_

■ 28.   What is a local variable and how does it behave?

■ 29.   What is a global variable and how can you create it?

■ 30. What is the Declarations section?

■ 31. What's an intrinsic constant. Cite some examples.

■ 32. What does the Const statement do?

■ 33. In the two procedures below, if you click Command1 and then Command2, what is printed to the screen? Explain why.

```
Private Sub Command1_Click ()
    Dim FName As String
    FName = "Joe"
    Print FName
End Sub
```

Joe

```
Private Sub Command2_Click ()
    Dim FName As String
    Print FName
End Sub
```

Nothing

■ 34. What happens to the above if Fname is declared at the form level but not inside each procedure? Explain.

Joe Joe

CHAPTER PROJECT

A. (5DIVIDE.FRM)

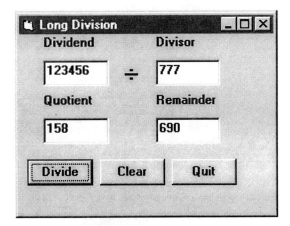

Figure 5.23   Long division results

This program lets the user enter two numbers and produces a quotient and a remainder (Figure 5.23). When Clear is clicked, the numbers in the four text boxes are cleared and the focus goes to the top-left box for another entry. (The ÷ sign is copied from a word processor to the label's edit field in the Properties window. If you cannot do it, use the / sign instead.)

B. (5COST.FRM)

Augie's Auto Body Shop charges $42 per hour for labor, plus costs of parts. Tax is 7%. Create an application (Figure 5.24) that will let the user enter hours and part costs and then calculate the result.

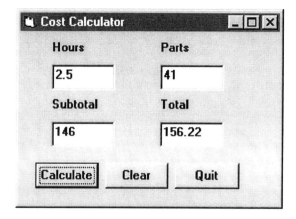

Figure 5.24   Calculating costs

C. (5ADDNUM1.FRM)

This program lets you add up numbers. Clicking Enter leads to an input box. After a number is entered, it appears in the text box, whose MultiLine property is set to True and ScrollBars to Vertical. Another input box also appears for another entry. If no entry is made, the text box adds the last two lines shown in Figure 5.25. Use For to create 100 loops; use Exit For to exit the loop when no entry is made.

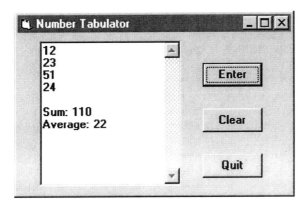

Figure 5.25   Adding up numbers

D. (5ADDNUM2.FRM)

Modified from the previous question, this project displays entries in two columns separated with the Tab character (Chr(9)). In each loop, the user is prompted to enter an item name and a number. When no entry is made, the last three items (Figure 5.26) are calculated and displayed. The tax amount is based on 7%. Print sends the text box's contents to the printer.

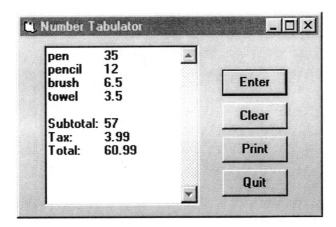

Figure 5.26   Two-column numbers

E. (5CALC.FRM)

Write a Form_Click procedure that will do the following:

1. Prompt the user to enter a number (operand 1).

2. Prompt the user to enter an operator (+, -, *, /). If no operator is entered, a beep is made and a message box appears; the procedure is then exited.

3. Prompt the user to enter a number (operand 2).

4. Calculate and display the result (Figure 5.27).

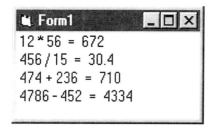

Figure 5.27   Calculated output

F. (5ABOUT.FRM)

Write a procedure that will display an About window as shown in Figure 5.28. Use the Now function to display the current date.

Figure 5.28   An About window

G. (5ADDLIST.FRM)

Write a program (Figure 5.29) that will behave as follows:

1. When Enter is pressed at run time, the Add command is executed.

2. Executing Add leads to an input box placed at 3000 twips from the top and 4000 twips from the left.

3. Entering a number in the input box adds it to the list box (left).

4. The sum of the numbers appear in the text box (top).

5. When no number is entered in the input box, the input box is cleared.

6. Pressing Esc executes Quit.

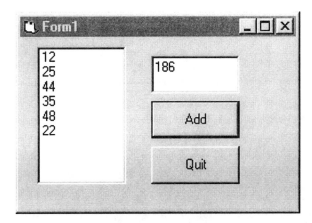

Figure 5.29   Adding numbers to a list box

FUN AND GAME

A. (SPIRAL1.FRM)

This program draws a spiral pattern (Figure 5.30) from the top right corner inward counterclockwise.

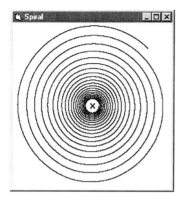

Figure 5.30   Spiral line

```
Private Sub Form_Load()
    Show            'show form
    Dim I As Single
    Dim Radius As Single
    Dim X As Single
    Dim Y As Single
    Dim Pi As Single

    Caption = "Spiral"
    Width = ScaleHeight      'square form
    Width = 2 * ScaleHeight - ScaleWidth
    Pi = 4 * Atn(1)              'get pi value
    Scale (-1, 1)-(1, -1)     'custom scale
        'from 1/4 pi pos till 20 circles
    For I = Pi / 4 To 40 * Pi Step Pi / 5000
        Radius = Exp(-I * 0.02)    'decrease radius
        X = Radius * Cos(I)  'get x axis
        Y = Radius * Sin(I)  'get y axis
        PSet (X, Y)       'set point
    Next I
    CurrentX = -0.02   'move left
    CurrentY = 0.04    'move up
    Print "X"          'bull's eye
End Sub
```

B. (SPIRAL2.FRM)

Modified from the previous, this program uses Circle instead of PSet to draw a pattern shown in Figure 5.31.

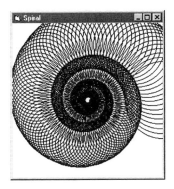

Figure 5.31   Snail

```
Sub Form_Load ()
    Show            'show form
    Dim I As Single
    Dim Radius As Single
    Dim X As Single
    Dim Y As Single
    Dim Pi As Single

    Caption = "Spiral"
    Width = ScaleHeight      'square form
    Width = 2 * ScaleHeight - ScaleWidth
    Pi = 4 * Atn(1)             'get pi value
    Scale (-1, 1)-(1, -1)      'custom scale
        'from inside out, counterclockwise
    For I = 8 * Pi To 0 Step -Pi / 50
        Radius = Exp(-I * 0.12)  'decrease radius
        X = Radius * Cos(I)  'get x axis
        Y = Radius * Sin(I)  'get y axis
        Circle (X, Y), Radius / 2
    Next I
End Sub
```

You can change many values to create different effects. Figure 5.32 is the result of changing the initial I value to 8 and dividing Radius by 4 in the Circle statement. The lines creating a square form are also commented out. A little more tinkering will produce Figure 5.33.

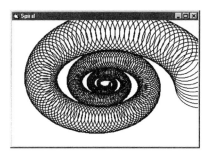

Figure 5.32   Winky slinky

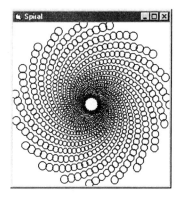

Figure 5.33   Mayan beads

Chapter 6
Program Flow

TOPICS

KEY TERMS

Branching   A programming technique of directing program execution to another location without returning to the original point. If, Select Case, and sometimes GoTo are used for branching.

Control structure   A block of statements that are executed if a condition is met. Such a block usually starts with If, Do, For, For Each, With, or Select Case. There are various ways to end each block.

Line label   A text string ending with a colon and placed at the beginning of a line. A line label has to conform to the rules for a variable name. A line label (or a line number) marks a location for GoTo or GoSub to branch execution to.

Line number   An integer placed by itself in a separate line or at the beginning of a code line. Like a line label, it is used as a place marker for branching.

Looping   A programming technique of repeatedly executing a group of statements until a condition is met. For and Do are commonly used for looping. The For Each and With commands are also useful in maneuvering some items.

Nesting   A programming technique of including a command or block of statements inside another command or control structure. After the nested command is finished, control returns to the nesting command.

When you learn to speak a foreign language, you need to learn its grammar. When you write a Basic program, you need to follow its syntax. This chapter covers some elementary concepts of how computer programs are put together and explores the commands used in Visual Basic to control the flow of program execution.

STRUCTURED PROGRAMMING

We use *program flow* or *control flow* to characterize the way a computer program is executed. This can be compared to the way physical objects move, such as air flow, water flow, or traffic flow. Just as you can control physical objects' flow, you can control program flow as well.

Programmers use **control structures** to control program flow. There are three types of control structures:

- Sequence
- Decision
- Iteration (looping)

Sequence denotes a straight-line pattern of flow; instructions are executed sequentially or linearly, one line after another. **Decision** involves a selection of two or more options to maintain or alter the sequential flow. **Iteration** repeats execution of a block of instructions.

Sequential execution was the only way you could control program flow in the old Basic. Any deviation requires complicated and difficult-to-follow sequence. It is still valid in Visual Basic, such as the following example:

```
Private Sub Command1_Click ()
10   Dim varX
20   varX = InputBox("Enter a number; use ""end"" to end.")
```

```
30   If varX = "end" Then GoTo 60
40   Print varX
50   GoTo 20
60   Print "That's all."
End Sub
```

This is an example of what is commonly called *spaghetti code*. It's like a pile of cooked spaghetti all intertwined, difficult to tell where one piece begins or ends.

This same procedure can be rewritten in a structured manner as shown below:

```
Private Sub Command1_Click ()
    Dim varX
    Do         'begin loop
      varX = InputBox("Enter a number; _
      use ""end"" to end")
      Print varX
    Loop Until (varX = "end")   'loop back if not end
    Print "That's all."
End Sub
```

This is the way a modern programming language works. If you have some rudimentary knowledge of computing, you can clearly see the pattern of program flow. If not, you'll learn from a section below.

Writing a computer program can be compared to writing an English essay. Treated as an essay, sentences in our first example are lumped together in a pattern whose logic is not immediately apparent. In the second example, related sentences are grouped into a distinct and well-constructed paragraph with a clear beginning and end. This is much easier to read and revise.

Visual Basic, being a modern computer language, comes with a full repertoire of commands to control program flow. Before we proceed to them, a few basic terms and concepts require explanation.

There are three common flow-control techniques: branching, looping, and nesting.

Branching directs execution to another location without returning to the original point. You can use If or Select Case to branch to one of two or more blocks of instructions. You can also use GoTo alone (for unconditional branching) or in combination with If (for conditional branching). You'll normally use If where options are limited to two or three and depend on Select Case where there are more options.

Looping repeats an operation a number of times. The statements in the loop are executed repeatedly—until a specified condition is met. After that, execution continues in the lines below the loop.

Nesting includes a command or block of statements inside another command or control structure. For example, a For can nest another For; the second For is placed between the first For and its matching Next. A procedure can also nest (call) another procedure. Unlike branching, nesting returns control to the original (nesting) command—after the nested command completes its course. Chapter 8 explains how you can create procedures and functions and make one call another.

This chapter concentrates on the techniques of looping, branching, and condition testing. We will cover various commands used for these purposes, including the following:

```
If-Then
Select Case
For-Next
For Each-Next
Do-Loop
With-End With
Goto, GoSub
```

These commands will be explained separately and accompanied by simple examples. The latter half of the chapter will provide more complex examples involving the use of two or more of these commands.

DECISION WITH IF-THEN

The If-Then command is as old as the first programming language. It is the simplest way to test a condition and then determine what the program is going to do next.

An If-Then control structure can be put in one line or constructed in a complex way taking up multiple lines. A one-line example may look like this:

```
If varA > 0 Then varA = varA + 1
```

If the conditional (Boolean) expression (varA > 0) evaluates to True, then the variable increases its value by 1. The above example can be rewritten this way:

```
If varA > 0 Then
   varA = varA + 1
End If
```

In such a multiline structure, an End If statement is required. Without this statement, the error shown in Figure 6.1 will appear.

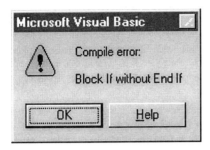

Figure 6.1 **Using If with no End If**

One way to avoid this error without using End If is to use the **line continuation character**. As explained in Chapter 5, it consists of a space followed by an underscore placed at the end of a line. So the following is legal:

```
If varA > 0 Then _
    varA = varA + 1
```

A more complex control structure can be arranged this way:

```
If condition1 Then
    statements
[ElseIf condition2 Then
    statements
ElseIf condition3 Then
    statements
Else
    statements]
End If
```

An optional **ElseIf** clause gives you another opportunity to test another condition. If the first condition is true, then it is ignored; otherwise, test the second, and so on. The optional **Else** clause is executed if all the above conditions are not true. If you wish, an If can **nest** another If, as shown in below.

```
Private Sub Command1_Click () '--Listing 1--
    Dim varA As Integer
    Dim varB As Integer

    varA = 1 : varB = -2
    If varA > 0 Then
```

```
        If varB > 0 Then
            Print "Both positive"
        Else
            Print "Second negative"
        End If
    ElseIf varB < 0 Then
        Print "Both negative"
    Else
        Print "First negative"
    End If
End Sub
```

Here we try to determine whether the two variables' values are positive or negative. So we use If-Then to go through a series of tests. If the first variable is positive, then another If-Then structure tests to see whether the second variable is positive. That could lead to the "Both positive" or "Second negative" output. If the first variable is negative, then the above lines are ignored and execution goes to the ElseIf statement. Here we provide another test. If the second variable is found to be negative, then "Both negative" appears; otherwise, "First negative" is the result. (Our procedure can't handle situations where either or both variables may have 0 value. That would lead to 9 possible alternatives. This scenario can be better handled by Select Case discussed in the next section.)

Our program could be simplified as shown below. The price we pay here is that we can no longer identify which one is negative.

```
Private Sub Command1_Click ()
    Dim varA As Integer
    Dim varB As Integer

    varA = 1 : varB = 2
    If varA > 0 And varB > 0 Then
        Print "Both positive."
    ElseIf varA < 0 And varB < 0 Then
        Print "Both negative."
    Else
        Print "One negative."
    End If
End Sub
```

An If statement tests to see whether an expression is true or false. In addition to the If keyword, you need to provide variables, values, and/or comparison operators. The remarks in Chapter 5 dealing with comparison operators can be applied here as well.

The following statements will all test true and thus return a True value:

```
    If True Then . . .
```

```
If 1 Then . . .
If 10 = 10 Then . . .
```

These will test false and return False:

```
If False Then . . .
If 0 Then . . .
If 10 = 11 Then . . .
```

If a conditional expression tests false, the statement(s) after Then are ignored. If ElseIf or Else follows, more testing is done and, depending on the result, a relevant block may or may not be executed.

TIP: Conditional Expressions

The **If** command (and other flow-control commands discussed later in this chapter) can use one of the following as an argument:

- A variable alone
- An expression combining variables and operators
- An equation involving an equal sign

If only a variable is involved, the If command determines program flow based on whether the variable has the value of 0 (false) or nonzero (true).

If an expression is involved, the result produced by the arithmetic operation determines the course of action. Consider this example:

```
If varX Mod 2 Then . . .
```

The statement is false if varX holds an even number (divisible by 2) because the arithmetic operation returns a 0 value. If varX has an odd number, the statement is true because the returned value is a nonzero.

If an equation is involved, both sides of the = sign must have an equal value for the If statement to be true. The following statement is true if varX is divisible by 2:

```
If varX Mod 2 = 0 Then . . .
```

If varX has an odd number, the statement is treated as follows:

```
If 1 = 0 Then . . .
```

Since the two sides are not equal, the statement is false.

An If-Then-Else control structure is most useful if options are limited to two or three. The code below provides a good example. Here the user is prompted to enter a text string (Figure 6.2). The entry is then compared with the string assigned to another variable. The If statement tests to see whether the two strings match and prints one or the other message.

```
Private Sub Command1_Click ()
    Dim Pass As String
    Dim varX As String

    Pass = "Open Sesame"
    varX = InputBox("Enter the password:")
    If Pass = varX Then
        Print "You got it."
    Else
        Print "You failed."
    End If
End Sub
```

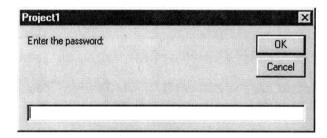

Figure 6.2   Prompting for a user input

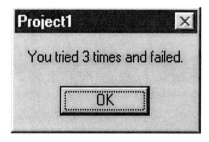

Figure 6.3   The message box after three failed tries

We can modify our program to limit the number of tries in entering a password. In the procedure below, we added a static variable to keep track of the number. After try 3, a message box pops up, shown in Figure 6.3. Upon clicking OK, the program ends.

```
Private Sub Command1_Click ()
    Dim Pass As String
    Dim varX As String

    Dim Title As String, Msg As String
    Static Tries As Integer 'keep track of try #

    Tries = Tries + 1          'increment try #
    Pass = "Open Sesame"
    Title = "Try #" & Tries
    varX = InputBox("Enter the password:", Title)

    If Pass = varX Then
        Print "You got it."
    Else
        Print "You failed."
    End If

    If Tries = 3 Then
        Msg = "You tried " & Tries & " times and failed."
        MsgBox Msg
        End       'end after try #3
    End If
End Sub
```

TIP: Case and String Comparison

By default, a string comparison operates in **Binary** mode and is thus case sensitive. The two compared strings must match not only in spelling but also in case. Otherwise, False will be returned. Here is an example:

```
Private Sub Form_Click ()
    If "Ace" = "ace" Then
        Print "true"
    Else
        Print "false"
    End If
End Sub
```

If you want a string comparison to be case insensitive, add the following in the Declarations section of the current form:

```
Option Compare Text
```

To add the text, go to the Code window's top portion (when Full Module View is on) and type the text as shown to change from the default **Binary** mode to **Text** mode. If you now run the program again, the two strings will be treated as equal.

Another technique is to use the **UCase** or **LCase** function to convert both strings to the same case before comparison. Our test line shown earlier could be rewritten this way:

```
If UCase(Pass) = UCase(varX) Then . . .
```

A practical application for the If command is in calculating wages. If a worker puts in 40 hours or less a week, his gross pay is the product of the hours multiplied by the hourly rate. If the hours exceed 40, then the additional hours are paid 1.5 times. A simple If-Else structure can handle this situation as shown in the procedure below.

```
Private Sub Form_Click ()
    Dim Hours As Single
    Dim Rate As Single
    Dim Gross As Single

    Hours = InputBox("Enter the hours")
    Rate = InputBox("Enter the pay per hour")

    If Hours <= 40 Then
        Gross = Hours * Rate      'regular
    Else
        Gross = Rate * 40 + Rate * (Hours - 40) * 1.5
    End If                        'overtime

    Print "hours = "; Hours       'output
    Print "rate = "; Rate
    Print "gross= "; Gross
    Print "------------------"
End Sub
```

This procedure produces the display shown in Figure 6.4. Each time you click the form, two input boxes will appear to prompt you for hours and pay rate. After you supply the second number, the screen shows three output items.

If you continue to click the form and enter the required numbers, the form will be filled up and the new entries will be invisible. If you intend to make many entries, place the **Cls** method at the beginning of the procedure. Every time the form is clicked, any previous display will be cleared first.

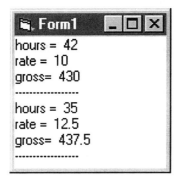

Figure 6.4   **Calculating gross pays**

This program will crash if you supply no number or click Cancel when an input box appears. You can set up a simple If-Then control structure to intercept such a situation. If either variable has no value, then the procedure is exited.

In situations where the available options are more than a few, an If-Then structure is no longer efficient. The Select Case command becomes a better alternative. This is discussed in the next section.

DECISION WITH SELECT CASE

The **Select Case** command is used to control program flow when there are multiple options. It follows this syntax:

```
Select Case test_expression
    Case expression1
        statements
    Case expression2
        statements
        . . .
    [Case Else
        statements]
End Select
```

The whole control structure must start with **Select Case** and end with **End Select**. The test expression is usually a variable whose value you want to match with any of the available Case expressions.

Each Case expression can contain the following:

- A list separated by commas
- The **To** keyword placed after a lower value and before a higher value
- The **Is** operator with comparison operators (use these with care)
- The same data type as the others

Let us use an example first. The procedure below shows a program soliciting a user input. Depending on the user input, a proper text string will be displayed in response.

```
Private Sub Command1_Click ()
    Dim varX As Variant

    varX = InputBox("Enter a letter or digit:")
    Select Case varX
        Case "a" To "z"
            Print "A lowercase letter."
        Case "A" To "Z"
            Print "An uppercase letter."
        Case "0" To "9"
            Print "A numeric digit."
        Case ""
            Print "You've entered nothing."
        Case Else
            Print "Not a valid entry."
    End Select
End Sub
```

The test expression placed after Select Case should normally be a variable whose value you want to test. You can also put an expression here on some occasions. If you do that, make sure you know what you are doing. Here is an example:

```
Select Case varX = 2
```

If varX has the value of 2, then the expression returns True, otherwise False. Do not consider this expression as assigning 2 to variable varX. Keep that in mind when you consider the following expression:

```
Select Case varX = InputBox("Enter a number:")
```

This can return only True or False. If you enter a number (in the input box) that matches the existing value of varX, the expression evaluates to True, otherwise False. Contrary to what you might expect, Visual Basic does not evaluate varX alone in this situation.

If you want limited options, the **Mod** operator can be very useful because it returns only a remainder. Here is an example:

```
Select Case varX Mod 3
```

No matter what the value of varX is, the expression can return only 0, 1, or 2.

The **Case Else** clause is optional. It is executed if the test expression does not match any of the Case expressions. It is similar to the Else clause in an If-Then control structure.

The **To** keyword lets you specify a range of values. When you use To, the value before it must be lower than the value after it. Here are two examples:

```
Case 0 To 9
Case -10 To -1
```

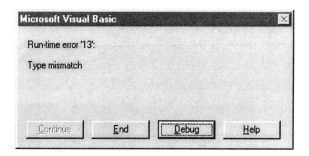

Figure 6.5   Mixing data types in Case expressions

If you reverse the two numbers in either case, you may sometimes trigger an error shown in Figure 6.5. Even if no error is triggered, such an expression is meaningless and will match nothing.

The error shown in Figure 6.5 may also appear if you mix data types in Case expressions. If a test expression contains a Variant variable, no error will be triggered. On the other hand, if the variable has been declared as a specific data type such as an integer, you cannot include a text string in a Case expression.

You can put a list of items after Case, with each separated from another by a comma. Here a comma serves a role similar to that of Or in the If command. Here is an example:

```
Case "zebra", "bird", "cat" To "hog"
```

The list does not require any particular order, except when To is involved.

Using a list in Case expressions can be an efficient way to handle numerous choices. In the following example, each Case expression provides a list of options.

```
Private Sub Command1_Click ()
    Dim varX As Variant

    varX = InputBox("Enter a character:")
    Select Case varX
        Case "a", "e", "i", "o", "u", "A", "E", _
            "I", "O", "U"
            Print "Vowel"
        Case "1", "3", "5", "7", "9"
            Print "Odd number"
        Case "2", "4", "6", "8"
            Print "Even number"
        Case Else
            Print "Don't know"
    End Select
End Sub
```

Select Case provides a speedy choice of multiple options. Unlike multiple If-Then statements, each of which is individually tested, Select Case finds a match and, after executing the statements in the matching block, leaves the control structure right away. When a match is found, the statements below the Case expression are executed until the next Case keyword is encountered. All other Case expressions, even if they match the test expression, are ignored. There is no need to do anything extra to break out of the structure.

Sometimes you can use the **To** keyword to include all the possible values in a bracket. Here is an example:

```
Case 80 To 89.99
    Print "Your grade is B."
```

If the variable turns out to have an odd value of 89.991, the above expression will not include it. The following expression, on the other hand, will not miss anything. Here anything from 80 to below 90 will be included.

```
Case Is < 90 And varX >= 80
    Print "Your grade is B."
```

The Is keyword cannot be placed after And. Reversing the two expressions before and after And will give you the *Expected: expression* error at design time and *Syntax error* at run time.

The following is legal but meaningless, because it will match anything.

```
Case Is < 90, Is >= 80
```

The following Case expression is also legal but meaningless. It won't work because of the absence of the **Is** operator. It will match only when varX has the value of 0. That's true regardless of how you arrange the two expressions or what you put after each comparison operator.

```
Case varX < 90 And varX >= 80
```

Beware of the following odd situation. This Case expression will be matching, resulting in a serious error.

```
varX = 75
Select Case varX
Case Is > 90 And varX >= 80
    . . .
```

The Tabulating Data section below has more details about the above situations.

If you need to do something more complex after finding a match, you can nest another Select Case structure or call a procedure (Chapter 8).

NOTE   if you use an input box or text box to supply a number, you may need to use the **Val** function to convert it to a numeric. If not, the entry may be matched to a comparable numeric or text string, thus producing an unpredictable result.

DRILL

Answers for questions 1-3:
    a. looping, b. nesting, c. branching

_____ 1.   Putting an If-Then structure inside another If-Then.

_____ 2.   Executing a block of statements a number of times.

_____ 3.   Diverting execution to another location without returning.

_____ 4.   The following statement is illegal because End If is missing. True or false?

```
If varX = 0 Then varY = 0
```

_____ 5.   The following statement is legal. True or false?

```
If varX > 100 Then Print "big" Else _
Print "small"
```

___1___ 6.   The following statement is legal. True or false?

```
If varX > 100 Then Print "big": _
Else Print "small"
```

___F___ 7.   If the user enters 100 in the following input box, it will be printed to the screen. True or false?

```
varX = InputBox("Enter a number:")
If varX > "99" Then Print varX
```

___F___ 8.   If the user enters any number except 0 in the following input box, it will be printed to the screen. True or false?

```
varX = InputBox("Enter a number:")
If varX = True Then Print varX
```

___T___ 9.   If the user enters any number except 0 in the following input box, it will be printed to the screen. True or false?

```
varX = InputBox("Enter a number:")
If varX Then Print varX
```

___F___ 10.   The following statement will match any number between 70 and below 80. True or false?

```
If varX < 80 Or varX >= 70 Then Print varX
```

___F___ 11.   If the user enters 95 in the following input box, it will match the first Case clause and be printed to the screen. True or false?

```
varX = InputBox("Enter a number:")
Select Case varX
    Case "90" To "100": Print varX
```

___d___ 12.   The following expression will match:
a. 0,   b. -1,   c. 70 to below 80,   d. anything

```
Case Is < 80, Is >= 70
```

___b___ 13.   If varX has the value of 2, Select Case varX = 2:
a.   directs execution to Case 0
b.   directs execution to Case -1
c.   directs execution to Case 2

d.   is illegal

Q 14.   If varX has the value of 4, Select Case varX Mod 2:
a.   directs execution to Case 0
b.   directs execution to Case -1
c.   directs execution to Case 2
d.   is illegal

F 15.   The following expression is illegal because the items are not arranged in alphabetic order. True or false?

```
Case "zebra", "bird", "cat" To "hog"
```

____ 16.   The following expression will trigger an error because the items before and after the To keyword are not arranged in alphabetic order. True or false?

```
Case "zebra", "bird", "hog" To "cat"
```

____ 17.   In the following expression, all the alphabetic letters will be included. True or false?

```
Case "a" To "z"
```

____ 18.   In the following expression, only alphabetic letters will be included. True or false?

```
Case "A" To "z"
```

____ 19.   The Case Else clause is not required in a Select Case control structure. True or false?

PRACTICE

■ 1.   What role does the following statement play?

```
Option Compare Text
```

■ 2.   Do the following two blocks produce the same result?

```
(1)   If varX > 100 Then Print "big" Else Print "small"

(2)   If varX > 100 Then Print "big"
      If varX < 100 Then Print "small"
```

3. In the following procedure, use Select Case to replace If.

```
Private Sub Command1_Click ()
    Dim Age As Integer
    Age = InputBox("Enter your age:")
    If Age < 21 Then Print "You're a minor."
    If Age >= 21 And Age <= 65 Then Print _
        "You're an adult."
    If Age > 65 Then Print "You're a senior citizen."
End Sub
```

4. Explain what the following expression does.

```
If varX <> "yes" Or varX <> "no" Then . . .
```

5. Write a Form_Click procedure that will let the user click the form window to show an input box, prompting for a number. If the user enters a number below 100, "small" is printed to the screen. If 100-200 is entered, "medium" is printed. And if a number larger than 200 is entered, "big" is printed.

6. Write a Form_Click procedure that will let the user click the window to show an input box, prompting for a character. If an alphabetic character (uppercase or lowercase) is entered, "alphabet" is printed to the screen. If the user enters a number, "digit" is printed. And if neither of the above is entered, "invalid" is printed.

7. Compare the following two expressions:

```
Case Is < 90, Is >= 80
Case varX < 90 And varX >= 80
```

8. What will happen to the following expression?

```
Select Case varX Mod 5
```

9. Explain what the following procedure is supposed to do. What happens if the last Case clause includes a single z and Z?

```
Private Sub Command1_Click ()
    Dim LName As String
    LName = InputBox("Enter your last name:")

    Select Case LName
    Case "a" To "h", "A" To "H"
        Print "You're in group 1."
    Case "i" To "p", "A" To "P"
        Print "You're in group 2."
```

```
        Case "q" To "zzzz", "Q" To "Zzzz"
            Print "You're group 3."
        End Select
    End Sub
```

■ 10. Is the following expression valid? Explain.

```
    Case 0 To -10
```

LOOPING WITH FOR-NEXT

The **For-Next** command is one of the most common and versatile tools available in every programming language. You can use it to repeatedly execute a block of statements until a specified condition is met.

In its most complete form, this command follows this syntax:

```
    For counter = start To end [Step increment]
        statements
        [Exit For]
        statements
    Next [increment]
```

When such a control structure is encountered, your program will behave this way:

* Check the starting and ending values and determine whether to enter the loop.

* If the loop is entered, assign the specified starting value to the counter and remember the ending and step values.

* Execute the statements in the loop structure.

* If the condition for exit exists, then execute Exit For to leave the loop.

* Increment the counter by the specified step value. If the counter's value does not exceed the ending value, the statements are executed again.

* When the counter's value exceeds the ending value, end the looping operation and execute the lines below Next.

Here is an example:

```
For I = 1 to 10
   Print I
Next I
```

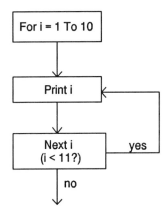

Figure 6.6   The flow of a For loop

The counter, which is also known as a **control variable**, starts out with the value
of 1. Since we did not specify a step value, it defaults to 1. Since the beginning
value is lower than the ending value, the loop is entered. The Print statement
sends 1 to the screen. The Next statement increments the counter value by 1 and
returns execution to the Print statement again. This process continues until the
counter exceeds 10, the ending value. This pattern is illustrated in Figure 6.6.

You can make the counter count downward rather than upward as we did earlier.
To do that, the beginning value must be higher than the ending value and the step
value must be negative. Here is an example:

```
For I = 10 to 1 Step -2
   Print I
Next I
```

Here we want to print 10, 8, 6, 4, and 2. We now decrement the counter value
by 2 in each looping operation. In this example, you must specify a step value,
which must also be negative. If these conditions are not met, the statement inside
the loop is ignored.

You can also use expressions for the counter's beginning and ending values, as
well as the step value. Fractional values can also be used as well. If 0 is the step

value and the condition for entering the loop is met, the loop becomes infinite and will lead to an *Overflow* error in our example. If we did not use Print in this situation, the program would be stuck.

The counter variable after Next is optional. If not specified, Visual Basic knows how to match it to the closest loop. Adding this counter, however, is a good idea. Your code becomes self-documenting and is easier to read and debug.

A For can **nest** another For, which in turn can nest another one. Here is such an example:

```
Private Sub Form_Click ()
    Dim I As Integer
    Dim J As Integer
    Dim K As Integer

    For I = 1 To 9
        For J = 1 To 9
            Print I * J;         'print on same line
            K = K + 8            'increment 8 tab stops
            Print Tab(K);        'move print head by 8
        Next J
        K = 0                    'go back to new position
        Print                    'a new line
    Next I
End Sub
```

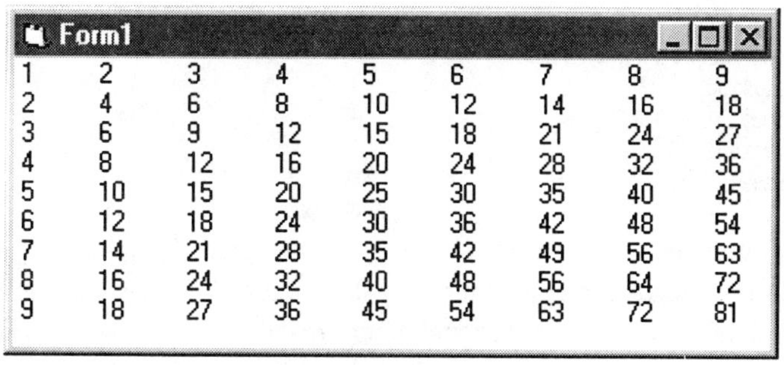

Form1								
1	2	3	4	5	6	7	8	9
2	4	6	8	10	12	14	16	18
3	6	9	12	15	18	21	24	27
4	8	12	16	20	24	28	32	36
5	10	15	20	25	30	35	40	45
6	12	18	24	30	36	42	48	54
7	14	21	28	35	42	49	56	63
8	16	24	32	40	48	56	64	72
9	18	27	36	45	54	63	72	81

Figure 6.7 **Using Tab to align text**

When a For nests another For, the nested (inner) loop completes its cycle before the nesting (outer) loop increments to its next step. In our example, when I has the value of 1, J goes from 1 through 9. Then I has the value of 2, and J goes through 1 to 9 again. This goes on until J finishes its 9th loop. By that time, I has

gone through 9 rounds, for each of which J goes through 9 rounds. By the time
the outer loop is through, 81 (9 x 9) numbers have been printed to the screen.

The **Tab** function determines the print head's column position on the screen. What
we do here is to move the print head to a specific column position before printing
each new number. The result is that the first digit of each number is eight
columns from the first digit of the previous number, as shown in Figure 6.7. Tab
was discussed in Chapter 5.

If you intend to exit a For-Next loop prematurely, use the **Exit For** command.
Here is an example:

```
For I = 1 to 100
    Print I * I
    If I = 5 then Exit For
Next I
```

Even though the ending value is 100, this loop will go through only five rounds.
At that point, the If statement becomes true, and the loop is terminated
prematurely.

LOOPING WITH FOR EACH-NEXT

There is a new (available since VB4) looping command called **For Each-Next**. It
is useful to maneuver arrays or collections (see Chapter 9). It follows this syntax:

```
For Each element In group
    statements
    Exit For
    statements
Next element
```

If there is at least one element in the group, the loop is entered. Looping
continues until the last element is encountered or the condition for Exit For is
true. The element name after Next is optional as in For-Next.

Here is a simple example:

```
Private Sub Form_Click()
    Dim Sum As Integer
    Dim Score As Variant
    Dim Counter As Integer
    Dim Test(5) As Integer

    Test(1) = 68
```

```
        Test(2) = 75
        Test(3) = 89
        Test(4) = 93
        Test(5) = 84

    For Each Score In Test()    '() optional
        Sum = Sum + Score       'add up sum
        Counter = Counter + 1   'track total count
    Next Score
    Print Sum / (Counter - 1)   'show average
End Sub
```

We use an array and assign five test scores to it. The For Each loop goes through each element from the beginning to the end; there is no need to use a control variable as in a For-Next loop. Since we specify six elements (0 to 5 by default) in the array, the For Each-Next loop goes through six rounds. When the loop is finished, the counter has the value of 6. So we need to subtract 1 in order to calculate the average score.

We can delete the parentheses after Test in the For Each line without affecting anything. We can also change Dim to ReDim to declare an array.

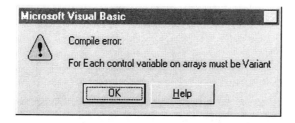

Figure 6.8   The control variable in a For Each loop

The element variable, Score in our example, must be a **Variant**. If we change it to another data type, Integer for example, Figure 6.8 will show up.

We can use the new **Array** function to simplify our procedure. The following code will produce the same result:

```
Private Sub Form_Click()
    Dim Sum As Integer
    Dim Score As Variant
    Dim Counter As Integer
    Dim Tests As Variant
```

```
        Tests = Array(68, 75, 89, 93, 84)
        For Each Score In Tests
            Sum = Sum + Score        'add up sum
            Counter = Counter + 1  'track total count
        Next Score
        Print Sum / Counter 'show average
End Sub
```

Notice that we did not subtract 1 from the counter value in the last line. Since there are only five elements in the array, the For Each-Next loop repeats only five times. The counter's final value is 5.

The multiplication table in the previous section can be modified by using the Array function for For Each-Next as follows. It will produce the same result as shown in Figure 6.7.

```
Private Sub Form_Click()
    Dim Num1 As Variant
    Dim Num2 As Variant
    Dim arrNum As Variant

    arrNum = Array(1, 2, 3, 4, 5, 6, 7, 8, 9)

    For Each Num1 In arrNum
        For Each Num2 In arrNum
            Print Num1 * Num2; Tab(Num2 * 8);
                'print product, move print head by 8
        Next Num2
        Print              'a new line
    Next Num1
End Sub
```

Chapter 9 will cover more issues related to arrays and the Array function.

TABULATING DATA

Sometimes you want to divide a group of numbers into a number of brackets. The commands explained so far can be combined to do that. Suppose you have a number of test scores and you want to know how many fall in each bracket (Figure 6.9). If you are familiar with the flow-control commands, this is a relatively easy task.

In the procedure below, we first put all the scores in an array. We then use a For Each loop to go through each element in the entire array. In each iteration of the loop, we use a Select Case control structure to place each element in a proper bracket. The Cnt array then increments accordingly. For example, if a score is in the 90s bracket, the first Case clause is executed. That adds 1 to Cnt(0). If a score is in the 80s bracket, then Cnt(1) is incremented instead.

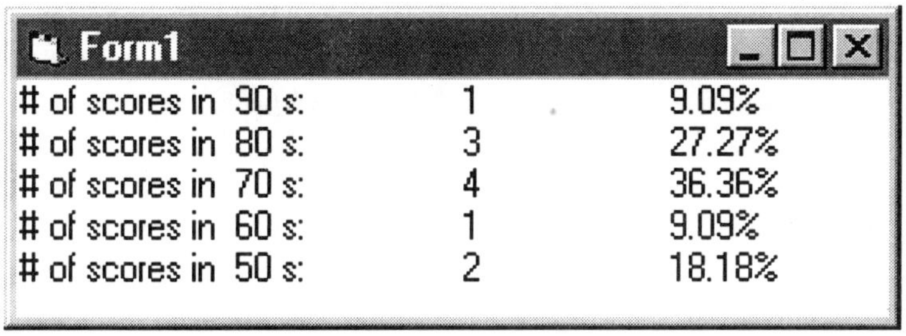

```
 Form1                          _ □ ×
# of scores in  90 s:      1          9.09%
# of scores in  80 s:      3          27.27%
# of scores in  70 s:      4          36.36%
# of scores in  60 s:      1          9.09%
# of scores in  50 s:      2          18.18%
```

Figure 6.9   Tabulating a group of numbers

(6TABULATE.FRM)

```
Private Sub Form_Click()
    Dim Grades As Variant
    Dim Score As Variant
    Dim I As Integer
    Dim Totcase As Integer
    Dim Cnt(4) As Integer

    Grades = Array(67, 98, 78, 76, 86, _
    79, 84, 56, 48, 80, 76) 'all the test scores

    For Each Score In Grades
        Select Case Score    'tabulate each bracket
        Case Is >= 90
            Cnt(0) = Cnt(0) + 1
        Case Is >= 80
            Cnt(1) = Cnt(1) + 1
        Case Is >= 70
            Cnt(2) = Cnt(2) + 1
        Case Is >= 60
            Cnt(3) = Cnt(3) + 1
        Case Else
            Cnt(4) = Cnt(4) + 1
        End Select
        Totcase = Totcase + 1
    Next Score

    For I = 90 To 50 Step -10
        Print "# of scores in "; I; "s:   "
    Next I      'print leftside labels

    CurrentY = 0            'move print head to top
    For I = 0 To 4
```

```
            Print , , Cnt(I), Format(Cnt(I) / Totcase _
            * 100, "#.00"); "%"      'calc % for each
                'print in 3rd & 4th columns
        Next I
End Sub
```

In the last For loop, we divide the value of each Cnt array element to get the
percentage figure. So the last two columns in the output display the count value as
well as its percentage of the total count.

Notice the descending order in the Case expressions. We place the highest score
bracket at the top and the lowest at the bottom. This is necessary to produce
accurate results. When a 90 or higher score is tested, the first Case expression is
true, so the count for 90 increments by one. But then other Case expressions are
also true, what happens to them? They never have a chance. After the first
expression returns true, all the others below are ignored so their counts are
unaffected.

Suppose we use 70 as another example. The first two Case expressions test false
and are thus skipped. The third expressions tests true, so its count increments by
one. The expressions below are also true, but they are ignored so their counts are
not affected.

If you change this order, the program won't provide accurate counts. Suppose
your reverse the order, putting 60 at the top and 90 at the bottom. The result is
that every score 60 or higher will be counted in the 60s bracket. The 70-90
brackets will be completely ignored.

If you don't want to follow the rigid order and don't want to exclude any possible
option, you need to supply more complex Case expressions. Consider the
following modifications to the previous Select Case structure:

```
Select Case Score    'tabulate each bracket
Case Is < 80 And Score >= 70
    Cnt(2) = Cnt(2) + 1
Case Is < 90 And Score >= 80
    Cnt(1) = Cnt(1) + 1
Case Is < 70 And Score >= 60
    Cnt(3) = Cnt(3) + 1
Case Is >= 90
    Cnt(0) = Cnt(0) + 1
Case Else
    Cnt(4) = Cnt(4) + 1
End Select
```

It will produce the same result as before. The order is now completely scrambled. But the Case expressions are mutually exclusive, with each expression limited to a range and not overlapping another range.

If you know statistics, you can easily adapt the above procedure to get the median, variance, standard deviation, and a host of similar numbers. You can also use similar techniques to tabulate poll data, such as finding out how many (number and percentage) of Democrats favored Ross Perot for president.

LOOPING WITH DO-LOOP

Another way of looping is to use the **Do-Loop** command. It can appear in the following syntactic variations:

```
Do
    statements
    If condition Then Exit Do
    statements
Loop

Do
    statements
Loop While | Until condition

Do While | Until condition
    statements
Loop
```

In the first syntax, the loop is entered and the statements are repeatedly executed until the If statement is tested true. In the second, the loop is entered, but the condition is specified after the Loop command. In the third, the loop is entered and repeated only when the beginning conditional expression is true. In the first two, the loop is entered at least once; in the third, the loop may be completely ignored—if the initial condition is not true.

There is a difference between **While** and **Until**. While means as long as the condition is true; do it as long as the condition remains true. Until, on the other hand, means until the condition is met; do it if the condition is not met.

In the procedure below, we intend to let the user enter a password three times (Figure 6.10). The program ends if a correct password is entered within three tries. Here we use If to specify two conditions; if either condition is met, the loop is exited. The If statement becomes true when a matching (including case) password is entered or after the loop repeats three times. A message box appears at the end (Figure 6.11); the message differs depending on whether a matching password has been provided.

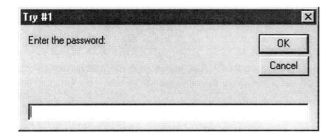

Figure 6.10   Prompting for an entry

Figure 6.11   Response after three tries

```
Private Sub Form_Click ()
    Dim Pass As String
    Dim varX As String
    Dim Msg As String
    Dim Title As String
    Dim Num As Integer

    Pass = "Open Sesame"
    Do
        Num = Num + 1                   'counter
        Title = "Try #" & Num        'title bar display
        varX = InputBox("Enter the password:", Title)
                'get user input, assign to x
        If varX = Pass Or Num = 3 Then Exit Do
                'exit if either condition met
    Loop        'loop back if condition not met

    If varX = Pass Then
        Msg = "You got it."
```

```
    Else
        Msg = "You failed."
    End If
    MsgBox Msg
End Sub
```

In the procedure below, we put the conditional expression at the beginning of the loop. In our case, this will work the same way as the previous arrangement. In some situations, the whole loop will be skipped if the initial condition is not met.

```
Private Sub Form_Click ()
    Dim Pass As String
    Dim varX As String
    Dim Msg As String
    Dim Title As String
    Dim Num As Integer

    Pass = "Open Sesame"
    Do Until varX = Pass Or Num = 3
        Num = Num + 1                    'counter
        Title = "Try #" & Num       'title bar display
        varX = InputBox("Enter the password:", Title)
                   'get user input, assign to x
    Loop          'loop back if condition not met

    If varX = Pass Then
        Msg = "You got it."
    Else
        Msg = "You failed."
    End If
    MsgBox Msg
End Sub
```

The following rearrangement will also work in our case. Unlike the previous case, this loop will be entered at least once.

```
    Do
        Num = Num + 1                    'counter
        Title = "Try #" & Num       'title bar display
        varX = InputBox("Enter the password:", title)
    Loop Until varX = pass Or Num = 3
```

The loop will also work if rearranged this way:

```
    Do While varX <> Pass And Num < 3
        Num = Num + 1                    'counter
        Title = "Try #" & Num       'title bar display
        varX = InputBox("Enter the password:", Title)
    Loop
```

What happens if we start our Do-Loop structure with the following line?

```
Do While varX <> Pass Or Num < 3
```

The loop will execute at least three times even if you supply the correct password. If no matching password is entered after the second round, the loop will continue indefinitely.

If you are familiar with an earlier version of Basic, you should be aware of the **While-Wend** structure, which is still available in Visual Basic. It follows this syntax:

```
While condition
    statements
Wend
```

This works the same as the Do While-Loop structure. The above syntax is the only one permitted with While-Wend; in contrast, Do-Loop gives you more choices.

LOOPING WITH WITH-END WITH

The **With-End With** statement can be used to maneuver objects. It can save you the trouble of having to repeatedly type the name of an object. Here is an example:

```
Private Sub Command1_Click()
    With Command1
        .FontSize = .FontSize * 2
        .Height = .Height * 2
        .Width = .Width * 2
        .Caption = "Larger"
    End With
End Sub
```

Each time you click Command1, you will double its height and width. Without using With, the same procedure would have to be written as shown below; the object's name would have to be repeated before each property.

```
Private Sub Command1_Click()
    Command1.FontSize = Command1.FontSize * 2
    Command1.Height = Command1.Height * 2
    Command1.Width = Command1.Width * 2
    Command1.Caption = "Larger"
End Sub
```

A With loop can nest another With loop. Here is an example:

```
Private Sub Command1_Click()
    With Text1
        .Height = .Height * 2
        .Width = .Width * 2
        .ForeColor = vbRed
        With .Font
            .Size = 20
            .Bold = True
        End With
        .Text = "Hello World"
    End With
End Sub
```

This procedure will double Text1's height and width, change its text color to red and font size to 20, and output a text string. The outer loop omits the object's name, and the inner loop omits an additional object name. Written the regular way, the font size would have to be specified this way:

```
Text1.Font.Size = 20
```

The With command can also be applied to a structure (user-defined type). This will be covered in Chapter 9.

BRANCHING WITH GOTO, GOSUB

Visual Basic continues to support three commands commonly used in earlier Basic versions: **GoTo, GoSub,** and **On-GoSub.** They were useful because they were the only tools available to steer program execution away from the sequential manner. These are no longer useful because the commands we have discussed earlier are more versatile and less prone to errors.

The use of the commands discussed in this section should be discouraged. They could lead to spaghetti code, as explained at the beginning of this chapter. Nevertheless, there may be some tight spots where GoTo may serve as the only logical and convenient way to get out. Also, when it comes to trapping run-time errors (Chapter 8), GoTo is the only choice you have.

GoTo can follow either syntax below:

```
GoTo LineNumber
GoTo LineLabel
```

A line number or line label marks a specific line which the GoTo command branches execution to. A **line number** is a unique number consisting of only numeric digits, just like a line number in Basic. A **line label** (different from a label control) is any text string that conforms to the rules of a variable name. A line label must have a colon (:) at the end, but a line number must not.

Both line number and line label must be at the beginning of a line. When you enter either item, it jumps to the left margin—regardless of the tab stop position you enter it. If you try to tab it to another position, it will go back to the left margin. A statement can also be placed to the right of a line number or line label.

Here are some examples of using GoTo:

```
GoTo SumLine          'branch to line label
If a > 10 GoTo 20     'conditional branching to number
. . .
SumLine:
. . .
20
. . .
```

The On-GoTo and On-GoSub commands were the most versatile tools in Basic. You could use them to pause program execution, present to the user a number of options, and branch execution to a proper line in response. They are, however, awkward and limited compared to Select Case explained earlier.

The procedure below shows a variety of ways to use GoSub. After the program is run and the form window is clicked, an input box appears. If the user enters 1, the last text string appears. The Sub procedure ends, but not the program. If 3 is entered instead, the same thing happens. Here we added Exit Sub to prevent the lines below from being executed.

If the user enters 2, the text string there is displayed and the Msg variable is assigned a new value. The **Return** command directs execution back to below the original branching line. A message box appears and the program ends.

```
Private Sub Form_Click ()
    Dim Msg As String
    Dim varX As String

    Msg = "Wrong choice!"
    varX = InputBox("Enter 1, 2, or 3:")
                            'get user selection
    On varX GoSub 1, 2, 3      'branching
    MsgBox Msg
    End
2
Two:
    Print "You have chosen 2 or Two."
    Msg = "That's all!"
    Return       'can't use with GoTo
```

```
Three:
3
     Print "You have chosen 3 or Three."
     Exit Sub
1
One:
     Print "You have chosen 1 or One."
End Sub
```

Notice that we purposely arranged the line numbers and labels in a disorderly way. This does not interfere with branching operation. Branching goes by specified line numbers or labels, not according to any specific order.

Since we place a line number and a line label at the beginning of each block of statements, our branching line could be written this way:

```
On varX GoSub One, Two, Three
```

As with any variable name, line labels can be in either case and not interfere with branching.

In the above procedure, you can replace GoSub with GoTo. In that case, you can no longer use Return to direct execution back to below the branching line. You need then to use something else, such as GoTo, to control program flow.

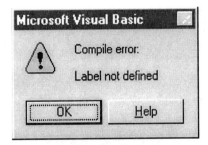

Figure 6.12   Branching to a label in another procedure

GoTo and GoSub cannot go beyond the current procedure. If you try to use either to branch execution to a line number or line label located in another procedure, the error shown in Figure 6.12 will appear. It shows that a line label is local in scope; a line label in one procedure is not visible to another procedure.

Another rule to remember is that line numbers and line labels must be unique within one procedure. If you use the same line number or line label the second time in the same procedure, the error shown in Figure 6.13 will appear. This won't happen if the duplicate is located in another procedure.

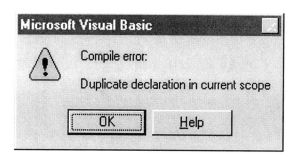

Figure 6.13   **Two identical labels in the same procedure**

GoTo is often used to trap run-time errors. This subject will be covered at the end of Chapter 8.

DRILL

____ 20.   The highest number printed in the following control structure is __ .

```
For I = 1 to 10 Step 3
    Print I
Next i
```

____ 21.   The highest number printed in the following control structure is __ .

```
For I = 0 to 10 Step 3
    Print I
Next I
```

____ 22.   The following loop will print 10 numbers. True or false?

```
For I = 10 to 1
    Print I
Next I
```

____ 23.   The following loop will print 10 numbers. True or false?

```
For I = 10 to 1 Step -1
    Print I
```

```
    Next I
```

____ 24. This loop will run infinitely. True or false?

```
    For I = 1 To 2 Step 0
    Next I
```

____ 25. This loop will run infinitely. True or false?

```
    For I = -1 To -2 Step 0
    Next I
```

____ 26. In a Do loop, you can specify a condition with While or with
_____ . Until

PRACTICE

■ 11. Write a Form_Click procedure that will prompt the user for a number and then a For-Next loop will print to the screen consecutive numbers from 1 to the supplied number.

■ 12. Modify the above so that the user is prompted to supply the beginning and the ending numbers.

■ 13. Modify the above so that the user is prompted to supply the step number as well.

■ 14. Construct a For-Next loop that will print consecutive even numbers from -20 to -10.

■ 15. What will be printed to the screen by this procedure? Explain.

```
Private Sub Form_Click ()
    Dim I As Integer, J As Integer, varX As Integer
    For I = 1 To 3
        For J = I To 3
            varX = varX + 1
        Next J
    Next I
    Print varX
End Sub
```

■ 16. What will be printed to the screen by this procedure? Explain.

```
Private Sub Form_Click ()
```

```
        Dim I As Integer, varX As Integer
        For I = 1 To 3
            varX = varX * I
        Next I
        Print I
        Print varX
    End Sub
```

■ 17. Write a Form_Click procedure that will display the numbers as shown
      below:

      1 2 3 4 5
      2 3 4 5 6
      3 4 5 6 7
      4 5 6 7 8
      5 6 7 8 9

■ 18. Modify the previous procedure so that the numbers are reversed, as
      shown below:

      9 8 7 6 5
      8 7 6 5 4
      7 6 5 4 3
      6 5 4 3 2
      5 4 3 2 1

■ 19. Construct a Do-While loop to print consecutive numbers 1-10. Place the
      condition at the beginning of the loop.

■ 20. Construct a Do-While loop to print consecutive numbers 1-10. Place the
      condition at the end of the loop.

■ 21 Replace While with Until in the above question and make other necessary
      changes.

■ 22. Modify the above so that the condition is placed inside the loop.

■ 23. Modify the above so that when the last number is printed, GoTo will
      direct execution to a line label to exit the procedure.

■ 24. How do the following two loops differ?

```
      Do While . . . Loop
      Do . . . Loop While
```

■ 25. Explain what the following procedure is trying to do.

```
Private Sub Command1_Click ()
    Dim varX
10
    varX = InputBox("What's the asking price?")
    If varX = "" Then GoTo 20
    If varX > 100 Then Print "It's too high."
    If varX <= 100 And varX >= 50 Then Print "OK."
    If varX < 50 Then Print "It's too low."
    varX = InputBox("Try again?")
    If varX = "yes" Then GoTo 10
20
End Sub
```

■ 26. Use Do-Loop to modify the previous procedure. The loop must be
        entered at least once. At the end, the user is prompted to enter "yes" in
        order to repeat the loop.

■ 27. Modify the above so that the loop is repeated unless the user supplies a
        "no" at the end of the loop.

■ 28. Modify the above so that the user must supply "yes" or "no" at the end.
        If not, a message box appears to show the message. Then the same
        prompt is repeated.

■ 29. Use two For-Next loops to produce a display like Figure 6.14. Hint: Use
        the Chr function to produce the letters, like this statement:

```
Print Chr(I + 64) & J;   'Chr(65) = A
```

Figure 6.14   Combining letters and numbers

■ 30. Use Array and For Each-Next to produce the same result as in the
        previous question. Hint: Use two Array functions, one for the numbers
        and the other for the letters.

■ 31. Modify 6TABULATE.FRM to tabulate the average and the counts above
        and below it. As shown in Figure 6.15, the scores should be printed

flush left but the items below should be horizontally centered according to length of the first line.

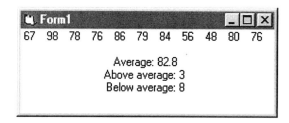

Figure 6.15   Tabulating arrays

BREAKING AN INFINITE LOOP

Sometimes you may want a program to run infinitely—until the user clicks the Quit button (if any) or the Close (X) button. Consider the following procedure:

```
Private Sub Form_Click ()
    Dim I As Long
    Do
        I = I + 1
        Caption = I
    Loop
End Sub
```

It will output each consecutive number to the form's caption. The loop runs infinitely. You cannot click the End button or a Quit button (with the End statement) to end program execution. In the Visual Basic environment, you can press **Ctrl + Break** to end. But if this were a compiled program, your computer would be frozen.

If you want the user to end such a program, you need to use the **DoEvents** statement or function. Consider the following modification:

```
Private Sub Form_Click ()
    Dim I As Long
    Do
        I = I + 1
        Caption = I
        DoEvents            'statement
    Loop
End Sub
```

The user can now click Quit or double-click the control box to terminate this procedure. The following arrangement will do the same thing:

```
Private Sub Form_Click ()
    Dim I As Long
    Do While DoEvents()     'function
        I = I + 1
        Caption = I
    Loop
End Sub
```

The While clause can also be placed after Loop, as demonstrated in a previous section.

The DoEvents function returns the number of visible forms. In the following statement, varX has the value of 1 if only one form is loaded and shown.

```
    varX = DoEvents()
```

You can specify a condition for DoEvents, such as below:

```
    If I > 5000 Then DoEvents
```

If you insert the above line inside the Do loop in our first example in this section, clicking the Quit button does not end the program until the condition is met.

When DoEvents is executed, the current procedure yields control to Windows. Other events in the Windows environment can then be executed. Putting DoEvents inside an infinite loop thus allows Windows to respond to the clicking of a command button.

VARIABLES AND PROGRAM FLOW

On some occasions you can use variables to fine tune program flow. When combined with the flow-control commands discussed so far, this technique can give you more precise control of program flow.

One example where this combination can be used is when a certain pattern is repeated. Green and red street lights alternate repeatedly. Three Chinese-checkers players take turns to play. Four bridge players take turns to shuffle the deck. How can you handle these common repetitive patterns?

To demonstrate how you can do it, we first simulate a two-player game in which the two players take turns. In the procedure below, player 1 starts, followed by player 2. The pattern is repeated until each has 12 turns.

```
Private Sub Form_Click ()
    Dim I As Integer, Player As Integer

    For I = 1 To 12
        Player = 1         'player 1
        MsgBox "Player " & Player
        Player = 2         'player 2
        MsgBox "Player " & Player
    Next I
End Sub
```

After running the program, the first message box shows "Player 1." After you press Enter, the second message box shows "Player 2." This pattern continues until the loop is repeated 12 times.

We can simplify the program by reducing one variable and one message box, from the original two each. In the modification shown below, variable Player's values alternate between -1 (True) and 0 (False). To make the message box display 1 and 2 alternately, we simply add 2 to the alternating values of -1 and 0.

```
Private Sub Form_Click ()
    Dim I As Integer, J As Integer
    Dim Player As Boolean

    Player = True
    For I = 1 To 12
        J = Int(I / 2 + .5)     'get round #
        MsgBox "Player " & Player + 2, , "Round " & J
        Player = Not Player
    Next I
End Sub
```

Figure 6.16   Using variables for program flow

This procedure also keeps track of rounds. Since each round requires two loops, we cannot use variable I for this purpose because it will display 1 to 12. The new variable J gets each consecutive value from a formula. The **Int** function simply chops off any decimal fraction (see Chapter 7). In the first round, I has the value of 1 and J that of 1. In the second round, I is 2 but J is still 1 (1.5 but with the decimal portion lopped off). In the next two rounds, J is changed to 2. This pattern is repeated until I reaches 12 and J arrives at 6. Variable J controls the number displayed in the message box's caption, as shown in Figure 6.16. At the time of round 3 and player 2, the loop will have repeated 6 times.

Instead of using the **Not** operator to alternate variable Player's values between -1 and 0, as shown above, we can use the **Mod** operator to switch its values between 1 and 2, as shown below. In the first round, Player has the value of 1; in the second round, it is changed to 2. This pattern is repeated until the end.

```
Private Sub Form_Click ()
    Dim I As Integer, J As Integer
    Dim Player As Integer

    For I = 1 To 12
        J = Int(I / 2 + .5)          'get round #
        Player = (I - 1) Mod 2 + 1   'get 1 or 2
        MsgBox "Player " & Player, , "Round " & J
    Next I
End Sub
```

The Mod operator can be used to alternate among any number. In the example below, we want the form's BackColor to alternate among 16 (0 to 15) colors. The **QBColor** function is discussed thoroughly in Chapter 11.

```
Private Sub Form_Click ()
    Dim I As Integer, J As Long
    Dim Color As Integer

    For I = 1 To 50
        Color = I Mod 16              'get 0 to 15
        BackColor = QBColor(Color)    'get backcolor
        J = Int(I / 16) + 1          'get round #
        Caption = "Round: " & J & ";  Color: " & Color
        For J = 1 To 100000: Next J    'idle loop
    Next I
    Caption = "Finished"
End Sub
```

In this case, variable J has the value of 1 during the first 16 rounds. It changes to 2 during the next 16 rounds. This goes on until variable I exceeds 50.

The above procedure includes an **idle loop,** which does nothing except whiling away time. Such a loop is normally used to pause program execution. In our case, execution is suspended for a while after each new color is shown. If your pause is too short or too long, increase or decrease the ending value accordingly.

Here is one final challenge. If you supply 0 (the lowest) or 15 (the highest) as an argument to QBColor, it returns black or white. What if you want all the other colors except these two? Replace the first line in the For loop with the following:

```
Color = ((I + 1) Mod 14) + 1      '1 to 14 only
```

No matter what the value of I is (as long as it is $> =0$), the expression will always return a value between 1 and 14, thus avoiding 0 and 15.

Let's use a more practical example to illustrate more variable tricks. Suppose you run a car rental business. Your basic rate is $50 per day. You want to give a 10% discount for each additional day. So the rate for the second day is 50 * 90%, for the third day 50 * 80%, and so on. The following procedure will print out a table for the first 10 days, shown in Figure 6.17.

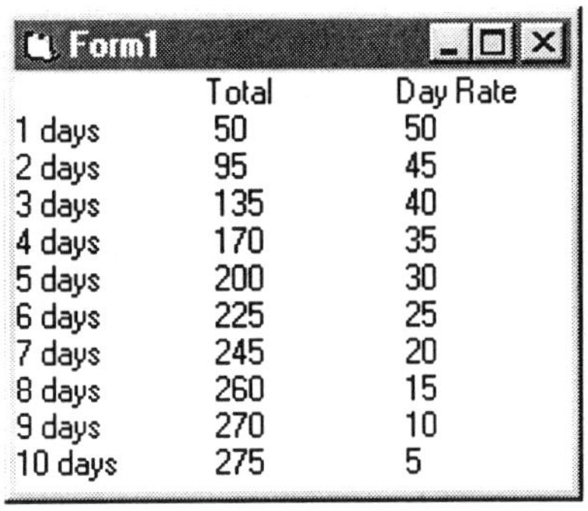

	Total	Day Rate
1 days	50	50
2 days	95	45
3 days	135	40
4 days	170	35
5 days	200	30
6 days	225	25
7 days	245	20
8 days	260	15
9 days	270	10
10 days	275	5

Figure 6.17   Discounting from a fixed rate

```
Private Sub Form_Click()
    Dim Rate As Single, Add As Single
    Dim Total As Single
    Dim I As Integer, Num As Integer

    Rate = 50        'rate
    Num = 10     'number of days
    For I = 0 To Num - 1
        Add = Rate * (1 - I / 10)      'addition
        Total = Total + Add    'total
```

```
        Print (I + 1) & " days", Total, Add
    Next I
End Sub
```

In the first pass of the For loop, I has the value of 0; both Add and Total have the same amount, namely 50. So the first day's rate is $50. In each ensuing pass, Add will decrease by 10% from 50.

If you go up to 11 days, the last day will be free and the total remains the same. If you go higher, the total begins to decrease because Add begins to have a negative value. If you want the total to remain the same, either line below (inserted before the total line) will do:

```
If I > 10 Then Add = 0
If Add < 0 Then Add = 0
```

Suppose you now want to change the formula to 10% discount from the previous day's rate. So the third day's rate is 90% of the second day's rate. The resulting rate will be higher than the previous formula. There is also no possibility of discounting beyond 100%.

In the following modification, we use variable Add to determine each additional day's rate. In the first pass in the For loop, Add is 50. In each ensuing pass, it is 90% of its previous value. The result is shown in Figure 6.18.

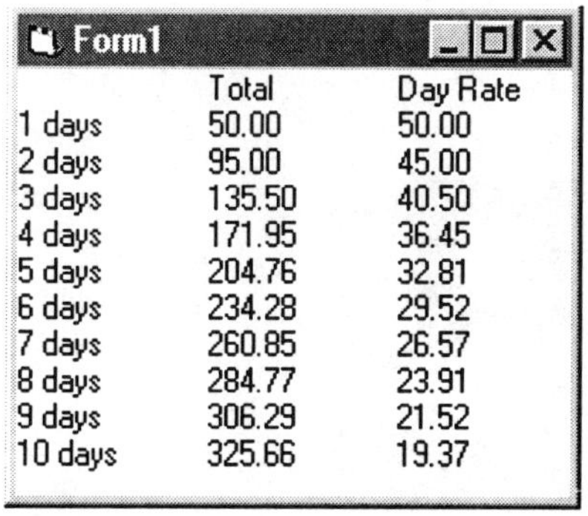

Form1	Total	Day Rate
1 days	50.00	50.00
2 days	95.00	45.00
3 days	135.50	40.50
4 days	171.95	36.45
5 days	204.76	32.81
6 days	234.28	29.52
7 days	260.85	26.57
8 days	284.77	23.91
9 days	306.29	21.52
10 days	325.66	19.37

Figure 6.18   Discounting from the previous rate

```
Private Sub Form_Click()
    Dim Rate As Single, Add As Single
    Dim Total As Single
    Dim I As Integer, Num As Integer
```

```
            Add = 50         'rate
            Num = 10         'number of days
            Print , "Total", "Day Rate"

            For I = 0 To Num - 1
                Total = Total + Add    'total
                Print (I + 1) & " days", Format(Total, "#.00"), _
                Format(Add, "#.00")    '2 decimal places
                Add = Add * 0.9           '10% reduction
            Next I
    End Sub
```

We also use the **Format** function to limit the numeric output to two decimal places. This function was explained in Chapter 5.

BOND PROJECT

This section presents a project that involves more challenging uses of variables. The project lets you figure out a new type of (inflation-indexed) bond that has a fixed interest rate throughout the bond's life, but the principal (face value) is adjusted upward or downward depending on the rate of inflation.

Suppose you invest $1000 at 3.5%. If this year's inflation rate is 4%, your earning will be $35 interest. The principal will be changed to $1040, which will be used to calculate next year's interest earning (1040 x 3.5%). Your total taxable income is $75, if this is a taxable security.

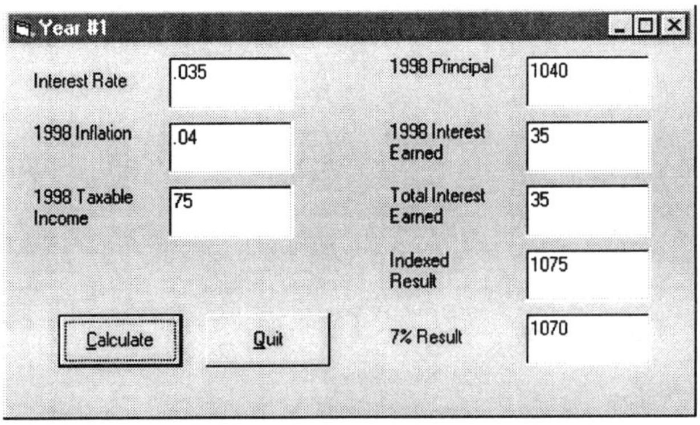

Figure 6.19   The first year's result of an inflation-indexed bond

Figure 6.19 shows our project's user interface. The properties are changed as shown below. Of the eight labels, only four have their names changed. These are used in code to dynamically change their captions; the others have fixed captions as shown in the figure.

Object	Property	Value
Text1	Name	txtIntRate
	TabIndex	0
Text2	Name	txtInflaction
	TabIndex	1
Text3	Name	txtTaxIncome
	TabStop	False
Text4	Name	txtPrincipal
	TabIndex	2
Text5	Name	txtIntEarn
	TabStop	False
Text6	Name	txtTotalInterest
	TabStop	False
Text7	Name	txtIndResult
	TabStop	False
Text8	Name	txtCompare
	TabStop	False
Label2	Name	lblInflation
Label3	Name	lblTaxIncome
Label4	Name	lblPrincipal
Label5	Name	lblIntEarn

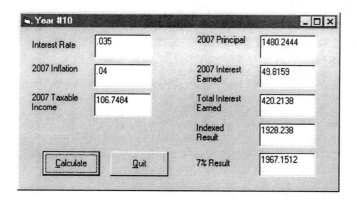

Figure 6.20   The results of two bonds after 10 years

Figure 6.19 shows the result at the end of the first year. The principal is changed to 1040. The interest earned for this year is $35, so is the total interest earned so far. Taxable income is $75. You can now change the inflation rate, if it's changed, and then click Calculate to calculate the following year's numbers.

To make it meaningful to compare this type of bond to one that has a fixed interest rate, our project includes a routine that adds 7% to the combination of the original principal and the interests earned so far. This result is changed each time you click the Calculate button. Figure 6.20 shows the result after 10 years, assuming no change in the rate of inflation. Here 7% fixed yield produces a better deal. But if inflation has gone up, you'd come out ahead with the other deal.

The code shown below are amply commented and quite self-evident. There are quite a few variables. They provide good examples of variable manipulation.

(6BONDINF.FRM)

```
Private Sub cmdCalculate_Click()
    'calculate inflation-indexed bond
    'adjusted annually
    Static YearNum As Integer
    Dim Principal As Currency
    Dim IntRate As Single
    Dim IntEarn As Currency
    Dim Inflation As Single
    Dim TaxIncome As Currency
    Static TotalInterest As Currency

    If txtIntRate.Text = "" Or txtInflation.Text = "" _
    Or txtPrincipal.Text = "" Then
        Beep    'if requisite numbers not supplied
        Exit Sub
    End If

    YearNum = YearNum + 1
    Caption = "Year #" & YearNum
    Principal = txtPrincipal.Text
    lblPrincipal.Caption = YearNum + 1997 & " Principal"
        '1997 is year 0
    lblInflation.Caption = YearNum + 1997 & " Inflation"
    lblIntEarn.Caption = YearNum + 1997 & _
    " Interest Earned"
    IntRate = txtIntRate.Text
    Inflation = txtInflation.Text

    If txtCompare.Text = "" Then
        'if no initial entry, use Principal
        txtCompare.Text = txtPrincipal
    End If
        'result of 7% interest compounded annually
    txtCompare.Text = CCur(txtCompare.Text * (1 + 0.07))
```

```
            'convert to currency data type

    IntEarn = Principal * IntRate
        'interest earned this year
    txtIntEarn.Text = IntEarn

    TaxIncome = Inflation * Principal + IntEarn
        'taxable income is interest earned,
        'plus increase in principal
    txtTaxIncome.Text = TaxIncome
    lblTaxIncome.Caption = YearNum + 1997 & _
    " Taxable Income"

    txtIndResult.Text = Principal + TaxIncome _
    + TotalInterest * (1 + IntRate + Inflation)
        'result of indexed calculation
        'current year's principal and interest, plus
        'previous interest earning the same rate
    txtIndResult.Text = CCur(txtIndResult.Text)

    TotalInterest = TotalInterest + IntEarn
        'all cumulative interests so far
    txtTotalInterest.Text = TotalInterest

    Principal = Principal * (1 + Inflation)
        'increase in principal
    txtPrincipal.Text = Principal
End Sub
```

INCOME TAX PROJECT

This section demonstrates a number of ways of using the commands we have covered in this chapter to calculate your income tax. We start with elementary techniques and move to simpler and more elegant solutions.

The current (1996) federal income tax brackets are as follows:

Married filing joint return

Up to 40,100	15%
Over 40,100 to 96,900	28%
Over 96,900 to 147,700	31%
Over 147,700 to 263,750	36%
Over 263,750	39.6%

Heads of household

Up to 32,150	15%
Over 32,150 to 83,050	28%
Over 83,050 to 134,500	31%
Over 134,500 to 263,750	36%

Over 263,700	39.6%
Singles	
Up to 24,100	15%
Over 24,100 to 58,150	28%
Over 58,150 to 121,300	31%
Over 121,300 to 263,750	36%
Over 263,750	39.6%

Since the total amount of tax depends on how much income falls in what bracket, we need to divide the taxable income amount into different categories and apply a different rate to each. The various commands you have learned in this chapter can be applied to tackle this problem.

We use the Married/Joint Return rates as our example. Our user interface is shown in Figure 6.21. The properties are set as shown below:

Object	Property	Value
Label1	Caption	Income
Label2	Caption	Tax
Text1	Text	(none)
	Name	txtInc
Text2	Text	(none)
	Name	txtTax
Command1	Caption	Calculate
	Name	cmdCalculate
Command2	Caption	Clear
	Name	cmdClear
Command3	Caption	&Quit
	Name	cmdQuit

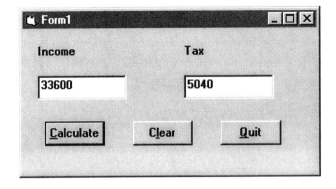

Figure 6.21   Interface for calculating tax

The three comm[...]   procedures are shown below. The code for the
cmdCalculate_Clic[...]   crudest version that requires little
imagination or expla[...]   [...]t up five If-Then control structures to
segregate any given tax[...]   specific brackets, calculate the rate for
each, and add them up.

(6TAX1.FRM)
```
Private Sub cmdCalculate_Click()
    Dim Income As Long, Tax As Long

    If txtInc.Text = "" Then
        Beep     'if no entry
        txtInc.SetFocus    'shift focus to Text1 for entry
        Exit Sub
    End If
    Income = Val(txtInc.Text)
        'get income amount from box 1
    If Income <= 40100 Then Tax = Income * 0.15
    If Income > 40100 And Income <= 96900 Then
        Tax = 40100 * 0.15 + (Income - 40100) * 0.28
    End If
    If Income > 96900 And Income <= 147700 Then
        Tax = 40100 * 0.15 + (96900 - 40100) * 0.28 + _
        (Income - 96900) * 0.31
    End If
    If Income > 147700 And Income <= 263750 Then
        Tax = 40100 * 0.15 + (96900 - 40100) * 0.28 + _
        (147700 - 96900) * 0.31 + (Income - 147700) * 0.36
    End If
    If Income > 263750 Then
        Tax = 40100 * 0.15 + (96900 - 40100) * 0.28 + _
        (147700 - 96900) * 0.31 + (263750 - 147700) * _
        0.36 + (Income - 263750) * 0.396
    End If
    txtTax.Text = Tax       'show result in box 2
End Sub

Private Sub cmdClear_Click ()
    txtInc.Text = ""
    txtTax.Text = ""
    txtInc.SetFocus    'shift focus to Text1 for entry
End Sub

Private Sub cmdQuit_Click ()
    End
End Sub
```

Suppose you run the program and enter 100,000. This number is assigned to
variable Income. The first two If-Then control structures are tested and skipped.
The third If statement is tested true and the structure is entered. The formula

applies 15% to the first 40100, 28% to the next 56800 (96900 - 40100), and 31% to the remainder. These amounts are added up and assigned to variable Tax.

The next two If-Then structures are tested and skipped. Finally, the amount is shown in Text2.

The above program contains quite a few fixed numbers. We can assign them to variables and use the variables to shorten and simplify the program. The procedure below shows this shortened version.

(6TAX2.FRM)

```
Private Sub cmdCalculate_Click ()
    Dim Income As Long, Tax As Long
    Dim T1 As Long, T2 As Long
    Dim T3 As Long, T4 As Long

    If txtInc.Text = "" Then
        Beep       'if no entry
        txtInc.SetFocus   'shift focus to Text1 for entry
        Exit Sub
    End If

    T1 = 6015        'tier 1
    T2 = 21919       'tier 2
    T3 = 37667       'tier 3
    T4 = 79445       'tier 4
    Income = Val(txtInc.Text)
    If Income <= 40100 Then Tax = Income * 0.15
    If Income > 40100 And Income <= 96900 Then
        Tax = T1 + (Income - 40100) * 0.28
    End If
    If Income > 96900 And Income <= 147700 Then
        Tax = T2 + (Income - 96900) * 0.31
    End If
    If Income > 147700 And Income <= 263750 Then
        Tax = T3 + (Income - 147700) * 0.36
    End If
    If Income > 263750 Then
        Tax = T4 + (Income - 263750) * 0.396
    End If
    txtTax.Text = Tax
End Sub
```

We use T1 to represent the fixed tax amount for the first tier (bracket). This amount is determined by 40100 x 15%. For people making more than 40100, they pay 15% for this, plus different rates for the remainder. For a person with an income higher than the second bracket, the first two brackets become fixed. The logic applies to the rest as well.

Each If-Then statement in a program is tested. By using many such statements, your program can slow down. In our example, the program tests five If-Then statements; testing continues even after a match has been found.

One way out in this situation is to add a line number or line label at the end of the last If control structure and then insert GoTo before each End If clause to direct execution to the designated line. If a match is found early, all the later If control structures are skipped, thus saving execution time.

With five possible choices, If-Then statements are not efficient. A better alternative is to set up a Select Case control structure. The procedure below shows this modification.

(6TAX3.FRM)

```
Private Sub cmdCalculate_Click ()
    Dim Income As Long, Tax As Long
    Dim T1 As Long, T2 As Long
    Dim T3 As Long, T4 As Long

    If txtInc.Text = "" Then
        Beep        'if no entry
        txtInc.SetFocus    'shift focus to Text1 for entry
        Exit Sub
    End If

    T1 = 6015        'tier 1
    T2 = 21919       'tier 2
    T3 = 37667       'tier 3
    T4 = 79445       'tier 4
    Income = Val(txtInc.Text)

    Select Case Income
        Case 1 To 40100
            Tax = Income * 0.15
        Case 40100.01 To 96900
            Tax = T1 + (Income - 40100) * 0.28
        Case 96900.01 To 147700
            Tax = T2 + (Income - 96900) * 0.31
        Case 147700.01 To 263750
            Tax = T3 + (Income - 147700) * 0.36
        Case Is > 263750
            Tax = T4 + (Income - 263750) * 0.396
    End Select
    txtTax.Text = Tax
End Sub
```

This last version is much shorter and easier to read. It is also quite efficient. Within the entire Select Case structure, only one Case expression and its accompanying block of statements are executed—quite unlike multiple If-Then statements, each of which has to be tested one after another.

Notice that we use new numbers (adding decimal fractions). This makes all the choices mutually exclusive. If we were to change the Long data type to Single, some numbers, such as 40100.15, could fall through the crack.

DRILL

____ 27.   The following is known as a(n):

```
For I = 1 To 5000 : Next
```

    a.   infinite loop
    b.   perpetual loop
    c.   idle loop
    d.   illegal

____ 28.   You can use GoTo to branch to this line:
    a.   0
    b.   10
    c.   abc:
    d.   abc
    e.   all except d

____ 29.   You can use GoTo to branch from one procedure to another. True or false?

____ 30.   The following control structure is:

```
Do While DoEvents()
       . . . .
Loop
```

    a.   illegal
    b.   never entered
    c.   infinite
    d.   terminable by the user
    e.   both c and d

PRACTICE

■ 32. Suppose you pay $3000 for a PC and its value declines by 30% each year. What's the PC's value at the end of the fifth year? Print to the screen a table showing the PC's value at the end of each year, as shown in Figure 6.22.

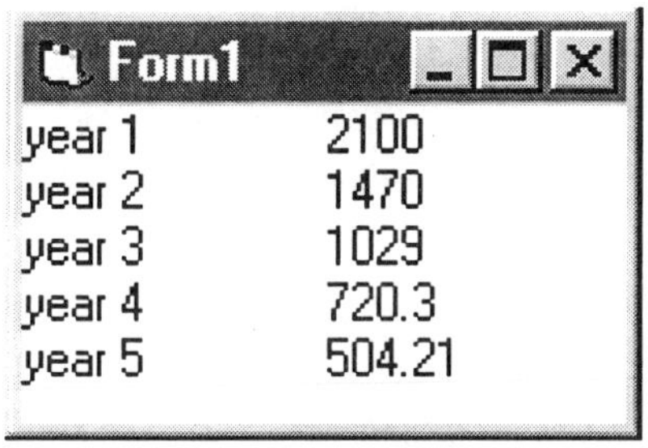

Figure 6.22   Depreciating a PC

■ 33. Modify Figure 6.21 and 6TAX3.FRM to allow the user to add a name and to print the name, income, and tax. The user interface should be as shown in Figure 6.21. When the user clicks Print, the above-mentioned items should be printed. The printout should show the following:

```
Joe Blow
Income          23456
Tax             3518.4
```

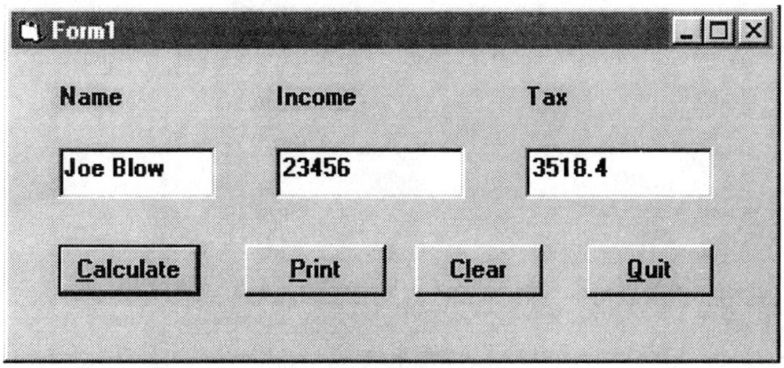

Figure 6.23   Modified from Figure 6.21

■ 34. In the above question, how can you make sure that the focus is in the leftmost (Text3) text box after the program runs? How can you do it at design time and at run time?

■ 35. In 6TAX3.FRM, modify the Select Case structure. The Case expressions should contain no decimal fraction, but should include all possibilities.

■ 36. In the **Fibonacci sequence**, each number is the sum of the two previous, as shown below:

1 1 2 3 5 8 13 21 34 55

Write a procedure to print the first 10 such numbers. Use a For-Next loop.

■ 37. In the previous question, use a Do-While loop.

■ 38. Modify the previous procedure so that the user will be prompted for a term, such as 19th, and the procedure will print to the screen the corresponding Fibonacci number.

■ 39. German mathematician Leibniz used the following series of numbers to derive the value of **Pi**:

Pi = 4/1 - 4/3 + 4/5 - 4/7 + 4/9 - 4/11 + 4/13. . .

Your mission: write a procedure containing an infinite loop to calculate Pi; the loop's iteration number and the current Pi value should be continuously shown in the form's caption.

■ 40. Modify Listing 1 (at the beginning of this chapter) by replacing If with Select Case and by expanding options to handle situations where either A or B can be 0, positive, or negative. The result should be something like these lines printed to the screen:

A is 0
B is negative

CHAPTER PROJECT

A. (6TEST.FRM)

This project lets you enter three numbers and compute the total, average, and letter grade. The user interface is shown in Figure 6.24. The program should behave as follows:

1. When you click Calculate, the fourth box shows the total, the fifth the average, and the sixth a letter grade. The letter grade is determined by the following scale:

   A >=90
   B <90, >=80
   C <80, >=70
   D <70, >=60
   F <60

2. When you choose Clear, all the text boxes are cleared and the focus goes to the first box.

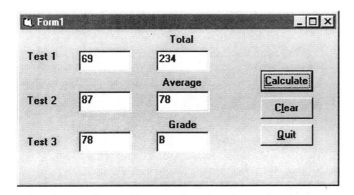

Figure 6.24 Computing grades

B. (6PAYROL1.FRM)

The project calculates a gross pay based on the rate and hours supplied. If hours exceed 40, each additional hour is paid 1.5 times. After entering the items in the first three text boxes, click Calculate to show the gross pay. The form caption (Figure 6.25) is set at design time.

Clicking Print produces a printout like this (use a comma to separate each printed item):

Name	Hours	Rate	Gross
Jimmy Locke	42	10	430

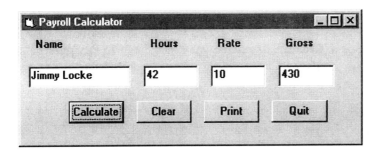

Figure 6.25   **Payroll calculator**

C. (6PAYROL2.FRM)

Modify the previous project so that the user can click Save to append each entered record to a file named PAYROLL in drive A. Clicking Open opens PAYROLL from drive A and displays all the saved records in a large text box (Figure 6.26).

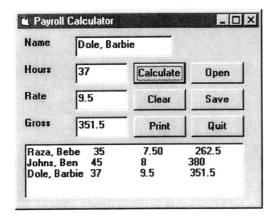

Figure 6.26   **Modified payroll calculator**

D. (6CALC.FRM)

This project lets the user two operands and one of the operators shown in Figure 6.27. Clicking Calculate displays the result. If any of the first three text boxes contains no entry, a beep is made and nothing else is done. (Use Select Case in this procedure to identify the operator used.) Clicking Print prints the four displayed numbers.

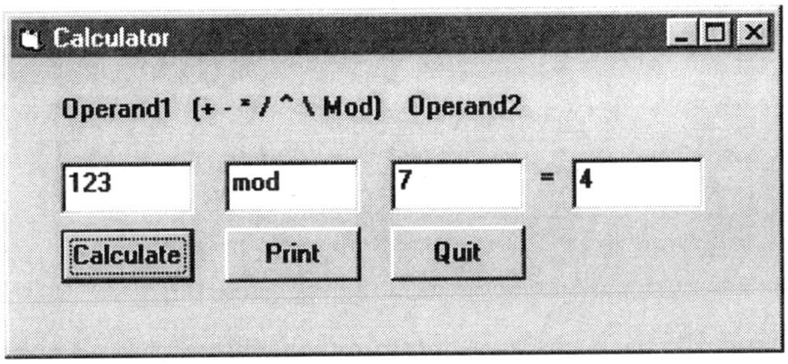

Figure 6.27   Calculator

E. (6RETIRE.FRM)

This project lets you calculate your retirement nest egg. Figure 6.28 shows that your initial sum is $10,000 and the interest rate is 8%. You are supposed to add $1,000 at the end of the years, for which you earn no interest for the year of the addition. Based on this method, the display shows that you'll have stashed away the total amount shown after 10 years. You can change any number in the left text boxes and click Calculate to show the new result.

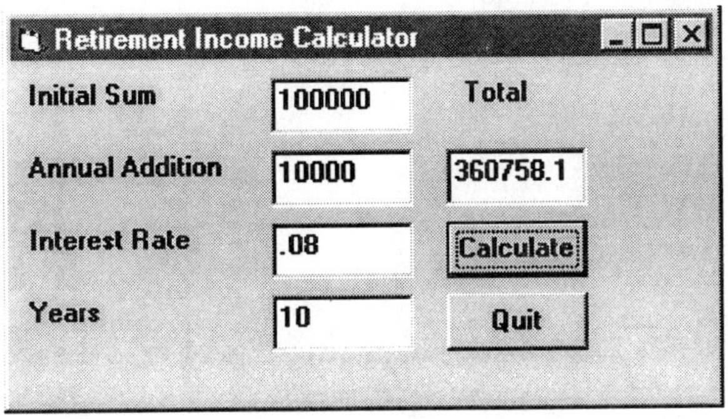

Figure 6.28   Calculating retirement fund

F. (6COMPND.FRM)

This project lets you enter a principal amount and interest rate to calculate the
results of three methods of compounding. Figure 6.29 shows the results.

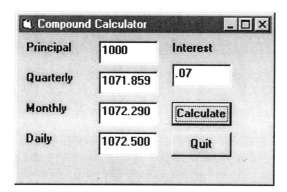

Figure 6.29   Three methods of interest compounding

G. (6PAUSE.FRM)

This project lets you display a running number after you click Start (Figure 6.30).
The display is slowed down with an idle loop. When Pause is clicked, the display
is paused. When Start is clicked again, the displayed picks up where it left off.
Clear clears the number. After the number is cleared, clicking Start starts the
display with 1 and increases by 1 each time. (Use a form-level variable to control
the stop and go mechanism.)

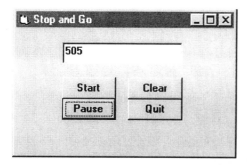

Figure 6.30   Stop and go

H. (6MOTEL.FRM)

Mo' Model Motel has decided to change its rates to $60 for a one-bed unit and $70 for each two-bed unit. To encourage longer-term guests, for each additional day a 10% discount is made from the previous day's rate. You are to change the code to implement the above changes. Also, add access keys to the command button, as shown in Figure 6.31.

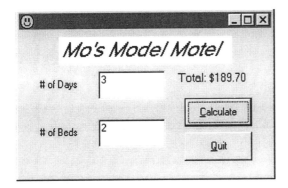

Figure 6.31   Adding access keys and changing rates

FUN AND GAME

A. (FLAGUS.FRM)

This program draws the flag shown in Figure 6.32. Whenever you resize the window, a new flag will be drawn to fill the window.

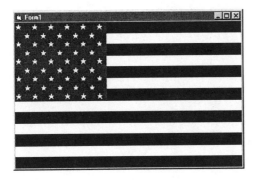

Figure 6.32   The U.S. flag

```
Private Sub Form_Resize()
    'activates when form is changed
    Dim I As Integer
    Dim J As Integer
    Dim PB As PictureBox

    Set PB = Picture1    'use PB for picture box
    BackColor = vbWhite 'form color white
    Cls            'clear form
    PB.Cls         'clear picture box
    AutoRedraw = True          'make drawing persistent
    PB.AutoRedraw = True
    PB.Width = 0       'reduce box size
    PB.Height = 0      'to prevent blank when reducing
    Scale (0, 0)-(1, 13)     '13 rows
    FillStyle = 0         'solid pattern
    ForeColor = vbRed    'fill color
    For I = 0 To 13 Step 2
        Line (0, I)-(1, I + 1), , BF
    Next I             '13 stripes, 7 red bands
    ScaleMode = 1    'restore twips mode
    PB.Width = Width * 0.4    'box width is 45% of form
    PB.Height = ScaleHeight * (7 / 13)
        'box height is 7/13 of form's scalable area
    PB.FontName = "wingdings"     'get star char
    PB.FontSize = PB.Width / 210
        'fontsize in proportion to box width
    PB.ForeColor = vbWhite
    PB.BackColor = vbBlue
    For I = 1 To 9       '9 rows
        If I Mod 2 Then
            For J = 1 To 6  '6-star rows
                PB.Print Chr(171); " "; 'star, space
            Next J
        Else
            For J = 1 To 5  '5-star rows
                PB.Print " "; Chr(171);  'space, star
            Next J
        End If
        PB.Print          'new line
        PB.CurrentY = PB.Height * I / 9
            'adjust new line printing position
    Next I
End Sub
```

B. (TWINKLE.FRM)

This program simulates a blue sky with white stars (Figure 6.33). Every second a
new star (with a random size) pops up at a random location within the form. The
window is cleared every 30 seconds, and a new form begins to show new stars.

Figure 6.33   Star gazing

```
Private Sub Form_Load()
    BackColor = vbBlue        'set form colors
    ForeColor = vbWhite
    FontName = "wingdings"    'select new font
    Timer1.Interval = 1000    '1 second interval
End Sub

Private Sub Timer1_Timer()
    Dim SW As Long
    Dim SH As Long
    Dim Star As String
    Dim CW As Integer
    Dim CH As Integer
    Static Counter As Integer

    Randomize    'get new random seed
    Counter = Counter + 1    'track count
    If Counter >= 30 Then
        Cls      'clear after 30 seconds
        Counter = 0
    End If
    SW = ScaleWidth        'get form's scalable area
    SH = ScaleHeight
    FontSize = Int(Rnd * 31) + 10
        'font size limited to 10 - 40 points
    Star = Chr(171)            'star character
    CW = TextWidth(Star)    'char width of star
    CH = TextHeight(Star)   'height of star
    CurrentX = Rnd * (SW - CW)
        'random pos of Counter and y within form
    CurrentY = Rnd * (SH - CH)
    Print Star      'output star to form
End Sub
```

Chapter 7
Built-In Functions

TOPICS

KEY TERMS

Built-in function   A subprogram that comes with Visual Basic's programming language. Each built-in function usually requires one or more arguments and returns a value. There are numerous built-in functions. The Help system's Contents tab has the Programming Language book. Opening it leads to a long alphabetic list of books. Opening each book results in one or more functions starting with that letter. You can double-click each to display more details.

Named argument   A feature that allows you to use names (like variables) in arguments for built-in functions as well as user-created general procedures. You can assign values to these names when you supply arguments to a function. If you use this arrangement, you can place arguments in any order rather than the required rigid order when names are not used.

Timer control   A control which will automatically execute a specific procedure at a preset interval. The interval, such as one second, can be set at design time or run time. At each interval, the Timer event will be triggered and the Timer procedure will be executed. You can use this mechanism to do something at a specific interval, such as displaying a digital clock. This arrangement does not interfere with your doing something with your PC.

A **built-in function** is a subprogram that is included in Visual Basic's programming language. There are numerous built-in functions in Visual Basic. We have used quite a few before, including InputBox, MsgBox, Val, Format, and so on. This chapter includes most of the functions available in Visual Basic and treats them in a more systematic manner.

The available functions can be divided into the following categories:

> Mathematic functions
> Financial functions
> String functions
> Date-Time functions

This chapter covers the built-in functions in the above order. Date-time functions are often used in conjunction with the timer control, a tool you can fetch from the Toolbox. We will cover the timer control before we deal with date-time functions.

(The items covered in this chapter are numerous and can be overwhelming. Depending on your need, you may want to emphasize some parts and skip others. If you are in a business-related major, you may want to skip math functions. If you are in math/science, financial functions may be less relevant to you.)

MATH FUNCTIONS

There are a dozen math functions. These can be used alone or combined to perform most number-related tasks you are likely to encounter. These can be divided into arithmetic and trigonometric functions.

Arithmetic Functions

Abs(X)   Returns the absolute (positive) value of X. If X is positive, the result is the same. If X is negative, the minus sign is eliminated.

Exp(X)   Returns e raised to the power of X; e is the base of natural logarithm, which is approximately 2.718282.

Fix(X)   Returns the integer portion of X. Regardless of whether X is positive or negative, any decimal fraction is discarded but the - sign is kept. Thus, Fix(1.2) and Fix(1.9) return 1; Fix(-1.2) and Fix(-1.9) return -1.

Int(X)   Returns the integer portion of X. If X is positive, any decimal fraction is discarded. Int(1.2) returns 1; so does Int(1.9). If X is negative and has a decimal fraction, however, Int rounds down and returns the integer portion. For example, both Int(-1.1) and Int(-1.9) return -2.

Log(X)   Returns the natural log (base e) of X; inverse of Exp.

Rnd   Returns a random number from 0 to below 1, including 0 but excluding 1.

Sgn(X)   Returns an integer indicating the sign of X. The returned integer can be 1 if X is greater than 0, -1 if X is less than 0, or 0 if X equals 0.

Sqr(X)   Returns the square root of X, which must be positive. If X is negative, the *Invalid procedure call* error appears. You can use X^(1/2) for the same purpose.

Fix and **Int** behave the same in dealing with positive numbers; both lop off the fractional portion. Fix does no rounding in negative numbers. Int, on the other hand, returns the lowest integer value. In a positive number, the fractional part is truncated; but in a negative number, it is rounded down.

The procedure below shows the program using five math functions. Running this program and clicking the window shows the result in Figure 7.1.

Form1	
Original	-47.57143
Abs	47.57143
Fix	-47
Int	-48
Sgn	-1
Sqr(-x)	6.8972045211302

Figure 7.1   Output by math functions

```
Private Sub Form_Click ()
    Dim varX As Single

    varX = -333 / 7
    Print "Original", varX
    Print "Abs", Abs(varX)
    Print "Fix", Fix(varX)
    Print "Int", Int(varX)
    Print "Sgn", Sgn(varX)
    Print "Sqr(-varX)", Sqr(-varX)
End Sub
```

TIP: Rounding Numbers

Most programming languages have a function named *round* to round off decimal fractions. Visual Basic's **Fix** and **Int** do not do rounding. What can you do?

One remedy is to add 0.5 to an argument. Here are some examples:

```
Fix(1.2 + .5)          '1
Fix(1.6 + .5)          '2
Int(1.1 + .5)          '1
Int(1.5 + .5)          '2
```

When it comes to negative decimal numbers, Fix will work if you add -0.5, but Int will not. Consider the following examples:

```
Fix(-1.2 - .5)        '-1, correct
Fix(-1.6 - .5)        '-2, correct
Int(-1.2 - .5)        '-2, wrong, rounded down
Int(-1.6 - .5)        '-3, wrong
```

The most logical solution is probably to use the **Format** function, which will correctly round positive or negative decimal numbers. Consider the following example:

```
Print Format(-1.23, "#")
```

The result is -1. If X has the value of -1.65, the result will be -2. If X is .23, the result will be nothing. To display 0 instead of nothing, change "#" to "0". If you want to round to two decimal places, use "0.00" or "#.00".

If all you want is to round to the next whole number, **CInt** and **CLng** are the simplest devices. These functions will be covered in another section below.

Exp and **Log** are used to manipulate natural-log numbers. Natural log has the base of e, which is approximately 2.718282. Exp and Log are inversely related. The following examples illustrate their relationship:

```
Exp(0) = 1                 Log(1) = 0
Exp(1) = 2.718282          Log(2.718282) = 1
Exp(Log(50)) = 50          Log(Exp(50)) = 50
```

An overflow error will be triggered if the argument for Exp exceeds 709. Also, if 0 is used as the argument for Log, the *Invalid procedure call* error will appear.

Keep in mind that we are dealing with base e math. Since e is constant, you can use it as a variable and assign a fixed value to it. The simplest way to do that is this:

```
e = Exp(1)

Private Sub Form_Click ()
    Dim X As Integer
    For X = 1 To 10
        Print "Exp("; X; ") = " & Exp(X),
        Print "Log("; X; ") = " & Log(X)
    Next X
End Sub
```

The procedure above produces the result shown in Figure 7.2. The left column can be interpreted this way:

```
Exp(1) = e ^ 1 = 2.718
Exp(2) = e ^ 2 = 7.389
```

The right column can be compared to the following:

```
e ^ Log(1) = e ^ 0 = 1
e ^ Log(2) = e ^ .693 = 2
```

Form1	
Exp(1) = 2.71828182845905	Log(1) = 0
Exp(2) = 7.38905609893065	Log(2) = 0.693147180559945
Exp(3) = 20.0855369231877	Log(3) = 1.09861228866811
Exp(4) = 54.5981500331442	Log(4) = 1.38629436111989
Exp(5) = 148.413159102577	Log(5) = 1.6094379124341
Exp(6) = 403.428793492735	Log(6) = 1.79175946922805
Exp(7) = 1096.63315842846	Log(7) = 1.94591014905531
Exp(8) = 2980.95798704173	Log(8) = 2.07944154167984
Exp(9) = 8103.08392757538	Log(9) = 2.19722457733622
Exp(10) = 22026.4657948067	Log(10) = 2.30258509299405

Figure 7.2   Log and Exp

Generating Random Numbers

The **Rnd** function can generate a sequence of single-precision random numbers ranging from 0 to below 1. The procedure below produces the result shown in Figure 7.3.

```
Private Sub Form_Click ()
    Dim I As Integer
    For I = 1 To 10
        Print Rnd
    Next I
End Sub
```

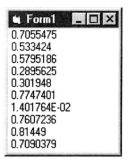

Figure 7.3   Random numbers generated by Rnd

You can use a number as an optional argument with Rnd. Such a number can be one of the following:

<0   Displays the same number every time—if the same negative number is used again.

=0   Displays the most recently generated number.

>0   Displays the next random number.

The last option is the same as having no argument.

To see what an optional argument can do, change Rnd to Rnd(0), Rnd(-5), Rnd(79), and back to Rnd(-5); run the program after you change the number. If you use 0 or a negative number, one number is repeated ten times in our case. If you return to the same negative number (or 0), the same number generated earlier will reappear. Each negative-number argument, however, generates a new number that is different from another negative-number argument. The following code will generate 10 different random numbers:

```
For I = 1 To 10
    Print Rnd(-I)
Next I
```

If you use no argument or a positive number, a sequence of different numbers are generated. If you run the program again, the same set reappears—even if you change to another positive-number argument.

What if you want to generate a new set of random numbers? Enter the **Randomize** statement at the beginning of the procedure, like this:

```
Private Sub Form_Click ()
    Dim I As Integer
    Randomize
    For I = 1 To 10
        Print Rnd
    Next I
End Sub
```

From now on, every time you run the program, a new set of numbers will appear.

You can limit random numbers to a fixed range. Follow this syntax:

```
Fix((high_number - low_number + 1) * Rnd) + low_number
```

Suppose we want to generate random numbers that are 10 to 100. In our example, the line can be written this way:

```
Print Fix((100 - 10 + 1) * Rnd) + 10
```

Rnd can go as low as 0. If Rnd returns 0, our formula will generate 10. Rnd can go as high as 0.9999. Multiplying this number by 91 produces 90, plus a high decimal fraction, which is lopped off by Fix. (We can also use Int here.) So the highest number could be 100.

Sometimes a range of options may not be in a sequential order. In that case, you can use Rnd in combination with Select Case to randomly pick one of the available options. In the following procedure, varX will be limited to the 0-3 range. After a random number is generated, Select Case determines which color will be used. Each time you click the form, the background color will be changed by the randomly generated number.

```
Private Sub Form_Click()
    Dim varX
    varX = Fix(Rnd * 4)
    Select Case varX
    Case 0
        BackColor = vbRed
    Case 1
        BackColor = vbYellow
    Case 2
        BackColor = vbBlue
    Case 3
        BackColor = vbCyan
    End Select
    Cls
    Print varX
End Sub
```

Converting Numbers

You can use a series of Visual Basic functions to convert data from one type to another. These include **CBool** (Boolean), **CByte** (Byte), **CCur** (Currency), **CDate** (Date), **CDbl** (Double), **CInt** (Integer), **CLng** (Long), **CSng** (Single), **CStr** (String), and **CVar** (Variant). These are shortened names for various data types, each preceded by the letter C. They simply convert a number to the specified data type. The available data types and how they differ were covered in Chapter 5.

The listing below shows a procedure that will convert a number to a specific type. It leads to Figure 7.4.

```
Private Sub Form_Click ()
    Dim varX
```

```
    varX = 22222 / 7
    Print "Original", varX
    Print "CBool", CBool(varX)
    Print "CByte", CByte(varX / 100)
    Print "CCur", CCur(varX)
    Print "CDbl", CDbl(varX)
    Print "CInt", CInt(varX)
    Print "CLng", CLng(varX)
    Print "CSng", CSng(varX)
    Print "CStr", CStr(varX) + " string"
    Print "CVar", CVar(varX) & " string"
End Sub
```

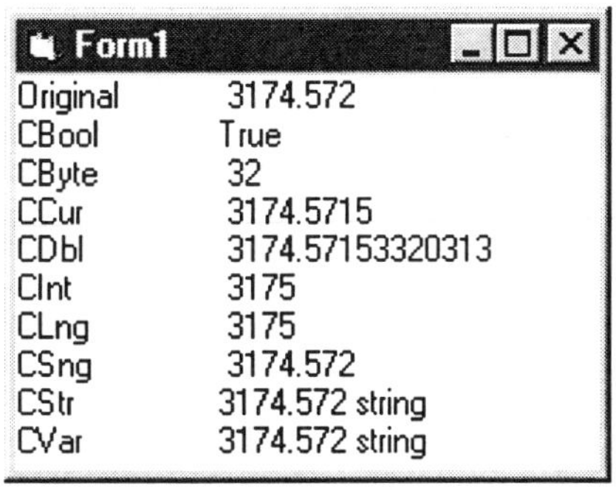

Form1	_ □ ✕
Original	3174.572
CBool	True
CByte	32
CCur	3174.5715
CDbl	3174.57153320313
CInt	3175
CLng	3175
CSng	3174.572
CStr	3174.572 string
CVar	3174.572 string

Figure 7.4   Functions that convert numbers

The **CBool** function converts a value to the Boolean data type. Here True is returned because varX has a nonzero value. If varX were 0, then this function would have returned False.

CByte converts a value to the Byte data type, which can hold values 0 to 255. Here we divide varX by 100 to result in 32 bytes. If we didn't do that, the *Overflow* error would appear.

Notice that the last example uses the & operator to concatenate two items. If we use a + here, the *Type mismatch* error will appear. Even though the first item, being a Variant, can be as a numeric or text string, it cannot be treated as a string in this situation.

These functions round off numbers when necessary. Positive numbers are rounded up and negative numbers rounded down. When a number is between 0.5 and -0.5, it may disappear in a rounding operation. Consider the following:

```
Print CInt(.5)              '0
Print CInt(-.5)             '0
Print CInt(.501)            '1
Print CInt(1.5)             '2
Print CInt(-1.5)            '-2
```

Notice that CInt(.5) is rounded down, but CInt(1.5) is rounded up.

Trigonometric Functions

Trigonometry, as the term implies, measures triangles. In its simplest form, it deals with right triangles. Visual Basic offers the typical trigonometric functions of **Sin** (sine), **Cos** (cosine), **Tan** (tangent), and **Atn** (arctangent).

The following trigonometric equations should help you understand Visual Basic's trigonometric functions (their returned values are shown in parentheses):

$\sin \Theta = y/r$ (-1 to 1)
$\cos \Theta = x/r$ (-1 to 1)
$\tan \Theta = y/x$ (a Double number)
atn (y/x) = angle value   ($-\pi/2$ to $\pi/2$ radians)
π = atn(1)*4
2π radians = 360 degrees

The Sin(*arg*), Cos(*arg*), and Tan(*arg*) functions take an angle expressed in radians as an argument, and return the ratios of two of these three items: X (coordinate), Y (coordinate), and R (radius). Atn is the inverse of Tan; it takes a ratio (Y/X) as an argument and returns the value of an angle expressed in radians.

An angle's degrees can be converted to radians this way:

degree * π / 180 = radians

Conversely, an angle's radians can be converted to degrees this way:

radians * 180 / π = degrees

Since there is no Pi function, you can assign it a fixed value before using it as a variable, such as:

```
Pi = 3.1416
```

You can also use a formula to get the value of Pi, like this:

```
Pi = Atn(1) * 4
```

This will give you a single-precision value, namely 3.141593. If you want a double-precision value, use Dim to declare variable Pi as Double. After that, the above assignment will give the variable a value that has 14 digits to the right of the decimal point.

The procedure below and Figure 7.5 provide a demonstration. You probably remember in your geometry or trigonometry class that when X and Y have the same value (see Figure 7.6), the two acute angles of a right triangle are 45 degrees each. In our program we assign 1 to both X and Y. The Atn function returns the radian value, which is then used to convert to 45 degrees.

```
Private Sub Form_Click ()
    Dim X As Integer, Y As Integer
    Dim Rad As Single, Deg As Single
    Dim Pi As Double            'use double for pi

    Pi = Atn(1) * 4             'get pi
    X = 1
    Y = 1
    Rad = Atn(Y / X)            'get radian
    Deg = Rad * 180 / Pi        'convert to degree
    Print "Pi", Pi
    Print
    Print "When x="; X; " and y="; Y
    Print
    Print "Radian", Rad
    Print "Degree", Deg
End Sub
```

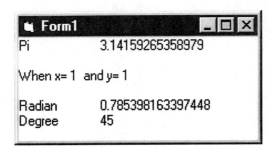

Figure 7.5   Trig functions

Try to change the values of X and Y and see what happens. When X is 0 and Y is 1, we can expect 90 degrees (see Figure 7.6). However, we will encounter the problem of division by zero and thus the *Invalid procedure call* error. To avoid this problem, you can give X a minute value, such as 0.0001. The Atn function will return a degree close to 90.

One way to envision trigonometry is to compare it to a two-legged compass, which you used to draw circles in your trig class. As you anchor down one leg and start drawing a circle from right to left counterclockwise, various items' values and relationships begin to change.

At the point where you start drawing, the angle's value is 0 (degree and radian), X equals 1, Y equals 0, and R equals X (see Figure 7.6). As you draw the circle counterclockwise, X decreases but Y increases in value. When the angle is 45 degrees ($\pi/4$ radians or 1/8 of the full circle), X and Y are equal in value (length). The triangle becomes isosceles.

Keep in mind that the values of X, Y, and R are not absolute, but relative to one another. Suppose we reach the 45-degree point and the value of R is 1. Do you know the value of X or Y? You can use this Pythagorean theorem to figure it out:

$$r\char`^2 = x\char`^2 + y\char`^2$$

Since X and Y are equal, and the sum of their squared values is 1, the answer is the square root of 0.5, or approximately 0.707.

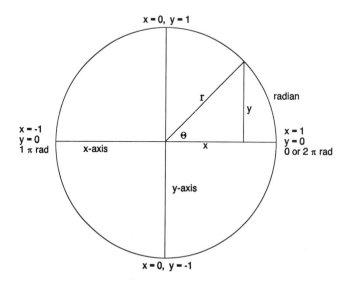

Figure 7.6   Cartesian coordinates and trig elements

The Sin, Cos, and Tan functions require an angle expressed in radians as an argument. They return various ratio values among X, Y, and R. The range of values returned by Sin and Cos is between -1 and 1. Tan could return an infinite value; if the number is too large, an *Overflow* (or *Invalid procedure call*) error will be triggered. (See a Fun and Game program at the end of this chapter for a demonstration of trig functions.)

DRILL

_____ 1. Abs(-1.5) returns:
    a.   1.5
    b.   1
    c.   -2
    d.   -1

_____ 2. Sgn(-1.5) returns:
    a.   1.5
    b.   1
    c.   -2
    d.   -1

_____ 3. Int(-1.5) returns:
    a.   1.5
    b.   1
    c.   -2
    d.   -1

_____ 4. Fix(-1.5) returns:
    a.   1.5
    b.   1
    c.   -2
    d.   -1

_____ 5. This function returns 0:
    a.   CCur(.5)
    b.   CDbl(-.5)
    c.   CInt(.5)
    d.   CLng(-.5)
    e.   both c and d

_____ 6. The highest value returned by Rnd(100) is:
    a.   0.9999
    b.   99

c.   9

d.   0

e.   none of the above

_____ 7.   The highest value returned by the following is:
           Int(Rnd(0)*100)

a.   0.9999

b.   99

c.   9

d.   0

e.   none of the above

_____ 8.   The following two statements will print two different numbers. True
           or false?

```
Print Rnd
Print Rnd(0)
```

_____ 9.   The following two statements will print two different numbers. True
           or false?

```
Print Rnd(-1)
Print Rnd(-2)
```

_____ 10. If X=1 and Y=1, Atn(Y/X) returns _____ radians:

a.   Pi

b.   Pi / 2

c.   Pi / 4

d.   Pi * 2

_____ 11. If X=1 and Y=1, Atn(Y/X) returns _____ degrees:

a.   0

b.   45

c.   90

d.   180

PRACTICE

■ 1. How do Int and Fix differ?

■ 2. Supply a formula that will return a random number that is between 1 and
       10, inclusive.

■ 3. What difference does it make if you supply to Rnd an argument that is greater than 0, 0, or less than 0?

■ 4. Assuming the data shown in the following right triangle, calculate Θ (expressed in degrees) and R.

FINANCIAL FUNCTIONS

Visual Basic includes 13 built-in financial functions for managing money matters. They closely resemble those found in Excel, 1-2-3, and other spreadsheet programs. We cover them in several sections below.

Calculating Depreciation Costs

DDB(cost, salvage, life, period[, factor])   Double-Declining Balance method of calculating depreciation expenses. The default *factor* value, if omitted, is 2 (double).

SLN(cost, salvage, life)   Straight-Line method of calculating depreciation expenses.

SYD(cost, salvage, life, per)   Sum-of-Years' Digits method of calculating depreciation expenses.

If you are in business, you need to figure out the annual depreciation amount for each piece of equipment you use for business. This amount is then deducted from income to determine income tax. There are three commonly used methods for calculating depreciation: straight line (SLN), double-declining balance (DDB), and sum-of-the-years' digits (SYD). Visual Basic provides a comparable function for each.

In calculating depreciation, you need to know the original cost, the life expectancy, and the salvage value. The last item is the expected resale value at the end of an asset's useful life.

The **SLN** method is the most straightforward. Each year's depreciation cost is the same. It is based on the original cost, minus salvage, divided by the years.

The **DDB** method produces a large depreciation for the first year, and decreases in each following year. The depreciation rate is twice that of the SLN method. For example, an asset that can last 10 years is depreciated by 10% each year using the SLN method. In the DDB method, the remaining value of the asset is depreciated by 20% each year. This results in large amounts in earlier years and much less for later years.

The **SYD** method produces results that are between the above two methods. The years of an asset's useful life are added up and the number serves as the denominator to determine each year's depreciation. For example, five years will add up to this number:

$$1 + 2 + 3 + 4 + 5 = 15$$

Thus the first year's depreciation will be the cost (minus salvage) multiplied by 5/15, the second year by 4/15, and so on.

These methods can be easily handled by simple arithmetic formulas. Visual Basic's functions make it even easier to find the desired answers.

Our application's user interface (Figure 7.7) contains three option buttons, four text boxes, and two command buttons. The option buttons let the user choose one of the three methods. The middle text boxes let the user enter the required numbers. The command buttons give the options of calculating the results or ending the program. The properties are set as shown below.

Object	Property	Value
Option1	Caption	SLN
	Name	optSLN
	Value	True
Option2	Caption	DDB
	Name	optDDB
Option3	Caption	SYD
	Name	optSYD
Label1	Caption	Cost
Label2	Caption	Salvage
Label3	Caption	Life

Text1	Name	txtCost
Text2	Name	txtSalvage
Text3	Name	txtLife
Text4	Name	txtResult
	MultiLine	True
	ScrollBars	2 - Vertical
Command1	Caption	&Calculate
	Name	cmdCalculate
	Default	True
Command2	Caption	&Quit
	Name	cmdQuit
	Cancel	True

The cmdCalculate_Click procedure is shown below. The first If structure is to prevent the program from going awry. If the user clicks Calculate when no entry is made in any one of the three text boxes, the program will return an error. When this happens, this If structure causes a beep and exits the procedure.

(7DEPRE.FRM)
```
Private Sub cmdCalculate_click ()
    Dim Cost As Single, Salv As Single
    Dim Life As Integer, Depre As Variant
    Dim Period As Integer, Temp As Variant

    If txtCost.Text = "" Or txtSalvage.Text = "" _
    Or txtLife.Text = "" Then
        Beep            'if no entry
        Exit Sub
    End If

    Cost = txtCost.Text             'cost of asset
    Salv = txtSalvage.Text          'salvage
    Life = txtLife.Text             'life

    If optSLN.Value Then            'if SLN is chosen
        Depre = SLN(Cost, Salv, Life) 'depreciation cost
        Depre = Format(Depre, "#,#.00")   'format number
    End If

    If optDDB.Value Or optSYD.Value Then
      For Period = 1 To Life        'control periods
        If optDDB.Value Then        'if Option2
            Temp = DDB(Cost, Salv, Life, Period)
        ElseIf optSYD.Value Then    'if Option3
            Temp = SYD(Cost, Salv, Life, Period)
        End If

        Temp = Format(Temp, "#,#.00")    'format temp
        Temp = Period & "    " & Temp & vbCrLf
        Depre = Depre & Temp            'accumulate
```

```
        Next Period
     End If
     txtResult.Text = Depre          'show result
  End Sub
```

Since we changed optSLN's Value property to True, this option is selected by default. The user, of course, is free to choose another option.

When an option button is chosen, its Value property (Value can be omitted) is True or -1. We can thus use If to find out whether a particular option is true or false and then handle program execution accordingly.

The SLN method is simple and is treated separately. For the other two methods, we set up a For loop to supply the needed periods. Since these two methods also differ from each other, we use another If to distinguish between them.

After running the program, you can type three numbers in the first three text boxes. Press Enter after the last number is typed; this has the effect of clicking Calculate because this command button's Default property is set to True. If you want another method of depreciation, choose it and then click Calculate or press Enter. The same numbers will produce different results. These are shown in Figures 7.7, 7.8, and 7.9.

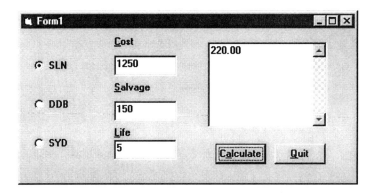

Figure 7.7   SLN function output

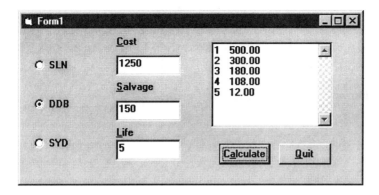

Figure 7.8   DDB function output

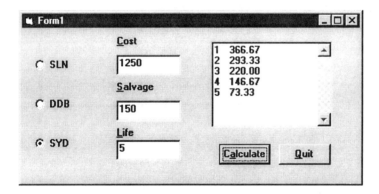

Figure 7.9   SYD function output

PRACTICE

■ 5. Assume that you paid $3,900 for a computer system with a life expectancy of 5 years and $500 salvage value. Calculate the annual depreciation amounts using the SLN, DDB, and SYD methods. Write down the numbers generated by each method.

■ 6. Modify the application in the above text section so that when one of the three option buttons is clicked, Text4 will automatically change without your clicking the Calculate button.

7. After the change made in the above question, what happens if you type a number in each of the first three text boxes and click the SLN option button—assuming its Value property is set to True at design time? How can you change this behavior?

8. What happens if no option button is preselected and you type the three numbers and press Enter at the end or click the Calculate button?

9. Add a command button named cmdPrint and captioned Print, as shown in Figure 7.10. When the button is clicked, the contents of the four text boxes should be sent to the printer.

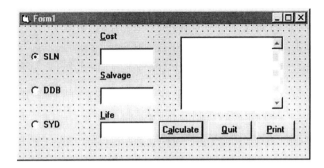

Figure 7.10   **Adding the Print button**

10. Modify the code for cmdPrint_Click in the above question so that the first three text boxes' contents will each be preceded by the caption of the label above it.

Calculating Payments

Visual Basic offers 10 built-in functions to handle matters related to interest. They require quite a few arguments. The following terms are used as arguments in the online help. They can also be used as **named arguments**; see another section below for this term.

rate   annual interest rate, such as 0.075 for 7.5%; divide the annual rate by 12 to derive the monthly rate

period   the number of years, or term; multiply it by 12 to derive the monthly figure nper   total number of periods

pv   present value in annuity; principal or loan amount

fv   future value; the total amount at the end of payments

type   either 0 (if payment is made at the end of the payment period) or 1 (if at the beginning)

pmt   payment made in each period

guess   your estimate of expected interest earning

Pmt(rate, nper, pv[, fv[, type]])   Payment amount for each period; calculates loan, mortgage, or annuity payment.

PPmt(rate, per, nper, pv[, fv[, type]])   Principal Payment of a particular period; calculates the principal portion of Pmt. The *per* argument specifies a period from 1 to *nper*.

IPmt(rate, per, nper, pv[, fv[, type]])   Interest Payment of a particular period; calculates the interest portion of Pmt. The *per* argument specifies a period from 1 to *nper*.

Calculating payments based on a constant interest rate and a target amount is a common financial transaction. Here are some hypothetical situations:

You arrange for a 3-year $15,000 car loan at 10% interest rate. What is your monthly payment?

You get a 30-year $100,000 mortgage at 8% interest rate. What is your monthly payment? What is your annual interest payment? This amount, as you know, is tax deductible.

You set a target of accumulating a $300,000 nest egg for your retirement. You have 15 years to go. Assuming that your money earns 8% interest rate, how much do you have to set aside each month?

Visual Basic's three related functions can handle numerous scenarios. **Pmt** returns the periodic payment amount. **PPmt** returns the principal portion and **IPmt** the interest part. So the three form the following relationship:

Pmt = PPmt + IPmt

A common and useful application is to let the user supply all the necessary numbers and the program will provide the monthly mortgage payment. Our current application is based on that concept. Its user interface appears in Figure 7.11. It has the following property values:

Object	Property	Value
Label1	Caption	&Principal
	TabIndex	0
Label2	Caption	&Interest Rate
	TabIndex	2
Label3	Caption	&Term
	TabIndex	4
Label4	Caption	Monthly Payment
Text1	Name	txtPrin
	TabIndex	1
Text2	Name	txtInt
	TabIndex	3
Text3	Name	txtTerm
	TabIndex	5
Text4	Name	txtPay
	TabStop	False
Command1	Caption	&Calculate
	Name	cmdCalculate
	Default	True
Command2	Caption	&Quit
	Name	cmdQuit
	Cancel	True

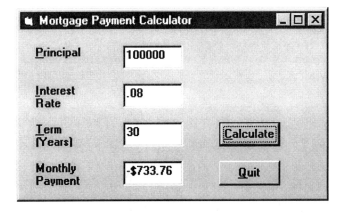

Figure 7.11   Mortgage calculator

After the program runs, the user can tab to each text box to type a number or press one of the label access keys to shift the focus to the right box. For example, you can press Alt+T to go to the third box. Since the label cannot receive the focus, the object with the next tab stop gets the focus.

After typing all the required numbers, you can click Calculate to show the result. Or you can simply press Enter to do the same thing because the Calculate command button's Default property is set to True. To quit, you can click Quit or press Esc.

The cmdCalculate_Click procedure is shown below:

(7MORT1.FRM)

```
Private Sub cmdCalculate_Click ()
    Dim Prin As Single, Intr As Single
    Dim Trm As Single, Ans As Single

    Prin = txtPrin.Text        'principal
    Intr = txtInt.Text / 12    'interest--monthly
    Trm = txtTerm.Text * 12    'term--year x month
    Ans = Pmt(Intr, Trm, Prin, 0, 0)    'answer
    Ans = Format(Ans, "$#,#.00")    'format number
    txtPay.Text = Ans          'show result
End Sub
```

The last argument for Pmt can be 0 or 1. We use 0 in our example. Most mortgage companies follow this practice of asking a mortgagor to pay at the end of each month. If you pay at the beginning instead, you need to change this argument to 1, which will reduce the payment because you are not paying the month's interest.

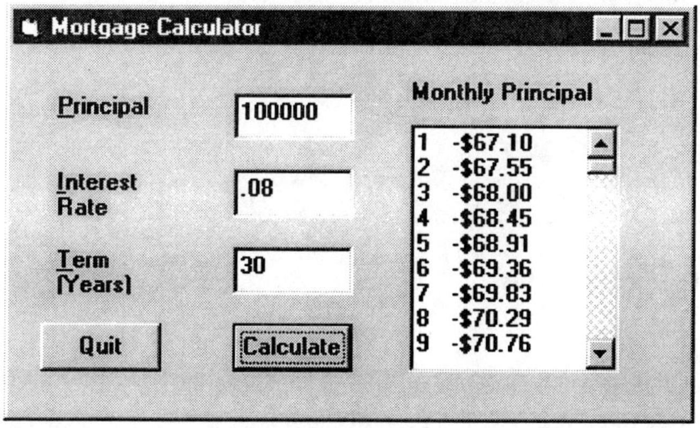

Figure 7.12   Beginning principal payments

Notice that a negative number is returned in Figure 7.11. This indicates a payment you need to make. On the other hand, we could produce a positive number here. That, however, has a different implication.

Suppose you now enter -100000 and press Enter (assuming the other numbers are as shown). What do you get? The same amount, except without the minus sign. You can interpret the result this way. You have $100,000 and the interest rate is 8%. You withdraw a fixed amount every month over the next 30 years. What is the amount? The positive sum is the amount you receive rather than pay.

You can use PPmt and IPmt to calculate a particular month's principal or interest payment. This process is slightly more complicated than finding out the total monthly payment because the principal and interest amounts vary from month to month.

Our user interface needs revision. In the revised version, shown in Figure 7.12, Text4 is enlarged and its MultiLine is set to True and ScrollBars to 2-Vertical. Running the program and supplying the same numbers result in Figure 7.12. You can use the mouse to scroll the resulting display. You can also click the text box to move the cursor there. Then press PgUp, PgDn, Ctrl+Home, or Ctrl+End to display different parts. Figure 7.12 shows the beginning portion, and Figure 7.13 the ending portion.

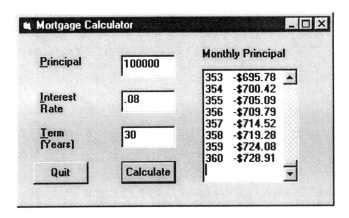

Figure 7.13   Last principal payments

The cmdCalculate_Click procedure is shown below. Here we set up a loop to calculate a result for each month. All the monthly numbers are then concatenated and vertically displayed in Text4.

(7MORT2.FRM)

```
Private Sub cmdCalculate_Click ()
    Dim Prin As Single, Intr As Single
    Dim Trm As Integer, Ans As Single
    Dim Period As Integer, Sum As String

    Prin = txtPrin.Text        'principal
    Intr = txtInt.Text / 12    'interest--monthly
    Trm = txtTerm.Text * 12    'term--year x month

    MousePointer = vbHourglass
    For Period = 1 To Trm           'to calc each period
        Ans = PPmt(Intr, Period, Trm, 0, Prin, 0)
        Ans = Format(Ans, "$#,###.00")    'format number
        Sum = Sum & Period & "    " & Ans & vbCrLf
    Next Period
    txtPay.Text = Sum          'show result
    MousePointer = vbDefault
End Sub
```

The above procedure can be easily modified to produce the results for monthly interest payments. Just change PPmt to IPmt.

Pmt, PPmt, and IPmt all have *pv* and *fv* arguments. The first is the amount you start out with and the second is the amount you end up with. Consider these two examples:

```
Print Pmt(.08, 10, 100000, 0, 0)      '14903
Print Pmt(.08, 10, 0, 100000, 0)      '6903
```

Here we intend to calculate the payment with an 8% interest rate and a 10-year term. In the first case, you start out with 100,000 and end up with 0. It means that you borrow this amount and need to reduce it to 0. So your annual payment is 14,903. By the time you finish, you will have paid 149,030. The difference between it and the original amount is interest.

In the second case, you start out with 0 and end up with 100,000. It means that in order to accumulate this amount you need to set aside 6,900 a year. By the time you finish, you will have paid (set aside) 69,000. The difference between this and the target amount is made up by interest earnings.

Some functions' ending arguments are optional; if omitted, they default to zeroes. So the above statements can also be written as shown below. The 0 in the middle, however, is required.

```
Print Pmt(.08, 10, 100000)
Print Pmt(.08, 10, 0, 100000)
```

Calculating Investment Returns

FV(rate, nper, pmt[, pv[, type]])   Future Value; returns the future sum of a
series of fixed payments.

NPer(rate, pmt, pv[, fv[, type]])   Number of Periods; returns the number of
periods necessary to pay off a loan or accumulate a target sum.

PV(rate, nper, pmt[, fv[, type]])   Present Value; calculates the current value of
future payments.

Money's nominal value changes due to inflation and other factors. Your $1 put in
a savings account may grow to $10 in 25 years due to interest earnings. If that is
the case, the $1 has the future value of $10, and the $10 has the present value of
$1. The money may not change in real value, but different numbers are used due
to the interest factor.

PV calculates the present value of fixed periodic payments. Scenario: You are due
$500 a month for the next 30 years, totaling $180,000 (500*12*30). Question:
Assuming 8% interest rate, what is that money worth in today's dollars? Answer:
$68,141. This is the formula:

```
PV(.08 / 12, 30 * 12, -500, 0, 0)
```

Here you use a negative number for the *pmt* argument, signifying the amount
deducted (received by you). We use 0 as the argument for *fv*; this is the amount
(balance) we intend to achieve at the end of the duration. If you specify an
amount here, the present value amount will be proportionally reduced. We also
use 0 as the *due* argument. That means you are paid at the end of each period. If
you use 1 here, the present value will increase because you earn interest on the
amount you receive earlier.

If you use 500 instead of -500, you pay into a fund. PV then returns -68141. By
the time you finish paying $500 for 360 months, you will have accumulated
$180,000, which is worth $68,141 in today's dollars.

FV calculates the future value of a series of fixed payments. Question: Assuming
8% interest rate and $500 monthly payment, how much do you accumulate at the
end of 30 years? Answer: $745,179. Here is the formula:

```
FV(.08 / 12, 30 * 12, 500, 0, 0)
```

NPer calculates the number of periods necessary to achieve a target amount. Scenario: You set aside $500 a month earning 8% interest. How long does it take you to reach $750,000? About 360 months, based on this formula:

```
Print NPer(.08 / 12, -500, 0, 750000, 0)
```

If you want to pay off a mortgage, specify it as the *pv* argument. Scenario: You have a 30-year $50,000 mortgage at 9.5% interest, for which you pay $420 monthly. Question: How long does it take to pay off the mortgage? About 362 months, according to the following formula:

```
Print NPer(.095 / 12, -420, 50000, 0, 0)
```

TIP: FV, PV, and Pmt

PV and **FV** are closely related. The latter is the former, plus additional interest. Their relationships can be expressed by these two formulas:

```
FV = PV * (1 + Rate) ^ N
PV = FV / (1 + Rate) ^ N
```

The following statements reflect the above formulas:

```
P = PV(.08 / 12, 30 * 12, 500, 0, 0)
   'P = 68,141
F = P * (1 + .08 / 12) ^ 360
   'F = 745,179
```

PV can nest Pmt to determine the present value of a loan. Scenario: You have a 30-year, $50,000 mortgage at 9.5% interest, and have made monthly payments for 10 years (with 20 years remaining). Question: How much do you still owe? Answer: $45,103. Here is how you get that number:

```
P = Pmt(.095 / 12, 30 * 12, 50000, 0, 0)
   'P = 420
V = PV(.095 / 12, 20 * 12, -P, 0, 0)
   'V = 45,103
```

Notice that we use 20 instead of 30 in PV's *nper* argument. Do you know what will be returned if we use 30? $50,000, the original principal. What if we change it to 0? The answer is $0. With 0 year remaining, the loan will be reduced to 0.

IRR(values ()[, guess])   Internal Rate of Return; calculates interest rate based on a series of cash flows and an estimated interest rate.

MIRR(values (), finance_rate, reinvest_rate)   Modified Internal Rate of Return. Two interest rates are used. The first is the rate you pay to get the capital to invest, and the second is the rate you earn from the returned profit.

NPV(rate, values ())   Net Present Value; returns an amount based on a specified interest rate and a series of periodic cash flows, the first of which, representing an initial investment, is negative.

Rate(nper, pmt, pv[, fv[, due[, guess]]])   Interest Rate per period; calculates interest rate based on a number of known factors.

The **Rate** function lets you figure out an interest rate. Scenario: You borrow $15,000 for a car loan and pay $400 per month for 48 months. Question: What is the annual interest rate? 13%. Here is how to figure it:

```
X = Rate(48, -400, 15000, 0, 0, .1) * 12
X = Format(X, "0.00")
Print X
```

The *guess* argument is an interest rate you supply to Visual Basic to get it started. A reasonable guess can be 0.1 for 10%.

The other functions, **NPV**, **IRR**, and **MIRR**, work in similar ways. Let us use IRR as an example. You are supposed to supply an interest rate and a series of cash flows. The first cash flow, representing an initial investment in business, is a negative number. Other cash flows may be positive or negative, depending on whether your business makes or loses money. Cash flows are assigned to an array.

Here is a scenario. You invest $2650 in a business. Over the next three years you receive $1000, $900, and $1200 annual incomes. What is the equivalent interest rate? Approximately 8.

```
Private Sub Form_Click ()
    Dim Cashflow(1 To 4) As Double   'cash flow
    Cashflow(1) = -2650          'initial investment
    Cashflow(2) = 1000           'periodic incomes
    Cashflow(3) = 900
    Cashflow(4) = 1200
    Print IRR(Cashflow(), 0.1)
End Sub
```

TIP: Double or Nothing

If a number grows at the compounded rate of 1%, it will double in approximately 70 periods. So if a country's population grows at 1% annually, it will double in 70 years. If the growth rate is changed, the period needs to be proportionally adjusted to achieve the same result. So at 2% rate, it will take only 35 years for the same population to double.

The following procedure will prompt you to enter a rate and then show how long it will take to double a number.

```
Private Sub Form_Click ()
    Dim Rate As Single, Prin As Integer

    Rate = InputBox("Enter the growth rate:")
    If Rate = 0 Then Exit Sub       'no entry
    If Rate >= 1 Then Rate = Rate * 0.01
        'convert to percent
    Do
        Prin = Prin + 1        'track periods
        If (1 + Rate) ^ Prin >= 2 Then Exit Do
    Loop                   'exit if doubled
    Print "The number will double in "; _
    Prin; " periods at "; Rate; " rate"
End Sub
```

If you don't have a computer to do the computing, you can achieve a similar result if you divide 70 by the growth rate.

Financial people use the rule of 69 (to be conservative) and rule of 72 (for easy calculation). So if your money grows at 6% annually, it will double in approximately 12 years (72 / 6).

NAMED ARGUMENTS

When you have to supply multiple arguments, you can take advantage **named arguments**. Normally, arguments are positional. You supply each required value in the specified order. In named arguments, you can arrange them in any order you want.

Let us use PV as an example. As explained earlier, it follows this syntax:

PV(rate, nper, pmt, fv, type)

We have also used the following example to return $68,141:

```
Print PV(.08 / 12, 30 * 12, -500, 0, 0)
```

Now consider this example:

```
Print PV(Rate:=0.08 / 12, NPer:=30 * 12, Pmt:=-500)
```

It will return the same amount as the previous statement. There are two differences. First, we deleted the last two arguments; they both default to 0. Second, we replaced the positional arguments with named arguments. If you use this latter approach, you are not required to place the arguments in any rigid order as in the case of positional arguments. Consider this change:

```
Print PV(Pmt:=-500, Rate:=0.08 / 12, NPer:=30 * 12)
```

This will also produce the same result. Here we move the last argument to before the other two. If we didn't use named arguments here, the result would be quite different.

Notice that we place := between an argument name and its value. This is similar to assigning a value to a variable. This arrangement does not obviate the need to supply all the required arguments. Omitting a required argument will lead to an error.

How do you know what names to use as required arguments? Use the online help. When required arguments are displayed as **bold and italic**, they are recognized names that can be assigned values. If they are shown only as italic, they cannot be used as named arguments.

All the functions discussed in this chapter are part of VBA (Visual Basic for Applications). They also belong in the VBA library when you use the **Object Browser**. Most of them permit named arguments when multiple arguments are required. Functions in the VB library, on the contrary, do not support named arguments. The Object Browser section in Chapter 8 provides more details.

Named arguments are also supported when you pass arguments to general procedures. This topic will be covered in Chapter 8.

DRILL

_____ 12.   This depreciation method yields the largest amount at the beginning:

a. SLN
b. DDB
c. SYD
d. none of the above

____ 13. If an asset has $1000 cost, 5 years of useful life, and salvage value of $100, the first year's depreciation expense using the DDB method is

_____ .

____ 14. If an asset has $1000 cost, 5 years of useful life, and salvage value of $100, the first year depreciation expense using the SYD method is

_____ .

____ 15. The following formula calculates the interest payment of the last of 10 periods. True or false?

```
IPmt(.08, 1, 10, 100000, 0, 0)
```

____ 16. Use a function to fill in the blank in the following equation:

PPmt + IPmt = _____

PRACTICE

■ 11. What is the monthly payment if you borrow $10,000 at 8% interest rate for 10 years? What is the formula to calculate that?

■ 12. What is the monthly amount you need to set aside if you aim to accumulate $10,000 in 10 years at 8% interest rate? What is the formula to calculate that?

■ 13. Modify 7MORT1.FRM so that the user can enter a percentage number, such as 8 instead of 0.08, for the interest rate.

■ 14. Modify the above so that the program can give a correct result regardless of whether the user enters 8 or 0.08 as the interest rate.

■ 15. Write a Form_Click procedure that will do the following:

a. Prompt the user to supply a principal amount.
b. Prompt the user to supply an interest rate.
c. Prompt the user to supply a mortgage term.
d. Show the results in a list box.

Figure 7.14 shows the results of supplying $100,000 principal, 0.08 interest
rate, and 30 years term. The Principal column shows each monthly principal
payment (use the PPmt function). The Interest column shows the monthly
interest payment (use IPmt). And the Balance is the remaining principal,
derived from the original principal minus all the previous monthly principal
payments. This amount should reach 0 at the end (360th month).

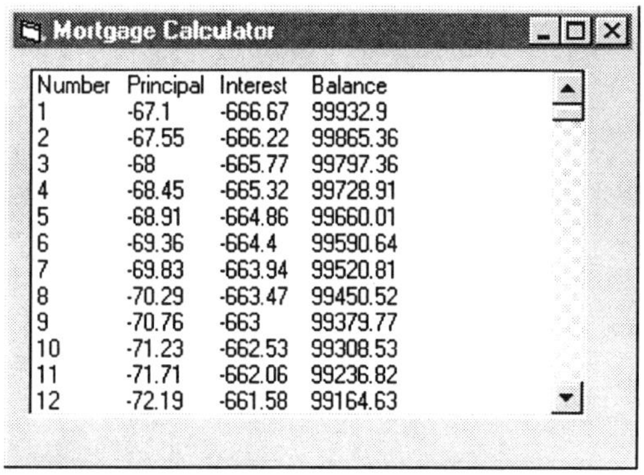

Number	Principal	Interest	Balance
1	-67.1	-666.67	99932.9
2	-67.55	-666.22	99865.36
3	-68	-665.77	99797.36
4	-68.45	-665.32	99728.91
5	-68.91	-664.86	99660.01
6	-69.36	-664.4	99590.64
7	-69.83	-663.94	99520.81
8	-70.29	-663.47	99450.52
9	-70.76	-663	99379.77
10	-71.23	-662.53	99308.53
11	-71.71	-662.06	99236.82
12	-72.19	-661.58	99164.63

Figure 7.14   Mortgage numbers

STRING FUNCTIONS

Visual Basic has about two dozen functions devoted to string manipulation.
Related functions are grouped together and explained in separate sections below.

In some functions, an optional $ character can be used. If it is included at the end
of a function name, the function returns a string; if not, it returns a Variant.

ANSI Conversion

Asc(string)   Returns the ANSI code value (a numeric) of the first character in
the string. The returned number can be 0 to 255. You can also use **AscB**
(byte) or **AscW** (wide) for similar results. Here is an example:

```
Print Asc("ace")      '97
```

Chr(number)   Returns the ANSI character corresponding to the number limited to the 0-255 range. You can also use **ChrB** (byte) or **ChrW** (wide) for similar results. For example,

```
Print Chr(97)          'a
```

You can search the online help for *character codes* or *character sets*. Both will lead to the same result. You can then choose to show either the 0-127 set or the 128-255 set.

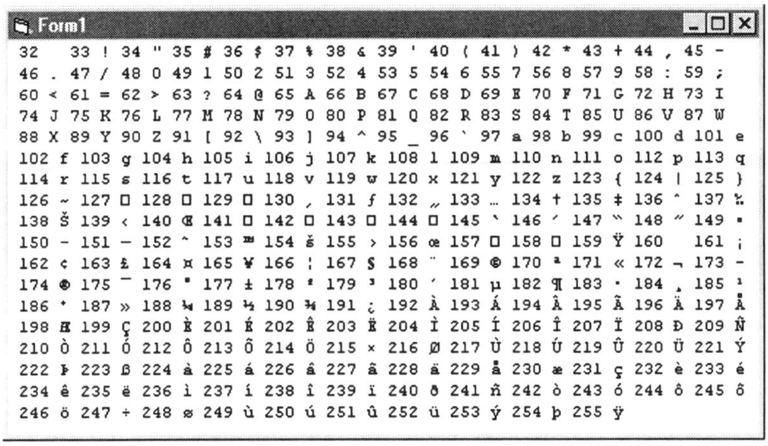

Figure 7.15   ANSI characters

You can also use the Chr function to display all the characters on the screen. In the procedure below, we supply 32 to 255 as arguments to Chr to show each related character as well as its ANSI code value. The result is shown in Figure 7.15. This display uses the monospaced Courier New font; if you use another font, the result may vary.

```
Private Sub Form_Resize ()
    Dim I As Integer
    Cls
    Font = "courier new"      'monospaced
    For I = 32 To 255
        Print I;              'print number
        Print Chr(I);         'print char

        If CurrentX + 600 >= ScaleWidth Then
            Print
```

```
                  'new line when 600 twips from border
         End If
    Next I
End Sub
```

Since we put the code in the Form_Resize procedure, we can resize the window to produce different results. In any event, no character will disappear to the right. When the print head reaches 600 twips from the right border, printing will go to the line below. If the window is too short, some characters may disappear to the bottom.

The Asc function is a remnant of DOS, which can maneuver **ASCII** (American Standard Code for Information Interchange) characters. ASCII uses 7 bits to code its characters, resulting in the total of 128 (0-127) standardized characters. IBM later used 8 bits to create an extended character set, but this is not a universal standard. **ANSI** (American National Standard Institute) has adopted an 8-bit standard character set. The initial 128 characters are the same in both ASCII and ANSI; ANSI simply standardizes the other 128 characters. This is the standard that Windows follows. However, as shown in Figure 7.15 and the related online help, many ANSI characters are not supported by Windows; these characters all appear as solid rectangular blocks if you try to display them.

Number-String Conversion

Val(string)   Returns the numeric of a string.
Str(number)   Returns the string of a number.

Here are some examples of the above two functions:

```
S = "123"
Print S + 123              '  246
Print Val(S) + 123         '  246
Print Str(123) + 123       '  246
Print Str(123) & 123       '  123123
Print S & 123              ' 123123
```

Here the variable S is treated as a Variant. It can be used as a numeric or string. Notice the leading space in the first four lines. They signify the numerics as being positive, with the + signs omitted; minus (-) signs will appear here if negative numbers are encountered.

The Val function can return a numeric if a supplied string argument contains one or more initial numeral digits. This can happen even if the digits are preceded by leading spaces. The following statement will print 246:

```
Print Val("   123abc456") + 123
```

A period is a valid decimal separator for both Val and Str. A comma's effect, as shown below, is unpredictable. Other characters may cause errors.

```
Print Val("123   .    456")   '123.456
Print Val("123   ,    456")   '123
Print Str("123.456")          '123.456
Print Str("123,,,456")        '123456
```

Hex and Octal Conversion

Hex(number)   Converts a number to a hex string or numeric.
Oct(number)   Converts a number to an octal string or numeric.

Here are some examples:

```
Print Oct(22)    '26; convert decimal to octal
Print &O22       ' 18; convert octal to decimal
Print &O26       ' 22
Print &H22       ' 34
H = Hex$(22)     'convert decimal to hex
Print H          '16
Print H + 1      ' 17
```

Octal and hexadecimal numbers are respectively base 8 and base 16 numerals (see Appendix B, Computer Math). You can use &O and &H to tell Visual Basic to go by octal or hex numbers. &O22 is 18 decimal (2 * 8 + 2) and &H22 is 34 decimal (2 * 16 + 2). Notice the leading space before each decimal numeric shown in the comments. When a number is negative, a - sign appears in this space instead. There is no extra space for a positive octal or hex numeric. Although Hex$ is supposed to return a string, our example shows that it returns a Variant, which can be manipulated arithmetically.

Figure 7.16 shows a simple user interface, which allows the user to enter a base 10 number and click an option button to show the equivalent base 8 or base 16 number. The code to convert a number is shown below.

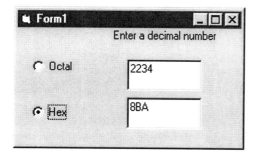

Figure 7.16   Converting decimal to octal and hex

```
Private Sub Option1_Click ()
    Dim varX
    varX = Text1.Text
    Text2.Text = Oct(varX)
End Sub

Private Sub Option2_Click ()
    Dim varX
    varX = Text1.Text
    Text2.Text = Hex(varX)
End Sub
```

You can ask Visual Basic to do arithmetic manipulation on octal or hex numbers. Here is an example:

```
Print &O123 + &O123
```

It will print 166 (O123 is 83 decimal), a decimal value. If you want Visual Basic to output the result in another format, you have to specify it, such as below; it will show 246:

```
Print Oct(&O123 + &O123)
```

Substring Manipulation

Len(string)   Returns the length (a numeric) of a string—the number of characters in the string.

Left(string, length)   Extracts the specified number of characters from the left side of the string.

Right(string, length)   Extracts the specified number of characters from the right side of the string.

Mid(string, start[, length])   Extracts a number of characters from the starting point up to the specified length (number of characters).

LTrim(string)   Strips off blank space(s) on the left side.

RTrim(string)   Strips off blank space(s) on the right side.

Trim(string)   Strips off blank space(s) on both sides.

The procedure below shows a string with 35 characters. The various functions return the results shown in Figure 7.17

```
Private Sub Form_Click ()
    Dim Strn As String
    Strn = "Purge the urge to merge and splurge"
    Print Strn
    Print "length: ", Len(Strn)
    Print "left 5: ", Left(Strn, 5)
    Print "right 7: ", Right(Strn, 7)
    Print "mid 11, 4: ", Mid(Strn, 11, 4)
    Print "left-12: ", Left(Strn, Len(Strn) - 12)
End Sub
```

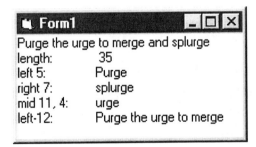

Figure 7.17   String functions

The last example shows a function nesting another function. In this case, we try to extract from the left side of the string. The specified length is the original length minus 12, resulting in 23 characters extracted.

All these functions have their byte equivalents that return byte numbers. Each equivalent byte function ends with the letter B. The following will print 70 to indicate the number of bytes in the string:

```
Print LenB(Strn)        '70 bytes in the string
```

You can use **Mid** as a statement to alter a string. As in Mid as a function (which can be used to extract characters), there are three arguments. The second argument specifies the position and the third determines how many characters to replace. The following statements will change the initial string to the one shown in the comment. Since the last argument specifies 2, only two digits are replaced. If it's greater than the number of available characters, the latter value is used. The same thing also happens if the last argument is omitted.

```
Strn = "1234567890"
Mid(Strn, 5, 2) = "aaa"
Print Strn               '1234aa567890
```

Case Conversion

LCase(string)   Converts a string to lowercase.
UCase(string)   Converts a string to uppercase.
StrConv(string, conversion)   Converts to the case according to the specified second argument.

Here are two examples:

```
Print UCase("ace")     'ACE
Print LCase("ACE")     'ace
Print StrConv("abc", vbUpperCase)    'ABC
Print StrConv("ABC", vbLowerCase)    'abc
Print StrConv("abc", vbProperCase)   'Abc
```

Instead of using the specified intrinsic constants in StrConv, you can use the numeric values of 1, 2, or 3.

If you want to capitalize a word without using the StrConv function, here is what you can do:

```
varX = "john"
varY = UCase(Left(varX, 1)) & LCase(Right(varX, _
Len(varX) - 1))
Print varY                    'John
```

The first (leftmost) character of the string is converted to uppercase and then concatenated to the lowercase of the rest of the string (the string minus the leftmost character).

Repeating and Aligning Characters

String(number, character) Returns a string consisting of a number of characters. The character (second) argument can be an ANSI code number or a string literal. In the following example, "*" can be replaced by 42:

```
S1 = String(3, "*")
S2 = 123.45
Print S1 & S2 & S1
```

The following shows the result:

```
***123.45***
```

The following procedure will produce a display of ANSI characters similar to those shown in Figure 7.15.

```
Private Sub Form_Click ()
    Dim I As Integer
    For I = 32 To 255
        Print I; String(1, I);
            'print 1 character
        If I Mod 10 = 0 Then Print
            '10 items per line
    Next
End Sub
```

Space(length) Returns the spaces according to the length specified in the argument. This assigns five spaces to a variable:

```
S = Space(5)
```

The variable can then be used to pad other strings. This function differs from **Spc**, which is used with Print to output spaces.

LSet string1 = string2 Left-aligns a string.
RSet string1 = string2 Right-aligns a string.

Before you can align *string2*, you must use Space to assign a value to *string1*. The procedure below results in Figure 7.18. We use the Courier New to produce the neat display; a proportional font will show a different result.

Since we use a Resize procedure, we can resize the window to produce different results. As you change the window's size, the font size will change and the display will move.

```
Private Sub Form_Resize()
    Dim I As Integer, J As Integer
    Dim strX As String, strY As String
    Dim strX1 As String, strY1 As String

    Cls
    Font.Name = "courier new"    'monospaced font
    Font.Size = ScaleWidth / 200
        'fontsize based on scalewidth
    strX1 = Space(8)   'set string width
    strY1 = strX1

    For I = 1 To 5
        For J = 1 To I    'concatenate line
            strX = strX & J    '123...
            strY = J & strY    '321...
        Next J
        RSet strX1 = strX       'right-align
        LSet strY1 = strY       'left-align
        Print strX1;            'print each
        Print strY1
        strX = "": strY = ""   'clear vars
    Next I
End Sub
```

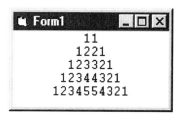

Figure 7.18   Left and right string alignment

Choose, Search, and Compare

IIf(exp, truepart, falsepart)   Immediate If; returns *truepart* if the expression is true; otherwise, *falsepart*.

Choose(index, string1, string2, string3...)   Returns the string corresponding to the index value.

Switch(exp1, val1[, exp2, val2...])   Returns the value corresponding to the matching the expression.

Here are some examples.

```
Print IIf(1 > 2, "true", "false")        'false
Print IIf(X > Y, X, Y)      'returns greater value
Print Choose(2, "one", "two", "three") 'two

ItemName = "book"
Print Switch(ItemName = "book", 34, ItemName = _
"pen", 12, ItemName = "other", "not available")  '34
```

Switch lets you match a series of pairs of items. When a matching item is found, its corresponding value is returned. In our example, since *book* matches the first expression in the list, 34 is returned. If no match is found, the Null value is returned.

InStr(start, string1, string2[, compare])   Searches string1 for a string matching string2 and returns the position of the first occurrence. If the starting position is not specified, the search begins with the first position. If the last argument is omitted, it defaults to the value specified by **Option Compare**. If Option Compare is not used, the default is **Binary** or 0. In that case, comparison is case sensitive. If you want comparison to be case insensitive, use Option Compare to specify **Text** or use 1 as the last argument in InStr. If you specify the last argument, you must also provide the first argument. Otherwise, the *Type mismatch* error will appear.

StrComp(string1, string2[, compare])   Compares two strings in Binary (0) or Text (1) mode and returns one of the following values:

-1	if string1 < string2
1	if string2 > string1
0	if string1 = string2
NULL	if one or both strings contain NULL value

Here is an example for InStr:

```
Strn = "Purge the urge to merge and splurge"
Print InStr(Strn, "merge")
```

The function returns 19, the position where the matching string is found.

You can use **InStrB** to return the **byte** position of the found string. If we use InStrB in the preceding example, the displayed value will be 37, or the 37th byte

from the beginning. Since each character in a 32-bit program consists of two
bytes, there are 36 bytes or 18 characters before the matching string and the
matching string is found in the 37th byte.

Here are some examples for StrComp:

```
S1 = "ace"
S2 = "Ace"
S3 = ""
S4 = Null
Print StrComp(S2, S1)        '-1
Print StrComp(S1, S2)        '1
Print StrComp(S1, S2, 1)     '0
Print StrComp(S1, "ace")     '0
Print StrComp(S1, S3)        '1
Print StrComp(S3, S4)        '#NULL#
```

The procedure below shows a program that you can use to count the number of
each letter in a string. Since we don't want to distinguish uppercase and
lowercase, we must add **Option Compare Text** in the Declarations section. We
also use an array Count( ) as a counter; arrays will be discussed in Chapter 9.
The reason we use 97 and 122 is because they are the ANSI values for "a" and
"z".

```
Option Compare Text
Private Sub Form_Click ()                '-- Listing 1 --
    Dim I As Integer, J As Integer
    Dim Strn As String
    Dim Count(97 To 122) As Integer

    Strn = "Purge the urge to merge and splurge"
    For I = 1 To Len(Strn)
        For J = Asc("a") To Asc("z")
            If Mid(Strn, I, 1) = Chr$(J) Then
                'match each successive char a-z
                Count(J) = Count(J) + 1
                    'if match, then add to counter
            End If
        Next J
    Next I

    Print Strn        'print the original string
    For J = Asc("a") To Asc("z")
        If Count(J) Then Print Chr$(J), Count(J)
                'if Count(j) <> 0, then print
    Next J
End Sub
```

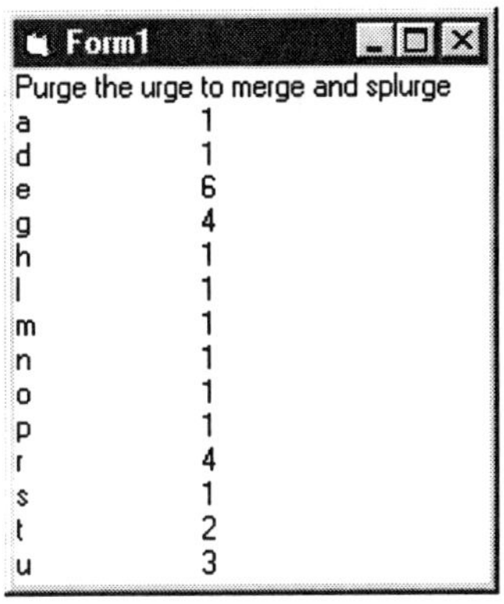

```
Form1                      [_][□][×]
Purge the urge to merge and splurge
a              1
d              1
e              6
g              4
h              1
l              1
m              1
n              1
o              1
p              1
r              4
s              1
t              2
u              3
```

Figure 7.19   Counted characters

Running the program and clicking the window shows the result in Figure 7.19. The top line shows the original string. The left column displays the letters found and the right column the number of occurrences for each.

You can use the **Like** operator to compare two strings, the second of which may contain wildcards. If the strings are alike, -1 is returned; otherwise, 0 is the result. Here is an example:

```
Private Sub Form_Click ()
    Dim varX
    varX = 12345
    Print "Ace" Like "a?e"
    Print varX Like "12###"
End Sub
```

The first Print statement will return 0 by default. If Option Compare Text is entered in the Declarations section, -1 will be returned instead. The second statement will return -1.

You can use the following characters to represent other characters:

?	a character in a fixed position
*	all the remaining characters
#	a digit in a fixed position.
[*charlist*]	any character in the character list
[*!charlist*]	any character not in the list

Special characters or ranges can be placed inside [ ].

DRILL

____ 17. Val("xyz123") returns:
a. 0
b. xyz
c. 123
d. an error

____ 18. Asc("alpha") returns the ANSI code values for all the characters in the string. True or false?

____ 19. Print Hex(10) will show:
a. 0
b. 1
c. 10
d. 12
e. A

____ 20. Print Oct(10) will show:
a. 0
b. 1
c. 10
d. 12
e. A

____ 21. Mid("wherewithal", 6, 4) returns:
a. wher
b. here
c. with
d. withal

____ 22. InStr("wherewithal", "with") returns:
a. 0
b. 6
c. -1
d. an error

____ 23. StrComp("Ace", "ace", 1) returns:
a. 0
b. 1
c. -1
d. an error

PRACTICE

■ 16. Modify Listing 1 so that the user will be prompted to enter a string and the program will count the letters in the string.

■ 17. Modify the above program so that it will count and display all the printable characters that appear on the keyboard.

■ 18. In Figure 7.16, how can you use an access key so that the user can press it to go to Text1 to enter data?

■ 19. Modify Figure 7.16 so that the user can press Alt+O to select the first option button and Alt+H to select the second. Explain the consequence of this change.

■ 20. Create an application shown in Figure 7.20. When the user types a character in Text1 (left), Text2 will show its ANSI code number.

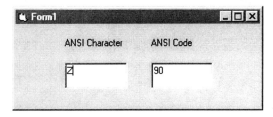

Figure 7.20   Converting character to code

■ 21. Modify the above application so that Text1 will receive an ANSI code number and Text2 will show the equivalent character.

TIMER CONTROL

The **timer control** shows a little old-fashioned stopwatch. Each time you double-click this tool in the Toolbox, a copy appears on the current form. The first one is named Timer1, second Timer2, and so on. Even though it is surrounded by sizing handles, it cannot be resized. It is also invisible at run time; you can thus place it anywhere on the form.

The timer has few properties, as shown in Figure 7.21. Enabled can be True (the default) or False. If set to False, the timer is disabled at run time.

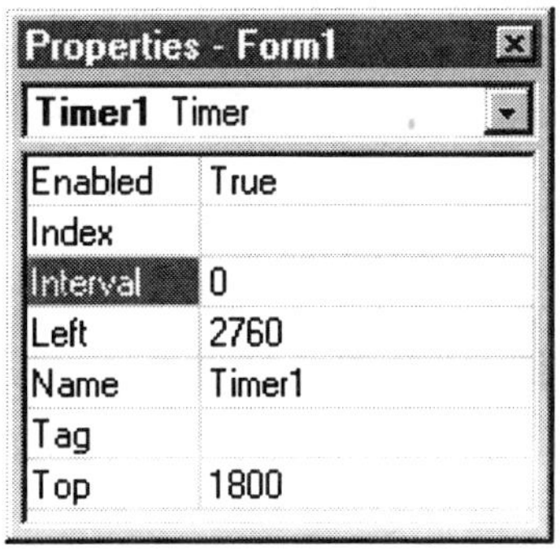

Properties - Form1   ☒

| **Timer1** Timer | ▼ |

Enabled	True
Index	
Interval	0
Left	2760
Name	Timer1
Tag	
Top	1800

Figure 7.21   Timer control's properties

The most important timer property is **Interval**, which is set to 0 by default. This value determines how often the timer is to respond. The value of 1 represents 1 millisecond (1000th of a second). If you set it to 1000, the timer responds every second. If you want it to respond every 5 seconds, set it to 5000. If Interval is 0, the timer is disabled.

The timer responds to a single event called **Timer**. When you double-click a timer on the form, the Timer1_Timer ( ) procedure template appears. If you click the down arrow in the Procedure box, there is nothing else.

To demonstrate how the timer control works, follow these steps:

1. On a new form, double-click the Timer tool. A little stopwatch symbol appears in the middle of the form.

2. Set its Interval property to 2000.

3. Double-click the timer on the form. The Code window appears and the Timer procedure template appears.

4. Enter the Beep command, as shown below:

```
Private Sub Timer1_Timer ()
    Beep
End Sub
```

5. Press F5 to run the program. Your PC now beeps every two seconds. The Timer event is triggered by the preset Interval value without your doing anything.

6. Click the X button to end.

An Interval value can be 1 to 65535. It can be set at design time or run time. The value of 0 will never trigger the timer at run time. You can change this value at design time, as we did above. You can also set it at run time with this procedure:

```
Private Sub Form_Load ()
    Timer1.Interval = 2000
End Sub
```

The timer's maximum Interval property allows for little more than one minute. It cannot be exceeded at design time or run time. Attempting to enter an excessive value will trigger the *Invalid property value* error.

What if you want to set a longer duration? You can use a counter to circumvent this limit. The code below shows the use of two Static variables named varX and varY; the Interval property is also set to 1000 at design time. In this arrangement, the value of varX never exceeds 10000, or 10 seconds. When varX reaches 10000, varX becomes 0 and varY increments by 1. When varY reaches 6, or 60 seconds, a beep is heard and varY is given the value of 0.

```
Private Sub Timer1_Timer ()
    Static varX As Long, varY As Long

    varX = varX + Timer1.Interval
    If varX = 10000 Then     '10 sec
        varX = 0  'x not exceed limit
        varY = varY + 1
    End If
    If varY = 6 Then
        Beep
        varY = 0
    End If
End Sub
```

You can create a timer program, compile it, and run it in the Windows environment. You can then run other programs concurrently. The timer program may remind you to do something at a fixed interval while you work with other programs.

DATE-TIME FORMATS

Visual Basic supplies a series of date-time functions to handle date-time numbers. These will be covered in the next section. They become more meaningful after you learn how to format date-time numbers, discussed in this section.

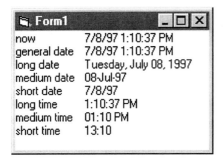

Figure 7.22   **Time formats**

The **Format** function, explained in Chapter 5, can be used to format date-time numbers as well. You can use either predefined formats or user-defined formats. The predefined formats' names and their effects are shown in Figure 7.22. These formats reflect the settings in Windows (Control Panel | Regional Settings | Date/Time). If you change the settings there, using the same format name here may lead to different results.

In the procedure below we use the **Now** function to show the current date and time. This function will be explained more fully in the next section.

```
Private Sub Form_Click ()
    Static Fmt(1 To 7) As String
    Dim varX As Double, I As Integer

    varX = Now           'assign current date-time to x
    Fmt(1) = "general date"
    Fmt(2) = "long date"
    Fmt(3) = "medium date"
    Fmt(4) = "short date"
    Fmt(5) = "long time"
    Fmt(6) = "medium time"
    Fmt(7) = "short time"
    Print "now", Now

    For I = 1 To 7
        Print Fmt(I), Format(varX, Fmt(I))
    Next I
End Sub
```

You can also use certain characters to create your own user-defined formats. The available characters are shown in Table 7.1.

Table 7.1   Characters for user-defined time formats

:	time separator
/	date separator
q	quarter (1-4) of the year
c	combining ddddd and ttttt
d	day with no leading 0; 1-31
dd	day with leading 0; 01-31
ddd	day abbreviation, Sun-Sat.
dddd	day full, Sunday-Saturday
ddddd	same as Short Date
dddddd	same as Long Date
w	day number of the week; 1=Sun, 7=Sat
ww	week number of the year, 1-53
m	month number (1-12) with no leading 0; display minute if m follows h or hh
mm	month number with leading 0
mmm	Jan-Dec
mmmm	January-December
y	day number of the year, 1-366
yy	year number in 2 digits
yyyy	year number in 4 digits
h/hh	hour without/with leading 0
n/nn	minute without/with leading 0
s/ss	second without/with leading 0
ttttt	same as Long Time
ampm, AMPM, AM/PM	uppercase AM or PM
am/pm	lowercase am or pm
A/P, a/p	uppercase or lowercase A or P

Here are three examples:

```
Print Format(Now, "h:mm:ss a/p")
Print Format(Now, "m/d/yy h:mm:ss ampm")
Print Format(Now, "mmmm dd, yyyy, dddd")
```

They produce these results:

```
9:39:45 a
3/14/97 9:39:45 AM
March 14, 1997, Thursday
```

DIGITAL CLOCK AND TIMER

What you have learned about the timer control and date-time formats in the two previous sections can be put together to create a digital clock. Follow these steps:

1. Start a new project.

2. Add a timer control to the form. Change its Interval property to 1000.

3. Add a text box. Stretch it wider (see Figure 7.23). Select a large font size.

4. Go to the Code window and write the following procedure:

```
Private Sub Timer1_Timer ()
     Text1.Text = Format(Now, "hh:mm:ss a/p")
End Sub
```

Figure 7.23   Digital clock

After you press F5 to run the program, the digital clock begins to display the current time. When you want to stop, click the X button.

Besides showing the current time, we can also create a digital timer and make it show elapsed time. The user interface is shown in Figure 7.24. It has a timer control, a command button, and a text box. The text box's font size is changed to 20 to display digits in a more visible way.

The listing below shows the code for various procedures. We use two form-level variables (entered in the Declarations section) to keep track of the beginning and elapsed time. As you learned in Chapter 5, form-level variables are visible to all the procedures in the same form.

Figure 7.24   Digital timer

Since Timer1's Interval is set to 1000 as soon as the program runs, the
Timer1_Timer procedure is executed every second. This triggers a change in the
number displayed in Text1. So every second a new number is displayed.

```
Dim StartTime As Double
Dim EndTime As Double
    'variables in Declarations section

Private Sub Form_Load ()
    Timer1.Interval = 1000     'set timer interval 1 sec
    StartTime = Now            'get start time
End Sub

Private Sub Timer1_Timer ()
    EndTime = Now - StartTime  'get and show elapsed time
    Text1.Text = Format(EndTime, "  hh:mm:ss")
End Sub
```

DATE-TIME FUNCTIONS

Visual Basic uses a Double number to handle all the date-time data. The integer
portion represents date and the decimal portion is used for time.

Microsoft chose midnight 12/30/1899 as point 0 and uses negative numbers to
represent the dates before that and positive numbers for the dates after it. A valid
date number can be from 1/1/100 to 12/31/9999.

NOTE   Lotus, which popularized the use of serial numbers to maneuver
date and time, set 12/31/1899 as 0 in its 1-2-3. If you use Lotus and
Microsoft products, you should be aware of the difference of 1 between
the two.

You can use the integer portion to maneuver date numbers. Each time you add 1, you move one day later; if you deduct 1, you move one day earlier. So Now is today, Now - 1 is yesterday, and Now + 1 is tomorrow.

The decimal portion can also be maneuvered. Visual Basic uses 0 to represent midnight and 0.99999 to represent 11:59:59 pm. If you add 0.5, you advance the clock by 12 hours (1/2 of 24 hours). On the other hand, if you deduct 0.25, you move the clock back by 6 hours (1/4 of 24 hours).

In the procedure below, we use 0 as the middle point and show the days and hours before and after that point.

```
Private Sub Form_Click ()
    Dim Fmt As String
    Dim I As Integer

    Fmt = "mm/dd/yyyy hh:mm:ss a/p"
    For I = -2.5 To 2.5 Step .5
        Print I, Format(I, Fmt)
    Next I
End Sub
```

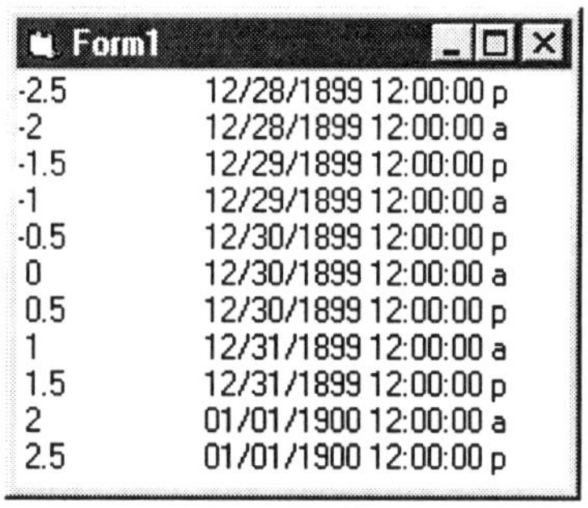

```
 Form1                        _ □ ✕
-2.5        12/28/1899 12:00:00 p
-2          12/28/1899 12:00:00 a
-1.5        12/29/1899 12:00:00 p
-1          12/29/1899 12:00:00 a
-0.5        12/30/1899 12:00:00 p
0           12/30/1899 12:00:00 a
0.5         12/30/1899 12:00:00 p
1           12/31/1899 12:00:00 a
1.5         12/31/1899 12:00:00 p
2           01/01/1900 12:00:00 a
2.5         01/01/1900 12:00:00 p
```

Figure 7.25   Time formats around 0

Figure 7.25 shows different date-time formats from the noon of day -2 to the noon of day +2. Each format is separated from another by 0.5, or half a day, or 12 hours.

Visual Basic offers more than a dozen functions and statements to maneuver date-time data. These are explained in separate sections below.

Current Time

Several functions let you display and maneuver the current date and time. These include Now, Date, Time, and Timer.

Now Returns the current date-time number. The number is a preformatted Variant type. If you use Print to output it to the screen, the General Date format of the current date-time appears.

Date Returns the preformatted date display representing the integer portion of the number in Now. (This portion is used to maneuver date numbers from 1/1/100 to 12/31/9999). Date displays 4/23/97 (same as Format(Now, "m/d/yy")) but Date$ shows 04-23-1997 (same as Format$ (Now, "mm-dd-yyyy")).

Time Returns the preformatted time display representing the decimal portion of the number in Now. Time and Time$ display different formats. Time$ shows the current time in the 24-hour format, just as Format(Now, "h:m:ss") does; on the other hand, Time shows the same thing as Format(Now, "h:m:ss AM/PM").

The following procedure produces the display shown in Figure 7.26.

```
Private Sub Form_Click ()
    Print "Date$", Date$
    Print "Date", Date
    Print "Time$", Time$
    Print "Time", Time
End Sub
```

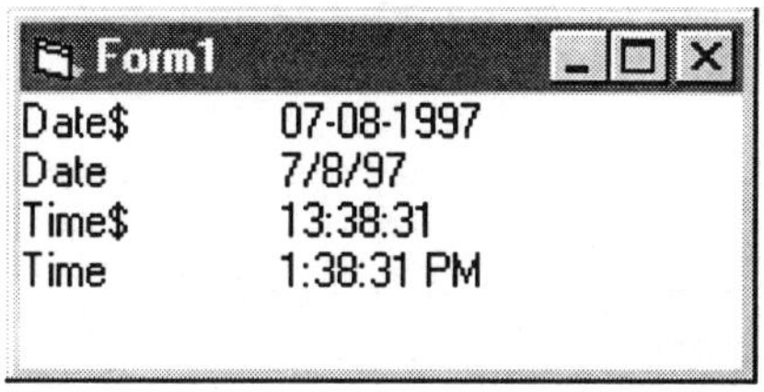

Form1	
Date$	07-08-1997
Date	7/8/97
Time$	13:38:31
Time	1:38:31 PM

Figure 7.26   Date and Time functions

Visual Basic uses a Double number to represent Now, Date, and Time. If you want to see the number causing the display, you can use the CDbl function to convert it to the unformatted state. The procedure below shows the conversion and Figure 7.27 shows the result.

```
Private Sub Form_Click ()
    Print "Now", Now
    Print "Double Now", CDbl(Now)
    Print "Date", Date
    Print "Double Date", CDbl(Date)
    Print "Time", Time
    Print "Double Time", CDbl(Time)
    Print "Date + Time", CDbl(Date) + CDbl(Time)
End Sub
```

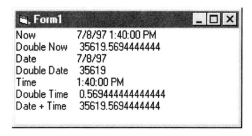

Figure 7.27   Time formats and numbers

TIP: The Many Faces of Now

The Now function stores the current date-time data in a Double number. This number comes preformatted. You can use a number of ways to convert it to an unformatted number. You can also isolate the integer or the decimal portion and display them in formatted or unformatted state. This can be done through simple arithmetic manipulations. The following procedure maneuvers Now without using other Visual Basic date-time functions.

```
Private Sub Form_Click ()
    Print CDbl(Now)            'number, unformatted
    Print Now / 1              'same as above
    Print Fix(Now)             'integer portion, formatted
    Print CDbl(Fix(Now))       'same as above, unformatted
    Print Now - CLng(Now)      'decimal portion, formatted
End Sub
```

Timer   Returns the number of seconds elapsed since midnight. This number can
be 0 to 86,400 because there are so many seconds in one day (24 x 60 x 60).
You can show the current second's number with this program:

```
Private Sub Form_Click ()
    Print Timer
End Sub
```

Run the program and click the window every few seconds. Each time you click,
the new number will reflect the elapsed seconds. Time the interval between clicking and see whether the number matches your watch. You can also write a Timer
procedure, like this:

```
Private Sub Timer1_Timer ()
    Print CLng(Timer)    'show long integer
End Sub
```

If you set Timer1's Interval property to 1000 and run the program, the current
second's number will be printed on the screen every second. The Timer function
has the Single data type. You can use CLng(Timer) to show only the integer
portion.

TIP: Pausing Program Execution

There are occasions when you want to pause program execution for a
while, perhaps to display some thing. Normally, you can use an idle loop to
do that. But such a loop is hardware dependent. A loop may induce a
pause that is too short on a fast PC and too long on a slow one. You can
use a timer control or the Timer function to provide a more precise interval.
Between the two, the Timer function is simpler, which is what we use here.
Consider this procedure.

```
Private Sub Command1_Click()
    Dim CurrTime As Single

    CurrTime = Timer
    Print 1
    Do While Timer < CurrTime + 2
    Loop      'pause 2 seconds
    Print 2
End Sub
```

The first number will be printed right away, but the second one 2 seconds
later.

You can put the pausing routine in a separate procedure and call it when necessary. Here is an example:

```
Private Sub Command1_Click()
    Print 1
    Pause 2         'call Pause and pass 2
    Print 2
    Pause 3         'pass 3
    Print 3
End Sub

Sub Pause(Sec As Integer)
    Dim CurrTime As Single
    CurrTime = Timer
    Do While Timer < CurrTime + Sec
        If Timer = 0 Then CurrTime = 0   'if midnight
    Loop     'pause based on passed number
End Sub
```

Here we call the Pause procedure twice, the first time passing 2 and the second time 3.

There is a rare chance that you might encounter midnight and get stuck in an infinite loop. The Timer function restarts from 0 after 86400. On such an occasion, we reset our variable to 0. Without this change, the loop will be stuck for 24 hours.

If you want to use a Timer event procedure to control a pause, check some of the Fun and Game programs for examples.

You can also use an **API** function called **Sleep**. Chapter 12 provides a concrete example.

Extracting Date and Time

Visual Basic supplies seven functions to extract a particular number from a date-time serial number. These are **Year, Month, Day, Weekday, Hour, Minute,** and **Second.** You supply a valid string or numeric expression as an argument and a proper number will be extracted. A valid numeric expression can be any serial number explained in the previous section. Valid string expressions for dates can be the following (they must be put inside double quotes if used directly):

```
2-1-98
2-1-1998
2/1/98
```

```
02/01/98
2/1/1998
Feb 1, 1998
February 1, 1998
1-Feb-1998
1 February 1998
```

Valid time string expressions can include a period (.) or colon (:) to separate hour, minute, and second—such as "5.30". Do not use minus (-) or slash (/) because they signify date numbers. You must supply at least two numbers separated by a valid separator. If only two parts are given, such as 3:45, the first is treated as hour and the second as minute.

The procedure below shows the ways to extract various numbers. Figure 7.28 shows the result.

```
Private Sub Form_Click ()
    Print "Now", Now
    Print "Year", Year(Now)
    Print "Month", Month(Now)
    Print "Weekday", WeekDay(Now)  '1=Sunday
    Print "Day", Day(Now)
    Print "Hour", Hour(Now)
    Print "Minute", Minute(Now)
    Print "Second", Second(Now)
End Sub
```

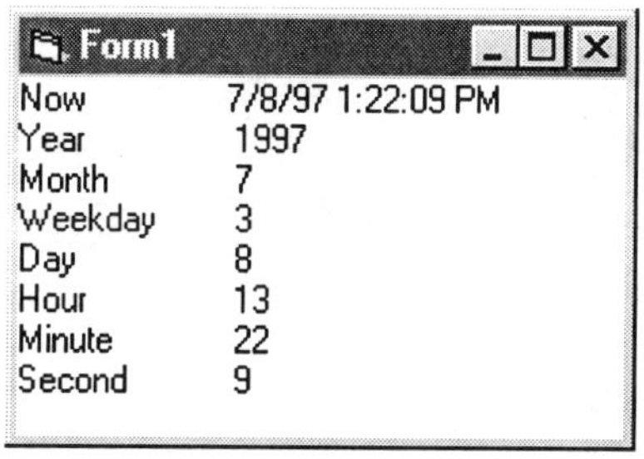

Form1	
Now	7/8/97 1:22:09 PM
Year	1997
Month	7
Weekday	3
Day	8
Hour	13
Minute	22
Second	9

Figure 7.28   **Extracted date-time numbers**

Converting Strings to Numerics

DateSerial, DateValue, TimeSerial, TimeValue are functions that can convert formatted date-time displays to numerics which can then be arithmetically maneuvered. DateValue and TimeValue will accept as arguments any valid date-time string expressions discussed in the previous section. DateSerial and TimeSerial follow these formats:

```
DateSerial(year, month, day)
TimeSerial(hour, minute, second)
```

They return preformatted date or time values. If you want to see the unformatted number, use CDbl as you do with Now and Time explained earlier.

You can perform arithmetic manipulation in the arguments. Here is an example:

```
Yr = 1997
Mn = 6
Print DateSerial(Yr + 1, Mn - 2, 12)
```

The **IsDate** and **CVDate** (or **CDate**) functions can respectively determine whether a string is a valid date string and convert a valid string to a date format (returning a Variant).

In Figure 7.29, we let the user type a text string in Text1 and Click the Convert button to show the result in Text2. If a valid expression is encountered, the CVDate function in the procedure below converts it to the m/d/yy format. IsDate does not consider a number a valid date. If you type a number in Text1, the Else clause will be executed. CVDate may or may not convert some numbers.

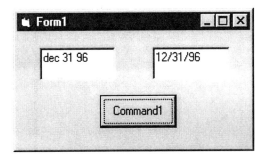

Figure 7.29   Converting string to date

```
Private Sub Command1_Click ()
    If IsDate(Text1.Text) Then
        Text2.Text = CVDate(Text1.Text)
    Else
        Text2.Text = "Not a valid date format"
    End If
End Sub
```

Calculating Date/Time Span

There are occasions when you need to know the time span between two points. Maneuvering such numbers can automate many computing tasks. For example, suppose today is June 20. Do you know how many days are left till Christmas? A worker checks in at 8:20 and leaves at 14:40; do you know how many hours and minutes he has stayed on his job? If you are an employer and pay your workers by the hour, such a number can let you quickly figure out wages.

Figure 7.30 lets you enter an hour value in Text1 and another in Text2. Clicking the Calculate button displays the difference in Text3. If an invalid entry appears in Text1 or Text2, a beep is made and a message appears in the form caption. The rest of the procedure is not executed. The procedures for the three command buttons are shown below.

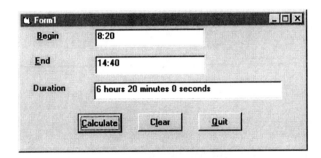

Figure 7.30   Calculating time span

```
Private Sub cmdCalculate_Click ()
    Dim Date1 As Date, Date2 As Date
    Dim Diff As Double

    If Not IsDate(txtBegin.Text) Or _
    Not IsDate(txtEnd.Text) Then
        Beep
        Caption = "Not Date1 valid date number"
        Exit Sub
    End If

    Date1 = DateValue(txtBegin.Text) + _
    TimeValue(txtBegin.Text)
        'begin date/time
    Date2 = DateValue(txtEnd.Text) + _
    TimeValue(txtEnd.Text)
```

```
              'end date/time
        Diff = Date2 - Date1     'difference

        txtDura.Text = Hour(Diff) & " hours " & _
        Minute(Diff) & " minutes " & _
        Second(Diff) & " seconds"
            'show result in txtDura
    End Sub

    Private Sub cmdClear_Click()
        Caption = ""
        txtBegin.Text = ""          'clear all
        txtEnd.Text = ""
        txtDura.Text = ""
        txtBegin.SetFocus           'for another entry
    End Sub
```

What if you want to calculate both date and time, as shown in Figure 7.31? All
we need to do is modify the cmdCalculate procedure as shown below.

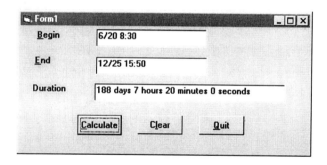

Figure 7.31   Calculating date and time span

(7SPAN.FRM)
```
Private Sub cmdCalculate_Click ()
    Dim Date1 As Date, Date2 As Date
    Dim Diff As Double

    If Not IsDate(txtBegin.Text) Or _
    Not IsDate(txtEnd.Text) Then
        Beep
        Caption = "Not Date1 valid date number"
        Exit Sub
    End If

    Date1 = DateValue(txtBegin.Text) + _
    TimeValue(txtBegin.Text)
        'begin date/time
```

```
      Date2 = DateValue(txtEnd.Text) + _
      TimeValue(txtEnd.Text)
          'end date/time
      Diff = Date2 - Date1    'difference

      txtDura.Text = Int(Diff) & " days " & _
      Hour(Diff) & " hours " & Minute(Diff) & _
      " minutes " & Second(Diff) & " seconds"
          'show result in txtDura
End Sub
```

We use the DateValue function to isolate the integer portion and the TimeValue to derive the decimal portion. These numeric values can then be arithmetically maneuvered.

The **Date** data type and a few date functions can be used to manipulate time spans as well.

DateAdd(*interval, number, date*)   Adds a number to the specified date at the specified interval and returns the new date.

DateDiff(*interval, date1, date2*)   Returns the difference between two specified dates at the specified interval.

DatePart(*interval, date*)   Returns the specified part (interval) of the specified date.

There are 10 possible *interval* arguments. They resemble those found in Table 7.1 and are all shown in the procedures below.

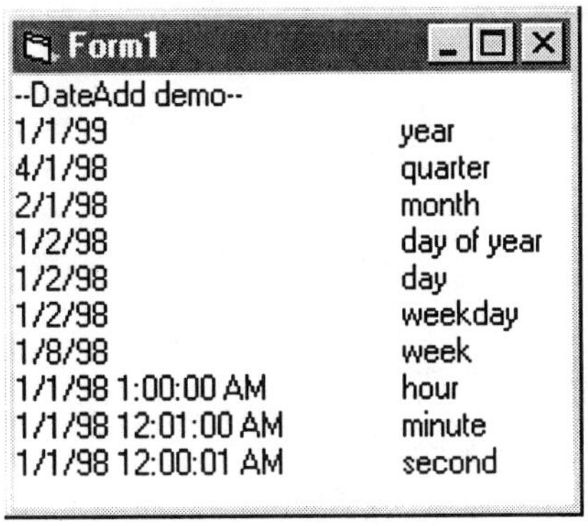

```
--DateAdd demo--
1/1/99                year
4/1/98                quarter
2/1/98                month
1/2/98                day of year
1/2/98                day
1/2/98                weekday
1/8/98                week
1/1/98 1:00:00 AM     hour
1/1/98 12:01:00 AM    minute
1/1/98 12:00:01 AM    second
```

Figure 7.32   Using DateAdd

You can add two additional arguments to the end of DateDiff and DatePart. You can use these arguments to specify the first day of the week and the first week of the year. The defaults are Sunday and the week in which January 1 occurs; these defaults may not be valid in some other countries.

The following procedure demonstrates using **DateAdd** to add 1 to various components of a date-time string. We declare the variable to be a Date data type. Using a Variant here will also produce the result shown in Figure 7.32.

```
Private Sub Form_Click()
    Dim VarX As Date

    VarX = "1/1/98 0:0:0"
    Print "--DateAdd demo--"  'add 1 to a date
    Print DateAdd("yyyy", 1, varX), , "year"
    Print DateAdd("q", 1, varX), , "quarter"
    Print DateAdd("m", 1, varX), , "month"
    Print DateAdd("y", 1, varX), , "day of year"
    Print DateAdd("d", 1, varX), , "day"
    Print DateAdd("w", 1, varX), , "weekday"
    Print DateAdd("ww", 1, varX), , "week"
    Print DateAdd("h", 1, varX), "hour"
    Print DateAdd("n", 1, varX), "minute"
    Print DateAdd("s", 1, varX), "second"
End Sub
```

You can also place a date value between a pair of # signs, as shown below. If the time portion consists of only 0 digits, it will automatically disappear.

```
    varX = #1/1/98 12:00:01 AM#
```

The following procedure uses **DateDiff** to compare the different components of two date-time strings. The result is shown in Figure 7.33.

```
Private Sub Form_Click()
    Dim X1 As Date, X2 As Date
    X1 = "1/1/97 0:0:0"
    X2 = "12/15/97 0:0:0"
    Print "--DateDiff demo--" 'difference between 2 dates
    Print DateDiff("yyyy", X1, X2), "year"
    Print DateDiff("q", X1, X2), "quarter"
    Print DateDiff("m", X1, X2), "month"
    Print DateDiff("y", X1, X2), "day of year"
    Print DateDiff("d", X1, X2), "day"
    Print DateDiff("w", X1, X2), "weekday"
    Print DateDiff("ww", X1, X2), "week"
    Print DateDiff("h", X1, X2), "hour"
    Print DateDiff("n", X1, X2), "minute"
    Print DateDiff("s", X1, X2), "second"
End Sub
```

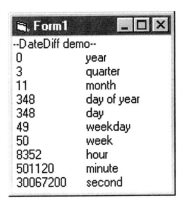

Figure 7.33 Using DateDiff

DateDiff can replace DateValue and TimeValue discussed earlier in this section. The following two statements are equivalent; both will return 366 days.

```
Print DateValue("2/21/98") - DateValue("2/21/97")
Print DateDiff("d", "2/21/97", "2/21/98")
```

The following procedure uses **DatePart** to extract various components of the current date-time. The result is shown in Figure 7.34.

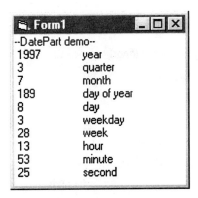

Figure 7.34 Using DatePart

```
Private Sub Form_Click()
    Print "--DatePart demo--"   'different date parts
    Print DatePart("yyyy", Now), "year"
```

```
        Print DatePart("q", Now),  "quarter"
        Print DatePart("m", Now),  "month"
        Print DatePart("y", Now),  "day of year"
        Print DatePart("d", Now),  "day"
        Print DatePart("w", Now),  "weekday"
        Print DatePart("ww", Now), "week"
        Print DatePart("h", Now),  "hour"
        Print DatePart("n", Now),  "minute"
        Print DatePart("s", Now),  "second"
End Sub
```

System Date and Time

Date and **Time** can be used as statements rather than functions as explained earlier. As statements, they can change your PC's clock. Do not do this unless you are using your own PC and intend to change its date and/or time.

Date will accept many valid date string expressions as explained in an earlier section. Date$ will accept mm-dd-yy, mm-dd-yyyy, mm/dd/yy, or mm/dd/yyyy.

Time and Time$ will accept hh:mm:ss. If only one number is provided, it is assumed to be the hour. You can use a 12-hour or 24-hour clock. The number can be separated by a colon or a period.

Here are two examples:

```
    Time = "8:30 p"
    Date = "7/23/97"
```

These statements will change this system's clock permanently—until the next change.

CALENDAR PROJECT

The various date-time functions discussed above can be used to create a simple calendar. The code to do that is shown in below and the result is shown in Figure 7.35.

The program starts by prompting the user to enter a date string. The current date also appears as the default entry; a form-level variable also saves this entry for future use. Since a weird string can be entered by the user, two safeguards are built in. The first If control structure tests to see whether the entry is a valid date. If not, a message box appears and the procedure is exited.

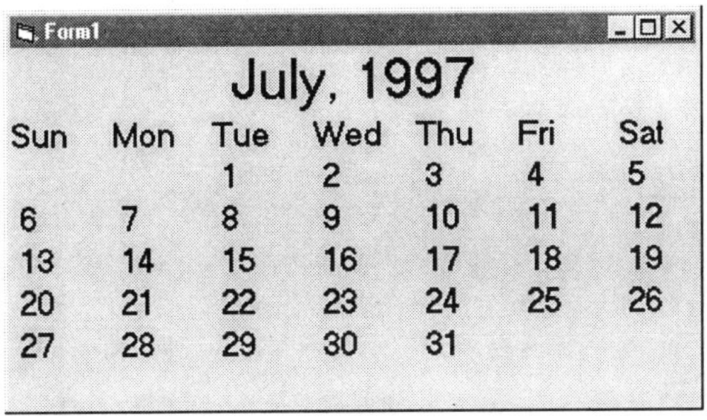

Figure 7.35   Monthly calendar display

The second If control structure deflects a valid date entry that could lead to a wrong result. For example, the user could enter 5/9/97, the result would be an inaccurate display. When such an entry is encountered, the date is changed to 5/1/97. If no date is supplied, such as 5/97, it is automatically added. This produces a correct result in any possible situation.

The program uses an array and the CurrentX property to position each number, which is 900 twips from the previous. The Weekday function is used to determine what weekday the first day of the month is. In our example, 2/1/95 happens to be a Wednesday. So the first number (1) is positioned in column four. When the column position reaches 7, it is changed to 1 again.

Determining how many days in a particular month is quite straightforward except for February, which is a little tricky because of the leap year factor. A leap year has 29 days in February. It occurs every four years (divisible by 4), with minor exceptions. Century years (those divisible by 100) are leap only if they are divisible by 400. We use a series of If statements to determine whether a particular February has 28 or 29 days.

We use the **ScaleWidth** property and the **TextWidth** function to center the first line whose length can vary. ScaleWidth reflects the current form window's scalable width; it will be explained more fully in Chapter 11. TextWidth returns the width (measured in twips) of a text string; if you want to know the height, use the **TextHeight** function instead.

If you want to display the calendar for another month, just click the form and enter another date string again. The previous display will be cleared and a new one displayed. If you want to print a hard copy, add Printer and a period (.) before Print, CurrentX, and FontSize. Also add Printer.EndDoc at the end to flush the printer buffer.

(7CALENDA.FRM)

```
Dim Entry As String
    'to save previous entry for future use

Private Sub Form_Load()
    Entry = Format(Now, "mm/yy")
        'initial default user entry is today
End Sub

Private Sub Form_Click()        '--Listing 2--
    Dim I As Integer      'counter
    Dim ColNum As Integer, Row As Integer
    Dim MaxDay As Integer, DayNum As Integer
    Dim Yr As Date, Mon As Date, WkDay As Date
    Dim Mon_Yr As Variant   'get user date
        'don't use Date; error if invalid entry
    Dim Col(1 To 7) As Integer  'control columns
    Dim Tmp As Variant  'store temp num or text
    Dim Wk As Variant      'used as an array

    Wk = Array("", "Sun", "Mon", "Tue", "Wed", _
    "Thu", "Fri", "Sat")
        'assign elements, element 0 is empty

    Mon_Yr = InputBox("Enter mm/yy, e.g., 3/98", , Entry)
        'prompt for entry
    If Mon_Yr = "" Then Exit Sub
        'if Cancel or no entry

    If Not IsDate(Mon_Yr) Then
        Beep
        MsgBox "Not a valid date"
        Exit Sub
    End If

    Cls     'clear previous display

    Entry = Mon_Yr   'default entry for next time

    WkDay = WeekDay(Mon_Yr)
        'get weekday for 1st day of month
    Mon = Month(Mon_Yr) 'get specified month
    Yr = Year(Mon_Yr)   'get year

    If Day(Mon_Yr) <> 1 Then   'if not 1st of month
        Tmp = Str(Mon) & "/" & "1" & "/" & Str(Yr)
```

```
        WkDay = WeekDay(Tmp)    'set to 1 of month
    End If

    Select Case Mon        'what month?
    Case 1, 3, 5, 7, 8, 10, 12
        MaxDay = 31
    Case 4, 6, 9, 11
        MaxDay = 30
    Case 2        'leap year
        If Yr Mod 4 = 0 Then
            If Yr Mod 100 = 0 And Yr Mod 400 <> 0 Then
                MaxDay = 28
                'if divisible by 100 but not by 400
            Else
                MaxDay = 29
            End If
        Else
            MaxDay = 28      'if not divisible by 4
        End If
    End Select

    FontSize = 24
    Tmp = Format(Mon_Yr, "mmmm, yyyy")
        'get month, year, spelled out, assign to var
    CurrentX = (ScaleWidth - TextWidth(Tmp)) / 2
        'to center text
    Print Tmp        'print Month/Year, centered
    Tmp = -900        'to control printing position
    FontSize = 15

    For I = 1 To 7
        Tmp = Tmp + 900        '900 twips apart
        Col(I) = Tmp      'assign 7 column positions
        CurrentX = Tmp
        Print Wk(I);        'print 2nd line
    Next I

    Print    'move down one line

    For Row = 1 To 6        'up to 6 rows
        For ColNum = WkDay To 7   '7 cols each row
            CurrentX = Col(ColNum)
                'move to proper weekday
            If ColNum = 7 Then WkDay = 1
                'new line start with col 1
            DayNum = DayNum + 1      'counter 1 to 31
            If DayNum > MaxDay Then Exit Sub
                'get out when max number exceeded
            Print DayNum;
        Next ColNum
        Print
    Next Row
End Sub
```

DRILL

____ 24. If a timer control's Interval property is initially set to 0, its Timer event will never be triggered. True or false?

____ 25. To trigger a timer control's Timer event every second, you need to set its Interval property to _____ .

____ 26. The _____ function returns the number of seconds elapsed since midnight.

____ 27. Used as a statement, Date permanently changes your system's date. True or false?

____ 28. Used as a function, Time will return the current time. True or false?

____ 29. Print DateSerial(1998, 3, 18) displays _____ .

____ 30. To show what day of the week a particular day is, you need to use the _____ function.

PRACTICE

■ 22. Write a program that will output to the window the following lines until the number reaches 10:

       1   second
       2   second
       . . .

■ 23. Write a program that will output a warning message to the screen after the program has run for 50 minutes. The program will then end after 60 minutes from the beginning.

■ 24. Explain how Visual Basic manages date-time data.

■ 25. Use Hour, Minute, and Second to display a digital clock that changes the display of current time every second.

■ 26. Display a timer in Text1 that will start with 0 and changes to the next higher number every second. The program ends when the number reaches 60.

■ 27. Modify the above so that the timer starts with 60 and goes down to 0.

■ 28. Write a Form_Click procedure that, when the form window is clicked, will show on the screen the number of seconds elapsed from the time the program starts. Each displayed number must be a whole number.

■ 29. Modify the above so that each time you click the form window, the displayed time represents the number of seconds elapsed since the last clicking.

■ 30. Write a program that will show a digital clock and a timer, as shown in Figure 7.36. The timer should start from 0 and go up by 1 every second. When the Stop button is clicked, the timer number should be frozen. When the Start button is clicked, the timer should start from 0 again.

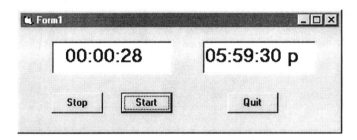

Figure 7.36   Digital clock and timer

■ 31. Modify the above so that the timer will start with 1 minute and count down. When 0 second is reached, the program ends.

■ 32. How many days are there between 3/20/96 to 4/1/97? Use both DateValue and DateDiff to calculate the result.

CHAPTER PROJECT

A. (7WORDS.FRM)

This program counts the number of words in a text box (Figure 7.37). Use a counter to count each space, period, and line break to determine the number of words.

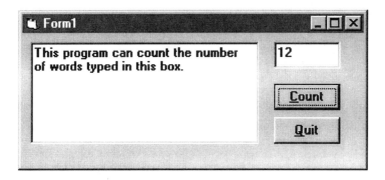

Figure 7.37   Word counter

B. (7GUESS1.FRM)

This program provides a number-guessing game. The user enters a number and
the program compares it to a randomly generated number and responds accordingly. The user interface is shown in Figure 7.38. The program should behave as
follows:

1. A random number is generated as soon as the program runs.

2. The focus goes to Text1 (the left text box).

3. When the user types a number and presses Enter (or clicks Calculate), the
    following should happen:

    a. A beep is made and nothing else happens if Text1 has no entry or its
        number is <1 or >10. If a valid number is entered, pressing Enter
        clears Text1.
    b. If the number matches the random number, Text2 (the right text box)
        shows a message, which should include a try number, as shown in the
        figure.
    c. If the number is too low, Text2 shows that number, together with "too
        low" and a try number.
    d. If the number is too high, Text2 shows that number, together with "too
        high" and a try number.

4. When the user selects Clear, the following should happen:

    a. Text2 is cleared.
    b. The focus is shifted to Text1.

c. A new random number is generated.

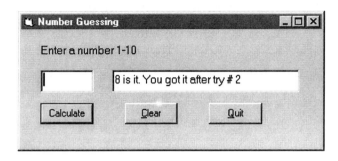

Figure 7.38   Number-guessing game #1

C. (7GUESS2.FRM)

This program lets you try your luck at gambling by rolling two imaginary dice. The user interface is shown in Figure 7.39. The program should behave as follows:

1. When the program starts, the focus goes to Text1 (the top box) for an entry. When you press Tab, it goes to Text2.

2. When you click Roll, the following activities occur:

    a. If either of the top two text boxes has no entry, a beep is made and nothing else happens. The same thing happens if the number in Text1 is 0 or negative.

    b. If the number in Text2 is <2 or >12, the same thing happens.

    c. A sequential number appears in the form's caption to indicate the current round.

    d. Two random numbers, each 1-6, are generated and displayed in Text3. The sum is also compared to the number in Text2. If the two do not match, Text3's number is reduced by the amount in Text1. If the two match, Text1's number is multiplied by one of the following factors and added to Text3:

        2 or 12   36
        3 or 11   36/2

4 or 10	36/3
5 or 9	36/4
6 or 8	36/5
7	36/6

For example, if you bet 100 on number 7, your payoff is 600; and if you bet on 2 or 12, your payoff is 3600.

3. When you click Clear, the entries in the top two text boxes are cleared and the focus goes to Text1 for another entry.

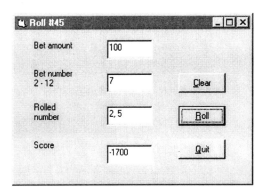

Figure 7.39   Gambling with two dice

If you want no change in the first two text boxes, you can continue to click Roll, press Alt+R, or press Enter (when Roll has the focus) without doing anything else. Figure 7.39 shows that I bet $100 on number 7. After trying this combination for 45 times, my total loss amounts to $1700. Gambling is addictive and expensive. Fortunately, this program costs you nothing while it entertains you.

D. (7ENCRYPT.FRM)

This program lets you enter a string in Text1 and the encrypted version automatically appears in Text2. Each encrypted character is the original character plus 1 in ANSI value, as shown in Figure 7.40. The program should erase the last character in both text boxes when the user presses the Del key to erase a character in Text1.

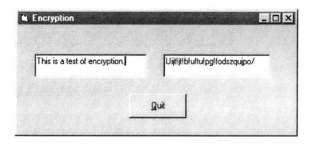

Figure 7.40   Encrypting a string

E. (7REVERS.FRM)

This program lets the user type a string in Text1 and reverses the string in Text2, as shown in Figure 7.41. Clicking Clear clears the two text strings and shifts the focus to Text1 for another entry.

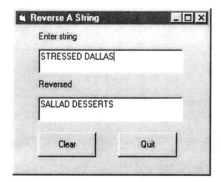

Figure 7.41   Reversing a string

F. (7PALIN.FRM)

This program determines whether a text string is a palindrome. When a string is entered in the top text box and the Test button clicked, the bottom text box shows a message. Case should be ignored in determining whether an entry is a palindrome, as shown in Figure 7.42 (this quote was attributed to Napoleon Bonaparte). Commas should also be ignored, as shown in Figure 7.43.

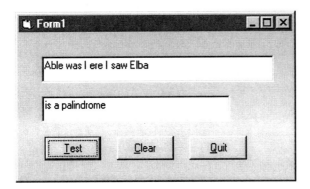

Figure 7.42   A palindrome

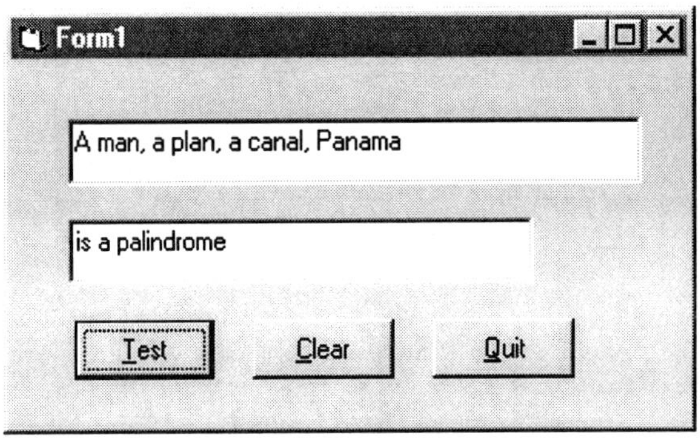

Figure 7.43   A palindrome with commas

G. (7CALC.FRM)

This program lets you type in Text1 a formula with two operands and an operator between them. When you press Enter, the result is displayed in Text2.

The program should accept and handle these operators:

    +   addition
    -    subtraction
    *   multiplication
    /   division
    ^   exponentiation
    \   integer division
    ~   modulus operation (returning remainder)

In typing a formula, you can optionally insert a space before and/or after an operator, as shown in Figure 7.44.

Use the InStr function to locate and extract the operator. Use other string functions to handle the operands. Use the Mod operator when ~ is encountered.

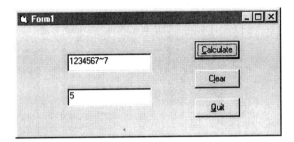

Figure 7.44   Converting a formula to a result

FUN AND GAME

A. (LIGHTS.FRM)

Figure 7.45   Traffic lights

This program (Figure 7.45) simulates traffic lights. There are two panels (frame controls), each with three circles (shape controls). When the program starts, the left panel's top circle shows green and the right panel's bottom circle shows red. After 2 seconds, both disappear and the middle circles show yellow for 1 second.

Then the left panel's bottom circle shows red and the right panel's top circle shows green for 2 seconds. The pattern is repeatedly indefinitely. The procedure shown below calls a timer procedure, which is the same as shown in the previous program.

```
Sub Form_Load ()
    Dim I As Integer
    Show            'show form
    Do
    For I = 0 To 2
        Shape1(I).FillStyle = 0        'solid
        Shape1(5 - I).FillStyle = 0    '2nd panel
        Select Case I
        Case 0
            Shape1(I).FillColor = vbGreen      '1st panel
            Shape1(5 - I).FillColor = vbRed    '2nd panel
            Timer1.Interval = 2000    '2 sec
            Timer1_Timer              'call timer proc
        Case 1
            Shape1(I).FillColor = vbYellow
            Shape1(5 - I).FillColor = vbYellow
            Timer1.Interval = 1000    '1 sec
            Timer1_Timer
        Case 2
            Shape1(I).FillColor = vbRed
            Shape1(5 - I).FillColor = vbGreen
            Timer1.Interval = 2000    '2 sec
            Timer1_Timer
        End Select
        Shape1(I).FillStyle = 1        'transparent
        Shape1(5 - I).FillStyle = 1    '2nd panel
    Next I
    Loop    'infinite loop
End Sub

Private Sub Timer1_Timer()
    Static Temp As Integer
        'track timer interval
    Temp = Temp + 1
    Do While DoEvents()
        If Temp Mod 2 = 0 Then Exit Do
            'exit after specified interval
    Loop
    Timer1.Interval = 0 'disable timer
End Sub
```

B. (TRIG.FRM)

This program demonstrates various aspects of trigonometry. It lets you draw a graph that resembles Figure 7.6 shown earlier in this chapter.

The graph in Figure 7.46 consists of a circle and two lines in the middle. These items are fixed. There are two additional lines, from a changing point on the circumference to the center and perpendicularly to the horizontal line. These two lines can be maneuvered by the user.

When you move the scroll bar between the 0 (Min) and 360 (Max) values, the two dynamic lines move accordingly. Moving the scroll bar up or down moves the two lines clockwise or counterclockwise. The four labels at the top right also show the changing values of X and Y coordinates and the angle's value in degrees and radians. Figure 7.46 shows the results when the angle is set to 45 degrees.

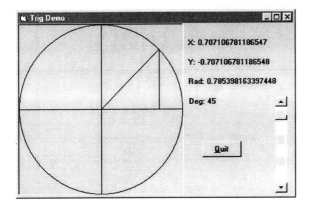

Figure 7.46   Showing trig ratios

```
Sub VScroll1_Change ()
    Dim Degree As Single
    Dim Radian As Single
    Dim Radius As Single
    Dim X As Single
    Dim Y As Single
    Dim Pi As Single
    Dim PB As PictureBox

    Set PB = Picture1    'use PB for Picture1
    lblRadian.Caption = "Deg: " & VScroll1.Value
        'show degree based on scroll value
    PB.Cls                      'clear each drawing
    Pi = Atn(1) * 4
    Radius = 1
    Degree = 360 - VScroll1.Value
        'angle in degree, counterclockwise
    Radian = VScroll1.Value * Pi / 180
        'convert to radian to show in label
```

```
        Degree = Degree * Pi / 180
            'convert to radian for calculation
        lblDegree.Caption = "Rad: " & Radian
            'show radian of angle
        PB.Scale (-1, -1)-(1, 1)
            'custom scale for picture box
        PB.Circle (0, 0), Radius    'draw full circle
        PB.Line (-1, 0)-(1, 0)      'hor line
        PB.Line (0, -1)-(0, 1)      'ver line
        X = Cos(Degree)             'get X, Y pos
        Y = Sin(Degree)
        PB.Line (0, 0)-(X, Y)       'from center to X, Y
        PB.Line (X, Y)-(X, 0)       'from X, Y to hor line
        lblX.Caption = "X: " & X    'show pos of X and Y
        lblY.Caption = "Y: " & Y
End Sub
```

Chapter 8
Managing Procedures,
Debugging, and Projects

TOPICS

A. General Procedures
B. Sub Procedures
C. Function Procedures
D. Sub and Function Compared
E. Passing By Value or Reference
F. Passing By Named Arguments
G. Recursion
H. Property Procedures
   a. Creating Property Procedures
   b. Using Property Set
   c. Declaring and Calling
   d. Read-Only and Custom Properties
I. Debugging Tools
   a. Watching Variables
   b. Debugging Windows
   c. Debugging Procedures
   d. Managing Variable Watch
   e. Menus and Debugging Buttons
J. Trapping Run-Time Errors
K. Modules and Scope
   a. Standard Modules
   b. Using Multiple Modules
   c. Scope of Procedures
   d. Managing Multiple Modules
L. Templates and Custom Controls
   a. Using Templates
   b. Adding/Removing Custom Controls
M. Browsing Objects
   a. Browsing Other Applications' Objects
   b. Browsing Your Own Objects
N. Making an EXE File

KEY TERMS

Calling   Diverting program execution to another procedure and, when the procedure is finished, returning to the original point.

Custom control   Also known as an OLE custom control or ActiveX control. It's stored in a separate file with the OCX extension. It can be added to the Toolbox and used like any other control. By adding custom controls to an application, you are using components (objects) created by others. The Learning Edition of Visual Basic comes with a few custom controls. The Professional and Enterprise Editions include many more. There are also numerous custom controls for sale by third-party vendors.

Function procedure   A user-defined general procedure that returns a value. A function procedure can also be used like a sub procedure.

General procedure   A procedure defined by the user; it can be a sub procedure a function procedure, or a property procedure.

Logic error   An error related to programming logic, occurring only at run time. Errors in variables, procedures, and arrays can lead to wrong results or unintended program flow.

Passing by reference   A programming technique of getting a procedure to pass (transfer) a variable's memory location to the called procedure. This allows the called procedure to alter the original value of the variable.

Passing by value   A programming technique of getting a procedure to pass (copy) a variable's value to the called procedure. The called procedure can maneuver the value but cannot alter the original copy.

Property procedure   A user-defined general procedure. There are three types: Property Get, Property Let, and Property Set. You use these to define and call property procedures. Property procedures can sometimes replace sub or function procedures. But mostly they are used to add properties to a class.

Recursion   A programming technique of getting a procedure to call itself. There is a limit as to how many times this can happen.

Run-time error   An error that occurs at run time, when a program is executed. It can be caused by a faulty program or user action such as not supplying a disk when saving data. You can make your program trap such an error at run time and handle it accordingly.

Sub procedure A user-defined general procedure that does not return a value.

Syntax error A programming error that occurs at design time. Incomplete or incorrect statements will trigger a syntax error. If Visual Basic's syntax checking feature is on (default), a brief error message appears, telling you what is wrong.

Template A reusable base module containing common elements to create applications. You add to this module the elements you commonly need for an application. After the module is saved as a template, it can be used again and again. For example, you can create and save an About form as a template. You can then add it to any application you develop.

Watch window A debugging window into which you can enter variables and expressions to observe their values in break mode. The expressions can be edited in break mode; their values will change accordingly.

This chapter covers three major topics in the following order:

- General procedures, including sub, function, and property procedures
- Debugging techniques, including watching variables and trapping run-time errors
- Managing projects and modules, including the Object Browser

GENERAL PROCEDURES

By now you should be thoroughly familiar with the concept that Visual Basic is object oriented and procedure based. You place objects on a form and attach procedure code to complete an application. When you double-click an object at design time, the Code window appears. In the Object box you can show all the objects. From the Procedure box you can display all the predefined event procedures for a specific object.

You may have noticed the **(General)** object in the Object box. In the past we have used it to declare variables that are accessible throughout a form. In this chapter we are going to use it as the key to general procedures.

A **general procedure** is a user-defined procedure. You tell Visual Basic what name you want to use and then write code for it. Writing a general procedure is not much different from writing an event procedure.

A general procedure can be a **sub procedure** or a **function procedure** (property procedure will be covered later). The major difference between the two is that the latter can return a value, but the former cannot. A function procedure can be likened to the numerous built-in functions we covered in the previous chapter. A sub procedure is comparable to an event procedure.

A general procedure and an **event procedure** differ in some important ways:

- An event procedure responds to an event such as a mouse click. A general procedure does not respond to events; it is instead invoked (called) by other procedures.

- An event procedure is always a sub procedure, not a function procedure, because it does not return a value.

- One procedure can call another, regardless of their type. You must, however, be aware of their scope, discussed in a section below.

- Although a function procedure created by you is similar to a built-in function, it can call other procedures while a built-in function cannot do that.

A **general procedure** is a subroutine or subprogram that contains instructions related to a task. If you have a lengthy and complex program, dividing it into multiple subprograms makes the program modular and gives you some advantages:

- The code is easier to read and debug. Since each procedure is limited to a well-defined task, the code is likely to be shorter and confined to a narrow purpose.

- The code is likely to be shorter because various procedures can call one another. For example, you may have a sorting routine confined to a procedure. Different procedures can then call this procedure to perform this task. Without this arrangement, the same code would have to be repeated in multiple procedures.

- The code can be recycled and put in another application. The above sorting routine, for example, can be put in a standard module. This module can then be incorporated into another application. This can save you the trouble of having to rewrite the same instructions.

Dividing a complex program into a number of subprograms can be compared to putting your papers (maybe related to your income tax) in different folders. If you organize them logically, you can easily find them when they are needed. If you dump the whole pile in a big box, you are likely to have a tough time finding what you need. In programming as well as in managing papers, a little planning and organization can go a long way and reap you tangible benefits. Sloppy as you go, so GIGO (garbage in, garbage out).

SUB PROCEDURES

Before explaining general procedures further, let us create one first. Follow these steps:

1. Start a new project.

2. Double-click the form to show the Code window.

3. Select Click from the Procedure box.

4. Add code as shown below:

```
Private Sub Form_Click ()
    Gobeep          'call a sub procedure
End Sub
```

In step **4**, you are asking Visual Basic to call a sub procedure. If you wish, you can add **Call** before the procedure's name, such as:

```
    Call Gobeep
```

A procedure's name must conform to the conventions for a variable name. Case makes no difference. The spelling of a called procedure's name, however, must match the calling statement.

If you run the program at this point, you'll get the *Sub or Function not defined* error. The reason is that Visual Basic cannot find a matching procedure to call and Gobeep makes no sense to it. You must create a general procedure named Gobeep.

Next, follow these steps to create a sub procedure named Gobeep:

1. From the Code window, choose the **Tools** menu from the menu bar. A list drops down.

2. Choose **Add Procedure**. A dialog box appears (Figure 8.1).

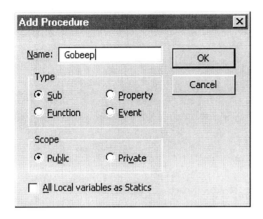

Figure 8.1   The Add Procedure dialog box

3. Type a name in the Name box and press Enter or click OK. The Code window appears and the Gobeep (the name you have provided) procedure template is displayed (Figure 8.2). Notice the top portion of the window. The Object box shows (General), and the Procedure box displays the name of the procedure.

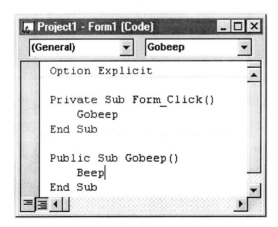

Figure 8.2   Coding a general procedure

4. Type Beep between the template lines.

You are now ready to run the program. Press F5 and click the form window. You should hear a beep each time you click the window.

You can make the calling statement pass a value to the called procedure. The calling statement may be like this:

```
Private Sub Form_Click ()
    Gobeep 5
End Sub
```

If you now run the program, you will get an error (*Wrong number of arguments or invalid property assignment*). You must modify the Gobeep procedure so that it will accept an argument. The modified version is shown below. (To display the procedure code in the Code window in **Procedure View**, you need to click (General) from the Object box, click the down arrow in the Procedure box, and then click the displayed procedure name.)

```
Public Sub Gobeep (J)
    Dim I As Integer
    For I = 1 To J
        Beep
    Next I
End Sub
```

The calling statement passes the value 5 to the called procedure. Variable J is then assigned this value. The For loop repeats 5 times. (To hear five beeps, you need to press F8 to begin. Then click the form. Then continue to press F8 to see the calling mechanism and the resulting five beeps.)

You can ask the user to supply a number. This number will then be passed to the called procedure to produce the specified number of beeps. The modified calling procedure is shown below.

```
Private Sub Form_Click ()
    Dim Num As Integer
    Num = InputBox("How many beeps?")
    Gobeep Num
End Sub
```

Suppose the user enters 5 after running the program. Variable Num holds this number. This number is then passed to J, the variable in the Gobeep procedure. This number is then used to control the looping operation.

TIP: Creating a New Procedure

You do not have to use the **Add Procedure dialog box** to create a general procedure. To bypass this dialog box. follow these steps:

1. With Full Module View on, move the cursor to an area outside of an existing procedure.

2. Type Sub or Function and a procedure name (if you wish, you can add Private, Public, or Static at the beginning).

3. Press Enter.

After step 3, the procedure template appears, and the cursor stays between the beginning and the ending lines. The screen is now ready for you to type your code. The Procedure box in the Code window also shows the name you have just entered.

FUNCTION PROCEDURES

A **function procedure**, like a sub procedure, is another form of a general procedure, which is created by the user. The major difference between a sub procedure and a function procedure is that a function procedure can return a value to the caller. We will discuss other differences in another section below.

Creating a function procedure follows the same steps as creating a sub procedure. The only difference is that you choose Function in the Add Procedure dialog box (Figure 8.1).

As a demonstration, start a new project and write the following procedures:

```
Private Sub Form_Click ()
    Print RandNum()  'call function and print result
End Sub

Public Function RandNum ()
    RandNum = Rnd 'generate a Rnd number and return
End Function
```

Now run the program and click the form window. Each time you click, a number appears.

Notice that the caller has a pair of parentheses at the end. This is optional in this situation; it's required only if an argument is passed.

We use the name RandNum three times, one to call a function, one as a function header, and one to return the call. When the first name is encountered, Visual Basic looks for a matching function name to call. After the matching function completes its course, the same name is used to respond to the caller. The two procedures are schematically linked this way:

```
Private Sub Form_Click ()
    Print RandNum() ──────────┐      'to call function
End Sub

    Public Function RandNum ()◄──┘  'function header
        RandNum = Rnd                'return to caller
    End Function
```

We can modify our program by making the caller pass two arguments and the function use the arguments. The calling program is changed as shown below.

```
Private Sub Form_Click ()
    Dim Lo As Integer, Hi As Integer
    Dim Num As Integer

    Lo = InputBox("Enter low number")
    Hi = InputBox("Enter high number")
    Num = RandNum(Lo, Hi)
    Print Num
End Sub
```

Here we prompt the user for a high and a low number so that the generated random number will be limited to this range. These numbers are then passed by the calling statement. When a value is returned, it is assigned to variable Num and then printed. This shows another way of manipulating the returned value; we could have bypassed the variable and directly printed the returned value, as we did earlier.

The function is also modified as shown below:

```
Public Function RandNum (LoNum, HiNum)
    RandNum = Fix((HiNum - LoNum + 1) * Rnd + LoNum)
End Function
```

The expression after the equal sign was explained in Chapter 7 when we discussed the **Rnd** function. It returns a random number between (and including) the low and the high numbers. This number is assigned to the function name, which in turn passes the value back to the calling statement.

Notice that we use two variables in the function header. This number must correspond to the one in the calling statement. Otherwise, An error will appear.

You can use the same variable names in the calling and the called procedures. We could have done it this way:

```
Public Function RandNum (Lo, Hi)
    RandNum = Fix((Hi - Lo + 1) * Rnd + Lo)
End Function
```

This will not cause conflict. These are local variables. They cease to exist once execution leaves the procedure where they reside. Another section below discusses procedure scope.

If you wish, you can specify a data type for a variable in a general procedure. In that case, do it this way:

```
Public Function RandNum (Lo As Integer, Hi As Integer)
```

NOTE   The **Procedure Attributes dialog box** (Tools | Procedure Attributes) is available after you have created at least one public variable or general procedure. All the public items can be pulled down from the Name combo box. You can then add some attributes, including a description. These can be read by the Object Browser. This subject will be explained later in this chapter.

SUB AND FUNCTION COMPARED

Sub and function procedures are similar in many ways but different in others. This section compares and contrasts them.

A sub procedure follows this syntax:

```
[Public|Private][Static] Sub name [(arglist)]
    [statements]
    [Exit Sub]
    [statements]
End Sub
```

Exit Sub works the same way as Exit For or Exit Do. When certain conditions are met, the procedure is exited and the statements below are ignored.

If you check *All Local variables as Statics* in the Add Procedure dialog box (Figure 8.1), the word **Static** will appear in the procedure header, following Private or Public. In that case, all local variables' values are preserved between calls; otherwise, they are erased. If you create a procedure manually (instead of using the Add Procedure dialog), you can manually add Static after Public or Private. You can delete this word if you change your mind.

A general procedure, like an event procedure, has the default **Public** scope. So the use of the keyword (Public) is optional. Such a procedure can be called from other modules. If you have a **Private** procedure instead, it can be called only from the same module, but not from another module. Suppose the RandNum function is in Form2 and changed to Private, using the following statement to call it from Form1 will result in the *Method or data member not found* error.

```
Print Form2.RandNum(Num1, Num2)
```

A function procedure follows a similar syntax:

```
[Public|Private][Static] Function name _
[(arglist)] [As type]
    [statements]
    [Exit Function]
    [statements]
    [name = expression]
End Function
```

The **As** keyword specifies the type of data returned, which can be any legal data type discussed in Chapter 5. Static, Public, Private, and Exit are the same as in a sub procedure.

A sub procedure caller is a complete statement and can thus stand alone with or without parameters. A sub procedure does not return a value, so the caller's name does not appear as part of a statement.

A function procedure is like a two-way street, in contrast to a sub procedure being a one-way street. A function name appears three times to provide for a two-way communication. A caller is a function name, it calls the function of the same name, and in the function body a function name returns a value to the caller.

A function procedure caller is an expression, not a complete statement (see below for an exception). Like Visual Basic's numerous built-in functions, it cannot be by itself. It can be used as a command's parameter or maneuvered as a value. Here are two examples:

```
Print FuncName (Num1, Num2)
RetVal = FuncName (Num1, Num2) * 10
```

In the first example, the returned value is printed. In the second, it is multiplied by 10 and then assigned to variable RetVal.

A function caller requires a pair of parentheses at the end—if an argument is passed and a value is to be returned by the function (this will be clarified at the end of this section). If no argument is passed, you can include nothing in the parentheses or get rid of them. If two or more arguments are used, separate them with commas. The number of arguments in the caller must normally correspond to those in the called function.

You can use two ways to call a sub procedure:

```
Call SubName [(argumentlist)]
SubName [argumentlist]
```

If **Call** is used, arguments, if any, must be enclosed in a pair of parentheses. If Call is not used, do not use parentheses to enclose arguments—unless you mean to pass them by value (see the next section).

A sub or function procedure's argument list can include the following optional keywords:

[Optional][ByVal | ByRef][ParamArray]

ByVal and **ByRef** will be covered in another section below. **ParamArray** is used to pass an arbitrary number of arguments and will be discussed shortly. **Optional** indicates an optional argument. Consider the following example:

```
Private Sub Form_Click()
    Print Sum(56, 75, 89)
End Sub

Function Sum(Optional Num1 As Integer, Optional Num2 _
As Integer, Optional Num3 As Integer) As Integer
    If IsMissing(Num1) Then Exit Function
    Sum = Num1 + Num2 + Num3
End Function
```

We specify Integer in the function header. VB5 allows you to specify data types. VB4 permitted only Variants here.

The caller passes three arguments. The function expects from zero to three arguments. If the passed arguments are within the limit, the passing mechanism will cause no error. If you pass a higher number of arguments, the *Wrong number of arguments* error will appear.

If you expect one argument, then take out the first Optional keyword and keep the rest. After an argument is specified as Optional, all the subsequent arguments must be Optional as well.

In our example, we use the **IsMissing** function to respond to the situation when no argument is passed. Even though the passing mechanism will cause no error when no argument is passed, our equation will cause the *Type mismatch* error. So when this happens, the function is exited without doing anything.

VB4/5 has added a number of Is functions. They include:

> **IsArray**
> **IsDate**
> **IsEmpty**
> **IsError**
> **IsMissing**
> **IsNull**
> **IsNumeric**
> **IsObject**

Each returns a Boolean value of True or False, as shown in the above IsMissing example and the IsDate function covered in Chapter 7. These can be used like **VarType** or **TypeName** functions (see Chapter 5) to determine data types.

You can use **ParamArray** followed by an array name to make a procedure receive an arbitrary number of arguments passed from a caller. Here is an example:

```
Private Sub Form_Click()
    Print Sum(1, 3, 4, 5, 9)
        'pass arguments, print returned total
End Sub

Function sum(ParamArray Nums())     '--Listing 1--
    Dim Item As Variant, Total As Integer

    For Each Item In Nums
        Total = Total + Item    'add up array elements
    Next Item
    Sum = Total       'return total
End Function
```

The Sum function passes five arguments to the Nums array (the parentheses are required here), which needs no declaration. We then use a For Each loop to add up all the values in the array and return the sum to the caller. This arrangement allows you to pass any number of individual arguments. However, you cannot pass an array in this situation; it will lead to the *Type mismatch* error.

A function call can follow the syntax of a sub call; this is new since VB4. In that case, no value is returned. The following two statements are identical:

```
FuncName Arg1, Arg2
Call FuncName(Arg1, Arg2)
```

Both are statements, not part of an expression like a typical function call. The values are passed to the function. The function can process the arguments as a sub does, but it cannot return a value as a function normally does. So our Randnum function in the previous section could be handled this way:

```
Private Sub Form_Click()
    RandNum   'call function like a sub
End Sub

Public Function RandNum()
    Print Rnd  'no return of value
End Function
```

The generated random number is printed in the called function. No value is returned to the caller. You can still place the following statement in the function to return a value to the caller. It will not cause an error. But the returned value is discarded because the caller has no mechanism to receive it.

```
RandNum = Rnd
```

PASSING BY VALUE OR REFERENCE

When a procedure is called, arguments are normally **passed by reference (ByRef)**. That means the memory addresses are given to the called procedure, sub or function. The procedure can change the original values. As a demonstration, let us write the following two procedures.

```
Private Sub Form_Click()
    Dim Num1 As Integer
    Dim Num2 As Integer

    Num1 = 100
    Print "before call,  Num1 = "; Num1
    Num2 = Half(Num1)         'call function
    Print "after call,  Num1 = "; Num1
```

```
        Print "after call,  Num2 = "; Num2
End Sub

Public Function Half(Num3)
        Half = Num3 / 2        'return to caller
        Num3 = 0               'assign new value
End Function
```

After running the program and clicking the window, the result is shown in Figure 8.3.

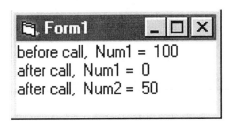

Figure 8.3   The effect of passing by reference

In the calling operation, the value of Num1, which is 100, is passed to the function by reference. Variable Num3 receives the value and returns half of it to Num2. Num3 is also assigned the new value 0. That means the memory location called Num1 and Num3 now holds the value 0. When the function completes its course, the calling procedure prints 0 for Num1.

If you do not want a called procedure to alter the original value, use the **ByVal** keyword to send a copy. This is called **passing arguments by value**. This does not allow the called procedure to access the original memory location. Whatever the procedure does to the value, the original remains intact.

To pass an argument by value, add the ByVal keyword before a variable name in a called procedure's header. Here is an example:

```
Public Function Half (ByVal Num3)
        Half = Num3 / 2        'return to caller
        Num3 = 0               'assign new value
End Function
```

After making the above modification, running the same program shows a different result in Figure 8.4. Even though Num3 is assigned 0, it does not affect the original value of Num1, which remains to be 100.

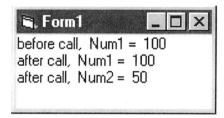

Figure 8.4   The result of passing by value

You can add the ByVal keyword in the calling statement, like this:

```
Num2 = Half(ByVal Num3)
```

But this will not change things. If you add it here but not in the called function's header, you will get the *Type mismatch* error.

The simplest way to pass an argument by value is to put it in a pair of parentheses in the calling statement. This does not require the use of ByVal anywhere, even though it will do no harm if you put it in the called function's header. So this is all you need to do:

```
Num2 = Half((Num1))
```

Notice the extra pair of parentheses. It is necessary if you intend to pass an argument by value.

Normally you need no parentheses when calling a sub procedure, and add them when combined with Call. If you want to pass arguments by value to a sub procedure, add an extra pair. Use one pair when Call is not involved and two pairs when Call is used.

If you pass several arguments, you can selectively pass them by value or by reference. If you use ByVal, just add it before a specific variable to the called function's header. If you use parentheses, selectively enclose the specific variables in the calling statement. Here are two examples:

```
Sub SubName(ByVal Num1, Num2)      'called sub's header
Call SubName ((Num1), Num2)        'calling statement
```

In both cases, Num1 is passed by value and Num2 by reference.

You can use a keyword called **ByRef**, which is intended to contrast the ByVal argument. This word's use is optional and redundant because it's the default. If you specify in a sub or function header that a variable is ByRef, you can still enclose a calling statement's variable in a pair of parentheses to pass the argument by value.

PASSING BY NAMED ARGUMENTS

Chapter 7 explained that you can use **named arguments** in many built-in functions. The same thing can be applied to a general procedure. Consider the following example:

```
Private Sub Form_Click()
    Print Pay(Rate:=12, Hours:=45)
End Sub

Public Function Pay(Hours, Rate)      '--Listing 2--
    If Hours <= 40 Then
        Pay = Hours * Rate    'regular
    Else
        Pay = Rate * (40 + 1.5 * (Hours - 40))
    End If            'overtime
End Function
```

Clicking the form will print 570 to the screen. Here we pass two values, the first is the number of hours and the second the pay rate. The function then returns the calculated result.

There is no need to declare the named variables in this situation—even though Option Explicit is specified. The undeclared variables are treated as Variants. You can optionally use Dim to declare a specific data type. If you want to use these variables outside of this context, you must declare them first.

Notice that in the calling statement we place Rate before Hours, but the function header reverses the two. When we use named arguments, order no longer makes a difference. If we don't use named arguments, the two pairs must match in position. If the function is not changed, the calling statement must be:

```
    Print Pay(45, 12)     'not Pay(12, 45)
```

When using named arguments, the corresponding names must be identical. Otherwise, the *Named argument not found* error will appear. This happens, for example, if we change one Rate to Rates.

RECURSION

A procedure can directly or indirectly call itself. This is known as **recursion**. There is, however, a limit as to the number of times a procedure can call itself. The number is determined by the operating system. As a demonstration, try the following procedure:

```
Private Sub Form_Click()
    Static staK As Integer     'retain value
    staK = staK + 1     'increment counter
    Debug.Print staK    'output to Immediate window
    Form_Click          'call itself
End Sub
```

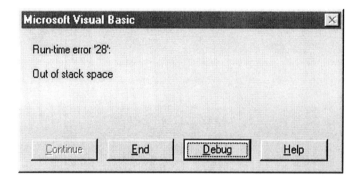

Figure 8.5   Error caused by recursion

Now press F5 to run the program. Expose the Immediate window so that its output can be visible. Click the form to execute the Click procedure. Eventually the program stops and Figure 8.5 appears.

Examine the numbers in the Immediate window. In my case, the last number is 5386. Yours may be different, depending on your PC. Your hard disk may also be busily clicking as it tries to handle the overload. (In VB3, the limit was quickly reached at 467. The hard disk was not activated. The difference reflects the way Windows 3.1 and Windows 95 manage memory.)

Each time a procedure calls itself, the procedure is executed from the beginning. What happens to the portion below the calling point? A copy, plus all the pertinent values, is stored in the memory area called the **stack**. If recursion occurs too many times, the stack space is exhausted and hence the error.

After the recursion ends, assuming no error, each of the previously stored copy is executed in reverse order. This order enables Visual Basic to keep the two parts (executed and unexecuted) in sync. This order is demonstrated in this procedure:

```
Private Sub Form_Click ()
    Static staK As Integer     'retain value
    staK = staK + 1            'increment counter
    Print staK
    If staK < 3 Then Form_Click 'call itself
    Print staK
    staK = staK - 1
End Sub
```

The above procedure will print the following numbers to the screen:

1
2
3
3
2
1

The procedure below provides a more elaborate demonstration. The result is shown in Figure 8.6.

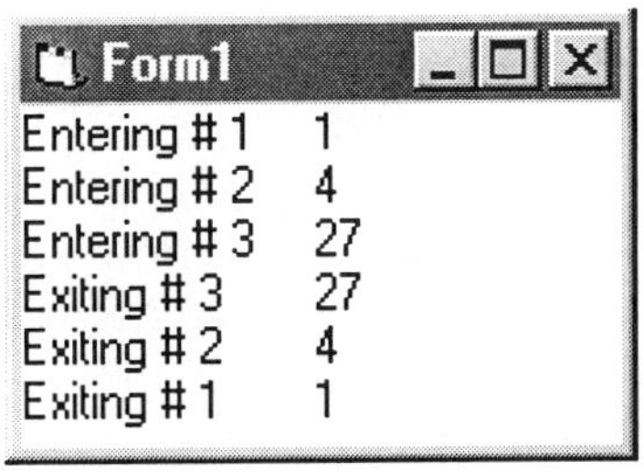

```
Form1                    _ □ X
Entering # 1    1
Entering # 2    4
Entering # 3    27
Exiting # 3     27
Exiting # 2     4
Exiting # 1     1
```

Figure 8.6   Recursion demonstration

```
Private Sub Form_Click ()
    ReDim Arr(3) As Integer          'local array
    Static staA As Integer           'retain value

    staA = staA + 1
    Arr(staA) = staA ^ staA       'assign power to arr. ele.
    Print "Entering #"; staA, Arr(staA)
    If staA < 3 Then Form_Click      'call itself
            'below is initially skipped
    Print "Exiting #"; staA, Arr(staA)
```

```
        staA = staA - 1
End Sub
```

We use **Static** to declare variable staA so that its value will be retained during run time. We can also use Dim to declare staA at the form level; the result will be the same. If we use **Dim** in the procedure instead, the If statement will never become true because each time Dim is executed, a new copy of the variable will be created and the current staA's value will be initialized to 0 (the previous copies are not accessible at this time); so the recursion will continue until the stack space is exhausted because staA's value is always either 0 or 1.

Since we use ReDim (we can also use Dim here) to declare a local array, each previously stored value is erased when ReDim is executed. So when the second Print statement is executed for the first time, Arr(3) has the value of 3, but Arr(2) and Arr(1) are both empty. In spite of that, the correct numbers are printed because they are retrieved from the stack where previous copies are saved. We could have used a static or form-level array here and produced the same result.

A little distinction between **Dim/ReDim** and **Static** is in order. A static variable has program-wide longevity. While the program is running, its value is not erased. In the case of recursion, no new copy is created. With Dim or ReDim, recursion results in creating a new local copy that is visible only during the appropriate iteration. So variable staA may hold a value. But when the procedure calls itself and encounters the Dim statement, the old staA is stored in the stack and a new staA with 0 initial value is created. The old staA's value is visible only when recursion rewinds itself backward from the last copy to the first copy.

Recursion is commonly used in calculating a **factorial** (Figure 8.7). To do that, we need to use a function procedure to call itself and pass a new argument in each call. Here is an example:

```
Private Sub Form_Click()
    Dim Num As Integer, RetVal As Long

    Num = 10
    RetVal = Fac(Num) 'call function and pass argument
    Print "Final tally:", RetVal
End Sub

Public Function Fac(Num As Integer) As Long
    Static Total As Long

    If Num = 1 Then
        Total = 1      'last factor; end recursion
    Else
        Total = Num * Fac(Num - 1)
```

```
            'call itself, decrement argument
      End If

      Print Num; "!  =  ", Total
      Fac = Total          'return total
End Function
```

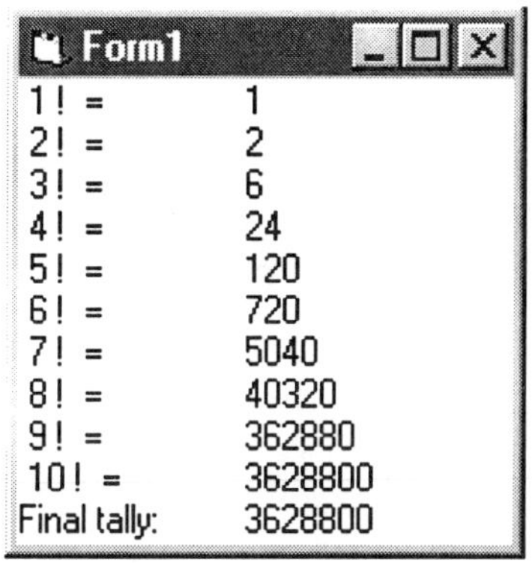

Figure 8.7   Factorials

When the Fac function is called, the initial argument passed is 10. In the function procedure itself, we use an If-Then control structure to get the function to call itself when Num is greater than 2. So when Num is 10, the Else clause is executed. The caller then passes the Num-1 argument to the function, resulting in 9 being passed. This continues until Num reaches 1.

Recursion ends when the If (rather than Else) branch is executed. Then the previously stored copies of the unexecuted portion are executed in reverse order. The proof of this order comes in the values of variables Total and Num. Notice we don't control them by incrementing or decrementing their values in the Print statement. But their values go from low to high by themselves.

Recursion is slow and limited by stack space; use it only as a last resort. To illustrate this point, you can press F8 continuously to see how a recursive function behaves. The following procedure can replace the above two procedures. Not only it is speedier, but also there is no possibility of triggering the *Out of stack space* error.

```
Private Sub Form_Click ()      '--Listing 3--
    Dim I As Integer, Total As Long
    Total = 1
```

```
        For I = 1 To 10
            Total = Total * I
            Print I & "! =", Total
        Next I
        Print "Final tally:", Total
End Sub
```

PROPERTY PROCEDURES

A **property procedure** a cross between a property and a general procedure. It can be created like any general procedure but is used (called) like a built-in property. You can use a set of matching property procedures (all sharing the same name) to create and manipulate custom properties.

There are three types of property procedures, as described below:

Property Get	Returns a property value; used like a function.
Property Let	Assigns a property value.
Property Set	References and processes objects.

You use Property Let or Property Set to assign and process a property value and Property Get to read the value. Property Let and Property Set follow the same syntax, which is slightly different from that of Property Get. In the next section, we use the Let-Get pair as examples. Property Set will be covered in another section.

Creating Property Procedures

Creating a property procedure is the same as creating a general procedure. You can manually enter a name in the Code window as explained earlier; after you enter a name, a procedure template will appear for you to enter code.

You can also use the Tools | Add Procedure command to do the same thing. After you choose this command, Figure 8.1 (shown at the beginning of this chapter) appears. Here you type a procedure name and check Property for Type. As before, you can change from Public to Private for Scope or enter a check to make all local variables static.

After you click OK, two procedure templates (the first two shown below) appear. The second template also has a default variable (vNewValue) automatically added. If you wish, you can change the variable's name or delete an unwanted template.

The Let procedure expects a Variant argument, and the Get procedure returns a Variant value. If you wish, you can omit or delete these parameters.

```
Public Property Get TextSize() As Variant
    Text1.Text = "width: " & Text1.Width & _
    "    height: " & Text1.Height
End Property

Public Property Let TextSize(vNewValue As Variant)
    Text1.Width = Text1.Width * vNewValue
    Text1.Height = Text1.Height * vNewValue
End Property

Private Sub cmdEnlarge_Click()
    TextSize = 1.2    'assign value to property; call Let
End Sub

Private Sub cmdShow_Click()
    Dim Txtsize    'return value
    Txtsize = TextSize()
        'assign procedure to a variable
        'call Get property procedure
End Sub
```

As a demonstration, we plan to let the user click a command button to enlarge a text box's size by 20% after each click, and click another button to show the size of this text box. The interface is shown in Figure 8.8. At design time, add a text box and place it at the top left corner. Also add two command buttons and place them some distance below the text box. Then write the procedures shown above.

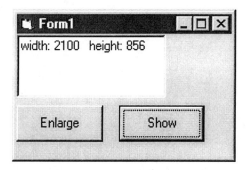

Figure 8.8   Demonstrating property procedures

At run time, when you click Enlarge, the value of 1.2 is assigned to the property named TextSize. This assignment in turn triggers the Property Let TextSize procedure. The value of 1.2 is passed to the vNewValue variable, which in turn is used to change the text box's Width and Height properties.

When the Show button is clicked, the Property Get TextSize procedure is called. Notice the calling mechanism—assigning the procedure name to a variable. This statement executes the procedure, which assigns the Width and Height values to the text box's Text property, thus displaying them in the box.

Our property procedures can be converted to sub procedures to achieve the same thing. The converted procedures are shown below. Property Get is changed to TextSize1 and Property Let to TextSize2. The default variable (vNewValue) is changed to show that it is not fixed. The calling mechanisms, shown in the last two procedures, are also changed to conform to a sub procedure's requirements.

```
Public Sub TextSize1()
    Text1.Text = "width: " & Text1.Width & _
    "   height: " & Text1.Height
End Sub

Public Sub TextSize2(Var)
    Text1.Width = Text1.Width * Var
    Text1.Height = Text1.Height * Var
End Sub

Private Sub cmdEnlarge_Click()
    TextSize2 1.2     'call procedure and pass argument
End Sub

Private Sub cmdShow_Click()
    TextSize1     'call procedure
End Sub
```

Using Property Set

Property Set can be used like the **Set** statement. The latter is normally used to assign an object such as a command button to a variable. Here is an example:

```
Dim Cmd                 'define a Variant variable
Set Cmd = Command1      'assign object to variable
Caption = Cmd.Caption      'use Cmd for Command1
```

The last statement will change the form's caption to Command1's caption. After the first two statements, we can use Cmd to reference Command1. (We will cover this subject more thoroughly in Chapter 9.) Here the Set statement does nothing other than setting a reference to an object. Property Set, on the other hand, can do more.

You can also use Set to call a Property Set procedure and pass arguments to the procedure. The procedure can process the passed arguments. This in effect expands the power of the Set statement.

As a demonstration, add a third command button to Figure 8.8 and name it cmdSet. Add a form-level variable named TxtObj so that we can use it in several procedures. Then write the Click procedure for the command button and the new Property Set procedure shown below. To write the Property Set procedure, just enter the header line below a procedure separator line; a template will automatically appear.

```
Dim TxtObj  'declare form-level Variant var

Private Sub cmdSet_Click()     '--Listing 4--
    Set TxtDemo = Text1
        'call TxtDemo procedure and pass Text1 as arg
    Caption = TxtObj.Text
        'assign processed object's text to form caption
End Sub

Property Set TxtDemo(Wid)
    Set TxtObj = Wid
        'assign passed arg to form-level variable
    With TxtObj   'use new var to reference object
        .Top = 0
        .Left = 0
        .Width = Width  'textbox and form same width
        .ForeColor = vbBlue
        .BackColor = vbCyan
        .FontSize = 20
        .Text = "This is a demo."
    End With
End Property
```

We use the Set statement in the Click procedure to call the Property Set procedure and pass Text1 as an argument. The Property Set procedure than processes the passed object by altering its original properties. In both places, a form-level variable is used to reference the object. This variable can be declared as an Object or Variant (or unspecified). This shows that a Property Set procedure can do more than the simple Set statement.

You can handle Property Set the way you use Property Let, with the following exceptions; the next section will provide more details:

- A calling statement must start with Set.
- The last passed argument must be an object.
- The last variable in the procedure header must be able to accept an object.

Declaring and Calling

You need to follow this syntax to declare a property procedure:

```
[Public|Private][Static] Property {Get|Let|Set} name _
[(arguments)][As type]
```

The arguments for Let and Set are the same, but are different from those for Get, as shown below:

Procedure	Syntax
Property Get	Property Get name(1,...,n) [As type]
Property Let	Property Let name(1,...,n, n+1)
Property Set	Property Set name(1,...,n, n+1)

Notice that Let and Set have the same number of arguments, which is one more than those for Get.

Property Get has an optional type specification at the end to specify the returned data type; if not specified, a Variant is returned. The others don't have this because they don't return a value.

Also, the last argument of each matching pair must be the same data type. So argument $n+1$ of Property Let (or Set) must be matching the data type specified by As in the Property Get header.

Calling a property procedure and passing arguments require special rules, as shown below:

Procedure	Syntax
Property Get	variable = [object.]propertyname[(arguments)]
Property Let	[object.]propertyname[(arguments)] = argument
Property Set	Set [object.]propertyname[(arguments)] = argument

Let's use a concrete example to illustrate these rules. Consider the following modifications of our previous project:

```
Public Property Get TextSize(Wid, Hi)
    Text1.Text = "width: " & Text1.Width & _
    "  height: " & Text1.Height & vbCrLf _
    & Wid & Hi
End Property

Public Property Let TextSize(Wid, Hi, BC)
    With Text1
```

```
            .Width = Text1.Width * Wid
            .Height = Text1.Height * Hi
            .BackColor = BC
    End With
End Property

Private Sub cmdEnlarge_Click()
    TextSize(1.2, 1.3) = vbRed 'call Let, pass arguments
End Sub

Private Sub cmdShow_Click()
    Dim Txtsize, Arg1, Arg2

    Arg1 = "arg 1    "
    Arg2 = "arg 2"
    txtsize = TextSize(Arg1, Arg2)
        'call Get, pass arguments
End Sub
```

Widen the Enlarge button is clicked in this new arrangement, three arguments are passed to the Let procedure. The text box is widened by 1.2 times and the height increased by 1.3 times, and the box's background color is changed to red.

When the Show button is clicked, two text-string arguments are passed to the Get procedure. They are then displayed at the end of the original string. If Text1's MultiLine property has been set to True, the arguments appear in a new line; otherwise, the line break (vbCrLf) characters will only appear as two solid rectangles and only one line of text is shown.

The cmdShow procedure passes two arguments to the **Property Get** procedure. The caller's arguments are enclosed in a pair of parentheses; these arguments in turn match the two variables in the procedure's header. The whole thing is then assigned to a variable.

Our cmdEnlarge procedure now passes three arguments, with the first two placed in parentheses and before the = sign and with the last argument placed after the = sign. These arguments are passed to the **Property Let** procedure as shown below:

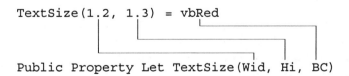

```
TextSize(1.2, 1.3) = vbRed




Public Property Let TextSize(Wid, Hi, BC)
```

So, when you are passing multiple arguments to a Property Let (or Set) procedure, remember this rule: Place the last argument after an = sign and all the others (separated by commas) before the = sign and enclosed in a pair of parentheses. If there is only one argument, place it after the = sign.

In the case of **Property Set**, the calling statement must start with Set. Also, since Set is used to maneuver objects, the last argument in both the caller and the procedure header must be an object, such as Text1 or Command1. So our Property Set procedure in the previous section can be called like this:

```
Set TxtDemo(1.2, 1.3) = Text1
```

This also requires the procedure header to have two additional arguments. The last argument is a object, but the others can be anything.

There is still one more rule to remember: the variables used in each Let-Get or Set-Get pair must be matching in names. In our example we use Hi and Wid in both procedures. If we change either one without doing the same in the matching procedure, the error message shown in Figure 8.9 will appear. Be prepared to see this ubiquitous message. It will also appear if the numbers of arguments in the matching pair don't match. (Remember that a Let or Set procedure has one more argument than its matching Get procedure.)

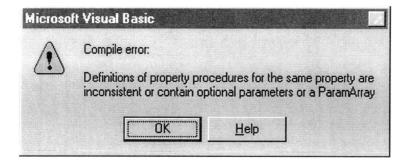

Figure 8.9   An error in calling a property procedure

Many of the rules related to sub or function can be applied to property procedures. As in a sub or function procedure, you can use ByVal or ByRef to pass values. You can use Exit Property as you use Exit Sub or Exit Function. Property procedures can also be put in an array and passed to a procedure. Arrays will be covered in Chapter 9.

Read-Only and Custom Properties

You can use a Property Get procedure to create a read-only custom property. If there is no matching Property Let or Property Set procedure, the contents in the Property Get procedure cannot be altered at run time, thus making it read-only. Consider the following example.

```
Private Sub Form_Click()
    Print Coder
End Sub

Property Get Coder()
    Coder = "Written by Minnie Smart"
End Property
```

When the form is clicked at run time, the Coder property will be printed to the form window. The property is defined in the Property Get Coder procedure, which returns a text string.

The Coder property is read-only because it cannot be changed by a user of this application. It can, however, be treated like any built-in property of the module (Form1 in our case) to which this custom property is attached. In the following two statements, the first will print the property and the second will display it as the form caption. In either case, the object before the dot is optional.

```
    Print Form1.Coder
    Form1.Caption = Coder
```

Since a property procedure is also a procedure, you can pass arguments to it. In the following example, a string is passed to the procedure, which returns it after combining it with another string.

```
Private Sub Form_Click()
    Dim Author As String
    Author = "Written by: "
    Print Coder(Author)
    Print Form1.Coder(Author)
    Form1.Caption = Coder(Author)
End Sub

Property Get Coder(Author)
    Coder = Author & "Minnie Smart"
End Property
```

You can create a custom property with True and False values. The user can then use the property to set either value. To demonstrate the following example, add

Text1 to a clear form and write the following procedures. When the form is clicked at run time, the CusBox property is set to True. The property procedure is called to change several of Text1's properties.

```
Private Sub Form_Click()          '--Listing 5--
    Form1.CusBox = True
End Sub

Property Let CusBox(blnTF As Boclean)
    If blnTF Then
        With Text1
            .BackColor = vbCyan
            .FontSize = 12
            .ForeColor = vbBlue
        End With
    End If
End Property
```

Property procedures are useful when you want to create classes. In that case, a property procedure becomes an object's property that can be maneuvered by code at run time. This will be covered in Chapter 12 when we discuss classes and OLE Automation.

DRILL

Choose the following options to answer questions 1-4:

       a.   general procedure
       b.   sub procedure,
       c.   function procedure
       d.   event procedure

_____ 1.   A procedure that will respond to a mouse click.

_____ 2.   A broad term for a user-defined procedure.

_____ 3.   A user-defined procedure that returns a value.

_____ 4.   A user-defined procedure that does not return a value.

_____ 5.   By default when a variable is passed to a procedure, the procedure has access to the address of the variable and can alter the original value. True of false?

_____ 6.   If 5 is passed to this function, five numbers will be printed to the screen. True of false?

```
Function Demo(Arg)
   Print Arg
   Arg = Demo(Arg - 1)
End Function
```

_____ 7. This function will be exited when Arg has the value of 0. True or false?

```
Function Demo(Arg)
   Print Arg
   Arg = Demo(Arg - 1)
   If Arg = 0 Then Exit Function
End Function
```

_____ 8. In the following function call, the XXX in the function header (last line below) should be:
a. erased
b. Optional
c. Array
d. ParamArray

```
Private Sub Form_Click()
    Print Sum (12, 3, 4, 5, 9)
End Sub

Function Sum(XXX nums())
```

_____ 9. To call a function and return a value, you need to use this statement:

a. Arg = Test (10)
b. Arg = Test ((10))
c. Arg = Test 10
d. Call Test (10)
e. both a and b

_____ 10. To create a read-only property, you use the _____ _____ procedure.

_____ 11. When you call a Property Set procedure, the last argument must be:

a. an object
b. a numeric
c. an array
d. any data type

PRACTICE

■ 1. How do sub and function procedures differ in their calling conventions?

■ 2. How do "passing by reference" and "passing by value" differ?

■ 3. How can you pass an argument by value?

■ 4. Change the Sum function in Listing 1 to Avg and make necessary modifications so that an arbitrary number of values can be passed to it and it will return the average. When the following statement is executed, it should return 88.

```
Print Avg(96, 93, 84, 79)
```

■ 5. Modify the Pay function in Listing 2 so that it will allow a calling statement to pass three named arguments like below. The returned amount should be 15% less than the original amount.

```
Print Pay(Rate:=12, Hours:=45, Deduct:=0.15)
```

■ 6. Suppose you are a real-estate agent. You get 3.5% commission for listing or selling a property and 7% for both. Write a function procedure that will accept three named arguments and return the commission amount based on the arguments passed. The following call should return 7000. If either of the first two arguments is False, the amount should be 3500. If both are False, the amount should be 0.

```
Private Sub Form_Click()
    Print Commission(List:=True, Sell:=True, _
    Price:=100000)
     'call function, pass named arguments
End Sub
```

■ 7. Change Listing 3 so that it will pass a value to a Fac function procedure, which will use a For loop to calculate the factorial and return it to the caller.

■ 8. Will the following procedure print the text string to the screen three times? Explain.

```
Private Sub Command1_Click ()
    Dim I As Integer
    I = I + 1
    Print "xxx"
```

```
      If I = 3 Then Exit Sub
      Command1_Click
End Sub
```

9. Assuming that I has been declared as a form-level variable, what happens when this procedure is executed.

```
Private Sub Command1_Click ()
    I = I + 1
    Print "xxx"
    If I = 3 Then Exit Sub
    Command1_Click
    Print I
End Sub
```

10. Explain what the following procedures do.

```
Private Sub Command1_Click()
  Test 5
End Sub

Sub Test(Arg)
  Print Arg
  If Arg > 0 Then Test (Arg - 1)
End Sub
```

11. Change the above to a function, which should return the sum of the digits of the passed value. For example, if 10 is passed, 55 is returned.

12. Write a read-only property procedure that will return your name when called by the procedure below

```
Private Sub Command1_Click()
    Print "My name is: "; MyName
End Sub
```

13. Explain what the following procedures do. Enter the procedures and press F8 continuously to observe and report the pattern.

```
Dim MeName As String

Private Sub Command1_Click()
    Dim NickName As String
    MyName = "John Smith"
    NickName = MyName()
    Print "My name is "; MeName; NickName
End Sub

Property Get MyName()
    MyName = ", also known as a genius."
```

```
End Property

Property Let MyName(Arg)
    MeName = Arg
End Property
```

■ 14. In Listing 4, add Text2 to the form and pass both text boxes to the
Property Set procedure. The procedure should process only Text2.

■ 15. Modify Listing 4 so that all the values controlling Text1 are passed from
the calling statement.

■ 16. In Listing 5, add Command1 and modify the project so that when
Command1 is clicked, Text1's default values will be restored.

DEBUGGING TOOLS

Errors come with programming; they are part of the game. Experienced
programmers make mistakes; inexperienced programmers make more mistakes.
The question is not whether you can make mistakes, but how to debug them when
they start bugging you.

While the bad news is that bugs are inevitable in programming, the good news is
that Visual Basic provides a host of tools to exterminate them. These techniques
will be discussed in the sections below, after we take an excursion to explore the
types of bugs you are likely to encounter.

Generally, you will encounter three kinds of errors:

- Syntax errors
- Logic errors
- Run-time errors

Syntax errors are the easiest to identify and rectify. It happens when you enter
something that is not what Visual Basic expects; it responds by showing you one
of the numerous error messages. For example, you might enter this line:

```
If varX = 0
```

As you move the cursor away, the line turns red (unless you have changed colors
in the Tools | Options | Editor tab) and the *Expected: Then or GoTo* error
appears. It tells you that you need to end this line with Then or GoTo.

You can press F1 to show more help. In our case, the *Expected: <value>* help topic appears. It is, however, not particularly helpful; it doesn't say that you need to end this line with Then. On such an occasion, you can move the cursor to the keyword (If in our case) and press F1 to show the pertinent help topic.

The Options dialog box (from the Tools | Options command) has the Editor tab. At the top left corner there is the **Auto Syntax Check** check box. It is checked by default. You can uncheck it to turn off syntax checking. After that, syntax errors will result in lines turning red but not triggering error messages. This arrangement is useful at the preliminary stage of writing code for a larger project.

Visual Basic cannot spot **logic errors** until a program is run. At that point, all the components are put together and checked. Only then can logic errors be identified. For example, you may have a function call. The caller may pass two arguments, but the function itself expects only one argument. In response, Visual Basic issues the *Wrong number of arguments* error.

Sometimes syntax errors and logic errors become blurred. For example, if you have an If control structure without End If, the error will not be detected until the program runs. This is a syntax error but Visual Basic cannot catch it until run time because the syntax involves multiple lines..

Another example is using a reserved word. Suppose you have this line without declaring the variable:

```
Right = 0
```

It will trigger the *Argument not optional* error at run time. Pressing F1 will show the *Argument not optional* help topic. It says that you need to supply missing arguments. It leaves you wondering, "What arguments?" If you knew that Right is a built-in function's name and that it cannot be used as a variable name, you might have avoided such a mistake. In this situation, you might want to press F1 when the cursor in on the word in the Code window. If a help topic matching the word appears, this is a reserved word. If the *Keyword Not Found* topic appears instead, this is not a reserved word.

Sometimes Visual Basic may be confused by your carelessness. Consider this scenario:

```
Do
    For I = 1 To 10
Loop
```

Figure 8.10 shows the result. Here you are missing the required Next statement. The error message says you are missing Do required to complete Loop. This erroneous error appeared in VB3 and is not corrected in VB4/5.

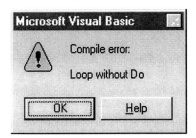

Figure 8.10   Wrong error message for missing Next

Now consider this situation:

```
For I = 1 To 10
     Do
Next I
```

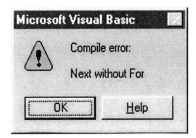

Figure 8.11   Wrong error message for missing Loop

Figure 8.11 shows another wrong error message; this was the same error shown in VB3. VB4 showed *Do without Loop* in this situation, which was correct. VB5 has reverted back to the same error as in VB3.

Logic errors frequently involve variables and procedures. These may receive no value or wrong values, resulting in mistakes. The next few sections will help you identify these errors.

Run-time errors occur at run time. There may be nothing wrong with your program. But the user may supply an unacceptable number or forget to put a disk in a drive when your program tries to save data. You can write code to trap such errors. We will cover various techniques in later sections.

Watching Variables

Chapter 2 demonstrated a break point and single stepping, plus the use of the **Stop** and **Assert** statements to get into break mode. This section provides more related details. We'll use the following example:

```
Private Sub Form_Click ()
    Dim I As Integer

    For I = 1 To 10
        Print I
        Debug.Print I
    Next I
End Sub
```

After writing the above procedure, place a **breakpoint** (F9) on the Debug line. Press F5 and click the form. You are now in **break mode** (examine the IDE's title bar). You can now watch I's value by doing any of the following:

- Move the mouse pointer over any I and a **data tip** pops up to show the variable's current value. This doesn't happen if **Auto Data Tips** is unchecked in the Tools | Options | Editor tab.

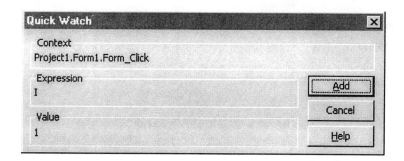

Figure 8.12 The Quick Watch dialog box

- Place the cursor on the desired variable (I in our case) and choose Debug | Quick Watch (Shift+F9). The **Quick Watch dialog box** appears (Figure 8.12). It shows the variable's name, its current value, and what procedure it's in. If all you want is to see a variable's current value, click Cancel to clear the dialog box. If you want to add this variable to the watch list, click Add. The Add Watch dialog box will appear (see below).

- If you want to add a variable to the watch list, right-click it and choose Add Watch from the shortcut menu. The **Add Watch dialog box** appears (Figure 8.13). Here you can accept the variable already entered in the top text box, or enter another one.

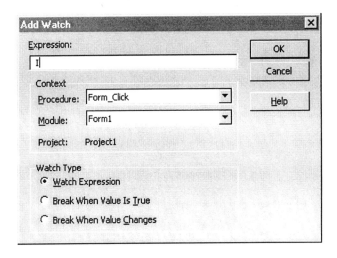

Figure 8.13   The Add Watch dialog box

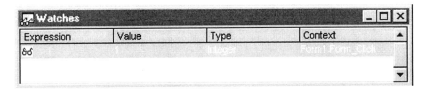

Figure 8.14   The Watch window with a watch variable

- After you add a variable to the watch list, the **Watch window** appears (Figure 8.14).

- As you use the Debug object to output to the **Immediate window**, display the window to show the output items (Figure 8.15).

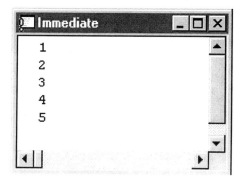

Figure 8.15   The Immediate window showing output by Debug

- You can use the View menu to display the **Locals window** (Figure 8.16) showing all the variables in the current procedure.

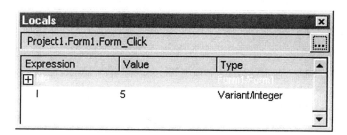

Figure 8.16   The Locals window showing the current procedure's variables

As you can see from the preceding discussion, there are multiple ways to show a variable's current value. Most of them are overlapping. The most convenient way to watch a variable's behavior is to use the **data tip**. Here's what you can do:

1. Set a breakpoint on the line where you want to watch a variable.

2. Move the mouse pointer over the variable.

3. Press 5 repeatedly and observe how the variable changes its value as shown in the popup data tip.

You can also show a data tip for an expression involving one or more operators. Consider this procedure:

```
Private Sub Form_Click()
    Dim I As Integer, J As Integer

    For I = 1 To 9
        For J = 1 To 9
        Print I * J
        Next J
    Next I
End Sub
```

Suppose you now want to observe the value of I * J. You can set a breakpoint on
that line. When execution reaches that line, highlight the expression and move the
pointer over it to pop up its data tip. As execution continues, however, the
highlight will disappear. If you want to see its next value, you'll have to select it
again. In this situation, it's better to enter the expression into the Watch window.

To enter a watch expression into the Watch window, just highlight it at design
time or in break mode and right-click it to pop up its shortcut menu. Choose Add
Watch from the list to display the dialog box. The selected expression will appear
in the top text box. If that's what you want, just press Enter or click OK to
accept. The expression will enter the Watch window at the bottom of the existing
list.

Debugging Windows

Previous versions included the Debug window. In VB5, this window has been
transformed into three separate windows: Immediate, Watch, and Locals.

The word **Debug** is still recognized as an object. When you use code to print
something to Debug, the output goes to the **Immediate window**; if it's not open,
you'll need to use the View menu to do it. You can also enter into this window a
statement at design time or in break mode to show an immediate result. Chapter 2
fully covered this topic.

The **Watch window** (Figure 8.17) displays in alphabetic order all the variables and
expressions you have added; it automatically opens when you add an item. You
use the Debug | Add Watch command to do it. If the cursor is located on a word
in the Code window, this word appears in the Expression text box of the Add
Watch dialog box. If a word or expression has been selected, the same thing
happens. If neither is the case, then the box is empty for you to type something.

A simpler way to add a watch variable or expression is to right-click a variable or selected expression. From the popup menu, choose Add Watch. You can now click OK to quickly enter the item into the Watch window.

Still another way is to drag from the Code window a selected variable or expression to the Watch window. This requires you to select an item first before you can drag it. This can be done at both design time and in break mode.

When you right-click a line in the Watch window, the resulting shortcut menu includes these options: Edit Watch, Add Watch, and Delete Watch. Choosing Delete removes the current item from the window. Choosing Add displays the Add Watch dialog box with the previously entered variable as the default. Choosing Edit shows the same dialog box but with the current variable (highlighted in the Watch window) as the default for you to make changes.

The Watch window has three column headers: Expression, Value, and Type. If a column is too narrow, some items in it may be covered by the next column. You can widen or narrow a column by dragging the border leftward or rightward.

You can directly add or delete items in the Watch window at both design time and in break mode. Values appear only in break mode. If you wish, you can edit these values. To do that, just click the displayed value. If the line has been selected, clicking the value highlights the value. If the clicked line was not selected, clicking that line highlights the entire line; you'll then need to click the value to highlight it. You can now change it to another legal value; other expressions may change their values to reflect the change. If you enter an illegal value, an error will appear; the original value is not changed.

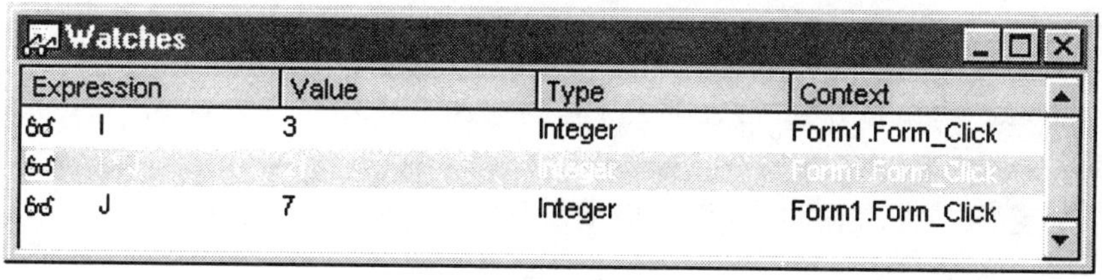

Expression	Value	Type	Context	
66 I	3	Integer	Form1 .Form_Click	
66		Integer	Form1 .Form_Click	
66 J	7	Integer	Form1 .Form_Click	

Figure 8.17   Watching and editing variables

Let's use the preceding procedure (also see Figure 8.18) as an example. We try to use two For-Next loops to watch two variables (I and J) and one expression (I * J). Suppose you set a breakpoint on the Print line and press F5 repeatedly. After a while, the Watch window resembles Figure 8.17 (assuming you have added the three displayed items as explained before).

The figure shows that when I is 3 and J is 7, I * J is 21. Now change the value of J to 1 and press Enter or click another line. I * J is changed to 3. Press F5 repeatedly to show that J increments from 1 to 2, 3, and so on.

Another way to change the course of execution is to drag the **Next Statement indicator**. It's an arrow on the **Indicator Bar** pointing to the line that is scheduled for execution (Figure 8.18). Move the mouse pointer over it to see it changing to another icon. You can now drag it to another line where you want to execute next. If you drag it to an unacceptable place, the icon changes to a No symbol; dropping the icon has no effect.

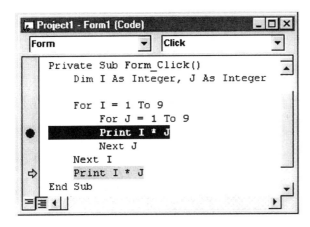

Figure 8.18   Next Statement indicator

As a demonstration, drag the indicator to the last Print line, just before the Next line. Press F8 repeatedly and see what happens. Execution no longer stays inside the For-Next loops as before, and the procedure is quickly exited.

The **Locals window** automatically shows, in break mode, all the variables in the current procedure. The display is similar to the Watch window. You can control column widths and change values as in the Watch window. When you change a value in one window, it will be reflected in the other. The Locals window won't let you add variables or expressions; you can add them only to the Watch window.

The first line in the Locals window is **Me** when a form or a class module is involved or a module name when a standard module is involved. In the case of a class or standard module, only variables are shown. In the case of a form, you can click the + sign appearing to the left of Me to expand it

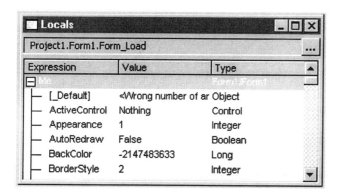

Figure 8.19   A form's Me variable expanded

Figure 8.19 shows a form's Me variable expanded. Here you find the form's properties and the controls you've added to the form. A series of + and - signs are available to expand or collapse various list of items.

All these three debugging windows are dockable. You can right-click each to pop up its shortcut menu to check/uncheck the **Dockable** option. When the screen becomes cluttered, you can close them. You can use the View menu to open them again. When a window is open at design time, it remains open at design time only. To keep it open in break mode, you'll have to open it in break mode.

There is also a three-dot button next to the Locals window. Clicking it brings up the Call Stack dialog box. This will be demonstrated in the next section.

Debugging Procedures

The **Debug menu** offers these options:

Step Into	F8
Step Over	Shift+F8
Step Out	Ctrl+Shift+F8
Run To Cursor	Ctrl+F8

. . .
Set Next Statement   Ctrl+F9
Show Next Statement

The first, second, and fourth are available at design time; all are available in
break mode.

Step Into was formerly known as Single Step. It executes one statement at a time.
Each statement scheduled for execution (**current execution point**) is marked yellow
by default. Pressing F8 will execute that and highlight the next to be executed.

Run To Cursor executes from the beginning to before the current line (where the
cursor is located) and highlights the current statement to be executed next. If a
breakpoint has been set, execution pauses before the breakpoint or the current
line, whichever occurs earlier. In break mode, you can use this command to skip
some lines.

There is a difference between **Step Into** and **Step Over** (formerly known as
Procedure Step). In Step Into, every line is executed. When calling a sub or
function, Step Into goes through the called procedure one statement at a time. In
Step Over, the called procedure is executed all at once. The screen does not show
the called procedure. When you are in a called procedure, you can use **Step Out**
to execute the remaining code in the procedure and return to the calling statement.

To change the current execution point, right-click the new line in break mode and
choose **Set Next Statement** from the shortcut menu. You can use this technique to
move forward or backward to skip some statements. But you cannot move to
another procedure; an error will appear if you do that. This has the same effect as
dragging the Next Statement indicator explained in the previous section.

The **Show Next Statement** command does nothing more than moving the cursor to
the current execution point. This command is also available from the shortcut
menu.

You can alternate between single step and procedure step. You start out with
single step. When you see a procedure you want to skip, press Shift+F8 to
execute it all at once. If you see a procedure you want to single-step through,
press F8 instead of Shift+F8. To step out of the called procedure in a hurry,
press Ctrl+Shift+F8.

As a demonstration, we are going to write three procedures, one event procedure
and two function procedures. The first step is to write the following procedures:

```
Private Sub Form_Click()
    Dim RetValue As Long

    RetValue = SOD(1, 10)    'sum of digits
    Print RetValue           'print returned value

    RetValue = Fac(1, 10)    'factorial
    Print RetValue
End Sub

Public Function SOD(I, J)
    Dim K As Integer, Temp As Integer

    For K = I To J
        Temp = Temp + K
    Next K
    Sod = Temp
End Function

Public Function Fac(I, J)
    Dim K As Integer, Temp As Long
    For K = I To J
        Temp = Temp + I * K
    Next K
    Fac = Temp
End Function
```

The first procedure calls two function procedures. So make sure you create these last two before you run the program. Running the program at this time will show 55 twice. The Fac function has bugs because 1*2*3...*10 should be much higher than 55.

We are going to debug the Fac procedure. Follow these steps:

1. Set a breakpoint on the Temp line in the Fac procedure.

2. Press F5 and click the form to run the program.

3. Open the Locals window if it's not.

4. Press F5 four times.

As you press F5 each time, notice the change in the Value column in the Locals window. Our example (Figure 8.20) shows that after going through 5 rounds, I remains 1. That means that in each round, K is multiplied by 1 and added to Temp. The effect is adding them up, not multiplying them as we intended. The formula is clearly faulty.

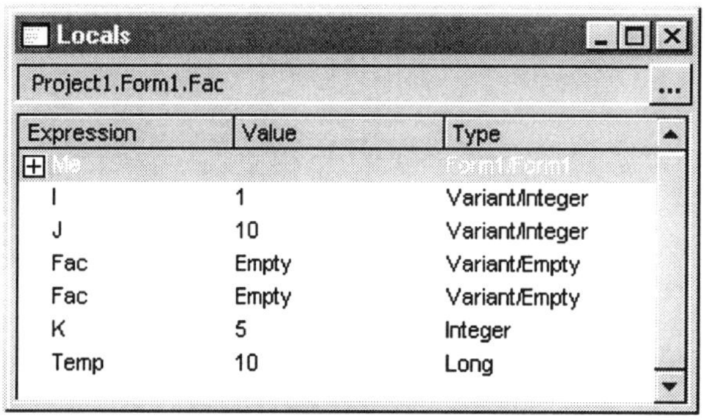

Figure 8.20   The Locals window with local variables and procedures

Now change the formula by taking out I, like this:

```
Temp = Temp * K
```

Try again. What happens? Variable Temp remains 0 throughout, and the final output is 0.

What's the remedy? Assign 1 to Temp before the For loop begins by adding this line before the For line:

```
Temp = 1
```

If you try again, the final result will be 3628800 rather than 0 or 55 as before.

Notice that the top of the Locals window has a box showing the current procedure's name and how it's connected to calling procedures. Our example, Project1.Form1.Fac, shows that we are in the Fac procedure, which is inside Form1, which is inside Project1.

The top-right corner of the Locals windows shows an ellipsis. This is known as the **Calls button**. Clicking this button displays the **Call Stack** dialog box; you can do the same thing by choosing View | Call Stack (Ctrl+L).

The **Call Stack dialog box** (Figure 8.21) is useful in finding out how the current procedure is connected to others. The current procedure is displayed in the first line and highlighted. The one below is the calling procedure. If that one is called by another, it'll appear below. So all the hierarchical procedures are stacked up with the current one on top; that's why it's called Call Stack. When you are done with this box, just click Close to close it; you'll be returned to where you came from. If you want to go to another procedure, just click it and click Show. You'll be taken to that procedure, but that doesn't alter the original course of execution.

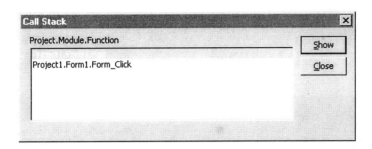

Figure 8.21   The Call Stack dialog box

The View menu has these two useful options:

Definition	Shift+F2
Last Position	Ctrl+Shift+F2

The first option moves the cursor to the first line of the specified procedure. If the cursor is not located on a valid procedure name, an error appears (*Identifier under cursor is not recognized*). If the cursor is on a variable name, pressing Shift+F2 will move the cursor to where variable was defined and highlight that variable. In either situation, pressing Ctrl+Shift+F2 will return the cursor to the line before you chose Definition.

Another useful technique to navigate lengthy code is to set a **bookmark** on a line you want to quickly go to. To do that, right-click the line to pop up a shortcut menu. Choose Toggle and then Bookmark; a rounded rectangle will appear on the Margin Indicator Bar. You can also do it by choosing Edit | Bookmarks | Toggle Bookmark. Both can be done at design time or in break mode. To move the cursor to a bookmark, choose Edit | Bookmarks and then one of the available options. A quicker way is to use the Edit toolbar (explained in another section below).

Managing Variable Watch

The Add Watch dialog box (Figure 8.22) lets you control a number of things. In addition to the text box at the top, there are two frames named Context and

Watch Type, the first with two drop-down lists and the second with three option buttons.

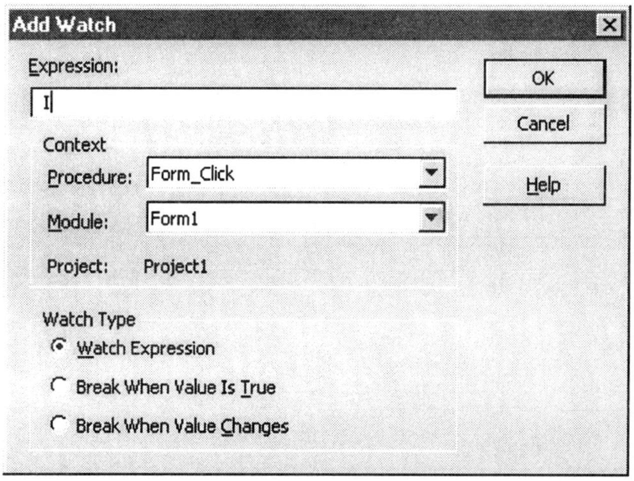

Figure 8.22   Add Watch's options

The Context frame shows the context of the selected variable (this context also appears in the Locals window as well). Our example shows that variable I belongs in the Form_Click procedure, which is in the Form1 module. The current project's name, shown at the bottom, is Project1. If you enter a watch expression now, you intend to watch an expression in the Form1_Click procedure that is in the Form1 module that is in the Project1 project. If that is not your intent, choose another procedure (or module) from the list boxes and then enter a watch expression in the text box. If the variable is at the module level, choose (All Procedures) from the Procedure box; if it's at the global level, choose (All Modules) from the Module box. If the variable is not linked to proper procedures or modules, the *Expression not defined in context* message will appear in the Value column in the Watch window. In that case, you cannot observe its changes.

The Watch Type frame offers three choices. You can make a choice here before you enter a watch expression. Watch Expression is the default. Visual Basic will simply display the expression and its value in the Watch window. A watch expression can be a variable name or a logical expression such as Num > 1. In that case, you want to know whether the condition is true or false.

The last two Watch Type choices tell Visual Basic to go into break mode when a watch expression is either changed or becomes true. Also, if either condition is met, the watch item in the Watch window is highlighted.

To demonstrate these Watch Type expressions, we will use the following procedure:

```
Private Sub Form_Click ()
    Dim I As Integer

    For I = 1 To 1000
        Print I
        If I = 10 Then Exit For
    Next I
End Sub
```

After starting a new project and writing the above code, follow these steps:

1. Add I as a watch expression.

2. Add I * I > 10 as a watch expression.

3. Add I > 5 as *Break When Value Is True*.

4. Add I as *Break When Value Changes*.

5. Press F5 to run the program. Expose the Watch window and examine it carefully.

6. Click the form window.

7. Press F8 to step through the code.

If you made a mistake, such as choosing a wrong option in the Watch Type frame, right-click the relevant item in the Watch window and choose **Edit Watch**. The dialog box will appear for you to edit the variable. This dialog is the same as the Add Watch dialog.

Figure 8.23 shows the result after the form window is clicked (step 6). Notice that the second item is highlighted, meaning its condition has been met. (Although we added this item last, it is moved up automatically.) Here we want Visual Basic to go into break mode when I is changed. So as soon as the procedure runs, I's value is changed and break mode begins. Now you can press F8 to step through the lines. As you do, notice the changes. When I reaches 4, the False in line 3 will change to True. When I gets to 6, the last line's False becomes True.

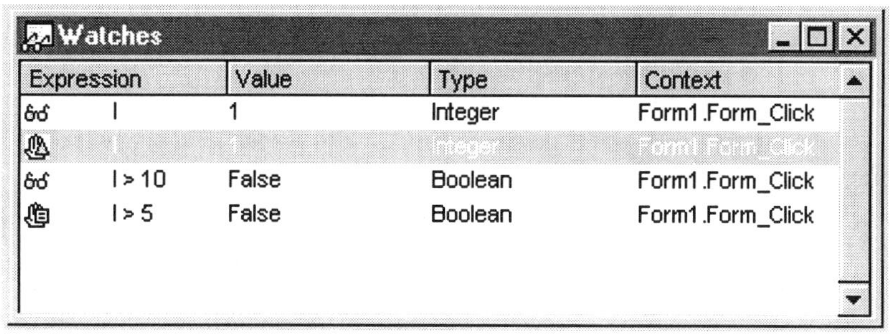

Watches				
Expression	Value	Type	Context	▲
I	1	Integer	Form1.Form_Click	
I	1	Integer	Form1.Form_Click	
I > 10	False	Boolean	Form1.Form_Click	
I > 5	False	Boolean	Form1.Form_Click	
				▼

Figure 8.23   Expressions in the Watch window

Menus and Debugging Buttons

You should take advantage of the **Debug toolbar** if you intend to speed up the debugging process. Figure 8.24 shows the buttons that can be used as shortcuts for debugging; the first three also appear on the Standard toolbar. These buttons represent various commonly used options from the Run, View, and Debug menus. Clicking a button here is faster than choosing an option from the menus. (In case you've forgotten, you can right-click the menu bar or any toolbar to bring up a list of available toolbars.)

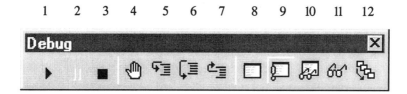

Figure 8.24   The Debug toolbar

The button names and their menu equivalents are shown below:

1. Start/Continue, from the Run menu
2. Break, from the Run menu
3. End, from the Run menu
4. Toggle Breakpoint, from the Debug menu
5. Step Into, from the Debug menu
6. Step Over, from the Debug menu

 7. Step Out, from the Debug menu
 8. Locals Window, from the View menu
 9. Immediate Window, from the View menu
10. Watch Window, from the View menu
11. Quick Watch, from the Debug menu
12. Call Stack, from the View menu

Some of these buttons may be dimmed under various circumstances. Most of them become available only in break mode. Since these buttons represent various menu options, the latter also reflect the same state of availability. That means that at run time or design time, many options in the Run and Debug menus are dimmed; they become available only in break mode.

The Run menu consists of these options:

Start	F5
Start With Full Compile	Ctrl+F5
Break	Ctrl+Break
End	
Restart	Shift+F5

At design time, only the first two options are available; the others are dimmed. F5 is used to run a normal program. Ctrl+F5 is for running an ActiveX server program. You can use the Professional (but not Learning) Edition to create an ActiveX server.

At run time, only the following three options are available. They allow you to go into break mode, end execution (return to design mode), or start execution from the beginning.

Break	Ctrl+Break
End	
Restart	Shift+F5

The following three options are available in break mode. The first option is also changed from Start to Continue.

Continue	F5
End	
Restart	Shift+F5

Continue means to execute the unexecuted portion of the code, but Restart means to begin from the beginning. You can of course use F8 to continue single stepping.

There are **shortcut menus** for the Code, Locals, Immediate, and Watch windows. Their options vary in various modes and circumstances. When you want to do something quickly, just right-click any part to see whether anything pops up.

TRAPPING RUN-TIME ERRORS

Run-time errors occur at run time. They could prematurely end a program and cause other more serious problems. The errors may be due to faulty code or user ineptitude. A good programmer anticipates such problems and writes robust code to prevent a program from going awry. You can use a series of tools in Visual Basic to trap numerous possible errors and prevent them from bombing your program.

To display a list of the errors that can be trapped at run time, use the online help's Index tab to search for *trappable errors*; various help topics can also lead to this topic. A long list appears. You can choose any one of them to show its details.

One common error is division by 0. It cannot be done because it will lead to an infinite quotient. The code below demonstrates such a scenario. We put an error-handling instruction just before where trouble is expected. Here we tell the program that if an error (any trappable error) is encountered from this point on, go to line 10.

```
Private Sub Form_Click ()
    Dim Temp As Variant

    On Error GoTo 10        'error trap
5   Temp = 10 / Temp        'division by 0
    Print Temp
    Exit Sub            'prevent spillover
10                      'error-handling routine
    Print "Error line:", , Erl
    Print "Error number:", , Err
    Print "Error message:", Error
    Temp = Erl & "   " & Err & "   " & Error
    Resume Next     'return to after error
End Sub
```

When line 5 (this is an arbitrary number to mark a particular line) is executed, a run-time error occurs. Normally program execution would have prematurely aborted and the pertinent error message displayed. Because of the error trap, however, execution next goes to line 10. Here we want to print the error's line number (where in the program the error occurred), the error number, and the error message. Three lines are now output to the screen. Next, Temp is assigned a new text string, and the **Resume Next** statement directs execution to the line below where this particular error occurred. Temp is printed, and Exit Sub ends the procedure. (If we did not put a stopper here, execution would continue below and cause problems.) The result is shown in Figure 8.25.

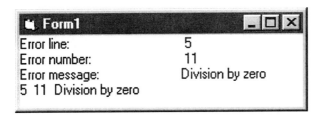

Figure 8.25   Various error items

TIP: Overflow and Division by Zero

In math, dividing any number by a 0 is considered meaningless. In Visual Basic, it could trigger one of the following errors:

```
Print 0 / 0      'Overflow
Print 1 / 0      'Division by zero
```

Each statement will trigger the error message shown in the comment.

When division by 0 is involved in a function call, these errors may also appear. That's what happens if you try Sin(1/0) and Sin(0/0). Sometimes the *Illegal function call* error may also be triggered.

Overflow happens when the result of an operation is too large to handle. It was common in the 16-bit Windows 3.x environment; it's no longer common in the 32-bit Windows 95 environment. The following procedure would lead to overflow in VB3; it leads to division by 0 in VB4/5:

```
Private Sub Form_Click ()
    Dim I As Single, J As Single

    I = 1
    J = 1
    Do
        I = I * 10
        J = J / 10
        Debug.Print I; " / "; J; " = ", I / J
```

```
    Loop  'show result in Immediate window
End Sub
```

The *Division by zero* error message will appear when the program tries to perform the following operation; go to the Immediate window and you will find this as the last line:

```
1E+19  /  1E-19  =  1E+38
```

You can use one of the following lines to trap run-time errors:

```
On Error Resume Next
On Error GoTo 0|line
```

In the first case, Next is the only legal option; you cannot place 0 or a line number or line label here. In this situation, any error is ignored and program execution continues with the next statement.

In the second case, using 0 after GoTo disables the active error trap. Here 0 does not signify a line number.

Using a line number or line label after GoTo is a common practice in this situation. In our previous example, we could have used a line label like below:

```
. . .
On Error GoTo ErrTrap
. . .
ErrTrap:
. . .
```

After you branch execution to a designated line (error-handling routine), you can use **Resume** to resume execution in a specific place. In our example, we use the **Next** keyword to resume execution after the error line. So the error line is skipped. You can also use two other permissible options: **0** and a line (number or label). If you use 0, execution resumes with the error line again (don't confuse **Resume 0** with **GoTo 0**). The same error will be triggered again unless you alter some values, such as changing the divisor in our case.

You should place an error trap as close to the suspect area as possible, preferably just before where you expect trouble. This will make the trap active to handle the expected error. If you place the trap after the offending line, then the trap is not active when an error occurs in that line. If you place a trap in one procedure which calls another procedure where an error occurs, Resume 0 or Resume Next will direct execution back to the caller and may lead to unpredictable results.

The functions commonly used to identify errors are: Erl, Err, and Error. **Erl** returns the line number at or before the point where the error occurred. If no line number is found, 0 is returned; a line label is not recognized in this case. **Err** returns a number that is associated with a specific error. **Error** returns the message text. The number and message correspond to those shown in the Trappable Errors and associated help topics.

When used alone, the **Error function** returns the error message of the most recent run-time error; if no error is encountered, it returns a zero-length string. Actually, this function is an array containing all the error messages. So you can supply a numeric value as an argument to make it return the corresponding error message. The following statement will print *Overflow*; if the argument is changed to 0, a zero-length string is returned. Error can also be used as a statement; this will be demonstrated shortly.

```
Print Error(6)
```

The code below shows another example of trapping an error. Here we expect a loop to refer to a nonexisting array element. Instead of letting the error bomb the program, we direct the error number and its message to a message box (Figure 8.26) and gracefully exit the procedure.

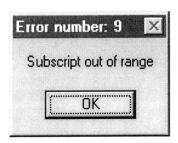

Figure 8.26   A message box showing error items

```
Private Sub Form_Click ()
    Dim I As Integer
    Dim FName(1 To 3) As String
    Dim Msg1 As String, Msg2 As String

    FName(1) = "Jon"
    FName(2) = "Tom"
    FName(3) = "Kim"

    On Error GoTo ErrorTrap
```

```
    For I = 1 To 10
        Print FName(I)
    Next I
    Exit Sub

ErrorTrap:
    Msg1 = Error
    Msg2 = "Error number: " & Err
    MsgBox Msg1, 0, Msg2     'show err # and msg
    I = 10                   'get out of loop
    Resume Next              'resume after error
End Sub
```

If you want the procedure to handle the error automatically and not bother the user, you can replace the On Error line with the following:

```
    On Error Resume Next
```

In this case, you can also get rid of the error-handling routine at the end of the procedure. When an error is encountered, execution proceeds with the next line and the user is not aware of anything.

Normally, you need the Resume command at the end of your error-handling routine to direct execution to a specified place. If this word is not used, the *No resume* error will appear in VB3 but not in VB4/5. If we erase Resume Next in our example, execution with continue with End Sub to end the procedure. In this situation, you can optionally use End, Stop, or Exit Sub to end the procedure.

An error trap should not leave any gap. Consider the following prototype:

```
Private Sub Form_Click ()
    On Error GoTo ErrorTrap
    . . .               'procedure body
    Exit Sub            'get out

ErrorTrap:
    . . .               'handle error
    Exit Sub            'get out, or Resume
End Sub
```

If no error occurs, the On Error line is ignored and the procedure ends when the first Exit Sub is encountered. If an error occurs, execution branches to the ErrorTrap line. After showing a message (or doing whatever you want to do), the second Exit Sub (optional in VB4/5, mandatory in VB3) ends the procedure. (If you wish, you can put Resume here to direct execution to another line.) If the first Exit Sub is not present, execution will spill over to the ErrorTrap line even if no error occurs. That will lead to undesirable side effects.

You can use a general procedure to handle errors that may occur in several other procedures. In the above model, put a calling routine before the second Exit Sub line. The called procedure will then provide a generic response by showing the canned error number and/or message. Whenever an error trap is needed in a procedure, just make a call to this error-handling routine.

Sometimes you can prevent an error without setting up an error trap. For example, if Text1 is empty when the user clicks a command button, your program will definitely lead to an error. In this situation, you may want to use an If-Then structure to prevent further execution.

```
If Text1.Text = "" Then
    Beep
    Exit Sub
End If
```

If you want to be more informative, you can use a message box to tell the user what to do.

TIP: Customized Error Response

Each trappable error is identified by a unique number. You can use this number to make a customized response to a specific error. This response may be more informative than the canned error message that comes with Visual Basic.

There are several ways to find out an error's number. The first is to use the **ERR** function in code to return the number, as shown earlier. The second is to use the number shown in a run-time error message. Still another way is to open the Trappable Errors book in the online help's Contents tab; all the trappable errors can be found here.

Suppose you want to supply a more meaningful message when the user enters a 0 as a divisor. Branch execution to a line and then place below that line the following code fragment to respond:

```
If Err = 6 Or Err = 11 Then
    Msg = "You can't use 0 as a divisor. Try again"
    MsgBox Msg
    Resume Next
End If
```

You can write a simple procedure to show most of the common error messages. To do that, add Text1 to a new form. Stretch the text box and change its MultiLine property to True and its ScrollBars property to 3 - Both. Then write the following code:

```
Private Sub txtShowError_Click() '--Listing 6--
    Dim I As Integer
    Dim Str1 As String, Str2 As String

    Str2 = "Application-defined or object-defined error"
    For I = 1 To 500
        If Error(I) <> Str2 Then   'if built-in message
            Str1 = Str1 & I & vbTab & Error(I) & vbCrLf
        End If        'add up found messages
    Next I
    txtShowError.Text = Str1    'put in text box
End Sub
```

Run the program and click the text box. Figure 8.27 will appear. It shows most, but not all, of the messages that you can see in various online help topics.

We use the **Error** function and each sequential number to identify each built-in error message. There are many numbers that have not been assigned error messages. This situation will normally return a generic string (the string assigned to variable Str2). In that case, we want it skipped. Only if a built-in message does not match the generic string do we accumulate it to variable Temp. Here we also use two intrinsic constants (**vbTab** and **vbCrLf**) to add a Tab character in each line and two line break characters at the end.

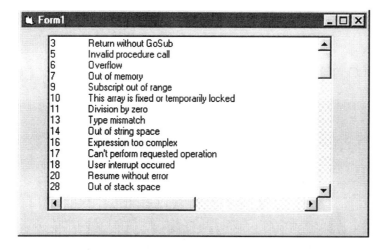

Figure 8.27   Showing trappable errors

Err has become an object (since VB4) with its own methods (Clear and Raise) and properties. The default property is Number. So Err and **Err.Number** will return the same value. **Err.Description** will also return the same message as the **Error function**. And **Err.Source** will show the project's name. The following procedure shows Err's properties in Figure 8.28.

```
Private Sub Form_Click()
    On Error GoTo ErrorTrap
    Print 0 / 0    'or Error 6
Exit Sub

ErrorTrap:
    Print "Number", Err.Number       'show each property
    Print "Source", Err.Source
    Print "Description", Err.Description
    Print "HelpFile", Err.HelpFile
    Print "HelpContext", Err.HelpContext
    Print "DLLError", Err.LastDllError
End Sub
```

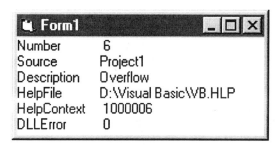

Figure 8.28   Showing Err's properties

You can also use **Error** as a statement (instead of function) to simulate an error situation. In our above example, we can replace the first Print line with the statement shown in the comment; it will produce the same results.

The **Tools | Options | General** tab has the following Error Trapping options:

Break on All Errors
Break in Class Module (default)
Break on Unhandled Errors

These have to do with how you want Visual Basic to handle errors in the development environment. Option 1 leads to break mode whenever an error occurs and in the resulting dialog box you can choose to end or go into break mode to show the offending line. This happens regardless of whether or not an error handler exists.

The last two options are identical under normal circumstances. If there is an error handler to deal with the error, it takes over and break mode is not entered. Break mode is entered only when an error is not properly handled. These two options differ only when a class module is involved.

DRILL

Syntax

____ 12. When Visual Basic tells you at design time that an error has occurred, this is a(n) _____ error. *Syntax*

_b_ 13. To move the cursor from a calling statement to where the called procedure is defined, you need to press:
   a. F2
   b. Shift+F2
   c. Ctrl+Shift+F2
   d. none of the above

_d_ 14. When program execution reaches a breakpoint,
   a. execution is halted
   b. the Immediate window is activated
   c. the Next Statement indicator appears.
   d. all of the above
   e. none of the above

_T_ 15. You can add a watch variable to the Watch window at both design time and in break mode. True or false?

_T_ 16. The following If-Then structure is illegal because there is no End If. True or false?

```
If Num <= 0 Then _
Num = Num + 1
```

_F_ 17. If you drag selected text from the Code window to the Immediate window, you make a duplicate in the target window. True or false?

_d_ 18. This window has the Call Stack button:
   a. Code window
   b. Immediate window
   c. Watch window

    d.   Locals window

19. This window has the Me expression:
    a.   Code window
    b.   Immediate window
    c.   Watch window
    d.   Locals window

20. This toolbar supplies most of the tools for catching program errors:
    a.   Standard
    b.   Edit
    c.   Debug
    d.   Format Editor
    e.   all of the above

21. When you want to show the message for a run-time error, use this function:
    a.   Err
    b.   Erl
    c.   Error
    d.   none of the above

22. If you want your program to ignore a run-time error and continue executing the rest of the code, you need to use On Error, followed by:
    a.   Resume 0
    b.   Resume 1
    c.   Resume Next
    d.   GoTo 0

23. Err.Number returns the same thing as:
    a.   Err
    b.   Error
    c.   Erl
    d.   none of the above
    e.   both a and b

PRACTICE

■ 17. What is a breakpoint? How can you set a breakpoint?

■ 18. What does the Stop statement do?

■ 19. How can you find out a variable's current value in break mode without opening any debugging window?

■ 20. Can you add a watch variable to the Watch window at design time?

■ 21. How can you use the shortcut menu to enter a bookmark on a line in the Code window?

■ 22. How can you remove a watch expression from the Watch window?

■ 23. What does the Call Stack dialog box do?

■ 24. Explain these terms related to trapping run-time errors: Erl, Err, and Error.

■ 25. What numbers are printed by the procedure below? Explain.

```
Private Sub Command1_Click()
    On Error GoTo ErrTrap
    Print 1 / 0
    Print 1
    Exit Sub

ErrTrap:
    Print 2
    Resume Next
End Sub
```

MODULES AND SCOPE

As briefly discussed in Chapter 4, there are three types of modules. These are described below:

Type	Purpose
Form	Contains visible objects and related procedures and declarations.
Class	Contains procedures and declarations to create a class or OLE object.
Standard	Contains declarations and procedures shared by all modules.

By now you should be thoroughly familiar with a form module because we have used it so often. (**User Control**, **Property Page**, and **User Document**—accessible from the Project menu, are variations of the standard form.) A **class module** lets you create a class; it will be covered in Chapter 12. A standard module, as explained in Chapter 5, contains the code that can be shared by the entire application.

An application may include multiple modules of different types. In such a situation, things can be quite complicated. Since VB5 allows multiple projects in one session, you can get into even more confusing situations. The sections below address some of the related issues.

Standard Modules

If a project becomes complicated, involving multiple forms and numerous procedures, you may want to make use of standard modules.

A **standard module**, known as a code module or a module for short, is a separate file saved to disk with the BAS extension. It may contain declarations and/or procedures. A standard module is basically a Basic source code file. This used to be the only file you had to handle in programming the old Basic. In Visual Basic, this can be added on top of forms.

A standard module can be compared to a form module. A form module is a container for objects, declarations, and procedures. A standard module, however, can contain everything except objects.

Why use standard modules to complicate things? Well, complicated projects require complicated measures. Here are some good reasons:

- Procedures in a standard module can be accessed by procedures in various modules. You can thus put one procedure in a standard module and call it from the procedures in other modules.

- Global (public) variables, which can be declared only in a standard module, are visible throughout the entire application and exist regardless of which procedure in which module is being executed.

- A standard module can be incorporated into another application. Since a module is saved as a separate file, it can be added to any project which could use it. You could write a standard module, and your friend could easily add it to his or her project.

As you can surmise from the above discussion, you need standard modules only if you use multiple forms in a project. By adding one or more modules on top of the forms, you can integrate the forms and enable various variables and procedures scattered in various forms to communicate with one another. Some of the repetitive routines can be put in a standard module to avoid repetitive coding.

Using Multiple Modules

A project can involve multiple modules. They can interact with one another in a variety of ways. To demonstrate such a scenario, we have modified a program shown earlier in this chapter. Our modified program has two forms and two standard modules. Form1 has the following code:

```
Private Sub Form_Click ()    'in Form1
    Dim RetVal As Long

    RetVal = SOD(1, 10)    'sum of digits
    Print RetVal
    RetVal = Fac(1, 10)    'factorial
    Print RetVal
End Sub
```

Form2 has the following code:

```
Private Sub Form_Click ()    'in Form2
    Dim RetVal As Long

    RetVal = SOD(1, 10) + 100
        'add 100 to returned value
    Print RetVal
    RetVal = Fac(1, 10) / 100
        'divide returned value by 100
    Print RetVal
End Sub
```

Module1 has the following code:

```
Function SOD(I, J)    'in Module1
    Dim K As Integer, Temp As Long
    For K = I To J
        Temp = Temp + K
    Next K
    SOD = Temp
End Function
```

Module2 has the following code:

```
Function Fac(I, J)    'in Module2
    Dim K As Integer, Temp As Long
    Temp = 1
    For K = I To J
```

```
        Temp = Temp * K
    Next K
    Fac = Temp
End Function
```

NOTE When you use multiple modules, which have procedures calling those in other modules, things can get really confusing. On such an occasion, make full use of the Shift+F2 (Definition) or Ctrl+Shift+F2 (Last Position) keys, both from the View menu. These were explained earlier.

To add Form2, Module1, or Module2, choose an appropriate option from the Project menu. You can also drop down the same options by clicking the little down arrow next to the second icon on the Standard toolbar.

If you now run the program, Form1 will appear. If you click it, two numbers will appear. This shows that the procedures in Form1 can call the procedures in Module1 and Module2.

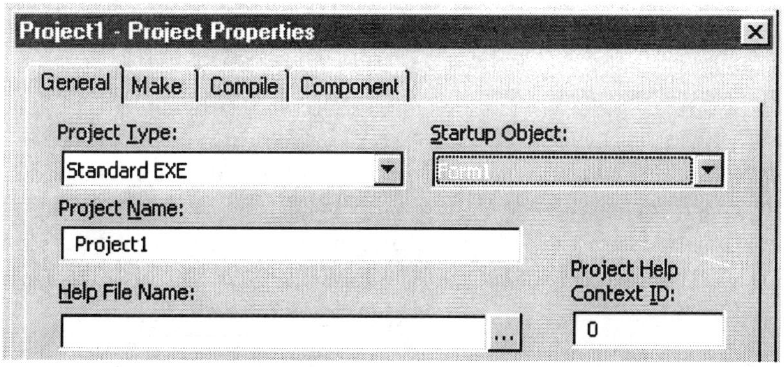

Figure 8.29   **The Project Properties dialog showing startup form**

What about Form2? It is ignored at this point. Choose Project | Project1 Properties, and you will see the General tab (Figure 8.29) showing the **Startup Object** as Form1; this is the default startup form.

If you want to start with Form2, open the combo box by clicking the down arrow. All the available options will appear. Select Form2 and click OK. If you run the program now, Form2 will appear for you to click. Two different numbers will appear after clicking. Compared to those in Form1, 100 is added to the first and the second is divided by 100. This shows that the procedures in Form2 can call those in Module1 and Module2.

Instead of a startup form, you can choose to start with the **Sub Main** procedure available in the Startup Object list. You can use this procedure to initialize some values for the project, just as a Form_Load procedure for a form. This procedure must be placed in a standard module for your project to find it. Placing it in a form module will lead to an error. This error also appears if you remove the startup form without creating a Sub Main procedure.

If you have multiple projects in the current session, you can right-click a project name in the Project window and choose Set as Start Up to make it the startup project. You can also choose Project Properties to open its dialog box.

Scope of Procedures

In Chapter 5 we discussed the scope of variables. A variable's scope is its visibility range, the area where it can be seen. The concept applies to procedures as well.

You have already seen **Public** or **Private** appearing at the beginning of a procedure. When you go through the regular way of creating a procedure, an appropriate word is automatically added. Private is automatically added to an event procedure, such as Private Command1_Click ( ). When you use Tools | Add Procedure to create a general procedure, the default Scope is Public (Figure 8.1). So unless you select another option, Public will be added at the beginning of the procedure.

Actually the word Public is redundant because a procedure has a public scope by default. If no scope is specified (neither Public nor Private appearing before a procedure name), this is a public procedure. Only when Private appears does a procedure become private.

In a **standard module**, a public (or unspecified) procedure, like a public (global) variable, is visible throughout the entire application. Another module can call this procedure the same way it calls a procedure in that module; there is no need to specify the module name in the calling statement. If two procedures share the same name, then the local procedure has precedence. If you want to call the one in the standard module in this situation, you need to specify the module.

In a form (or class) module, a public (or unspecified) procedure, like a public (module-level) variable in that module, can be called from another module by specifying the module and the procedure. Suppose Sub Fac is in Form2, you can call it from Form1 or another module this way:

    Call Form2.Fac

Here Call is optional. You can also pass arguments as discussed earlier in this chapter. If the Sub Fac procedure is in a standard module, there is no need to specify the object. You can do it with either statement below:

    Call Fac
    Call Module1.Fac

When a procedure is specified as **Private**, it can be called by any procedure from the same module, but not from another module. Attempting to do the latter will result in an error. This is true regardless of the type of module where the procedure is stored.

Managing Multiple Modules

Modules can be added or deleted. At the outset, a form module with the default Form1 name is automatically supplied. You can remove it or add others. To add a module, just open the Project menu and choose Add Form, Add Module, or Add Class Module. You can also use the second button on the Standard toolbar to add these modules (click the down arrow to open the list of options). Either list will give you several other options; these will be covered in Chapter 12.

A form module comes with a form and a Code window. A standard module or class module has a Code window but no form. So you cannot add visual objects to these.

A form or an object on it each sports a Properties window. You can use this window to change an object's numerous properties at design time. A standard module also has a Properties window, but it has only one property, namely Name. This allows you to change a standard module's Name property at design time.

When you have multiple modules, you should take advantage of the **Project window**. Since modules can cover up one another, you may be wondering how to get from one module to another. The simple solution is to use the Project window to do it. You can dock it to one side of the IDE and use the inside border to control the window's size as necessary. You can also make it dockable but let it float on top of the other windows, which can also be maximized. Since the Project window is always available in this arrangement, you can use it to go to any of the hidden windows.

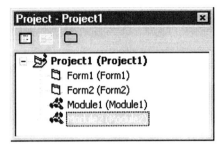

Figure 8.30   The Project window's components

Figure 8.30 shows the Project window with one project name and four module names. The highlighted one is the one with the focus. As you bring each to the top, the highlight will change. Notice that there are two names for each. The one inside a pair of parentheses is the file name; it will change to the name you use to save the object. The one outside is the Name property; it will change when you use the Properties window to change it.

After you click a name in the Project window, you can then click the View Form or View Code button to move the focus to the specified object. A standard or class module has no form, so the View Form button is dimmed. If you double-click a form module name, the form appears; if you do the same to a class module or standard module, its Code window will appear instead.

You can use the Project window to manage its components. When you right-click a project name, you can choose Save Project and Remove Project. When you right-click a module name, you'll have the Save, Save As, and Remove options. Both will give you these options: Properties, Add, Print. Use the first to open the Project Properties dialog box (for a project) or the Properties window for a module. Use Add to add a module to the current project. Use Print to print the selected object. If you don't use these shortcut menus, you'll have to look for their pertinent commands from the File and Project menus.

If you work on a complex module, you should periodically save it to minimize data loss due to computer mishap. The easiest way to save a module is to right-click its name in the Project window and choose Save File (or Ctrl+S). If you are saving a file for the first time, you will be prompted to enter a name. If this file has been saved to disk before, the Save File option does not prompt you. The current version is saved over the old one on disk. This happens even if you have not changed anything in the module.

If you intend to keep the old disk version, you should use the Save File As option. You will be prompted to enter a new file name. This allows you to save multiple copies of one file. If you enter a name matching an existing file on disk, you will be prompted with Yes/No to overwrite it.

You can add a file to the current project by choosing Add File (Ctrl+D) from the Project menu. Visual Basic displays all the files that can be added, as shown in Figure 8.31.

The display in Figure 8.31 is confusing. You can limit the displayed items to those matching *.FRM, *.BAS, or *.CLS—instead of all of them, which is the default. The combo box at the bottom lets you choose any pattern you want.

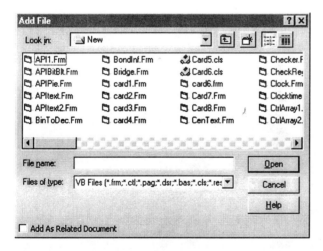

Figure 8.31   The Add File dialog box

If a project has multiple modules, it's convenient to save a project file to manage those modules. When you choose **File | Save Project** the first time, you are prompted to save each module and then the project. When you use the same command again, all the related items will be saved automatically. If nothing has been changed since the last saving, no action is taken.

You can choose **File** | **Save Project As** to save a new project (VBP) file. This saves only the project file, but not the component module files. This file contains the names and locations of the component module file names. When you open this file, attempts will be made to open the specified files in the specified drive/folder. If a specified file is not available, an error appears. You'll be prompted to quit or to continue loading others.

If opening a project file fails to load one of the component module files, you can use **Project** | **Add File** (this option is also available from the Project window's shortcut menu) to load it. If fact, if a project consists of multiple modules, you can use this command to individually load all of them without involving a project file. You can also drag a module file name from Windows Explorer or My Computer to the Project window to add it to the current project. If a module's Name property conflicts with a loaded one, the new one will not open; a new log file with the **LOG** extension will be created to record the error message.

You can also use **Edit** | **Insert File** to add text to a procedure in the Code window. Just move the cursor to where you want to insert text and then choose this command. The Insert File dialog box will appear for you to open a file.

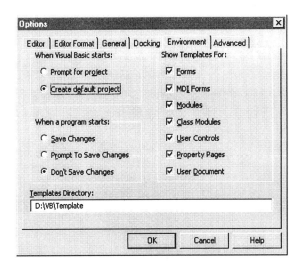

Figure 8.32   **The Environment tab of the Options dialog box**

The **Environment tab** (Figure 8.32) in the Tools | Options dialog box can save you lots of time if you want to add default items. When you use the File menu to add a project or the Project menu to add a form or module, an Add dialog box will appear for you to select an item, with the default item preselected. If you want to add the default item without opening this dialog box, uncheck the item in the Show Templates For frame. Suppose you uncheck Forms. Next time you choose Project | Add Form a form will be automatically added, thus bypassing the Add Form dialog box.

The top left frame ("When Visual Basic starts") in Figure 8.32 reflects what you did in the New Project dialog box. If you check the bottom check box ("Don't show this dialog in the future") in the New Project dialog box (see Figure 1.1 in Chapter 1) which appears when you start Visual Basic, then "Create default project" will be selected here. In that case, the New Project dialog box doesn't appear at startup. If you want to display this dialog box next time, select "Prompt for project."

TEMPLATES AND CUSTOM CONTROLS

If you develop long and complex projects, you may want to consider enlisting the help of two tools discussed here: templates and custom controls. The former let you reuse some of the work you or other people have done, and the latter let you incorporate programs others have written.

Using Templates

Previous versions of Visual Basic used to include an **Autoload** file that would load itself whenever Visual Basic was started. The file would set various initial values, including loading custom controls. This file is no longer used. A series of templates have replaced it.

A **template** is a module file that can serve as a base for a new module. When you load a template, you have a module that may contain controls or procedures. You can then add new items to create a new application. You can reuse one template to create multiple applications. This can speed up application development because you don't have to redo some of the common chores shared by all the applications.

VB5 comes with quite a few templates. Consider Figure 8.33. This dialog box appears when you choose Project | Add Form. The items shown here are all form templates. So far we have limited ourselves to the Form1 template at the top left. On some occasions you may want to load other templates. If you load the About

Dialog template, for example, you'll get a form, several controls, and some prewritten procedures. By changing a few things, you can quickly create an About dialog box for your application.

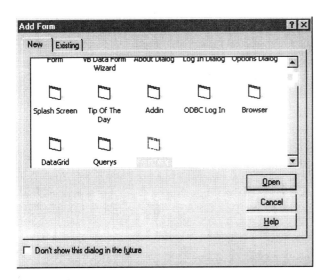

Figure 8.33   The Add Form dialog box showing form templates

When you try to add another type of module, a different list of templates may or may not appear. That depends on what you have done with the **Environment tab** in the Tools | Options dialog box (Figure 8.32). Notice the Show Templates For frame on the right. If an item is checked here, the next time you try to load a module, the Add . . . dialog box will appear and the available templates will be displayed. Otherwise, the default module will be added automatically.

Notice the bottom of Figure 8.32. The \VB\Templates directory is the default location for Visual Basic to show all the available templates. (You can use another directory to store and access your own templates). This directory has several subdirectories for specific modules. When you try to add a form, all the available form templates located in the \VB\Templates\Forms directory will appear in the Add Form dialog box. If you want to use your own form template, create one and save it to this particular directory. Every time you open the Add Form dialog box, this template will be made available. Figure 8.33 shows FormTemp, a user-added template.

If you want to use your own project template, add all the necessary items (forms, standard module, custom controls, etc.) and save the component modules to any directory you want but save the project file to the \VB\Templates\Projects directory. In the future when you use File | New Project to open a new project, the ensuing dialog box will show your project template. Opening that project will open all the related items. When you save files, you'll be prompted to save to new names. If you then save over the same files after doing more work, you'll replace the old template. When you no longer want a template, delete or remove it from the specified directory.

Adding/Removing Custom Controls

Custom controls are controls that you can add to the Toolbox to provide you additional functionality beyond the standard controls. Custom controls used to be called **OLE controls**. Now they are often referred to as **ActiveX controls**. The Learning Edition comes with a few custom controls. The Professional and Enterprise Editions include many more. There are also many custom controls marketed by third-party vendors.

You can use the Controls tab of the **Components dialog box** (Figure 8.34) to add or remove custom controls. This dialog appears after you choose Project | Components; you can also right-click the Toolbox and choose Components.

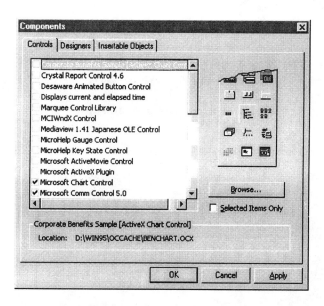

Figure 8.34   The Components dialog box

As you click each name in the middle list box, the bottom panel of the dialog box will show where the related file is located. If you don't find the desired control, use the Browse button to find it. Custom control files carry the name extension of OCX (OLE Custom Controls). They are usually stored in the WINDOWS\ SYSTEM directory. If there are too many displayed files, check Selected Items Only to show only those items that have been checked.

To add a custom control, check the check box to the left of the control's name. To remove it, just uncheck the check box. When you are done, click OK. The Toolbox will reflect your new settings.

After a custom control is added to the Toolbox, you can use it just as you do any standard control. You can show its tooltip by pointing to it. You can double-click it to get a copy to the form. You can also click it and press F1 to show its online help. Chapters 10 and 12 show concrete examples of using some custom controls.

If you use the Professional Edition, the New Project dialog box (File | New Project) should show a template named VB Professional Edition Controls. Opening this template will automatically check all the necessary check boxes in the Components dialog box and add more than two-dozen controls to the Toolbox.

BROWSING OBJECTS

Besides the Project window, you can also use the **Object Browser** to manage multiple modules. The Object Browser has many uses, some of which we have explored before. This section provides a more thorough coverage.

The Object Browser can be opened with any of the following ways:

- Press F2.
- Choose View | Object Browser.
- Click the Object Browser icon (second from the right) on the Standard toolbar.

The Object Browser (Figure 8.35) has interlocking parts. They work as follows:

- **Project/Library** (top left)   Click the down arrow to drop down a list. Click a displayed item. All the classes appear in the Classes box.

- **Classes** (left)   All the browsable objects in the selected project/library appear here. Click an item here, and the right box changes to reflect the selection.

- **Members** (right)   All the pertinent events, methods, and properties are shown in this box. Click an item here, and the bottom panel changes to reflect the selection.

- **Details pane** (bottom)   The selected member's details appear here. If you want the pertinent online help, press F1 or click the ? icon on the menu bar.

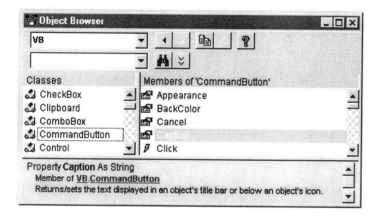

Figure 8.35   The Object Browser

Browsing Other Applications' Objects

Figure 8.35 shows that we're showing the VB library; if no selection is made here, < All Libraries > is the default. We've clicked CommandButton in the Classes box. We've also clicked Caption in the Members box. The Details pane shows a brief description of Caption and where it comes from.

When the focus is in a list box, you can type one or more letters to move to the matching item—the same way you can select an item in the Properties window.

You can display the items in the two list boxes in alphabetic order or according to groups. Just right-click either box and check/uncheck Group Members. If checked, items are displayed in groups; otherwise, in alphabetic order. In a group display, properties are placed at the top, followed by methods, and with events at the bottom.

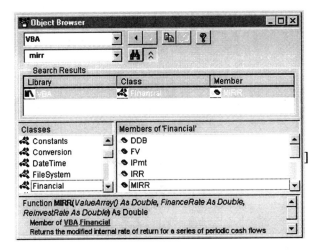

Figure 8.36   Searching for an item

The second combo box shows the tooltip of **Search Text** when the mouse pointer is over it. Here you type a search string, which can include wildcards, and press Enter or click Search (the binocular icon) to find matching entries. The Search Results box opens up to tell you the results. Here you may see *No items found* or a list of one or more matching items. Figure 8.36 shows that we are searching for the VBA library for the Mirr item. Since it's found, all the related details appear below. The Search Text combo box saves up to four search strings in the current session. You can drop down the list to reuse a previous search string.

Next to the Search (binocular) icon, there is an icon with two arrows that can point upward or downward. You can use it to show the search results or close this extra pane.

You may find multiple **split bars**. You can use one to shrink or enlarge a pane vertically or horizontally. When the mouse pointer goes over a dividing line and transforms itself into a two-headed arrow, just drag it to one side or the other.

The first two buttons on the toolbar are called **Go Back** (◂) and **Go Forward** (▸). You can use these to quickly move to previously selected items.

The next (third from left) button is named **Copy to Clipboard**. It sends the selected text to the Clipboard; you can then paste the string to a Code window. You can also right-click a displayed item and choose Copy to do the same thing. If you want to copy the text in the Details pane, you need to select it first.

The Object Browser window can be dockable. To make it dockable, right-click the window and check **Dockable**. The dockable state is also reflected in the Tools | Options | Docking tab. You can also use this tab to change the window's dockable state.

If you want to browse another application's library (such as Excel's), right-click anywhere in the Object Browser window and choose References. The **References dialog box** (Figure 8.37) will open; it's also available from the Project menu. Check any of the displayed items to show its library or uncheck one to clear it. The checked ones will appear in the Project/Library combo box in the Object Browser.

You can use the up or down arrow in the References dialog box to set priority. As you click it, the selected (highlighted) file will go up or down in the list box. The order shown in this list will be reflected in the Object Browser list. If a conflict is found (two identical names in two different libraries) during compiling, the library at the top is used.

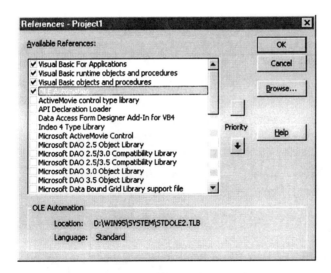

Figure 8.37   The References dialog box

You can use the Browse button in the References dialog box to search for the files not shown. The Add References dialog box appears. There you can specify the types of files to display, and go to various folders to find desired files. Double-click it when one is found. You may get the *Can't add a reference to the specified file* error. If this error doesn't appear, you can press F2 to go to the Object Browser. Your new addition will appear in the Libraries/Project list.

If custom controls (see the next section) appear in the Toolbox, their names will also appear in the Object Browser's Project/Library list. In that case, you can view each control's methods and properties. If they don't appear in the Toolbox, they are not shown in the Object Browser. In that case, you can still view their methods and properties. To do that, just use the Browse button in the References dialog box and open the desired OCX file, usually located in the \WINDOWS\ SYSTEM directory. No additional button appears in the Toolbox, but a new name will be added in the Object Browser. It will disappear from the Object Browser after you start a new project.

When a library is not needed, it should be removed from the References dialog box. Leaving many here may slow down compiling (running the program or making an EXE file) because Visual Basic needs to check all the libraries while converting your source code to executable instructions.

Browsing Your Own Objects

You can use the Object Browser to browse and manage the objects you create in Visual Basic. Your objects may be lumped together with Visual Basic's intrinsic objects. But you can easily tell them apart because your objects are displayed in boldface. For example, your Project1 may include Form1 which may have a Form_Click procedure. Choosing Project1 in the Project/Library box will display Form1 in the Classes box. Clicking Form1 will show lots of items in the Members box. Form_Click will appear here in boldface to distinguish it from the intrinsic form-related items.

When you select a project from the Project/Library box, the Classes box displays all the modules, plus <globals>. Clicking <globals> displays in the Members box all the global variables (declared with Public or Global, but not Dim or Private) in a **standard module**. Public **Enum** variables (see Chapter 9), regardless of where they are declared, also appear here.

When you click a module in the Classes box, its methods (sub and function procedures) and properties (property procedures and module-level variables) will appear in the Members box; these are identified by different icons. If you click a member, its details will appear in the Details pane. Details may include a constant value that you have used Const to assign, a procedure's parameters, or a procedure's attributes that you have used **Tools | Procedure Attributes** dialog box to enter.

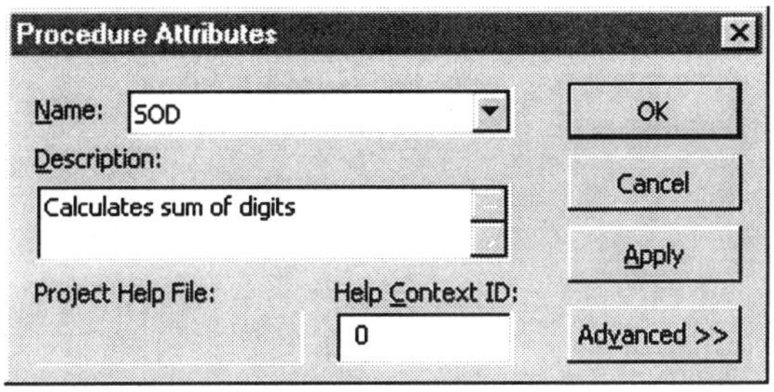

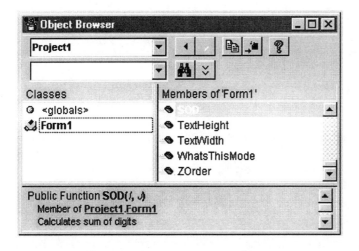

(Procedure Attributes dialog box)

Figure 8.38   **The Procedure Attributes dialog box**

You can use the Object Browser to access the Procedure Attributes dialog box. When you right-click a public variable or a procedure name in the Members box, the Properties option becomes available (it's not available when you click something else). If you choose it, the **Procedure Attributes dialog box** (Figure 8.38) appears. This is the same box shown when you choose Tools | Procedure Attributes. You can use this dialog box to make a new entry or alter an existing one. What you enter here will appear in the Details pane of the Object Browser, as shown in Figure 8.39.

Figure 8.39   **Adding a description to a procedure**

If you right-click a class name (in the Classes box) or a private procedure name (in the Members box) and then choose Properties, the **Member Options dialog box** (Figure 8.40) will appear instead. You can now add a description as in the Procedure Attributes dialog box, which will also appear in the Details pane of the Object Browser. Both dialog boxes let you designate a help file, which appears when the user click the ? button in the Object Browser. The difference between these two is that the Procedure Attributes dialog box has the Advanced button to let you designate a member as the default. Clicking this button adds a pane to bottom of the Procedure Attributes dialog box. Different features become available depending on whether you have selected a sub, function, or property (procedure or variable).

The button next to the ? (second from the right) is known as **View Definition**. It comes to life when an item created by you has been selected in the Classes or Members box. If a procedure has been selected, clicking this button takes you back to the beginning of that procedure in the Code window. If a module has been selected instead, the cursor goes to the previous position in the Code window. This option is also available when you right-click an item created by you.

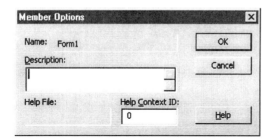

Figure 8.40   The Member Options dialog box

A quicker way to go back to the Code window is to double-click one of your items in the Object Browser window. The browser window remains open, but the cursor goes to the location as explained before.

If you compile a class into an **ActiveX** component file (see Chapter 12), it can be browsed by the Object Browser. Go to the References dialog box and use the Browse button to open the file. When it appears in the list, check it and then click OK to exit. It should now appear in the Project/Library list.

MAKING AN EXE FILE

You can compile a project into an executable file. Such a file can be run directly from Windows. To compile the current project, just choose File | Make Project.exe. The **Make Project dialog box** appears for you to enter a file name. You supply the file name and Visual Basic will automatically add EXE. You can use the Save-in box to determine where to save the file; if there is a duplicate, you'll be asked Yes/No to overwrite it.

The Make Project dialog box has the Options button. Clicking it opens the **Project Properties dialog box** (Figure 8.41). The two tabs shown here are similar to those shown when you choose Project | Project Properties, which has two additional tabs.

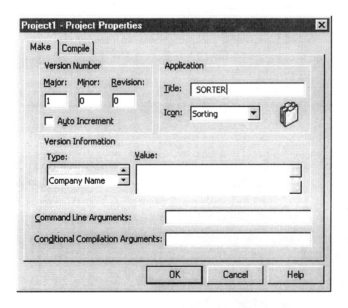

Figure 8.41   The options for making an EXE file

You can enter various version numbers from 0 to 999. If you check **Auto Increment,** the Revision number will increment by 1 every time you compile. You can choose an icon to represent this executable file. All the form modules' names can be pulled down from the Icon box, and you can select one to make its icon appear as the default icon. (To change a form's icon, you need to use its **Icon property** and open a desired icon, as explained in Chapter 3.) Fill in various

Application and Version entries as you deem necessary. These entries will appear in the property sheet of this file. When you right-click this file in Windows and choose Properties, you can click the General or Version tab to display these items. Users of your application will then know more about its background.

The information entered in Figure 8.41 can also be read with the **App** object's properties. For example, you can use App.Title, App.EXEName, App.LegalCopyright, etc. to read them. The App object has many properties, most of them are related to OLE.

You can open the **Compile tab** and select an option to compile your project. Here you can choose to create a speedier or smaller executable file. If you wish, you can click the Advanced Optimizations button to tweak your code during compiling. A message tells you that this is a dangerous venture.

When you open a project and the Open Project dialog box appears, you can right-click a project (VBP) or project group (VBG) file to pop up a shortcut menu that includes the Make and Make EXE File options to create an executable file. These options are not available when you right-click another type of file.

A compiled file does not require Visual Basic to run. However, Windows must be able to find the **MSVBVM50.DLL** file (run-time module) before it will run a standalone program compiled by Visual Basic. If your system has Visual Basic 5 installed, this file is installed in the WINDOWS\SYSTEM directory and Windows can find it there.

DRILL

Sub Main

____ 24. A startup object can be a form or a ____ ____ procedure.

____ 25. A procedure whose name is not preceded by Public or Private is by default a public procedure. True or false?

____ 26. To call a public procedure in a standard module from another module, you must specify the module name in the calling statement. True of false?

Envornment ____ 27. The _____ tab lets you determine whether templates are displayed.

____ 28. You can load a custom control by using the Toolbox. True or false?

___ 29. The Project window displays:
   a. a module's Name property
   b. a module's file name
   c. custom controls used in the project
   d. all of the above
   e. both a and b

___ 30. Procedure attributes appear in the:
   a. Object Browser
   b. Components dialog box
   c. Toolbox
   d. Project window

PRACTICE

■ 26. At the beginning of a new project, what happens if you select Form1 in the Project window and select Remove Form1 from the Project menu? What happens if you then choose Add Form from the Project menu?

■ 27. Explain the role of a project file.

■ 28. How can you use the Project window to manage multiple modules.

■ 29. How can you use the Object Browser to move the cursor from the current procedure to a procedure in another module.

■ 30. How can you browse another application's methods or properties?

■ 31. Create a function named Rept that will return a number of specified characters. For example, the following will print 10 times the specified character (X):

```
Print Rept("X", 10)
```

■ 32. Create a function named Faht that will return a number that is the Fahrenheit equivalent of a passed Centigrade number. For example, the following will print 212:

```
Print Faht(100)
```

■ 33. Create a function that will return the Fibonacci number of the specified term. (See a Practice question near the end of Chapter 6.) For example, this will print 55:

```
Print Fibon(10)
```

■ 34. Create a function that will return a passed string in reverse order.

■ 35. Modify the procedure for the last Practice question in Chapter 6. The nested Select Case lines should all be put in a function procedure. This function should be called and B's value should be passed to it. The function then returns the proper string matching B's value.

CHAPTER PROJECT

A. (8TAX1.FRM)

Modify the 6TAX3.FRM program in Chapter 6. When the Calculate button (Figure 8.42) is clicked, a user-defined function is called and the number in the left text box is passed to the function. The function calculates the tax amount and returns it to the caller, which displays it in the right text box.

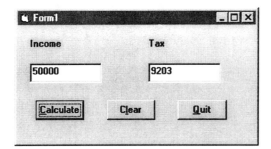

Figure 8.42   Calculating tax with a function

B. (8TAX2.FRM)

Convert the above function procedure to a property procedure. The project should do the same thing as before.

C. (8ADDRIL.FRM)

This program provides a drill for addition of two randomly generated numbers. The user interface is shown in Figure 8.43. It has five text boxes, five labels, three command buttons, and a timer.

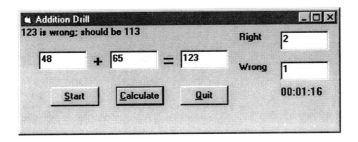

Figure 8.43   Addition drill

The program should behave as follows:

1. When the Start button is clicked, two two-digit random numbers 10-99 appear in Text1 and Text2. The focus goes to Text3 for an entry.

2. When the user types a number and presses Enter (or clicks Calculate), the top left corner of the screen displays "You got it" or an answer as shown in Figure 8.43.

3. Text4 and Text5 keep the score of right and wrong answers.

4. Label5 (bottom right corner) displays the elapsed time.

5. When Start is selected again, the first three text boxes are cleared, two new random numbers are generated and displayed, and the focus goes to Text3 for another entry.

D. (8BINDEC.FRM)

This program lets the user convert a binary number to a decimal number and vice versa. The program should behave as follows.

1. Selecting each option changes the form's caption and the two labels, as shown in Figures 8.44 and 8.45.

2. Typing a number in Text1 immediately results in it being converted to the other number and displayed in Text2.

3. Clicking Clear clears the displays in the text boxes.

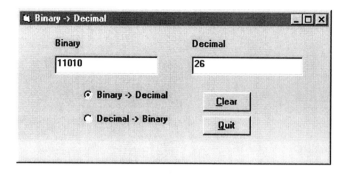

Figure 8.44   Converting from binary to decimal

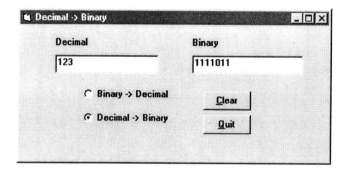

Figure 8.45   Converting from decimal to binary

E. (8CALENDA.FRM)

This program creates a perpetual calendar. The user interface is shown in Figure 8.46. The program should behave as follows:

1. The display in Figure 8.46 (January, 1997) automatically appears at the beginning of run time.

2. You can move the Month scroll bar from 1 to 12 and the Year scroll bar from 1000 to 3000. When each is moved, the text box display changes accordingly.

3. Each displayed column is separated from the next by a Tab character.

4. Clicking the Print button sends the displayed calendar to the printer.

(Use the Calendar project in Chapter 7 to create each monthly display. Write a general procedure that can be called at the beginning and when a scroll bar is changed.)

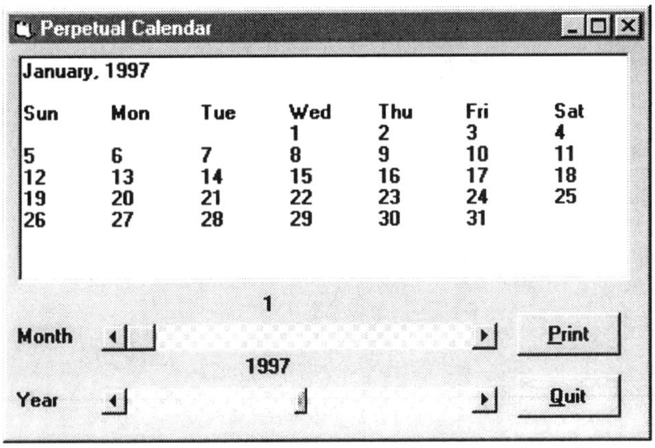

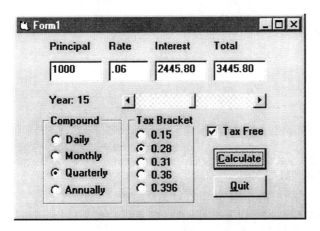

Figure 8.46   **A perpetual calendar**

F. (8INVEST.FRM)

This program lets you calculate returns from a fixed-income investment, such as CDs and bonds. The Principal and Rate boxes contain numbers entered by the user. The program returns the numbers in Interest and Total.

Figure 8.47   **Calculating investment returns**

The user can choose a compound option from the left frame and use the scroll bar to set a year number from 1 to 30. At the beginning of run time, Year is 1 and Annual is chosen by default. If the user enters Principal and Rate and clicks Calculate, annual compounding for one year is the default. If no entry is made in either Principal or Rate, a beep is made and nothing else happens.

Use the following formula for compounding. Put it in a function procedure and call it when Calculate is clicked.

   total = principal * (1 + rate / term) ^ (term * year)

If the Tax Free check box is checked and an option is selected in Tax Bracket, the tax equivalent yield is returned by using the following formula:

   tax equivalent yield = (tax free yield) / (1 - tax rate)

If either option is not checked, the program ignores both options and returns the regular yield.

Figure 8.47 shows the results based on the following factors:

   initial investment: 1000
   interest rate: 6%
   taxable status: tax free
   tax bracket: 28%
   years: 15
   compound: quarterly

You can change some or all of these factors and click Calculate to show a different result. For example, you might use 8.5% and taxable to see whether this combination will bring you a higher income.

FUN AND GAME

A. (ARROW.FRM)

This program simulates a yellow arrow sign (Figure 8.48) you see on highways when construction crews close a lane. There are 11 circles (shape controls) that form a control array at design time. When the program starts, the left circle lights up. Each of the next circle takes turn to light up after half a second. Finally, the 5 circles forming the arrow head light up at the same time. All the lights stay on for 1 more second and then disappear together. The cycle repeats itself infinitely.

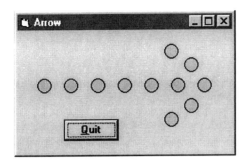

Figure 8.48   Lighted arrow

```
Private Sub Form_Load()
    Dim I As Integer

    Show      'show form
    Do
        For I = 0 To 5          'arrow body
            Shape1(I).FillStyle = 0        'solid
            Shape1(I).FillColor = vbYellow
            Timer1.Interval = 500          '1/2 sec
            Timer1_Timer      'call timer to delay
        Next I

        For I = 6 To 10         'arrow head, no delay
            Shape1(I).FillStyle = 0
            Shape1(I).FillColor = vbYellow
        Next I
        Timer1.Interval = 1000          '1 sec
        Timer1_Timer      'call timer to delay

        For I = 0 To 10   'transparent, no color
            Shape1(I).FillStyle = 1
        Next I
        Timer1.Interval = 500          '1/2 sec
        Timer1_Timer      'call timer to delay
    Loop
End Sub

Private Sub Timer1_Timer()
    Static Turn As Integer    'track timer interval

    Turn = Turn + 1
    Do While DoEvents()
        If Turn Mod 2 = 0 Then Exit Do
            'exit after specified interval
    Loop
    Timer1.Interval = 0 'disable timer
```

```
End Sub
```

B. (FLAGUK.FRM)

This program draws the British flag (Figure 8.49). You can also resize the form
to redraw the flag to fit in the new window. This program demonstrates a series
of calls to a procedure. This greatly reduces the length of the code.

Figure 8.49   The U.K. flag

```
Private Sub Form_Load()
    Dim I As Integer
    'At design time, Line1's Name changed to linBar
    'Index changed to 0 for cloning
    linBar(0).Visible = False     'hide original
    For I = 1 To 8
        Load linBar(I)           'create line clones
    Next I
    BackColor = vbBlue  'set form back color
End Sub

Private Sub Form_Resize()
    Dim SH As Long
    Dim SW As Long

    SH = ScaleHeight      'get form dimensions
    SW = ScaleWidth
    Call SetBar(1, SW * 0.006, vbRed, 0, SH / 2, SW, _
    SH / 2)
        'middle, left to right bar, red
    Call SetBar(2, SW * 0.006, vbRed, SW / 2, 0, _
    SW / 2, SH)
        'middle, top to bottom
    Call SetBar(3, SW * 0.008, vbWhite, 0, SH / 2, _
    SW, SH / 2)
        'middle, left to right, white
    Call SetBar(4, SW * 0.008, vbWhite, SW / 2, 0, _
    SW / 2, SH)
        'middle, top to bottom, white
```

```
        Call SetBar(5, SW * 0.002, vbRed, 0, 0, SW, SH)
            'top-left to bot-right, narrow red
        Call SetBar(6, SW * 0.004, vbWhite, 0, 0, SW, SH)
            'top-left to bot-right, wide white
        Call SetBar(7, SW * 0.002, vbRed, 0, SH, SW, 0)
            'bot-left to top-right
        Call SetBar(8, SW * 0.004, vbWhite, 0, SH, SW, 0)
End Sub

Private Sub SetBar(I, BW, BC, X1, Y1, X2, Y2)
        linBar(I).BorderWidth = BW    'line width in pixels
        linBar(I).BorderColor = BC    'line color
        linBar(I).X1 = X1
        linBar(I).Y1 = Y1
        linBar(I).X2 = X2             'position line
        linBar(I).Y2 = Y2
        linBar(I).Visible = True      'show line
End Sub
```

Chapter 9
Arrays, Control Arrays, and Collections

TOPICS

KEY TERMS

Array   A group of related variables that share the same name. The individual variables are known as elements. Each element is distinguished from another by an index number. An array may have one or more ranges of elements; each range is a subscript. Multiple subscript ranges make multidimensional arrays.

Array function   A function that lets you assign an arbitrary number of Variant-type elements to a Variant variable. The variable can then be maneuvered like an array. This function combines the DATA and READ commands available in most versions of Basic.

Collection   An array-like object that can contain members of different data types. Visual Basic maintain many internal collections to handle objects. Users can create their own collections and manipulate them like arrays.

Control array   An array of multiple controls of the same type. They all share one name but are distinguished by different index numbers.

Dynamic array   An array with no fixed subscript range. When needed, the range can be specified dynamically, by the program or the user. This arrangement can make better use of memory.

Enum   An enumeration (list) of constants that can share the same name and be tied together as a unit. In the Object Browser, enumerations are treated as classes and their variable (member) names and values are visible.

Option Base   A statement in the Declarations section of a module specifying the base (lowest) number of an array's range.

Object variable   A variable that can be used to maneuver objects (forms and controls). It must be specifically declared with an appropriate command such as Dim, ReDim, Static, or Global. Use the Set command to assign an object to an object variable at run time.

User-Defined Data Type   A data type, also known as a structure, that can contain multiple elements of different data types. It must be created with Type...End Type in the Declarations section of a module. After a structure has been created, you can declare a variable to be that type. Combine the structure name and each individual element name with a period, and use this combination as you would an ordinary variable.

Instead of using one variable to hold one piece of information as we have done most of the time so far, we can use a variable to hold multiple pieces. We can use an array, a structure (user-defined type), a control array, or a collection to do that. The first half of this chapter explains these items and the second half provides more complex applications for arrays, the most common and versatile of the these.

AN ARRAY EXAMPLE

Let's use a concrete example before we proceed further. Let's suppose that you work five days a week and earn a different amount each day. If you use regular variables to maneuver those numbers, you can do it this way:

```
Private Sub Form_Click()
    Dim Day1 As Integer, Day2 As Integer
    Dim Day3 As Integer, Day4 As Integer
    Dim Day5 As Integer
    Dim Total As Integer
    Dim Average As Single

    Day1 = 90: Day2 = 110: Day3 = 89
    Day4 = 95: Day5 = 98

    Total = Day1 + Day2 + Day3 + Day4 + Day5
    Print Total
    Average = Total / 5
    Print Average
End Sub
```

We use five variables, Day1, Day2, etc., to store five values. We also use all the five variables to get the total. As the number of variables increases, this approach can become inefficient and unmanageable.

Now consider the alternative of using a single array to store and maneuver all five values:

```
Private Sub Form_Click()
    Dim Day(1 To 5) As Integer      'declare array
    Dim Total As Integer
    Dim Average As Single
    Dim I As Integer

    Day(1) = 90: Day(2) = 110: Day(3) = 89
    Day(4) = 95: Day(5) = 98

    For I = 1 To 5
        Total = Total + Day(I)
```

```
     Next I

     Print Total
     Average = Total / (I - 1)
     Print Average
End Sub
```

Instead of adding up all the individual variables, we use a simple For-Next loop to do it. This new arrangement is very efficient when you have a large number of variables.

We can make the whole thing even simpler by using the **Array function**:

```
Private Sub Form_Click()
     Dim Total As Integer
     Dim Average As Single
     Dim Item As Variant
     Dim Days As Variant

     Days = Array(90, 110, 89, 95, 98)

     For Each Item In Days
         Total = Total + Item
     Next Item

     Print Total
     Average = Total / 5
     Print Average
End Sub
```

The Array function will be discussed further, after we cover other array topics below.

ARRAY FUNDAMENTALS

An **array** is a group of related variables that share the same name. The individual variables are known as **elements**. Each element is identified by an **index** number, which is also known as a **subscript**. If Arr is an array name, *Arr* or *Arr( )* is an array that contains multiple elements. Arr(1), Arr(2), etc. are individual elements, each of which can be assigned a separate value; the index numbers of 1, 2, etc. distinguish one element from another. Arr(1) is a subscripted variable and is commonly read as "Arr sub 1."

For example, you may want to maneuver the seven days of the week. Instead of using seven separate variables to represent those names, you can use one array name with seven elements. Suppose you use WkDay as the array name. You may then have the following possibilities:

WkDay(0)	'Sunday
WkDay(1)	'Monday
WkDay(2)	'Tuesday
. . .	

When you want to refer to Sunday, use WkDay(0) instead. This way, you can maneuver seven different items with just one name. This arrangement can be visualized as shown in Figure 9.1.

Sunday	Monday	Tuesday	Wednesday	Thursday	Friday	Saturday
WkDay(0)	WkDay(1)	WkDay(2)	WkDay(3)	WkDay(4)	WkDay(5)	WkDay(6)

Figure 9.1   A one-dimensional array

The above example is a **one-dimensional array** because we use one subscript range. We can use two or more subscript ranges to create **multidimensional arrays**. This arrangement can make your arrays even more versatile.

Suppose you manage three convenience stores and need to tabulate their weekly incomes. You can use a two-dimensional array to handle such a situation. Here are some possibilities:

WkDay(0, 0)	'day 0, store 0
WkDay(0, 1)	'day 0, store 1
. . .	
WkDay(1, 0)	'day1, store 0
WkDay(1, 1)	'day1, store 1
. . .	

You can now use one array to handle 21 items. If you use individual variables, you will have to use 21 names.

This arrangement can be visualized as shown in Figure 9.2. This figure shows a grid with 7 rows (0-6) and 3 columns (0-2). Each array element contains two numbers. The first number represents the row (day) subscript and the second number is for the column (store) subscript.

Stores

Days	0	1	2
0	WkDay(0,0)		WkDay(0,2)
1			
2			
3		WkDay(3,1)	
4			
5			
6	WkDay(6,0)		WkDay(6,2)

Figure 9.2   A two-dimensional array

Visual Basic requires you to declare an array before you can use it. Otherwise, the *Sub or Function not defined* error will appear. This is true regardless of whether Option Explicit is on or off.

To declare an array, you also need to specify a subscript range. This range determines the lowest to the highest index numbers the array can handle. You can specify a range or just the maximum number.

Declaring an array sets aside a block of memory whose size depends on the specified subscript and the data type. When values are assigned or retrieved, your program uses the allocated memory.

You can declare a **local array** in a procedure by using the **Dim**, **ReDim**, or **Static** (for a static array) statements. Here are two examples:

```
ReDim WkDay(6)        'subscript range 0-6
Static WkDay(1 To 7) 'range 1-7, static
```

In the first example, the subscript range is presumed to be from 0 to 6. The assigned values are also erased between calls. In the second, the range is from 1 to 7, and the values are kept between calls. The **To** keyword is used to specify the lowest and highest elements' index values.

To declare an array with two or more dimensions, separate each subscript range with a comma. Here is an example:

```
ReDim WkDay(5, 1 To 5) As Single
```

The first subscript has range 0 to 5 and the second 1 to 5.

You can specify a data type for all the elements in an array, as shown in our example above. If no data type is specified, the elements are Variants, capable of holding any type of data.

You can also use the **Dim** or **Private** statement to declare a **module-level array** in the **Declarations section**. If Full Module View is on, go to the top of the Code window and enter the declaration. If not, you need to make sure that (General) appears in the Object box and (Declarations) in the Proc box. If Option Explicit is on, it can be placed before or after an array or variable.

The rules concerning variable scope also apply to arrays. An array declared in the Declarations section of a form is visible throughout all the procedures in that form, and those declared in a procedure are not visible outside the procedure.

You can declare **global arrays** only in the Declarations section of a **standard module** by using **Global** or **Public**. These two words are not allowed in a form module; they will both lead to errors. Global arrays are visible throughout the entire application.

You can use the **Option Base** statement in the Declarations section to specify the base number for all the arrays. By default, the base (first) number is 0. So if you declare an array with Num(4), it can handle five elements, from 0 to 4. If you want the base number to be 1 (this is the only legal alternative), put this in the Declarations section:

```
Option Base 1
```

If you now declare an array with Num(4), it can handle only four elements, 1 to 4. Of course, you can always use the **To** keyword to specify a range regardless of what the base number is. Here you are allowed to start with any integer and end with any higher integer. In fact, you can start or end with a negative value. But keep in mind that the value before To must be lower than the one after it.

An array index can be any integer or expression that returns an integer. We use an expression in this example:

```
Private Sub Form_Click ()
    Static I As Integer
    Dim Arr(2) As Integer

    Arr(I Mod 3) = I
    Print I, I Mod 3, Arr(I Mod 3)
    I = I + 1
End Sub
```

Running the procedure and clicking the form nine times will lead to Figure 9.3. The middle column shows that the array's index numbers rotate among 0, 1, and 2—one of the values returned by an expression.

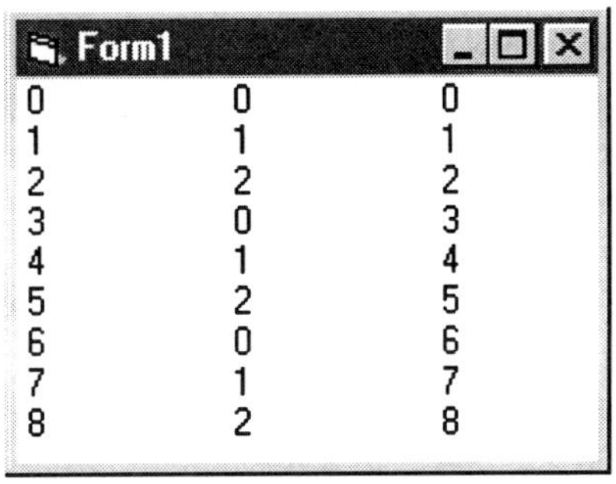

Figure 9.3   Using an expression as an array index

You can use a decimal number for an array index, such as Arr(.2) or Arr(1.5). Since only integers are allowed as index numbers, Visual Basic will round off the decimal values and convert the former to Arr(0) and the latter to Arr(2). This practice should normally be avoided because it will cause confusion and may result in invisible errors.

MORE ARRAY EXAMPLES

This section provides more concrete examples of using one-dimensional and multidimensional arrays. The first example is shown below. After the program runs, a blank window appears. Clicking the window leads to an input box to prompt you to enter each day's amount (we are using the convenience store example discussed earlier). After you enter five numbers, the screen shows those numbers and their sum and average (Figure 9.4).

```
Private Sub Form_Click ()
    Dim I As Integer
    Dim Sum As Single
    Dim Prompt As String
    Dim Num(1 To 5) As Single

    For I = 1 To 5
        Prompt = "Enter day " & I & " amount"
        Num(I) = Val(InputBox(Prompt)) 'get input numeric
        Print "Day " & I, Num(I)    'print each number
        Sum = Sum + Num(I)             'tabulate total
    Next I

    Print "Sum: ", Sum
    Print "Average: ", Sum / (I - 1)
End Sub
```

Notice how we use a single variable name to hold five different values. When the For loop goes through the first round, our variable name becomes Num(1) and holds the first value supplied by the user. The index number inside the parentheses increments by 1 each time the loop is repeated. This is an efficient programming technique when there are numerous related variables.

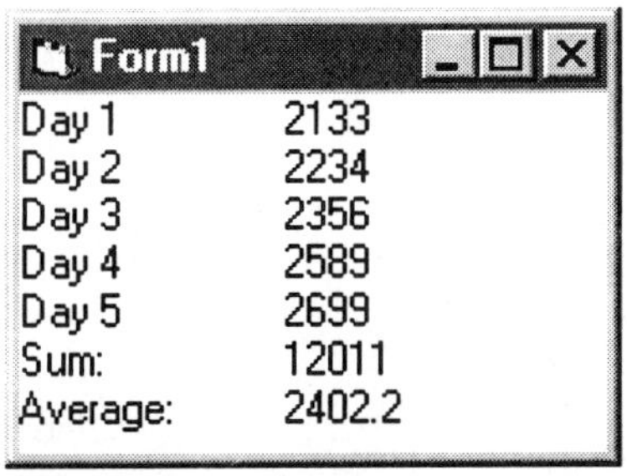

Form1	_ □ ✕
Day 1	2133
Day 2	2234
Day 3	2356
Day 4	2589
Day 5	2699
Sum:	12011
Average:	2402.2

Figure 9.4   Output by an array

The formula in the last Print statement returns the result of dividing the total by 5. The counter variable (I in our case) in the For loop has the value of 1 higher than the upper limit at the end of the looping operation. Since variable I goes from 1 to 5, at the end of the looping operation it has the value of 6. We need to subtract 1 from it to get the number of rounds (this won't be necessary if we use 0 as our base number). So the following formula returns the average:

```
Sum / (I - 1)
```

In the procedure below, we use a two-dimensional array to provide a concrete example for Figure 9.5. The elements consist of three strings and three numerics. This illustrates the versatility of Variant variables which can hold any type of data. The values are also assigned in the procedure, in contrast to being entered from the keyboard as shown before. The procedure produces the result shown in Figure 9.5.

```
Private Sub Form_Click ()
    Dim I As Integer
    Dim Avg As Single
    Dim Sum As Single
    Dim City(2, 1) As Variant
        '2-dimension: 0-2 & 0-1
    City(0, 0) = "New York"     'assign values
    City(0, 1) = 67
    City(1, 0) = "Chicago"
    City(1, 1) = 52
    City(2, 0) = "Seattle"
    City(2, 1) = 65

    Print "City", "Temperature"     'print headline
    For I = 0 To 2
        Sum = Sum + City(I, 1)   'get total
    Next I

    Avg = Sum / I          'get average
    For I = 0 To 2         'print each value
        Print City(I, 0), City(I, 1)
    Next I
    Print "Average", Format(Avg, "#.00")
End Sub                         'print last line
```

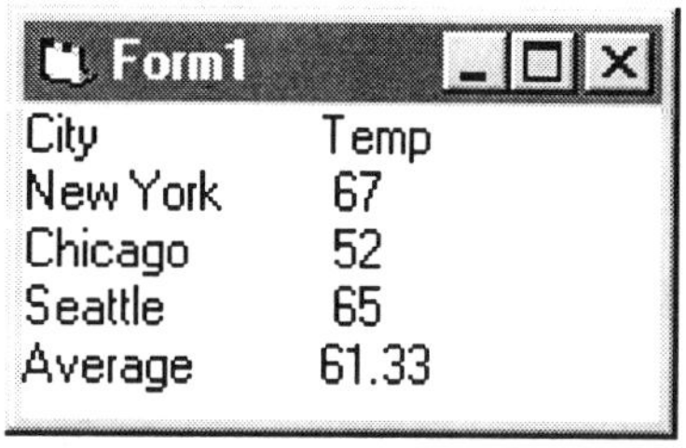

Figure 9.5   Output by a two-dimensional array

When numbers are arranged orderly, it's logical to maneuver them with an array. Consider Figures 9.6 and 9.7.

Column

	1	2	3
1	1	2	3
Row 2	4	5	6
3	7	8	9

Figure 9.6   An orderly set of numbers

The numbers are orderly and flow from one row to the next, resembling a telephone dial. How can we put their numbers in an array? You can do it manually, like below:

```
Num(1, 1) = 1 : Num(1, 2) = 2 : Num(1, 3) = 3
Num(2, 1) = 4 : Num(2, 2) = 5 : Num(3, 3) = 6
Num(3, 1) = 7 : Num(3, 2) = 8 : Num(3, 3) = 9
```

On the other hand, you can easily use a couple of loops to accomplish the same thing, as shown in this procedure:

```
Private Sub Form_Click ()        '--Listing 1--
    Dim Col As Integer
    Dim Row As Integer
    Dim K As Integer
    Dim Num(1 To 3, 1 To 3) As Integer
    For Row = 1 To 3          'row
        For Col = 1 To 3      'col
            K = K + 1          'digit counter
            Num(Row, Col) = K  'assign to element
            Print Num(Row, Col),
                'print element, same line
        Next Col
        Print            'new line
    Next Row
End Sub
```

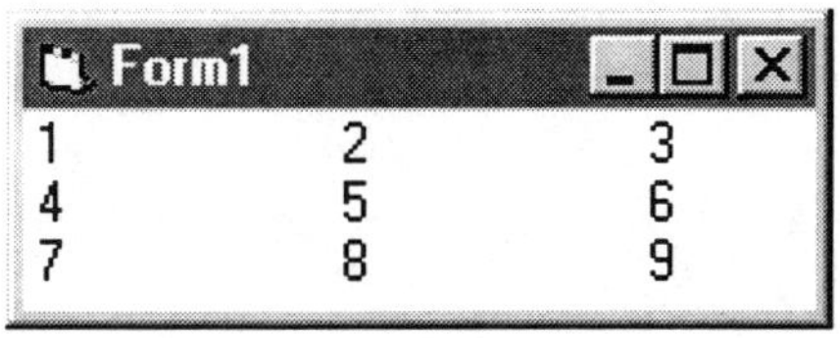

```
Form1                    _ □ X
1            2            3
4            5            6
7            8            9
```

Figure 9.7   Output by a two-dimensional array

DYNAMIC ARRAYS

An array's subscript range limits the number of elements an array can handle. If you specify a large range, you may waste a big chunk of unused memory. If you specify a small one, it may not be enough to do the job. One solution is to declare a **dynamic array** and fill in the needed subscript as the situation calls for.

A module-level dynamic array can be declared in the Declarations section with the Dim statement without a subscript. Here is an example:

```
Dim Num()
```

This is an empty array that sets aside no memory. The needed memory can be dynamically set in one or more procedures.

If you need only a local array, you can dimension it with a number supplied by the user or passed from another procedure. Here is an example of using a local array:

```
Private Sub Form_Click ()
    Dim I As Integer
    Dim EleNum As Integer

    EleNum = InputBox("How many elements?")
    ReDim Num(EleNum)        'specify subscript
    For I = 1 To EleNum
        Num(I) = I       'assign values to array
        Print Num(I)   'print array elements
    Next I
End Sub
```

The user is prompted to specify the number of elements. The Dim statement then sets aside the correspondent amount of memory. This arrangement can handle any number of elements without wasting memory.

The **ReDim** keyword cannot be replaced by **Dim** in this situation because Dim does not allow a variable as an argument. The *Constant expression required* error will be triggered by using Dim with a variable.

There are occasions when you want to expand an array's subscript range without erasing the existing values. You need to use the **Preserve** keyword to preserve any existing values and expand the array's subscript range. Here is an example:

```
Private Sub Form_Click()
    Dim I As Integer
    Dim EleNum As Integer
```

```
    Dim Entry As Variant

    ReDim Num(0)      'initial subscript
    EleNum = 0

    Do
        Entry = InputBox("Enter element #" & EleNum)
        If Entry = "" Then Exit Do  'no entry, get out
        Num(EleNum) = Entry
            'assign value to each element
        EleNum = EleNum + 1
            'increment subscript range
        ReDim Preserve Num(EleNum)
            'redim subscript
    Loop

    For I = 0 To EleNum - 1
        Print Num(I)  'print array elements
    Next I
End Sub
```

We start out with ReDim Num(0) to supply the first (0) subscript. Using Dim Num(0) either at the module or procedure level will lead to the *Array already dimensioned* error. Using Dim Num( ) at the module level will cause the *Subscript out of range* error.

We use the Preserve keyword to preserve the data already stored in the array. If this word is not present when we use ReDim, all the existing data will be erased.

ARRAY COMMANDS

The following commands are commonly used to maneuver arrays:

LBound   Returns the lowest index number in the array
UBound   Returns the highest index number in the array
Erase   Erases array elements

LBound (lowerbound) and UBound (upperbound) are functions that can read an array's subscript range. They follow this syntax:

LBound(*ArrayName*[, *dimension*])

The returned value is determined by the declaration. The following procedure leads to the result shown in Figure 9-8.

```
Private Sub Form_Click()
    Dim Arr(3, 2 To 5, -10 To 10)
```

```
        Print "LBound", "UBound"
        Print LBound(Arr, 1),
        Print UBound(Arr, 1)
        Print LBound(Arr, 2),
        Print UBound(Arr, 2)
        Print LBound(Arr, 3),
        Print UBound(Arr, 3)
End Sub
```

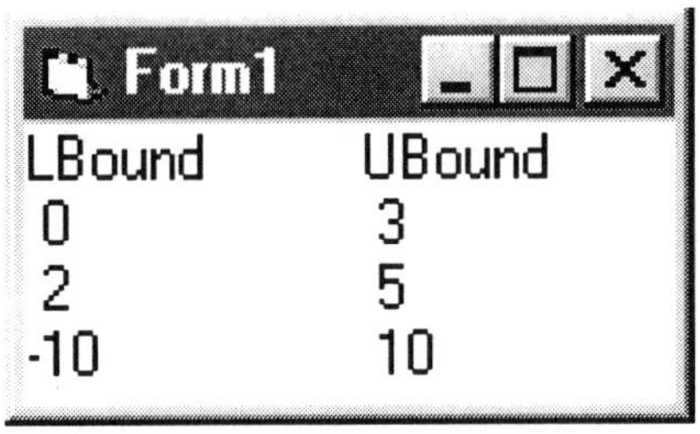

Figure 9.8   Showing LBound and UBound

If you omit the optional dimension-number argument in LBound or UBound, the default is the first dimension. So LBound(Arr) returns 0 in our example.

The **Erase** statement erases an array's contents. The statement below will erase any existing contents in the specified array name:

```
    Erase ArrayName
```

It can do different things to different types of arrays. The following table shows its effects on ordinary (fixed-size) arrays.

Array type	Effect
Fixed numeric	Sets each element to 0.
Fixed string (fixed length)	Sets each element to 0.
Fixed string (variable length)	Sets each element to 0-length.
Fixed Variant	Sets each element to Empty.
User defined	Sets each element to a separate variable.
Object	Sets each element to Nothing.

When a **dynamic array** is involved, Erase frees the memory previously allocated to the array. In effect, the array no longer exists. If you want to use it again, you have to use ReDim to declare it again.

The following procedure demonstrates ArrA as a fixed-size array and ArrB as a dynamic array. ArrB is a dynamic array because its subscript is specified by a variable, not a fixed value as in ArrA. After its erasure, ArrA(0) has the value of 0. After its erasure, ArrB(0) is no longer recognized. Instead, the *Subscript out of range* error will appear.

```
Private Sub Form_Click()
    Dim ArrA(3) As Integer          'fixed array
    ArrA(0) = 1: Print ArrA(0)      '1
    Erase ArrA: Print ArrA(0)       '0

    Dim Num
    Num = 3
    ReDim ArrB(Num) As Integer      'dynamic array
    ArrB(0) = 2: Print ArrB(0) '2
    Erase ArrB: Print ArrB(0)       'error
End Sub
```

ARRAYS AND PROCEDURES

Arrays can be passed to a procedure, which can then do something to the array. Pass an array to a sub procedure if you intend to manipulate the array without returning a value. Pass it to a function procedure if you expect it to return a value. The example below involves a sub procedure.

```
Private Sub Form_Click()
    Dim I As Integer
    Dim FName(2) As String

    FName(0) = "Jon"        'assign names to array
    FName(1) = "Tom"
    FName(2) = "Kim"

    For I = 0 To 2
        Print FName(I) 'print names
    Next I

    GoArray FName              'call sub, pass array
    For I = 0 To 2
        Print FName(I)    'no more, erased
    Next I
End Sub

Private Sub GoArray(ArrName)
    Dim I As Integer

    For I = 0 To 2
        ArrName(I) = "" 'erase each element
```

```
    Next I
End Sub
```

What do you think will be printed to the screen? The three names are printed only once, by the first For loop but not by the second. When the second For loop is executed, the elements are all assigned nothing, so nothing is printed after the call. This shows that an array is normally passed to a procedure **by reference**. That allows the called procedure to alter the array's contents.

What if you want to **pass by value**? The simplest way is to add a pair of extra parentheses to the array in the calling statement. The following two statements are equivalent:

```
GoArray(FName)
Call GoArray((FName))
```

As explained in Chapter 8, you need to enclose an argument in a pair of parentheses when Call is used. Adding an extra pair signifies passing an argument by value.

When you expect a called procedure to return a value, pass an array to a function, not a sub, procedure. In the following example, the calling procedure passes a local array to a function, which returns the highest value in the array.

```
Private Sub Form_Click ()
    Dim HiNum As Integer
    Dim Num(2) As Integer       'local array

    Num(0) = 123
    Num(1) = 456
    Num(2) = 789
    HiNum = MaxNum(Num)     'call func, pass by reference
    Print HiNum             'print highest value
End Sub

Private Function MaxNum(Num)
    Dim I As Integer
    Dim Temp As Integer

    Temp = Num(0)     'assign 1st element to x
    For I = LBound(Num) + 1 To UBound(Num)
        If Temp < Num(I) Then Temp = Num(I)
    Next I            'change if element higher

    MaxNum = Temp     'return highest value to caller
End Function
```

The above example can be used to replace the DEF FN command in Basic, which is no longer available in Visual Basic (see Chapter 8). The following provides another example in which a local array is passed to a function, which in turn returns the average.

```
Private Sub Form_Click ()
    Dim Ave As Single
    Dim Num(2) As Integer    'local array, index 0-2

    Num(0) = 83
    Num(1) = 75
    Num(2) = 78
    Ave = Avg(Num)    'call func, pass by reference
    Print Ave         'print average
End Sub

Private Function Avg(Sum)
    Dim I As Integer
    Dim Tot As Integer
    For I = LBound(Sum) To UBound(Sum)
        Tot = Tot + Sum(I)   'add elements
    Next I
    Avg = Tot / I   'get average, return
End Function
```

In all the above examples, we pass whole arrays to procedures. You can also pass an array element by specifying an array's index number in a calling statement; the called procedure will receive the element as a regular variable. The passing can also be done by value or by reference. See Chapter 8 for more details.

If you have a module-level array, any procedure within that module can access or alter the array without any passing arrangement.

ARRAYS WITHIN AN ARRAY

An array element of the Variant type can be assigned another array. Values of different data types can be assigned to different such elements. This can make a one-dimensional array behave like a multidimensional array, with each element storing a different type of data. Such an array can be very flexible.

In the example below, we declare ArrA to be Integer type, ArrB String type, and ArrC unspecified type. ArrX, on the other hand, must be of the Variant data type. If you specify it as another type, you'll get the *Type mismatch* error.

```
Private Sub Form_Click()        '--Listing 2--
    Dim ArrA(1 To 5) As Integer
```

```
Dim ArrB(1 To 5) As String
Dim ArrC(1 To 5)    'Variant by default
Dim ArrX(1 To 3) As Variant
Dim I As Integer
Dim J As Integer

For I = 1 To 5
    ArrA(I) = I          'assign numbers
    ArrB(I) = "hello"    'assign strings
    ArrC(I) = "there"    'same
Next I

ArrX(1) = ArrA() 'assign array of numbers to element
ArrX(2) = ArrB() 'strings, all () optional
ArrX(3) = ArrC() 'Variant

For I = 1 To 3
    For J = 1 To 5
        CurrentX = (I - 1) * 500
          'move print head right by 500 twips
        Print ArrX(I)(J)  'see text
    Next J
    CurrentY = 0      'move to top
Next I
End Sub
```

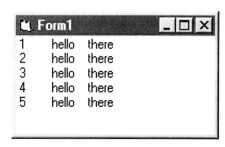

Figure 9.9   Demonstrating arrays inside another array

The procedure tries to maneuver each of ArrA's elements. That produces a column-oriented result (Figure 9.9). So column 1 is printed first, followed by columns two and three. A practice question below lets you maneuver rows to print one line at a time.

The ArrA array is originally a one-dimensional array with three elements. By assigning an array to each element, it behaves like a two-dimensional array. Notice the unusual expression in the following statement. This C-like expression appeared in VB4 for the first time. A similar C expression is used to reference a two-dimensional array; here it is used in a one-dimensional array (Visual Basic's elements in a multidimensional array are enclosed in a single pair of parentheses and separated by commas).

```
Print ArrX(I)(J)
```

This is how the one-dimensional ArrX array references each subelement in each of the array's elements. The referencing can also be done as shown below. If you replace the inner For-Next loop with the following For Each-Next loop, the result will be identical.

```
For Each J In ArrX(I)
    CurrentX = (ArrX(1)(I) - 1) * 500
      'move print head right by 500 twips
    Print J
Next J
```

Here we use the numbers in the first dimension of the X array to control the display of columns. We can also use the ArrA array for the same result, such as:

```
CurrentX = (ArrA(I) - 1) * 500
```

We are also using variable J to represent each subelement of each of ArrX's elements. J is not part of the array and cannot be used to alter the array's contents. If you want to change the array, you need to use the referencing mechanism shown earlier; this will be further demonstrated below.

THE ARRAY FUNCTION

We have used the new Array function on several occasions. This section provides a more thorough coverage.

The **Array** function lets you use a single statement to assign a group of values to a Variant variable. This resembles the arrangement in the C language that lets you declare an array variable and assign values in a single statement. It is also similar to the combination of the READ and DATA commands in Basic. Using this function, you can quickly make a Variant variable behave like a one-dimensional array, which in turn can be made to behave like a two-dimensional array, and so on. Here is an example:

```
Dim ArrX as Variant
ArrX = Array("one", 2, "three")
Print ArrX(0)
```

The above statements will result in "one" (the first element) being printed to the screen. Notice that we can mix data types here. Here ArrX is declared to be a single-value (also known as **scalar**) variable. But we can use Array to assign multiple values to it, thus making it into an array.

The variable ArrX can only be the **Variant** data type. If you don't specify a data type or don't declare it when Option Explicit is not on, then the variable is a Variant by default. Specifying another data type will lead to a variety of errors.

What we have here is actually a **Variant** variable holding an array of Variant elements. So ArrX is a Variant; each element in the array is also a Variant. You can thus assign any type of data to an element in the array.

Since an array consists of a group of elements, you can use the **For Each-Next** command to maneuver them. Here is an example:

```
Private Sub Command1_Click()
    Dim Item As Variant
    Dim Group As Variant
    Dim Sum As Single
    Group = Array(3.4, 8.6, 9.5)
    For Each Item In Group
        Sum = Sum + Item
    Next Item
    Print Sum
End Sub
```

Here we use Group as an array to store a group of values and Item to represent each element. The For Each-Next loop goes through each element from the first to the last and add it to Sum. This arrangement is simple but lacks flexibility. If you want to do more complex manipulation, such as looping from the last to the first element, you need to use index numbers, as shown below.

Keep in mind that Item in this situation is a variable representing an element in an array; it's not an element in the array. The array is not altered by the following:

```
For Each Item In Group
    Item = 0          'array unchanged
Next Item
```

On the other hand, the following will replace all the values in the array with zeroes:

```
I = 0
For Each Item In Group
    Group(I) = 0                  'replace element values
    I = I + 1
```

```
Next Item
```

We can convert the For Each-Next control structure to the For-Next control structure as below. It will produce the same result as in the original procedure.

```
For Item = 0 To UBound(Group)
    Sum = Sum + Group(Item)
Next Item
```

We now use the conventional Group(Item) expression to represent each element in the array. We also use UBound to determine the last index number in the array. We can also use LBound(group) to replace 0. LBound has the default 0 value if the base value is not changed by **Option Base**. So the LBound value of an array created by the Array function can be 0 or 1, depending on the value specified by Option Base.

Once you know the index number of the last element in an array, you can use it to maneuver the array. For example, if you want to return the average, you can divide the sum by UBound(Group).

An array created by the Array function can also be passed to a general procedure. We can thus call a function and pass the array as follows:

```
Print Avg(Group)     'call function and pass argument
```

The function procedure can be written this way:

```
Private Function Avg(Ary)
    Dim I As Integer
    Dim Sum As Single
    Dim Mem As Variant

    For Each Mem In Ary
        Sum = Sum + Mem
        I = I + 1
    Next mem
    Avg = Sum / I          'return call with average
End Function
```

Array Group is passed to a Variant variable named Ary. If you wish, you can add As Variant after Ary in the function header to specify variable Ary's data type. You can also use the same array name in both places.

Keep in mind that Ary is an array and must be treated as such. An error will result if you treat it as a single-value variable.

The For Each-Next loop in our example can be replaced with the For-Next loop this way:

```
For I = 0 To UBound(Ary)
    Sum = Sum + Ary(I)
Next I
```

The above demonstration shows that we can pass an array to a Variant variable. If fact, you can also assign an array to a Variant variable. So if ArrX is an array, you can assign it to Variant variable ArrY this way:

```
ArrY = ArrX
```

Now ArrY becomes an array containing all the elements in ArrX. You can use the **VarType** and **TypeName** functions to verify ArrY's transformation from a Variant to an array.

Used in this situation, ArrY must be a Variant. If it's of another data type, the above assignment will lead to the *Type mismatch* error.

After you convert a Variant variable to a multidimensional array, you can resort to a number of ways to reference the individual values. In the first example below, we use Array to assign a list of values to each element in the one-dimensional array. It leads to Figure 9.10.

```
Private Sub Form_Click()        '--Listing 3--
    Dim I As Integer
    Dim Total As Integer
    Dim Element As Variant
    Dim Names(4) As Variant

    Names(0) = Array("Joe", 67, 77, 65)
    Names(1) = Array("Jane", 87, 76, 80)
    Names(2) = Array("Tim", 97, 85, 89)
    Names(3) = Array("Jim", 69, 87, 80)
    Names(4) = Array("John", 88, 79, 65)

    For I = 0 To UBound(Names)
        Total = 0        'start each person with 0
        For Each Element In Names(I)
            If VarType(Element) = vbString Then
                Print Element,
                'if string type, print name
            End If        'use Val to avoid type mismatch
            Total = Total + Val(Element)
        Next Element
        Print "Total = "; Total,
        Print "Average = "; Format(Total / 3, "#.00")
    Next I
```

```
End Sub
```

We declare Names as a one-dimensional array. Each element in this array is assigned another array of four elements. We use For-Next and an index number to maneuver the elements in the Names array. We then use For Each-Next to manipulate each of the four elements in each Names element.

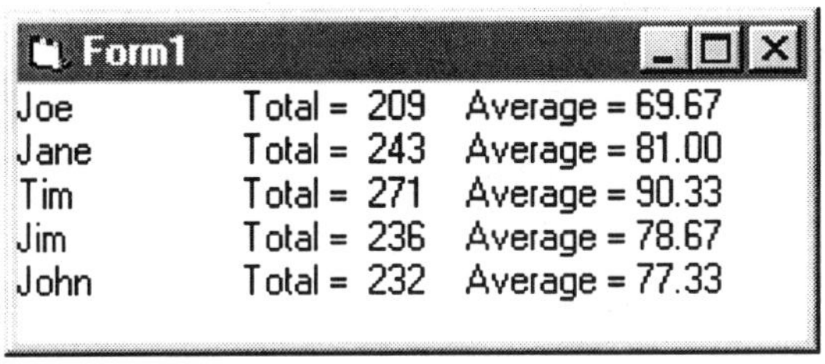

```
Form1                                    _ □ ×
Joe        Total = 209   Average = 69.67
Jane       Total = 243   Average = 81.00
Tim        Total = 271   Average = 90.33
Jim        Total = 236   Average = 78.67
John       Total = 232   Average = 77.33
```

Figure 9.10   Referencing a multidimensional array

We can alter our assignments at the beginning of the procedure as shown below. We change Names from an array to a Variant; this is required for our modification. We then assign each Array list to a regular Variant variable. We then assign these variables as elements in the Names variable. These changes will produce the same result without changing anything else in the rest of the procedure.

```
Dim Names        'changed from array to Variant
Dim N0, N1, N2, N3, N4
N0 = Array("Joe", 67, 77, 65)
N1 = Array("Jane", 87, 76, 80)
N2 = Array("Tim", 97, 85, 89)
N3 = Array("Jim", 69, 87, 80)
N4 = Array("John", 88, 79, 65)
Names = Array(N0, N1, N2, N3, N4)
   'assign arrays to be elements of another array
```

We can also use the new referencing technique demonstrated in the previous section—enclosing two index numbers in two separate pairs of parentheses. The inner For-Next loop in Listing 3 can be changed to the following to produce the same result. This requires a new variable named J, which you must declare first if Option Explicit is on.

```
For J = 0 To UBound(Names(0))
    If VarType(names(I)(J)) = vbString Then
        Print names(I)(J),
        'if string type, print name
    End If      'use Val to avoid type mismatch
```

```
    Total = Total + Val(Names(I)(J))
Next J
```

STRUCTURES (USER-DEFINED TYPES)

You can define a variable that can contain multiple elements of different types. This is a **user-defined data type** commonly called a **structure** (known as a record in Pascal).

Normally an array must contain elements of the same data type. **Variants**, however, have changed that rule. Unless you specify data types for the elements in an array, the elements can hold different types of data at different times. This versatility now makes structures less useful.

To create a structure (user-defined data type), you must use the Type-End Type statement placed in the Declarations section of a module, such as the following:

```
Type StructName
    ElementName [(subscripts)] As TypeName
    [ElementName [(subscripts)] As TypeName]
    . . .
End Type
```

You start with **Type** followed by a structure name and end with **End Type**. In between, you declare individual elements by specifying a data type after **As**. This As is required, although you can use it to specify a Variant, which can hold any type of data.

Each individual element can be an array if you specify it. So you can enter this:

```
    ElementName(10) As Integer
```

In that case, this array has 11 elements of its own by default.

A structure can be public or private in scope. When it's created in a **standard module**, the default scope is public. You can make it private by placing Private before the structure name. If you want to create a structure in a form or a class module, you must specify **Private**; otherwise, an error will appear.

In the **Object Browser,** a structure is treated as a class and displayed in the Classes box with its own unique icon. The variables in a structure appear in the Members list. The variables of a public structure are not global and don't appear in the <global> list.

In our example, *StructName* is not a variable, but a **data type** defined by you. Before you can use the structure, you must declare a variable to be of that type. You can enter something like this, just below End Type:

```
Dim VarName As StructName
```

In that case, *VarName* is a variable of the StructName type. If you use Global or Public instead of Dim, the variable's scope will be widened. If you put the above statement inside a procedure, then VarName is a local variable.

Using a variable of a structure requires you to specify both the declared variable name and the element name, and connect them with a dot, like this:

```
VarName.Element1 = 123
```

This assigns a value to an element in the specified structure.

After a structure is declared, you can use it to declare an array, each element of which is a separate structure, like this:

```
Dim ArrayName (10) As StructName
```

This creates a local array of 11 elements, each of which is a duplicate of the declared structure.

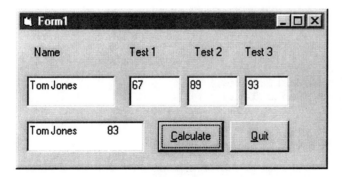

Figure 9.11   Using a structure

In the listing below, we use Grades as the structure name. Then we declare Gd in the cmdCalculate_Click procedure to be of the Grades type. This variable is local in scope. It is tied to the individual elements by a period. This combination is then used like an ordinary variable. So after we enter the items in the top text boxes (Figure 9.11) and click Calculate, the bottom text box displays the result.

```
'In the form's Declarations section
Private Type Grades
    Name As String * 20
    T1 As Integer
    T2 As Integer
    T3 As Integer
End Type

Private Sub cmdCalculate_Click ()
    Dim Gd As Grades      'declare variable
    Dim Avg As Single

    Gd.Name = txtName.Text  'assign values to elements
    Gd.T1 = Val(txtTest1.Text)
    Gd.T2 = Val(txtTest2.Text)
    Gd.T3 = Val(txtTest3.Text)
    Avg = (Gd.T1 + Gd.T2 + Gd.T3) / 3 'get avg
    txtOutput.Text = Gd.Name & Avg    'put in text box
End Sub
```

The above demonstration shows that a structure can unnecessarily complicate things. We could have done it in a much simpler way. A structure, however, can be useful to control records in a random-access file. This will be demonstrated in Chapter 10. We'll also use a structure array when we demonstrate sorting a multidimensional array in another section below.

Chapter 6 discusses the new **With-End With** command. It can be used to maneuver a structure as well as an object. The last part of the above procedure can be changed to below without affecting the outcome.

```
With Gd
    .Name = txtName.Text        'assign values to elements
    .T1 = Val(txtTest1.Text)
    .T2 = Val(txtTest2.Text)
    .T3 = Val(txtTest3.Text)
    Avg = (.T1 + .T2 + .T3) / 3    'get avg
    txtOutput.Text = .Name & Avg 'put in text box
End With
```

ENUMERATED (ENUM) CONSTANTS

If you have a series of related constants, you can use the **Enum** statement to tie them together as a unit. This is not particularly useful if you are writing an independent executable file. But if you create a class (Chapter 12), users can easily use the **Object Browser** to find out the available constants of an object.

To create a list of **enumerated constants** (or **enumeration** for short), go to the module level of the current form or module and enter a list of variable names inside Enum and End Enum, such as this:

```
Enum Alphabet
    Alpha
    Beta
    Gamma
End Enum
```

You can now access the constants like this:

```
Sub Form_Click()
    Print Alpha              '0
    Print Alphabet.Beta      '1
    Print Gamma              '2
End Sub
```

Notice that we used the Enum name only in the second Print line. The use of this name is optional. If you have several Enum lists, using this name can avoid confusion and reduce the chances of conflict.

Take advantage of the **IntelliSense** feature. Notice that after you type the dot in the second Print line, a list of three constants pops up for you to make a selection. You can also show the list by right-clicking the Code window and choose **List Properties/Methods** (or **Ctrl+J**). Our three constants will be included among the intrinsic items if you press Ctrl+J with the cursor over Alphabet. If you do it with the cursor over Beta (after Alphabet), only three constants will pop up.

Since we didn't assign values to the variables in the Enum statement, the default values are used. The first variable in the list has the default 0 value. Each ensuing variable has one greater value. At design time, you can find out each constant's value by moving the cursor over it and pressing **Ctrl+I**. If you do it over Gamma, for example, 2 will pop up. In break mode, you can point to each constant and a **data tip** will pop up.

Consider the following change. Beta will change to 10 and Gamma to 11.

```
Enum Alphabet
    Alpha
    Beta = 10
    Gamma
End Enum
```

In the following change, Gamma will have the value of 20.

```
Enum Alphabet
    Alpha
    Beta = 10
    Gamma = Alpha + 20
End Enum
```

An enumeration variable has a Long data type. Decimal numbers are rounded off. No string is permitted.

An enumeration can be private or public in scope; public is the default if it's not specified.[1] A private enumeration is visible inside the attached module. A public enumeration is global in scope, regardless of what type of module (form, class, or standard) it is placed in.

In the **Object Browser**, an enumeration (like a user-defined type discussed in the preceding section) is treated as a class and appears in the Classes list. Its variables appear in the Members list. Clicking each displays its value in the Details pane at the bottom. A public enumeration's members are also included in the <globals> class.

The Object Browser treats an enumeration and an individual constant (declared with Const) the same and marks each with an icon that is a rounded rectangle with an = sign inside. In contrast, a public scalar variable is treated as a property, marked with a different icon.

After you have declared an enumeration type, you can declare a variable of that type, just as you do with the Type statement explained in the preceding section. The first line below declares Letter to be the Alphabet type. After you type = in the second line, our constants pop up for you to make a selection. After this assignment, Letter and Alpha have the same value.

```
Dim Letter As Alphabet
Letter = Alpha
```

In this situation, variable Letter is a Long data type and can store any value of that type without generating an error. On the other hand, an original variable in the enumeration list cannot change its assigned or default value. In the following statements, the first is legal but the second will generate an error:

---

[1]In contrast, a constant declared (with **Const**) in a standard module's module level defaults to private, unless Public is specified. The word Public is not allowed in any other module.

```
    Letter = 9999
    Alpha = 9999
```

It's a common practice to use **Enum General** as a general-purpose enumeration for a list of disparate constants. Here General can be used just like any enumeration identifier; in the following example, Profit and General.Profit are equivalent.

```
Enum General
    Profit = 256000
    PartnerA = 50    'A's share 50%
    PartnerB = 30
    PartnerC = 20
End Enum

Private Sub Form_Click()
    Print "Total profit", , General.Profit
    Print "Partner A's profit = ", _
    Profit * PartnerA / 100
    Print "Partner B's profit = ", _
    Profit * PartnerB / 100
    Print "Partner C's profit = ", _
    Profit * PartnerC / 100
End Sub
```

Since an enumeration variable can hold no decimal values, we need to take extra steps. PartnerA's share is assigned 50 instead of 0.5. The value 50 is the result of 0.5 * 100. To get PartnerA's profit, we need to divide it by 100. The result is shown in Figure 9.12.

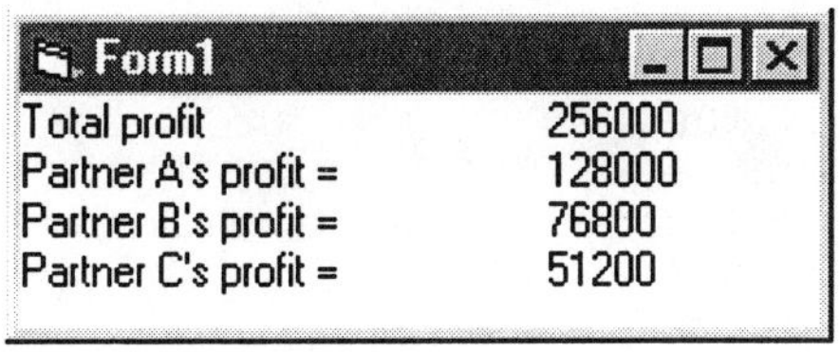

Form1	
Total profit	256000
Partner A's profit =	128000
Partner B's profit =	76800
Partner C's profit =	51200

Figure 9.12   Demonstrating Enum

There is a program at the end of Chapter 6 that lets you calculate your federal income tax. There we used a lot of fixed numbers. Those are best put in an enumeration. That program can be modified as follows:

(9TaxEnum.frm)
```
Enum FedTax
    T1Bracket = 150    'tier 1 tax bracket
    T2Bracket = 280    '1000 times of actual value
```

```
        T3Bracket = 310
        T4Bracket = 360
        T5Bracket = 396

        T2Income = 40100        'tier 2 income
        T3Income = 96900
        T4Income = 147700
        T5Income = 263750

        T2Tax = 6015            'tier 2 tax amount
        T3Tax = 21919
        T4Tax = 37667
        T5Tax = 79445
End Enum

Private Sub cmdCalculate_Click()
    Dim Income As Long
    Dim Tax As Long

    If txtIncome.Text = "" Then
        Beep      'if no entry
        txtIncome.SetFocus
            'shift focus to Text1 for entry
        Exit Sub
    End If

    Income = Val(txtIncome.Text)

    Select Case Income
      Case Is >= FedTax.T5Income
        Tax = FedTax.T5Tax + (Income - FedTax.T5Income) _
        * (FedTax.T5Bracket / 1000)
            'extra brackets to avoid overflow error
      Case Is >= FedTax.T4Income
        Tax = FedTax.T4Tax + (Income - FedTax.T4Income) _
        * FedTax.T4Bracket / 1000
      Case Is >= FedTax.T3Income
        Tax = FedTax.T3Tax + (Income - FedTax.T3Income) _
            * FedTax.T3Bracket / 1000
      Case Is >= FedTax.T2Income
        Tax = FedTax.T2Tax + (Income - FedTax.T2Income) _
            * FedTax.T2Bracket / 1000
      Case Else
        Tax = Income * FedTax.T1Bracket / 1000
    End Select
    txtTax.Text = Tax
End Sub

Private Sub cmdClear_Click()
    txtIncome.Text = ""
    txtTax.Text = ""
    txtIncome.SetFocus    'shift focus to Text1 for entry
End Sub
```

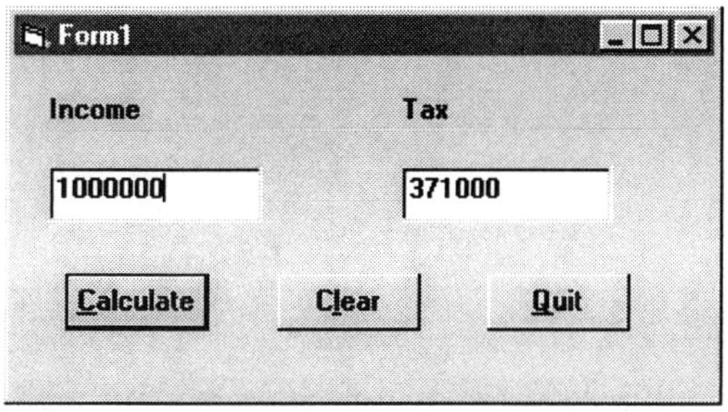

Figure 9.13   Calculating tax with Enum

This program (Figure 9.13) will work as before. We've now moved all the fixed numbers to the Enum statement. Constants are now used instead of numeric literals. (This looks laborious to type, but you can do it quickly with copy and paste.) These constants are now visible in the Object Browser. If you compile this program into an **ActiveX component,** users can still see these constants.

Another change you may have noticed is that we have reversed the order in the Case expressions. We now put the highest value first. This arrangement lets us simplify the Case expressions, as explained in Chapter 6.

DRILL

_____ 1.   A one-dimensional array has one:
  a.   element
  b.   variable
  c.   subscript
  d.   index number

_____ 2.   The following statement is legal. True or false?

```
Dim ArrX(-1 To -2)
```

_____ 3.   The ReDim statement below is legal. True or false?

```
Dim varX, varY
varX = 1: varY = 10
ReDim varX(varX To varY)
```

_____ 4.   Option _____ determines the number for the lowest element of an array. _base_

_____ 5. Assuming default values, the Name(5, 6) array has a total of _____ elements.

_____ 6. All the elements of an array must be of the same data type. True or false?

_____ 7. Passing an array to a procedure allows the procedure to alter the original array. True or false?

_____ 8. The second statement below will print _____ .

```
ReDim ArrX(5)
Print UBound(ArrX)
```

_____ 9. In the following statements, if the user enters three numbers, the number 10 will be printed to the screen. True or false?

```
ReDim ArrX(10)
For I = 1 To UBound(ArrX)
    ArrX(I) = InputBox("Enter a number.")
    If ArrX(I) = "" Then Exit For
Next I
Print UBound(ArrX)
```

_____ 10. If the user enters three numbers, the following statements will return the correct average. True or false?

```
ReDim ArrX(10)
For I = 1 To UBound(x)
    ArrX(I) = InputBox("Enter a number.")
    If ArrX(I) = "" Then Exit For
    Sum = Sum + Val(ArrX(I))
Next I
Print "Average = "; Sum / UBound(ArrX)
```

_____ 11. The second statement below is illegal because variable varA is not declared as an array. True or false?

```
Dim varA
varA = Array(44, 65, 69)
```

_____ 12. The last line below will print _____ .

```
Dim varX, varA, varB
varA = Array(1, 2)
varB = Array("A", "B")
varX = Array(varA, varB)
Print varX(1)(1)
```

___ 13.   The Type-End Type command can be entered at the Declarations
          section of a form. True or false?

___ 14.   By default, the following structure sets aside _____ bytes of
          memory.

```
Type Books
    Novel(10) As String * 25
    Prose(10) As String * 25
End Type
```

___ 15.   After the following declaration, Tim has the value of _____ .

```
Enum Names
    Jim
    Kim
    Tim
End Enum
```

PRACTICE

■ 1.   What is an array? Explain its various components.

■ 2.   Explain what the following procedure will do.

```
Sub Command1_Click ()
    Dim I As Integer
    ReDim ArrX(-10 To -1)
    For I = -10 To -1
        ArrX(I) = I
        Print ArrX(I)
    Next I
End Sub
```

■ 3.   What is a dynamic array? How do you use a dynamic array?

■ 4.   In Listing 1 in the text, change the code so that the numbers will appear
        as below:

```
A    B    C
D    E    F
G    H    I
```

■ 5.   In Listing 1 in the text, change the code so that the numbers will appear
        as below:

```
1       4       7
2       5       8
3       6       9
```

■ 6. The PC's numeric keypad has the following arrangement:

```
7       8       9
4       5       6
1       2       3
```

Modify the previous procedure so that it will print this pattern.

■ 7. Write a procedure to do the following:

    a. Prompt the user to enter an integer number.
    b. Use the number to define an array.
    c. Prompt the user to enter an integer value for each element.
    d. Print to the screen each element and the lowest value.

■ 8. In step c above, if the user enters no value, the procedure will stop prompting for another entry and proceed to print to the screen each element and the highest value.

■ 9. In the previous procedure, add a function procedure which will return the highest value.

■ 10. In the previous procedure, use the function to return the average. Make provision for a situation where the actually number of elements may be different from the number specified at the beginning. For example, the user may specify 10 element, but actually enters only 5. So the program must use 5 to calculate the average.

■ 11. Explain the mechanism of passing an array to a sub procedure.

■ 12. Explain the mechanism of passing an array to a function and returning a value.

■ 13. Create a structure as shown below:

```
Private Type Sportshoes
    Kind(2) As String * 10
    Cost(2) As Integer
End Type
```

Then in the Command1_Click procedure, declare a variable to be of this type and assign the individual elements (shown in Figure 9.14) to the arrays. When Command1 is clicked, these elements are printed to the screen, together with the last line shown.

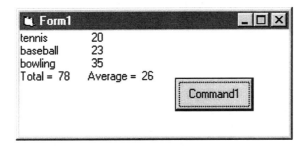

Figure 9.14 Output by a structure

■ 14. Use a single one-dimensional array to create a multiplication table shown in Figure 9.15. Each column must be right-justified. The array is created with the Array function, as shown below.

```
Arr = Array(1, 2, 3, 4, 5, 6, 7, 8, 9)
```

```
 Form1                                    _ □ ✕
  1   2   3   4   5   6   7   8   9
  2   4   6   8  10  12  14  16  18
  3   6   9  12  15  18  21  24  27
  4   8  12  16  20  24  28  32  36
  5  10  15  20  25  30  35  40  45
  6  12  18  24  30  36  42  48  54
  7  14  21  28  35  42  49  56  63
  8  16  24  32  40  48  56  64  72
  9  18  27  36  45  54  63  72  81
```

Figure 9.15 Multiplication created with an array

■ 15. In Listing 2, change the two For-Next loops so that rows rather than columns will be printed from top to bottom.

■ 16. Use the Array function to assign a series of values to a variable and use a statement to call a Max function that will return the highest value. The

Max function should return 11.2 when called by the following statements:

```
All = Array(11.2, 6.99, 3.4, 8.6, 9.5)
Print "highest value: "; Max(All)
```

■ 17. Change the Max function to Min. It should return 3.4 when called by the following statements:

```
All = Array(11.2, 6.99, 3.4, 8.6, 9.5)
Print "lowest value: "; Min(All)
```

■ 18. Write a sub procedure that will take the values passed to it and compute (and print to the screen) the average and count the number above and below the average. The values should be passed to the procedure by these statements:

```
All = Array(11.2, 6.99, 3.4, 8.6, 9.5)
Call Above(All)
```

CONTROL ARRAYS

You can use a one-dimensional array to tie together multiple controls of the same type; such an array is known as a **control array**. You can then use one name in combination with a sequence of index numbers to manipulate these controls. A control array can be created at design time or at run time.

Design-Time Creation

There are three ways to create a control array at design time:

- Copy a control to the Clipboard and then paste it on the same form.

- Give the same Name (not Caption) property to two or more controls.

- Set a control's Index property to an integer value. Then change control names.

Each technique is explored separately below.

One efficient way of maneuvering multiple option buttons is to use control arrays to tie them together. Follow these steps to create a control array of option buttons:

1. Add an option button to a blank form by double-clicking the option button tool.

   (Examine the Properties window. Notice the Option1 value for both Caption and Name properties. Check the **Index** value; there is nothing there.)

2. With the option button still selected, choose Copy from the Edit menu. (You can use shortcut keys here; you can also use the shortcut menu by right-clicking an object.)

3. Choose Paste from the Edit menu. A prompt, shown in Figure 9.16, appears.

4. Choose Yes. Another option button appears at the top left corner of the form.

   (Examine the properties of this new object. It has Option1, or the name given by you earlier, as its Name and Caption properties. Notice the **Index** property; it is 1. The Index property of the original option button is also changed to 0.)

5. Paste more copies if you wish to add more option buttons; each will also be sequentially indexed.

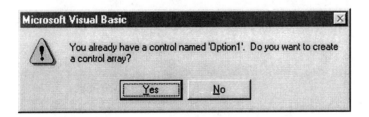

Figure 9.16   Creating a control array

In step 4, if you choose No instead, the Caption property will be the same as the original copy, but the Name property keeps the default value assigned by Visual Basic. In that case, the default Index property for both objects does not change.

Another method of creating a control array is by assigning the same Name
property value to two or more objects of the same type. You will also provoke a
display of the prompt shown in Figure 9.16. After answering Yes, the Name (not
Caption) property will be changed. The Index property becomes 1 while the
object of the original name will have the Index property of 0. You can proceed to
change other objects' Name properties and no more prompt will appear. The
Index property of each will be properly adjusted.

Still another way of creating a control array is by changing the Index property
first. Suppose you have created Option1 and Option2 and you want to create a
control array of the two. Follow these steps:

1. Change Option2's Index property to 1.

2. Change Option2's Name property to Option1.

Step 2 does not cause the display of Figure 9.16. However, after making the
change, the original Option1's Index property will be changed to 0. The two now
have become a control array. You can also change Option1's Index to 0 and then
change Option2's Name to Option1. The result will be the same.

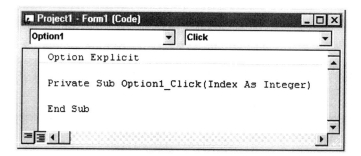

Figure 9.17   The Click procedure of a control array

One way to find out whether a control is part of a control array is to double-click
it to show the Code window. Figure 9.17 appears. Notice that the Object box
shows only one object, Option1, to represent all the controls. Regardless of which
option button you double-click, the result will be the same. How can Visual Basic
distinguish one object from another? The answer lies in the variable named Index.
(This is a suggested variable, which you can change to another name if you
wish.)

As an experiment, add two option buttons to the form. Keep their original Caption properties. Change Option2's Index property to 1 and Name property to Option1. Then follow these steps:

1. Double-click either control. The Click procedure template appears.

2. Add the following statement between the template lines.

    ```
    Print Index
    ```

3. Press F5 to run the program; 0 appears and Option1 is automatically selected (because it has the TabIndex property of 0).

4. Click the two buttons alternately. The result is shown in Figure 9.18.

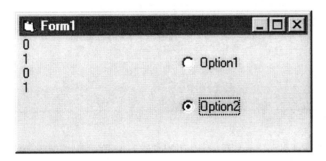

Figure 9.18   Showing a control element's index number

If you click Option1, 0 appears; if you click Option2, 1 is shown. These numbers reflect the value of the variable named Index. This variable changes value depending on which button is chosen.

Figure 9.19 shows how you can click either option to convert a text string to uppercase or lowercase. Both option buttons have the Name property of Option1, but the first (left) has the Index property of 0 and the second that of 1.

The code to respond to an option selection is shown below. Double-click either option to go to the Code window; the same procedure template appears regardless of which object you double-click. Enter the following lines.

```
Private Sub Option1_Click (Index As Integer)
    If Index = 0 Then
```

```
        Text1.Text = UCase(Text1.Text)
    Else
        Text1.Text = LCase(Text1.Text)
    End If
End Sub
```

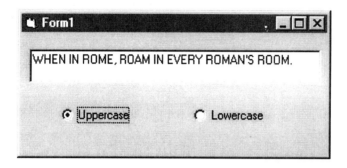

Figure 9.19   Using a control array for two option buttons

After you run the program, enter a text string in the text box, and click an option button, the string is converted. The Index variable determines which option button is clicked and which case to convert to. When Uppercase is clicked, Index has the value of 0 and the text string is converted to uppercase. If Lowercase is clicked, the Index has the value of 1 and the string is converted to lowercase.

Figure 9.20 shows another way of maneuvering a control array. Here we intend to let the user enter numbers in two text boxes and click an option button to calculate the result. The option buttons are a control array. The code for it is shown below.

```
Private Sub Option1_Click (Index As Integer)
    Dim Result As Single

    Select Case Index
    Case 0
        Result = txtOp1.Text * txtOp2.Text
    Case 1
        Result = txtOp1.Text / txtOp2.Text
    Case 2   'use Val to avoid concatenation
        Result = Val(txtOp1.Text) + txtOp2.Text
    Case 3
        Result = txtOp1.Text - txtOp2.Text
    End Select
    txtOutput.Text = Result
End Sub
```

In our example, the option buttons must not have the first four (0-3) TabIndex values. This will lead to the *Type mismatch* error as soon as you run the program. The error results if there are no entries in the text boxes and the Click procedure is executed. A simple remedy is to assign at design time 0 and 1 TabIndex values to the first two text boxes. That way, when one of the option buttons is clicked or tabbed to, there are already entries for the Click procedure to process.

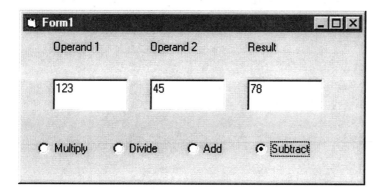

Figure 9.20   Interface for two control arrays

We can replace Click with **GotFocus**, such as shown below, to get the same result. A GotFocus event occurs when the pertinent object is clicked, tabbed to, or its access key pressed.

```
Private Sub Option1_GotFocus(Index As Integer)
```

Run-Time Creation

A control array can be created at run time. To do that, you need to follow these steps:

1. Add a control to the form at design time—if you intend to create a control array of that control.

2. Change the control's Index property to 0 at design time. This cannot be done at run time.

3. Use the **Load** statement in code to load additional copies of the control, each with a different Index value.

4. Maneuver the **Visible** property of each new copy to show or hide it on the form.

5. Move each new copy to a new location so that the copies will not cover up each other.

Our demonstration project leads to a display of 9 command buttons, each showing a number, as shown in Figure 9.21. When the user clicks one of the buttons, its number appears in the form's caption.

At design time, the user interface consists of a form and a single command button. This button can be placed anywhere on the form. To reduce typing, the Name property is changed at design time to Cmd (you can use any acceptable name). The Index property must also be changed to 0 to signify it as one of the array elements.

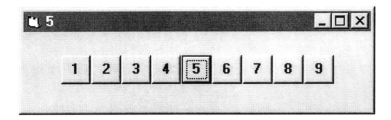

Figure 9.21   A control array created at run time

The procedures to create the control array and to display a number in response to clicking a button are listed below. The Form_Load procedure automatically creates and displays the control array. The Cmd_Click procedure is attached to the command button at design time; it responds to the clicking of one of the displayed command buttons.

(9CTRAY1.FRM)

```
Private Sub Form_Load ()
    'Command1 Name changed to Cmd
    'Index changed to 0
    Dim I As Integer

    Cmd(0).Left = 100      'move original button to top left
    Cmd(0).Top = 300
    Cmd(0).Visible = False  'hide the original button
    Cmd(0).Width = 400      'each 400 twips in width

    For I = 1 To 9
```

```
    Load Cmd(I)      'create 9 copies of the button
    Cmd(I).Left = Cmd(I - 1).Left _
    + Cmd(I - 1).Width + 20
        'space each 20 twips apart
    Cmd(I).Caption = Cmd(I).Index
        'put index value in caption
    Cmd(I).Visible = True      'show result
    Next I
End Sub

Private Sub cmd_Click (Index As Integer)
    Caption = Index  'put button index in form caption
End Sub
```

Notice that we did not declare an array in the procedure. This neglect, however, does not cause an error as it normally does. Visual Basic recognizes an array's existence when you change an object's Index property to 0 at design time.

NOTE　You can add an underscore character (access key) to each displayed number. To do that, modify the Caption line as follows:

```
Cmd(i).Caption = "&" & Cmd(i).Index
```

After that, you can, at run time, hold down the Alt key and press a number key to choose a corresponding button.

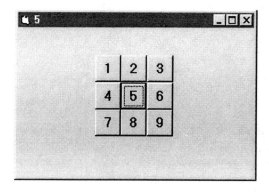

Figure 9.22　**Using variables to control objects**

What if you want to arrange the buttons in three columns and three rows (Figure 9.22)? You can use For alone to do that. But combining For and Select Case provides a more efficient way, as shown below.

(9CTRAY2.FRM)

```
Private Sub Form_Load ()
    'Command1 Name changed to Cmd
    'Index changed to 0
    Dim I As Integer

    Cmd(0).Visible = False  'invisible
    Cmd(0).Width = 500      'each 500 twips square
    Cmd(0).Height = 500
    Cmd(0).FontSize = 12    'button's font size

    For I = 1 To 9
        Load Cmd(I)      'create 9 copies of button
        Select Case I        'horizontal position
        Case 1, 2, 3                 '1st row
            Cmd(I).Top = 500
        Case 4, 5, 6                 '2nd row
            Cmd(I).Top = 1000
        Case 7, 8, 9                 '3rd row
            Cmd(I).Top = 1500
        End Select
        Select Case I       'vertical position
        Case 1, 4, 7                 '1st col
            Cmd(I).Left = 1500
        Case 2, 5, 8                 '2nd col
            Cmd(I).Left = 2000
        Case 3, 6, 9                 '3rd col
            Cmd(I).Left = 2500
        End Select
        Cmd(I).Caption = I
                'show number in button caption
        Cmd(I).Visible = True        'show button
    Next I
End Sub

Private Sub Cmd_Click (Index As Integer)
    Caption = Index       'show index num in form caption
End Sub
```

We use For to loop nine times. In each round, the Top and Left position of each button is determined. After the ninth round, all the nine buttons are neatly arranged in a grid of three columns and three rows.

OBJECTS AND VARIABLES

Visual Basic's objects (forms and controls) can be maneuvered by code at run time. New copies (clones or instances) of an existing object can be created. Object names can be assigned to variables. These **object variables**, variables to reference Visual Basic objects, can be maneuvered in ways similar to, but not exactly the same as, data variables.

Object Aliases

As you already know, the first command button that you place on a form has the default name of Command1. At design time, you can change this Name property to something else. At run time, you cannot use the regular way to assign a new name to it. However, you can use the **Set** command to assign it to an alias. You can then use this alias to reference the original object.

As a demonstration, add Command1 to a new form. Move this button to the top left corner. Then write the following procedure:

```
Private Sub Command1_Click ()
    Dim CB As CommandButton    'declare object variable
    Set CB = Command1          'assign object to var
    CB.Caption = "Bigger"      'use alias
    CB.Width = CB.Width * 2
    CB.Height = CB.Height * 2
    CB.FontSize = CB.FontSize * 2
End Sub
```

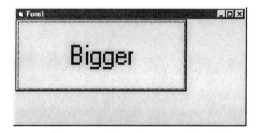

Figure 9.23   Using an object variable

Now run the program and click the button twice. The result is shown in Figure 9.23. Each time you click it, the button and the font are doubled in size.

We use the Dim command to declare a variable named CB as an object type called CommandButton. How do you know what object type name to use? Ask Visual Basic. When you add a control to the form and click the control to choose it, the Object box in the Properties window shows the object's type (class) name.

You can also point to the command button tool in the Toolbox to show the CommandButton tooltip.

We also use the Set command to assign a value (object) to this variable. After the assignment, CB (the variable name) can be used whenever reference to Command1 (the original name) is needed. If you wish, you can still use the original name; both will refer to the same object.

The CommandButton object type refers to a specific type of object, namely a command button. After you declare a variable to be a specific object type, you can no longer use the variable to refer to another object of a different type. If you want a variable to refer to any type of object (control), you need to use the word **Control**, such as:

```
Dim Ctl As Control  'declare generic object type
```

After that, variable Ctl can be used to reference any type of control. Suppose you now add a label to the above form and replace the second line in the procedure with the following:

```
Set Ctl = Label1    'assign Label1 to var Ctl
```

Running the program and clicking Command1 will enlarge Label1 instead. Variable Ctl can now reference any type of object. To make it refer to another object, just use Set to assign an existing object's Name property to Ctl.

The distinction between a specific object type and a generic object type (using Control) is comparable to that between a local variable and a global variable. The former is narrower in scope but more memory efficient. The latter is broader in scope but consumes more memory and can create side effects.

After you have assigned an object to a variable (and possibly get confused as to what you have done), you can use the **TypeOf** keyword with If to determine whether it is of a certain object type. Follow this syntax:

```
If TypeOf varname Is objecttype
```

In the following modified procedure, If Ctl is a Label, then the statements in the If control structure is executed; otherwise, it is ignored.

```
Private Sub Command1_Click ()
    Dim Ctl As Control  'declare generic object type
    Set Ctl = Label1            'assign object to var
    If TypeOf Ctl Is Label Then         'test type
        Ctl.Caption = "Bigger" 'use alias
```

```
        Ctl.Width = Ctl.Width * 2
        Ctl.Height = Ctl.Height * 2
        Ctl.FontSize = Ctl.FontSize * 2
    End If
End Sub
```

You can declare multiple object variables and use Set to assign one's value to another. The following declares two control variables:

```
Dim CtlB As Control, CtlC As Control
```

After that, you can assign what's in CtlC to CtlB this way:

```
Set CtlB = CtlC
```

Notice that Set is mandatory here; without it an error will result. This is somewhat like the use of Let in the first-generation Basic to make an assignment.

NOTE   As discussed in Chapter 5, You can now assign an object to a **Variant** variable. So you are no longer required to declare a variable to be a **Control** or **Object** type. On the other hand, be aware that Variant variables generally consume more resources.

Cloning and Removing Forms

You can use the **New** command to create copies of a form. After that, you need to use Set to assign the new copy to a variable name. Finally, use the **Show** method to display the new copy. Either technique below will do:

(1)   ```
        Dim Frm As New Form1   'not Form
        Frm.Show
        ```

(2)     ```
        Dim Frm As Form1         'can be Form
        Set Frm = New Form1
        Frm.Show
        ```

In the first example, New creates a copy and Show displays it; there is no need to use **Set**. In the second, Set and New are required in the second line.[2] In the second (but not the first) example, you can use **Form** instead of Form1 in the first line. In that case, you are using a generic type similar to the use of Control

---

[2]If New is not used here, no new form is created but the variable becomes an alias for the original form.

discussed in the previous section. The variable (Frm) can then be used to reference either a regular form or an MDI form (see Chapter 12).

In the following procedure, we use both techniques. Each creates a new copy of the original form. Clicking Command1 once results in two new forms, as shown in Figure 9.24.

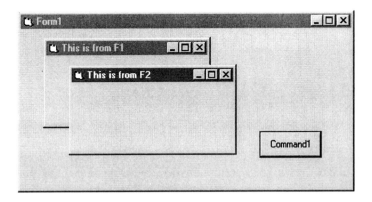

Figure 9.24   Two clone forms

```
Private Sub Command1_Click ()
    Dim F1 As New Form1        '1st clone

    F1.Caption = "This is from F1"
    F1.Top = Top + 500
    F1.Left = Left + 500
    F1.Height = Height / 2
    F1.Width = Width / 2
    F1.Show

    Dim F2 As Form1            '2nd clone
    Set F2 = New Form1
    F2.Caption = "This is from F2"
    F2.Top = F1.Top + 500
    F2.Left = F1.Left + 500
    F2.Height = Height / 2
    F2.Width = Width / 2
    F2.Show
End Sub
```

We use a number of properties to shrink and move the clones; without these steps, the latest copy will cover up each previous one. Since we specify no objects for these properties, Form1 (the original form) is assumed. We must specify a form, such as F1 or F2, if it is not the default.

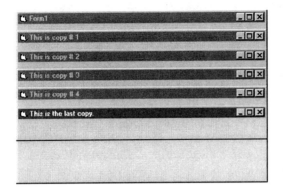

Figure 9.25   Creating form clones

We can use an array to reference objects. The procedure below creates five copies of the original form. The result is shown in Figure 9.25. (If the **Startup Position** is set to other than Manual, the clone forms will appear in different positions. Right-click the **Form Layout window** and choose Startup Position to make changes.)

```
Private Sub Form_Click ()
    Dim I As Integer
    Dim Frm(1 To 5) As Form1
        'declare an array as object type

    Set Frm(1) = New Form1      'create 1st copy
    Frm(1).Show                 'show 1st copy
    Frm(1).Top = Form1.Top + 500
        'top is 500 twips lower
    Frm(1).Height = Form1.Height / 5
        '1/5 original height
    Frm(1).Caption = "This is copy # 1"
        'show caption

    For I = 2 To 5              'control copies 2-5
        Set Frm(I) = New Form1
        Frm(I).Show
        Frm(I).Height = Form1.Height / 5
        Frm(I).Top = Frm(I - 1).Top + 500
        Frm(I).Caption = "This is copy # " & I
    Next I

    Frm(I - 1).FontSize = 12
    Frm(I - 1).Caption = "This is the last copy."
End Sub
```

We use five elements in an array to reference five objects (clone forms). Such an array can be used just like an array for data. Depending on the circumstances, you can also use Dim, Static, Global, or Public to declare an array of objects.

In the last two lines of the above procedure, we reference the last copy of the new forms. If we did not specify this particular form, output would by default go to the original form. The value of I is 6 (1 higher than the last number) after the For loop is completed. We need to subtract 1 from it in order to refer to copy 5.

You can use a statement like below to output text to a specific window. This statement will print to the last window:

```
Frm(I - 1).Print "This is the last copy."
```

Like the original form, each displayed clone form can be independently maneuvered. It can be moved, resized, or made active by clicking its visible portion.

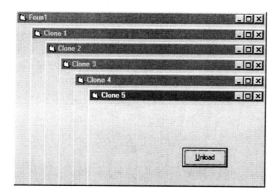

Figure 9.26   Five clone forms

A clone form inherits the controls, procedures, and variables that are in the original form. Figure 9.26 shows five clone forms, each of which has a command button, just like the original.

The Form_DblClick procedure shown below creates five clone forms (Figure 9.26) when the original form is double-clicked:

```
Private Sub Form_DblClick ()
    Dim I As Integer
    Dim Frm(4) As Form1
```

```
        Set Frm(0) = New Form1 'create 1st clone
        Frm(0).Top = Top + 400
        Frm(0).Left = Left + 400
        Frm(0).Height = Height - 400
        Frm(0).Width = Width - 400
        Frm(0).Caption = "Clone " & 1
        Frm(0).Show

        For I = 1 To 4          'create 4 clones
            Set Frm(I) = New Form1
            Frm(I).Top = Frm(I - 1).Top + 400
            Frm(I).Left = Frm(I - 1).Left + 400
            Frm(I).Height = Frm(I - 1).Height - 400
            Frm(I).Width = Frm(I - 1).Width - 400
            Frm(I).Caption = "Clone " & (I + 1)
            Frm(I).Show
        Next I
End Sub
```

The procedure below, which is attached to the Unload button, demonstrates the use of the **Me** property. When the Unload button is clicked (and you supply OK in response to the input box), the current form will be removed by the **Unload** statement.

```
Private Sub cmdUnload_Click ()
    Dim Ok As String
    Dim Msg As String

    Msg = "Unload " & Me.Caption & "?"
    Ok = InputBox(Msg, , "Ok")
    If Ok = "Ok" Then Unload Me
End Sub
```

The **Me** property refers to the current form. You can also use **Screen.ActiveForm** (or ActiveForm alone) for the same purpose under most circumstances. If you want to reference the active control, use **Screen.ActiveControl** instead.

NOTE   The variables used in a form (original or clone) are visible only in that form. If you want a variable to be visible from another form, you must use a global variable declared in a standard module with the Global or Public keyword.

Cloning and Removing Controls

Notice that we use **Set** in combination with New to create a new form clone. This combination cannot be applied to controls such as command buttons or text boxes.

When you use Set on a control, you merely assign an existing control to an alias. To create control clones, as demonstrated earlier, you need to use the **Load** statement to create a copy and the Visible property to make it visible.

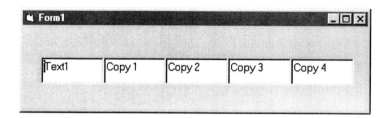

Figure 9.27   Creating control clones

The following code produces the display shown in Figure 9.27. At design time, we add Text1 to the form and drag it to the top left. Its Index property is also changed to 0. The rest is handled by code.

```
Private Sub Form_Load ()
    Show                    'show form1
    Dim I As Integer
    Dim TB(4) As Control    'declare control array

    Set TB(0) = Text1(0)        'assign original to TB(0)
    TB(0).FontSize = 10         'set original fontsize

    For I = 1 To 4
        Set TB(I) = Text1(I)  'set alias for each
        Load TB(I)                'load each copy
        TB(I).Left = TB(I - 1).Left + TB(I - 1).Width
                '1000 twips from one Left to another
        TB(I) = "Copy " & I  'show Text property
        TB(I).Visible = True  'show each copy
    Next I
End Sub
```

Instead of using the original name of Text1 to refer to the object, we use the TB control array and its various elements to reference the clones. Notice also that the properties of the original object, such as Top, Height, Width, and FontSize, are inherited by the clones.

When you no longer need a clone object, you can assign **Nothing** to the variable. This frees up the memory occupied by the object. To demonstrate how you can do that, add Command1 to the form. Erase the Dim line in the above procedure. Add the following form-level array (we need to reference it from Command1):

```
    Dim TB(4) As Control
```

Finally, add this procedure:

```
Private Sub Command1_Click ()
    Dim I As Integer
    For I = 1 To 4
        TB(I).Visible = False 'hide
        Set TB(I) = Nothing    'erase
    Next I
End Sub
```

When the clone objects are displayed, clicking Command1 will erase them. We could use the Visible line alone. But that would only hide them, not erase them from memory. Also, if you reverse the order of the two lines, the *Object variable or With block variable not set* error will occur. It proves that the objects have been set to Nothing. A simpler alternative to the above two lines is the line below; it will erase the object from memory and clear it from the screen.

```
    Unload TB(I)
```

Collections of Objects

To keep track of clone objects created at run time, Visual Basic maintains two internal array-like objects called **collections**; these are **forms collection** and **controls collection**. While an ordinary array's elements do not change their order at run time, a collection's elements can change as objects are added or deleted. The two collections follow these syntactic formats:

```
    Forms(Number)                'form array
    FormName(Number)             'control array
    FormName.Controls(Number)       'same as above
```

Each collection has a **Count** property which returns the number of loaded objects. The total count is Count minus 1 because counting starts with 0; if there are 10 objects, they number from 0 to 9.

Let's use Figure 9.25 in the previous section as an example. Suppose we now add the Command1 button to the form and attach the following procedure:

```
Private Sub Command1_Click ()
    Dim I As Integer

    For I = 0 To Forms.Count - 1
        Debug.Print Forms(I).Caption
```

```
      Next I   'forms collection
End Sub
```

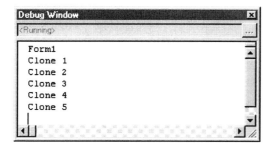

Figure 9.28   Showing all form captions

Figure 9.28 appears after we double-click the original form to create five clones
and then click Command1. The captions of the six forms that constitute the forms
collection are printed to the Immediate window.

Now add Label1 and Option1 to the form and modify the procedure as shown
below. Clicking Command1 results in Figure 9.29. The controls' captions are
now displayed.

```
Private Sub Command1_Click ()
    Dim I As Integer

    For I = 0 To Form1.Count - 1
        Debug.Print Form1(I).Caption
    Next I   'controls collection
End Sub
```

Figure 9.29   Showing all control captions

Notice that we use Form1, not Forms, to reference the controls. We can add Controls(i) to do the same thing, as shown below:

```
Private Sub Command1_Click ()
    Dim I As Integer

    For I = 0 To Form1.Controls.Count - 1
        Debug.Print Form1.Controls(I).Caption
    Next I
End Sub
```

COLLECTION OBJECTS

You can create a **Collection** object of your own. Such an object can contain members (elements) of the Variant data type, so you can assign anything to them. An internal indexing system is automatically maintained, which allows you to access each member's value. Such a collection behaves similar (but not identical) to an array.

Since a collection is an object, you need to create an instance before you can manipulate it. The following statement creates a new instance of the Collection class (it's a common practice to use plurality in a collection identifier):

```
Dim colNames as New Collection
```

Once a collection object is created, you can use the **Add** method to add members, the **Remove** method to remove members, and the **Item** method to access members. These are the only methods of this object.

The Collection class has only one property, namely **Count**. It returns the total number of members currently in the collection. As you add or remove members, the number will change. Suppose there are 10 members in a collection. The first is treated as number 1 (not 0) and the last as number 10 (not 9). So Count in this situation returns 10, not 9. This system makes the value different from the Count property of Visual Basic's intrinsic collections discussed in the previous section.

```
Private Sub Form_Click()
    'demo Collection, Add, Remove, Item
    Dim colNums As New Collection
    Dim Temp As Variant
    Dim Member As Variant
    Dim I As Integer

    Temp = "one"
    colNums.Add (Temp)      'using var to add
```

```
colNums.Add ("two")    'no variable
colNums.Add 23 / 3     'numeric
colNums.Add "four"     'string
colNums.Add "5555"

For Each Member In colNums
    Print Member     'show each member
Next

Print String(60, "-")
    'print character 60 times
colNums.Remove 2      'remove 2nd member

For I = 1 To colNums.Count   'use Count property
    Print I, colNums.Item(I)
        'can be shortened to: colNums(i)
Next I

On Error GoTo ErrTrap
Print colNums(5)        '"Item" omitted
    'error; member gone
Exit Sub

ErrTrap:
    Print String(60, "-")
    Print Err.Number, Err.Description
End Sub
```

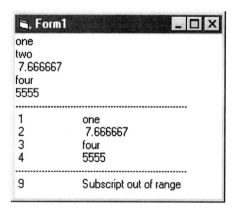

Figure 9.30   Demonstrating collection members

The procedure above produces the display shown in Figure 9.30. Notice that you can put a variety of values after Add. You can optionally enclose a value in a pair of parentheses. Removing a member is quite simple—just specify its index number. After a member is removed, those below are moved upward, thus leaving no employ space. This is what makes a collection different from an array, whose elements don't change their positions.

Our procedure removes a member in the middle and then tries to access the last member of the unaltered collection, thus leading to an error. This is the same error you encounter when you go beyond an ordinary array's range.

The **Item** method is the default method. Like anything default, it can be omitted. The above procedure demonstrates its use in both situations.

The **Add** method has the following syntax:

```
object.Add(Item, Key, before | after)
```

The first argument is the only one required. If you supply a name for the **Key argument**, you can use this name to access the first argument. This name can replace an index number as a way of accessing a member's value. Here is an example:

```
colNums.Add 99, "Jim"
Print colNums("Jim")        '99
```

So you can now access 99 by using Jim. However, you cannot access Jim by using 99.

The arguments shown in the syntax line are all **named arguments**. That means you can use them to alter the shown order or skip an optional argument. The following statements will add a numeric to the first member of the collection and then print that value.

```
colNums.Add before:=1, Item:=99.99
Print colNums(1)      '99.99
```

If you don't specify a position, an item is added at the end. By using *before* or *after*, you can specify a position (index number) to add an item. Specifying an illogical index number, such as specifying 3 when the collection has no existing member, will lead to a number of errors. The *before* and *after* arguments cannot coexist. If you use one, you must not use the other. Use the one that is the most appropriate for the occasion. The following two examples achieve the same thing, adding a member to the one before the last member of the existing collection.

```
colNums.Add Item:="last", before:=colNums.Count
colNums.Add Item:="last", after:=colNums.Count - 1
```

You can use the **Key argument** as a textual (rather than numeric) index to access the corresponding Item's value. A Key argument must be different from an existing Key argument; otherwise, an error will result (*This key is already associated with an element of this collection*). In the following arrangement, we can use John (case is irrelevant) to show 100; we don't need to know the numeric index of the 100 value.

```
colNums.Add Key:="John", Item:=100
Print colNums.Item("john")        '100
```

This arrangement allows you to use a member's name to access its value. You can now use the **!** (bang) operator to access that member, as in this example:

```
Print colNums!John + 10     '110
```

In this situation, you can use a member's name to get its index value in order to add a new member. Here is an example:

```
colNums.Add before:="john", Item:=80, Key:="Joe"
```

A new member named Joe with the value of 80 is added before the member named John. You can now access the 80 value by using the name Joe.

You can also remove a member by using its name, like below:

```
colNums.Remove "John"
```

After the removal, accessing it with either statement shown below will lead to the *Invalid procedure call* error:

```
Print colNums!John
Print colNums("John")
```

There is no Clear (as in a list box) or Erase (as in an array) method for the Collection object to remove all the members at once. If you want to do that, you need to use the Remove method to remove each individual member one at a time. In the following routine, the removal order is from last to first:

```
Do While colNums.Count > 0
    colNums.Remove colNums.Count
Loop
```

If you want to remove from the beginning to the end, change the above middle line to this:

```
colNums.Remove 1
```

A collection can contain multiple other collections. This is comparable to putting several arrays inside an array. The procedure below demonstrates how to do that. It produces the display shown in Figure 9.31.

```
Private Sub Form_Click()
    'demo collections inside a collection
    Dim ABCcorp As New Collection
    Dim DivA As New Collection
    Dim DivB As New Collection
    Dim DivC As New Collection
    Dim Member As Variant
    Dim I As Integer

    ABCcorp.Add DivA
    ABCcorp.Add DivB
    ABCcorp.Add DivC
    Print "ABCcorp now has "; ABCcorp.Count; "members."

    DivA.Add "Division A-" & 1
    DivA.Add "Division A-" & 2
    DivA.Add "Division A-" & 3
    Print "Division A now has "; DivA.Count; "members."

    DivB.Add "Division B-" & 1
    DivB.Add "Division B-" & 2
    DivB.Add "Division B-" & 3

    DivC.Add "Division C-" & 1
    DivC.Add "Division C-" & 2
    DivC.Add "Division C-" & 3

    For Each Member In DivA
        Print Member,
    Next
    Print    'new line
    For I = 1 To ABCcorp.Count
        'access each member in ABCcorp
        For Each Member In ABCcorp.Item(I)
            'access each member in each division
            Print Member,
        Next
        Print
    Next I
End Sub
```

In this arrangement, ABCcorp has three members, each of which is a collection that in turn contains three string values. After adding all the members, ABCcorp(1) (Item is optional) contains the same items as in the DivA collection.

Figure 9.31   **Collections inside a collection**

How can you access an individual item in this situation? Suppose we want to access ABCcorp's DivA's second item. I wondered about that and tried many tricks. Many errors and much frustration later, I remembered the peculiar (and new) way of addressing an array inside another array. That did it, and here it is:

```
Print ABCcorp(1)(2)
```

This gives us the second member of the collection that is the first member of the ABCcorp collection. So the last part of the above procedure can be changed to the following without altering the outcome.

```
For I = 1 To ABCcorp.Count
    'access each member in ABCcorp
    For J = 1 To ABCcorp.Item(i).Count
        'access each member in each division
        Print ABCcorp(I)(J),
    Next J
    Print
Next I
```

DRILL

_____ 16.   When multiple controls of the same type share the same name, they become a _____ _____.   *control array*

_____ 17.   If you have Command1 and Command2 on a form, changing Command1's Index to 0 and then changing Command2's Name to Command1 will lead to a prompt asking whether you want to create a control array. True or false?

___ 18.   The following will create and show a new copy of Command1. True or false?

```
Load Command1(1)
Show Command1(1)
```

___ 19.   The ___Type Of___ keyword can be used with If to determine what type of object a variable is referencing.

Answers for questions 20 - 24:
   a. Set,   b. New,   c. Load,   d. Show,   e. Visible,

___ 20.   Used to create a form clone.
___ 21.   Used to create a control clone.
___ 22.   Used to display a form.
___ 23.   Used to display a control.
___ 24.   Used to assign an object to a variable name.

___ 25.   When you want to remove a control, you can assign ___Nothing___ to an object variable.

___ 26.   You can use ___Me___ to reference the form being executed.

___ 27.   The following statement will:

```
ActiveControl.Visible = 0
```

   a.   make the current form invisible
   b.   make the current control invisible
   c.   make the current control visible
   d.   lead to an error

___ 28.   The following statement will:

```
Caption = Form1(0).Caption
```

   a.   print all the control captions
   b.   put a form caption in a control caption
   c.   put a control caption in a form caption
   d.   lead to an error

___ 29.   The following four statements will all print the same thing. True or false?

```
Print Me.Caption
Print Screen.ActiveForm.Caption
```

```
Print ActiveControl.Caption
Print Screen.ActiveControl.Caption
```

____ 30. A user-created collection has an index value of ____ for its first item.

PRACTICE

■ 19. How can you create a control array at design time?

■ 20. What is an object variable? How can you use an object variable?

■ 21. How can you create a clone form at run time?

■ 22. How can you create clones (copies) of a control (such as a command button) at run time?

■ 23. Create a metric conversion application shown in Figure 9.32.

The conversion should be done in a sub procedure named Result. Use a control array for the four option buttons. Use Select Case to determine which option button is selected. The conversion ratios are as follows:

1 meter = 3.281 feet
1 kilometer = 0.621 mile
1 liter = 0.264 gallon

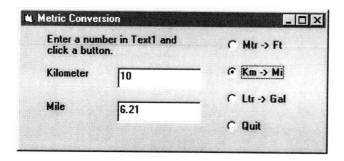

Figure 9.32   Metric converter

■ 24. This project creates at run time five copies of a text box. They are arranged in a straight column, as shown in Figure 9.33. Each box shows a sequential number. The form's caption also shows the number of loaded controls.

When you double-click a displayed text box, it is erased. The form's caption also updates the number of available controls.

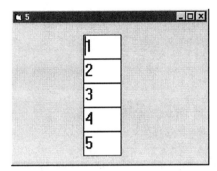

Figure 9.33   Text box clones

SORTING ARRAYS

One of the most common computing tasks is to sort a series of numeric or text entries. This task requires the use of an array. The routine for such a task is best put in a separate general procedure, which can be called by other procedures.

There are many ways to sort data. The best known include **exchange sort, bubble sort** (the slowest), and **Shell sort** (the speediest). The exchange sort is fairly fast; it's also simple to understand. That's what we use here.

In an exchange sort, you try to put the lowest value in the first location, then the second lowest value in the second location, and so on. As an example, let us assume that there are five numbers stored in five memory locations as shown below:

Memory position	p1	p2	p3	p4	p5
Original order	4	5	1	3	2
After pass 1	1	5	4	3	2
After pass 2	1	2	5	4	3
After pass 3	1	2	3	5	4
After pass 4	1	2	3	4	5

The first thing you do is to put the lowest value in p1 (assuming you want an ascending order), then the second in p2, and so on. To put the lowest value in p1, compare its value (4) to p2, p3, and so on. In the first pass, you go through four comparisons. First, compare 4 to 5; no switch is made here. Then compare 4 to 1; the two are switched. Then compare 1 (the new value in p1) to 3 and 2; no switch is made. This completes pass 1. In pass 2, compare p2 to those on the right, thus making only three comparisons. In the last pass, only one comparison is made.

One-Dimensional Arrays

We first show how to sort a one-dimensional array. Our demonstration program lets you enter a series of numbers and, at the end, print the numbers in sorted order. Two form-level declarations (shown at the beginning) make it unnecessary to pass the array; we can just call the general procedure to alter the array.

```
Dim Counter As Integer     'counter throughout app
Dim Entry() As Single      'track entries

Private Sub Form_Load()    '--Listing 4--
    Dim Temp As Variant
    Dim I As Integer

    Show
    Do
        Temp = InputBox("Enter a number")
        If Temp = "" Then Exit Do    'if no entry
        Counter = Counter + 1         'increment index num
        ReDim Preserve Entry(Counter)
          'redim dynamic array and preserve previous value
        Entry(Counter) = Val(Temp)
          'assign to each element
    Loop

    Sort     'call sub to sort

    For I = 1 To Counter
        Print Entry(I)     'print sorted entries
    Next I
End Sub

Private Sub Sort()
    Dim I As Integer
    Dim J As Integer
    Dim Temp As Single

    For I = 1 To Counter - 1
        For J = I + 1 To Counter
```

```
              If Entry(I) > Entry(J) Then
                  Temp = Entry(I)  'switch
                  Entry(I) = Entry(J)
                  Entry(J) = Temp
              End If
        Next J
    Next I
End Sub
```

We use a dynamic array to handle user entries. This array is first declared with Dim without specifying a subscript. Then we use ReDim to continuously redimension the subscript as necessary. To preserve any previously assigned values, we also use the **Preserve** keyword.

In the Form_Load procedure, we use an input box to prompt for a series of entries. Each entry is assigned to an element in the array; this allows us to sort all the elements. When Cancel is chosen or Enter is pressed without typing anything, the Do loop is exited. Then the Sort procedure is called.

In the Sort procedure, we use two For-Next loops to compare each successive array element to the rest. If the second entry has a lower value than the first, the two are swapped. To swap the two, we assign the first to the Temp variable, the second to the first, and finally Temp to the second. By the time the two loops end, each successive element in the array has been compared to the rest and, if necessary, swapped.

After the Sort procedure is finished, execution returns to the Form_Load procedure. We then use another loop to print the sorted entries.

TIP: Swapping Data

How do you tell a computer to swap data? Suppose 1 is stored in memory (variable) A and 2 in B. Now you want to tell the computer to exchange them, namely putting 1 in B and 2 in A. You might be tempted to do the following:

```
A = B    'A = 2
B = A    'B = 2
```

Do you know what will happen if you do that? Both will have the same value, namely 2. In the first statement, you assign 2 (the value of B) to A; A holds 2 after the statement. In the second, you also assign 2 (the new value of A) to B.
What's the solution? Use a temporary variable. Consider the following:

```
Temp = A          'Temp = 1
A = B             'A = 2
B = Temp          'B = 1
```

First, we assign A to Temp; Temp has 1 as the result. Then we assign B to A; A now holds 2. Finally, we assign Temp (A's original value) to B, which results in B having the value of 1.

Passing And Sorting

Instead of using a form-level array, we can use a local array and pass it to a general procedure that will return the sorted array. This arrangement is slower to execute because passing arguments require more time. On the other hand, it is more versatile because various procedures can call the general procedure to perform the sorting task.

Our first procedure below uses the Array function to assign six elements to the All variable, prints all the values, calls the Sort procedure, and prints the sorted array after the call.

```
Private Sub Form_Click()        '--Listing 5--
    Dim All As Variant
    Dim Item As Variant

    All = Array(33, 21, 66, 90, 64, 45)

    For Each Item In All
        Print Item; "  ";   'print each before sort
    Next Item
    Print
    Sort All     'call sort and pass array

    For Each Item In All
        Print Item; "  ";   'print after sort
    Next Item
End Sub

Private Sub Sort(Entry)
    Dim I As Integer
    Dim J As Integer
    Dim K As Integer
    Dim Temp As Variant

    K = UBound(Entry)              'highest index value

    For I = 0 To K - 1
        For J = I + 1 To K
            If Entry(I) > Entry(J) Then
```

```
                    Temp = Entry(I)    'switch
                    Entry(I) = Entry(J)
                    Entry(J) = Temp
                End If
            Next J
        Next I
    End Sub
```

The called procedure is the same as shown in the previous section, except that it is modified to accept an argument. It also uses the UBound function to determine the highest index number in the passed array.

Since an array is passed by reference, the called procedure has access to the array elements' addresses. After the rearrangement is made, the calling procedure has access to the new addresses. Even though no value is returned, the elements are rearranged. If you wish, you can change the Sort routine to a function procedure that will return a sorted array.

Finding the Median

The median is the middle value in a sorted number of values. Half of the values fall above and half fall below it. It is commonly used to indicate many things such as median SAT score, median house price, median household income, and so on.

If there is an odd number of values, five for example, then the median is the one in the middle, the third of the five. If there is an even number instead, six for example, the median is the average of the two middle values, third and fourth.

Finding the median of a series of values requires sorting them first. After that, you need to determine whether the number of values is odd or even. If even, you need to calculate the average of the two middle values.

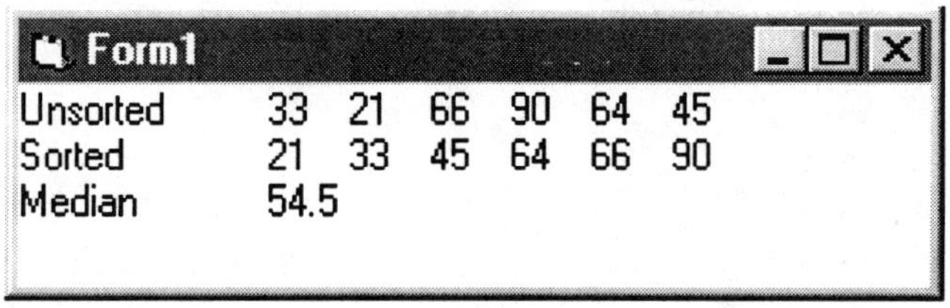

Figure 9.34   Calculating the median

Figure 9.34 shows three lines. The first consists of the unsorted values. These are assigned to a Variant variable by using the Array function, as we have done before. The array is then passed to a function procedure. This Sort procedure is changed from the original sub procedure because we intend to make it return a value, the median.

(9MEDIAN.FRM)

```
Private Sub Form_Click()
    Dim All As Variant
    Dim Item As Variant
    Dim Median As Single

    All = Array(33, 21, 66, 90, 64, 45)
    Print "Unsorted",

    For Each Item In All
        Print Item; "   ";    'print each before sort
    Next Item
    Print
    Median = Sort(All)    'call function and pass array
    Print "Sorted",

    For Each Item In All
        Print Item; "   ";    'print after sort
    Next Item
    Print
    Print "Median", Median   'print returned value
End Sub

Private Function Sort(Entry)
    Dim I As Integer
    Dim J As Integer
    Dim K As Integer
    Dim Temp As Variant

    K = UBound(Entry)             'highest index value
    For I = 0 To K - 1
        For J = I + 1 To K
            If Entry(I) > Entry(J) Then
                Temp = Entry(I)    'switch
                Entry(I) = Entry(J)
                Entry(J) = Temp
            End If
        Next J
    Next I

    If K Mod 2 Then 'if even count, avg of 2 middle
        Sort = (Entry(K / 2) + Entry((K + 1) / 2)) / 2
    Else             'return call
        Sort = Entry(K / 2)
    End If           'if odd count, return the mid value
End Function
```

The If control structure added at the end of the Sort procedure returns a value depending on whether the passed array contains an odd or even number of cases. If the remainder of this number divided by 2 has a remainder, then we have an even number. So if we have six cases (0 - 5), the highest index value in the array is 5. Five divided by two results in a remainder of one. So the If branch is executed, but the Else branch is ignored. If we have seven cases (0 - 6) instead, the fourth value will be returned; that happens to be the value with the index of 3, the result of dividing 6 by 2.

Structures and Multidimensional Arrays

If you want to sort a multidimensional array, you need to switch all the corresponding pairs of elements, not just one single pair. If not, the previously connected elements will become disconnected. For example, a person's name may be connected to another person's Social Security number. This can lead to serious consequences.

To demonstrate sorting a multidimensional array, we'll use a structure array to illustrate a point discussed earlier. Our structure is declared at the form level with Private, which is required. The structure is named Student and has three elements. In Form1 we also declare at the form level a one-dimensional array named Stu to be the Student type; this in effect makes Stu comparable to a two-dimensional array.

The Form_Click procedure assigns elements to each element, prints the original elements, calls the Sort procedure to sort according to grades, and finally prints the sorted array (Figure 9.35).

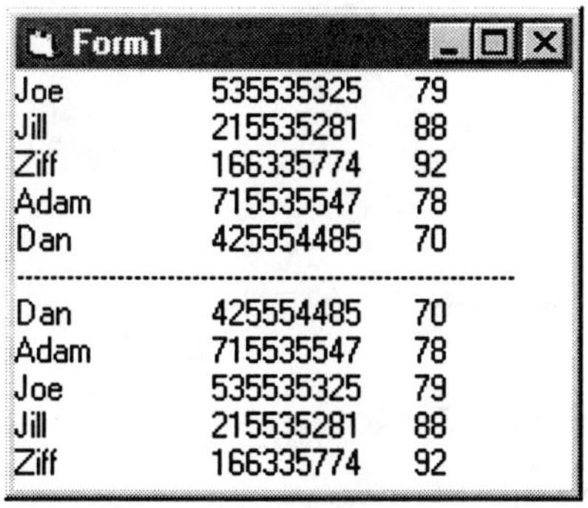

Figure 9.35   Sorting a structure

(9SORTSTRUCT.FRM)

```
Private Type Student
    Name As String * 10
    SSNum As String * 9
    Grade As Integer
End Type

Dim Stu(4) As Student      'form-level declaration

Private Sub Form_Click()
    Dim I As Integer

    Stu(0).Name = "Joe"    'assign each element
    Stu(0).SSNum = "535535325"
    Stu(0).Grade = 79
    Stu(1).Name = "Jill"
    Stu(1).SSNum = "215535281"
    Stu(1).Grade = 88
    Stu(2).Name = "Ziff"
    Stu(2).SSNum = "166335774"
    Stu(2).Grade = 92
    Stu(3).Name = "Adam"
    Stu(3).SSNum = "715535547"
    Stu(3).Grade = 78
    Stu(4).Name = "Dan"
    Stu(4).SSNum = "425554485"
    Stu(4).Grade = 70

    For I = 0 To 4         'before sort
        Print Stu(I).Name, Stu(I).SSNum, Stu(I).Grade
    Next I
    Print String(60, "-")    'separator line
    Call Sort

    For I = 0 To 4          'after sort
        Print Stu(I).Name, Stu(I).SSNum, Stu(I).Grade
    Next I
End Sub

Private Sub Sort()
    Dim I As Integer
    Dim J As Integer
    Dim K As Integer
    Dim Temp As Variant

    K = UBound(Stu)         'upperbound of array
    For I = 0 To K - 1
        For J = I + 1 To K
            If Stu(I).Grade > Stu(J).Grade Then
                'compare grades
                Temp = Stu(I).Grade    'switch grades
                Stu(I).Grade = Stu(J).Grade
                Stu(J).Grade = Temp
```

```
                    Temp = Stu(I).Name     'switch names
                    Stu(I).Name = Stu(J).Name
                    Stu(J).Name = Temp

                    Temp = Stu(I).SSNum    'switch SSNum #
                    Stu(I).SSNum = Stu(J).SSNum
                    Stu(J).SSNum = Temp
                End If
          Next J
      Next I
End Sub
```

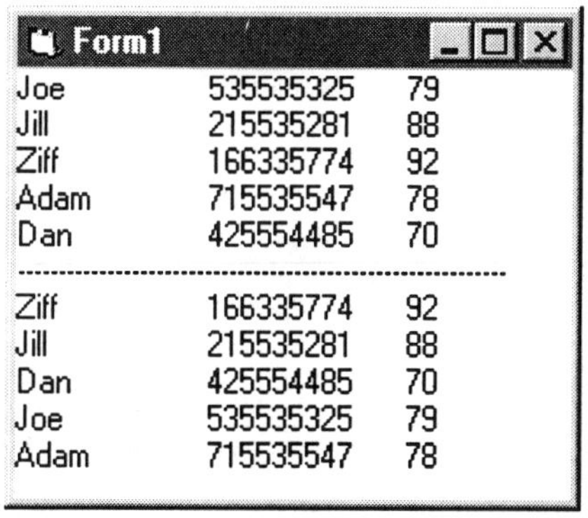

Figure 9.36   Sorting by the second field

The Sort procedure compares grades. When a switch is necessary, the corresponding names and Social Security numbers are switched as well. If we didn't switch these last two, the original grades would be disconnected from their related items. If you want to sort by names or Social Security numbers, you need to make necessary changes in the If line and other corresponding items. Figure 9.36 shows the result of sorting by Social Security numbers.

We declare our array variable at the form level. That obviates the need to pass an argument to the Sort procedure. We can also use a local variable. To do that, move the declaration line to the beginning of the Form_Click procedure. In the calling statement, use the line below; if you want to use Call, put the argument inside a pair of parentheses:

```
    Sort Stu()
```

In the Sort procedure's header, you need to change to this:

```
    Private Sub Sort(Stu() As Student)
```

If you don't specify As Student in the header, various errors will appear, including the one shown in Figure 9.37.

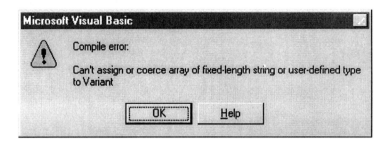

Figure 9.37   Failing to declare a user-defined type

Notice the empty pairs of parentheses. The one in the calling statement is optional. The one in the Sort procedure header is mandatory. I tried many times without this and always got the *Type mismatch* error. I tried many remedies and could not shake off this error. By chance I tried the parentheses and finally shook off the bug.

The If control structure in the Sort procedure requires us to specify each element of our data structure that requires switching. This is rather clumsy. If we use an array (instead of a structure) here, we can do it in three lines (instead nine). A chapter project at the end of this chapter will let you try to use a two-dimensional array to provide a simpler and more elegant solution.

SEARCHING ARRAYS: SEQUENTIAL AND BINARY

An array can be searched. You specify a search value and check to see whether there is anything matching it in the array. There are two common search algorithms: **sequential search** and **binary search**. Our application (Figure 9.38) supplies both.

We use a series of general procedures to perform a number of tasks. The Generate procedure generates a series of random numbers in the 1-999 range and puts them in List1 (the left list box); these numbers are used to demonstrate searching techniques. You can change the 500 value specified in the procedure. You can also use an input box to get a user-supplied number.

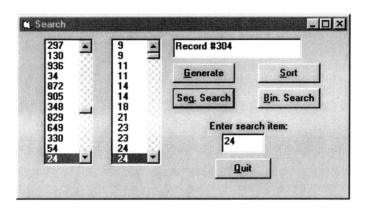

Figure 9.38   Searching arrays

After you run the application and click Generate, the random numbers appear in List1. Then supply a search value in the middle text box and click Seq. Search. (If no search value is supplied, clicking the button just makes a beep.) If no matching number is found, a message appears in the top text box. If a matching value is found, its index value in the list box is displayed in the top text box and the first matching item is also highlighted in List1.

Since a list box is an array, we do not put the items into another array. Instead, as shown below, we simply go through each item in the list box from the beginning to the end to find a matching value. The procedure is exited when the first matching item is found.

(9SEARCH.FRM)

```
Dim TopNum As Integer
    'higher array number throughout app
Dim Entry() As Integer
    'track entries, dynamic array

Private Sub cmdGenerate_Click()
    'generate random numbers, put into 1st list box
    Dim I As Integer
    Dim Num As Integer

    MousePointer = vbHourglass
    TopNum = 500    'InputBox("Enter a number")
    ReDim Entry(TopNum - 1) 'specify elements
```

```
        lstRandom.Clear 'clear list box previous entries
        Randomize          'get new seed

        For I = 0 To TopNum - 1
            Num = Fix(999 * Rnd) + 1  'random 1 - 999
            lstRandom.AddItem Num        'add to lstRandom
        Next I
        MousePointer = vbDefault
End Sub

Private Sub GetData()
        'put 1st list box numbers into array
        Dim I As Integer

        lstSorted.Clear        'clear previous entries
        For I = 0 To TopNum - 1
                '1st index num in listbox is 0
            Entry(I) = Val(lstRandom.List(I))
                'get listbox to array
        Next I          'convert to numeric
End Sub

Private Sub ShowData()
        'put sorted numbers into 2nd list box
        Dim I As Integer

        For I = 0 To TopNum - 1
            lstSorted.AddItem Str(Entry(I)) 'put in lstSorted
        Next I
End Sub

Private Sub cmdBSearch_Click()
        'binary search
        Dim Half As Integer
        Dim First As Integer
        Dim Last As Integer
        Dim Num As Integer
        Dim Flag As Boolean

        First = 0          '1st record index
        Last = TopNum - 1     'last record index
        Flag = False     'not found
        Num = Val(txtItem.Text)  'search entry

        If Num = 0 Or lstSorted.List(0) = "" Then
            Beep          'if no entry in text or list box
            Exit Sub
        End If

        Do
            Half = (First + Last) \ 2    'half, middle index
            Select Case Val(lstSorted.List(Half))
            Case Num                'if matching
                Flag = True          'get out
```

```
                    Case Is < Num           'if lower than Num
                        First = Half + 1    'search 1st half
                    Case Is > Num           'if higher than Num
                        Last = Half - 1     'search 2nd half
                End Select
            Loop While (Last >= First) And (Flag = False)

            If Flag = True Then
                txtMsg.Text = "Record #" & (Half + 1)
                    'show found item in text box
                lstSorted.Selected(Half) = True
                    'highlight item in list box
            Else
                Beep
                txtMsg.Text = "Not found"
            End If
    End Sub

    Private Sub cmdSort_Click()
        'sort entries in the array
        Dim I As Integer
        Dim J As Integer
        Dim Temp As Integer

        MousePointer = vbHourglass
        Call GetData    'get data to array
        For I = 0 To TopNum - 2  'from 1st to next to last
            For J = I + 1 To TopNum - 1
                'from 2nd to each next
                If Entry(I) > Entry(J) Then
                    Temp = Entry(I)
                    Entry(I) = Entry(J)
                    Entry(J) = Temp
                End If
            Next J
        Next I
        Call ShowData  'show sorted array
        MousePointer = vbDefault
    End Sub

    Private Sub cmdSSearch_Click()
        'sequential search
        Dim I As Integer
        Dim Flag As Boolean

        If txtItem.Text = "" Then
            Beep            'if no search entry
            Exit Sub
        End If

        Flag = False     'assume not found
        For I = 0 To lstRandom.ListCount - 1
            If lstRandom.List(I) = txtItem.Text Then
                Flag = True       'found
```

```
            Exit For       'get out
        End If
    Next I

    If Flag = True Then
        txtMsg.Text = "Record #" & (I + 1)
            'show found item in text box
        lstRandom.Selected(I) = True
            'highlight item in list box
    Else
        Beep
        txtMsg.Text = "Not found"
    End If
End Sub

Private Sub cmdQuit_Click()
    End
End Sub
```

A binary search, shown above, may be speedier if the array to be searched is large. This algorithm requires a sorted array. So our application includes the sort routine. After you generate random numbers, click Sort to sort the numbers and put them in List2. Supplying a search value and clicking Bin. Search will search List2 for a matching value. The first matching value's index number will appear in the top text box. If there is nothing in List2 or if you supply no search value, a beep is made and nothing else is done.

The Sort procedure is carried over from the previous section. We need a sorted array to do a binary search. This procedure sorts the random numbers in List1 and puts the result in List2. The Sort procedure uses the Get_data procedure to put the List1 data into the array. After sorting the array, it calls the Show_data procedure to put the array data into List2 to show the sorted result.

The binary search algorithm follows a logic of "divide and conquer." You divide the array into two halves and see whether the item in the middle is the matching one. If so, the search is over. If not, the program decides whether to search the top half (if the search value is lower than the middle value) or the bottom half (if the search value is greater than the middle value). Then the identified half is halved again. And the process continues until a matching value is found or all the items are exhausted.

PRACTICE

■ 25. This project (Figure 9.39) lets you continuously enter numbers. When you press Enter after typing a number in the text box, the number goes to the list box on the right, the text box is cleared, and the focus remains in the text box for another entry.

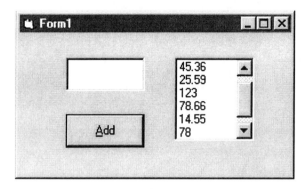

Figure 9.39   Entering numbers

■ 26. Add the Sort command button to the previous question. When this button is clicked, the list box numbers will be sorted and redisplayed in the sorted (ascending) order.

■ 27. In Listing 4, delete all form-level variables and use local variables to do the same thing. Also add two text boxes. Text1 should display each number as it is entered from the input box. When no number is entered, the sorting procedure is called and the sorted numbers are displayed in Text2, as shown in Figure 9.40.

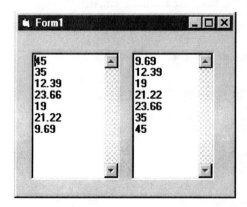

Figure 9.40   Showing original and sorted numbers

■ 28. Modify Listing 5 so that the Sort procedure is changed to a function procedure. It should accept an array passed by value and return a sorted array.

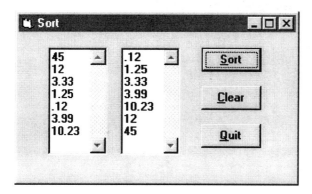

Figure 9.41   Sorting a text box

■ 29. This project (Figure 9.41) lets the user enter numbers in the left text box. When Sort is clicked, the sorted numbers appear in the second text box. Keep in mind that each text line ends with Chr(13) and Chr(10), or vbCr and vbLf. You need to use some string functions to extract each line, convert it to a numeric, and assign it to an array element. After that you can sort the array.

■ 30. Modify the previous project to calculate and display the items shown in the middle text box (Figure 9.42). Clear clears the contents in both text boxes and shifts the focus to the first box for more entries.

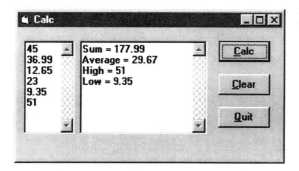

Figure 9.42   Tabulating a text box

■ 31. Write a procedure to display the numbers in **Pascal's triangle** (Figure 9.43). Each row starts and ends with 1, and each number in the middle is the sum of the two directly above it. There should be nine rows, and each row should be centered. (Use a two-dimensional array to maneuver the numbers and control the display.)

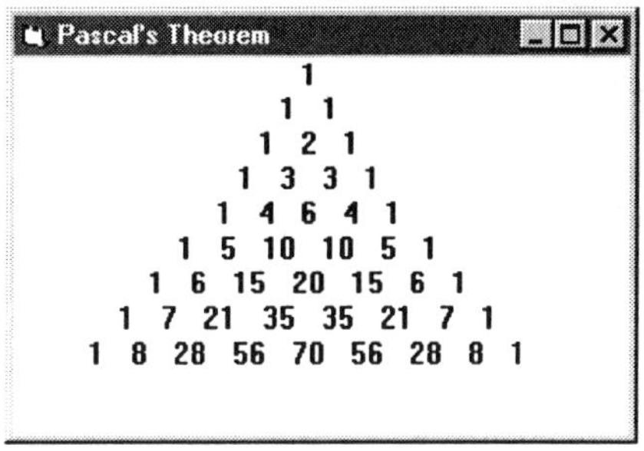

```
Pascal's Theorem                    _ □ ×
                      1
                     1  1
                    1  2  1
                   1  3  3  1
                  1  4  6  4  1
                 1  5  10  10  5  1
                1  6  15  20  15  6  1
              1  7  21  35  35  21  7  1
            1  8  28  56  70  56  28  8  1
```

Figure 9.43   Pascal's Triangle

■ 32. Write a procedure that uses an array to manipulate and print the first ten **Fibonacci** numbers as shown below. (Each number is the sum of the two before.)

1 1 2 3 5 8 13 21 34 55

■ 33. Write a function that will return the Fibonacci number based on the passed term. For example, if 10 is passed, 55 will be returned. If 0 or a negative value is passed, an error message appears. If 1 or 2 is passed, then 1 is returned. Use an array to maneuver the numbers.

```
Form1                    _ □ ×
1              19  times
2              16  times
3              20  times
4              15  times
5              12  times
6              18  times
```

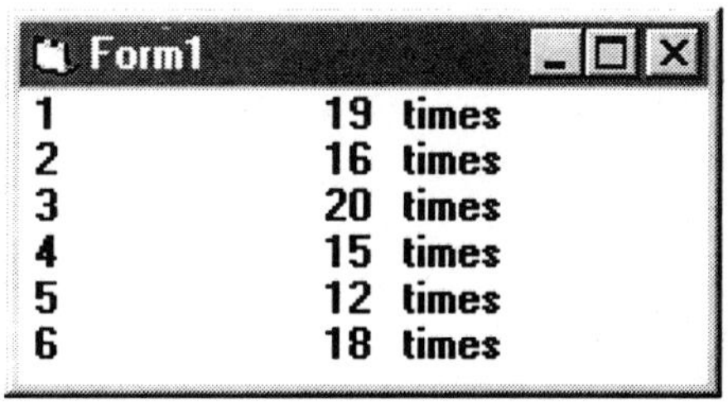

Figure 9.44   Rolling one die 100 times

■ 34. Write a Form_Click procedure that will simulate rolling a die 100 times. The procedure should call a function procedure 100 times to generate

100 random numbers in range 1-6. The frequency of each number should be tabulated and printed to the screen at the end, as shown in Figure 9.44.

■ 35. Modify the above so that it will simulate rolling two dice 100 times (Figure 9.45).

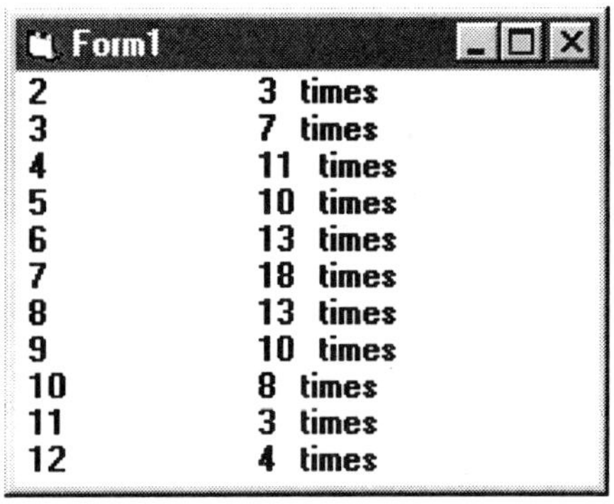

```
■ Form1                    _ □ ×
2              3  times
3              7  times
4              11 times
5              10 times
6              13 times
7              18 times
8              13 times
9              10 times
10             8  times
11             3  times
12             4  times
```

Figure 9.45   Rolling two dice 100 times

■ 36. Modify the above so that the caption shows the total passes and the last column displays the total numbers. Figure 9.46 shows the results after clicking the form 70 times.

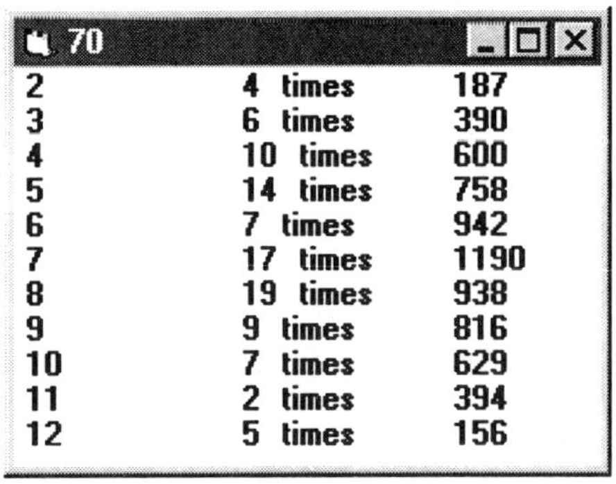

```
■ 70                       _ □ ×
2          4  times    187
3          6  times    390
4          10 times    600
5          14 times    758
6          7  times    942
7          17 times    1190
8          19 times    938
9          9  times    816
10         7  times    629
11         2  times    394
12         5  times    156
```

Figure 9.46   Tracking totals

CHAPTER PROJECT

A. (9CALC1.FRM)

Do the following in this project (Figure 9.47):

1. At design time, make the first four command (operator) buttons into a control array, all sharing Command1 as their name and caption.

2. As soon as the program starts, the operators appear as shown.

3. The font size for the four operators are also changed to 12 points at run time.

4. Write one single procedure, Command1_Click, to respond to all four operator buttons.

5. If either of the first two text boxes is empty when an operator button is clicked, a beep is made and nothing else happens.

6. When an operator button is clicked, the operator sign (caption) should appear between the two entered numbers and the result of the arithmetic operation should be shown in the last text box.

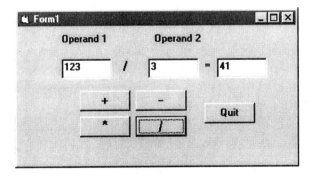

Figure 9.47   Calculating two numbers

B. (9CALC2.FRM)

This project lets the user click displayed digits and operators to calculate the result, as shown in Figure 9.48. The program should behave as follows:

1. The digits and operators form a control array, which is created at run time.

2. The display at the bottom consists of five labels added at design time.

3. The user is supposed to enter the first operand (with one or more digits), an operator, and then the second operand. Each entry is made by clicking proper items displayed.

4. Before an operator is selected, clicking a digit makes its number appear before the operator at the bottom line. After an operator is clicked, future selected digits appear after the operator and the results are immediately displayed; if more digits are selected, the result changes accordingly.

5. The Clear button clears the display at the bottom. The Quit button ends the program. These are added at design time.

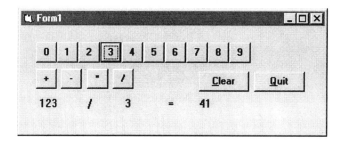

Figure 9.48   A calculator with digits and operators

C. (9CLONE1.FRM)

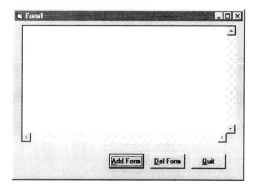

Figure 9.49   The original form

This project lets you create and delete copies of the original form that contains a text box (with scroll bars) and three command buttons, as shown in Figure 9.49. When the Add Form button is clicked, a new clone form appears. The Top and Height are limited as shown in Figure 9.50. Future clones are of the same size but the Top is similarly distanced from one another. The maximum clone number is 5. After the limit is reached, clicking Add Form does nothing except making a beep. Clicking Del Form displays an input box. The last clone number appears in the default line. If you press Enter or click OK, that clone is removed. You can enter another number to remove that particular clone form. Clicking Cancel just clears the input box.

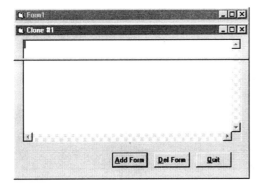

Figure 9.50   The first clone form

E. (9COLOR.FRM)

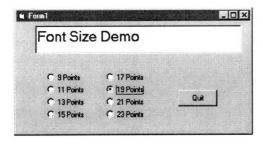

Figure 9.51   Creating clones at run time

This project (Figure 9.51) consists of three controls at design time: a text box, an option button, and a command button. At run time, eight clones of the option button are created and arranged in two columns. Their captions show their font size numbers, each 2 points higher than the previous. Clicking an option changes the font size of the text in the text box.

D. (9CLONE2.FRM)

This project creates at run time a collection of objects, namely 16 clones of Text1. They are neatly arranged in four rows and four columns; these are done by code. When a text box is clicked, a corresponding QBColor color appears. For example, clicking the first box (top left) leads to color 0 (the box's background becomes black) and clicking the second (row 1, column 2) shows blue (1). Figure 9.52 the next to the last box displayed in yellow.

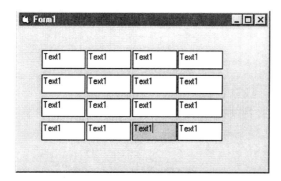

Figure 9.52   Clones and colors

F. (9colPHONES1.FRM)

This project (Figure 9.53) lets the user enter a name in the left text box to show a corresponding phone number in the right text box. It should behave as follows:

1. A form-level declaration creates a collection object.

2. A Form_Load procedure adds half a dozen members to the collection, using the Item and Key named arguments.

3. When the user types a name in the left text box and presses Enter, the Show button's Click procedure is called. This procedure uses the supplied text string to find a corresponding phone number and show it in the right text box.

4. If the supplied name does not match any existing member in the collection, an error trap should display a message box with a proper message.

5. When the user presses Esc, the Clear button's click procedure is called to clear the two text boxes and the focus goes back to the left text box for another entry.

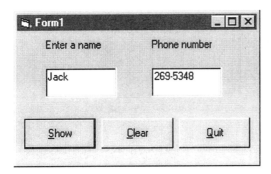

Figure 9.53   Typing a key to retrieve data in a collection

G. (9colPHONES2.FRM)

Modify the previous project by using a list box to display all the names (Figure 9.54). When a name is clicked, its corresponding phone number appears in the text box. (The names need to be separately loaded to the list box from the Form_Load procedure.)

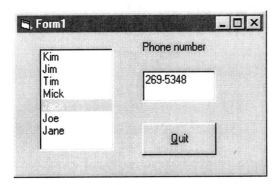

Figure 9.54   Clicking a key name to retrieve data from a collection

H. (9SORT2.FRM)

Modify 9SORTSCTRUCT.FRM (Figure 9.35) as follows:

1. Replace the structure array with a two-dimensional local array. Remove the standard module.

2. Assign the same elements to this new array.

3. In the calling statement, pass the array to the Sort procedure, plus an optional second argument specifying which column (field) to sort by.

Modify the Sort procedure as follows:

1. Make the procedure accept an optional second argument. (Use the **Optional** keyword in the header)

2. If the second argument is missing, sorting is done by the first field. (Use the **IsMissing** function to determine whether this argument is missing.)

3. If an acceptable column number (0-2) is passed, sorting is done by that column.

4. If an unacceptable column number is passed, a message appears and no sorting is done.

Figure 9.55 shows the array sorted by column 0, which is passed from the calling statement.

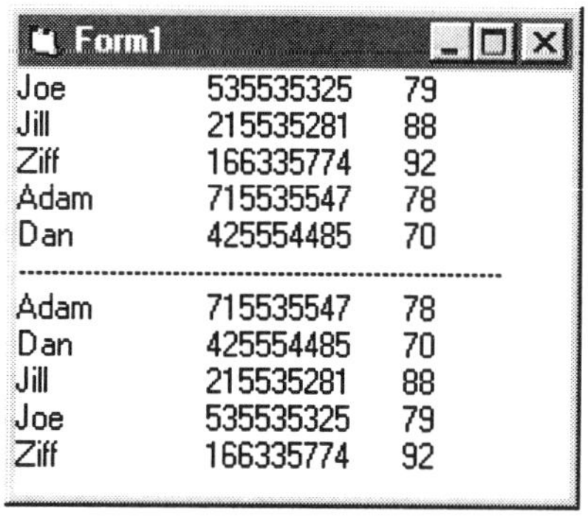

Figure 9.55   Sorting by the first column

I. (9ADD.FRM)

This program is a modified version of the one found at the end of Chapter 4. The user interface is shown in Figure 9.56; it includes three new text boxes at the right side, txtSorted, txtMean, and txtMedian. The program should behave as explained in Chapter 4, plus the following:

1. The entered numbers are displayed in txtSorted in sorted order.

2. The mean (average) of all the numbers is shown in txtMean.

3 The median (middle) of all the numbers appears in txtMedian.

4. When Clear is clicked, all the text box displays are cleared.

5. When Print is clicked, the txtList (middle), txtSum, txtMean, and txtMedian contents are printed, each preceded by a proper label text.

6. Use a dynamic array that can accommodate any number of entries.

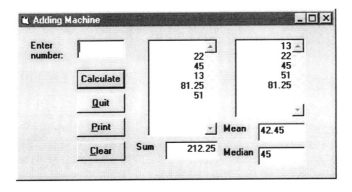

Figure 9.56   Tabulating numbers

FUN AND GAME

A. (RADAR.FRM)

This program simulates a radar screen with a hand sweeping counterclockwise (Figure 9.57). Each time a circle is completed, a new random color is generated. The new color covers up the old color as the hand continues its endless motion.

```
Private Sub Form_Click()
    Dim I As Single
    Dim Pi As Single
    Dim X As Single
    Dim Y As Single

    Pi = 4 * Atn(1)
    X = ScaleWidth / 2          'center
    Y = ScaleHeight / 2
    FillStyle = 0               'solid

    Do        'infinite loop
        Randomize                   'new random seed
        FillColor = RGB(Rnd * 256, Rnd * 256, Rnd * 256)
            'random fill color
        For I = 0 To 2 * Pi Step 0.02
            Circle (X, Y), Y, , -2 * Pi, -I
                'widening wedge with rnd color
        DoEvents            'allow break
        Next I
    Loop
End Sub
```

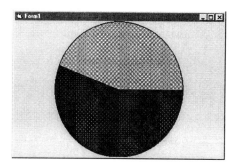

Figure 9.57   Radar screen

B. (COLORPANEL.FRM)

This program shows a circle with twelve pie slices (Figure 9.58), each showing a randomly generated color. There is a timer controlling the continuous counterclockwise motion. The timer is set at 100 Interval value, which is 1/10 of a second. When a panel is displayed, there is a pause of 1/10 of a second. Then the next panel is displayed. This continues indefinitely. You can set the timer's Interval value higher to slow down the motion.

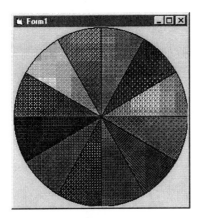

Figure 9.58   Color panels

```
Private Sub Form_Click()
    Dim Pi As Single
    Dim I As Single
    Dim StepVal As Single

    Width = ScaleHeight      'set perfect square
    Width = 2 * ScaleHeight - ScaleWidth
    Scale (0, 0)-(1, 1)
    Randomize        'get new random seed
    Pi = 4 * Atn(1)
    FillStyle = 0          'solid fill
    StepVal = Pi / 6      'number of slices
    Do
        DoEvents      'allow break
        For I = 0.00001 To 2 * Pi - StepVal Step StepVal
                'full circle, counterclockwise
            FillColor = RGB(Rnd * 255, Rnd * 255, _
            Rnd * 255)
                'random fill color for each slice
            If I + StepVal >= 2 * Pi - StepVal Then
                I = I - 0.001    'last slice
            End If
            Circle (0.5, 0.5), 0.5, , -I, -(I + StepVal)
            Timer1.Interval = 100
                'set timer interval, 1/10 sec
            Timer1_Timer     'call timer event procedure
        Next I
    Loop     'infinite loop
End Sub

Private Sub Timer1_Timer()
    Static Turn As Integer
    Turn = Turn + 1
    Do While DoEvents()
        If Turn Mod 2 Then Exit Do
```

```
    Loop      'loop in 1 timer cycle
    Timer1.Interval = 0      'disable timer
End Sub
```

Chapter 10
File and Data Management

TOPICS

KEY TERMS

Combo box   A control that combines a list (display) box at the bottom and a text (edit) box at the top. To select an item in the list, the user can type text in the edit box or click a displayed item.

Common dialog control   A custom control that provides uniform dialog boxes for five common tasks: opening a file, saving a file, printing text, selecting a color, and selecting a font.

Directory list box   A control that displays all the available directories. At run time, the user can double-click any directory to make it current.

Drive list box   A control that displays all the available disk drives. At run time, the user can click a displayed drive letter to change to that drive.

File list box   A control that displays a list of file names matching the attributes set in the Pattern property.

List box   A control that displays at run time a list of items from which the user can make one or more selections.

Random-access file   A file consisting of uniform records. All the records have the same length and number of fields. All the comparable fields have the same length and data type. Such a file allows manipulation of individual records—unlike an unstructured sequential file.

Sequential file   Disk data that is saved and read in sequential order. Like a piece of music or movie saved to a cassette tape, a sequential file is saved to disk or read from it one byte after another in a prearranged order.

This chapter is all about permanent data, the information you want Visual Basic to save, read, and manipulate. The data could range from well defined records (such as an employee payroll) to text and numbers without any regularity.

Visual Basic provides many tools to manage data. You can use them to create and manipulate different kinds of files. These include five standard controls shown in the Toolbox (list box, combo box, drive list box, file list box, and directory list box), plus a custom control called common dialog control. There are also numerous statements that can be used to maneuver files. We start with the controls.

LIST BOX

List boxes and combo boxes are similar in major ways and different in minor ways. We will first discuss list boxes in detail. What you learn in this section will mostly apply to combo boxes discussed in another section below

A **list box** displays at run time a list of items from which the user can make one or more selections. To display such a list and respond to a user selection, you need to understand quite a few rules. We will first explain the important rules, and then provide some concrete examples later.

A list box has the default Name property of List1 for the first, List2 for the second, and so on. This name appears at the top left corner of the box at design time but not run time. A list box has no Caption property. There is a Text property, but it is available only at run time.

A list box has these unique properties at design time:

Columns	0 (default)
	n
IntegralHeight	True (default)
	False
MultiSelect	0 - None (default)
	1 - Simple
	2 - Extended
Sorted	True
	False (default)
Style	0 - Standard (default)
	1 - Checkbox

IntegralHeight determines whether a large item (with a large font) is completely displayed or partially displayed. The default is to display complete items. So if there is no room to display another item, it's not displayed—rather than partially displayed.

The default 0 value for **Columns** means that all the items are displayed vertically. If there is not enough room to show all the available items, a vertical scroll bar appears. You can then scroll the items up and down. But if the width of the box is not enough to display wider items, there is nothing the user can do at run time since there is no horizontal scrolling and the box borders cannot be altered.

If you change 0 to another value, the items will be displayed in the specified number of snaking columns. A horizontal scroll bar appears if there is not enough space to display all the available items. If the items cannot be displayed in one column, they flow from one column to the next and from left to right. If the width of the box is not enough to display the specified columns, different columns overlap each other and the resulting text may not be legible.

If **MultiSelect** is 0, the default, the user can select only one item at a time. If another item is selected, the previous one is deselected. If you change 0 to 1, multiple items can be selected. The user can click each item to toggle between selecting or deselecting it. You can also select/deselect an item by pressing the space bar on the keyboard.

If MultiSelect is changed to 2, you can hold down the Shift key and move a cursor key (or the mouse pointer) to select a block of items, just like the way you select multiple lines of text in the Code window. You can also hold down Ctrl to select another item without deselecting the previous block(s). To select another block, hold down the Ctrl+Shift key combination and move the cursor.

The **Sorted** property is set to False by default. That means the items are displayed in the order they are entered. If this property is set to True, the items are displayed in alphabetic order. This property must be set at design time. Trying to set it at run time will lead to an error.

Numbers in a list box are sorted according to their ASCII values. So 11 will be placed before 9. To display numbers sorted according to their numeric values, use a sorting algorithm explained in Chapter 9 and add them to a list box whose Sorted property must be False.

When **Style** is set to 1 - Checkbox, a check box appears on the left of each item in the list box. Clicking an item (or pressing the spacebar when an item is highlighted) toggles between selecting and deselecting it. Multiple items can be selected (checked) one at a time.

Changing Style to 1 - Checkbox will automatically change MultiSelect to 0 - None. In this setting, you are not permitted to change MultiSelect to another option. If you try, Figure 10.1 will show up.

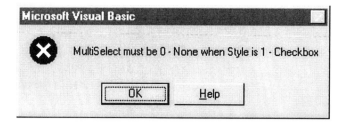

Figure 10.1   Changing MultiSelect to 1 or 2 when Style is 1

At run time, a list box has these useful properties:

ItemData	An array of long integers; elements correspond to those in the List array.
List	A string array containing all the items in a list box.
ListCount	An integer representing the total count of the items.

ListIndex	An integer representing the index value of the selected item.
NewIndex	Specifies the position to insert an item at run time.
Selected	Boolean True or False indicating whether an item is selected.
Text	A text string representing the selected item's name, the same as List(ListIndex); read-only at both design time and run time; ".Text" is optional in code.
TopIndex	Returns the index value of the topmost item or scrolls to the top of the list box the item matching the specified index value; run time only.

A list box has the following important methods:

AddItem	Adds a specific item to the list box.
RemoveItem	Removes a specific item from the list box.
Refresh	Updates the listed items after a change.
Clear	Removes all the items from the list box.

A list box has more than a dozen events, including the most common **Click** and **DblClick**. You can add procedure code to respond to these events. There is the **Scroll** event, which is triggered whenever the scroll box in the scroll bar is moved by whatever means. This behavior applies to all the similar controls discussed later in this chapter.

A list box has the unique **ItemCheck** event. It's triggered if the style is set to 1 - Checkbox and the user clicks a displayed check box at run time. Clicking a check box also triggers the Click event, which follows the ItemCheck event. Clicking a displayed item outside of the check box triggers only the Click event (but if you click it a another time, you'll also trigger the ItemCheck event). If the style is 0 - Standard, there is no check box to click, and any existing ItemCheck event is ignored.

The procedures below show a concrete example involving many of the terms discussed so far. The Form_Load procedure uses AddItem to add four items to the list box shown in Figure 10.2.

```
Private Sub Form_Load ()
    List1.AddItem "beta"
    List1.AddItem "gamma"
    List1.AddItem "delta"
    List1.AddItem "alpha"
End Sub

Private Sub List1_Click ()
    Print List1.TopIndex,      'show topmost index
    Print List1.ListIndex,     'index of selected item
    Print List1.ListCount,     'total number of items
```

```
        Print List1.Text,      'selected item; .Text optional
        Print List1.List(List1.ListIndex),    'same as above
        Print List1.Selected(0)
            'True if 1st item selected, False if not
End Sub
```

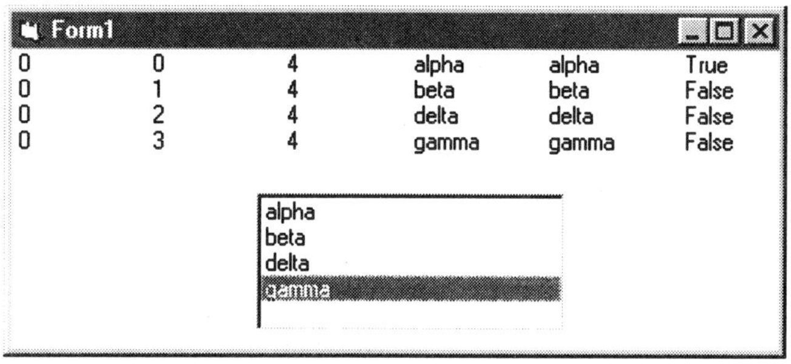

Figure 10.2   After clicking "alpha" and "delta"

We added items in a haphazard way. The items in the list box appear in alphabetic order because its Sorted property was set to True at design time. The four lines at the top of Figure 10.2 are the result of clicking each item in the list box one by one. Notice that the returned values (such as ListIndex) are related to the items displayed on the screen, not necessarily the same as those in the source code.

You can add an index value after AddItem to specify the position of the item in the list box. Here is an example:

```
    List1.AddItem "alpha", 0
```

This will place this item at the top; 0 is the first index value, 1 the second, and so on. This method takes precedence over the Sorted property when it is set to True. The above statement will place "alpha" before "ace" (if it exists) even though the latter is normally placed before the former; the existing first item will be pushed down to the second. If you try to insert an item with an improper index value, an error will occur.

You can also use the **List** property to add items. In the following example, the item will be inserted at the top. If there is already an existing item matching the index value (0), it will be replaced, not pushed downward. If you try to insert an item with an improper index value, an error will occur just as doing it with AddItem.

```
List1.List(0) = "alpha"
```

You can use the **RemoveItem** method to remove from the list box an item of the specified index value. It expects as its argument a number that is an index value, similar to the way AddItem can use an index value to place an item in a specific position. Consider the following examples:

```
List1.RemoveItem 0        'remove the first in the list box
List1.RemoveItem List1.ListIndex    'remove the selected
```

The first example removes a fixed item, in our example, the first of the displayed items. The second removes the one selected by the user. If you want to let the user remove selected items, put this statement in a command button's Click procedure. The user can then select an item and click the command button to remove it. If you want to let the user clear everything in a list box, use this method:

```
List1.Clear
```

The **TopIndex** property can be used at run time to designate the item to be displayed at the top of the list box; the portion above it is scrolled beyond view. In the demonstration below, each time the Scroll button is clicked, the displayed items scroll up by five; after the end is reached, the top portion is displayed again. The Top button simply scrolls the display to the top.

Figure 10.3 shows the list box displaying numbers in three columns because the Columns property was set to 3 at design time. Notice that a horizontal (rather than vertical) scroll bar automatically appears when there are undisplayed items.

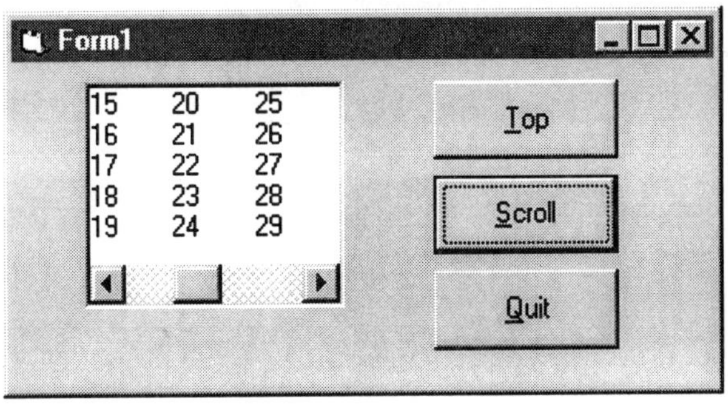

Figure 10.3   3-column list box and TopIndex property

```
Private Sub Form_Load()
    Dim I As Integer

    For I = 0 To 50        'fill box with 0-50
        List1.AddItem I
    Next I
End Sub

Private Sub cmdScroll_Click()
    Static Temp As Integer

    Temp = Temp + 5
    If Temp >= List1.ListCount Then
        Temp = 0    'after end, go to top
        Beep
    End If
    List1.TopIndex = Temp   'scroll up by 5
End Sub

Private Sub cmdTop_Click()
    List1.TopIndex = 0         'goto top
End Sub
```

Our next application has the user interface shown in Figure 10.4. The list box's Sorted property is set to True and the text box's font size is change to 20.

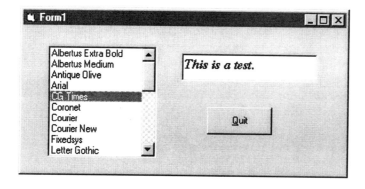

Figure 10.4   Clicking a font name to show the result

```
Private Sub Form_Load ()
    Dim I As Integer

    For I = 0 To Screen.FontCount - 1
        List1.AddItem Screen.Fonts(i)
            'show all fonts in list box 1
    Next I
End Sub
```

```
Private Sub List1_Click ()
    With Text1
        .FontName = List1.Text
        .FontSize = 12
        .Text = "This is a test."
    End With
End Sub
```

The Form_Load procedure shown above loads all the available screen fonts and displays them in the list box. When you click one of them, the List1_Click procedure selects that font and uses it to display the text. As you click a new name, the text changes to reflect the new font.

Our next application is slightly modified from the previous. It requires two list boxes and two command buttons (Figure 10.5). The first list box has the Sorted property set to True. The procedures are shown below.

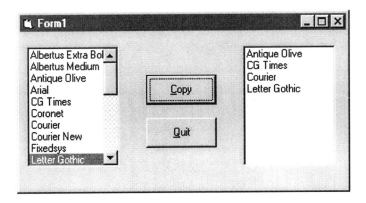

Figure 10.5   Copying from one list box to another

```
Private Sub Form_Load ()
    Dim I As Integer

    For I = 0 To Screen.FontCount - 1
        List1.AddItem Screen.Fonts(I)
    Next I
End Sub

Private Sub cmdCopy_Click ()
    Dim I As Integer

    For I = 0 To List1.ListCount - 1
        If List1.Selected(I) Then
            List2.AddItem List1.List(I)
```

```
            Exit For      'exit when match found
        End If
    Next I
End Sub
```

The Form_Load procedure loads and displays the available fonts in the first list box. You can now click a name and then click the Copy button to copy it to the second list box. As you add more items than the box can display, a vertical scroll bar will appear.

Now, as an experiment, change List1's **MultiSelect** property from 0 to 1 and run the program again. You can now select multiple items and toggle between selecting and deselecting. Change the MultiSelect property to 2 and see how things change.

A list box has the **List** and **ItemData** properties. These were available before VB4 only at run time; List was also read-only to read the items added with the AddItem method. They are now available at design time as well. The Properties window shows (List) as the default value for both properties. When you click the down arrow in the Settings box, a rectangular box will pop up for you to make entries. You can make multicolumn and multiline entries here. If you open either List or ItemData box and enter nothing, the default List1 text will disappear from the list box, although the (List1) notation remains in the Properties window.

As you enter List items, a matching number of 0's will also be automatically entered in the ItemData entry box in the Properties window. For example, if you enter five lines in the List box, you can go to the ItemData box and five 0's will be there (this also happens if you use AddItem at run time). You can change these to sequential numbers so that each will be unique and can be used to identify the corresponding item in the List box. Then you can use statements like below to pull out the (first) matching pair:

```
Print List1.List(0)
Print List1.ItemData(0)
```

You can also use code to add matching pairs to both List and ItemData. Our demonstration project (Figure 10.6) shows a list of names in the list box. You can click a name to display (in the label) the ListIndex value, the name (List), and its companion ItemData (Social Security number).

In the code below, we also use the run-time **NewIndex** property to keep track of the position where each item is inserted in the list box. If the list box's Sorted property is set to True, this is necessary to maintain an accurate order.

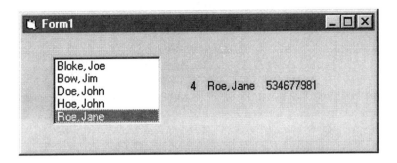

Figure 10.6   **Showing List, ItemData, and New Index**

```
Private Sub Form_Load()
    List1.AddItem "Doe, John"
    List1.ItemData(List1.NewIndex) = 543678990
    List1.AddItem "Bloke, Joe"
    List1.ItemData(List1.NewIndex) = 243648961
    List1.AddItem "Hoe, John"
    List1.ItemData(List1.NewIndex) = 443578697
    List1.AddItem "Roe, Jane"
    List1.ItemData(List1.NewIndex) = 534677981
    List1.AddItem "Bow, Jim"
    List1.ItemData(List1.NewIndex) = 143658810
End Sub

Private Sub List1_Click()
    Dim strA As String
    Dim strB As String
    Dim strC As String

    strA = List1.ListIndex
    strB = List1.List(List1.ListIndex)
    strC = List1.ItemData(List1.ListIndex)
    Label1.Caption = strA & "    " & strB & "    " & strC
End Sub
```

Besides the **AddItem** method, you can use the **List** property at run time to add items to the list in a list box. Our first line in the preceding procedure can be replaced by the line below. To change other comparable lines, adjust the index number accordingly.

```
List1.List(0) = "Doe, John"
```

If you use ListIndex property instead of a fixed index value in this situation, each subsequent item will replace the previous, resulting in only the last item being available. If you have entries made at design time, an error may also occur.

Using AddItem can avoid these problems because it will add to the bottom of existing entries and automatically adjust the ListIndex value.

If you want to tie multiple items together, you need something more complex than the ItemData property alone. Our next demonstration project tries to keep four items (a name and three test scores) in sync. It has the user interface shown in Figure 10.7. It lets you click a name in the list box, and the five text boxes will show three test scores, their total, and the average. The list box's Sorted property is set to True at design time so that the names will appear in alphabetic order even though they are added haphazardly in the procedure.

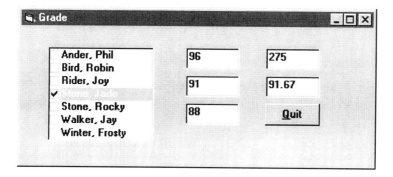

Figure 10.7   Clicking a name to show test scores

The user interface's objects have their properties changed as shown below:

Object	Property	Value
List1	Name	lstScores
	Style	1 - Checkbox
Text1	Name	txtTest1
Text2	Name	txtTest2
Text3	Name	txtTest3
Text4	Name	txtTotal
Text5	Name	txtAvg
Command1	Name	cmdQuit

(10GRADE1.FRM)

```
Private Sub Form_Load ()        --Listing 1--
    lstScores.AddItem "Winter, Frosty"
    lstScores.AddItem "Stone, Rocky"
    lstScores.AddItem "Walker, Jay"
```

```
        lstScores.AddItem "Ander, Phil"
        lstScores.AddItem "Rider, Joy"
        lstScores.AddItem "Stone, Jade"
        lstScores.AddItem "Bird, Robin"
End Sub

Private Sub lstScores_Click()
    Select Case lstScores.Text    'selected in list box
    Case "Ander, Phil"  'test scores
        txtTest1.Text = 70
        txtTest2.Text = 78
        txtTest3.Text = 85
    Case "Bird, Robin"
        txtTest1.Text = 69
        txtTest2.Text = 76
        txtTest3.Text = 89
    Case "Rider, Joy"
        txtTest1.Text = 89
        txtTest2.Text = 87
        txtTest3.Text = 90
    Case "Walker, Jay"
        txtTest1.Text = 97
        txtTest2.Text = 89
        txtTest3.Text = 90
    Case "Stone, Jade"
        txtTest1.Text = 96
        txtTest2.Text = 91
        txtTest3.Text = 88
    Case "Stone, Rocky"
        txtTest1.Text = 67
        txtTest2.Text = 59
        txtTest3.Text = 68
    Case "Winter, Frosty"
        txtTest1.Text = 59
        txtTest2.Text = 68
        txtTest3.Text = 87
    End Select

    txtTotal.Text = Val(txtTest1.Text) + _
    Val(txtTest2.Text) + Val(txtTest3.Text)
    txtAvg.Text = Format(txtTotal.Text / 3, "##.00")
End Sub

Private Sub cmdQuit_Click()
    End
End Sub
```

When the program runs, the Form_Load procedure automatically adds the items to the list box. When you click a displayed item, the lstScores_Click procedure sends the numbers to the text boxes. You can also check a check box to do the same thing.

LIST BOX AND TEXT BOX

A list box and a text box are similar in some ways but different in others. Each can do things the other cannot. You can combine them to do things which each is unable to do separately.

Although a list box's display resembles that of a text box, there is one major difference. Each line in a list box is distinct and can easily be isolated. On the other hand, lines in a text box are lumped together and cannot be easily isolated. With each line separated from the next only by Chr(13) and Chr(10), a text box's contents require a great deal of string functions and lengthy formulas to isolate a particular line. If you intend to maneuver each individual displayed line, use a list box rather than a text box to output or display data.

The user interface shown in Figure 10.8 resembles the one in Chapter 4 when we discussed the text box control. There we demonstrated how you can display multiple lines in a text box. Here we demonstrate how you can add multiple lines to a list box and maneuver each displayed item. The two Click procedures for the list box and the Enter command button are shown below.

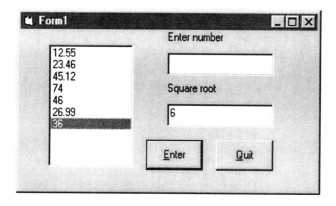

Figure 10.8   Maneuvering a list-box item

```
Private Sub cmdEnter_Click ()
    List1.AddItem Text1.Text 'add each new entry to List1
    Text1.Text = ""           'clear Text1
End Sub

Private Sub List1_Click ()
    Text2.Text = List1.Text ^ (1 / 2)
        'square root value
```

```
End Sub
```

At run time, the focus goes to Text1 because its TabIndex property is set to 0. When you type a number and press Enter, it is automatically added to the bottom of List1's existing numbers. This happens because the Enter button's **Default** property was set to True at design time.

When you click a number displayed in List1, its square-root value appears in Text2. Clicking an item displayed in List1 triggers the List1_Click procedure. The selected number's square-root value is then assigned to Text2.

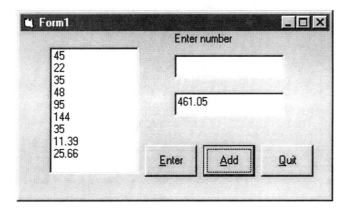

Figure 10.9   Adding list-box items

We can modify our user interface to the one shown in Figure 10.9. The new Add command button's Click procedure is shown below.

```
Private Sub cmdAdd_Click ()
    Dim I As Integer
    Dim Temp As Single

    For I = 0 To List1.ListCount - 1
        Temp = Temp + Val(List1.List(I))
            'add up all items in List1
    Next I
    Text2.Text = Temp    'show total in Text2
End Sub
```

After you enter some numbers in List1, clicking Add will display the sum in Text2. You can also add more numbers and click Add another time to display the new sum.

The items displayed in a list box cannot be altered from the display itself. On the other hand, you can copy an item to a text box where you can edit the contents. Then you can replace the original version with the edited one.

Figure 10.10 shows an interface with a list box (left), a label (top middle), two text boxes, and three command buttons. At the beginning, we can enter items in the text boxes and then click Add to add to the list box. When you want to change an item in the list box, click it to copy it to the two text boxes. Clicking Replace replaces the old version with the new one.

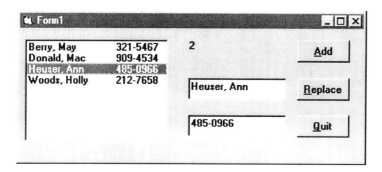

Figure 10.10   Using a text box to edit list-box items

The objects' properties are changed as shown below.

Object	Property	Value
List1	Name	lstItems
	Sorted	True
Label1	Name	lblIndex
Text1	Name	txtName
Text2	Name	txtPhone
Command1	Name	cmdAdd
Command2	Name	cmdReplace
Command3	Name	cmdQuit

To make the displayed items appear in two columns, we embed a Tab character between the two original text-box items. In the lblItems_Click procedure shown below, we use some string functions to separate the selected item into two parts, one before the Tab character and one after it. In the cmdReplace_Click procedure, we use the number displayed in lblIndex to identify the number of the record being edited. After this record is removed, the edited one is added to the list box.

(10LISTX.FRM)
```
Private Sub cmdAdd_click()
    'add an entry to the list box
    lstItems.AddItem txtName.Text & _
    vbTab & txtPhone.Text
        'add to lstItems a Tab between
        'txtName and txtPhone
    txtName.Text = ""          'clear
    txtPhone.Text = ""
End Sub

Private Sub cmdReplace_Click()
    'replace the selected item with revised one
    Dim CurList As Integer

    CurList = Val(lblIndex.Caption) 'get current item #
    lstItems.RemoveItem CurList      'remove current item
    cmdAdd_click              'call proc to add a new one
End Sub

Private Sub lstItems_Click()
    'copy clicked item to text boxes
    Dim StrLen As Integer
    Dim TabPos As Integer

    StrLen = Len(lstItems.Text)  'get length of string
    TabPos = InStr(lstItems, vbTab)  'get pos of Tab
    txtName.Text = Left(lstItems, TabPos - 1)
        'get left of Tab
    txtPhone.Text = Right(lstItems, StrLen - TabPos)
        'get right of Tab
    lblIndex.Caption = lstItems.ListIndex
        'show item #
End Sub

Private Sub cmdQuit_Click()
    End
End Sub
```

After you have entered and revised items in a list box, you may want to save them for future use. The Sequential Files section below will explain how to do that.

 ## TIP: Design-Time List Property

A list (and combo) box has a List property. This is a run-time read-only property in VB3; in VB4/5 it is available at design time as well. It is comparable to the Text property in a text box, as explained in Chapter 4. You can use it to enter multicolumn and multiline text at design time. The entries here will also be saved to an **FRX** file, together with any multiline text-box entries made at design time.

The List items entered at design time appear in the list box at both design time and run time. If the Sorted property is False, the order entered at design time remains the same at run time. Changing Sorted to True doesn't immediately affect the order in the list box or entry box. But running the program will change the items to the sorted order in both places.

If you use the AddItem method to add items to a list box, the new items will be added at the bottom of the existing entries made at design time—if Sorted is False. If Sorted is True, then the two groups will be mixed and the sorted order will appear in the list box. Of course, the items added with AddItem appear only at run time; they don't show up in the entry box, nor are they saved to the corresponding FRX file.

COMBO BOX

A **combo box** combines a list (display) box at the bottom and a text (edit) box at the top. It's commonly used to replace a list box when an interface is crowded because a combo box takes much less room. The user can open up a list of items, make a selection, and then close up the box again. To select an item in the list, the user can type text in the edit box or click a displayed item after clicking the down arrow to open up the list. In addition to those properties shared with a list box, it has this unique property:

Style	0 - Dropdown Combo (default)
	1 - Simple Combo
	2 - Dropdown List

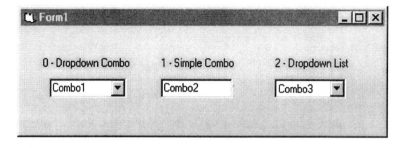

Figure 10.11   The combo box control's three styles

Figure 10.11 shows the combo box control's three different styles at design time. (These cannot be set at run time.) In all the three styles, a combo box can be stretched horizontally. But only style 1 allows you to stretch vertically. No matter how you stretch styles 0 and 2 vertically, they always bounce back. After you choose style 1 and vertically stretch a combo box, choosing style 0 or 2 will reduce the box to the default one-line size.

Figure 10.12 shows the contrast among the three styles at run time. When the pointer moves to the edit box in styles 0 and 1, it changes to an I beam. You can type and edit text here. If you press up, down, PgUp, or PgDn keys, the display scrolls vertically. If you press left or right arrow keys, the cursor moves in the edit box. Home and End move the cursor in the edit box only.

In style 0, when the list box is open (click the down arrow to do that), typing one or more letters and pressing Enter (or clicking the down arrow) displays the matching item (if any) in the edit box and closes the list box. The displayed item, however, is not selected. Only clicking an item in the list box leads to a selection. If the list box is not open or if no match is found, entering text in the edit box produces no effect.

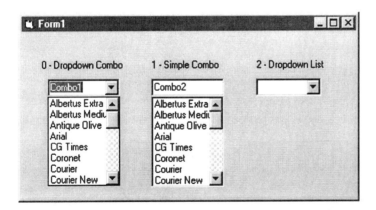

Figure 10.12   Three combo box styles at run time

In style 1, if the combo box is vertically stretched so that it can display at least two lines of text, you can type a letter in the edit box to control the list box display. The first matching item will appear at the top of the list box. This behavior is similar to the way you type letters to search for an online help topic. No item is selected until you click one in the list box. If the combo box is not vertically stretched and can display only one line of text, you can click the box to move the focus there. Then press an up or down arrow key from the keyboard to display a new item in the box. Each time a new item appears, it is considered selected.

In style 2, a combo box behaves like a shrunken list box. The top portion (text box) is disabled; you cannot enter text here. The down arrow lets you open up the displayed items. Upon clicking one, it is selected and the box closes again. From the keyboard, you can tab to the combo box to give it the focus; you can then press an up or down arrow key from the keyboard to display (and select) each subsequent item. The left arrow key is the same as the up arrow key and the down arrow key the same as the right arrow key; they all move to another item. Home and End moves the cursor respectively to the first and last item. If you want to drop down the list, hold down Alt and press the down arrow key; Alt+up arrow key closes the box.

The display area in style 1 is always open—if you have vertically stretched the combo box at design time. On the other hand, styles 0 and 2 close the displayed area when they lose the focus. This is useful if the screen space is crowded.

You can use the List property at design time to make entries in a combo box. When Style is 1, the entries will immediately appear in a combo box, just as they do in a list box.

The following list box properties are also available for a combo box:

    IntegralHeight
    ItemData
    List
    ListCount
    ListIndex
    Sorted
    Text

The only difference is that a combo box's Text property is available at both design time and run time (see the TIP below); it is available for a list box only at run time.

A combo box does not have these list box properties:

    MultiSelect
    Selected

You can select only one item from a combo box. That being the case, there is no need to use Selected to see whether multiple items are selected. As in a list box, you can use either of the following properties to designate a selected item:

```
Combo1.Text
Combo1.List(Combo1.ListIndex)
```

Both return the name of the selected item. In the first case, you can simply use Combo1 and omit the Text part.

A combo box has the **Locked** property, which is shared by a text box but not by a list box. When it's set to True, you cannot make a run-time selection from the displayed list. You can drop down the list and use the mouse to scroll the list, but the control won't respond to typing or clicking.

A combo box and a list box share the same methods and similar events. One exception is that a combo box can respond to a Change event (when the Text property is changed; see the TIP below), which a list box cannot.

We can easily change our application in Figure 10.5 by changing all List1 to Combo1 and List2 to Combo2. The cmdCopy_Click procedure requires only this line:

```
Combo2.AddItem Combo1.Text
```

Since only one item can be selected in a combo box, only one item will be added to Combo2. Also, Since Selected is not a property, we can no longer use it here.

TIP: A Combo Box's Text Property

A combo box has the **Text** property. It's available for styles 0 and 1 at both design time and run time. In these two styles, a combo box behaves like a text box. The Text property set at design time or run time appears at the beginning (edit box) of the combo box. It cannot be selected at run time because it is not added by the AddItem statement.

In style 2, a combo box behaves like a list box. At both design time and run time, the Text property reflects the Name property. Here you are not allowed to manipulate the Text property separately. You cannot edit the value at design time; the keyboard is disabled. If you try to erase its value at design time, Figure 10.13 appears. At run time, if you assign a value that matches an item in the list, it will be selected; otherwise, a similar error message will appear. This does not happen in style 0 or 1.

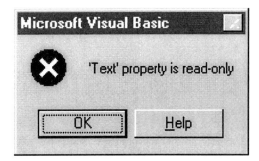

Figure 10.13   Changing the Text property in combo style 2

So, if you want to display a heading in a combo box that is not part of the items to be selected by the user, choose style 0 or 1 and assign a text string to the Text property at design time or run time.

Once the user selects an item from a combo box (or a list box), the name of this item is assigned to the Text property. So you can use Combo1.Text (the extension is optional) to read the selection. The selected item also replaces your initial text string in the edit box at the top.

In style 0 or 1, you can select a combo box's text displayed at the top and pop up a shortcut menu as you can with a text box.

A combo box has both **Click** and **Change** events (a list box has Click and ItemCheck). The former is triggered when the user clicks an item in the list. It also occurs when the box has the focus and the user presses an up or down arrow keyboard key. This changes a selection and triggers the Click event. The Change event occurs when the user types something in the text (top) box. Each keystroke triggers the Change event once.

Two properties can also trigger these events at run time. The **Text** property triggers the Change event, and the **ListIndex** property does the same to the Click event. So if you assign a new value (not the same value) to the Text property, this action will execute an existing Change procedure. If you assign a new value to the ListIndex property, the action will execute the Click procedure (if any).

Assigning a Text property by code causes the text to enter the top text box. This may cause problem. If the text matches one of the existing items (names), this item is displayed in the text box. If there is no match, the text entered by code appears in the text box without an error when the combo box's Style is 0 or 1. If the Style is 2, an error will occur.

There is still one more twist. Changing the Text property does not scroll the internal list's display, but changing the ListIndex property does. After changing the Text property and thus showing the matching item in the text box, pressing an up or down arrow key when the combo box has the focus always leads to the first item in the list, not the next. Since ListIndex scrolls the list, doing the same will lead to the next item in the list.

If you are totally confused by the above discussion, try the following demonstration. After running it, try different things to see what triggers what. The copious comments in the code may help you out. Figure 10.14 is the result of clicking the two top command buttons.

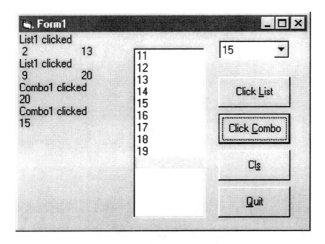

Figure 10.14   Demonstrating combo box events and properties

(10ComboDemo.Frm)

```
Private Sub Form_Load()
    Dim I As Integer
    For I = 11 To 20
        List1.AddItem I
        Combo1.AddItem I
    Next I
End Sub

Private Sub cmdList_Click()
    List1.ListIndex = 2    'select 3rd item from top
    'error if outside of index range
```

```
                'triggers List1_Click if selection is changed
            List1.Text = 20
            'selects item matching "20"
            'no selection if there is no match
            'triggers List1_Click regardless of match
        End Sub

        Private Sub List1_Click()
            Print "List1 clicked"        'to prove triggered
            Print List1.ListIndex, List1.Text
            'print selected index and item
            'or Print List1.List(List1.ListIndex)
        End Sub

        Private Sub cmdCombo_Click()
            Combo1.ListIndex = Combo1.ListCount - 1
            'selects an item matching index number, last here
            'error if outside of index range
            'triggers Combo1_Click
            Combo1.Text = 15
            'enters a item in top of combo box
            'error if in Style 2 (Dropdown List)
            'and there is no matching item in list
            'if there is match, it's selected
            'triggers Combo1_Change
        End Sub

        Private Sub Combo1_Click()
            Print "Combo1 clicked"        'to prove triggered
            Print Combo1.Text             'print selected item
            'or Combo1.List(Combo1.ListIndex)
        End Sub

        Private Sub Combo1_Change()
            Print "Combo1_Change triggered"
        End Sub

        Private Sub cmdCls_Click()
            Cls       'clears screen display
        End Sub

        Private Sub cmdQuit_Click()
            End
        End Sub
```

DRILL

_____ 1.   This line will return the name of the item selected at run time.
        a.   List1.List(List1.ListIndex)
        b.   List1.Text
        c.   List1.ListIndex

d. both a and b
e. none of the above

_T_ 2. Both list box and combo box controls have the Style property. True or false?

____ 3. When a check box (in a list box or combo box) is checked/unchecked at run time, the action triggers the Click event and the _____ event.

____ 4. To display a list of items but not allow the user to select one, you need to set a combo box's _____ property to True.

_T_ 5. When a list box or a combo box has the Sorted property set to True, numbers are sorted according to their numeric values. True or false?

____ 6. This property allows you to enter items into a list box or combo box at design time.
a. Text
b. List
c. ListIndex
d. none of the above

____ 7. To let the user select multiple items that are not adjacent to one another, you need to set a list box's MultiSelect property to:
a. 0 - None
b. 1 - Simple
c. 2 - Extended
d. none of the above

____ 8. This event is shared by both list boxes and combo boxes:
a. Change
b. Click
c. ItemCheck
d. all of the above

_T_ 9. If the first item in a list box is selected, List1.Selected(0) returns -1. True or false?

____ 10. The following statement will place "zebra" before "ape" in a list box. True or false?

```
List1.AddItem "zebra", 0
```

PRACTICE

■   1.   Explain the MultiSelect property of a list box.

■   2.   Explain the following statement.

         ```
         List1.AddItem "ace", 1
         ```

■   3.   Explain the List and ItemData properties.

■   4.   Write a Form_Load procedure that will display a list box with the items
          shown in Figure 10.15.

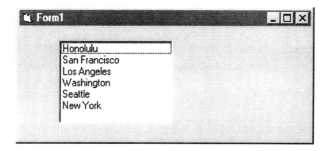

Figure 10.15   A list box with six items

■   5.   Modify the above so that when you click an item, it will be removed
          from the list box.

■   6.   Make necessary changes in question 5 so as to display the cities in
          alphabetic order and the first line shown in Figure 10.16 always on top.

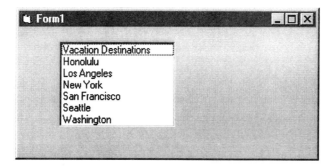

Figure 10.16   A list box with a head line

7. Modify the above so that when the user clicks a city, Text1 (Figure 10.17) will show the chosen city.

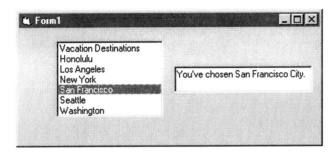

Figure 10.17   Selecting a list box item

8. Modify the above so that if the user clicks the title in the list box, nothing will happen (instead of displaying it in the text box).

9. What does the following property do?

```
List1.List(List1.ListIndex)
```

10. Change the above List1 to Combo1 (Figure 10.18), and make all the necessary changes.

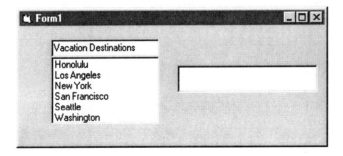

Figure 10.18   Changing a list box to a combo box

11. Modify the above so that when the user clicks an item in the combo box, the text box will show an associated cost, as shown in Figure 10.19. The Form_Load procedure should not be changed; control the output with the Combo1_Click procedure. Use the following numbers:

New York	1200
Seattle	500
San Francisco	700
Los Angeles	750
Washington	900
Honolulu	1500

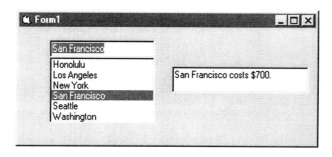

Figure 10.19   Selecting a combo box item

■ 12. Modify the above by entering the List and ItemData properties from the Form_Load procedure. When a displayed List item is clicked, its associated ItemData is used to produce the display in the text box.

■ 13. Explain the Text property of a list box and a combo box.

■ 14. Modify Listing 1 so that a new text box will show a letter grade based on the average score (A for 90%, B for 80%, C for 70%, and D for 60%). Also change the Style property. The result should be as shown in Figure 10.20.

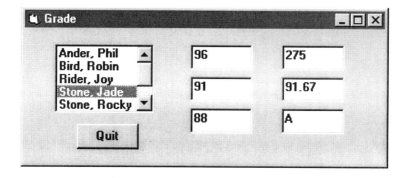

Figure 10.20   Selecting a list box item to show a grade

FILE SYSTEM CONTROLS

Visual Basic offers three standard controls to manage files. These are **drive list box**, **directory list box**, and **file list box**. Lots of functionality has been programmed into them. They are easy to use and can do lots of work with a minimum of programming on your part.

These controls have the default Name property of Drive1, Dir1, and File1. Unlike other objects, there is no need for you to have a second copy of the same control on the same form.

All the three controls have the following run-time properties shared by list and combo boxes discussed earlier:

> **List**
> **ListCount**
> **ListIndex**

They also work the same way as previously explained, with some minor exceptions (see the TIP below).

Drive1 has the **Drive** property to read and display a drive. Dir1 and File1 have the **Path** property to read and display directory paths and file names. They are available at run time only.

Drive1 responds to the **Change** event, which is triggered when a displayed drive letter is clicked. There is no Click event, so you cannot write code for it.

Dir1 responds to **Change** and **Click** events, but not DblClick. Change is triggered when a directory path is double-clicked.

File1 has the following unique properties at both design time and run time; their default values are shown on the right:

> | | |
> |---|---|
> | **Pattern** | *.* |
> | **Archive** | True |
> | **Hidden** | False |
> | **Normal** | True |
> | **ReadOnly** | True |
> | **System** | False |

The default pattern is to show everything; you can use wildcards to change it (you can also set multiple patterns separated by semicolons). Other default properties reflect the DOS DIR command of showing all except hidden and system files. If you set both Hidden and System to True, you will see the hidden files the way you can use the /A switch with the DIR command to show them. (The /A switch is available in DOS version 5 or later.)

File1 also has **MultiSelect** and **Selected** properties. They behave the same way as those found in a list box discussed at the beginning of this chapter.

File1 shares the **TopIndex** property with a list box. This property is shared by only these two controls. It behaves the same way for both. It can be used at run time to scroll displayed items without making a selection.

We are going to build a simple application that will let you read directory contents. First add Drive1 (bottom left), Dir1 (top left), and File1 (right) to the form. As you double-click each icon, the object on the form begins to show its contents. Stretch each and rearrange them as shown in Figure 10.21.

Notice that before you write code the contents of the current drive or folder are already displayed. An open-folder icon indicates an open directory. In our example, D:\ and D:\Visual Basic are open and the others are closed.

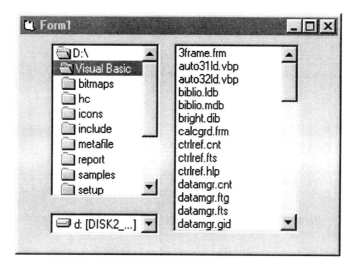

Figure 10.21   Drive1, Dir1, and File1 controls

Now you need to write code for Drive1 and Dir1 so that when one is changed, others will reflect the change and show new results. Double-click each and add one line to each procedure shown below.

```
Private Sub Drive1_Change ()
    Dir1.Path = Drive1.Drive   'assign new drive to Dir1
End Sub

Private Sub Dir1_Change ()
    File1.Path = Dir1.Path     'assign new path to File1
End Sub
```

When you are done, press F5 to run the program. Open the Drive1 combo box and click another drive (make sure the drive is ready for reading files). If a drive has directories, they will appear in the Dir1 box. The current directory's files will also appear in the File1 box. To change a directory, double-click a displayed directory name. Remember: a single click triggers the Change event in Drive1 and a double click activates the Change event in Dir1.

If you click or double-click a displayed file at this time, nothing will happen because we have not written code to respond to these events. We will address this issue in later sections in this chapter.

TIP: ListCount and ListIndex Variations

The ListCount and ListIndex properties are shared by all the five controls we have discussed so far: List1, Combo1, Drive1, Dir1, and File1. They, however, may return different values when used with different controls.

ListCount returns for Drive1 the number of installed drives, for Dir1 the number of subdirectories in the current directory, and for File1 the number of files matching the Pattern property in the current directory. For List1 and Combo1, it returns the number of the items in the list box.

When used with List1, Combo1, and File1, **ListIndex** returns the absolute position of the selected item. For example, if the user selects item number 3, ListIndex returns 2 (0 is the first). The highest ListIndex value is ListCount minus 1 because ListIndex starts with 0, not 1. **If -1 is returned, it means no item is selected**.

When used with Dir1, ListIndex returns -1 for the current directory, -2 for the parent directory, -3 for the next higher directory, and so on. In the current directory structure, 0 represents the first subdirectory, 1 the second, and so on.

For Drive1, ListIndex returns the current drive's index number and ListCount the number of available drives. If you have a hard disk and two floppies and start Visual Basic from drive C, ListIndex returns 2 and ListCount 3.

COMMON DIALOG CONTROL

In addition to the above controls, you can use the **common dialog control** to manage files. This control provides uniform dialog boxes for five common tasks: opening a file, saving a file, printing text, selecting a color, and selecting a font. This control makes it easy for the programmer to handle some common chores and gives the user a familiar interface.

Keep in mind that this is a custom control. If it doesn't appear in the Toolbox, you need to use Project | Components to add it to the Toolbox. When you double-click this tool in the Toolbox, the control appears in the middle of the form. Like the timer control, it cannot be resized. It also becomes invisible at run time. Its default name is CommonDialog1. It has no Caption property.

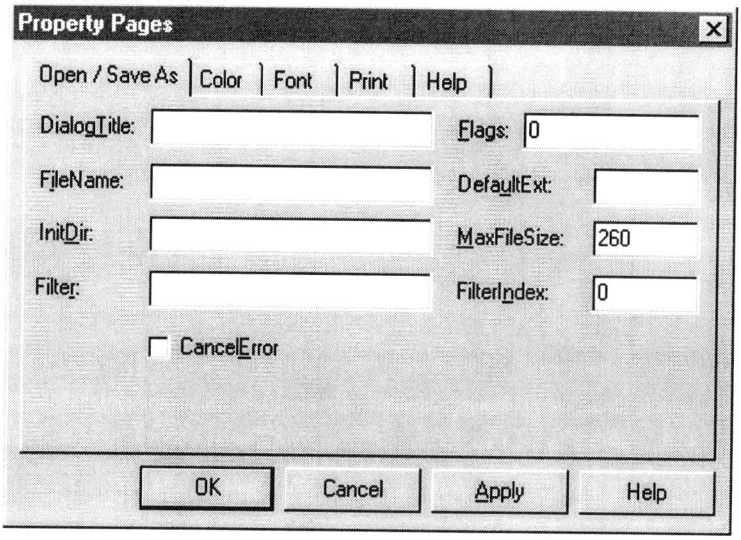

Figure 10.22   The Common Dialog's Property Pages dialog

The control allows you to set many properties at design time. The **Custom** property opens the **Property Pages** dialog box shown in Figure 10.22. You can set a few properties here as well as in the regular Properties window. Either place leads to the same result. Many of these properties can also be set at run time. Most of these items will be explained below.

How can one control handle five tasks? The answer lies in the control's run-time property called **Action** (this word can be omitted in code). For example, this statement opens the **Open** dialog box:

```
CommonDialog1.Action = 1
```

The assigned value can be one of the following:

0   No action
1   Open
2   Save As
3   Color
4   Font
5   Printer
6   Invokes WINHLP32.EXE

The above provides the only mechanism to open a dialog box in earlier versions. It is still available. In VB4/5 you can also use the following methods:

ShowOpen
ShowSave
ShowColor
ShowFont
ShowPrinter
ShowHelp

So, the following statement will show the Open dialog box:

```
CommonDialog1.ShowOpen
```

The old mechanism of using numbers is easier to manage programmatically. The simple lines below can give the user all the options and handle all possible circumstances. If you use the new methods, you'll need a more elaborate control structure to handle the same situation.

```
intX = Val(InputBox("Enter 1-6"))
If intX < 1 Or intX > 6 Then Exit Sub
CommonDialog1.Action = intX
```

When a dialog box opens, the user is allowed to select an option or supply the required information. You need to use the **Flags** property in code to find out what the user has done and to respond accordingly. Consider the following lines:

```
CommonDialog1.ShowPrinter
If CommonDialog1.Flags = 1 Then . . .
```

The first line opens the **Print** dialog box. The box lets the user check the Selection option to print only selected text. If this option is selected, Visual Basic returns 1 Flags value. The code then determines what to do.

The online help on CommonDialog (click the tool and press F1) shows the Properties jump. Clicking it leads to a Topics Found dialog box with many properties. Included are four Flags properties. Opening each leads to a list of intrinsic constants and their equivalent values. You can also type Flags in the Code window and press F. You can then click one of the four displayed options to show the related Flags values.

We are going to use these options of the common dialog control to create a text processor, allowing you to open, save, and print text files. The user interface, shown in Figure 10.23, has a text box whose MultiLine property is set to True and ScrollBars set to 3 - Both. There is a common dialog control which is invisible at run time. There are four command buttons to perform specific tasks. The procedures for these command buttons are shown in below.

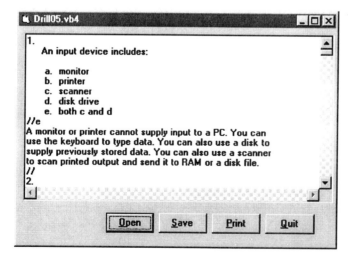

Figure 10.23   A text processor

(10COMDIA.VBP)

```vb
Private Sub cmdOpen_Click()
    Dim Lines As String
    Dim Line1 As String

    On Error GoTo ErrTrap
    CommonDialog1.Filter =
"Text Files *.txt|*.txt|All Files *.*|*.*"
        'dialog box file display pattern
    CommonDialog1.ShowOpen
    txtEditor.Text = ""        'clear previous display
    Open CommonDialog1.FileName For Input As #1
        'open file
        Caption = CommonDialog1.FileTitle
            'show file name
        Do While Not EOF(1)
            Line Input #1, Line1
              'read each line, assign to line1
            Lines = Lines & Line1 & vbCrLf
              'add each line to lines and add Enter at end
        Loop
    Close #1
    txtEditor.Text = Lines     'show in text box
    Exit Sub     'exit if no error

ErrTrap:
    ErrMsg         'call sub
End Sub

Private Sub cmdPrint_Click()
    On Error GoTo ErrTrap
    CommonDialog1.Flags = 0
        'set dialog box selection to All
        'this ensures the dialog box to open
    CommonDialog1.ShowPrinter
    If CommonDialog1.Flags = 1 Then
            'if Selection in the dialog box is checked
        Printer.Print txtEditor.SelText
            'print only selected text
    Else
        Printer.Print txtEditor.Text
            'print all--if All is selected (Flags = 0)
    End If
    Printer.EndDoc  'flush buffer
    Exit Sub

ErrTrap:
    ErrMsg         'call sub
End Sub

Private Sub cmdSave_Click()
    Dim FilName As String

    On Error GoTo ErrTrap
```

```
        CommonDialog1.Flags = 2
            'prompt for Yes/No if file exists
            'determines behavior of ShowSave
        CommonDialog1.ShowSave
        FilName = CommonDialog1.FileName
            'get file name & path
        Open FilName For Output As #1
            Print #1, txtEditor.Text
        Close #1
        Exit Sub

ErrTrap:
        ErrMsg        'call sub
End Sub

Private Sub ErrMsg()
        If Err.Number = cdlCancel Then    'or 32755
            Exit Sub                      'if Cancel chosen
        Else
            MsgBox Error              'show error msg
        End If
End Sub
```

Our application allows you to open a file. Clicking the Open button leads to Figure 10.24. The display pattern is controlled by the following line:

```
    CommonDialog1.Filter =
    "Text Files *.txt|*.txt|All Files *.*|*.*"
```

We specify two choices. The first choice is this:

```
    Text Files *.txt|*.txt
```

The string before the pipe (|) symbol appears in the Files-of-type combo box (bottom in Figure 10.24). The files matching the pattern specified after the | sign (plus all the subfolders) appear in the large list box.

Our second choice is determined by this string:

```
    All Files *.*|*.*
```

The user can click the down arrow in the Files-of-type combo box to show this option and then click it to display all the files in the current folder.

The Open dialog (and the others in the common dialog control) behaves the same as the Open dialog in Windows 95. It can be used as explained in Chapter 0. You can right-click the large list box in the middle to pop up a shortcut menu. You can use the ? button to show you what you are supposed to do with each item.

When the user double-clicks a displayed file or clicks a file and then clicks OK, the file is retrieved to the text box. We use the CommonDialog1.**FileName** property to identify the full path of the selected file. It is different from the **FileTitle** property, which contains only the file name but not directory string. We use the FileTitle property to get the file name of the selected file and assign it to the form's caption.

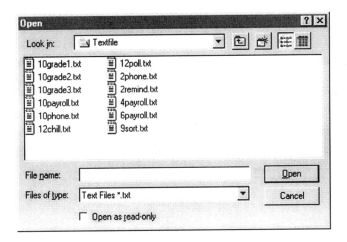

Figure 10.24   The Open dialog box

The Open dialog box displays by default the matching files in the current folder. At design time, you can set CommonDialog1's **InitDir** property to a specific folder. The following statement sets the initial directory to drive A's root directory at run time:

```
CommonDialog1.InitDir = "a:\"
```

To allow us to trap Cancel (to generate an error when Cancel is selected), we have set CommonDialog1's **CancelError** property from the default False to True at design time. If you did not do that, you can enter the following line in the Form_Load procedure or at the beginning of each pertinent procedure:

```
CommonDialog1.CancelError = True     'to trap Cancel
```

When the Cancel button is selected, Visual Basic returns error 32755 (or cdlCancel). We set up a trap to respond to this selection. If Cancel is selected in our case, nothing happens (the procedure is exited). If another error is encountered, the ErrMsg general procedure displays the pertinent error message.

The three error traps we set up are necessary. The program may bomb without these traps. For example, the user may try to save data to a drive that is not ready. In this situation, our trap will show an error message without aborting the program.

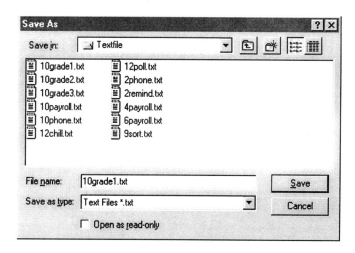

Figure 10.25   The Save As dialog box

You can use the text box to type new text and edit the text retrieved from disk. You can then save or print text. Clicking the Save button leads to the Save As dialog box shown in Figure 10.25. In the cmdSave_Click procedure, we use the Flags property to see whether it returns the 2 value (this number is supplied by the online help). If this value is returned, it means that a matching disk file is found. A message box (Figure 10.26) appears with the Yes and No options. Only if Yes is selected will the saving proceed.

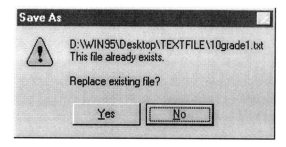

Figure 10.26   Prompting to replace an existing file

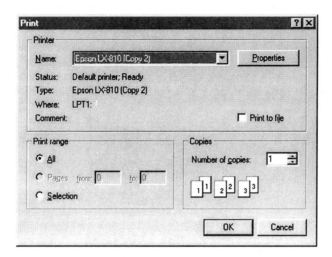

Figure 10.27   The Print dialog box

Selecting the Print command button leads to the Print dialog box shown in Figure 10.27. If you select All (the default) and click OK, Text1's entire contents will be printed. If you select text lines in Text1 and then select Selection in the Print dialog box, only the selected text (contained in Text1.**SelText**) will be printed.

If you want to display the Color or Font dialog box, set the Action property to 3 or 4. The Color dialog box lets the user choose a default color or define a custom color. The process resembles the one when you choose Palette from Visual Basic's Window menu, as explained in Chapter 3. After the user selects a color, your code then assigns it (the Color property) to an object. The following statements will assign the selected color to the text in Text1:

```
CommonDialog1.ShowColor
    'or CommonDialog1.Action = 3
Text1.ForeColor = CommonDialog1.Color
    'assign selected color to text
```

When CommonDialog1's Action property is set to 4, the Font dialog box appears (Figure 10.28). We need to set the Flags property to 1 as shown below; otherwise an error (no fonts installed) will appear.

```
CommonDialog1.Flags = 1      'show system fonts
CommonDialog1.ShowFont
    'or CommonDialog1.Action = 4
Text1.FontName = CommonDialog1.FontName
            'assign selected font to Text1
```

The last line above assigns CommonDialog1's FontName property to Text1's FontName property. Any existing and future text will appear in the specified font style and size.

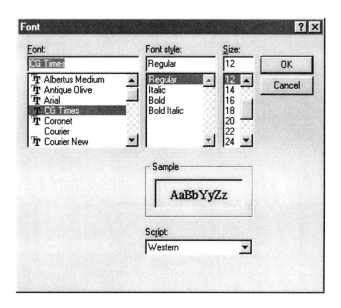

Figure 10.28   The Font dialog box

FILE and DIRECTORY MANAGEMENT

Visual Basic comes with quite a few functions and statements that can be used to manipulate existing files and directories. Most of these resemble DOS commands. If you are familiar with the basic DOS commands, you can easily master these.

Managing Directories

You can use the following commands in code to handle directories; most of them emulate comparable DOS commands:

ChDir   Changes directory (CD in DOS).
ChDrive   Changes drive (the same as entering a drive letter followed by a colon in DOS).
MkDir   Makes a directory (MD in DOS).

RmDir	Removes an empty directory (RD in DOS).
CurDir	A function that returns the current directory's path name (in DOS, same as CD with no argument).
Dir	A function that returns the file or directory names matching certain conditions.

The procedure below demonstrates how you can use most of these commands. The instructions here will create a directory named ABC in drive A, change the name to XYZ, remove it, and restore the original drive and directory.

```
Private Sub Command1_Click ()
    Dim D1 As Variant
    Dim D2 As Variant

    D2 = CurDir             'assign current dir to d2
    D1 = Left(D2, 2)        'get current drive
    Print CurDir            'show current dir
    ChDrive "a:"            'change to drive A
    ChDir "\"               'go to root dir
    MkDir "abc"             'make new dir abc
    ChDir "abc"             'go to new dir
    Print CurDir            'show current dir
    ChDir ".."              'back to root, 1 level up
    Name "abc" As "xyz"        'change dir abc to xyz
    Print CurDir
    RmDir "xyz"             'remove dir
    ChDrive D1              'restore drive
    ChDir D2               'restore dir
    Print CurDir
End Sub
```

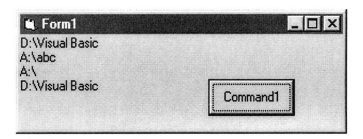

Figure 10.29   Managing directories

Figure 10.29 shows the current directory at various points. If you run this program, make sure drive A is ready and it does not contain directories named ABC and XYZ. You can change A to B if drive B is more convenient for you.

Dir returns a variety of names stored in DOS directories. You need to specify two arguments, like this:

```
Dir(FileSpec, AttrMask)
```

In the first argument, you specify the directory or matching pattern of the items you want shown. In the second argument, you specify an attribute mask by using one of the following numbers (you can also use an intrinsic constant by adding vb to the first words in the text lines shown below):

0	Normal files
2	Hidden files
4	System files
8	Volume label
16	Directory names

Here Normal means any file not having any of the other attributes.

When Dir is used with arguments, it returns the first matching item. If you keep using the same arguments, the same item will be returned. To return subsequent matching items, use Dir with no argument.

The procedure below will return all the items stored in drive C's root directory. By using 30 (0 + 2 + 4 + 8 + 16), we instruct Visual Basic to show everything. Notice that we use Dir alone for subsequent calls. Without this change, only one item will be shown repeatedly.

```
Private Sub Form_Click ()
    Dim I As Integer
    Dim strDir As String

    strDir = Dir("c:\*.*", 30)      '1st time with arguments
    Print strDir                    'print 1st call
    On Error GoTo ErrTrap

    For I = 1 To 200
        strDir = Dir       'call with no argument
        Print strDir
    Next I
    Exit Sub

ErrTrap:
    Caption = Error      'show error
End Sub
```

Figure 10.30 shows the result. In the code, we want to loop 200 times. When there is nothing left for Dir to read, the error shown here will appear. Our error trap guides execution to show the error message in the form's caption and exit the procedure.

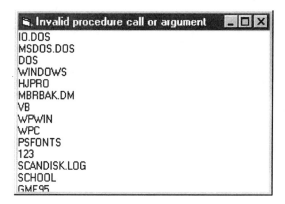

Figure 10.30   The Dir function

Managing Files

The following commands can be used to manage files:

Name	Renames a directory; moves or renames a file (combines REN and MOVE in DOS).
FileCopy	Copies one file from one place to another; no wildcards permitted.
Kill	Deletes a file (DEL in DOS); wildcards allowed.
Shell	Shells out to the DOS command line to run a specified external program.

Where appropriate, you can use wildcards just as you do in DOS. Consider this DOS command:

```
A>del *.bak
```

It will delete all the files in the current directory with the BAK extension. In Visual Basic, the equivalent command is:

```
Kill "*.bak"
```

Unlike DOS COPY, **FileCopy** does not permit wildcards. It follows this syntax:

```
FileCopy source, target
```

Notice the comma separating the two arguments; DOS COPY does not allow this.

Visual Basic's **Name** statement is not the same as the DOS REN command. REN can only change an existing file name to a new one and nothing else. Name can do more. It follows this syntax:

```
Name oldspec As newspec
```

The arguments are string expressions. These arguments can do the following:

- If the first argument is a directory, its name is changed to the second argument.

- If the first argument is a file and the second a file name, the file name is changed.

- If the first argument is a file and the second argument a directory, the file is moved to the new directory and the file name is not changed.

- If the first argument is a file and the second argument combines directory and file names, the file is moved and renamed.

A file opened by Visual Basic cannot be renamed. Attempting to do that will lead to an error.

Name cannot move a file to another drive. You need to use the **FileCopy** command to do that.

Shell is a function that lets you run a program stored on disk. It follows this syntax:

```
varX = Shell(command [, windowstyle])
```

The program's name has to be fully spelled out, including its extension; if an extension is EXE, it can be omitted. Visual Basic will give you the *File not found* error if you run a DOS internal command or if Visual Basic fails to find a matching program to run.

In the following code, Visual Basic will load FORMAT.COM and pause for you to act (check the taskbar to see the DOS program in operation). You can press Ctrl+Break to abort when the instruction appears on the DOS screen, or you can put in a new disk in drive A to format it.

```
Private Sub Form_Click ()
    Dim varX As Long
    varX = Shell("format.com a:")
    Print varX
End Sub
```

Shell returns a number that identifies the program.

Shell's second argument is optional. It can be any of the following values (integers or constants):

0	vbHide
1	vbNormalFocus
2	vbMinimizedFocus
3	vbMaximizedFocus
4	vbNormalNoFocus
6	vbMinimizedNoFocus

All these have to do with the state of the program after its execution. The executed program becomes part of the Windows environment.

File Attributes

You can use the following three functions and one statement to manage file data:

FileDateTime	Returns a file's date and time.
FileLen	Returns a disk file's length in bytes.
GetAttr	Returns a file's attributes.
SetAttr	Sets a file's attributes.

`FileLen("filename")` returns the length of the specified file. For example, the following statement will show 1862416:

```
Print FileLen("c:\vb\vb5.exe")
```

To set a file's attribute, follow this syntax:

```
SetAttr "filename", attribute
```

Here an attribute can be one of the following values:

0	vbNormal
1	vbReadOnly
2	vbHidden

4	vbSystem
32	vbArchive

When a file is saved or resaved, DOS automatically adds the A attribute (archive bit) to the directory where all the file attributes are stored. This attribute is used by BACKUP (version 5 or before) or MS Backup (version 6 or later) to back up files. This attribute is removed when a file is backed up so that it will not be backed up again in the future.

In Visual Basic, Normal (0) here means that the file has been backed up and its A attribute is taken out. A newly created or modified file will be identified as Archive (32).

You can use various combinations to find out whether multiple attributes have been set. The number 3 (1 + 2), for example, means that both Read-only and Hidden attributes are present.

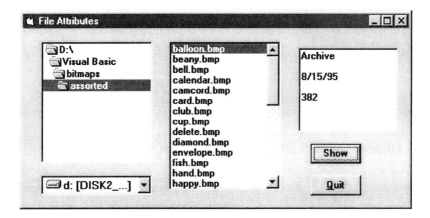

Figure 10.31   Showing file attributes

We can modify our program shown earlier in Figure 10.21 so that a selected file's attributes can be shown. In our modified user interface shown in Figure 10.31, we have added a text box and two command buttons. The text box's MultiLine property is set to True at design time so that multiple lines can be displayed in the box.

The listing below shows the procedures to run Figure 10.31. The Form_Load procedure changes File1's Hidden and System properties to True so that all files will be displayed; if you wish, these properties can also be set at design time. The

File1_DblClick procedure is added so that when a displayed file is double-clicked, it will activate the Show button's Click procedure.

(10FILATT.FRM)

```
Private Sub Form_Load()
    File1.Hidden = True
    File1.System = True
End Sub

Private Sub cmdShow_Click()
    Dim Str1 As String
    Dim Str2 As String
    Dim Str3 As String

    txtAttr.Text = ""              'clear text box

    On Error GoTo ErrTrap
    ChDrive Drive1        'change to current drive
    ChDir Dir1            'change to current dir
    Str1 = GetAttr(File1)  'get attr of selected file
    Select Case Str1
        Case 0
            Str1 = "Normal"
        Case 1
            Str1 = "Read-only"
        Case 2
            Str1 = "Hidden"
        Case 3
            Str1 = "Read-only and Hidden"
        Case 4
            Str1 = "System"
        Case 5
            Str1 = "Read-only and System"
        Case 6
            Str1 = "Hidden and System"
        Case 7
            Str1 = "Read-only, Hidden, System"
        Case Else
            Str1 = "Archive"
    End Select

    Str2 = FileDateTime(File1) & vbCrLf    'add new line
    Str3 = FileLen(File1) & vbCrLf
    txtAttr.Text = Str1 & vbCrLf & vbCrLf & _
    Str2 & vbCrLf & Str3
    Exit Sub

ErrTrap:
    MsgBox Error        'show error message
End Sub

Private Sub Drive1_Change()
    Dir1.Path = Drive1.Drive
```

```
End Sub

Private Sub Dir1_Change()
     File1.Path = Dir1.Path
End Sub

Private Sub File1_DblClick()
     cmdShow_Click
End Sub

Private Sub cmdQuit_Click()
     End
End Sub
```

DRILL

11. The MultiSelect property is available for:
    a.   List1
    b.   File1
    c.   Combo1
    d.   Dir1
    e.   both a and b

12. The Drive1.ListCount property returns the total number of drives available in your system. True or false?

13. The File1.ListCount property returns the count of all the files stored in the current directory. True or false?

14. Visual Basic's equivalent command for DOS CD is _____ .

15. Visual Basic's equivalent command for DOS DEL is _____ .

16. The Shell command lets you run a DOS internal command. True or false?

17. A file you create normally carries the attribute value of:
    a.   0
    b.   1
    c.   2
    d.   4
    e.   32

18. If GetAttr(filename) returns the value of 1, it means that the file is:
    a.   read-only

b.   hidden
c.   system
d.   archive
e.   all of the above

____   19.   If GetAttr(filename) returns the value of 39, it means that the file is:
a.   read-only
b.   hidden
c.   system
d.   archive
e.   all of the above

____   20.   The _____ function returns the byte count of a disk file.

PRACTICE

■   15.   Explain the results of adding Dir1 to the form and enlarging it.

■   16.   What happens when you add a File list box to the form and enlarge it? How can you display hidden files with the others?

■   17.   What is the default Pattern property for File1? How can you make it display only the files with the FRM and MAK extensions?

■   18.   How does the ListIndex property behave with the List1, Combo1, File1, and Dir1 controls?

■   19.   Explain various Visual Basic commands available to manage drives and directories.

■   20.   How does Visual Basic's Name command differ from DOS's REN command?

■   21.   What happens after this statement is executed?

```
SetAttr "filename", 7
```

■   22.   In Figure 10.31, add a command button captioned ReadOnly and named cmdReadOnly. Each time this button is clicked, the currently selected file should be changed to read-only (if it is not read-only) or not read-only (if it is read-only). Use the Show command button to prove the change.

- 23. In Figure 10.31, add a command button captioned Name and named cmdName. When this command button is clicked, the currently selected file will be renamed. An input box should prompt the user for a new name, with the old path and name appearing as the default string for editing. When a new name is supplied, the File1 box should immediately reflect the name change (use File1.**Refresh** to refresh the screen).

- 24. In Figure 10.31, add a command button captioned Kill and named cmdKill. When it is clicked, the currently selected file should be deleted. The user should be prompted with a message box with the name of the file to be deleted and Yes and No options. Save a test file (using Save File As from the File menu). Then run this program and use this command button to erase it. The File1 box should immediately reflect the deletion.

- 25. Add to Figure 12.21 a command button captioned Font and named cmdFont. Clicking the button should lead to the Font dialog box. The font style and size selected by the user should be used to display Text1.

- 26. Modify the above so that if Italic is selected, the text will change accordingly.

- 27. Add to Figure 12.21 a command button captioned Color and named cmdColor. Clicking the button should lead to the Color dialog box. After the user selects a color, an input box should appear to let the user choose 1 for ForeColor and 2 for BackColor used to display Text1.

SEQUENTIAL FILES

A **sequential file** contains data stored sequentially, one byte after another the way you sent it to disk. It can be compared to a song stored on a cassette tape. To reach song number three, you have to go through number one and two. When you play the song, you have to play from the beginning to the end. This arrangement is different from that of a random-access file discussed in another section below.

Creating Sequential Files

Creating a sequential file is very easy. You probably remember using COPY CON in DOS to create a file, such as the following:

```
A>copy con testfile
line 1
line 2
line 3
^Z
```

The above keystrokes entered on the DOS command line will create a file in drive A named TESTFILE. You can then use the TYPE command to show it on the screen. This is a sequential file because the file stores data in the exact order you entered it.

In Visual Basic, the comparable procedure to create an identical file is shown below:

```
Private Sub Form_Click ()
    Open "a:testfile" For Output As #1
            'open file for output
        Print #1, "line 1"              'send a line to file
        Print #1, "line 2"
        Print #1, "line 3"
    Close #1                            'close file
End Sub
```

After you created the file, you can use the following procedure to show it:

```
Private Sub Form_Click ()
    Dim I As Integer
    Dim Strn As String

    Open "a:testfile" For Input As #1
    For I = 1 To 3                  'go through 3 rounds
        Line Input #1, Strn
            'pull data from disk and put it in a variable
        Print Strn                 'print the line
    Next I
    Close #1
End Sub
```

If you want to create a file and show it immediately, the above two procedures can be combined into one, as shown below:

```
Private Sub Form_Click ()
    Dim I As Integer
    Dim Strn As String

    Open "a:testfile" For Output As #1
        Print #1, "line 1"
        Print #1, "line 2"
        Print #1, "line 3"
    Close #1
```

```
Open "a:testfile" For Input As #1

For I = 1 To 3
    Line Input #1, Strn
    Print Strn
Next I
Close #1
End Sub
```

In our example, we use a For loop three times to read three lines. If you loop twice or less, the file will be partially read. If you loop more than three times, an error will occur. We will soon explain a way to read till the end of an entire file.

Tools for Sequential Files

The following tools are available to handle sequential files (the number after # specifies a file number; the # symbol is mandatory where it is shown in all the following situations):

Open	Opens a file for input, output, or append.
Close	Closes an open file.
Print #1	Prints to disk the same way Print prints to the screen.
Write #1	Writes to disk with quotes.
Input #1	Reads data until (not including) a comma or carriage return; strips off leading spaces.
Input	Reads all characters, excluding nothing.
InputB	Same as above, except reading bytes rather than characters.
Line Input #	Reads data until (not including) a carriage return.

The **Open** statement follows this syntax:

```
Open file [For mode] [Access access] As [#] filenumber
```

where the following parameters have various options:

file   A text-string argument signifying a file name. A new file will be created or an existing file overwritten if Output is the specified *access*.

mode   Can be Random, Binary, Input, Output, or Append; if not specified, Random is the default.

access Can be Read, Write, or Read Write (default).

You must use the Open command to open a file before you can access a disk drive. After a file is opened, a disk buffer is supplied, and the file number you have specified directs input and output activities to the specified file. You can open multiple files. The maximum allowed is 511.

After you are through with a file, you must close it. Otherwise, the data stored in that file may be lost, or the disk directory structure may be damaged. Specify a number such as Close #1 to close a specific file. If no argument is supplied (Close is used alone), all the files opened by the program are closed. Exiting a program automatically closes all the files opened by it.

When Open or Close is involved, the # notation before a file number is optional. Adding it, however, makes your code more readable.

You can use the *mode* argument to specify a type of file to create. If this argument is absent, Random is the default. Random-access and binary files (together with *access*) will be covered later. The other options have the following meanings:

Input	Opens an existing sequential file to read.
Output	Opens a sequential file to write to, creating a new file or overwriting a matching existing file.
Append	Adds new data to a sequential file. If the specified file does not exist, it will be created.

The following functions return valuable information which you can use to manage open files (in contrast to existing disk files discussed in previous sections):

EOF	End of file; returns Boolean True or False; True if the end of file is reached, otherwise False.
FreeFile	Returns the next available file number for the Open statement.
LOF	Length of a file; returns the number of bytes in an open file.
FileAttr	Returns the attribute (represented by a number) of an open file.

After you open a file, you can use **FileAttr** to find out its file attributes with the following syntax:

```
FileAttr(filenumber, attribute)
```

The first argument is the number you used to open this file. You can use 1 or 2 as the second argument, like the following:

```
varF = FileAttr(filenumber, 2)
varM = FileAttr(filenumber, 1)
```

The first returns a number that is a file handle assigned by the operating system for the file you opened. This number is not related to the one you use to open a file. The second statement above returns one of the following numbers:

    1   Input
    2   Output
    4   Random
    8   Append
    32 Binary

The returned number reflects the mode you used to open this file.

EOF is most useful in finding out whether the entire file has been read. You can use the following control structure to read the entire file #1:

```
Do While Not EOF(1)
      . . .
Loop
```

This loop will continue as long as the end of file #1 is not reached. Use another number if you opened a file with it.

If you open multiple files, you can use the **FreeFile** function to ask Visual Basic to give you the next available file handle, like this:

```
varN = FreeFile
Open "testfile" for Output as #varN
. . .
Close #varN
```

If you have already opened two files, Visual Basic will assign 3 to varN. As usual, the # symbol is optional. The value returned by FreeFile changes as more files are opened or closed.

The **LOF** function returns the byte count in a specified file. The number is the same as when you use the DIR command on the DOS command line. To show the length of file #1, you can use either line below:

```
varN = LOF(1) : Print varN
Print LOF(1)
```

For a disk file that is not currently open, use `FileLen("filename")` to return the length of the specified file. This was explained earlier.

Comparing Input/Output Commands

There are two commands to write sequential data to disk:

```
Print #
Write #
```

The **Print #** statement operates exactly the way the Print method behaves when it outputs to the screen. You can use it with a comma, semicolon, Spc, or Tab. What you learned in Chapter 5 can be applied here. The only difference is to add # to signify writing to disk rather than to the screen.

Write #, a remnant from the past, works in a slightly different manner. It saves quotation marks but not extra spaces. Consider the following:

```
Print #1 "one", "two", 1, 2, 3
Write #1 "one", "two", 1, 2, 3
```

Print # will save the five items stretched out, as they would appear on the screen. The two text strings are not enclosed in quotes. Commas are not saved. A carriage return is added to the end of the line. Write #, on the other hand, saves comma-delimited items. Commas are also added to separate items. It also inserts quotes around strings. The above statement will save to disk a line like below (plus a carriage return):

```
"one","two",1,2,3
```

One advantage of this format is that it can be imported to spreadsheet or database management programs with a minimum of hassle. If you import such a file to Lotus 1-2-3, for example, the quotation marks will disappear and the separate items will enter separate cells without your having to parse a long string. This format is also useful in creating a database where records are of uneven lengths.

There are three commands to pull sequential data from a disk file:

```
Line Input #
Input #
Input
```

Line Input # is the easiest to use. It reads one line at a time and pulls characters before the carriage return, which is not included in the reading. If you want to display data (read by Line Input #) in a text box, you need to take an extra step. In order to place each subsequent line below the previous, you need to add two extra characters, Chr(13) and Chr(10) (or vbCrLf); we will demonstrate this shortly.

Input # reads text up to a comma or carriage return each time. Quotation marks, commas, or carriage returns are not read. In the above example saved by Write # ("one", "two", 1, 2, 3), it will read two text strings and three numbers.

When you open a file for input, you can use the **Input** or **InputB** function to read data. It follows this syntax:

```
varX = Input(n , [#]filenumber)
```

The first argument is the number of characters (or bytes for **InputB**) you want to read at one time, and the second is simply the file number specified in the Open statement.

The number of characters read at one time can be between 1 and up to 65535. If you specify a higher number, the reading process is faster. If you use 1 to read one character at a time, the process is slower but the read character can be compared to any character to see whether it exists in the file or whether it should be filtered out. Here is an example:

```
Do While Not EOF(1) 'not end of file
    varX = Input(100, #1)
         'read 100 characters at one time
    Print varX                 'print a line
    varB = varB & varX         'add to varB
Loop
```

Input and **Input #1** (the # is mandatory and the number is the file number specified in the Open statement) are different. Input is a function. The characters read are assigned to a variable placed before the = sign. Input # reads characters until a delimiter (a comma or carriage return) and assigns each to the variable list placed after the command. Compare the following:

```
varX = Input(10, #1)
Input #1, varX, varY, varZ
```

The first pulls in 10 characters and assigns them to a variable. The second pulls in three fields of a record and assigns the first to the first variable and the other two to the next two variables.

Input # should most of the time be used with Write #. Write # saves data by enclosing each text string with quotation marks and separating each field with a comma. Each record is also saved in a separate line. This orderly structure can be manipulated with Input # to pull in records one at a time. When Input # reads data, it does not pull in quotation marks and treats a comma as a field delimiter and a carriage return as a record delimiter. It can thus separate one field (piece of information) from another and one record (a line) from another.

Input and **Line Input #** are different. The latter pulls in one line (not including a carriage return) at a time. The former pulls in the number of characters (including carriage returns) specified by you. Input, unlike Input # or Line Input #, can read files opened in Binary mode. If you open a file in Binary mode and try to read it with the other two, an error will occur.

You can use **LOF** as an argument for **Input** to pull in an entire file all at once. In the following example, Text1's MultiLine is set to True at design time. The Input function reads the entire length of the specified text file and assigns it to the text box. The length of the file is also shown in the Immediate window.

```
Private Sub Form_Click()
    Open "a:\textfile\10grade1.txt" For Input As #1
    Text1.Text = Input(LOF(1), #1)
    Debug.Print LOF(1)
    Close #1
End Sub
```

Input returns a Long integer. So you can use a Long variable to store the length of the file read. In the following change, we use variable FileLen to store the read file's length and use this value to pull in all the text.

```
Private Sub Form_Click()
    Dim FileLen As Long

    Open "a:\textfile\10grade1.txt" For Input As #1
    FileLen = LOF(1)
    Text1.Text = Input(FileLen, #1)
    Close #1
End Sub
```

User-Controlled Sequential Files

When we started discussing sequential files earlier, we put text lines in a program to create a file containing the fixed lines. A more flexible way is to present the user a text box, which can be used to show text from an existing disk file or to enter text lines to be saved to disk. Figure 10.32 is an example.

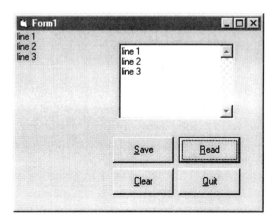

Figure 10.32   Using a text box to read and save text

Here the user can choose Clear to clear the text box (and the form window), enter text in the text box and choose Save to send the text to disk, or click Read to show the specified file (TESTFILE) in the text box (and the form window). The procedures are shown below.

```
Private Sub cmdSave_Click()
    Dim FileName As String

    On Error GoTo ErrTrap
    FileName = "a:\testfile"            'file name to open
    Open FileName For Output As #1     'open for output
    Print #1, Text1.Text      'send from text box to file
    Close #1                            'close file
    Exit Sub

ErrTrap:
    MsgBox Error
End Sub

Private Sub cmdRead_Click()
    Dim FileName As String
    Dim TextLines As String
    Dim Temp As String

    On Error GoTo ErrTrap
    FileName = "a:\testfile"           'file name
    Open FileName For Input As #1      'open for input

    Do While Not EOF(1)            'not end of file
        Line Input #1, Temp
        'pull from disk and assign each line to var
```

```
        Print Temp              'print a line
        TextLines = TextLines & Temp & vbCrLf
    Loop     'add up each line & carriage return
    Close #1                    'close file
    Text1.Text = TextLines      'show in text box
    Exit Sub

ErrTrap:
    MsgBox Error
End Sub

Private Sub cmdClear_Click()
    Text1.Text = "" 'clear text box
    Cls            'clear screen
End Sub
```

Sequential Records

At the beginning of this chapter, we used a list box to keep track of test scores. There the data had to be entered in the source code, a rather inflexible arrangement. We can store data separately on disk. The program can then pull the data from disk to show it on the screen. Our current project is based on this idea.

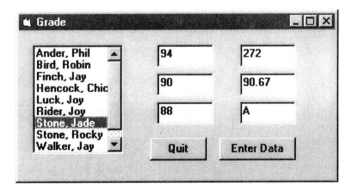

Figure 10.33   Form1, to show grades

To make it easy to enter data as well as show it, we use two forms shown in Figures 10.33 and 10.34. The first (Form1, Figure 10.33) is a modification of the one shown earlier in Figure 10.7 except here we added another text box to show a letter grade. Also, The Enter Data command button (cmdEnter in Name property) is to switch to the other form to enter data.

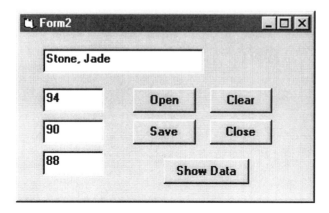

Figure 10.34   Form2, to enter grades

Form2 (Figure 10.34) allows entry and saving (appending of data). Enter the items shown, then click Open and Save. Click Clear to clear the entries. Enter more records and click Save and Clear each time. When you are done, click Close to close the file. If you want to show the old data, click Show Data to switch to the other form. To read the records you just entered, you need to quit and start again so that the Form_Load procedure can add the updated items to the list box. Another alternative is to add a command button in Form1 and add the following lines to its Click procedure:

```
List1.Clear      'clear list box
Form_Load        'run procedure
```

When this button is clicked, the list box will be cleared and the updated list will appear.

(10GRADE2.VBP)
```
Dim Grade(1 To 30, 3) As Variant

Private Sub Form_Load()    '1st form
    Dim I As Integer
    Dim J As Integer

    On Error GoTo ErrTrap
    Open "a:\textfile\10grade1.txt" For Input As #1

    Do While Not EOF(1)
        I = I + 1
        For J = 0 To 3
        Input #1, Grade(I, J)
```

```
                    'pull in each name and 3 test scores
            Next J
            List1.AddItem Grade(I, 0)
        Loop      'add names to list box
        Close #1
        Exit Sub

    ErrTrap:
        MsgBox Error
    End Sub

    Private Sub List1_Click()
        Dim I As Integer
        Dim J As Integer
        Dim Avg As Single
        Dim T(1 To 3) 'temp grade score
            'up to max of 1st index num in array
        For I = 1 To UBound(Grade, 1)
            If List1.Text = Grade(I, 0) Then
                'if a name is selected in list box
                For J = 1 To 3
                    T(J) = Grade(I, J) 'get scores
                Next J
                Exit For   'get out if found
            End If
        Next I

        txtTest1.Text = T(1)          'show test scores in boxes
        txtTest2.Text = T(2)
        txtTest3.Text = T(3)

        txtTotal.Text = Val(T(1)) + Val(T(2)) + Val(T(3))
        txtAvg.Text = Format(txtTotal.Text / 3, "##.00")

        Avg = Val(txtAvg.Text)
        Select Case Avg
            'convert to letter grade
            Case Is >= 90
                txtGrade.Text = "A"
            Case Is < 90 And Avg >= 80
                txtGrade.Text = "B"
            Case Is < 80 And Avg >= 70
                txtGrade.Text = "C"
            Case Is < 70 And Avg >= 60
                txtGrade.Text = "D"
            Case Else
                txtGrade.Text = "F"
        End Select
    End Sub

    Private Sub cmdEnter_Click()
        Close #1
        frmShowData.Hide        'hide form 1, show form 2
        frmEnterData.Show
```

```
End Sub

Private Sub cmdQuit_Click()
    Close #1
    End
End Sub

Private Sub cmdOpen_Click()        '2nd form
    On Error GoTo ErrTrap
    Open "a:\textfile\10grade1.txt" For Append As #1
    Exit Sub

ErrTrap:
    MsgBox Error
End Sub

Private Sub cmdSave_Click()
    Dim T1 As Integer
    Dim T2 As Integer
    Dim T3 As Integer

    T1 = txtTest1.Text
    T2 = txtTest2.Text
    T3 = txtTest3.Text
    Write #1, txtName.Text, T1, T2, T3
        'write records
End Sub

Private Sub cmdShow_Click()
    Close #1      'close this file
    frmEnterData.Hide  'hide form 2, show form 1
    frmShowData.Show
End Sub

Private Sub cmdClear_Click()
    txtName.Text = ""
    txtTest1.Text = ""
    txtTest2.Text = ""
    txtTest3.Text = ""
End Sub

Private Sub cmdClose_Click()
    Close #1
End Sub
```

In the code show above, we use a two-dimensional array, Grade(I, J) to keep track of names and scores. This array is declared in the form's Declarations section. as follows:

```
Dim Grade(1 To 30, 3)
```

This allows us to track 30 records (1 to 30) and four (0 to 3) fields (pieces of information) in each record, namely one name and three tests.

We also use UBound(Grade, 1) to get the first subscript's upper limit. (If you want to get the second subscript's maximum number, use 2 instead of 1.) If you change the array's subscript range (increase to accommodate more records or decrease to reduce memory consumption), UBound can reflect the new number.

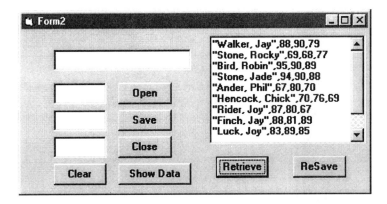

Figure 10.35   Form2 modified to allow editing of records

Our program has some shortcomings. What if you make a mistake in entering data? What if you want to record the first test now and second and third later? These can be remedied by adding one text box and two command buttons, as shown in Figure 10.35.

This arrangement allows the user to click Retrieve to pull the existing records to Text5, whose MultiLine property is at design time set to True and ScrollBars set to 2 - Vertical. You can then edit and make any necessary changes, including adding new records. Click the ReSave button to save over the same file.

The two new procedures for the two new command buttons are shown below.

(10GRADE3.VBP)

```
Private Sub cmdRetrieve_Click ()
    Dim I As Integer
    Dim Lines As String
    Dim Line1 As String

    On Error GoTo ErrTrap
```

```
        Open "a:\textfile\10grade1.txt" For Input As #1
        Do While Not EOF(1)
            Line Input #1, Line1
            I = I + 1          'keep track of line number
                               'i Dimmed at form level
            Lines = Lines & Line1 & vbCrLf
        Loop
        txtShowAll.Text = Lines
        Close #1
        Exit Sub

ErrTrap:
        MsgBox Error
End Sub

Private Sub cmdResave_Click()
        On Error GoTo ErrTrap
        Open "a:\textfile\agrade1.txt" For Output As #1
        txtShowAll.Text = Left(txtShowAll, _
        Len(txtShowAll) - 2)
        Print #1, txtShowAll.Text
        Close #1
        Exit Sub

ErrTrap:
        MsgBox Error
End Sub
```

When you use Print # to save the text in a text box, an extra carriage return is
automatically added to each line. We use the Left and Len functions to strip off
the last two bytes, namely Chr(13) and Chr(10). Before you click the ReSave
button, make sure the last line in the text box ends with a single carriage return.
Otherwise, the extra carriage returns will cause the reading to go beyond the last
record and trigger an error. To prevent the error from aborting the program, you
can also set up an error trap here as we have done in several places.

TIP: Saving & Opening List-Box Items

You can save the items in a list box to a disk file. Doing so, however,
requires you to specify each item to be saved—unlike the case when a text
box is involved. After a file is opened, the following For-Next loop will save
all the items in List1:

```
For I = 0 To List1.ListCount -1
    Print #1, List1.List(I)
Next I       'save all records
```

The saving will start with the first item (0) and end with the last, whose index value is ListCount minus 1.

Since we are using a loop to control the items to be saved, we can do all sorts of tricks here. For example, we can save only the first half, the last half, every other item, from last to first, and so on.

Retrieving a file to a list box is the same as doing it to a text box. The only difference is that you don't need to add Chr(13) and Chr(10) to the end of each line. After opening a file, use the following routine to load everything in the file to List1:

```
Do While Not EOF(1)
     Line Input #1, varA     'assign each line to var
     List1.AddItem varA      'assign to list box
Loop
```

RANDOM ACCESS AND BINARY

If you want to store rigidly structured data, you should create a random-access file, instead of a sequential file.

A **random-access file** contains uniform records, each of which holds uniform fields—separate pieces of related information. For example, you may maintain an address book. Each entry may contain a person's name, an address, and a phone number. What you have here are three fields. All the related fields put together constitute a record.

A random-access file requires uniformity. Each record has the same length as the next and contains the same number of fields as well. Each field, Name for example, is of the same data type and of the same length as the next comparable field. If the data you supply exceeds the specified length, the excess is discarded. If it is less, extra spaces are added.

Such uniformity allows you to access a particular record, alter it, and save it over the original. You can open such a file for reading and writing at the same time. These things cannot be done to a sequential file because the data is not uniformly structured.

To create a random-access file, you use the Open statement with the following syntax:

```
Open file [For mode][Access access] As [#] _
filenumber [Len = reclen]
```

This is the same syntax used for opening a sequential file,[1] except the Len argument, which we will return to shortly.

If you omit all the optional arguments, you can end up with this statement:

```
Open "a:testfile" As #1
```

This is legal. Since you do not specify anything, the following default values kick in:

mode	Random is the default.
access	Read Write is the default.
reclen	Record length is 128 bytes.

If you want to specify a mode, you can use Read or Write. If it is not specified, you can read from and write to the open file.

Use Len to specify the maximum length for each record. If not specified, 128 bytes is the default. You can go up to 32767.

To maneuver the records in a random access file, use these two commands:

Get	Pulls a record from disk.
Put	Saves a record to disk.

Either command requires three arguments: file number, record number, and variable name. Here is an example:

```
Get #1, 5, varA
```

Here you read file 1 (the number specified with Open), record 5, and assign it to variable varA. If you want to save the same information, use Put instead of Get.

You can use the **Seek statement** and the **Seek function** to position reading or writing at a specified record. They are used like the following:

```
Seek #1, 3              'statement; move to 3rd record
Get #1, Seek(1), varA   'function; read next record
```

---

[1]If your PC is networked, you can use Lock, Unlock, and Lock combined with Open to permit or restrict access to an opened file. Check these terms in the online help for details.

Each time a record is written or read, Seek(1) changes its value. If you read or write records sequentially, there is no need for you to worry about the read/write position. If you want to move to a particular record, use the Seek statement to set the record number. After that, you can omit the first argument for Get or Put. Here is an example:

```
Get #1, , varA
```

Here we omit the record number and use the default position. The default position can be set by the Seek statement.

The procedure below demonstrates the use of Get, Put, and Seek (both function and statement). Here we use Arr1( ) and Arr2( ) arrays to write and then read records.

```
Private Sub Form_Click ()
    Dim I As Integer
    Dim J As Integer
    Dim Arr1(1 To 5) As Integer
    Dim Arr2(1 To 5) As Integer

    Open "a:\xxx" For Random As #1
    For I = 1 To 5
        Arr1(I) = I * I
        Put #1, I, Arr1(I)        'save arr1(i) to rec i
        Print Arr1(I)             'show on screen
    Next I
    Close #1
    Open "a:\xxx" For Random As #1
    Seek #1, I - 1               'seek last record
    For J = Seek(1) To 1 Step -1 'from last to 1st
        Get #1, J, Arr2(J)        'assign to arr2(j)
        Print Arr2(J)             'show
    Next J
    Close #1
End Sub
```

Running the program and clicking the form window leads to the result shown in Figure 10.36.

Figure 10.37 resembles some figures shown earlier. It has six text boxes to show a name, three test scores, an average score, and a letter grade. It has a label to show the number for the current record. The Open, Close, Clear, Save, and Quit buttons and their procedures are inherited from the past but with modified procedure code shown in AGRADE2.VBP. The Add button and the horizontal scroll bar are new.

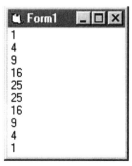

Figure 10.36   Showing Seek and Get

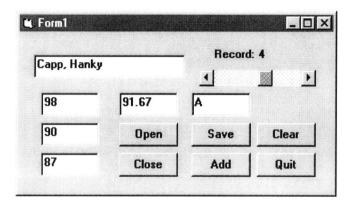

Figure 10.37   Using a scroll bar to show records

The scroll bar allows the user to scroll left or right to show the contents of each record. At design time, enter 1 as its Min value and the highest record number as its Max value. Do not change the default 1 value for LargeChange and SmallChange. If you have a large number of records, you might want to change LargeChange to 10 or a higher number.

This project involves a form and a standard module (Module1). The module is necessary because we are demonstrating the use of a user-defined data type (structure). A structure, because of its fixed length, is well-suited for a random-access file.

As explained in Chapter 9, the **Type-End Type** command is used to declare a structure. It can be entered only in the Declarations section of a standard module.

We specify 30 bytes for each name and an Integer for each grade score. That means each record will have 36 bytes in length, 30 bytes for the name and 2 bytes for each score.

(10GRADER.FRM)

```
Private Type TestScores
    Name As String * 30
    T1 As Integer
    T2 As Integer
    T3 As Integer
End Type
    'user type declaration at form level

Dim TS As TestScores
    'declare a form-level var of the user type

Private Sub cmdOpen_Click()
    On Error GoTo ErrTrap
    Open "a:\textfile\10grade3.txt" For Random _
    Access Read Write As #1 Len = Len(TS)
    HScroll1.Max = LOF(1) / Len(TS)
        'set scroll bar max value based on record number
    HScroll1.Value = 1  'assign 1st record to scroll bar
    HScroll1_Change      'show 1st record
    Exit Sub

ErrTrap:
    MsgBox Error
End Sub

Private Sub cmdSave_Click()
    On Error GoTo ErrTrap
    SaveRec Loc(1)   'call sub to save
    Exit Sub

ErrTrap:
    MsgBox Error
End Sub

Private Sub cmdAdd_Click()
    SaveRec HScroll1.Max + 1
        'call sub to add record
End Sub

Private Sub SaveRec(RecNum)
    On Error GoTo ErrTrap

    TS.Name = txtName.Text            'text
    TS.T1 = Val(txtTest1.Text)        'numerics
    TS.T2 = Val(txtTest2.Text)
    TS.T3 = Val(txtTest3.Text)
    Put #1, RecNum, TS
    Exit Sub
```

```
ErrTrap:
    MsgBox Error
End Sub

Private Sub HScroll1_Change()
    'process data when scrolled
    Dim Total As Integer
    Dim Score As Integer

    On Error GoTo ErrTrap
    Get #1, HScroll1.Value, TS
        'use scroll value to get rec
    Label1.Caption = "Record: " & HScroll1.Value
    txtName.Text = TS.Name           'put name in txtName
    txtTest1.Text = TS.T1            'scores 1, 2, 3
    txtTest2.Text = TS.T2
    txtTest3.Text = TS.T3            'total
    Total = Val(txtTest1.Text) + Val(txtTest2.Text) _
    + Val(txtTest3.Text)
    txtTotal.Text = Format(Val(Total) / 3, "##.00")
                            'average
    Score = Val(txtTotal.Text)
    Select Case Score        'convert to letter grade
        Case Is >= 90
            txtGrade.Text = "A"
        Case Is < 90 And Score >= 80
            txtGrade.Text = "B"
        Case Is < 80 And Score >= 70
            txtGrade.Text = "C"
        Case Is < 70 And Score >= 60
            txtGrade.Text = "D"
        Case Else
            txtGrade.Text = "F"
    End Select
    Exit Sub

ErrTrap:
    MsgBox Error, 0, "You must click Open first."
End Sub

Private Sub cmdClear_Click()
    txtName.Text = ""
    txtTest1.Text = ""
    txtTest2.Text = ""
    txtTest3.Text = ""
    txtTotal.Text = ""
    txtGrade.Text = ""
End Sub

Private Sub cmdClose_Click()
    Close #1
End Sub
```

```
Private Sub cmdQuit_Click()
    End
End Sub
```

The cmdSave_Click and cmdAdd_Click procedures call the general procedure named SaveRec. When the user clicks Save, Loc(1) is passed to SaveRec and the number is used to save the record. In a random access file, the **Loc**(1) function (1 is the number used in the Open statement) returns the current record's position. You can thus alter the currently displayed record and click Save to replace the old one on disk; other records will not be affected.

When the user clicks Add, 1 is added to the Max property of HScroll1. That means the record that is currently displayed is added at the end of the random access file. This will expand the file and not replace any existing record.

The cmdOpen_Click procedure has this crucial line:

```
HScroll1.Max = LOF(1) / Len(ts)
```

This assigns to the Max property of the scroll bar a value that represents the number of records available in the opened file. That way, the scroll bar will not scroll to a higher value and cause error due to reading a nonexisting record. This value is determined by dividing the length of the file by the number of bytes in each record. Since a random access file is rigidly structured, these numbers can be easily obtained.

If the user starts moving the scroll bar right after running the program, an error will be triggered because the file to read is not yet open. So our error trap directs execution to a message and exits the procedure. The user is then instructed to click Open first. If you wish, you can move the lines currently in the cmdOpen_-Click procedure to the Form_Load procedure. In that case, the file will open and the first record will be shown as soon as the program is run. However, the user will have less control as to when and what file to open.

You can open a file in binary mode and manipulate it similar to the way you manipulate a random-access file. You can then use Get to read a specific byte and Put to change a specific byte.

In the procedure below, we use **Binary** instead of Input to open a file. Since we do not specify *access*, the default is Read Write, which allows us to read and alter disk data.

```
Private Sub cmdRead_Click ()
    Dim strA As String
    Dim strB As String
```

```
    Dim Temp As String

    strA = "a:testfile"            'file name
    Open strA For Binary As #1    'open binary mode
    Do While Not EOF(1)           'not end of file
        Temp = String(1, " ")     'get 1 byte at strA time
        Get #1, , Temp
        Print Temp;               'print strA byte
        strB = strB & Temp                'combine
    Loop
    Close #1                      'close file
    Text1.Text = strB            'show in text box
End Sub
```

Before you can assign incoming data to a variable, you must assign one or more spaces to this variable. This creates a placeholder for storing characters. You can also use **String** function to do the same thing. Consider the following examples:

```
    Temp = "   "                   '3 spaces
    Temp = String(10, " ")        '10 spaces
```

In the second example, make sure there is a space between the quotes. The specified spaces determine the number of characters read at one time, similar to the number specified with Input.

You can also use Input to read a file opened in Binary mode. In the above procedure, the Temp and Get lines can be replaced by this single line:

```
    Temp = Input(1, #1)
```

The first 1 is the number of characters you want to pull in at one time; you can specify a higher number. The second 1 is the number used to open this file; the # sign is optional. When you use Input, there is no need to pre-assign spaces to a variable—contrary to using Get in Binary mode.

Notice that in the above procedure we do not use new line characters, namely Chr(13) and Chr(10). The reason is that both Get and Input read every character and skip nothing—quite unlike Line Input # and Input #, both of which skip carriage returns.

If you open an ASCII file (saved with Print # and Write #) in Binary mode, every character is read and legible. If you instead open a binary file (saved with Put or a form file saved by Visual Basic), not all the characters are read and those that are may be mostly incomprehensible.

In a random-access file the **Seek** and **Loc** functions return a record's position, but in a Binary mode or a sequential file they return a byte position instead. In either case, Seek returns the next byte position, where reading or writing will be done next. In Binary mode, Loc returns the last (read or written) byte position. In a sequential file, Loc returns the current byte position divided by 128, the default record length.

DRILL

____ 21. The _____ function returns the byte count of a open file.

____ 22. The _____ function returns the next available file handle.

____ 23. If you use Write #1 to create a sequential file, you need to use this to read it:
    a.   varX = Input(10, #1)
    b.   Input #1, varX, varY, varZ
    c.   Line Input #1, varA
    d.   none of the above
    e.   any of the above

____ 24. The _____ function returns the byte count of a record in a random-access file.

____ 25. In an open file, the _____ function returns the position of the last read/written byte or record.

____ 26. In an open file, the _____ function returns the position where reading or writing will next take place.

____ 27. This statement reads a record from a random-access file:
    a.   Get
    b.   Put
    c.   Input
    d.   none of the above

____ 28. This statement can read data from a file opened in Binary mode:
    a.   Get
    b.   Put
    c.   Input
    d.   both a and b
    e.   both a and c

____ 29. This statement saves a record to a random-access file:
    a.   Get

b.   Put
c.   Print #
d.   Write #

____ 30.   An ASCII text file can be opened in Binary mode. True or false?

PRACTICE

■ 28.   Compare and contrast Print #1 and Write #1.

■ 29.   Compare and contrast Line Input #, Input #, and Input.

■ 30.   Add a text box (Text2) to Figure 10.32. Modify the cmdSave_Click procedure so that when this command button is clicked the file name entered in Text2 will be used to save the text typed in Text1.

■ 31.   In the above question, if the user clicks the Save button without entering a file name in Text2, show a message box without executing the saving process.

■ 32.   In the above question, if the user enters a path in Text2 without starting with A or B, show a message box without executing the saving process —to prevent the user from saving a file to drive C.

■ 33.   How do the following statements differ?

varX = Input(1, #1)
Input #1, varX

■ 34.   Explain what the following statement does.

Open "a:testfile" As #1

■ 35.   Explain what the following statement does.

Get #1, , varA

CHAPTER PROJECT

A. (10FILEMAN.FRM)

This project provides a number of tools to manage existing files. The user interface, shown in Figure 10.38, contains six command buttons, a text box (far left), a drive list box, a directory list box, and a file list box. When the program is run, it should behave as follows:

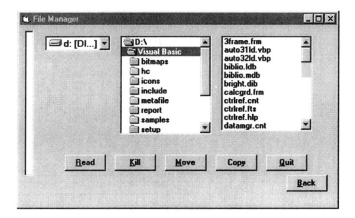

Figure 10.38   The file manager interface

1. When a drive is clicked, its directories appear in the directory list box.

2. When a directory is double-clicked, its files appear in the file list box.

3. When a file name is double-clicked (or when a file is clicked and then the Read button is clicked), its contents are displayed in the text box. The text box is invisible at the beginning. When the Read button is selected, it becomes visible and stretched out to display text.

4. The Back button is invisible at the beginning. It becomes visible when Read is clicked. Clicking Back makes the text box and the Back button invisible again.

5. When Kill, Move, or Copy is clicked, an input box appears with the current file name and path appearing as the default value for editing. When the user presses Enter or clicks OK, the file selected in the file list box is moved to

the supplied path (or changed to the supplied name), copied to the supplied location, or erased. If the user clicks the Cancel button instead, no action is taken. If a file is targeted for deletion, a message box with Yes and No buttons appears. If No is selected, the file is not deleted; if Yes is chosen, it is deleted. The screen is immediately refreshed to reflect the deletion. Refreshing also happens when a file is moved, renamed, or copied.

B. (10CHECK.FRM)

This project simulates check writing, printing, and saving. The user interface consists of four labels, five text boxes, and four command buttons. Four of the labels are set at design time. At run time, the program should behave as follows:

1. The current date is automatically displayed in Label1, as shown in Figure 10.39.

2. At the outset, the focus goes to Text1 (top right). Pressing Tab moves the focus to Text2 (top middle), Text3 (right middle), Text5 (bottom) for making entries.

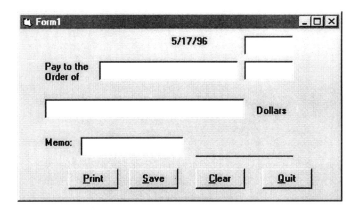

Figure 10.39   A blank check

3. Enter check number in Text1, payee in Text2, amount in Text3, and memo in Text5.

4. When a number is typed in Text3, the spelled-out version automatically appears in Text4.

5. When Print is clicked, the relevant items are sent to the printer. The output resembles a written check. The numeral amount appears on paper as follows:

   \$123.69

6. When Save is clicked, the following items are saved (appended) to the CHECKS file in a single line. Each item is separated from the next by a Tab character.

   100   5/17/96   Joe Blow   123.69   fix auto air

7. Clear clears all the text boxes and moves the focus to Text1 for making another entry.

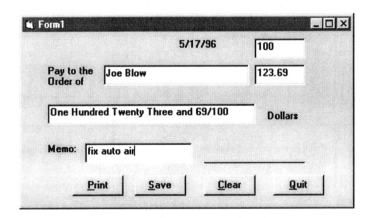

Figure 10.40   A completed check

C. (10PHONE.FRM)

This project lets you manage a phone book. The user interface is shown in Figure 10.41. The program should behave as follows:

1. When you click Add, the entries in the three text boxes are added to the list box and the text boxes are cleared. If Text1 contains nothing when Add is clicked, a beep is made and nothing else happens. The items in List1 are displayed in alphabetic order.

2. When you click an item displayed in the list box, the three parts (separated by Tab) are displayed in the three text boxes. You can edit them and click Add to add to the list box.

3. Clicking Delete deletes the item selected in the list box. If no item is selected, a beep is made and nothing else happens.

4. Clicking Clear clears the entire list box.

5. Clicking Save saves all the items in the list box to a file named PHONE.

6. Clicking Open retrieves the PHONE file to the list box. (Set up error traps for possible file errors during saving and opening a file.)

7. Clicking Prn Text prints the three text boxes' contents. Clicking Prn List prints all the items displayed in the list box. If there is no content to print, a beep is made and nothing else happens.

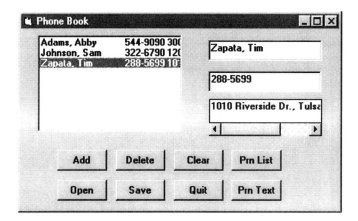

Figure 10.41   Managing a phone book

D. (10PUNCH.FRM)

This project simulates a punch-card machine, which records the check-in and check-out time of each worker. The initial user interface is shown in Figure 10.42. The program should behave as follows:

1. At run time, the current time is displayed at the top and the workers' names appear in List1 on the left.

2. When a worker comes in, he clicks his name and clicks the In button. When that happens, the name is moved from List1 to List2, with a tab and the current time (with the hh:mm format) added, as shown in Figure 10.43. If nothing is selected in List1 or if the title item is selected, clicking the In button makes a beep and nothing else happens.

3. When a worker clicks his name in the Check Out box (List2) and clicks the Out button, the current time is added to the end of the item, as shown in Figure 10.44. If nothing is selected in List2 or if the title item is selected, clicking the Out button makes a beep and nothing else happens.

4. When the Save button is clicked, an input box appears to prompt you for a file name. The items displayed in List2, except the title, are saved to disk. The saved items are also removed.

5. When the Open button is clicked, an input box appears to prompt you for a file name. The file is retrieved and displayed in List2, as shown in Figure 10.44.

6. When the Print button is clicked, List2's items, except the title, are printed.

(You should, in the morning, save a file named 10PAYROLL.TXT after moving some or all of the items from List1 to List2. This file should consist of two columns, one for names and the other for the time numbers, as shown in List2 in Figure 10.43. In the afternoon, open this file and add the current time to the items in List2, as explained in step 3 above. Use this file for the next project.)

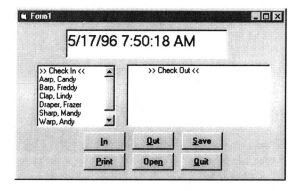

Figure 10.42   The initial run-time interface

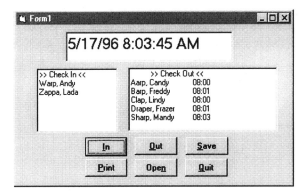

Figure 10.43   After some workers checked in

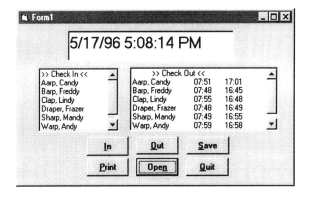

Figure 10.44   Opening and checking out

E. (10PAY.FRM)

This project lets you use the saved time numbers to quickly calculate the pay due to each worker. The user interface is shown in Figure 10.453. The program should behave as follows:

1. When the Open button is clicked, an input box prompts you to enter a file. The opened file's contents are displayed in the large list box. Use the 10PAYROLL.TXT file saved in the previous project (a demo file can be found in the \TEXTFILE directory of the companion disk).

2. When you enter a number in the Rate text box and click an item displayed in the list box, the numbers in the Hours and Pay text boxes are computed and

filled in automatically. The Hours value is calculated by subtracting the beginning time number from the ending time number in the selected list-box item. In calculating time, minutes should be converted to an hourly fraction. For example, 6 minutes should be treated as 0.1 hour. The Pay amount is determined by the Rate and Hours values.

3. When the Print button is clicked, the selected item and the calculated results are printed in the format shown below:

Barp, Freddy	07:55	16:48
Rate:	12.50	
Hours:	8.88	
Pay:	111.00	

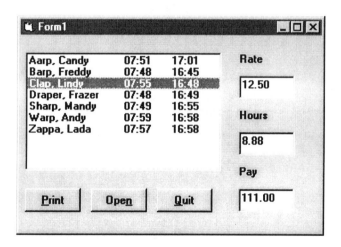

Figure 10.453   Calculating pay

F. (10MOTEL.FRM)

Mo's Model Motel has decided to change its rates as shown in the frame on the right of Figure 10.46. The rates during the popular season are 50% higher than the normal season. In addition, the 10% discount for each additional day will be limited to the first 10 days; after that, the lowest rate applies to the remainder of the stay. The total charge will be displayed in a larger font and in bright red for easier reading. Clicking a different option should also lead to an immediate change in the total charge.

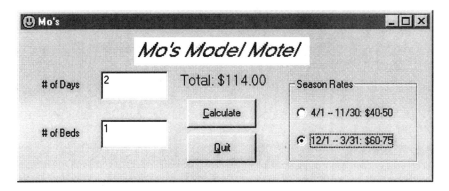

Figure 10.46   Changing daily rates

FUN AND GAME

A. (TURBAN.FRM)

This program continuously draws the shape shown in Figure 10.47. The drawing
of each semicircular line begins at 0 radian and moves counterclockwise. There is
a pause of 2/10 second from one line to the next. After all the lines are drawn,
there is a pause of 1 second. Then the screen is cleared and the whole cycle
renews. Each cycle also generates a new foreground color and a new background
color. Double-click the form to end. Clicking the X button clears the screen and
starts a new cycle.

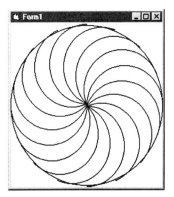

Figure 10.47   A turban in perpetual motion

```
Private Sub Form_Load()
    Dim I As Single
    Dim X As Single
    Dim Y As Single
    Dim Pi As Single
    Dim Begin As Single

    Show
    Pi = 4 * Atn(1)
    DrawWidth = 2
    Width = ScaleHeight      'square
    Width = 2 * ScaleHeight - ScaleWidth
    Scale (-1, 1)-(1, -1)    'Cartesian scale
    Do
        ForeColor = RGB(Rnd * 255, Rnd * 255, Rnd * 255)
        BackColor = RGB(Rnd * 255, Rnd * 255, Rnd * 255)
        Circle (0, 0), 1          'outer circle
            'use "Step pi" to get 2 iterations
        For I = 0 To 2 * Pi Step Pi / 8 'counterclockwise
            X = 0.5 * Cos(I)     'get x,y on circumference
            Y = 0.5 * Sin(I)
            If I <= Pi Then       'top half
                Circle (X, Y), 0.5, , I, I + Pi
            Else                  'bot half
                Circle (X, Y), 0.5, , I, I - Pi
            End If

            Begin = Timer    'begin time
            Do While Timer < Begin + 0.2
            Loop     'pause 2/10 second
            DoEvents
        Next I

        Begin = Timer    'begin time
        Do While Timer < Begin + 1
        Loop     'pause 1 second
    Loop
End Sub

Private Sub Form_QueryUnload(Cancel As Integer, _
UnloadMode As Integer)
    'this is triggered when you click X
    Dim Temp As Integer

    Temp = MsgBox("Do you want to quit?", vbYesNo)
    If Temp = vbYes Then
        Cancel = 0
        Unload Me     'close form, end code execution
        End
    Else
        Cancel = 1 'cancel closing; continue
    End If
End Sub
```

B. (MAGIC.FRM)

This program lets you specify a number to create a **magic square**, which has the same and odd-numbered columns and rows. Each column, row, or diagonal also shares the same sum. To create a magic square, enter 1 in the middle of the first row and then enter each subsequent number in each adjacent upper-left cell (it can also be made to go upper-right). If the target cell lies beyond a border, you continue on the other side, such as 2 and 5 in Figure 10.48. If a target cell is already filled, you enter the next number below the original cell and continue from there. For example, 8 is supposed to go to 1; but since it's occupied, it goes to below 7 instead.

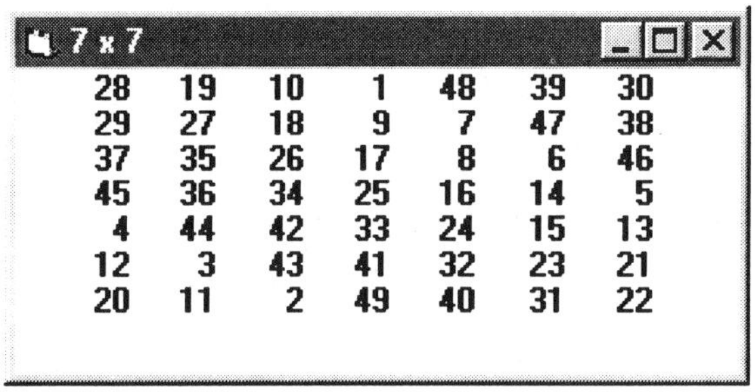

Figure 10.48   A 7 x 7 magic square

```
Private Sub Form_Click()
    Dim Num As Integer
    Dim I As Integer
    Dim J As Integer
    Dim Row As Integer
    Dim Col As Integer
    Dim CurrX As Long
    Dim Elm As Integer

    Num = Val(InputBox("Enter an odd number:"))
    If Num = 0 Then Exit Sub    'no entry
    If Num Mod 2 = 0 Then
        Beep
        MsgBox "An even number is illegal."
        Exit Sub
    End If

    Cls      'clear for a new form

    ReDim Arr(1 To Num, 1 To Num)    'dynamic array

    I = 1                            'row 1
```

```
J = (Num + 1) / 2                'mid column
Arr(I, J) = 1                    '1st element
Elm = 2                          '2nd element

Do While Elm <= Num ^ 2          'up to num square
    Row = (I - 1) Mod Num        'next row
    If Row < 1 Then Row = Row + Num
        'wrap around if 0 or less
    Col = (J - 1) Mod Num        'next col
    If Col < 1 Then Col = Col + Num
        'wrap around if over left
    If Arr(Row, Col) <> 0 Then   'if already assigned
        I = I + 1
        If I > Num Then I = I - Num
    Else        'move down 1 row, wrap if needed
        I = Row        'move up & left
        J = Col
    End If
    Arr(I, J) = Elm   'assign next element
    Elm = Elm + 1
Loop
Caption = Num & " x " & Num
                'show dimension in caption
For I = 1 To Num
    CurrX = 100                  'left margin
    For J = 1 To Num
        CurrX = CurrX + 500      '500 twips apart
        CurrentX = CurrX - TextWidth(Arr(I, J))
                'move printhead right
        Print Arr(I, J);         'print element
    Next J
    Print                        'new line
Next I
End Sub
```

Chapter *11*
Graphics and Animation

TOPICS

KEY TERMS

Absolute/Relative coordinates   An absolute coordinate is a point in a graphics container measured from the top and left margins. A relative coordinate, in contrast, is a point measured from the current position.

Bitmap   A picture containing a series of predetermined dots. If you stretch it, the dots become bigger and farther apart and the picture becomes coarse. A bitmap file has the BMP extension.

Graphical controls   Four controls—label, line, shape, and image—that serve mostly decorative purposes, to make a user interface more attractive or informative. They cannot receive the focus (you cannot tab to them) and have few related methods, events, or properties.

Graphics container   A control that can contain graphics. They include form, image control, and picture box control.

Icon   A bitmap picture limited to 32 by 32 pixels. They are most commonly used to graphically represent an application in the Windows environment. An icon file has the ICO extension.

Last Point Referenced (LPR)   A point in a graphics container where drawing last occurred. You can use CurrentX and CurrentY to move the print head to a specific point or tell you where the LPR is.

Line control   A control that appears as a straight line inside a graphics container. It has coordinate properties that can be set at design time or run time to control the line's length and position. You can use various border styles to determine the line's appearance.

Metafile   A picture file with the WMF (Windows metafile) extension that stores graphics in vector format. Instead of predetermined dots, the algorithm for those dots is saved. When such a file is stretched, more dots will fill up the expanded space. The picture's integrity is thus preserved. This mechanism also makes metafiles mostly larger.

Shape control   A control that can appear inside a graphics container as a rectangle or circle. You can choose different colors or hatch patterns to fill the inside.

Visual Basic provides two kinds of tools for you to maneuver graphics: objects and programming commands.

There are five objects pertinent to graphics: form plus four controls—line, shape, image, and picture box. Among these five objects, line and shape controls serve mostly decorative purposes. Form, image control, and picture box can contain predrawn graphics. Form and picture box can have graphics drawn in them.

At run time, you can use a number of commands to draw straight lines, circles, boxes (rectangles), arcs, and other variations. You can mix these shapes with a huge variety of colors. These shapes can be drawn in a form or a picture box; they can also be sent to the printer or saved as a bitmap file.

The supplied pictures and the graphics you draw with Visual Basic can be animated. When you throw in colors and various motions, the result can be quite captivating. Anyone young at heart can enjoy hours of making colorful screen objects move in fanciful ways.

This chapter starts with line and shape controls, then colors, then various programming commands to draw your own shapes, and then the graphics containers where you can place and show the numerous pictures that come with Visual Basic. Then, we will attempt to make things come alive with some animation techniques. Finally, we'll graph data by creating line, pie, and bar graphs.

LINE CONTROL

A **line control** is a simple tool that lets you add lines to your interface. It has limited methods, events, and properties, and serves mostly decorative purposes. It can be placed in three graphics containers: forms, frames, and picture boxes.

A line control has only a dozen properties. The following properties are significant:

BorderStyle	0 - Transparent
	1 - Solid (default)
	2 - Dash
	3 - Dot
	4 - Dash-Dot
	5 - Dash-Dot-Dot
	6 - Inside Solid
BorderWidth	1

X1	variable
X2	variable
Y1	variable
Y2	variable

When BorderWidth is set to higher than 1, a line becomes solid—if you choose any option other than Transparent, which is invisible.

When you double-click the line control in the Toolbox, a slanted line appears on the form. A sizing handle also appears on either end of the line. If you move the pointer to either handle, it becomes a cross. You can now stretch the line in any direction you want. As you do, the values of X1, X2, Y1, or Y2 properties may change.

These properties represent a line's coordinates in the form (or another container). X1 indicates the column position of the beginning end of the line, and X2 the other end. Y1 and Y2 reflect the row position of the line. If a line is vertically straight, X1 and X2 have the same value because they are of equal distance from the left margin. In that case, subtracting the lower value of Y1 or Y2 from the higher one produces the length of the line. For example, if Y2 is 1200 and Y1 is 1000, then the line is 200 twips in length.

At run time, a line cannot be moved with the Move method. However, the X and Y properties can be manipulated to simulate motion. By increasing or decreasing their values, the line can change its length and/or position. Here is an example:

```
Line1.X1 = Line1.X2
Line1.Y1 = Line1.Y1 - 100
```

X1 will be moved to the same column position as X2; the line thus becomes vertical. Y1 will move closer to the top by 100 twips.

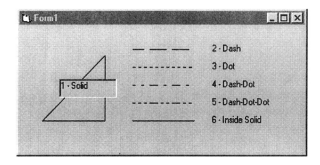

Figure 11.1   A line control's border styles

Figure 11.1 shows the results of various **BorderStyles**. The triangle is a good example of what you can do with lines. Notice that when a label (with Fixed Single BorderStyle) is superimposed on the lines, it covers up some portions. The reason for that is that the label was added after the lines. If you reverse the order, the lines would cover up portions of the label.

SHAPE CONTROL

The **shape control** offers six options for enclosed two-dimensional shapes. The options are provided in the **Shape** property. They are as follows:

> 0 - Rectangle (default)
> 1 - Square
> 2 - Oval
> 3 - Circle
> 4 - Rounded Rectangle
> 5 - Rounded Square

The enclosed area of a shape can be filled with one of the eight options available in the **FillStyle** property. These options are:

> 0 - Solid
> 1 - Transparent (default)
> 2 - Horizontal Line
> 3 - Vertical Line
> 4 - Upward Diagonal
> 5 - Downward Diagonal
> 6 - Cross
> 7 - Diagonal Cross

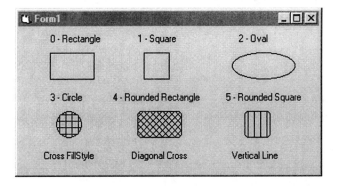

Figure 11.2   A shape control's Shape and FillStyle properties

Figure 11.2 shows the results of all the Shape property options. The last three shapes are also filled with the specified options from the FillStyle property.

A shape control's BorderWidth and BorderStyle properties are the same as those of a line control.

A shape control's **BackStyle** property can be 0 - Transparent (default) or 1 - Opaque. With the Transparent setting, the background objects show through and the shape control's BackColor property has no effect. When the BackStyle property is changed to Opaque, the shape control's BackColor takes effect and covers up any object underneath.

NOTE   The **BackStyle** property is available to only the shape, label, and OLE controls. For a shape control, the default value is Transparent; for a label or OLE control, it is Opaque. In Figure 11.1, if we change the label's BackStyle property to Transparent, the triangle lines underneath will show through.

A shape control's **FillColor** property affects the hatch lines set with the FillStyle property. The lines are displayed in the color chosen in the color palette available when you double-click the FillColor property. If **FillStyle** is Transparent, the color has no effect. If FillStyle is Solid, then the color fills the entire shape. This color also prevails over any color you may have chosen for the BackColor property.

A shape control is not a container like a form, frame, image control, or picture box. Text or pictures can be placed on, above, or underneath it—but not inside. It lacks container properties to hold other items.

NOTE   Four controls—label, line, shape, and image—are classified by Visual Basic as **graphical controls**. They serve mostly decorative purposes—to make a user interface look more attractive or informative.They cannot receive the focus and have few associated methods, events, and properties. Since they do little, they also consume fewer resources.

A shape control has no X or Y property. Instead, like a form, it has Top, Left, Height, and Width properties to identify its position and dimensions. These properties can be changed at design time or run time.

Unlike a line control, a shape control can be moved with the **Move** method. It follows this syntax:

```
object.Move left[, top, width, height]
```

The only required argument is the first. It designates the object's left-side distance from the container's left-side border. The default measuring unit is twip, but it can be changed by the ScaleMode property. The *top* argument designates the distance from the top margin. The last two arguments specify the objects size.

The Move method will be used to animate objects. The following statement will move Shape1 to the top left corner and double its size.

```
Shape1.Move 0, 0, Shape1.Width * 2, Shape1.Height * 2
```

TIP: Centering an Object

The **Move** method can be used to move (and animate) all the visible controls. One practical use for it is to automatically center one or more objects when the user resizes a form. In the following procedure, Command1 will always stay in the center:

```
Private Sub Form_Resize()
    Command1.Move (ScaleWidth - Command1.Width) / 2, _
    (ScaleHeight - Command1.Height) / 2
End Sub
```

If you want to change the command button's size based on the form's size, try the following:

```
Private Sub Form_Resize()
    Dim HorSize As Long
    Dim VerSize As Long

    HorSize = ScaleWidth / 5   'get Command1's horizontal
    VerSize = ScaleHeight / 5 'and vertical size
    Command1.Move (ScaleWidth - HorSize) / 2, _
    (ScaleHeight - VerSize) / 2, HorSize, VerSize
End Sub
```

You can use the Left and Top properties to replace Move. The following statement will center Command1 on the form:

```
Command1.Left = (ScaleWidth - Command1.Width) / 2
Command1.Top = (ScaleHeight - Command1.Height) / 2
```

SHOWING COLORS

Visual Basic uses a long integer number to represent a color. When a color argument is expected, you can use a number—assuming you know what color that number presents. If you do not know that, you can use two functions, RGB and QBColor, to show you.

RGB Colors

Visual Basic uses the **RGB** function to manipulate three color elements, red, green, and blue. By mixing the three, each of which can have the intensity of 0 to 255, a huge number of results can be produced.

The RGB function can control up to 16,777,216 (0 to 16,777,215) color pixels. A 24-bit graphics card used in Super VGA systems can take advantage of this large selection.

The RGB function follows this syntax:

```
varX = RGB(rednumber, greennumber, bluenumber)
```

Each color number can be 0 to 255. This scheme can produce 256^3 (256 * 256 * 256) possible mixtures.

In this numbering system, 0 is no color or black. Thus when all the three components have the value of 0, black is the result. If one component has the highest possible value and the other two have 0, then a primary color is produced. Here are three examples:

```
BackColor = RGB(255, 0, 0)  'red
BackColor = RGB(0, 255, 0)  'green
BackColor = RGB(0, 0, 255)  'blue
```

When all the components have the highest value (255), the result is white.

Many objects, such as forms and text boxes, allow you to change their ForeColor and BackColor properties at design time. You will be given a color palette from which you can make a choice. The hex value representing the chosen color then appears in the Properties window. This number is determined by Windows.

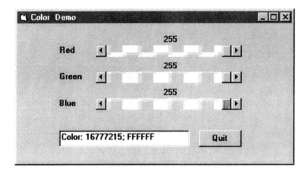

Figure 11.3 Using three scroll bars to show colors

If you want to change a color at run time, you can create your own color mix by combining amounts of red, green, and blue. The application with the user interface shown in Figure 11.3 will let you quickly find out the number you need for a specific displayed color.

Visual Basic uses two bytes to manage each of the three RGB components. The first number specified in the function represents red. This number reflects the lowest two bytes of the six bytes used to manage the three components. Conversely, the last number (the blue component) is represented in the highest two bytes. This arrangement can be demonstrated in our application.

As you move the Red scroll bar, you are changing the lowest two bytes (the R component). If you move this scroll box to the far right, the text box at the bottom shows the red color as well as 255 decimal and FF hex numbers. If you move only the Green bar to the end, the hex value is FF00. If only the Blue bar is moved to the end, the hex value becomes FF0000. If all the three bars are at the end, the hex value is FFFFFF and the resulting color is white, as shown in Figure 11.3.

The application's properties are shown below:

Object	Property	Value
Label1	Caption	Red
Label2	Caption	Green
Label3	Caption	Blue
Label4	Caption	0
	Name	lblRed
Label5	Caption	0

	Name	lblGreen
Label6	Caption	0
	Name	lblBlue
HScroll1	Name	hsbRed
HScroll2	Name	hsbGreen
HScroll3	Name	hsbBlue
HScroll1/2/3	Min	0
	Max	255
	SmallChange	1
	LargeChange	20
Text1	Text	(none)

The procedures below respond to the scroll bars. The first procedure moves the initial position of the three scroll boxes to the middle and calls the Color procedure to set the initial color based on the scroll values.

(11COLOR.FRM)

```
Private Sub Form_Load()
    hsbRed.Value = hsbRed.Max / 2     'scroll to midpoint
    hsbGreen.Value = hsbGreen.Max / 2
    hsbBlue.Value = hsbBlue.Max / 2
    GetColor   'call procedure to get initial display
End Sub

Private Sub hsbRed_Change()
    lblRed.Caption = hsbRed.Value
                'show scroll value in label
    GetColor   'call GetColor sub procedure
End Sub

Private Sub hsbGreen_Change()
    lblGreen.Caption = hsbGreen.Value
    GetColor
End Sub

Private Sub hsbBlue_Change()
    lblBlue.Caption = hsbBlue.Value
    GetColor
End Sub

Private Sub GetColor()
    Dim R As Integer
    Dim G As Integer
    Dim B As Integer
    Dim Color As Long

    R = hsbRed.Value
    G = hsbGreen.Value
    B = hsbBlue.Value
```

```
      Color = RGB(R, G, B)
      Text1.BackColor = Color
          'assign RGB colors to text box
      Text1.Text = "Color: " & Color & "; " & Hex(Color)
          'show decimal and hex values in box
End Sub

Private Sub cmdQuit_Click()
      End
End Sub
```

QBColor

If mixing three separate numbers to get a color is too complicated for you, you can use an older and simpler method to get a color. The **QBColor** function was available in Quick Basic and is still available in Visual Basic. The advantage is that it is very simple to get a color. The disadvantage is that there are not too many choices. These are shown in Table 11.1.

Table 11.1   QBColor arguments

0	Black	8	Gray
1	Blue	9	Light Blue
2	Green	10	Light Green
3	Cyan	11	Light Cyan
4	Red	12	Light Red
5	Magenta	13	Light Magenta
6	Brown	14	Light Yellow
7	White	15	Bright White

Using the QBColor function is very simple. Just specify one of the 16 numbers and assign it to an object. Here are some examples:

```
ForeColor = QBColor(4)
Form1.ForeColor=QBColor(4)
Text1.ForeColor = QBColor(4)
```

All the examples specify the dark red color. The first two are identical. Since no object is identified in the first example, it defaults to the current form. In the third case, the Text1 text box will use the red color to display text.

The QBColor function actually returns the same value as the RGB function—when the same color is involved. For example, QBColor(12) returns 255; so does RGB(255, 0, 0). Both will also set the red color. By the same token,

QBColor(15) and RGB(255, 255, 255) both set the white color and return 16777215.

We can create a simple application to show all the colors available with QBColor. Figure 11.4 shows the interface and the procedure is shown below.

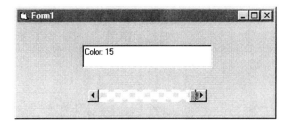

Figure 11.4   Showing QBColor colors

```
Private Sub HScroll1_Change ()        'Listing 1
    HScroll1.Min = 0                  'set scroll min value
    HScroll1.Max = 15                 'set scroll max value
    Text1.Text = "Color: " & HScroll1.Value
        'show text and number
    Text1.BackColor = QBColor(HScroll1.Value) 'show color
End Sub
```

Our application consists of a text box and a horizontal scroll bar. Just add those to a form and stretch them out a little bit. The code will take care of the rest.

When you run the program and move the scroll bar back and forth, the text box will show the current background color and its corresponding number.

The following procedure lets you repeatedly click the form to show each of the 16 QBColor options and display in the form caption the pertinent QBColor option, its decimal value, and the hex equivalent. When QBColor option is 15, the background color is white and the hex value is FFFFFF.

```
Private Sub Form_Click()
    Static staX As Integer

    BackColor = QBColor(staX Mod 16)   '0 to 15
    Caption = staX Mod 16 & " : " & BackColor _
        & " : " & Hex(BackColor)
        'QBColor val : decimal : hex
    staX = staX + 1    'control variable
End Sub
```

NOTE The easiest way to add a common color to an object is to use the intrinsic constants, instead of messing with RGB or QBColor. You should take advantage of this feature available since VB4. You can search the online help for *color constants* to display numerous intrinsic constants and their numeric equivalents. These constants are to be used alone, not as arguments for RGB or QBColor. The following three statements are equivalent; they all make the form's background color red. The last one is obviously the easiest to remember.

```
BackColor = RGB(255, 0, 0)
BackColor = QBColor(12)
BackColor = vbRed
```

RANDOM COLORS

You can use the Rnd function to generate a random color. This color can then be used to display whatever you have in mind. You can also use a timer control to change the color at a set interval. This can result in a continuous display of changing colors.

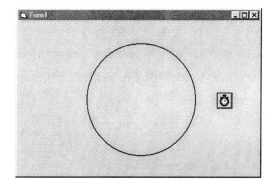

Figure 11.5   A timer and shape control

Our simple project involves a shape control and a timer control. The shape is enlarged as shown in Figure 11.5. Their properties are set at run time in the Form_Load procedure.

The procedures are shown below. The Timer event procedure calls the RandomColor function procedure every second to get a random number for the form's BackColor property and another number for the shape control's FillColor property. So every second a new color fills the circle and another color fills the form.

```
Private Sub Form_Load()
    Timer1.Interval = 1000      '1 sec
    Shape1.FillStyle = vbFSSolid
End Sub

Private Sub Timer1_Timer()      'Listing 2
    BackColor = RandomColor()
        'get backcolor for form
    Shape1.FillColor = RandomColor()
        'get random color to fill Shape1
End Sub

Function RandomColor()
    Dim R As Integer, G As Integer, B As Integer
    Randomize               'get new seed
    R = Rnd * 255           'generate random numbers
    G = Rnd * 255           '0 - 255
    B = Rnd * 255
    RandomColor = RGB(R, G, B)   'return new random color
End Function
```

The RandomColor function procedure is a handy general-purpose procedure. It can be called by any procedure when a random RGB number is needed. If you find it useful, you can put it in a module. You can then incorporate it into any other project without recoding.

You can manipulate RGB colors to create 3-D looks. A later section will provide concrete demonstrations.

DRILL

____ 1.   If a line control's BorderStyle property is set to Transparent, the line becomes invisible. True or false?

____ 2.   It is possible to use the line control to create a thick dotted line. True or false?

____ 3.   A shape control cannot appear as a:
          a.   triangle
          b.   square
          c.   circle
          d.   rectangle

e.   oval

____ 4.   If a shape control's BorderStyle property is set to Transparent, the shape is always invisible. True or false?

____ 5.   This statement concerning a default shape control is true:
a.   BackStyle is Transparent
b.   FillStyle is Transparent
c.   BorderStyle is Solid
d.   all of the above
e.   none of the above

____ 6.   To fill a shape control with the color set in the FillColor property, these conditions must exist:
a.   FillStyle is Solid
b.   BackStyle is Opaque
c.   BorderStyle is Transparent
d.   both a and b

____ 7.   To fill a shape control with the color set in the BackColor property, these conditions must exist:
a.   FillStyle is Transparent
b.   BackStyle is Opaque
c.   both a and b
d.   neither a nor b

____ 8.   The four graphical controls are: line, shape, image, and
_____ .

____ 9.   The shape and label controls are the only two controls that share the _____ property.

Choose one of the following options to answer questions 10-14.
a. black,   b. white,   c. red,   d. green,   e. blue

____ 10.   BackColor = RGB(255, 0, 0)

____ 11.   BackColor = RGB(0, 255, 0)

____ 12.   BackColor = RGB(0, 0, 255)

____ 13.   BackColor = RGB(0, 0, 0)

____ 14.   BackColor = RGB(255, 255, 255)

PRACTICE

■ 1. Explain a line control's X1, X2, Y1, and Y2 properties.

■ 2. What kinds of images can you create using the shape control?

■ 3. How do RGB and QBColor differ?

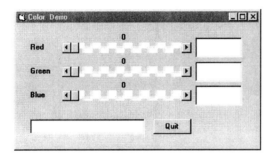

Figure 11.6   Showing RGB numbers in text boxes

■ 4. In Figure 11.3, add three text boxes, Text2, Text3, and Text4 (shown in Figure 11.6). Modify the accompanying code so that when the user moves a scroll bar, the related text box will show a color and a number to reflect the scroll bar. The number in each text box must be in white so that it is visible no matter what the background color is.

■ 5. Modify Listing 1 so that the text box will display a background color based on the scroll bar, but also a foreground color whose number is one higher than the number for the background color. If the background color is 15, then the foreground color should be 0.

■ 6. In Listing 2, use the BackColor (instead of FillColor) property to control the circle's colors.

DRAWING LINES

In addition to the line control discussed earlier, you can use the **Line** method at run time to draw a straight line in a form, in a picture box, or to a printer. The line will appear in the specified ForeColor property, in the style specified in the DrawStyle property, and in the width specified in the DrawWidth property.

Drawing graphics requires you to know lots of rules and specifications. We will demonstrate how to draw lines first and then cover some of the basic principles. These principles can then be applied to drawing other shapes.

The Coordinate System

To draw a line with **Line**, you normally need to specify the beginning and the ending points. Here is an example:

```
Line(200, 100)-(1640, 100)
```

This statement will draw a straight line that is one inch in length. The beginning point is 200 twips from the left margin of the current form window and 100 twips from the top. The ending point is 1640 twips from the left margin and 100 twips from the top. Since both points' distances from the top are the same, the result is a straight horizontal line. By subtracting 200 from 1640, we get 1440 twips, or one inch. The resulting line may not be exactly one inch on the screen due to variations in hardware standards. But if you send the line to the printer, it will be very close to one inch. To send the line to the printer, specify Printer, such as:

```
Printer.Line(200, 100)-(1640, 100)
```

When you want to tell Visual Basic to draw a line, you need to tell it each point's distances from the left margin and the top margin. In order to instruct Visual Basic to draw a line from point X to point Y, you have to let Visual Basic know where point X is and where point Y is. So you need to say point X is 200 twips from the left and 100 twips from the top, and point Y is 1640 twips from the left and 100 twips from the top.

Visual Basic has certain built-in form (and picture box) properties to control positioning of graphics. A form's coordinates for the four corners are shown in Figure 11.7. The top and left numbers are 0 by default, but the others depend on the size of the form.

You probably remember the discussion in Chapter 3 dealing with a form's dimensions. A form has Top, Left, Width, and Height properties. Their values are shown in the Properties window and on the menu bar. As you move or resize the form, these numbers change to reflect the new locations and dimensions.

(ScaleLeft, ScaleTop)   (ScaleWidth, ScaleTop)

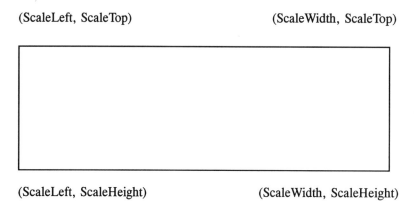

(ScaleLeft, ScaleHeight)   (ScaleWidth, ScaleHeight)

Figure 11.7   The default coordinate values

The above numbers reflect the form's position against the screen. They also include the borders and the title bar. They are thus different from the numbers for their counterparts for the form's scalable portion, namely ScaleTop, ScaleLeft, ScaleWidth, and ScaleHeight. You can scrutinize all these eight numbers in the Properties window or print them out (using the Print method) to compare them.

Take advantage of the numbers in the **ScaleWidth** and **ScaleHeight** properties to position lines and circles. Here are two examples:

```
Line (ScaleLeft, ScaleHeight / 2)-(ScaleWidth, _
ScaleHeight / 2)
Line (ScaleWidth / 2, ScaleTop)-(ScaleWidth / 2, _
ScaleHeight)
```

The first will draw a horizontal line and the second a vertical line, both in the middle of the window. Study them carefully and make sure you understand the logic. Instructing the computer to draw graphics is a great way to learn programming and understand programming logic. Besides, it's fun to watch the result—if you can get your program to do what you have in mind.

Instead of drawing single lines, you can use loops to draw lines forming a pattern. The procedure below is an example. It produces the pattern shown in Figure 11.8.

```
Private Sub Form_Click ()
    Dim X1 As Long
    Dim X2 As Long
    Dim Y1 As Long
    Dim Y2 As Long
    Dim LeftPoint As Integer
```

```
    Dim RightPoint As Long
    Dim StepVal As Integer

    X1 = 0
    Y1 = 0
    Y2 = 3000   '3000 twips from top
    StepVal = 200
    LeftPoint = 0
    RightPoint = 6000
    For X2 = LeftPoint To RightPoint Step StepVal
        Line (X1, Y1)-(X2, Y2)
    Next X2
End Sub
```

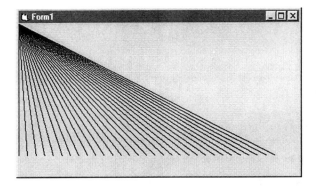

Figure 11.8   A line pattern

The first two lines in our procedure are not necessary because the default starting point is (0, 0). On the other hand, they provide flexibility. What if you want to start somewhere else, say midpoint at the top? What if you want to end each line 100 twips above the bottom margin? You can manually control them by trial and error. On the other hand, you may want to make Visual Basic control the precise position. Our next example will demonstrate this shortly.

Line Styles

By default, when you use Line to draw a line, a solid line appears. If you wish to change, you can use a form's **DrawStyle** property to do that. These are the available options:

0 - Solid (default)
1 - Dash

2 - Dot
3 - Dash-Dot
4 - Dash-Dot-Dot
5 - Transparent
6 - Inside Solid

You can also change the thickness of a line drawn by changing the default value of a form's DrawWidth property. By default, the DrawWidth property is set to 1. You can change it to a higher number.

If DrawWidth is set to higher than 1, then options 1 to 4 of the DrawStyle property produce a solid line instead of the specified styles.

Figure 11.9 shows lines drawn using the Dot style. The procedure below specifies each line to start from the top middle and 200 twips above the bottom margin.

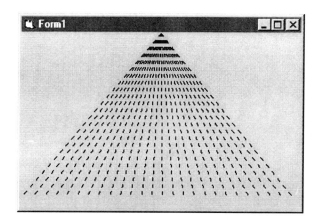

Figure 11.9   A modified line pattern

```
Private Sub Form_Click ()            'Listing 3
    Dim X1 As Long
    Dim X2 As Long
    Dim Y1 As Long
    Dim Y2 As Long
    Dim LeftPoint As Integer
    Dim RightPoint As Long
    Dim StepVal As Integer

    DrawStyle = 2             'change to dot
    X1 = ScaleWidth / 2       'horizontal midpoint
    Y1 = 0
    Y2 = ScaleHeight - 200    '200 twips above bottom
```

```
      StepVal = 200
      LeftPoint = 0
      RightPoint = ScaleWidth
      For X2 = LeftPoint To RightPoint Step StepVal
          Line (X1, Y1)-(X2, Y2)
      Next X2
End Sub
```

CUSTOM SCALES

Visual Basic's default scaling system explained above can be changed. To do so, make a selection from a form's **ScaleMode** property. These are the available options:

0 - User
1 - Twip (default)
2 - Point
3 - Pixel
4 - Character
5 - Inch
6 - Millimeter
7 - Centimeter

An inch (option 5), as you already know, has 72 points. A point (2) has 20 twips. So an inch has 1440 twips. If you find twips too difficult to maneuver, you are free to choose one of the available measuring units. As you do, watch various property values change to reflect the new selection.

A character (option 4) is 120 twips in width (horizontal) and 240 twips in height (vertical).

Changing to a different measuring unit (options 2 to 7) affect only the ScaleTop, ScaleLeft, ScaleWidth, and ScaleHeight properties, not Top, Left, Width, and Height properties. The latter properties are still expressed in the default twips.

If you change one of the four Scale properties, Visual Basic will automatically change the ScaleMode property to 0 - User. This indicates that the user is controlling the scaling system. You can choose 1 - Twip to return to the default measuring unit. At run time, you can use the **Scale** method to create your own scaling system. This will be demonstrated shortly.

The **Pixel** (contraction of *picture element*) option uses your monitor's screen dots as the measuring unit. How many pixels your monitor has depends on the hardware. The twip system, on the other hand, is independent of hardware. You can use the procedure below to show your monitor's twips and pixels. The result is shown in Figure 11.10; your result may be different from what is shown here.

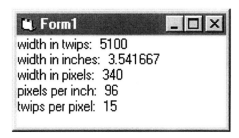

width in twips: 5100
width in inches: 3.541667
width in pixels: 340
pixels per inch: 96
twips per pixel: 15

Figure 11.10   Showing twips and pixels

```
Private Sub Form_Click ()
    Dim X1 As Long
    Dim X2 As Long

    X1 = ScaleWidth
    Print "width in twips: "; X1
    Print "width in inches: "; X1 / 1440
    ScaleMode = 3
    X2 = ScaleWidth
    Print "width in pixels: "; X2
    Print "pixels per inch: "; X2 / (X1 / 1440)
    Print "twips per pixel: "; X1 / X2
End Sub
```

You can also use the **TwipsPerPixelX/Y** property to show the number of horizontal (X) and vertical (Y) twips per pixel for two objects: **Screen** and **Printer**. Use the following statements to show your system:

```
Print Screen.TwipsPerPixelX
Print Screen.TwipsPerPixelY
Print Printer.TwipsPerPixelX
Print Printer.TwipsPerPixelY
```

You can use **Scale** to create a custom scale at run time. In such a scale, you specify the top-left corner and the bottom-right corner. You can then more easily maneuver the numbers in between.

A **Cartesian coordinate system**, which is commonly used in mathematics, can be easily created with Scale. In such a system, the center is point (0, 0). As you move to the right, the X axis increases and the Y axis does not change. On the other hand, if you move to the left, X decreases in value. Moving up or down a straight line increases or decreases Y but does not affect X.

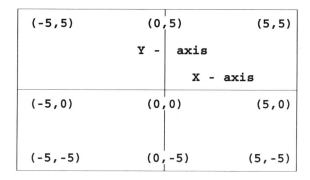

Figure 11.11   Cartesian coordinates

Figure 11.11 shows the values of X and Y at various points in Cartesian coordinates. At the left edge, X is always -5 (the arbitrary number we set); at the right edge, it is 5 instead. Y is 5 at the top and -5 at the bottom.

To set up such a system in Visual Basic, all you need to do is this statement:

```
Scale (-5, 5) - (5, -5)
```

This specifies the top-left corner as point (-5, 5) and the bottom-right corner as point (5, -5). These numbers express X and Y ratios; they are not based on twips or any other measuring unit.

If you set up the above scale system, then ScaleTop becomes 5 and ScaleLeft -5, meaning 5 units from point (0, 0). ScaleWidth is changed to 10 and ScaleHeight to -10. Beware of these changes when you maneuver these properties.

You can use Scale several times to set up multiple custom scales. These scales can control different parts of the screen or be used to draw something else over the same area. If you use Scale with no parameter, you restore Visual Basic's scaling system, with (0, 0) at the top left corner and the rest measured in twips. This is useful in manipulating a form's default properties.

In some situations, a Cartesian coordinate system is much easier to maneuver than Visual Basic's. All you need to remember is to increase Y as you go up and increase X as you go right; decrease them as you go the opposite. This makes programming logic simpler and program code easier to write.

The procedure below shows a simple program that will produce the display in Figure 11.12. Here we use several variables to maneuver quite a few numbers. Should you decide to experiment with different numbers, all you need to do is to assign different initial values to the variables.

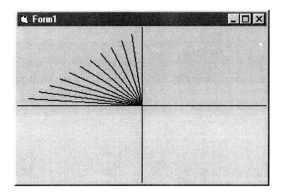

Figure 11.12   The top-left quadrant

```
Private Sub Form_Click ()
    Dim I As Integer
    Dim J As Integer
    Dim X As Integer
    Dim Y As Integer

    X = 120             'scale values for x, y
    Y = 120
    Scale (-X, Y)-(X, -Y)      'scale to x, y
    Line (-X, 0)-(X, 0)        'horizontal line
    Line (0, Y)-(0, -Y)        'vertical line

    For I = -X To 0 Step 10
        Line (0, 0)-(I, J)     'top left quad
        J = J + 10
    Next I
End Sub
```

How can we draw the top-right quadrant, as shown in Figure 11.13? Once we have the system set up, the rest is very easy. The following fragment added at the end of the procedure will do the trick:

```
    J = Y         'start from 120
    For I = 0 To X Step 10
        Line (0, 0)-(I, J)  'top right quad
        J = J - 10
    Next I
```

Form1

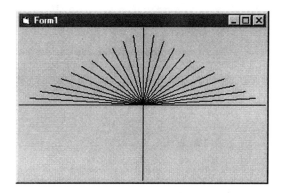

Figure 11.13 The top-right quadrant

(0,0)
(100,0)
(0,50)
(100,50)

Figure 11.14 A custom scale

Another custom scale you can use is to designate the top-left corner as point (0, 0) and use simple numbers for the rest. Figure 11.14 shows an example. Here X has twice the value of Y, and all the numbers can be easily remembered and maneuvered.

Form1
Invoice

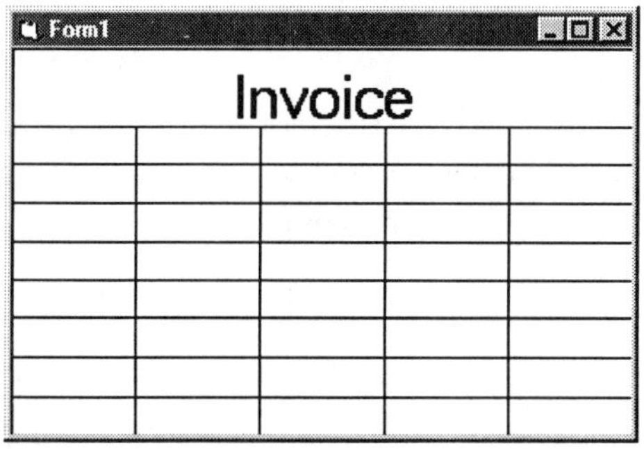

Figure 11.15 A custom-scale output

Using our custom scale, we can easily create a form shown in Figure 11.15. The code to draw these lines is shown below.

(11CUSFRM.FRM)

```
Private Sub Form_Click ()
    Dim I As Integer
    Dim X1 As Integer
    Dim X2 As Integer
    Dim Y1 As Integer
    Dim Y2 As Integer
    Dim Strn As String
    Dim Txt As String

    X1 = 0
    Y1 = 0
    X2 = 100
    Y2 = 50
    Scale (X1, Y1)-(X2, Y2) 'custom scale

    Line (X1, Y1)-(X1, Y2)   'top
    Line (X2, Y1)-(X2, Y2)   'right
    Line (X1, Y2)-(X2, Y2)   'bottom
    Line (X1, Y1)-(X2, Y1)   'left

    FontSize = 24            'set font size
    Txt = "Invoice"          'text to be printed
    Strn = TextWidth(Txt)    'get text width
    CurrentY = 2            'move print head down 2/50
    CurrentX = (ScaleWidth - Strn) / 2
            'move print head to horizontal midpoint
    Print Txt               'print text

    For I = 10 To Y2 Step 5
        Line (X1, Y1 + I)-(X2, Y1 + I)
    Next I                   'horizontal lines

    For I = 20 To X2 Step 20
        Line (X1 + I, 10)-(X1 + I, Y2)
    Next I                   'vertical lines
End Sub
```

After setting up the custom scale, the code draws four border lines from the top clockwise. Then two For loops respectively draw the horizontal and then vertical lines. A few lines of code can thus accomplish a fairly complex task.

If you want thicker lines, add this at the beginning:

```
    DrawWidth = 3
```

This will triple the original line's width. This value can also be set at design time.

If you want to print the form, add Printer where appropriate. Any output directed to the form will be channeled to the printer.

Depending on your printer, the result may not be satisfactory. You may need to adjust some of the numbers to get a decent printout. One adjustment you can make is to change the custom scale this way:

```
Printer.Scale (-20, 0)-(120, 60)
```

This will force the border lines to be printed closer to the center (rather than along the paper's edges), thus creating page margins and adjusting the printout accordingly. If you wish, you can keep the original custom scale but adjust the other numbers.

You can play many tricks with Scale. In the following example, we use Scale twice to define two different custom scales. After each definition, calling the same routine draws different lines (Figure 11.16). Since we use a Form_Resize event, we can resize the form to draw new lines.

```
Private Sub Form_Resize()
    Dim Num As Integer

    Cls
    ForeColor = vbWhite
    BackColor = vbRed
    DrawWidth = 20

    Num = 10      'you can change this number
    Scale (0, 0)-(Num / 2, Num / 2)
        'custom scale based on total lines
    Draw Num      'call sub and pass num

    Scale (Num / 2, 0)-(0, Num / 2)
        'top-right=(0,0), bot-left=(num/2,num/2)
    Draw Num
End Sub

Sub Draw(Num)
    Dim I As Integer
    For I = 1 To Num
        Line (0, I)-(I, 0)
            'first, left to top
            'then top to right
    Next I
End Sub
```

The first Scale is common. The top left is (0, 0) and the bottom right is (Num/2, Num/2). So the Draw procedure draws slanted lines from the left border to the top border.

The second Scale changes the top left to (Num/2, 0) and the bottom right to (0, Num/2). As a result , the top right becomes (0, 0) and the bottom left becomes (Num/2, Num/2). So the Draw routine draws lines from top border to the right border.

Figure 11.16   Drawing slanted lines

The Scale method is quite versatile, and you can do many tricks with it. The Fun and Game programs at the end of various chapter provide lots of examples.

LPR AND RELATIVE COORDINATES

In drawing a line, Visual Basic requires only one argument. The following is the bare minimum:

```
Line -(2000, 1000)
```

Since there is no beginning point, how can a line be drawn? Visual Basic uses something called the **Last Point Referenced** (LPR) to keep track of the default beginning point. At the beginning, the beginning point is (0, 0) or the top left corner. After the above statement, the LPR becomes point (2000, 1000)—2000 twips from the left and 1000 twips from the top. Suppose you now execute this statement:

```
Line -(5000, 3000)
```

A line will be drawn from point (2000, 1000) to point (5000, 3000).

You can also use **CurrentX** and **CurrentY** to specify the LPR. Here is an example:

```
CurrentX = 2000
CurrentY = 1000
Line -(5000, 3000)
```

This will draw a line from point (2000, 1000) to point (5000, 3000). Furthermore, CurrentX, CurrentY, and the LPR will all be changed to reflect the new location. This is how Visual Basic can keep track of the latest position.

You can also use CurrentX and CurrentY to tell you where the LPR is. You can use Print to show their twip numbers and assign them to variables to maneuver them.

In all our examples so far, we have used only **absolute coordinates** by specifying fixed positions. There is another way, and that is **relative coordinates**. Instead of specifying so many twips from the left or top, we can tell Visual Basic to add so many twips to the current point.

To specify relative coordinates, you use the **Step** keyword and the additional twip numbers you want to add to (or subtract from) the current point. Suppose the LPR is at point (2000, 1000). You now want to use relative coordinates to draw a line to point (5000, 3000). This statement will do:

```
Line -Step(3000, 2000)
```

Here we omit the beginning point for the Line statement and tell Visual Basic to draw from the LPR to 3000 twips to the right and 2000 twips further down. What happens if you use negative numbers, such as below?

```
Line -Step(-200, -100)
```

This tells Visual Basic to draw a line beginning at the LPR to 200 twips to the left and 100 twips closer to the top.

You can use Step in the beginning point or the ending point or both. Whenever Step is encountered, the specified twips are added to or subtracted from the current point's twip numbers. When Step is not used, Visual Basic starts measuring from the left and top. Here is an example:

```
Line Step(100, 50) - Step(200, 300)
```

The beginning point of this line is 100 twips to the right and 50 twips to the bottom of the current point. And the ending point is 200 twips to the right and 300 points to the bottom of the current point.

DRAWING BOXES

The Line statement can be given additional arguments to draw boxes, which can be filled with a specified color or hatch lines. Here is the syntax:

```
Line (X1, Y1)-(X2, Y2)[, color, B|F]
```

If you supply only the color argument, a line will be drawn in the specified color. A color number can be specified using RGB or QBColor.

If you add the B argument, a box (rectangle) will be drawn based on the specified coordinate numbers. If a color is specified, the box lines will be in that color. If you provide no color before B, you must add an extra comma to signify its absence. In that case, the default ForeColor of the form will be used. You can change the default DrawWidth of 1 to a higher number to use a thicker line.

The F argument must be used with B, not alone. If both B and F are specified, the box will be filled with the specified color. If no color argument is supplied, the form's ForeColor value will be used to fill the box.

You can use B without F to fill a box with hatch lines. You need to change the form's FillStyle property from the default Transparent to one of the available options (these options are the same as those found in a shape control discussed at the beginning of this chapter). If both B and F are specified, then the box will be filled with the specified color rather than the pattern specified with FillStyle.

Here is an example of drawing a box:

```
Private Sub Form_Click ()
    Line (100, 100)-(1540, 1540), QBColor(4), BF
End Sub
```

This will draw a one-inch square box that is located 100 twips from the top and left. The box will also be filled with the dark red color. If we take out the color parameter, the box will be black (filled with the default ForeColor of the form). If we take out the F argument, the box will be hollow. If you want to fill the box with a hatch pattern, take out the F argument; then set a different FillStyle value in the Properties window, or add this line at the beginning of the procedure:

```
FillStyle = 6   'or vbCross
```

This will fill the box with cross hatch lines. The color of the hatch lines depends on the FillColor property of the form.

DRILL

_____ 15. The second line below will draw a:

```
Scale (-1, 1)-(1, -1)
Line  (-1, 1)-(1, -1)
```

    a.   diagonal line, top-left to bottom-right
    b.   diagonal line, bottom-left to top-right
    c.   one-inch horizontal line
    d.   one-inch vertical line

_____ 16. If you draw a line without specifying a point, the _____ (use abbreviation) is presumed.

_____ 17. The following statement is legal. True or false?
Line -(ScaleWidth, ScaleHeight)

_____ 18. This statement will draw:
Line -Step(1440, 0)
    a.   a one-inch vertical line
    b.   a one-inch diagonal line
    c.   a one-inch horizontal line
    d.   nothing; illegal

_____ 19. After the following statements, the print head goes to the:

```
Scale (-1, 1)-(1, -1)
CurrentX = 0 : CurrentY = 0
```

    a.   Top left
    b.   center
    c.   bottom right
    d.   nowhere; is not moved

_____ 20. To draw a rectangle and fill it with a color, you need to add the _____ parameters to the end of a Line statement.

PRACTICE

■ 7. Explain how these properties differ: Top, ScaleTop, Left, and ScaleLeft.

■ 8. Explain how these properties differ: Width, ScaleWidth, Height, and ScaleHeight.

■ 9. Give two Line statements that will draw two diagonal lines from top-left to bottom-right and from bottom-left to top-right. Do not use any number.

■ 10. Write a Form_Click procedure that will use four Line statements to draw a rectangle with each side positioned one inch from the form window's corresponding border.

■ 11. Draw 20 rectangles, each of which is 100 twips inside the previous. The result should be as shown in Figure 11.17.

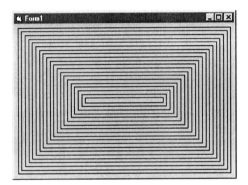

Figure 11.17   Drawing 20 rectangles

■ 12. Draw 20 diamonds, each of which is 100 twips inside the previous. The result should be as shown in Figure 11.18. (Hint: Use Cartesian coordinates.)

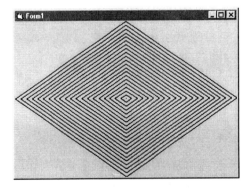

Figure 11.18   Drawing 20 diamonds

■ 13. In Listing 3, change the drawing to begin each line from the top right corner.

■ 14. Complete drawing in all the four quadrants shown in Figure 11.13. The result should be as shown in Figure 11.19.

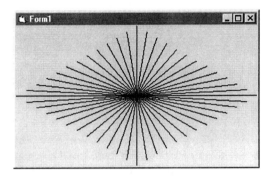

Figure 11.19   Drawing lines in all four quadrants

■ 15. What does the following procedure do?

```
Sub Form_Click ()
    FillStyle = 7
    Line (100, 100)-(1540, 1540), , B
End Sub
```

■ 16. Write a Form_Click procedure that will use the Line statement to draw a one-inch square box located in the middle of the form window and fill it with diagonal-cross hatch lines.

■ 17. Write a Form_Click procedure that will use the Line statement to draw a one-inch square box located at the bottom right corner and fill it with diagonal-cross hatch lines.

■ 18. Modify the above so that the box has the same size as the form.

PSET AND POINT

PSet and **Point** are two methods that you can use to set a point (dot) on a form or return the color number at a specified point. PSet turns on a **pixel** of the specified location by giving it a specified color. Here is an example:

```
Private Sub Form_Click ()
    Dim Dot As Long

    PSet (100, 100), QBColor(12)
    Dot = Point(100, 100)
    Print Dot
End Sub
```

The first line sets a bright-red dot at point (100, 100). The second line returns the RGB color number for point (100, 100). Line 3 prints out 255, the RGB value for the color number.

If the form's DrawWidth property remains the default value of 1, the dot set by PSet may not be visible. You may need to increase this value so that the resulting dot can be seen by the naked eye.

If no color is specified with PSet, the default ForeColor is used to set the dot.

Executing a PSet statement moves the LPR to the specified coordinates. The CurrentX and CurrentY properties also reflect the location.

You can use Step to designate relative coordinates as you can in drawing lines. Here is an example:

```
PSet Step(50, 50)
```

This will set a point 50 twips to the right and 50 twips further down.

You can use PSet to erase a dot set by PSet. To do that, you assign the background color to the specified pixel, which makes the pixel invisible. Here is an example:

```
PSet Step(0, 0), BackColor
```

This will turn on the background color at the current point. Whatever color you may have assigned to the pixel, it is now the same as the background and thus indistinguishable from the rest.

DRAWING CIRCLES

The **Circle** method can be used to draw circles. You need to supply the coordinates for a center and specify a radius value. In its simplest form, Circle follows this syntax:

```
Circle [Step](x, y), radius
```

Use the optional **Step** to specify relative coordinates; otherwise, you need to supply absolute coordinates. The following procedure draws 10 concentric circles, with all sharing the same center point and with each subsequent ring 150 twips wider in radius, as shown in Figure 11.20.

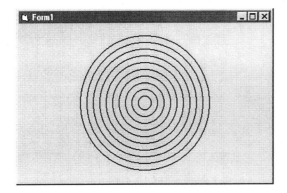

Figure 11.20   Drawing 10 concentric circles

```
Private Sub Form_Click ()
    Dim I As Integer
    Dim X As Long
    Dim Y As Long

    X = ScaleWidth / 2    'get horizontal midpoint
    Y = ScaleHeight / 2   'get vertical midpoint

    For I = 1 To 10
        Circle (X, Y), 150 * I
    Next I
End Sub
```

 ## TIP: A Perfect Square

The typical form is a rectangle in which the ScaleWidth property is larger than the ScaleHeight counterpart. What can you do if you want to make both equal in the number of twips? There are occasions when you must do that in order to make your drawing appear balanced. In Figure 11.20, for example, you may want to draw the circles in a perfectly square form to make the result look better.

You may have in mind the idea of assigning each an equal value, such as:

```
ScaleWidth = 3000
ScaleHeight = 3000
```

Or you may have in mind assigning the latter to the former, such as this:

```
ScaleWidth = ScaleHeight
```

These statements (or similar moves at design time) only set the internal (and invisible) area for drawing graphics. They don't change the form's physical dimensions.

You can assign ScaleHeight to Width, such as this:

```
Width = ScaleHeight
```

But Width is slightly larger than ScaleWidth. The above statement will make ScaleWidth less than ScaleHeight by 120 twips. So, in order to create a perfectly square form, you can use a line like below:

```
Width = ScaleHeight + 120
```

If you don't want the bother of adding a specific number, the following two lines will do the trick:

```
Width = ScaleHeight   'this line is required
Width = ScaleHeight + (ScaleHeight - ScaleWidth)
   'or Width = 2 * ScaleHeight - ScaleWidth
```

The procedure below will create a perfect square and draw a circle filling up the square. Here ScaleHeight can be substituted with a variable, but ScaleWidth cannot.

```
Private Sub Form_Click ()
    Dim SH As Long

    SH = ScaleHeight
    Width = SH
    Width = 2 * SH - ScaleWidth
    Circle (SH / 2, SH / 2), SH / 2
End Sub
```

This arrangement uses the default ScaleHeight for the square. If you want to have a larger or smaller square, you can manually set the height at design time or add before the above two lines a line like below:

```
Height = 6000
```

Replace the above line with the following lines if you want the largest possible square for drawing:

```
Top = 0          'move form to top left of screen
Left = 0         'can be a higher value here

Height = Screen.Height
```

The procedure below produces the Olympic rings shown in Figure 11.21. Here we use two arrays as well as ScaleWidth and ScaleHeight to maneuver the rings' positions.

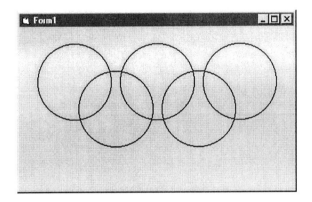

Figure 11.21   Olympic rings

(11OLYMPIC.FRM)
```
Private Sub Form_Load ()
    Show  'show Form1
    Dim I As Integer
    Dim SH As Long
    Dim SW As Long
    Dim X(1 To 5) As Single
    Dim Y(1 To 2) As Single
        'get coordinates for x & y using
        'the form's height and width
    SW = ScaleWidth
    SH = ScaleHeight
    X(1) = SW * 0.2
    X(2) = SW * 0.5
    X(3) = SW * 0.8
    X(4) = SW * 0.35
```

```
    X(5)  =  SW  *  0.65
    Y(1)  =  SH  /  3
    Y(2)  =  SH  /  2

    For  I  =  1  To  3        'draw top rings
        Circle  (X(I),  Y(1)),  800
    Next  I

    For  I  =  4  To  5        'draw bottom rings
        Circle  (X(I),  Y(2)),  800
    Next  I
End  Sub
```

As mentioned earlier, a form's FillStyle property has eight options, the same as
those in a shape control. If you set this to Diagonal Cross (7), the result of
running the same procedure is shown in Figure 11.22.

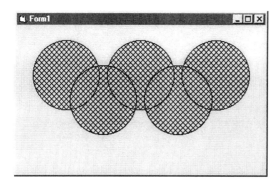

Figure 11.22   Rings filled with diagonal-cross lines

ARCS, ELLIPSES, AND PIE SLICES

In its complete form, the **Circle** statement can follow this syntax:

```
Circle(x, y), radius, color, start, end, aspect
```

The color argument is the same as in Line; it specifies the color for drawing the
circle line or the hatch lines.

The aspect argument governs the vertical to horizontal ratio. There are three
distinct scenarios: higher than 1, between 1 and -1, and lower than -1. Each

scenario leads to very different results. Their differences are best illustrated with some concrete examples shown below.

```
Private Sub Form_Click ()
    Dim I As Single
    Dim J As Integer

    For I = 2 To -2 Step -0.5
        J = J + 600
        Circle (J, 1000), 400, , , , I
        Print I
    Next I
End Sub
```

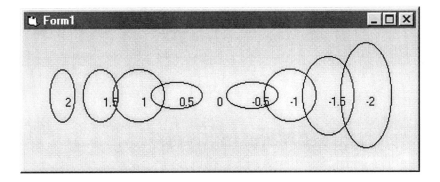

Figure 11.23   Results of using different aspects

Our program attempts to test various aspect ratios. Based on the results shown in Figure 11.23, we can draw the following conclusions:

- If the value is 0, no circle is drawn. Only the LPR is moved.

- If the value increases from 1, the height does not change, but the width decreases proportionally. With the value of 2, the width is 1/2 of the height; if the value goes to 4, the width is only 1/4 of the height.

- Both 1 and -1 produce the same perfect circle. If you go to lower fractions, the width remains the same but the height gets smaller. So with .5 (1/2) or -.5 (-1/2), the height is only half of the width. If you use 1/5 or -1/5, the height will be only 1/5 of the width.

- If the value decreases from -1, the width does not change, but the height increases. So at -2, the height is twice that of the width, and at -5 five times.

So, the numbers seem to work opposite of what they imply. If you go up from 1, you squeeze the waistline without raising the height. If you go from 1 or -1 to smaller fractions, you flatten the ring without widening its width. If you decrease from -1, you heighten the ring without changing its width.

Circle's start and end arguments specify the beginning and ending points of an arc (incomplete circle). You can control these arguments to produce partial circles with or without sides. For a complete circle, you can omit the arguments or respectively specify 0 and 2 Pi radians. (Actually if both arguments are the same and do not exceed 2 Pi, a complete circle will be drawn.) So if you have 0 and Pi, the upper half is drawn. If you use Pi and 2 Pi, the bottom half will be drawn.

To add a side (radius) to a particular circle, add a minus (-) sign. If you want both sides drawn, add - to both start and end numbers.

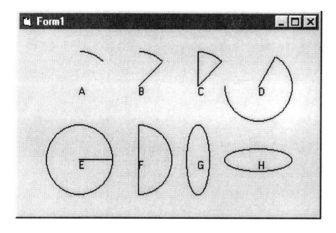

Figure 11.24   Circle variations

The procedure below produces the shapes in Figure 11.24.

(11CIRCLES.FRM)

```
Private Sub Form_Click ()
    Dim Pi As Single
    Dim SH As Long
    Dim SW As Long
```

```
        Dim R As Integer

        Pi = 4 * Atn(1)
        R = 600      'radius
        SW = ScaleWidth
        SH = ScaleHeight
        Circle (SW * 0.2, SH * 0.3), R, , Pi / 4, Pi / 2
        Print "A"
        Circle (SW * 0.4, SH * 0.3), R, , -Pi / 4, Pi / 2
        Print "B"
        Circle (SW * 0.6, SH * 0.3), R, , -Pi / 4, -Pi / 2
        Print "C"
        Circle (SW * 0.8, SH * 0.3), R, , Pi, -Pi / 3
        Print "D"
        Circle (SW * 0.2, SH * 0.7), R, , -2 * Pi, -0
        Print "E"
        Circle (SW * 0.4, SH * 0.7), R, , -Pi * 1.5, -Pi / 2
        Print "F"
        Circle (SW * 0.6, SH * 0.7), R, , Pi, Pi, 3
            'vertical
        Print "G"
        Circle (SW * 0.8, SH * 0.7), R, , 1, 1, 1 / 3
            'horizontal
        Print "H"
End Sub
```

After a Circle statement is executed, the resulting circle's center becomes the LPR as well as the coordinates for CurrentX and CurrentY. The letters in Figure 11.24 are each placed at the LPR of each object.

You can fill a completely enclosed drawing (ellipses, circles, and pie slices) with a specified color or hatch pattern. The rules are the same as those dealing with boxes and circles; this was explained in previous sections.

3-D SIMULATION

You can manipulate RGB colors to produce a 3-D look. One way to do it is to keep one color element in full strength and gradually increase the other two from 0 to create the fading effect. The result is like shining light on an object.

Figure 11.25 is created by the procedure below. In the FillColor statement, we keep R at 255 and gradually increase G and B from 0. So as the circle gets smaller, the fill color becomes less intensely red.

```
Private Sub Form_Click()
    Dim I As Integer
    Dim X As Single
```

```
    Dim Y As Single

    On Error GoTo ErrTrap
    DrawStyle = 5    'Transparent
        'to prevent line from messing up effect
        'try without it and see the difference
    X = ScaleWidth / 2
    Y = ScaleHeight / 2
    For I = 0 To 255
        FillColor = RGB(255, I, I)
        'full red, increase G & B to reduce red
        Circle (X, Y), Y - I * 8, FillColor
        'I*lower to fade faster
    Next I

ErrTrap:
    'if invalid procedure call, just exit sub
    'triggered by a negative radius value in Circle
End Sub
```

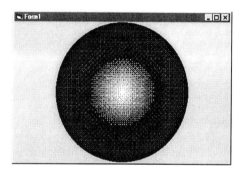

Figure 11.25   Reducing color intensity to create a 3-D look

We use I*8 to control the degree of color fading. If you use a lower factor, the fading will go faster. If you use a higher value, the opposite is true. That could reduce the radius to less than 0, which will trigger an error. Our error trap then directs execution to the trap to exit the procedure without showing the error.

You can change the display's red to another color. The following change will lead to a blue ball:

```
FillColor = RGB(I, I, 255)
```

Instead of fading the color to the center, you can make it fade to a corner. Replacing the previous Circle statement with the following will shift the faded part to the upper right corner, producing the effect shown in Figure 11.26.

```
Circle (X + I * 5, Y - I * 4), Y - I * 10, FillColor
    'shift center upward and rightward
```

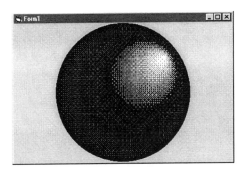

Figure 11.26   Fading to the upper right

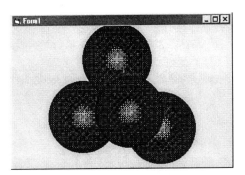

Figure 11.27   3-D looking balls

Figure 11.27 shows a bunch of 3-D looking balls (oranges). Each ball appears when you click a spot inside the window. The Form_MouseUp procedure shown below responds to each click by drawing a ball; mouse events will be fully covered in Chapter 12.

The Form_Load procedure produces the initial red ball in the middle. If you then click a point inside this ball, you'll produce a 3-D effect on this ball. If you delete this procedure, the MouseUp procedure will let you add a pile of oranges to the window without the original red ball.

```
Private Sub Form_Load()
    Dim X As Long, Y As Long
```

```
        Show
        X = ScaleWidth / 2
        Y = ScaleHeight / 2
        FillStyle = 0    'solid fill
        FillColor = vbRed
        Circle (X, Y), Y, FillColor
            'draw middle circle and fill with red
    End Sub

    Private Sub Form_MouseUp(Button As Integer, Shift As _
    Integer, X As Single, Y As Single)
        Dim I As Integer
        On Error GoTo ErrTrap

        FillStyle = 0    'solid fill
        DrawStyle = 5    'transparent line

        For I = 1 To 255
            FillColor = RGB(255, I, I)
            'reduce red by increasing green & blue
            Circle (X, Y), 1000 - I * 5, FillColor
            'exit if radius < 0
            'center is click point (X,Y)
            'radius is decreased from 1000 twips
        Next I

    ErrTrap:
        'if invalid procedure call, just exit sub
    End Sub
```

RETAINING & SAVING SCREEN DISPLAYS

As explained in Chapter 5, a form has the **AutoRedraw** property, which is set to False by default. When screen output reaches beyond the existing window's boundaries, it is lost. The same thing happens when you cover up a display. If you change this property to True, a copy of the output is saved to RAM. When the window is redisplayed, the screen is repainted. This necessarily requires hardware overhead and slows down your computer.

A form can also respond to a **Paint** event. This event, just as the Load event, is triggered when a form is loaded. Furthermore, it is also activated when the form is uncovered (re-exposed). If you want to keep your output to a form persistent, put output statements by Print, Line, and Circle in a Form_Paint procedure.

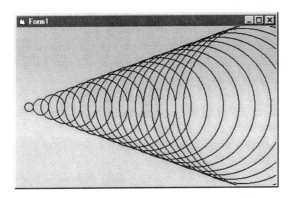

Figure 11.28   A persistent graphic

The Form_Paint procedure shown below starts out with the **Cls** statement to clear any previous drawing. We then instruct Visual Basic to draw a series of larger circles—until the LPR (CurrentX) reaches the right border (Figure 11.28).

```
Private Sub Form_Paint ()            'Listing 4
    Dim I As Integer
    Dim SH As Long
    Dim SW As Long

    Cls                      'clear previous drawing
    SW = ScaleWidth              'get width
    SH = ScaleHeight             'get height
    For I = 0 To SW Step 300
        Circle (I, SH / 2), I / 3
    Next I
End Sub
```

If you now enlarge the window or cover and then uncover it, the screen will be repainted. However, repainting does not happen if you reduce the window's size. Also, the Paint event is not triggered when AutoRedraw is on.

If you want a window to be repainted whenever it is resized, use the **Resize** event. This event is triggered whenever the size of the window is altered. This happens regardless of the state of AutoRedraw. If AutoRedraw is not on, covering up the window will erase any drawing in the covered area.

The simplest way to clear the screen for another drawing is to use the Cls method, which we have done many times. In addition, executing the **Refresh** method will also clear the existing drawing. The same thing will also happen when you assign a new BackColor property.

A from has the **ClipControls** property which is set to True by default. In this state, drawing in the form does not cover the controls already placed on the form. This requires extra overhead and time because the controls' locations have to be retained and not painted over. Changing ClipControls to False can marginally speed up drawing graphics on the screen but will paint over existing controls.

You can use the **SavePicture** statement to save a screen drawing to a bitmap file on disk. Execute this statement after the picture appears:

```
SavePicture Form1.Image "PicName.bmp"
```

Form1 can be changed to Me or omitted; change it to the picture box's name if the drawing appears in it. **Image** can be changed to **Picture** and make no difference in most situations. You can also change BMP to ICO, CUR, or WMF. Based on my experience, these names don't affect the picture's quality or file size, which can be huge for a simple color picture.

The **AutoRedraw** property must be on for SavePicture to save a display. Otherwise, you'll have a huge file with no picture in it.

If you use the **Picture** property of a form, picture box, or image control to load a picture at design time or run time, you can also use SavePicture to save it to another disk file of the same format. In case of conflict, the picture in the Picture property is saved, not the one drawn at run time.

You can use the Windows Paint program to paint something and then select an area to copy to the Clipboard. You can then select a form, image control, or picture box (or even an OLE control) and choose Edit | Paste to make the picture appear. The picture is then loaded. The involved object's Picture property will change from (None) to (Bitmap) in the Properties window. You can highlight (Bitmap) and press Del to erase it; the picture will disappear. If you save the form with a picture loaded, a separate binary file of the same name but the FRX extension will also be saved. This file stores the picture loaded at design time. When you load the form, the picture will be loaded as well. If you erase this file from disk, loading the form will lead to an error and no picture.

The bitmap file you save to disk can also be loaded to a command button, check box, or option box—if their Style property is changed from Standard to Graphical. But you can't paste to these what you copy from Paint; the Paste option is simply not available.

GRAPHICS CONTAINERS

Visual Basic comes with three containers which you can use to display predrawn pictures. These graphics containers are: form, image control, and picture box control.

The graphics containers can display five types of graphics files. These are bitmaps, icons, Windows metafiles (standard and enhanced), GIF, and JPEG. The WINDOWS and VB\GRAPHICS directories contain many files with the BMP, ICO, CUR, and WMF extensions. These can all be used by Visual Basic.

A **bitmap** picture contains a series of predetermined dots. If you stretch it, the dots become bigger and farther apart and the picture becomes coarse. You can use Windows Paintbrush to draw bitmaps and copy them to Visual Basic as discussed in the preceding section.

Icons are bitmaps limited to 32 by 32 pixels. They are most commonly used to graphically represent an object or application in the Windows environment.

Metafiles store graphics in vector format. Instead of predetermined dots, the algorithm for those dots is saved. When such a picture is stretched, more dots will fill up the expanded space. The picture's integrity is thus preserved. This mechanism also makes most metafiles larger.

The C:\VB\GRAPHICS directory contains three subdirectories, BITMAPS, CURSORS, ICONS, and METAFILE. Each contains numerous picture files. The C:\WINDOWS directory also has quite a few bitmap files.

Forms and Pictures

To display a picture in the current form, double-click **Picture** in the Properties window. The Load Picture dialog box appears, shown in Figure 11.29.

Double-click the desired folder to show its pertinent file names. In our example, go to GRAPHICS, METAFILE, and then ARROWS. Double-click the first file shown in Figure 11.29. The picture appears in the form, shown in Figure 11.30.

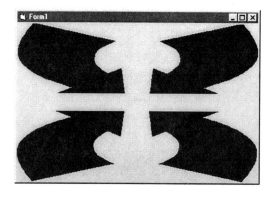

Figure 11.29   The Load Picture dialog box

After the above steps, the Picture entry in the Properties window shows
(Metafile), replacing the original (None). If you now erase this entry (just
highlight it and press Del), (None) will return and the picture will disappear from
the form.

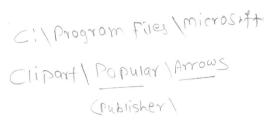

C:\Program Files \microsift

Clipart\ Popular \Arrows

(publisher\

Figure 11.30   A loaded picture

Another way of bringing a picture to the current form is by using the **LoadPicture**
function at run time. Our above steps could be replaced by the following
procedure:

```
Private Sub Form_Load ()
    Picture = LoadPicture _
    ("graphics\metafile\arrows\2darrow1.wmf")
```

```
End Sub
```

When the program runs, the specified picture (the same as shown in Figure 11.30) will be displayed.

To unload a picture at run time, supply an empty string as the argument, such as:

```
Picture = LoadPicture("")   'to unload form picture
```

When you save a form with a picture loaded at design time, the picture will be saved to a separate FRX file. This file is used to load the picture in the future. If you use code to load a picture at run time, you must make sure that the picture is available for the program to find and load.

Image Control

An image control is used primarily to display pictures. It has the **Picture property** just like a form. You can use it to load a picture at design time. You can also use **LoadPicture** to load a picture to an image control at run time. If you want to load a picture to an image control rather than to a form, make sure to specify the object, such as:

```
Image1.Picture = LoadPicture(". . .")
```

If you did not specify Image1 (the default name) and used Picture alone, the picture would be loaded to the current form instead. In the above statement, you can use Image1 alone and omit Picture; this applies to Picture1 (next section) as well.

An image control has the unique **Stretch** property. It is by default set to False. In this state, the picture stays in its original size and the control is resized to fit the picture. If you resize the control, the picture remains the same. If you set this property to True, a picture can be stretched or shrunken to fit within the control's borders. As you resize the control, the picture will change to fit. The Stretch property is not available for a form or picture box.

Picture Box

A picture box combines some properties of a form and an image control. You can display a picture in it as in an image control. You can print text and draw lines or circles in it as in a form; this cannot be done in an image control. Inside a picture box you can place any control, including another picture box. Since a picture box has many properties and supports many methods, it requires more resources. If you just want to display a picture, use an image control, which requires much less overhead.

When you add an image control or a picture box to a form, there are no words to identify them. Both show a rectangular box. The only distinction between them is the style of borderlines. An image control is framed by dotted lines, but a picture box by solid lines. At run time, an image control shows no borderlines and the background items show through. A picture box has single-line borders by default, which you can change to None; any background display is also covered up.

A picture box has the **AutoSize** property, which is set to False by default. In this setting, the control is fixed and the picture inside may change to fit the control's size and shape. A metafile will be resized to fit in. A bitmap may be clipped or occupy only part of the control. If you change this property to True, the original picture determines the display; the control's borders may be changed to accommodate the picture.

Figure 11.31   Output to a picture box

Much of what is said about a form can be applied to a picture box as well. You must, however, specify Picture1 or another name in order to do something to it—just as you specify Printer in order to use Print to send text to the printer rather than the form. The procedure below shows where you need to add Picture1 in order to output to the picture box shown in Figure 11.31. Without these additions, the output would go to the form as shown earlier (Figure 11.21).

```
Private Sub Form_Load ()
    Show   'show Form1
    Dim I As Integer
    Dim SH As Long
    Dim SW As Long
    Dim Txt As String
    Dim PicWidth As Long
    Dim X(1 To 5) As Single
    Dim Y(1 To 2) As Single
        'get coordinates for x & y using
        'the form's height and width
    SW = Picture1.ScaleWidth
    SH = Picture1.ScaleHeight
    X(1) = SW * 0.2
    X(2) = SW * 0.5
    X(3) = SW * 0.8
    X(4) = SW * 0.35
    X(5) = SW * 0.65
    Y(1) = SH / 3
    Y(2) = SH / 2

    For I = 1 To 3      'draw top rings
        Picture1.Circle (X(I), Y(1)), 800
    Next I

    For I = 4 To 5      'draw bottom rings
        Picture1.Circle (X(I), Y(2)), 800
    Next I

    Picture1.FontSize = 24     'pic box font size
    Txt = "Picture Box Demo"
    PicWidth = Picture1.TextWidth(Txt)
        'pic box text width
    Picture1.CurrentX = (SW - PicWidth) / 2
        'center of pic box
    Picture1.CurrentY = SH * 0.8   '80% from top
    Picture1.Print Txt
End Sub
```

We use variables SW and SH to respectively represent its ScaleWidth and ScaleHeight. We also use a formula to make the text appear in the center of the picture box.

NOTE   You can create a perfectly square picture box at design time or run time. Just set its Height and Width to the same twip value. When this happens, the Scale properties will also be equal—quite unlike a form.

You can use the **LoadPicture** method to load a picture to an image control or a picture box, just as you do to a form. Once a picture is loaded to an object, either at design time or at run time, you can use assignment statements to copy it to another graphics container. Here are some examples:

```
Image1 = Picture              'from form to image control
Picture = Picture1            'from picture box to form
Form1.Picture = Picture1.Picture        'same
```

If the original object has no picture, then no picture is assigned. You can assign an empty string to an object to erase a previous assignment.

You can also use the **Picture object** to store a picture. In the following procedure, a picture is loaded to Picture1 at design time. An object named objPic is created from the Picture class. This object is assigned the picture loaded at design time. It is then assigned to the Picture property of the form.

```
Private Sub Form_Click()
    Dim objPic As Picture  'can be Variant or Object
    Set objPic = Picture1.Picture
    Me.Picture = objPic    'load pic to form
    Print objPic.Type      'integer for pic type
End Sub
```

The Picture object has, among others, a **Type property**. You can use it to designate the type of picture to store in the object or tell you what type of picture is stored in the object. Check the online help for Picture Object and Picture Object Constants for details.

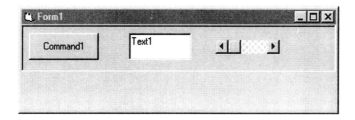

Figure 11.32   Adding controls in a picture box

A picture box can contain other controls. You can thus add a picture box to a form and then add other controls in the picture box. To make the picture box fit in the form across the top, change the picture box's **Align** property from the default 0 - None to 1 - Align Top. To add another control to this box, click a tool and then draw inside the box—the same way you handle a frame control. Figure 11.32 shows three controls added to Picture1.

TIP: Toolbar, Status Bar, and Alignment

You can add to an application a toolbar at the top and/or a status bar at the bottom. To do that, you add to a form two picture boxes and set one's Align property to Top and the other's to Bottom. The two picture boxes will then appear respectively at the top and the bottom. You can then add controls to the separate picture boxes. If you wish, you can use the bottom box to respond to a user action by showing an instruction or error message. To do that, add a label or text box to it and write code to respond to user actions; you can also use the Print statement to output text directly to a picture box. This arrangement lets you channel to the status bar messages that will normally appear in a message box, which can be quite obtrusive. To make the status bar (picture box) less obtrusive, you can use the Visible property to hide it when it is not in use.

When you add a picture box to a form, its default **Align** property value is 0 - None. This allows you to resize the picture box and drag it to any location on the form. You can change this value to 1 - Align Top or 2 - Align Bottom. After you do that, the picture box goes to the designated location and you can no longer move or size it.

If you have multiple picture boxes aligned at the top or bottom, you can rearrange their relative positions by dragging one to above or below another. The boxes will change their relative positions

Picture Viewer

Wouldn't it be convenient if we could click one file name after another to see each successive picture? After all, it is hard to judge a picture by its file name and it is inconvenient to load a file just to see its picture. We can create such an application by combining an image control and the file and directory tools you learned in Chapter 10.

Our user interface (Figure 11.33) has Drive1, Dir1, File1, Text1, a command button named cmdQuit, and an image control.

File1's **Pattern property** is set at design time to the following:

    .ico;.bmp;*.wmf;*.emf;*.cur;*.gif;*.jpg

The list includes all the file types that can be displayed in Visual Basic. Your system is likely to include many pictures of the first three types and very few of the others.

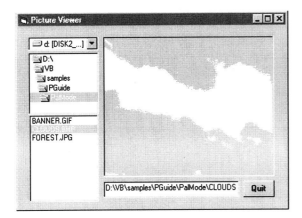

Figure 11.33   **Viewing a picture**

The image control's **Stretch property** must be set to True at design time. If not, you should do it in code at run time. If this property is not changed to True, some pictures, particularly icons and cursors, may appear in a tiny square and thus illegible.

The procedures below show all the procedures for the application. They are to respond to your double-clicking Drive1 and Dir1, and single-clicking File1 and Quit.

(11 VIEWPIC.FRM)

```
Private Sub Drive1_Change()
    On Error GoTo ErrTrap

    Dir1.Path = Drive1.Drive
        'change dir path when drive is changed
    Exit Sub

ErrTrap:
    MsgBox Error
End Sub

Private Sub Dir1_Change()
    File1.Path = Dir1.Path
        'change file list when dir is changed
```

```
End Sub

Private Sub File1_Click()
    On Error GoTo ErrTrap

    If Right(File1.Path, 1) = "\" Then
        Text1.Text = File1.Path & File1.FileName
            'show root directory in text box
    Else
        Text1.Text = File1.Path & "\" & File1.FileName
            'if not root directory
    End If
    Image1.Picture = LoadPicture(Text1.Text)
            'load image
    Exit Sub

ErrTrap:
    MsgBox Error
End Sub

Private Sub cmdQuit_Click()
    End
End Sub
```

Drive1's Change event is triggered by clicking a drive. Dir1's Change, however, is activated only when you double-click a directory. To open a file, you can use Click or DblClick. Click, the one we use, seems more convenient in this situation because this allows quicker action to see a picture. As you click each file displayed in the File1 box, its picture will appear in the Image1 box. You can thus see many pictures very quickly.

Painting Pictures

You can use the **PaintPicture** method to copy a picture or part of it from a form, image control, or picture box to a form, a picture box, or a printer. It has this syntax:

```
obj.PaintPicture pic destX, destY[, destWidth[, _
destHeight[, srcX[, srcY[, srcWidth[, _
srcHeight[, opcode]]]]]]]
```

The first three arguments are mandatory, but the others are all optional. Basically, you need to specify where the original picture is, where the picture should be copied to, the size of the destination picture, the beginning X and Y coordinates of the original picture to be clipped, and the ending point of the area to be clipped.

To demonstrate how to use the PaintPicture method, add Image1 to a clear form
and write the following procedure.

```
Private Sub Form_Click()
    Dim I As Integer
    Dim J As Integer
    Dim Pic As Image

    Set Pic = Image1     'use Pic for Image1
    Pic.Picture = LoadPicture _
    ("graphics\bitmaps\assorted\beany.bmp")
        'load picture to image box
    Pic.Left = -10000 'move original out of view

    For I = 1 To 3
        For J = 1 To 5
            PaintPicture Pic.Picture, J * Pic.Width, _
            I * Pic.Height, Pic.Width, Pic.Height
        Next
    Next
End Sub
```

We use the LoadPicture method to load a bitmap to Image1 at run time. This
picture is then copied to the form (Figure 11.34). We use only the required
arguments for PaintPicture and omit all the rest; so the default values are used
here.

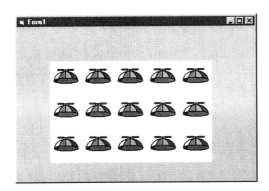

Figure 11.34   Using PaintPicture

We can flip a destination picture horizontally or vertically by adding a - sign
before a pertinent argument. If we add a - (minus) before our last two arguments,
the result is shown in Figure 11.35. Each destination picture is flipped from right
to left and bottom to top. As a result, the whole group is moved closer to the top
left.

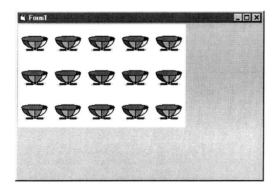

Figure 11.35   Flipping pictures

We can change our PaintPicture statement to the following. Here we want to start at 10% from the top and left of the source picture and copy only 1/2.. The result is shown in Figure 11.36.

```
PaintPicture Pic.Picture, J * Pic.Width, _
I * Pic.Height, Pic.Width, Pic.Height, _
Pic.Width / 10, Pic.Height / 10, Pic.Width / 2, _
Pic.Height / 2
```

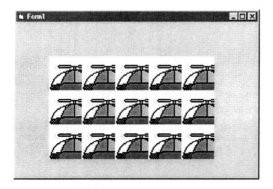

Figure 11.36   Cropping pictures

ANIMATION TECHNIQUES

It is common to use trigonometric formulas to create animation and moving patterns. If you throw in colors, the result could be spectacular and entertaining. Besides trigonometry, there are many other ways to generate patterns and animation. In the sections below, we use a variety of techniques to generate patterns and simulate motion.

Flapping Wings

Sine and Cosine waves can be used to generate patterns. The procedure below shows how to use PSet and Cos in a custom scale to generate the display shown in Figure 11.37.

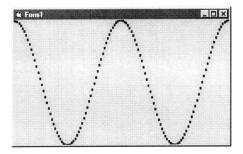

Figure 11.37   A cosine wave

```
Private Sub Form_Click ()
    Dim I As Single
    Dim Pi As Single

    DrawWidth = 3
    Pi = 4 * Atn(1)
    Scale (-Pi * 2, 1)-(Pi * 2, -1)
        '-2 pi to 2 pi

    For I = -Pi * 2 To Pi * 2 Step 0.1
        PSet (I, Cos(I))
    Next I
End Sub
```

We can change PSet to Line, such as:

```
    Line (0, 0)-(I, Cos(I))
```

The same shape remains, but a line connects each dot to the center. The result is shown in Figure 11.38.

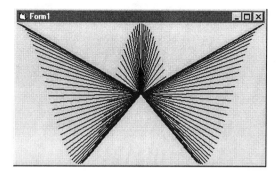

Figure 11.38   Using Line instead of PSet

We can change Cos to Sin, such as:

```
Line (0, 0)-(I, Sin(I))
```

The pattern is changed to that shown in Figure 11.39.

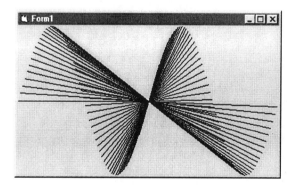

Figure 11.39   Changing Cos to Sin

Sine and Cosine waves can be used to simulate waving motions. The previous procedure can be modified as shown below. The difference is that we now use an infinite loop to keep the motion going.

To provide for a way to end the program, you need to add the DoEvents statement (or the DoEvents( ) function). It allows other Windows applications to get the CPU time. Without this statement, the loop monopolizes the CPU and

other applications cannot be accessed. In our arrangement, you can click the End
icon to break out of the loop and end the program.

```
Private Sub Form_Click ()
    Dim I As Single
    Dim Pi As Single

    DrawWidth = 1
    Pi = 4 * Atn(1)
    Scale (-Pi * 2, 1)-(Pi * 2, -1)
        '-2 pi to 2 pi
    Do      'beginning of infinite loop
        For I = -Pi * 2 To Pi * 2 Step 0.05
            Line (0, 0)-(I, Cos(I))
        Next I

        If I >= Pi * 2 Then
        Cls
        For I = Pi * 2 To -Pi * 2 Step -0.05
            Line (0, 0)-(I, Cos(I))
        Next I
        End If
        Cls
        DoEvents    'can break out
    Loop    'infinite loop
End Sub
```

When the program runs, the screen shows an object resembling a butterfly
flapping its wings.

There are a number of ways you can modify the program to simulate different
illusions. These are the items you can tinker with:

- The DrawWidth value can be increased.
- Step values can be increased or decreased.
- Cos can be changed to Sin.

Furthermore, colors can be added to make the resulting illusions more attractive.

Glittering Flower

Our next project uses Sin, Cos, and RGB to generate varying patterns and colors.
One result is shown in Figure 11.40.

(11FLOWER.FRM)
```
Private Sub Form_Click ()
    Dim I As Single
```

```
    Dim Pi As Single
    Dim R As Single
    Dim X As Single
    Dim Y As Single

    Pi = 4 * Atn(1)
    DrawWidth = 3
    Scale (-1, 1)-(1, -1)          'Cartesian scale

    Do
        BackColor = RndCo()     'call function
        ForeColor = RndCo()     'get random color
        For I = 0 To 4 * Pi Step 0.01
            R = Cos(I * 6)          'get radius
            X = R * Cos(I)          'get x axis
            Y = R * Sin(I)          'get y axis
            PSet (X, Y)
        Next I
        DoEvents     'allow End button to work
    Loop
End Sub

Function RndCo()
    Dim R As Integer
    Dim G As Integer
    Dim B As Integer

    Randomize
    R = Rnd * 255          'generate random numbers
    G = Rnd * 255
    B = Rnd * 255
    RndCo = RGB(R, G, B)        'get new random color
End Function

Private Sub cmdQuit_Click()
    End
End Sub
```

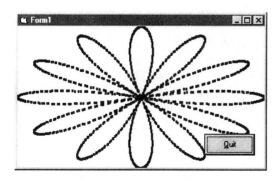

Figure 11.40   A flower pattern

You can change many items in this project to produce a wide variety of fascinating results. For example, we use 6 in Cos to produce 12 petals in the flower. You can increase or decrease this number to change the number of petals.

To create attractive graphics and animation, you need to know the circumference. Study the following procedure carefully and you'll find many ways to create balanced patterns and move an object along an imaginary circumference:

```
Private Sub Form_Click ()
    Dim I As Single
    Dim R As Single
    Dim X As Single
    Dim Y As Single
    Dim Pi As Single

    Pi = 4 * Atn(1)
    Scale (-1, 1)-(1, -1)
    R = 1        'radius
    For I = 2 * Pi To 0 Step -0.01 'clockwise
        X = R * Cos(I)        'get x axis
        Y = R * Sin(I)        'get y axis
        PSet (X, Y)           'draw point
    Next I
End Sub
```

If you run this procedure as shown, an oval will be drawn from 2 Pi radian point (far right) clockwise back to the same point. If you have a square form, a circle will be the result. If you change the I control variable from 0 to 2 * pi, the motion will be reversed, namely counterclockwise. If you increase the Step value, fewer dots will be drawn; more dots if you decrease it.

If you decrease the R value, a smaller circle or oval will be drawn. If you decrease its value by a small fraction and create several circles, the result will be a spiral.

If you change I's value as an argument for Sin and Cos, the resulting pattern or motion will be distorted in many possible ways.

Armed with the above observations, you can now go back to some of the Fun programs appearing in earlier chapters, alter some variables, and test the result. These rules will also be helpful when you try to tackle some of the chapter projects below.

GRAPHING DATA: BAR, LINE, AND PIE

Numbers can be represented by lines, bars, and pie slices. These graphs make it easy to visually compare numbers. There are numerous ways to graph data. We present a generic program that can accept and handle any numbers supplied by the user.

Our application's interface consists of a picture box to display a graph, a text box to enter data, three option boxes to choose a graph type, and three command buttons. After entering the data, select a graph type and click Draw to draw the graph. If you want to use the same data for another graph type, click Clear to clear the previous drawing, click a graph type, and click Draw again. If you don't clear the previous drawing, a new graph will be superimposed on the previous. It's common to have a line graph and a bar graph superimposed on each other.

Figures 11.41 to 11.43 show three graphs using the same data. The procedures are shown below. The Draw procedure first calls the Get_num procedure to get the numbers in the text box into an array. It then determines what graph option has been selected and calls a proper procedure to draw the graph.

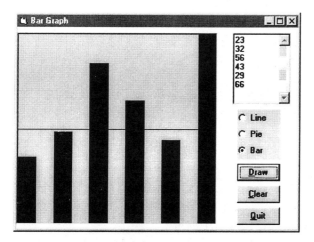

Figure 11.41   A bar graph

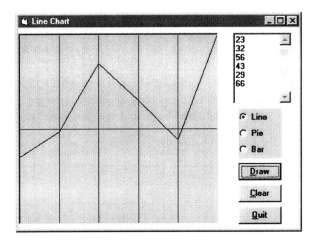

Figure 11.42   A line graph

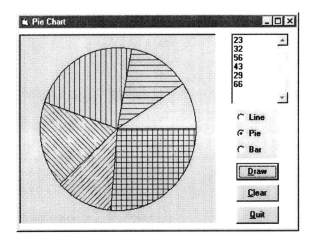

Figure 11.43   A pie chart

(11GRAPH.FRM)

```
Dim NumArray(20) As Variant 'hold text box entries
Dim Pic As PictureBox     'use Pic for pic box
Dim Indx As Integer       'track total number of items
Dim Sum As Single         'track total value
Dim Max As Single         'track highest value

Private Sub Form_Load()
    Set Pic = Picture1       'use Pic for pic box
    Pic.ForeColor = vbBlue
```

```
        Pic.FillColor = vbMagenta
End Sub

Private Sub cmdDraw_Click()
    Dim I As Integer

    On Error GoTo ErrTrap
    Call GetNum      'call sub to get text box numbers
    For I = 0 To 2
        If optGraphType(I).Value Then Exit For
    Next I          'which is selected?

    Select Case I    'the index of selected item
    Case 0
        Call DrawLine   'call sub to draw line graph
    Case 1
        Call DrawPie
    Case 2
        Call DrawBar
    End Select
    Exit Sub

ErrTrap:
    Beep
    MsgBox Error      'show error message
End Sub

Private Sub GetNum()
    Dim I As Integer
    Dim Temp As String

    Erase NumArray   'erase array contents
    Indx = 0         'restart at 0

    Do While Right(Text1, 1) = Chr(10)
        Text1 = Left(Text1, Len(Text1) - 2)
    Loop     'rid ending carriage returns

    For I = 1 To Len(Text1)
        Temp = Mid(Text1, I, 1) 'get each char
        If Temp = Chr(13) Then  'if chr 13
            I = I + 1           'skip next char
            Indx = Indx + 1     'add index
        Else
            NumArray(Indx) = NumArray(Indx) & Temp
        End If    'add (concatenate) each to array
    Next

    Max = Val(NumArray(0)) 'put 1st value in array
    Sum = Max              'in max and sum

    For I = 1 To Indx
        Sum = Sum + Val(NumArray(I))      'get total
        If Val(NumArray(I)) > Max Then
```

```
                    Max = Val(NumArray(I))   'get highest value
             End If
        Next
End Sub

Private Sub DrawBar()
    Dim I As Integer
    Dim BarWidth As Single

    Caption = "Bar Graph"
    BarWidth = 0.5       'width of bar, 50% of each slot
    Pic.Scale (0, Max)-(Indx + BarWidth, 0)
         'adjust scale so bars can fit inside pic box
    Pic.Line (0, Max / 2)-(Indx + BarWidth, Max / 2)
         'hor. middle line
    For I = 0 To Indx
         Pic.Line (I, 0)-(I + BarWidth, NumArray(I)), , BF
              'print box
    Next I
End Sub

Private Sub DrawLine()
    Dim I As Integer

    Caption = "Line Chart"
    Pic.Scale (0, Max)-(Indx, 0)
         'scale based on number of items and highest value
    Pic.ForeColor = vbBlue
    Pic.Line (0, Max / 2)-(Indx, Max / 2)
         'horizontal line
    For I = 1 To Indx
         Pic.Line (I, 0)-(I, Max)        'vertical lines
    Next I

    Pic.ForeColor = vbRed
    For I = 0 To Indx
       Pic.Line (I, NumArray(I))-(I + 1, NumArray(I + 1))
    Next       'draw data lines
End Sub

Private Sub DrawPie()
    Dim I As Integer
    Dim R As Integer
    Dim Pi As Single
    Dim Slice1 As Single
    Dim Slice2 As Single

    Caption = "Pie Chart"
    Pi = Atn(1) * 4
    Pic.Scale (-10, -10)-(10, 10)
        'custom scale for picture box
    R = 8     'radius

    For I = 0 To Indx
```

```
                    NumArray(I) = NumArray(I) / Sum * 2 * Pi
                        'convert to 2 Pi scale
                    If I = 0 Then            'beginning angle
                        Slice1 = 0.001       '1st slice = 0
                        Slice2 = NumArray(I)
                            'ending angle for 1st slice
                    Else
                        Slice1 = Slice1 + NumArray(I - 1)
                            'previous angle--cumulative
                        Slice2 = Slice2 + NumArray(I)
                            'ending angle--cumulative
                    End If
                    Pic.FillStyle = (I + 1) Mod 7
                        'hatch lines, alternate among 7
                    Pic.Circle (0, 0), R, , -Slice1, -Slice2
                Next I       'draw slices
            End Sub

            Private Sub cmdClear_Click()
                Picture1.Cls    'clear drawing
                Caption = ""    'clear form caption
            End Sub

            Private Sub cmdQuit_Click()
                End
            End Sub
```

The three drawing procedures are quite flexible. They can handle with equal aplomb any numbers you can throw at them. The key to this flexibility lies in the use of **dynamic scaling**.

The DrawLine procedure is probably the easiest to understand. We designate the bottom left of the drawing area as point (0, 0) and the top right as point (indx, max). Max is the highest value entered by the user and Indx is the total number of items. So, in setting up the custom scale, we designate the top left as point (0, max) and the bottom right as point (indx, 0). The highest value reaches the top border and the last item appears at the right border. Everything in between is scaled to fit. Using the numbers entered in the text box as examples, the first line is drawn from point (0, 12) to point (1, 45), the second from point (1, 45) to point (2, 19), and so on.

The DrawBar procedure's custom scale has a provision to make extra room for the last bar. Without this adjustment, the last bar will start from the right border and extend to outside of the picture box (invisible). We use a factor of 0.5 and assign it to variable W. This value is used to widen the scalable area and determine the width of each bar and the distance between two bars. You can increase this value to widen each bar and narrow the area between bars. Each bar is distanced from the previous at the interval of 1. So the factor of 0.5 makes each bar and the ensuing gap to have the same distance. If you increase it to 0.8, the bar will be 0.8 wide and the gap 0.2.

The DrawPie procedure draws pie slices from 0 degree (far right) counterclockwise. The size of each slice is its percentage of 2 Pi radians (360 degrees). We use a Cartesian scale with the top left as point (-10, -10) and the bottom right as point (10, 10). An earlier section in this chapter and the Trigonometric Functions section in Chapter 7 explain the reason for negative values. The radius (R) value is set at 8. You can increase or decrease it to change the size of the pie.

DRILL

_____ 21.   This event is triggered when the form window is enlarged:
        a.   Paint
        b.   Click
        c.   DblClick
        d.   Load

_____ 22.   To load a picture to the current form at design time, you use the
        _____ property in the Properties window to do it.

_____ 23.   This control cannot contain a picture:
        a.   form
        b.   frame
        c.   image
        d.   picture box

_____ 24.   This file supplies the best picture quality:
        a.   icon
        b.   bitmap
        c.   metafile
        d.   cursor

_____ 25.   This control has the Stretch property:
        a.   image
        b.   frame
        c.   form
        d.   picture box

_____ 26.   A picture box can contain another picture box, which in turn can contain another picture box. True or false?

____ 27. A picture box's _____ property lets you determine whether the control itself or the loaded picture controls the appearance.

____ 28. This control can contain nothing but a picture:
a. form
b. image
c. picture box

____ 29. The _____ word (property) should appear before = if you want to load a picture to a form at run time.

```
? = LoadPicture(". . .")
```

____ 30. The _____ property allows you to blend a variety of colors and hatch lines.

PRACTICE

■ 19. What happens if you change Cos to Sin in the code for Figure 11.37.

■ 20. What happens if you change the value of X from 2 to 4 in the code for Figure 11.37.

■ 21. What happens if you change the Step value to a higher or lower number in the code for Figure 11.40.

■ 22. In the code for Figure 11.40, what happens if you increase or decrease the value of R, such as changing the 6 to 3 or 8?

■ 23. In the code for Figure 11.40, change PSet to Line and report the resulting difference.

■ 24. In the code for Figure 11.40, what happens if you change the value for the Y axis, such as this:

```
Y = R * Sin(I / 2)      'get y axis
```

■ 25. Draw a spiral pattern shown in Figure 11.44.

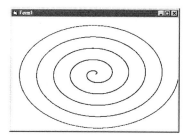

Figure 11.44   Counterclockwise spiral

■ 26. Write a procedure to draw a pie chart with the first piece (top-right quarter) exploded as shown in Figure 11.45.

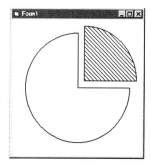

Figure 11.45   Top-right slice exploded

■ 27. Modify the above procedure so that the top-left slice is exploded Figure 11.46).

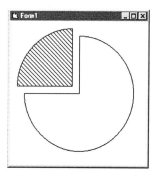

Figure 11.46   Top-left slice exploded

■ 28. Modify the Graph project (Figures 41-43) so that the user can click an option to immediately draw a graph.

■ 29. Modify Figure 11.28 so that the spring will spring out from left and then from right continuously; each display is cleared before the next display appears. Use the Timer function to pause for 1/10 second from one circle to the next and 1 second from one side to the next. Put the pausing routine in a sub procedure. The calling statement should pass the amount of time for pausing. The statement below will delay 1/10 second:

```
Delay 0.1
```

■ 30. Use custom scales to draw the display shown in Figure 11.47.

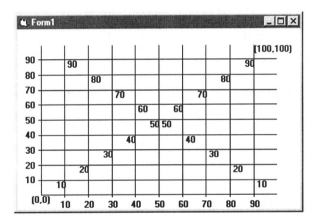

Figure 11.47   Using custom scales

CHAPTER PROJECT

A. (11PATTRN1.FRM)

This project draws a pattern in a picture box, shown at the left side of Figure 11.48. When the Draw button is clicked, a circle is drawn in the perfectly square box. Then from 0 radian (right corner; middle of the right border) and at the interval of 1/8 Pi, four lines are drawn from each point to the four corners. This continues counterclockwise until the drawing point returns to 0 radian.

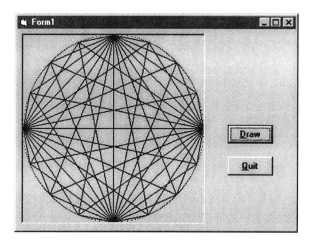

Figure 11.48   Drawing in a picture box

B. (11PATTRN2.FRM)

Modified from the previous project, this project continuously draws a circular pattern, as shown in Figure 11.49. At the beginning, 4 lines are drawn from 0 radian (right) to the middle of the four borders. Then the point is moved to 2 degrees counterclockwise along an imaginary circle and four lines are drawn again. When the drawing point returns to 0 radian (degree) again, the picture looks like a round ball of yarn. At that point, the drawing is cleared and another round begins. When Quit is clicked, the program ends. Use an idle loop to slow down the drawing so that you can enjoy the mesmerizing motion.

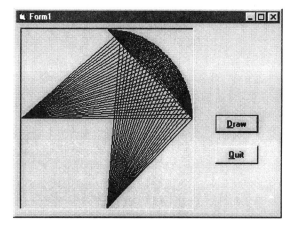

Figure 11.49   Beginning of a circular pattern

C. (11PATTRN3.FRM)

This project continuously draws (using PSet) the pattern shown in Figure 11.50. For the first time, the pattern is drawn from the center towards the borders. It is then cleared. The same pattern is drawn again, this time from outside inward. This process is repeated indefinitely—until the user double-clicks the control box to end.

The drawing shown consists of a single pattern repeated four times. Use Sin and Cos functions with incremental (or decremental) values to create the distortion.

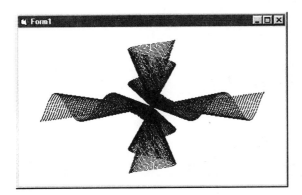

Figure 11.50   A pattern with four iterations

D. (11PATTRN4.FRM)

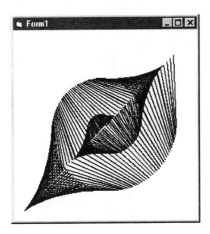

Figure 11.51   Untitled pattern

Use the Line statement and tinker with various variables in the previous program to produce the pattern shown in Figure 11.51.

E.   (11PATTRN5.FRM)

This project draws a pattern shown in Figure 11.52. When the form is changed to a perfect square, the drawing appears in Figure 11.53. The drawing consists of a series of circles whose radius is half of the form's ScaleHeight and whose centers move along an imaginary circumference. (The radius and centers can be changed to achieve different effects.)

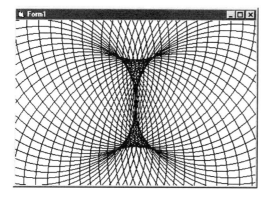

Figure 11.52   Swirling circles

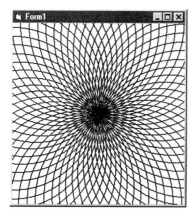

Figure 11.53   Swirling circles in a square form

Modify the project to simulate a gyrating motion. The drawing of circles starts from 0 degree and rotates clockwise. After the rotation completes two rounds, the drawing is cleared and another round begins. A new QBColor is used for the circles after every two rounds. The user can click the End icon on the toolbar to end.

F. (11PATTRN6.FRM)

This project draws a doughnut (tire?) shown in Figure 11.54. It consists of a series of circles with centers located along the imaginary circumference.

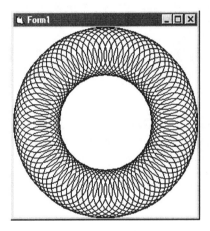

Figure 11.54   A doughnut

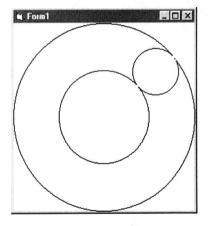

Figure 11.55   A rotating ring

Modify the drawing to simulate animation. The small ring shown in Figure 11.55 continuously moves counterclockwise along the track—until the user clicks the End icon.

FUN AND GAME

A. (SLOT.FRM)

This program simulates a slot machine (Figure 11.56). You enter a wager amount and click Turn to show three flags. If they all match, your payoff is 30 times; otherwise, you lose your bet. The caption shows three numbers reflecting your performance (luck). If you don't want to change the wager amount, you can just click Turn to continue betting. When this button has the focus, you can also continue to press the Enter key to keep going. If you want to improve your odds, you can increase the 30 factor.

This program uses two image control arrays. At design time, Image1's Index value is changed to 0. At run time, its Visible property is set to False and five invisible clones are created. Each is also loaded with an icon. These icons are copied at run time to three members of the Image2 control array. These members are properly arranged at design time and their Stretch properties are also set to True so that the icons can be enlarged at run time.

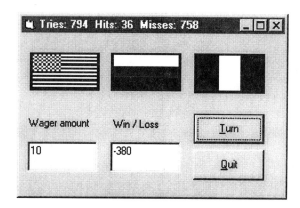

Figure 11.56   Simulating a slot machine

```
Private Sub Form_Load()
    Dim I As Integer
```

```
        Image1(0).Visible = False    'hide original image
        On Error GoTo ErrTrap         'if fail to load icons
        For I = 1 To 5
            Load Image1(I)   'load five clones
        Next I
            'load a picture to each image box
        Image1(0).Picture = LoadPicture _
        ("graphics\icons\flags\flgcan.ico")
        Image1(1).Picture = LoadPicture _
        ("graphics\icons\flags\flgfran.ico")
        Image1(2).Picture = LoadPicture _
        ("graphics\icons\flags\flggerm.ico")
        Image1(3).Picture = LoadPicture _
        ("graphics\icons\flags\flgitaly.ico")
        Image1(4).Picture = LoadPicture _
        ("graphics\icons\flags\flgrus.ico")
        Image1(5).Picture = LoadPicture _
        ("graphics\icons\flags\flgusa02.ico")
        Exit Sub

ErrTrap:
    MsgBox Error
End Sub

Private Sub cmdTurn_Click()
    Dim I As Integer
    Dim Amt As Integer
    Dim RndNum As Integer
    Dim Sum As Integer
    Static Try As Integer
    Static Hit As Integer
    Dim Num(2) As Integer

    Randomize
    If Text1.Text = "" Then
        Beep    'if no bet
        Text1.SetFocus
        Exit Sub
    End If

    For I = 0 To 2
        RndNum = Fix(6 * Rnd)    'random number 0 - 5
        Image2(I).Picture = Image1(RndNum).Picture
            'load 1 of 6 images to 1 of 3 boxes
        Num(I) = RndNum       'put random number in array
    Next I

    If Num(0) = Num(1) And Num(1) = Num(2) And _
    Num(0) = Num(2) Then
        'if all 3 numbers match, 30 times payoff
        Text2.Text = Val(Text2.Text) + Text1.Text * 30
        Hit = Hit + 1
    Else
        Text2.Text = Val(Text2.Text) - Text1.Text
```

```
      End If        'deduct wager amount
      Try = Try + 1
      Caption = "Tries: " & Try & "  Hits: " & Hit & _
      "  Misses: " & (Try - Hit)
      'show in caption number of times
End Sub
```

B. (TRAIN)

This program continuously moves a train of five characters counterclockwise
along a track bounded by two circles (Figure 11.57). Each time a round is
completed, the number in the middle increases by 1. Click the X button to start
from round 1 again. Double-click the form to end.

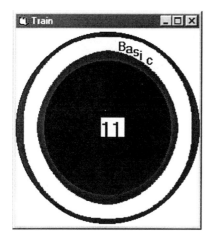

Figure 11.57   A train of five characters

```
Private Sub Form_Load()
      Dim I As Single
      Dim SH As Long
      Dim SW As Long
      Dim Pi As Single
      Dim X As Single
      Dim Y As Single
      Dim Radius As Single
      Dim Counter As Integer

      Show              'show form
      Pi = 4 * Atn(1)

      'Label1 name changed to lblBasic and
```

```
'Index to 0 at design time
lblBasic(0).Visible = False    '1st copy not shown
lblBasic(0).BackStyle = 0      'transparent
lblBasic(0).Font.Size = 12     'label font size

For I = 1 To 5
    Load lblBasic(I)      'load and show clones
    lblBasic(I).Visible = True
Next I

lblBasic(1).Caption = "B"
lblBasic(2).Caption = "a"
lblBasic(3).Caption = "s"
lblBasic(4).Caption = "i"
lblBasic(5).Caption = "c"

SW = ScaleWidth           'get perfect square form
SH = ScaleHeight
Width = SH
ScaleWidth = 2 * SH - SW
    'scale for 2nd label and two circles
Scale (-1, 1)-(1, -1)
lblCounter.Move -0.07, 0.1 'center 2nd label
lblCounter.Font.Size = 20    'label font size
FillStyle = 0             'solid fill
FillColor = vbRed
Circle (0, 0), 1          'outer circle

FillColor = vbBlue

Circle (0, 0), 0.7        'inner circle
    'custom scale, adjusted for printing chars
Scale (-0.88, 0.88)-(1, -1)
Radius = 0.8

Do      'infinite loop
    Counter = Counter + 1
    lblCounter.Caption = Counter
        'put number in lblCounter
    For I = 0 To 2 * Pi Step 0.02
        DoEvents     'allow break
        'from 0 degree counterclockwise,
        'change Step value to adjust speed
        X = Radius * Cos(I + 0.5) 'get x coordinate
        Y = Radius * Sin(I + 0.5) 'get y coordinate
        lblBasic(1).Move X, Y
            'move 1st label clone with "B"
        X = Radius * Cos(I + 0.4)
        Y = Radius * Sin(I + 0.4)
        lblBasic(2).Move X, Y       '"a"
        X = Radius * Cos(I + 0.3)
        Y = Radius * Sin(I + 0.3)
        lblBasic(3).Move X, Y       '"s"
        X = Radius * Cos(I + 0.2)
```

```
            Y = Radius * Sin(I + 0.2)
            lblBasic(4).Move X, Y     '"i"
            X = Radius * Cos(I + 0.1)
            Y = Radius * Sin(I + 0.1)
            lblBasic(5).Move X, Y     '"c"
        Next I
    Loop
End Sub

Private Sub Form_DblClick()
    End
End Sub
```

Chapter 12
Advanced Tools

TOPICS

KEY TERMS

ActiveX   The new name for expanded OLE. ActiveX components are individual programs that follow Microsoft's COM (Common Object Model) standard. These components may be ActiveX controls that appear in Visual Basic's Toolbox, ActiveX servers that provide functions for other applications, or ActiveX documents that can be run by a Web browser. VB5 allows you to create all these.

API (Application Programming Interface)   The gateway to let a Windows application access dynamic-link libraries (DLLs) available in Windows and other packages. You can use the Declare keyword to call many external functions included in various Windows DLL files.

Bound controls   Controls that can bind (link) database records and fields to the screen. They include label, image, text box, check box, and picture box. Also known as data-aware controls, they are used to display data stored in a file.

Custom menu   A menu you use the Menu Design window to design and attach to an application. The menu bar at the top of a form displays all the menu options. The user can select a menu option to do something. You need to write code to respond to such a selection.

DAO   Data access objects; a series of object classes defined in the Microsoft Jet database engine and included in Visual Basic. The objects derived from the classes can be used in code to programmatically maneuver databases.

Data control   A control that includes the database engine of Microsoft Access. It can be used to view the records of databases created by Access and other popular programs. A companion Visual Data Manager can be used to create a simple database, which can be viewed with a data control.

Database   A collection of information on related items. A computer database consists of one or more tables, each of which consists of multiple records, each of which contains multiple fields. A record can be compared to a row and a field to a column in a spreadsheet.

Dynamic Data Exchange (DDE)   A mechanism through which two Windows applications can engage in a conversation. One can send data and the other can receive it.

Grid control   A custom control that supplies columns and rows, and stores data in cells as in a spreadsheet program.

MDI form   Multiple-document interface form, a super (parent) form that can contain other (child) forms. It allows an application to have multiple windows as in many Windows programs. The user can then open new windows or close and manipulate existing ones.

OLE (object linking and embedding)   A technology created by Microsoft for computer users to create compound documents. Based on this technology, a word processing document may contain a spreadsheet or a graph created by other applications. Visual Basic provides many OLE tools. You can create an application that lets users access Word, Access, Excel, and so on. The availability of this technology is what makes Visual Basic a popular front-end programming tool.

SQL   Structured Query Language. A common and simple language used to query databases. Most remote databases are SQL databases. They follow the ODBC (Open Database Connectivity) standards which allow users to use SQL commands to maneuver their records.

This chapter covers a series of Visual Basic features that we have neglected so far. These features are less commonly used. Some of them can also be quite complex, involving external programs as well.

Some of the features covered here can do some complicated and sophisticated jobs. If you can master them and incorporate them into your applications, you'll be amply rewarded. Due to space limitations, some features are not covered in great detail. However, there is plenty of online help available—if you want to know more. Some of these topics, particularly ActiveX, API, and database, are more fully covered in another book—*The Visual Basic 5 Advanced Coursebook*.

KEYBOARD EVENTS

Any object that is capable of receiving the focus can respond to three keyboard events, namely KeyPress, KeyDown, and KeyUp. If you wish, you can write a procedure to respond to each event.

Among these three events, **KeyPress** is the simplest to understand and use. A KeyPress event occurs when a keyboard key (with some exceptions as explained below) is pressed. Your procedure can intercept such an event and respond accordingly.

To write a KeyPress event, go to the Procedure box in the Code window and click KeyPress. A procedure template like below appears:

```
Sub Form_KeyPress (KeyAscii As Integer)

End Sub
```

The **KeyAscii** argument is already supplied. If you dislike verbosity, you can change this suggested variable name to a single letter, such as K.

One use for such a procedure is to show the ANSI code for a letter pressed. The following procedure will do that:

```
Sub Form_KeyPress (K As Integer)
    Print Chr(K), K
End Sub
```

When the program is run, pressing a keyboard (ANSI) key leads to the corresponding character and its code number being printed to the screen. You can use this to quickly find out the ANSI code value for any character or keyboard key. Each time a key is pressed, the entire procedure is executed.

A procedure can be written to reject certain keys or respond to some keys in a special way. In the following procedure, pressing Esc will do nothing—the procedure is exited. Pressing Enter will end the program.

```
Sub Form_KeyPress (K As Integer)
    If K = 27 Then Exit Sub    'or vbKeyEscape
    Print Chr(k), K
    If K = 13 Then End         'or vbKeyReturn
End Sub
```

NOTE There are numerous **intrinsic constants** related to keyboard keys. The simplest way to access the popup list is type *vbKey* and then press **Ctrl+J** or **Ctrl+spacebar**.

We can use a KeyPress procedure to simulate an adding machine. Our user interface is shown in Figure 12.1. It consists of three text boxes, txtEntry, txtSum, and txtList. txtList's MultiLine is set to True and ScrollBars set to 2 - Vertical. txtEntry's KeyPress procedure is shown below.

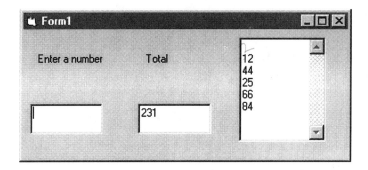

Figure 12.1   A calculator that responds to keyboard events

```
Private Sub txtEntry_KeyPress (K As Integer)
            '--Listing 1--
    If K = 13 Then        'if Enter
        txtSum.Text = Val(txtSum.Text) + _
        Val(txtEntry.Text) 'total
        txtList.Text = txtList.Text & vbCrLf _
        & txtEntry.Text
            'show all entered numbers
        txtEntry.Text = ""  'clear for a new entry
    End If

    If K < 48 Or K > 57 Then     'if non-digit
        Beep
        K = 0  'not display number
    End If
End Sub
```

Keep in mind that Visual Basic intercepts a key press and returns its ANSI (ASCII) value. Thus, when you press the 0 key, the K variable is given the integer value of 48; it has 57 when the 9 key is pressed.

In Listing 1, we use two If control structures to respond to a variety of keys. When you press Enter with or without a number in txtEntry, the number in txtEntry is added to the existing number in txtSum and the result is displayed in txtSum. txtEntry is also cleared for another entry. If you type anything other than number keys, the second If structure causes a beep and assigns 0 to K; the typed character is not displayed.

A KeyPress event can respond to only ANSI keys. **KeyUp** and **KeyDown**, on the other hand, can intercept ANSI keys as well as other keyboard keys and their numerous combinations, including cursor (navigation) keys, editing keys, and function keys alone or in combination with Shift, Ctrl, and Alt. KeyDown is triggered when a key is pressed. KeyUp, on the other hand, occurs when a pressed key is released.

When you select KeyDown (or KeyUp) from the Procedure box in the Code window, the procedure template appears with two integer arguments as shown below:

```
Private Sub Form_KeyDown (KeyCode As Integer, _
Shift As Integer)

End Sub
```

Again, you can change each suggested argument to a single letter, such as K or S. The KeyCode argument represents a number designated for a particular keyboard key. Shift is a bit-field argument that reflects the Shift, Ctrl, or Alt key.

The **Shift argument** can be 1 (001 binary; Shift), 2 (010; Ctrl), or 4 (100; Alt).[1] Visual Basic uses three least-significant bits to represent these arguments. When the last bit is turned on, 1 is assigned to Shift. That means when the Shift key is pressed, the Shift argument has the value of 1. The three keys can be combined in a variety of ways. For example, when Shift has the value of 7 (111 binary), all the three keys are pressed and all the three bits are turned on.

The following procedure will show the key code value of each key pressed, plus the Shift value. Run it and try various key combinations.

```
Private Sub Form_KeyDown (K As Integer, S As Integer)
    Cls
    Print K        'show key code value
    Print S        'show Shift, Ctrl, Alt
End Sub
```

If you prefer to show a key code in hex, change the pertinent line to this:

```
    Print Hex(K)
```

It makes no sense to show a Shift argument in hex because the highest possible value is only 7. Using Hex returns the same number as not using it.

You can use code to intercept certain keys or key combinations and respond in a special way. In the following procedure, the program ends when the user presses Ctrl+F1.

---

[1]You can replace these numbers with **vbShiftMask**, **vbCtrlMask**, or **vbAltMask**.

```
Private Sub Form_KeyDown (K As Integer, S As Integer)
    Cls
    Print Hex(K)
    Print S
    If K = vbKeyF1 And S = 2 Then End          'Ctrl+F1
End Sub
```

The online help provides many key code constants; search for *Key Code constants* and a long list will appear. You can use the intrinsic constant strings or their equivalent numeric values. According to this list, the equivalent of vbKeyF1 is 112. You can also use 112 or its hex number, &H70.

Objects capable of receiving the focus can respond to the **GotFocus** and **LostFocus** events. The GotFocus event occurs when an object has the focus, such as your clicking it, tabbing to it, or pressing a pertinent access key. If you have written a relevant procedure, it will be executed.

To demonstrate how these two events happen, add two text boxes or one text box and another object capable of receiving the focus. Then write the following two procedures:

```
Private Sub Text1_GotFocus ()
    Text1.BackColor = vbRed
End Sub

Private Sub Text1_LostFocus ()
    Text1.BackColor = vbGrayText
End Sub
```

After running the program, you can shift the focus between the two objects and see how things change. When Text1 has the focus, its background color is changed to red. When it loses the focus, the color is changed to gray.

If a form contains no object, the form responds to keyboard events. However, if there is an object that is capable of receiving the focus, the form itself cannot receive the focus or respond to keyboard events. For example, if you place a text box or command button on a form, the Form_KeyPress procedure will never be triggered. This pattern can be changed by you.

KeyPreview, a form property available only at run time, can be used to make the form (rather than a control) respond to keyboard events first. This property is set to False by default. That means when the user presses a key, the control with the focus responds to the event. If you want the form to do that also, change this value to True.

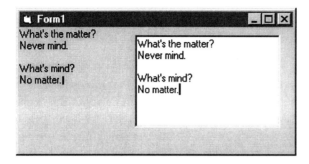

Figure 12.2   KeyPreview demonstration

Consider Figure 12.2. It has a form and a text box. At run time, the text box has
the focus; the cursor stays inside the box. If you type something, it appears in the
box. The following procedures can make any typed text appear in both places:

```
Private Sub Form_Load ()
    KeyPreview = True    'make form respond to keys
End Sub

Private Sub Form_KeyPress (K As Integer)
    Print Chr(K);         'print to form
End Sub
```

Without the first procedure, the Form_KeyPress procedure will not be executed.
If you want only the form to respond to ANSI keys, add the following statement
to the end of the second procedure:

```
    K = 0
```

If you want only the form to respond to other keys, such as functions keys, assign
0 to the KeyCode variable in the Form_KeyDown procedure.

TIP: Tab in a Text Box

Have you ever pressed the **Tab key** when the cursor is in a text box? The
focus shifts to another object if such an object exists. This behavior is
controlled by Windows. What if you want to tab the cursor to the next tab
stop in the same text box? You can press Ctrl+Tab or Ctrl+I.

Another alternative is to substitute another key for the Tab key. Suppose you want to use the ` key (just above the Tab key on the PC keyboard). All you need is to add this procedure:

```
Private Sub Text1_KeyPress (K As Integer)
    If K = 96 Then K = 9     'change ` to tab
End Sub
```

Also, you must set the MultiLine property of Text1 to True at either design time or run time; if not, pressing the above key will only lead to a beep and nothing else.

If you are more comfortable with another key or key combination, use its ANSI value. Suppose you want to use Ctrl+T. Replace the 96 value with 20, which happens to be the ANSI value for this key combination.

PRACTICE

■ 1. Figure 12.1 does not allow the use of a minus sign or decimal point. Modify the program so that the two characters will be accepted and the program can handle negative as well as decimal numbers.

■ 2. Modify the above so that the Backspace key can be used to erase a typed character.

■ 3. Modify the above so that the program will end when the Esc key is pressed.

■ 4. In Listing 1, use characters instead of integers to handle keys being pressed by the user.

■ 5. How do KeyPress, KeyDown, and KeyUp differ?

■ 6. Explain the KeyCode and Shift arguments of a KeyDown or KeyUp procedure.

MOUSE EVENTS

There are five mouse-related events. In the list below, their names appear on the left and the time of their occurrence on the right:

MouseDown	When a mouse button is pressed.
MouseUp	When a pressed button is released.
MouseMove	When the mouse pointer is moved.
DragDrop	When a control is dropped on the object.
DragOver	When a control is dragged over the object.

The first three events follow the same syntax and have the same arguments. When **MouseMove** is clicked in the Procedure box of the Code window, the following template appears:

```
Private Sub Form_MouseMove (Button As Integer, _
Shift As Integer, X As Single, Y As Single)

End Sub
```

The Shift argument is the same as discussed earlier. The **Button argument** indicates whether or not one or more mouse buttons are pressed. Here, as in Shift, Visual Basic uses three bits to handle the three mouse buttons. If the left button is pressed, Button has the value of 1 (001 binary). If the right button is pressed, it is assigned 2 (010). If the middle button (if any) is pressed, it has 4 (100).[2] If all the buttons are pressed, then Button has the value of 7 (111).

The X and Y arguments are coordinate values similar to the CurrentX and CurrentY properties discussed in Chapter 3. X represents the horizontal position of the mouse pointer and Y the vertical position. These values are expressed in twips by default. They can be changed by the **ScaleMode** property.

In the following procedure, you can move the pointer and its current X and Y coordinates will be printed to the screen:

```
Private Sub Form_MouseMove (B As Integer, S As Integer, _
X As Single, Y As Single)
    Print B, S, X, Y     'Button, Shift, X, Y
    If CurrentY >= ScaleHeight Then Cls
       'clear if screen full
End Sub
```

You can hold down mouse buttons and/or Shift, Ctrl, or Alt keys as you move the pointer. As shown in Figure 12.3, the Button and Shift arguments will change as you try various combinations.

---

[2]You can replace these numbers with **vbLeftButton**, **vbRightButton**, or **vbMiddleButton**.

```
Form1                        _ □ ✕
0        0        3765        480
1        0        3750        480
0        0        3750        480
0        6        3750        495
0        6        3750        495
2        6        3765        495
0        6        3765        495
3        6        3765        510
0        6        3765        510
1        1        3780        510
0        1        3780        510
2        1        3780        525
2        1        3780        540
0        1        3780        540
0        4        3795        540
0        4        3795        540
2        4        3780        540
0        4        3780        540
0        0        3780        525
```

Figure 12.3   Showing Button, Shift, X, and Y

You can use the **Move method** with a mouse-related event to move an object. In the following procedure, the Command1 button will move to the pointer location where you press and release a mouse button. The moving does not occur until the pressed button is released because we use **MouseUp**. If **MouseDown** is used instead, the moving occurs when a mouse button is pressed.

```
Private Sub Form_MouseUp (B As Integer, S As Integer, _
X As Single, Y As Single)
    Command1.Move X, Y
End Sub
```

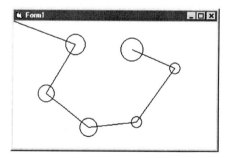

Figure 12.4   MouseDown demonstration

You can use a mouse-related event to trigger drawing a line or circle. The following procedure will draw a line and a circle when a button is pressed. The initial point is (0,0), or the top left corner. As you move the pointer and click a new location, a line will be drawn from the previously clicked point to the current point; the current location will also be used as the center to draw a circle that has the radius of 50 to 350 twips. The result is shown in Figure 12.4.

```
Private Sub Form_MouseDown (B As Integer, S As Integer, _
X As Single, Y As Single)
    Line -(X, Y)  'line from LPR to current point
    Circle (X, Y), Rnd * 300 + 50
End Sub
```

In the following procedure, we start each drawing from the middle of the bottom border. The result is shown in Figure 12.5.

```
Private Sub Form_MouseDown (B As Integer, S As Integer, _
X As Single, Y As Single)
    CurrentX = ScaleWidth / 2 'middle of X
    CurrentY = ScaleHeight    'bottom border
    Line -(X, Y)
    Circle (X, Y), 300
End Sub
```

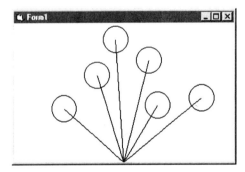

Figure 12.5   Drawing from the bottom middle

You can use **MouseMove** for the above procedures. The result is continuous drawing whenever the mouse is moved.

You can specify the condition for drawing to occur. The following modification leads to drawing only when the left mouse button is held down:

```
If B = 1 Then Line -(X, Y)
```

This is useful when combined with a MouseMove event.

Do you like to doodle something on the screen, maybe using the mouse to create your signature? Try the following procedures and you can draw the Chinese characters shown in Figure 12.6 (it means Beautiful Country, or America). If you want thick strokes as shown here, change the form's DrawWidth property to 5.

```
Private Sub Form_MouseDown (B As Integer, S As Integer, _
X As Single, Y As Single)
    CurrentX = X           'move the current point
    CurrentY = Y
    If B = 2 Then Cls      'right button to clear
End Sub

Private Sub Form_MouseMove(B As Integer, S As Integer, _
X As Single, Y As Single)
    If B = 1 Then Line -(X, Y)    'left button, draw line
End Sub
```

In this arrangement, when you click a point on the screen, the current point is moved to the pointer position. When you hold down the left mouse button and move the pointer, a line is continuously drawn. Drawing ceases when you release the button. You can then move the pointer to another location and start drawing again. If you want to clear your doodle art, press the right mouse button to do that.

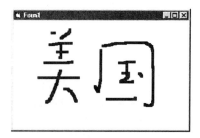

Figure 12.6   America in Chinese

At design time, all the objects except a custom menu can be dragged and dropped in any place inside a form. At run time, you can let the user drag any object except a menu and invisible controls such as a timer or common dialog (see another section below).

An object that can be dragged has the **DragMode** property. It is by default set to 0 - Manual. With this setting, the object cannot be dragged at run time. You need to set it to 1 - Automatic at design time or run time—if you want to let the user drag this object at run time.

When a control is dragged at run time, an outline of the control appears for you to move to a new location. This outline can be replaced by an icon of your choice. You can use the **DragIcon** property from the Properties window to load a specific icon; the process is the same as loading a picture explained in Chapter 11. You can also use the LoadPicture function to do the same thing at run time; this technique was also explained in Chapter 11.

DragDrop and **DragOver** are two events that can be triggered in a dragging operation. DragDrop occurs when an object being dragged is dropped on the current control. DragOver occurs when the dragged object moves over the control.

You need to write code to respond to dragging. To do that, you need to attach a DragDrop or DragOver procedure to the target object. In our demonstration, we assume that the current form has two controls, Command1 and Text1. We intend to drag the two controls and drop one onto the other.

When you click DragDrop in the Code window's Procedure box, the following procedure template appears:

```
Private Sub Form_DragDrop (Source As Control, X As _
Single, Y As Single)

End Sub
```

Here we use Form as our target object because we intend to drop something onto it. The Source argument signifies an object which you want to drop onto the target. The X and Y arguments are coordinates expressed in twips.

To let the user drag our two controls (Command1 and Text1), you need to set their DragMode property to 1 either at design time or at run time as explained earlier. Then you need to insert the following line in the above DragDrop procedure template:

```
Source.Move X, Y
```

Here Source is any object that can be dragged and whose DragMode property is changed to 1. When such an object is dragged and dropped on the form, the form's DragDrop procedure is executed, resulting in the Source object (the one being dragged) moving to point (X, Y).

Point (X, Y) is where the pointer is located. If the pointer is located at the top left corner of the object being dragged, the object will stay in the target location. If the pointer is in the middle of the dragged object, its top left corner will be positioned at the pointer location, resulting in inaccurate positioning. One remedy to that is to use the midpoint (rather than top left) of the source object for positioning. The following code will do just that:

```
Source.Move X - Source.Width / 2, Y - Source.Height / 2
```

To further demonstrate dragging techniques, try the following procedure:

```
Private Sub Command1_DragDrop (Source As Control, X As _
Single, Y As Single)
    Source.Visible = False
End Sub
```

If you now run the program and drag Text1 and drop it onto Command1, Text1 will become invisible. If you now click Command1, it will also become invisible because it becomes the Source object, whose Visible property will be set to False. In the following procedure, you can press a key to make Text1 reappear, assuming that Command1 is visible and has the focus.

```
Private Sub Command1_KeyPress (KeyAscii As Integer)
    Text1.Visible = True
End Sub
```

The DragOver event has a State argument. It can be 0 (entering the object's borders), 1 (leaving), or 2 (over). In the following procedure, Text1 will change color when you drag it over Command1.

```
Private Sub Command1_DragOver (Source As Control, X As _
Single, Y As Single, State As Integer)
    If State = 0 Then Source.BackColor = vbBlue
    If State = 1 Then Source.BackColor = vbRed
    If State = 2 Then Source.BackColor = vbYellow
End Sub
```

In the above arrangement, blue will never appear. On the other hand, if you comment out the last State line, blue and red will appear. If you comment out the first line, red and yellow will be displayed.

If you enjoy colors, try the following:

```
Private Sub Form_MouseMove (B As Integer, S As Integer, _
X As Single, Y As Single)
    Scale (0, 0)-(255, 255)    'custom scale
    BackColor = RGB(X, Y, (X + Y) / 2)
```

```
        'set backcolor based on X, Y coordinates
    Caption = "Red = " & X & "; Green = " & Y & _
    "; Blue = " & (X + Y) / 2
        'show values in caption
End Sub
```

As you move the pointer to various parts of the form window, the background color will continuously change. Our custom scale (see Chapter 11) limits the values of X and Y to the 0-255 range; this limit gives us all the possible values for RGB's first two components, but not the third (blue). You can change these variables' values or positions to create different effects. The RGB function was also explained in Chapter 11.

You can use the Drag method to manage drag and drop operations. You can supply three arguments: 0 (cancel dragging), 1 (begin; default), and 2 (drop). The following procedure lets you drag Text1; this procedure obviates the need to change the DragMode property at design time or run time.

```
Private Sub Text1_MouseDown (B As Integer, _
S As Integer, X As Single, Y As Single)
    Text1.Drag     'enable dragging
End Sub
```

You can add 1 after Drag without making any difference. The above procedure is executed when you move the pointer to Text1 and hold down a mouse button. The procedure's execution enables you to drag Text1. As you drop Text1, the previous Form_DragDrop procedure will implement a moving action.

✓DRILL

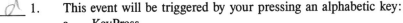

1.   This event will be triggered by your pressing an alphabetic key:
   a.   KeyPress
   b.   KeyDown
   c.   KeyUp
   d.   all of the above
   e.   none of the above

2.   This event will be triggered by your pressing a function key:
   a.   KeyPress
   b.   KeyDown
   c.   KeyUp
   d.   both a and b
   e.   both b and c

_6_ 3. If Ctrl and Alt keys are pressed at the same time, the Shift argument in a keyboard or mouse event returns _____ (number).

_e_ 4. When you click a control at run time, this event of the control occurs:
a. GotFocus
b. MouseDown
c. KeyDown
d. KeyUp
e. both a and b

_b_ 5. At run time when you use Tab to move the focus away from a control, this event of the control occurs:
a. GotFocus
b. LostFocus
c. MouseDown
d. MouseUp

key preview 6. If you want the form to respond to keyboard events when there are controls that can receive the focus, you must set the form's _____ property's value to True.

____ 7. The first argument in a MouseMove procedure is:
a. Button
b. Shift
c. X
d. Y

____ 8. In the following statement in a Form_MouseDown procedure, the program ends if the Shift key is held down and the right mouse button is pressed. True or false?   _True_

```
If Shift = 1 And Button = 2 Then End
```

_F_ 9. In the following statement in a mouse-related event procedure, the center of Command1 is moved to point (x, y). True or false?

```
Command1.Move X, Y
```

____ 10. The first argument in a DragDrop or DragOver procedure is called _Source As Control_

_F_ 11. By default an object appearing on the screen can be dragged at run time. True or false?

PRACTICE

7. Write procedures that will do the following:

   1. Command1 moves to the position where you press a mouse button.
   2. Command1 returns to the original position when the mouse button is released.

8 Modify Figure 12.5 so that each drawing will start from the middle of the form window.

9. Modify the above so that a consecutive number starting from 1 will appear in the middle of each circle.

10. Modify the above so that a circle with a radius of 30 twips will be drawn inside each larger circle.

11. In the above drawing, fill each smaller circle with the default fill color.

12. In Figure 12.5, modify the code so that the screen is cleared when you hold down Ctrl and press the right mouse button.

13. Modify the Command1_DragDrop procedure (discussed in the text) so that when Text1 is dropped onto Command1, the text will be erased.

14. Modify the Form_MouseMove procedure showing RGB colors (discussed in the text) so that the current R, G, and B values will appear in the form's caption.

CUSTOM AND POPUP MENUS

When an application becomes complex and the user interface gets congested, you can use a **custom menu** to alleviate the congestion. The options normally appearing on the screen, such as command buttons or option buttons, can then be converted to menu options. Since menu options are not displayed until they are pulled down (as in a combo box), they do not crowd the user interface.

To design a menu structure, when the form or a control has the focus, select **Menu Editor** (Ctrl+E) from the Tools menu. The Menu Editor window (Figure 12.7) appears. You can click the Menu Editor button on the toolbar to show this window. You can also right-click the form to pop up a shortcut menu; the Menu Editor option is included in this menu.

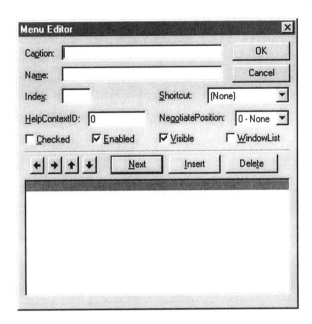

Figure 12.7   The Menu Design window

Supply various required items in the Menu Editor window. As you type something or make various selections in various boxes, the large list box at the bottom will show your menu outline. Click OK when you are done; click Cancel if you want to abort. After clicking OK, a menu bar will appear at the top of the form.

The four arrow buttons in the middle can be used to move a particular menu option left or right, up or down in the menu's hierarchy. Each time you click the left or right button, you move the selected menu item closer to the left margin or further away (indented) from it. Those menu captions appearing flush left in the list box will all be displayed on the menu bar after you click OK. If you want a submenu, use the right arrow button to indent it to the proper position in the menu system's hierarchy. When a menu item is clicked from the menu bar at design time or run time, its submenus or options, if any, will open up. A menu system can have up to five levels of submenus, making it six levels altogether if we include the main menu.

The up and down arrow buttons move the current item (highlighted) in the list box up or down, thus exchanging it with the item above or below. This allows you to change the order of the existing menu items.

The Next button lets you select the next menu item and thus highlight the next item in the list box. You can use an arrow key to do that as well; you can also click any item in the list box to select it. The selected item's properties all appear in proper places above the list box.

The Insert button lets you insert an extra space above the current item. You can then add a new item. If you want to delete an item or extra space, select it and click Delete.

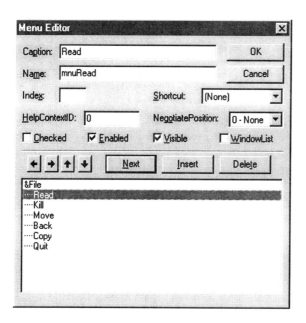

Figure 12.8   A completed menu

To create the menu system shown in Figure 12.9, follow these steps:

1. Press Ctrl+E to show the window.

2. Enter &File in the Caption box and File in the Name box.

3. Click Next to add a submenu. The highlight in the list box goes to the next empty line.

4. Click the right arrow button. Four dots are added in the current line in the list box to signify this item as a submenu.

5. Click the Caption box and enter Read.

6. Tab to the Name box and enter mnuRead.

7. Open the Shortcut box and choose Ctrl+R.

8. Repeat steps 3-7 and enter the items shown in the bottom list box in Figure 12.8. In each case the Name property should be preceded by *mnu*; this is a common convention.

9. Click OK and the File menu appears on the menu bar above the form, as shown in Figure 12.9.

Figure 12.9 comes from a chapter project in Chapter 10. As you may remember, the screen was very cluttered. The new user interface is less congested than before. What can we do with all the procedures attached to the command buttons? Move them to the menus we just created.

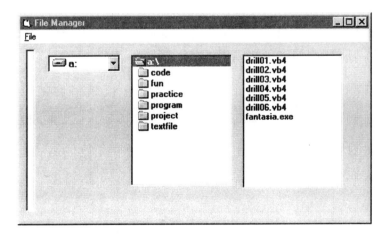

Figure 12.9   A menu at design time

Visual Basic treats a menu as a control, even though it has no pictorial existence like other controls. You can search the online help for Menu Control to see more details. You can even display a menu control's Properties window. To do that, open the Object box in the Properties window. Click one of the displayed menu items. The resulting Properties window will display only the properties available for a menu, as shown in Figure 12.10.

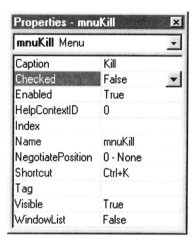

Figure 12.10   A menu's Properties window

A menu control can respond to only one event, namely Click. A menu can be activated by clicking it. Pressing a shortcut key or access key, if any, also triggers the Click event. To respond to the user selecting a menu option, you need to write a Click procedure for it.

When you click a menu option at design time, its Click procedure template appears. The following appears when we click the menu option named mnuRead:

```
Private Sub mnuRead_Click ()

End Sub
```

The code in this procedure will be executed when the user clicks this menu option at run time.

To complete our File Manager application's conversion, we can move the code from a command button to a menu option. For example, we can move the code lines from the original cmdRead_Click procedure to the mnuRead_Click procedure. A simpler way is to change all *cmd* prefixes to *mnu* in the procedures. So cmdRead_Click will become mnuRead_Click. After you finish making the changes, select all the command buttons and press Del to remove them.

Now run the program and see what happens. If your code refers to the erased buttons, errors will occur. In that case, delete those lines and run the program again. Without the command buttons, the screen is much cleaner. To do something to a file, you need to pull down the menu and choose an option, or you can press a designated shortcut key.

If you are unhappy with your menu structure, you can change it at will. Just use the arrow buttons to move each item up or down, left or right. Our menu outline looks like this in the list box of the Menu Editor window:

&File
....Read
....Kill
....Move
....Copy
....Back
....Quit

Suppose you now want to move Back to after Read. It's very simple. Click Back to select it. Then click the up arrow button three times. Each time you click this button, the selected item moves up by one position.

If there are too many options in one menu, you can separate them with **separator bars**. These are horizontal lines that appear when a menu is pulled down. If you pull down Visual Basic's File menu, for example, you will find six separator bars.

Suppose you now want to insert a separator bar after the Back option (which has been moved to after Read). Click the item below Back in the list box. Click Insert to insert a new line; four dots appear automatically to indent the new item to the second level. Click the Caption box and type a hyphen (-). Click the Name box and type a name, maybe xxx. The menu outline in the list box appears as shown below:

&File
....Read
....Back
....-
....Kill
....Move
....Copy
....Quit

If you now click OK and the pull down the File menu, a horizontal line will appear after the Back option.

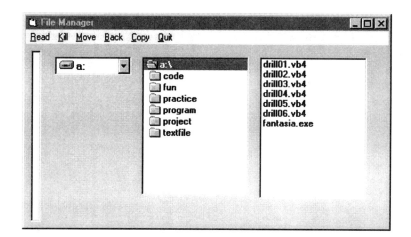

Figure 12.11   The menu bar with six menus

Our simple menu structure results in the user interface displaying only one menu. The user is then required to pull down the menu to choose an option. A simpler way is to display all the options on the menu bar so that the user will have an easier time choosing an option, as shown in Figure 12.11.

Converting to this new system is easy. In the Menu Editor window, delete the &File item by selecting it and then clicking Delete. Select each subsequent item and click the left arrow button to move it to the left margin. Add access keys by adding an & before each appropriate caption letter. If you click OK now, you will get the *Can't assign shortcut key to a top-level menu* error. The remedy is to select each item, click the down arrow in the Shortcut combo box, and select (none) at the top of the long list. The original shortcut keys will disappear from the menu outline. If you now click OK, no more error will appear and the menu bar will be as shown in Figure 12.11.

If you want to put some menu options in a **control array**, enter their **Index** numbers in the Menu Editor. You can then use these numbers to maneuver the options (see Chapter 9). Check and uncheck other boxes as you see fit. The WindowList box will be explained in the MDI section below.

Another way to make it convenient for the user is to use the **PopupMenu** method to create a popup menu, which pops up on the screen when a designated mouse button is pressed. A popup menu must have one or more options; these options appear when the menu is popped up. Our original File menu is suitable for this operation. Assuming you have not changed it, all you need now is the following procedure:

```
Private Sub Form_MouseDown (B As Integer, _
S As Integer, X As Single, Y As Single)
    If B = 2 Then PopupMenu file
        'if right button pressed, open File menu
End Sub
```

After adding the above code, running the program and clicking any area on the form with the right mouse button will bring up the File menu at the pointer location. Clicking anything other than the displayed menu will clear the menu. The *PopupMenu method* topic in the Help system can provide more details.

Visual Basic has a feature that allows you to mimic a Windows 95 shortcut menu with a bolded option. The bolded item signifies the default option. When you double-click a displayed item, that option will be automatically executed. Consider the following modifications:

```
Private Sub File1_MouseDown (B As Integer, _
S As Integer, X As Single, Y As Single)
    If B = 2 Then PopupMenu File, , , , mnuRead
End Sub
```

We've changed Form to File1 in the procedure header. That means right-clicking anywhere inside the File1 box will trigger the popup menu. We've also added one more argument to PopupMenu. This method has five arguments. The first is the menu name, the last is the default-option name, and the three middle ones designate the menu's popup location (we use default values here). With this new arrangement, the default Read option will be bolded. Double-clicking a file in the File1 box will automatically execute this option.

The Checked check box in the Menu Editor window lets you designate a menu option as preselected at run time. A selected option has a check mark appearing on its left. In code you can use the Checked property to handle a selected menu option. You can also let the user toggle between selecting and deselecting an option.

Consider the following two statements:

```
mnuSave.Checked = Not mnuSave.Checked
If mnuSave.Checked Then . . .
```

The first will toggle the Save menu between checked and unchecked. The second will do something if the Save menu is checked.

CLIPBOARD INTERACTION

Windows maintains a **Clipboard**, which is a memory area set aside for temporary storage of data. Any Windows-compliant program can use the Clipboard to send or receive data.

The data sent to the Clipboard can be text and/or pictures. Each time you send a text string or picture to the Clipboard, it replaces the previous counterpart, if any. The second text string replaces the first text string; the second picture replaces the first picture. A picture and a text string, however, can coexist in the Clipboard—although only one of each is allowed.

Visual Basic recognizes the keyword Clipboard as an object just like Screen or Printer. When you want to do something with the Clipboard, you need to specify this name.

The Clipboard can be manipulated with the following methods:

Clear	Clears the Clipboard.
GetData	Gets a picture from the Clipboard.
GetText	Gets text from the Clipboard.
SetData	Sends a picture to the Clipboard.
SetText	Sends text to the Clipboard.
GetFormat	Checks Clipboard data type and returns True or False.

GetData and GetFormat can use a number as an argument, such as the following:

```
GetData(format)
GetFormat(format)
```

An argument for GetData can be 0, 2 (bitmap), 3 (metafile), 8 (DIB or device-independent bitmap), or 9 (color palette). If the argument is 0 or omitted (nothing is placed inside the parentheses), Visual Basic automatically finds the appropriate format.

An argument for GetFormat is mandatory. It can be &HBF00 (DDE data transfer), &HBF01 (Rich Text format), 1 (text), 2 (bitmap), 3 (metafile), 8 (device-independent bitmap), or 9 (color palette).

GetFormat returns either True or False, depending on whether the Clipboard contains data of the specified format. In the following procedure, True will be returned if the Clipboard contains text; otherwise, False will appear.

```
Private Sub Form_Click ()
    Print Clipboard.GetFormat(1)
End Sub
```

On the other hand, the following procedure produces False because the Clipboard is cleared first.

```
Private Sub Form_Click ()
    Clipboard.Clear
    Print Clipboard.GetFormat(1)
End Sub
```

In the following procedure, the first line loads a picture to the Clipboard and the second returns True because the Clipboard contains a bitmap picture.

```
Private Sub Form_Click ()
    Clipboard.SetData LoadPicture _
    ("graphics\bitmaps\gauge\dome.bmp")
    Print Clipboard.GetFormat(2)
End Sub
```

In the following procedure, we use the first two lines to send a bitmap picture and a text string to the Clipboard. The next two lines copy the Clipboard contents to the screen. The last two lines return True to indicate the existence of the above items.

```
Private Sub Form_Click ()
    Clipboard.SetData LoadPicture _
    ("graphics\bitmaps\gauge\dome.bmp")
    Clipboard.SetText "This goes to the Clipboard."
    Picture = Clipboard.GetData()      'show pic
    Print Clipboard.GetText()          'show text
    Print Clipboard.GetFormat(1)       'text?
    Print Clipboard.GetFormat(2)       'bitmap?
End Sub
```

Near the end of Chapter 11, there is a Picture Viewer application which lets you click a file name to display its picture on the screen. In that application, we used the following line to load each selected picture:

```
Image1.Picture = LoadPicture(Text1.Text)
```

We can replace it with the following:

```
Clipboard.Clear
Clipboard.SetData LoadPicture(Text1.Text)
Image1 = Clipboard.GetData()
```

The first line is to clear the existing contents in the Clipboard; without this line, a new metafile will not be displayed. The second line is to load the selected picture to the Clipboard. The third line is to copy from the Clipboard to the image control.

One disadvantage of this arrangement is that an icon file (ICO) cannot be loaded to the Clipboard. If you attempt to load such a file, you will get the *Invalid Clipboard format* error.

Figure 12.12 shows a user interface with two command buttons (Command1 on the left and Command2 on the right) and two text boxes whose MultiLine properties are set to True. The procedures for the two command buttons are shown below.

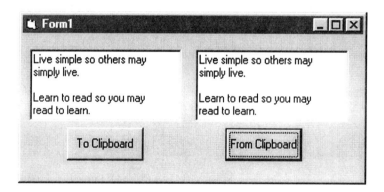

Figure 12.12   Copying text to and from the Clipboard

```
Private Sub cmdToCB_Click ()
    Clipboard.SetText txtToCB.Text   'to Clipboard
End Sub

Private Sub cmdFromCB_Click ()
    txtFromCB.Text = Clipboard.GetText(1) 'from Clipboard
End Sub
```

When the left button is clicked, the content in the left text box is sent to the Clipboard. When you click the right button, the text in the Clipboard is copied to the right text box.

Text box and combo box controls have the following properties at run time. These properties can be used to interact with the Clipboard.

SelText   Selected text string.
SelStart   The starting position of selected text.
SelLength   The length (number of characters) of selected text.

The following procedure is modified from the previous one. The first line sends the selected block of text in Text1 to the Clipboard. The last two lines return numbers indicating the starting position of the selected block of text and its length or number of characters.

```
Private Sub cmdToCB_Click ()
    Clipboard.SetText txtToCB.SelText
      'send selected text to Clipboard
    Print txtToCB.SelStart
    Print txtToCB.SelLength
End Sub
```

Let us use the example shown in Figure 12.12. If we select the second paragraph from the first character to the end of the second line (not including the line break), this paragraph will be sent to the Clipboard and the screen will show two numbers, 42 and 39. The first number indicates the selected text to begin in the 42nd character. The second number shows the text length to be 39 characters. A line break is counted as two characters.

NOTE   No code is needed to transfer text between two text boxes at run time. Just select the text in one box and right click the selected text to pop up the shortcut menu. You can then choose Cut or Copy. Move the cursor to the desired location in the other box. Right-click the box to pop up the shortcut menu and choose Paste.

DYNAMIC DATA EXCHANGE (DDE)

A Windows program can engage in a conversation (exchange of data) with another Windows program. This arrangement is known as DDE (dynamic data exchange). To do that, you need to run both applications (source and destination) and establish a few basic rules.

We are going to create two Visual Basic applications and make one send data and the other receive the data. Start a new project. Add a text box to the form. Change the form's LinkMode property to 1 - Source. Change the form's Caption

to Source; this is optional. Create an EXE file and name it SOURCE. The source
application is now complete.

Next, we need to create a destination application. Start a new project; there is no
need to save the old source file. Add a text box. If you wish, change the form's
Caption to Target. Add the following event procedures:

```
Private Sub Form_Load ()
    Dim varX As Variant
    varX = Shell("source", 1)   'load source program
    varX = DoEvents()           'wait till end of loading
    Text1.LinkTopic = "source|form1"
      'program name, container name
    Text1.LinkItem = "Text1"    'control on source
    Text1.LinkMode = 1          'automatic link
End Sub

Private Sub Form_DblClick ()
    Text1.LinkMode = 0  'close the link
End Sub

Private Sub Text1_LinkClose ()
    MsgBox "The link is closed."
      'show message after closing
End Sub
```

Press F5 to run the Target program. The Source program is also loaded by the
Shell statement. Resize the two windows so that they appear side by side. Go to
the Source text box and type something. As you type, the text appears in both text
boxes.

When you are done, double-click the Target form. The DblClick event is
triggered. The link is severed. This in turn triggers the LinkClose event. A
message is then displayed. The LinkClose event is also triggered when you
double-click the control box to close either form.

If you want to send or receive data manually, you need to use some special
properties, events, and methods. The online help on various Link items can give
you lots of information.

OLE: INSERTABLE OBJECTS AND CONTAINER

If you want to link two applications more closely, try object linking and embedding (**OLE**). Using this technology, you can place (embed or link) an object (document, database, picture, worksheet, etc.) in a Visual Basic application (known as destination or client). At design time or run time, you can open the original application (known as source or server) and edit the object. This mechanism lets you use Visual Basic to access other applications and work on compound documents.

OLE is considered a strategic product and is heavily promoted by Microsoft. This feature is leading more people to use Visual Basic as a front-end development tool that serves as a glue to bind together various OLE-compliant applications. Using this feature, a Visual Basic programmer can quickly put together a simple application that can use other existing applications (word processor, spreadsheet, database, graphics) to do many things.

An OLE object can be added to a Visual Basic project as an **insertable object** or placed in an OLE container control. We discuss the first approach first.

Inserting Objects

An insertable (OLE) object can be added to the Toolbox like a custom control. Choose Project | Components | Insertable Objects. You can also right-click the Toolbox and click Components to open the **Components** dialog box and then open the Insertable Objects tab. The result is shown in Figure 12.13. For our demonstration, check Microsoft Excel 5.0 Worksheet (your version may be different) and click OK. The Excel icon now appears in the Toolbox, added at the bottom. Double-click this icon, and Figure 12.14 appears.

A small worksheet area appears in the middle, which you can enlarge. You can now enter data. Right-clicking the worksheet pops up a shortcut menu with limited editing options. If you shift the focus to another object, the worksheet disappears; entries, if any, remain. If you want to activate the worksheet, right-click the object and choose Edit from the popup menu to show Figure 12.14. Choose Open if you want the full version of Excel opened in a separate window.

An object inserted into your project becomes part of (embedded in) the project. At run time you can double-click the embedded object to activate it. A menu bar with limited options (Figure 12.15) will appear. You can also use the sizing handles (available when the object is activated) to move or change the window.

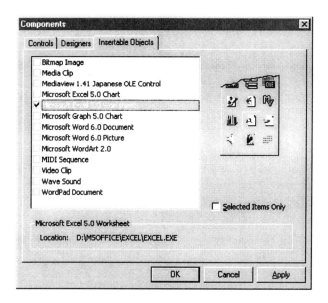

Figure 12.13   The Insertable Objects tab of the Components dialog box

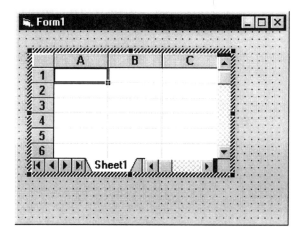

Figure 12.14   Inserting an Excel worksheet

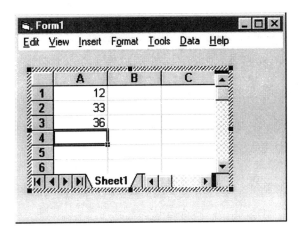

Figure 12.15   Excel with scaled-down menus

TIP: Sound and Sight

If you want to make your application come alive, you can add the Media Player explained in Chapter 0. To do that, check Media Clip in the Components dialog box's Insertable Objects tab; its icon enters the Toolbox after you click OK to close the dialog box. When you move the pointer to this new icon, the *mplayer* tooltip appears.

Double-clicking this icon adds it to the form and opens the Media Player dialog box. You can use the Device menu to select a device and then choose Open to show all the available files for that device. After you open a file, you can use this dialog box to play the clip.

After a file is open, you can also right-click the icon on the form to pop up a shortcut menu and choose to Play, Edit, or Open. The first will start playing the clip. The last two options will open the dialog box for you to edit.

At run time, you can double-click the icon (showing the title of the selected clip) on the form to start playing the clip.

If you develop your own multimedia clip, you can use the Media Player to play it. If you don't need multiple devices, choose one of these from the Insertable Objects tab of the Components dialog box: MIDI Sequence, Video Clip, or Wave Sound. These don't give you a choice of device.

OLE Container

To place an OLE object inside an OLE container at design time, just double-click the OLE container tool. OLE1, the default name, appears on the form. The Insert Object tab (Figure 12.16) also appears. All the OLE-capable applications appear in the middle box. For our demonstration, double-click Microsoft Excel 5.0 Worksheet. Excel is loaded, and an empty sheet is ready for you to add entries; the resulting display is the same as shown earlier in Figure 12.15.

An OLE container has several properties which you can use to change its appearance. These include BackColor, BackStyle, and BorderStyle. They can make the OLE container look different from an insertable object. Other than that, the two behave the same at both design time and run time.

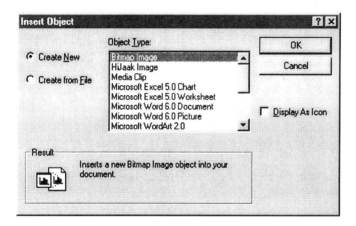

Figure 12.16   The Insert Object dialog box

If you click Cancel when Figure 12.16 is shown, nothing is entered into the container. If you want to insert an object later, right-click the object and choose Insert Object; Figure 12.16 will reappear for you to insert an object. If you check Create from File (instead of Create New), the dialog box will change to Figure 12.17. You're here asked to enter a file name. You can use the Browse button to look for a desired file. When you find one, click it and then click the new Insert button. Figure 12.15 will reappear.

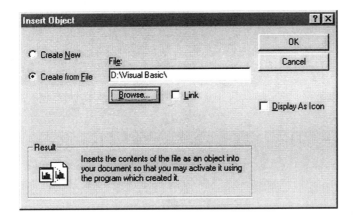

Figure 12.17 Linking or embedding a data file

Figure 12.17 shows a new **Link** check box. If you check it, the file will be linked instead of embedded. An embedded object is included in your project and excluded from other applications. This can make your project larger. A linked object, on the other hand, has a separate existence and can be shared by other applications. It can be altered by any of the sharing applications. Your Visual Basic application is smaller this way because it contains only references to the object, not the object itself.

If you have cut data from another application at design time, you can right-click an OLE container and choose Paste or **Paste Special** from the popup menu; these options are available only when the Clipboard contains data. Paste inserts the data into the container; this is object embedding. Paste Special leads to a dialog box from which you can choose Paste or Paste Special. If you choose the latter, you are doing object linking.

For an application that supports drag and drop, you can drag selected data to an OLE container at design time or run time. Suppose at design time you highlight some lines in WordPad and drag it to OLE1, the lines will be moved to the container; this is cut and paste as well as object embedding. If you want to do copy and paste, use the popup menu instead of drag and drop. To do the same thing at run time, you must change the **OLEDropAllowed** property from the default False to True.

After you insert an object, OLE1's Properties window will automatically have entries in the **Class** (object type), **SourceDoc** (file name and its directory path), and/or **SourceItem** (e.g., worksheet range) properties; if OLE1 contains a database, the **DataSource** and **DataField** properties will have entries too. If you wish, you can make changes here. Each will open a dialog box for you.

When you link or embed a database file (such as BIBLIO.MDB) to an OLE container, an icon with the file name appears. Right-clicking it at design time pops up a shortcut menu with, among other things, the Activate Contents option. Choosing this option opens Access and retrieves the database; the same thing happens if you double-click the object at run time.

The OLE container control has many methods and properties. If you want to know more, check the Properties window and the online help topic called OLE Container Control.

OLE at Run Time

There are many ways to maneuver OLE objects at run time. One way to find out what you can do is to type the word **Action** in the Code window and press F1. You'll find a long list of arguments for this OLE run-time property and their new equivalent methods. You can also click the See Also jump to show the related items.

Here we provide two concrete examples of manipulating OLE objects. Our first example (Figure 12.18) lets you click the Insert Object button to open the Insert Object dialog box, click Open to open an existing data file, and click Save to save the data in the container. At design time an empty OLE container is added. The listing below shows the procedures for the command buttons.

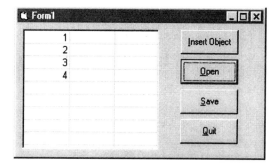

Figure 12.18   **Inserting an OLE object (Excel worksheet) at run time**

(12OLEDEMO.FRM)

```
Private Sub cmdInsObj_Click()
    OLE1.InsertObjDlg     'open Insert Object box
End Sub

Private Sub cmdOpen_Click()
    Dim FilNum As Integer

    On Error GoTo ErrTrap
    FilNum = FreeFile   'get available file number
    Open "a:\textfile\12olefile" For Binary As #FilNum
        'open file for action
        OLE1.ReadFromFile FilNum
            'read data to OLE container
    Close #FilNum   'close file
    Exit Sub

ErrTrap:
    MsgBox Error
End Sub

Private Sub cmdSave_Click()
    Dim FilNum As Integer

    On Error GoTo ErrTrap
    FilNum = FreeFile    'get available file number
    Open "a:\textfile\12olefile" For Binary As #FilNum
        'open file for action
        OLE1.SaveToFile FilNum   'save OLE contents
    Close #FilNum    'close file
    Exit Sub

ErrTrap:
    MsgBox Error
End Sub
```

The **InsertObjDlg** method simply opens the Insert Object dialog box for you to choose an action. Our figure shows the result of opening a new Excel sheet and manually entering some numbers. Clicking Save executes the **SaveToFile** method to save all the entries to the specified file. Clicking Open executes the **ReadFromFile** method to read the data to the worksheet, replacing any existing data. These two methods are used to save and open embedded objects. If you link a file, you need to use the server application's File | Save command to save changed data.

Below we supply a simple demonstration program (Figure 12.19) that will let you enter a few numbers (the numbers shown have been entered at design time) and enlist Excel to add them up. The middle box shows Excel with all the numbers in the left text box, plus the sum at the bottom. At design time an empty Excel worksheet is added to the OLE1 container. At run time the numbers shown in the worksheet are entered by the procedure below.

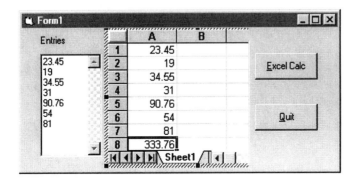

Figure 12.19   Using Excel to add up numbers

(12EXCEL1.FRM)

```
Private Sub cmdExcel_Click()
    Dim I As Integer
    Dim Row As Integer
    Dim Char As String

    Row = 1
    For I = 1 To Len(Text1.Text)
        If Mid(Text1.Text, I, 1) = vbCr _
        Then Row = Row + 1        'get num of rows
    Next I
    ReDim Txt(1 To Row) As String
        'dynamic array based on row num
    Row = 1    'row starts with 1
    For I = 1 To Len(Text1.Text) - 2
            'ignore last 2 chars
        Char = Mid(Text1.Text, I, 1)
            'go through each char
        If Char = vbCr Then      'if Chr(13)
            Row = Row + 1    'go to next row
            I = I + 1    'skip Chr(10)
        Else
            Txt(Row) = Txt(Row) & Char
        End If        'combine each char
    Next I

    OLE1.DoVerb vbOLEShow
        'activate OLE object for editing
    For I = 1 To Row
        SendKeys Val(Txt(I))     'send entry to cell
        SendKeys "{Enter}"       'send Enter key
```

```
Next I   'put array values in col 1 cells

SendKeys "=sum{(}a1: a" & Row & "{)}" & "{enter}"
        'formula: sum of A1 to col A & last row
End Sub
```

When the Excel Calc button is clicked, the entries in Text1 are put into an array. Each element in the array is sent to the each subsequent cell starting from A1. A formula is then entered in the cell below to calculate the sum. The **DoVerb** method activates an OLE object. It has seven available arguments; see the online help for detail. The **SendKeys** statement lets you send keystrokes to any Windows-compliant program. If a keystroke does not lead to a character being displayed, you need to enclose it in a pair of curly braces.

CLASS MODULES and ActiveX SERVERS

OLE has assumed a bigger role and, as a result, is often called by a different name, namely ActiveX. ActiveX has become Microsoft's major tool to compete against Java to dominate the Internet. ActiveX is Microsoft's technology to create software components that can compete against Java applets.

ActiveX components are individual programs that follow Microsoft's **COM** (Common Object Model) standard. These components may be **ActiveX controls** that appear in Visual Basic's Toolbox, **ActiveX servers** that provide functions for other applications, or **ActiveX documents** that can be read and run like an **HTML** (hypertext markup language) page by a Web browser such as Microsoft Internet Explorer 3.0 or later. VB5 allows you to create all these.

ActiveX servers (formerly known as OLE servers) are applications that expose their properties (public variables and property procedures) and methods (sub and function procedures) to other applications (OLE clients). Users of a client application can programmatically manipulate a server's properties and methods without having to do lots of programming. This is a major advantage that has made OOP (object-oriented programming) so popular.

An object is derived from a class. A **class** is a template or definition for an object. You use a class module to create a class. Users of the class can create instances, which become objects. Through an object, users can access the methods and properties contained in the original class.

Creating and Using Classes

A **class module** is a cross between a form module and a standard module. Public variables and procedures in a class, like those in a form, can be accessed only by providing references to them. Those in a standard module can be accessed directly (no reference is needed). Like a standard module, a class module can contain only code, but not visual objects.

A class module can be added by choosing Project | Add Class Module. You can also click the down arrow next to the second icon on the Standard toolbar to display a list of the available modules and then click Class Module.

Examine the Properties window. It has Class1 as its Name property and there is no other property. This is true if you add a class module to a Standard EXE project. This will change if you open (or change an existing project to) a different type of project. If you choose Project | Project Properties to open the **Project Properties dialog box**, the General tab has the Project Type combo box. You can use it to change to **ActiveX DLL**, **ActiveX EXE**, or **ActiveX Control**. If you do that, the Properties window will add an **Instancing** property with as many as the following options:

    1 - Private
    2 - PublicNotCreatable
    3 - SingleUse
    4 - GlobalSingleUse
    5 - MultiUse
    6 - GlobalMultiUse

An ActiveX EXE module will have all of the above. An ActiveX DLL module will have 1, 2, 5, and 6. An ActiveX Control module will have 1 and 2. A Standard EXE module, with no Instancing property, has the same effect as having only 1.

The Instancing property determines whether the class allows creation of objects. The Private option lets you create an instance only inside the same project, but not by other applications. The other options provide different degrees of accessibility. The online help on *Instancing property* has details.

You might want to know the differences among **ActiveX DLL**, **ActiveX EXE**, **ActiveX Control** modules. You create an ActiveX control for use by Visual Basic, Microsoft Office 97 suite, Microsoft Internet Explorer, and many other applications that can run them; this will be covered in another section below. You create the other two to provide services for other applications. ActiveX DLL runs in the client's memory space and is thus known as an **in-process server.** ActiveX EXE runs in its more memory space and is known as an **out-of-process server.** Between these two, each has its own pluses and minuses; the more common is DLL.

We are going to create a class. Then we will use an object derived from this class. This object will contain one property (a property procedure) and two methods (a sub procedure and a function procedure). We'll then call these methods from a regular Visual Basic procedure.

To insert a class module to a project, choose Insert | Class Module. Class1 appears. Go to its Properties window and change the Name property to SortData. This name is similar to the name you give to a form or a standard module. Go to its Code window and add the general procedures shown below. (This project consists of two modules, 12SORTDATA3.CLS and 12SORT3.FRM. If you open 12SORT3.VBP, both modules will open.)

(12SORTDATA3.CLS)

```
Public Function ToSort(Tex1, Tex3)
        'accept 2 arguments from text boxes
    Dim Rows As Integer
    Dim Cols As Integer
    Dim Col As Integer
    Dim Row As Integer
    Dim I As Integer
    Dim J As Integer
    Dim SrtCol As Integer
    Dim Txt As String
    Dim Temp As Variant

'--get col and row numbers--
    Col = 0: Row = 0     'start with 0 col and 0 row
    For I = 1 To Len(Tex1) 'go thru all chars in text box
        Txt = Mid(Tex1, I, 1)     'get each char
        If Txt = Chr(9) Then Col = Col + 1
            'add col if tab
        If Txt = Chr(13) Then        'if chr 13
            I = I + 1       'skip next char (10)
            Row = Row + 1  'get total num of lines (rows)
        End If
    Next I

    Cols = Col / Row       'num of columns
    Rows = Row             'num of rows
    ReDim TxtArr(0 To Rows, 0 To Cols)
        'dim dynamic array

'--if no valid entry in box 3--
```

```
    SrtCol = Val(Tex3)          'sort col
    If SrtCol < 0 Or SrtCol > Cols Then
        Beep
        MsgBox "Invalid column to sort." & vbCr _
        & "Enter: 0-" & Cols
        Exit Function
    End If

'--read text box and put in array--
    Row = 0: Col = 0    'start with row 0 and col 0
    For I = 1 To Len(Tex1)
        Txt = Mid(Tex1, I, 1)       'get each char
        Select Case Txt
        Case Chr(9)        'tab
            Col = Col + 1  'get col
        Case Chr(13)       'carriage return
            I = I + 1      'skip next char (10)
            Row = Row + 1     'increment row
            Col = 0           'start a new col
        Case Else
            TxtArr(Row, Col) = TxtArr(Row, Col) & Txt
                'add (concatenate) each to array
        End Select
    Next I

'--call sorting routine to sort
    SortArr TxtArr(), Cols, SrtCol
        'call procedure within class
        'pass array, total col #, col to sort by

'--display sorted lines--
    Txt = ""        'clear and reuse var
    For I = 1 To Rows        'from 1st to last row
        For J = 0 To Cols  '1st to last col
            Txt = Txt & TxtArr(I, J)
                'concatenate each char
            If J < Cols Then
                Txt = Txt & vbTab  'add tab if not end
            End If
        Next J
        Txt = Txt & vbCrLf  'add line break
    Next I
    ToSort = Txt            'return sorted array to caller
End Function

Private Sub SortArr(ArrTxt(), Col, SortBy)
    Dim I As Integer, J As Integer
    Dim K As Integer, M As Integer
    Dim Temp As Variant

    K = UBound(ArrTxt)          'upperbound of array
    For I = 0 To K - 1
        For J = I + 1 To K
            If ArrTxt(I, SortBy) > ArrTxt(J, SortBy) Then
```

```
            For M = 0 To Col
                Temp = ArrTxt(I, M)
                    'change each element
                ArrTxt(I, M) = ArrTxt(J, M)
                ArrTxt(J, M) = Temp
            Next M
        End If
    Next J
    Next I
End Sub

Public Property Get MsgDemo()
    MsgDemo = "This demonstrates class property."
End Property
```

Our class has one function procedure, one sub procedure, and one property procedure. The function procedure will be called by a regular procedure which we'll cover shortly. The sub procedure is called by the function procedure. The property procedure can be called by another procedure also discussed below.

We can now write procedures that will call the class's one method (function procedure) and one property procedure. These procedures (shown below) are attached to the interface shown in Figure 12.20. It consists of a form, three text boxes, and two command buttons. We intend to let the user type multicolumn text in Text1 (left text box) and specify a column number in Text3 (bottom) to sort the text lines. The sorted lines are then displayed in Text2 (right). Our demo data is already entered in Text1 at design time. You can alter the items shown by adding columns or lines, and then click Sort to sort the new data.

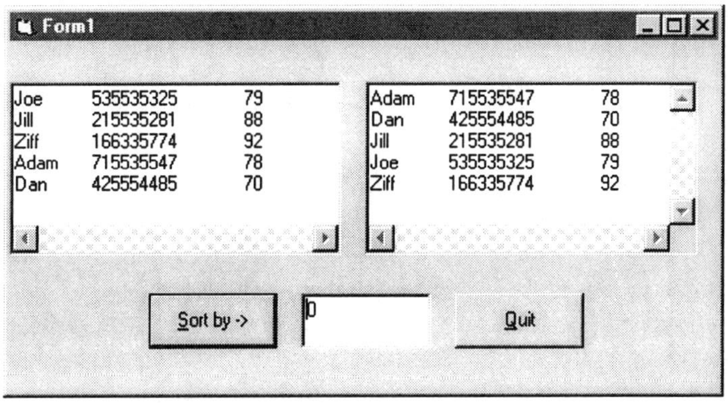

Figure 12.20   Using a class

We create a form-level Object variable named clsSort as an instance of the
SortData class (the class we put in the class module). The cmdSort_Click
procedure then calls the ToSort function procedure in the clsSort object; two
arguments are also passed to this function procedure. The data returned from the
call is then assigned to T, which in turn is shown in Text2.

If you click the form, the Form_Click procedure calls the MsgDemo property
procedure in the clsSort object; the returned text string (property) is then
displayed in a message box.

(12SORT3.FRM)

```
Dim clsSort As New SortData
    'create a new instance of class

Private Sub cmdSort_Click()
    Dim Txt As String

    On Error GoTo ErrTrap
    Txt = clsSort.ToSort(Text1.Text, Text3.Text)
        'call class.method, pass 2 arguments

    Text2.Text = Txt    'put in text box
    Text3.SetFocus   'for another col num
    Exit Sub

ErrTrap:
    MsgBox Error     'show error msg
End Sub

Private Sub Form_Click()
    Dim Msg As String

    Msg = clsSort.MsgDemo()
        'call class.property procedure
    MsgBox Msg  'show property in message box
End Sub
```

Most of the work is done in the SortData class, particularly in the ToSort function.
This function takes two arguments from a caller from outside the class. It breaks up
all the entries in the first argument (Text1) and puts them in a dynamic array. It
then determines whether the second passed argument is within the available fields to
be sorted. If not, a message is displayed and the procedure is exited. If so, it calls
the SortArr procedure to sort the array. This call is within the same class, so in the
calling statement there is no need to specify an object before the procedure name.

The SortArr procedure takes three arguments, one array and two Variants. The first
Variant supplies the total number of available columns (fields) in the array. The
second Variant specifies which column to sort the data by. This procedure returns

no data, but it alters the order of the array passed to it by reference. So when the caller returns the returned data to its caller, the array has already been sorted.

Using External Objects

An OLE server or an application that complies with OLE standards can expose its properties and methods to an OLE client. We'll provide two examples of calling the methods of these external objects, one is an OLE server created with VB5 Professional Edition and the other is Microsoft Excel.

On the disk that comes with this book, there is a DLL file in the \PROGRAM directory. This file (12SORT3.DLL) has been compiled as an in-process server. It is the same as shown in 12SORTDATA3.CLS. Since it's an external server, it can be called by a Visual Basic project.

The calling project is the same as Figure 12.20 and 12SORT3.FRM shown at the end of the previous section. If you want to try this, first load 12SORT3.FRM from a new project. Or, if the previous section's project is still in place, remove 12SORTDATA3.CLS.

To call the 12SORT3.DLL file, choose Project | References. The References dialog box appears. If the list does not show "Sort 2-dimension array passed from a text box," then use Browse to show the A:\PROGRAM directory. When the description appears, check it and then click OK. The OLE server is now registered and ready for call.

Press F5 to run 12SORT3.FRM and proceed as described in the previous section. This simple project can now do a fairly complex job because it enlists a DLL file. This DLL file can be used by other projects as well. This is an example of code reuse.

Even if you don't create an OLE server, you can still use many application's methods and properties. Here we demonstrate how to use Microsoft Excel. Our project (Figure 12.21) lets you enter some numbers (the numbers shown here have been entered at design time) and click a button to calculate the sum and show it in the smaller text box.

(12EXCEL2.FRM)
```
Private Sub cmdExcel_Click()
    Dim I As Integer
    Dim Row As Integer
    Dim Char As String
```

```
Row = 1
For I = 1 To Len(txtEntries.Text)
    If Mid(txtEntries.Text, I, 1) = vbCr _
    Then Row = Row + 1        'get num of rows
Next I

ReDim Txt(1 To Row) As Variant
    'dynamic array based on row num
Row = 1    'row starts with 1
For I = 1 To Len(txtEntries.Text) - 2
       'ignore last 2 chars
    Char = Mid(txtEntries.Text, I, 1)
       'go through each char
    If Char = vbCr Then      'if Chr(13)
       Row = Row + 1   'go to next row
       I = I + 1    'skip Chr(10)
    Else
       Txt(Row) = Txt(Row) & Char
    End If         'combine each char
Next I

Dim Ex As Object     'get object reference
MousePointer = 11    'hour glass
Set Ex = CreateObject("excel.sheet")
    'open Excel and a sheet
'Ex.application.Visible = True
    'if you want to show Excel screen

For I = 1 To Row
    Ex.Cells(I, 1).Value = Val(Txt(I))
Next I  'put array values in col 1 cells

Ex.Cells(I, 1).Formula = "=sum(a1" & ":a" & Row & ")"
    'formula: sum of row 1 col A to row last col A
txtSum.Text = Ex.Cells(I, 1).Value
    'put sum in box 2
Ex.Application.Quit  'close Excel
MousePointer = 0     'default
Set Ex = Nothing     'free variable
End Sub
```

In the first half of the procedure, we try to put the numbers into a one-dimensional array. This array is then passed to Excel to get the sum.

We use Ex as a Variant; you can also declare it as an Object. We then use the **CreateObject** function to assign an object to Ex. We then assign each array element to each subsequent cell in column 1. We then enter a formula in the last cell to get the sum of all the numbers. This sum is then transferred back to a text box in our project.

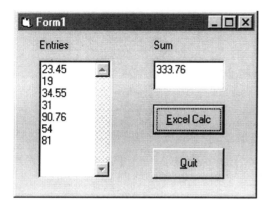

Figure 12.21   Calling Excel to add up numbers

Calling an external method is a cumbersome process and can sometimes take a long time. So we change the **MousePointer** property to the hourglass sign. We change it back to the default shape at the end.

If you want to see Excel's screen and single-step through the procedure, take out the Visible line's apostrophe and continue to press F8. When Excel appears, resize the two windows so that the two can both been seen at the same time. When it's done, close the Excel window manually by clicking the X button.

CREATING ActiveX CONTROLS

You can use VB5 to create **ActiveX controls**. Such controls can be added to the Visual Basic Toolbox or run by many other programs such as Microsoft Internet Explorer and any of the Office 97 suite components.

Creating an ActiveX control involves a **UserControl**. This module, like a regular form, serves as a container for other regular controls. When you close the UserControl, it transforms itself into an ActiveX control and is automatically added to the Toolbox. You can then add this new control to a regular project.

The first step in creating an ActiveX control is to add a UserControl module. Choose File | Add Project. Double-click ActiveX Control in the ensuing Add Project dialog box. This will add a project and a UserControl. A simpler way for this is to use the second icon on the Standard toolbar. Click the down arrow to drop down a list and then choose User Control. This will add a UserControl to the current project without adding a new project. A designer window labeled "Project1

- UserControl1 (UserControl)" is added to the current project. This name is also added to the Project window.

The UserControl resembles a form in most respects. It is enclosed in a designer window. It comes with its own Properties window and Code window. You use these accessories to create an interface and write code just as you would with a standalone program. The major difference is that when you close the UserControl's designer window, a control is added to the Toolbox.

As a demonstration, we are going to create an ActiveX control that will show the current time whenever the control is added to the current project. Follow these steps:

1. Choose File | New Project and double-click Standard EXE. This is the default setting for creating a standalone program.

2. Add a UserControl by using the second icon on the Standard toolbar. "Project1 - UserControl1 (UserControl)" is added. Notice that two dimmed icons are added to the Toolbox, one for the designer window and the other for the UserControl. If you click the X button to close the designer window, the designer icon disappears from the Toolbox and the UserControl icon is activated. If you want to remove the module, right-click it in the Project window and choose Remove UserControl1; the corresponding icons will also disappear from the Toolbox.

3. Use the Properties window to change the name from UserControl1 to CurrentTime. This is optional, just like changing a form's name.

4. Use the Toolbox to add Label1 and Timer1 to the UserControl. Move the label to the top left corner and stretch it horizontally. Change the UserControl's size to be just slightly larger than the label. The label needs to be long enough to display the current time and some text. The UserControl's size determines its run-time size of the resulting control.

5. Go to the UserControl's Code window and add the following procedures. The **Initialize** event is triggered whenever the control is used. It sets the timer's Interval property to 1000 or 1 second. So the Timer event of Timer1 is triggered every second to display the current time.

```
Private Sub UserControl_Initialize()
    Timer1.Interval = 1000
    Label1.FontSize = 15
    Label1.ForeColor = vbRed
    Label1.BackColor = vbCyan
End Sub
```

```
Private Sub Timer1_Timer()
    Label1.Caption = "Current Time = " & Now
End Sub
```

6. Close the UserControl's designer window by clicking the X button. Notice that the corresponding icon in the Toolbox is now visible.

7. Double-click the CurrentTime icon in the Toolbox. The control is added to Form1 and the current time is displayed immediately. The control now goes into run mode without your doing anything else. (The top portion of Figure 12.22 shows the result.) You can now resize the control or delete it as you would with any regular control.

8. Select CurrentTime in the Project window and click View Object. This opens the control's designer window and freezes the control in Form1.

9. Close the UserControl's designer window, and the control in the form starts running again.

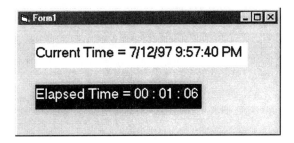

Figure 12.22   Using two UserControls

To create the bottom half of Figure 12.22, add a new UserControl, change its name to ElapsedTime (optional), add Label1 and Timer1 as before, and add the following procedures:

```
Dim StartTime As Date
Private Sub UserControl_Initialize()
    Timer1.Interval = 1000
    Label1.FontSize = 15
    Label1.BackColor = vbRed
    Label1.ForeColor = vbCyan
    StartTime = Now
End Sub

Private Sub Timer1_Timer()
```

```
    Label1.Caption = "Elapsed Time = " & _
    Format(Now - StartTime, "hh : mm : ss")
End Sub
```

NOTE   The companion disk, in the PROGRAM directory, contains a file
named **12TIMER.VBP**. Opening this file will load two modules:
12CurrentTime.ctl and 12ElapsedTime.ctl. Two new icons will also enter
the Toolbox. The controls are now available to be added to a regular
form that you can add to this project.

If you now close ElapsedTime's designer window, it becomes available in the
Toolbox. If you add this control to Form1, the timer begins to function right
away.

We now have two designer windows. If we open either one, the two displays in
Form1 are frozen. If both designer windows are open, closing one will also close
the other as well as activate the two controls.

A UserControl has the **ToolboxBitmap** property. You can use it to load a picture
that will replace the default icon appearing in the Toolbox.

When you save a UserControl file, the name you've given at design time (or the
default module name) will be the default file name; you can change it to another
name. The extension name is **CTL**. If you've saved a project file with one or
more UserControls, opening the project file will open all the UserControl files. If
you wish, you can open an individual UserControl file.

You can compile a UserControl project into an OCX file, which in turn can be
shared by other users. Before you compile, you must change each UserControl's
Public property from the default False to True. Then choose Project | Project
Properties to change the project's properties. In the General tab (Figure 12.23),
specify ActiveX Control (you can use this to convert from another type of project
an to ActiveX control, or vice versa). Specify (None) for Startup Object, unless
you have code in the **Sub Main** procedure. Enter a description in **Project
Description**; this is important because this description will be exposed to users. In
the Make tab, enter the application's title, version number, and other optional
information.

After you have taken care of project properties, choose **File | Make Project1.ocx**.
After you supply a name, your screen will go through a series of convulsions and
a file will be saved to the specified (or current) directory.

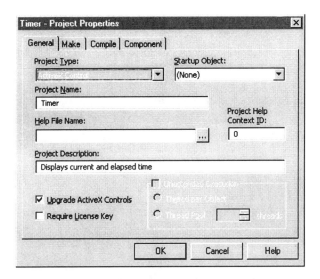

Figure 12.23   Entering ActiveX properties

To use the ActiveX controls created earlier, start a new project, right-click the Toolbox and choose Components. In the **Components dialog box**, use the Browse button to load the compiled file (with the OCX extension). The file enters the dialog box and is automatically checked. The description you've supplied earlier now appears in this middle list box. After clicking OK in this dialog box, the two controls are added to the Toolbox. You can now use them as you would any regular control.

You can use an **add-in** called **ActiveX Control Interface Wizard** to add standard (built-in) or custom (user-defined) properties, methods, and events to your controls. Like a data form designer discussed later in this chpater, it will generate the underlying code for you. After using the add-in manager to add this wizard to the IDE, you can find more from the relevant online help.

WINDOWS API FUNCTIONS

In addition to the numerous built-in functions discussed in Chapter 8, you can use Visual Basic to access the functions (and sub procedures) contained in some dynamic-link libraries (DLLs). Windows comes with numerous DLL files. They can have the DLL, EXE, or other extensions. Some of these compiled program files contain routines that can be called by other Windows applications.[3] A routine is loaded to memory only when it is called; it can also be called by multiple applications. This arrangement makes programs smaller and uses memory more efficiently.

The gateway to these Windows functions is known as the API (application programming interface). The key to open the gate is the **Declare** statement. You use this keyword to tell what function in what API library you want to access. You must also specify the required arguments. The listing below provides an example. Here we call the Pie function in the GDI32.DLL file to draw the display shown in Figure 12.24.

(12DLLPIE.FRM)

```
Private Declare Function Pie Lib "gdi32" (ByVal hdc As _
Long, ByVal X1 As Long, ByVal Y1 As Long, ByVal X2 As _
Long, ByVal Y2 As Long, ByVal X3 As Long, ByVal Y3 _
As Long, ByVal X4 As Long, ByVal Y4 As Long) As Long

Private Sub Form_Click()
    Dim SW As Long
    Dim RetVal As Long
    Dim X1 As Long
    Dim X2 As Long
    Dim X3 As Long
    Dim X4 As Long
    Dim Y1 As Long
    Dim Y2 As Long
    Dim Y3 As Long
    Dim Y4 As Long

    Width = ScaleHeight      'square
    Width = 2 * ScaleHeight - ScaleWidth
    ScaleMode = vbPixels
    SW = ScaleWidth     'get scalewidth in pixels
    FillStyle = vbFSSolid
    FillColor = vbRed  'fill with red

    X1 = 0      'top-left x of rectangle
    Y1 = 0      'top-left y of rectangle
    X2 = SW     'bot-right x of rectangle
    Y2 = SW     'bot-right y of rectangle
    X3 = SW     'beginning of pie
    Y3 = SW / 3
    X4 = SW     'ending of pie
    Y4 = SW
```

---

[3]A Windows application can call the functions contained in the following major libraries that come with Windows 95: KERNEL32.DLL, GDI32.DLL, and USER32.DLL.

```
      RetVal = Pie(Form1.hdc, X1, Y1, X2, Y2, X3, Y3, _
      X4, Y4)
End Sub
```

The **Declare** statement has to be a single logical line. It can be entered at the module level of a standard module with or without **Public** preceding it; Public is the default if omitted. You can also put it at the module level of a form. In that case, you must precede it with the **Private** keyword. You can type everything in lowercase; Visual Basic will convert case where appropriate. In the new 32-bit version, however, procedure names are case sensitive. So we can no longer use *pie* as we could in the past; we must now use *Pie*.

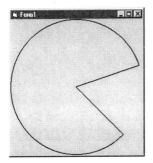

Figure 12.24   A Pie drawing

The Pie function has 9 arguments. The first, hDC, gets the handle for Device Context. This is one of the three handles available to Visual Basic and is required to access this function.

The other arguments represent various coordinate points. These points are by default measured in pixels (rather than twips) and from the left and top borders; they are not affected by the Scale statement (custom scale). X1/Y1 and X2/Y2 specifies the drawing area, similar to the ScaleWidth and ScaleHeight properties. X3/Y3 and X4/Y4 are adjusted so that they are relative to each other. We specify X3 as ScaleWidth and Y3 as 1/3 of that. So the starting point of the pie has the X coordinate value that is three times that of the Y coordinate. You can change these arguments to create a variety of effects.

You can use the Arc function to draw an arc, but you cannot fill it with a color since it is not enclosed.

Chapter 7 discusses a technique of pausing program execution. In addition to that, you can use an API function called **Sleep** to do the same thing. Here is the procedure declaration:

```
Declare Sub Sleep Lib "kernel32" _
(ByVal dwMilliseconds As Long)
```

To call this procedure, you need to pass a timer Interval (millisecond) value as an argument. The example below pauses for one second; the Call keyword can also be omitted:

```
    Call Sleep(1000)      'pause 1 second
```

You can call thousands of Windows functions. How do you know what to call? If you are using the Professional Edition, you are in luck. You should have a directory named WINAPI. This directory contains several related files, including APILOAD.EXE, WIN32API.TXT, and maybe more.

APILOAD.EXE is known as the **API Viewer**. You can use it to view all the available API functions. The easiest way to run this program is to use the **Add-Ins menu**. If API Viewer appears in this menu, just click it. If not, choose **Add-In Manager**, Figure 12.25 appears. Check VB API Viewer and click OK. If you open the Add-Ins menu again, API Viewer should appear there. APILOAD.EXE can also be run from Windows.

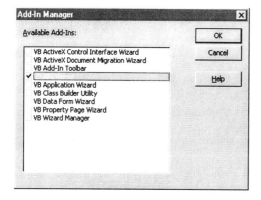

Figure 12.25 The Add-In Manager

From the API View's File menu, choose Load Text File or Load Database File. Try the second option first. If you can find WIN32API.MDB, double-click it to open. If not, click Cancel and then choose Load Text File from the File menu. Find the WIN32API.TXT and load it. This is a huge file and takes a long time to load. You'll be asked whether to convert it to a database to speed up future loading.

If you load a text file, an extra Search button appears (Figure 12.26). Clicking it leads to an input box. You can enter a string to search. This button doesn't appear if you load a database file. You can use the scroll bar to scroll the desired item to view. You can also click a displayed item and then start typing the desired search string to bring it to view.

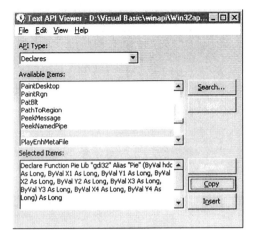

Figure 12.26   The API Viewer

When you find the desired item, click it and click Add to add it to the bottom list box. If you want to remove an item here, click it and then click Remove.

After adding the desired items, click Copy to copy to the Clipboard or Insert to insert directly into the current module. If you choose Copy, then you need to move the cursor to the Declarations section of the desired module and choose Paste from the File menu. This mechanism eliminates typing errors. The Declare statements in our previous examples were both copied from the API Viewer.

You can search the online help for API to get more information. You can also type Declare in the Code window and press F1 to show related information.

If you are serious about using the Windows API functions, you should get a book marketed by Microsoft. It's called *Microsoft Windows Programmer's Reference*. Another popular book is *Dan Appleman's Visual Basic 5.0 Programmer's Guide to the Win32 API*, published by ZD Press. There are many other books that cover this subject.

DRILL

12. A menu's Click event is triggered only when the menu is clicked. True or false?

13. When a menu's Checked property is set to True at design time, running the program automatically executes the menu's Click procedure. True or false?

14. Complete the following statement to send Text1's contents to the Clipboard:

```
Clipboard._____ Text1.Text
```

15. Complete the following statement to send selected text in Text1 to the Clipboard:

```
Clipboard.SetText Text1._____
```

16. Complete the following statement to display in the current form the picture stored in the Clipboard:

```
Picture = Clipboard._____ ()
```

17. A UserControl's _____ property must be set to True if the procedures in it are to be called by other applications.

18. To create a program that can be added to Visual Basic's Toolbox, you need to create this type of project:
    a. Standard EXE
    b. ActiveX EXE
    c. ActiveX DLL
    d. ActiveX Control

19. To let the user of your application insert an object at run time, you need to use the _____ method.

20. This statement is needed to access an API function:
    a. Dim
    b. ReDim
    c. Static
    d. Declare
    e. any of the above

PRACTICE

■   15. How can you display the Properties window of a menu?

■   16. Create a menu that looks like the following when it is pulled down:

    Menu
      Option 1
      Option 2

      Option 3
      Option 4

    At run time, when an option is selected, the form caption should display
    "Option" plus an appropriate number.

■   17. Modify the above so that the Menu options will pop up when the right
        mouse button is pressed on the form.

■   18. Modify the above so that the menu will pop up when the left mouse
        button is pressed. Explain the difference with the previous procedure.

■   19. Modify the above so that the menu will pop up when Ctrl is held down
        and the left mouse button is pressed.

■   20. Modify the above so that the menu bar will disappear at run time but the
        user is allowed to pop up the menu.

■   21. How can you disable the menu at design time and at run time? What is
        the consequence?

■   22. How can you check-mark a menu option at design time?

■   23. Use code to designate Option 1 as checked at run time. Then allow the
        user to check and uncheck this option.

■   24. How can you use code to display the form caption as "Option 1" if it is
        checked at the beginning of run time?

GRID CONTROL

The **MSFlexGrid control** is a simple spreadsheet program. It supplies columns and rows. The intersection of a column and a row becomes a cell. A cell is a miniature container where you can store a text string or a picture.

The grid control is a custom control. If your Toolbox shows it, double-click it to add a grid to the current form. If it is not there, choose Project | Components. Check Microsoft FlexGrid Control and click OK. The grid tool is now added to the Toolbox.

When you double-click the grid control tool, MSFlexGrid1 appears in the middle of the current form. The grid has two default columns and rows. You can stretch it horizontally and vertically. You can use the Properties window to change the number of cells. You can have multiple grids in an application.

The grid control's Properties window shows a Custom property. It leads to the **Property Pages** dialog box (Figure 12.27). You can use this to set many properties. You can also use the regular Properties window to do the same thing.

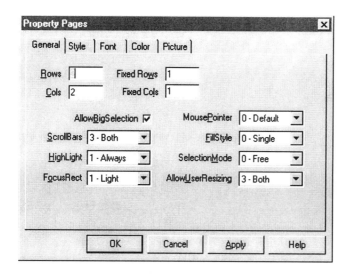

Figure 12.27   The Grid Control's Property Pages dialog box

The Properties window shows many properties. The following are unique or significant:

Cols	2
FixedCols	1
FixedRows	1
GridLines	1 - flexGridFlat
GridLineWidth	1
HighLight	1 - flexHighlightAlways
Rows	2
ScrollBars	3 - flexScrollBarBoth

The default columns and rows are both 2. If you want to change, use **Rows** or **Cols** at design time or run time and assign a value.

Use **FixedCols** and **FixedRows** to specify the number of title columns and rows. You can change the default 1 to 0 or a higher number. When you scroll columns or rows at run time, some may be out of sight, but the fixed ones always stay. At run time, a fixed column/row also lets you click it to select the entire column/row. This can be changed by changing the default True value of the **AllowBigSelection** property to False.

Horizontal and vertical scroll bars will by default appear if there are more cells than there is room to display them. You can change the Both value to None, Horizontal, or Vertical. In that case, scroll bars will not appear. The user can still move to undisplayed cells by pressing a proper cursor key. The cursor keys used in the Code window can be applied here as well.

By default grid lines appear to separate cells. If you change the **GridLines** property's value from True to False, grid lines will disappear. If grid lines are on, you can set the line width, which is 1 twip by default.

HighLight is to highlight selected cells. If it is set to True (default), the selected cells are highlighted. If you change it to False, the user cannot tell which cells are selected.

All the properties discussed above are also available at run time. There are also about a dozen more properties available only at run time; some of these will be covered below.

Two events are unique to a grid control. These are **RowColChange** and **SelChange**. Both occur when a cell is clicked. Dragging the pointer, however, triggers only the latter event.

You can use the **AddItem** and **RemoveItem** methods to add or remove rows and text entries in cells—the same way you use them with a list or combo box. The following statement will add a new row and fill the first three cells of the row with the specified letters:

```
MSFlexGrid1.AddItem "A" & Chr(9) & "B" & Chr(9) & "C"
```

Chr(9) is the Tab character (you can also use **vbTab**). It is used to separate one cell's content from the next in the same row.

The following statement will remove row 1, including its contents:

```
MSFlexGrid1.RemoveItem 1
```

A more versatile way is to use the **Text** property at run time to assign an entry to a cell. The Text string can be omitted just as in Text1, List1, or Combo1. So MSFlexGrid1 is the same as MSFlexGrid1.Text.

Figure 12.28 shows a grid with a fixed column and a fixed row. In addition, there are nine other columns and rows where a multiplication table is displayed. To create this display, add a grid control to a blank form. Stretch the grid both ways so that enough cells can be displayed. The rest is taken care of by the Form_Load procedure shown below.

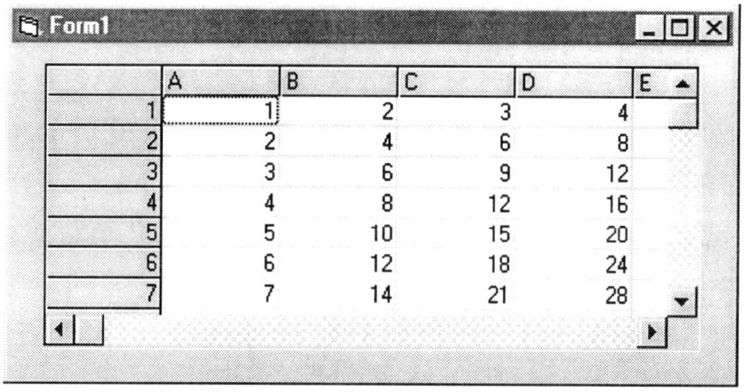

Figure 12.28   A grid with a multiplication table

(12GRID1.VBP)
```
Private Sub Form_Load ()            '--Listing 2--
    Dim I As Integer
    Dim J As Integer

    MSFlexGrid1.Rows = 10                '10 rows
    MSFlexGrid1.Cols = 10                '10 cols
```

```
    For I = 1 To 9
        MSFlexGrid1.Col = I
        MSFlexGrid1.Row = 0
        MSFlexGrid1.Text = Chr$(I + 64)
            'letters for top row
        MSFlexGrid1.Col = 0
        MSFlexGrid1.Row = I
        MSFlexGrid1.Text = I          'numbers for left col
    Next I

    For I = 1 To 9
        For J = 1 To 9
            MSFlexGrid1.Row = I    'write multiplication
            MSFlexGrid1.Col = J    'table to grid
            MSFlexGrid1.Text = I * J
        Next J
    Next I

    MSFlexGrid1.Row = 1              'move cursor to cell A1
    MSFlexGrid1.Col = 1
    Form1.Show
    MSFlexGrid1.SetFocus
End Sub
```

Figure 12.28 shows two scroll bars. These bars automatically appear when there are undisplayed items. These bars allow you to use the mouse to scroll the display.

You can now move the pointer to any displayed cell. The current cell is enclosed in an outline. The current cell is selected. You can select an entire column or row by clicking a fixed cell at the top or left. You can also select a block of cells by dragging the mouse pointer or by holding down the Shift key and moving the pointer. Clicking the top-left fixed cell selects all the cells. We will shortly write a procedure to handle selected cells.

By default the column and row sizes cannot be resized at run time. You can make the title lines respond to dragging; this may be necessary to display some large items. Use the **AllowUserResizing** property at design time or run time from 0 (not allowed) to one of the other three options (column, row, or both). In code you can do it this way:

```
MSFlexGrid1.AllowUserResizing = flexResizeBoth
```

After you type the =, a list will pop up for you to select.

You can also use the **ColWidth** or **RowHeight** properties in code to specify the number of twips. These properties are not available at design time. In the following example, column 0 will have 500 twips:

```
MSFlexGrid1.ColWidth(0) = 500
```

Our procedure will do nothing to respond to a new cell being selected. The following procedure, however, will do that:

```
Sub MSFlexGrid1_Click()
    Dim R As String
    Dim C As String

    R = MSFlexGrid1.Row        'get current row
    C = MSFlexGrid1.Col        'get current col
    Caption = R & " X " & C & " = " & MSFlexGrid1.Text
        'show result in form caption
End Sub
```

We use the Click event here. It is triggered which you click a cell. In response, our procedure will display in the form's caption the selected cell's value and its column and row position, as shown in Figure 12.29.

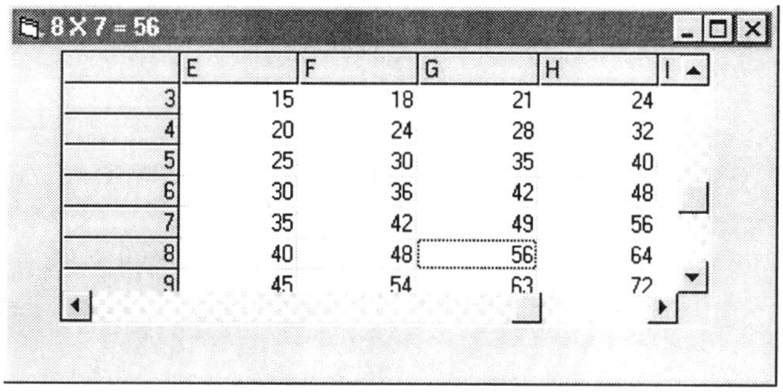

Figure 12.29   Showing cell data in the form caption

You can also use **RowColChange** or **SelChange** events in this situation. The former is triggered whenever the current column or row is changed. The latter occurs when a new cell is clicked or a keyboard key is pressed to change the current cell. Executing Col or Row property to change the current cell will also trigger these events.

Don't confuse between **Col/Row** and **Cols/Rows**. The latter are available at both design time and run time; they control the number of columns and rows in the grid. The former are available only at run time. They can return numbers representing the current cell's location or move the pointer to a designated location. They are used like CurrentX and CurrentY.

In counting column and row numbers, you need to start with 0. So the first row is row 0; the second, row 1; and so on. By default column 0 and row 0 are fixed. If you want to change that, you can use **FixedCols** or **FixedRows** properties at run time to assign higher or lower values. Clicking a fixed column/row at run time selects the entire column/row (unless the default value is changed). If the column/row is not fixed, clicking it just selects the cell.

The **Clip** property, available only at run time, returns the contents of the selected cells. You can write procedures to handle these cells, such as saving data, erasing entries, or copying them to the **Clipboard**. The following procedure will copy them to the Clipboard, and from the Clipboard to Text1, whose MultiLine property has been set to True.

```
Private Sub cmdCopy_Click ()
    Clipboard.SetText MSFlexGrid1.Clip
        'copy selected cells to Clipboard
    Text1.Text = Clipboard.GetText()
        'copy from Clipboard to text box
End Sub
```

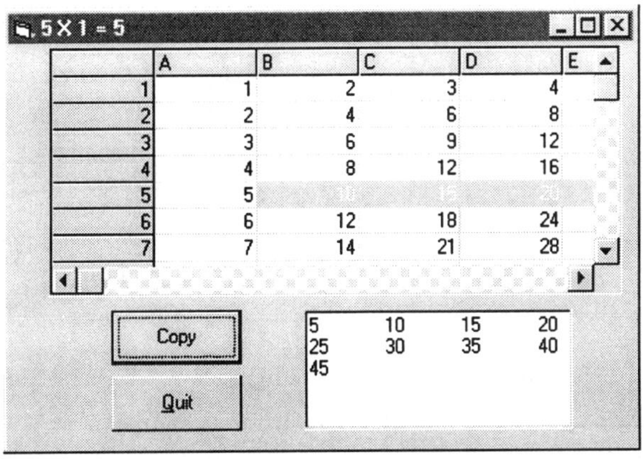

Figure 12.30   Copying selected cells

Figure 12.30 shows the result when we click row 5 to select the entire row and then click Copy. The entire row is copied to the Clipboard and then to the text box. The text box shows that each cell entry is separated from another by a tab, or Chr(9). Furthermore (not shown here), each row is separated from another by a carriage return, or Chr(13). Such data can be imported to a spreadsheet program with a minimum of adjustment. You can save data to the Clipboard and then retrieve it to your spreadsheet. Or you can save data to a file and then import it to the spreadsheet.

You can load an ICO or BMP picture to a cell by using **Set** to assign the picture to the **CellPicture** property. Here is an example:

```
Set MSFlexGrid1.CellPicture = Icon
```

This will load the current form's icon to the current cell. If you have loaded an icon or bitmap picture to the current form, you can also copy it to the current cell this way:

```
Set MSFlexGrid1.CellPicture = Picture
```

You can also use the **LoadPicture** function. If you want to load a bell picture to the top left cell in Figure 12.30, add the following lines to before the first For statement in Listing 2.

```
MSFlexGrid1.Row = 0          'cursor to top-left cell
MSFlexGrid1.Col = 0
Set MSFlexGrid1.CellPicture = LoadPicture( _
"graphics\bitmaps\assorted\bell.bmp")
```

A cell's content cannot be edited directly. You can, however, enlist the help of a text box. The following procedure will copy the current cell's content to Text1:

```
Private Sub MSFlexGrid1_SelChange ()
    Text1.Text = MSFlexGrid1.Text
End Sub
```

Then you need to add this procedure:

```
Private Sub Text1_Change ()
    MSFlexGrid1.Text = Text1.Text
End Sub
```

In this arrangement, when you click a cell, its content is automatically copied to Text1. If you want to change it, click Text1 and make any necessary change. Any change is automatically reflected in the current cell.

Another trick you can do is to double-click a cell to move the pointer to the text box to edit the entry. The following procedure will respond to that:

```
Private Sub MSFlexGrid1_DblClick ()
    Text1.Text = MSFlexGrid1.Text
    Text1.SetFocus        'move cursor to Text1
    SendKeys "{End}"      'move cursor to end of line
End Sub
```

DATABASE TOOLS

"Information is power." "This is the information age." "We're suffering from information overload." You have no doubt read or heard remarks like these. We collect tons of information and try to access lots of information. Your mortgage company tries to get lots of information from you when you apply for a mortgage. Your life insurance company tries to access all the available information about you before writing a policy for you. How do we do all these things? Mostly with computer databases.

Visual Basic is marketed as a RAD tool for developing business applications. Since businesses nowadays depend heavily on databases for many functions, VB5 supplies a series of tools to create and manipulate databases. Before we explore Visual Basic's database tools, we need to clarify a few basic terms and concepts.

Basic Terms and Concepts

A **database** is a collection of information about related items. A telephone directory is a database. So is the address book you keep of your friends. A bank keeps a database of its depositors' accounts. A company keeps a database of its employees' pays (including deductions of all kinds). The examples can go on and on.

If you have a small business, you're likely to have used a Rolodex to record and retrieve information about your clients, suppliers, contacts, and so on. If you arrange their names in alphabetic order, you can easily look up a name when you need to know something about that person. This is quick and easy if your operation is small or your needs are simple. On the other hand, if your want to do something unusual, you'll be out of luck. Suppose you want to look up a particularly telephone number, a specific ZIP number, or a person you contacted a month ago. You're going to have a tough time if you depend on nothing but the Rolodex.

If you have a computer database, on the other hand, you can do the above and even more esoteric tasks. Suppose you want to mail personalized letters and fliers to those who have purchased something in the past 12 months. If you have a computer database, this is a relatively easy job. All you need to do is to select the records meeting certain conditions and insert each record in the proper place in the letter you've prepared. In no time a pile of mail will be ready to go out. (The down side of this is that many of us are annoyed by unwanted and unsolicited junk mail easily produced by computers and laser printers.)

To keep a large amount of data manageable, a computer database is organized into logical parts. These include tables, records, and fields—with each getting into smaller pieces of information. A **field** is a piece of information, such as a name or telephone number. Multiple pieces of related information are put together to form a **record**. So a record may have a name, a phone number, an address, and so on—all related to one person. A record is a row, and a field is a column. A worksheet consisting of rows and columns can also be maneuvered as a database. Multiple related records are put together to form a **table**. Your Rolodex may be divided into several sections, one for clients, one for suppliers, and so on. Each such a section can be compared to a table. One or more tables are put together to form a **database**.

Multiple tables can be related to one another. The result is a **relational database** (rather than a flat database). For example, your database may have an Inventory table and a Suppliers table. The Inventory table may include all the merchandise you have in stock. Each merchandise item may have a field identifying the supplier. This field can then relate to the Suppliers table. So when you want to know the supplier of a merchandise, you can quickly look up the related table for more information.

A computer database is organized in such a way that a computer program can manipulate. There are many such programs, which are commonly called **DBMS** (database management system) programs; a program that can manipulate multiple related tables is also known as RDBMS (relational database management system). **Microsoft Access** is a late comer in this burgeoning field, but is gaining a large market share. Access is based on the Microsoft **Jet** database engine. This engine, the program routine used to manipulate database items, is also included in Visual Basic. So a database you create with Visual Basic can be manipulated by Access, and vice versa.

NOTE In the PROGRAM directory of the disk that accompanies this book, there are two database files named 12GRADES1.MDB and

12GRADES2.MDB. They are used for demonstration in the sections below.

Accessing Data with Data Control

The **data control** is a miniature DBMS program. It contains the same engine as Access. You can use a data control to display databases created by Access and other popular packages. The data control won't let you create a database, but you can do that with some tools explored in later sections.

When you double-click the data control tool in the Toolbox, Data1 appears. You can stretch it horizontally and/or vertically as you do with a scroll bar. The control has four VCR-type buttons (arrows). From left to right, they let you move to the first, previous, next, and last record.

To display the records of an existing database, you need to use the data control's **DatabaseName** and **RecordSource** properties to specify what file name and what table to use (these can also be set at run time). When you double-click DatabaseName in the Properties window, a dialog box appears and all the files with the MDB (Microsoft Database) extension are also displayed. After you select a file and click OK, it is loaded and its name appears in the Properties window (DatabaseName).

After a database file is loaded, its tables appear in the RecordSource property list in the Properties window. You can go to the Settings box to pull down all the available tables. If there are multiple tables, you need to make a selection here.

To display the records of a database, you need to use one or more of the eight available **bound controls**: label, image, text box, check box, picture box, list box, combo box, and OLE container; the last three are made data aware since VB4. (The Professional Edition includes more such controls.) These data-aware controls can bind (link or connect) data in a field to the screen. These controls have the **DataSource** and **DataField** properties. You use the former to connect to the name of a data control (default Data1) and the latter to a field name of the database to be displayed. After making these intertwining connections at design time, you can at run time click the arrows of a data control to display each record. This is done with little or no programming.

The VB (or Visual Basic) directory contains a sample database file named BIBLIO.MDB. We are going to write a project to display the file's records. The

user interface is shown in Figure 12.31 and the properties are set below. This
project is a more elaborate version of the one shown at the end of Chapter 4.

(12DATA1.FRM)

Object	Property	Value
Data1	DatabaseName	Biblio.mdb
	RecordSource	All Titles
Label1	Caption	Author
Label2	Caption	Title
Label3	Caption	Publisher
Label4	Caption	Year / ISBN
Text1	DataSource	Data1
	DataField	Author
Text2	DataSource	Data1
	MultiLine	True
	DataField	Title
Text3	DataSource	Data1
	DataField	Company Name
Text4	DataSource	Data1
	DataField	Year Published
Text5	DataSource	Data1
	DataField	ISBN

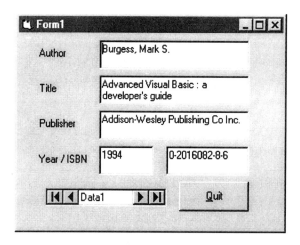

Figure 12.31   Using a data control to show database records

There is no code, except that the Quit button has the usual End statement. When
you run the program, the first record appears automatically. You can then click

one of Data1's four available buttons to display any record. The linking is done internally, not by any user-written code.

At design time, when you select Data1 and double-click its **DatabaseName** in the Properties window, a dialog box appears and all the files with the MDB extension are displayed. After you double-click BIBLIO.MBD, the name enters the MDB Properties window. The database's tables also enter the **RecordSource** property in the Properties window. There are five tables in this database; you can display them by clicking the down arrow in the Properties window's Settings box.

To link the three text boxes to the database, we set their **DataSource** properties to Data1. When you select Text1 and then DataSource, you can click the down arrow in the Properties window's Settings box. All the available data control names (Data1, Data2, etc.) will appear for you to select. After making a selection, you can click **DataField** and then the down arrow in the Settings box. All the available fields will appear for you to select. These selections establish connections necessary to display records.

The **Connect** property of a data control lets you determine what type of file to connect a data control to. The default setting is Access. In this case, when you try to enter a DatabaseName property value, all the files matching the MDB extension will appear. You can select a Connect property from a list of nearly 20 options. Suppose you select Excel 5.0. When you try to open a database file, all the files with the XLS extensions will be shown. If you connect to a worksheet or a text file, each row is a record and each column is a field. In a text file, each field is separated from the next by a Tab character. In a worksheet, each sheet is also treated as a table.

A data control's **BOFAction** (beginning of file) and **EOFAction** (end of file) properties can be used to tell your application what to do when either end is exceeded. One possible action is to let the user add a new record after the last record is displayed. This will allow the database to expand. You can also use the Data1.**Recordset.AddNew** method in code to add a record or Data1.**Recordset.Delete** to delete a record.

The data control has the **ReadOnly** property whose value is set to False by default. In this state, if you change a displayed item and move to another record, the change is saved to the disk file. When you return to the previous record, the revised version will appear. If you want to prevent any change, change the ReadOnly property to True. If you want to permit no change in a specific displayed item, use the **Validate** event to intercept such an action and add code to negate a change. This event can be used in combination with the **DataChanged** property available at run time to a bound control.

Mail Merge with a Database

When you have a database, you can easily do **mail merge** to quickly produce a large number of personalized letters discussed earlier. Figure 12.32 shows the result. You can click an arrow on the data control to go to each record. Edit the comment in the bottom text box. Click Print to send the result to the printer.

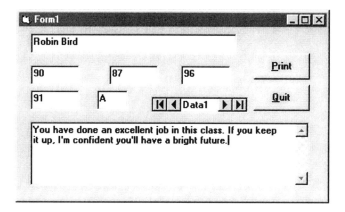

Figure 12.32   Doing a mail merge

Object	Property	Value
Data1	DatabaseName	A:\PROGRAM\12GRADES1.MBD
	RecordSource	Class1
Text1	DataSource	Data1
	DataField	Name
Text2	DataSource	Data1
	DataField	Grade1
Text3	DataSource	Data1
	DataField	Grade2
Text4	DataSource	Data1
	DataField	Grade3

The properties are shown above, and the two procedures are shown below. The **Reposition** event occurs when the user clicks an arrow on the data control to move to another record. When this happens, the procedure uses the newly displayed numbers (in the middle text boxes) to produce and display an average number and a letter grade in the two middle text boxes.

(12DATA2.FRM)

```
Private Sub Form_Load()
    Data1.Refresh
    'show first record's results
End Sub

Private Sub Data1_Reposition()
    Dim Temp As Variant

    txtAvg.Text = Format((Val(txtTest1.Text) + _
Val(txtTest2.Text) + Val(txtTest3.Text)) / 3, "#.00")
        'format to 2 decimal points
    Temp = Val(txtAvg.Text)

    Select Case Temp        'convert to letter grade
        Case Is >= 90
            txtGrade.Text = "A"
        Case Is >= 80
            txtGrade.Text = "B"
        Case Is >= 70
            txtGrade.Text = "C"
        Case Is >= 60
            txtGrade.Text = "D"
        Case Else
            txtGrade.Text = "F"
    End Select
End Sub

Private Sub cmdPrint_Click()
    Printer.Print txtName.Text
    Printer.Print "Test 1 score: "; txtTest1.Text
    Printer.Print "Test 2 score: "; txtTest2.Text
    Printer.Print "Test 3 score: "; txtTest3.Text
    Printer.Print "Average: "; txtAvg.Text
    Printer.Print "Letter grade: "; txtGrade.Text
    Printer.Print
    Printer.Print txtComment.Text
    Printer.EndDoc
End Sub
```

Visual Data Manager

VB4 included a Data Manager and Data Form Designer. In VB5, they are changed to **Visual Data Manager** and **Date Form Wizard**. Both are add-in programs. (The Professional Edition includes the VISDATA.VBP file stored in the SAMPLES\VISDATA directory. There are more than 200 associated files.)

You can use it to create and edit a database, and create a data form out of an existing database.

To open Visual Data Manager, choose Visual Data Manager from the **Add-Ins** menu. The VisData window (Figure 12.33) appears with nothing inside. There is a menu bar and a toolbar with nine buttons. From this window you can create a new database or open an existing one to alter it.

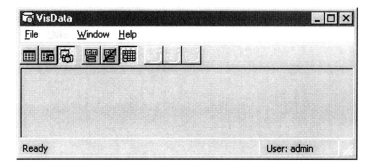

Figure 12.33   Visual Data Manager

You should spend sometime getting familiar with the Visual Data Manager environment. The menu bar includes four menus. The Help menu takes you to the VB5 Help system, where you may find some but not much help related to Visual Data Manager.

The **File menu** lets you open a new or existing database or compact and repair an existing (but not opened) database. If a database has been altered a great deal, compacting it can make it smaller and run faster. If a database won't open, repairing it may make it work again.

The **Utility menu** lets you build a query or design a data form. These will be covered in separate sections below.

The **Windows menu** acts the same as any typical Windows menu. You can use it to arrange open windows and bring one to the top.

The toolbar has the following nine buttons divided into three groups, each consisting of three buttons:

Table type Recordset   Opens the actual records from a single table.

Dynaset type Recordset Opens a dynamic set of records from one or more tables resulting from a query.

Snapshot type Recordset Opens a static set of records from one or more tables resulting from a query.

Use Data Control on New Form
Uses a data control when displaying data.

Don't Use Data Control on New Form
Uses a scroll bar control rather than a data control when displaying data.

Use DBGrid Control on New Form
Uses a databound grid control when displaying data.

Begin a Transaction Begins a data transaction.

Rollback current Transaction
Rolls back a transaction and restores the previous conditions.

Commit current Transaction Commits a transaction.

The first group determines what kind of records will be made available. You need to make a choice here before you open a table. Making a choice here doesn't affect an open table.

When Snapshot-type Recordset button is selected, you can open a table only to show the contents but not alter them. If you open the table with Table-type Recordset, you cannot use the Sort or Filter button. These two functions are available if you open the table with the other two options. If you click Sort, you'll be asked to supply a column name to sort by. A simpler way is to click the column heading to sort by it.

The second group determines how data will be presented to the user. Some figures below show their differences. Again, you need to make a choice here before opening a table.

The third group determines what to do when you change data in a table.

To open a database, choose File | Open DataBase | Microsoft Access from Visual Data Manager and double-click BIBLIO.MDB when you find it. Two windows open up: Database Window and SQL Statement. When you are done with a window, just click the X button to close it.

The Database Window displays all the tables available in the opened database (Figure 12.34). This window works like Windows Explorer. You can click + or - to open (expand) and close (collapse) various subitems. You can right-click any displayed item to pop up a list of options. Some commands are not available from the menu bar, so you have to depend on the popup menus. You can use these popup menus to change many properties or open a database.

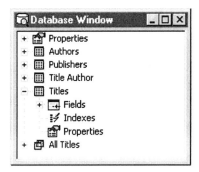

Figure 12.34   The Database Window in VisData

You can open a table by double-clicking it. The resulting display is determined by what you have chosen in the first two groups of button on the toolbar. To show Figure 12.35, follow these steps:

1. Choose Snapshot-type Recordset in the first group on the toolbar.

2. Choose Use DBGrid Control on New Form in the second group.

3. Double-click the Authors table in the Database Window.

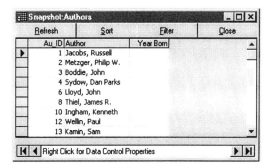

Figure 12.35   Records from a table displayed in a grid

On the other hand, Figure 12.36 will be the result if you change to Dynaset-type Recordset in step 2 and to Use Data Control on New Form in step 3. You can open multiple windows to display data in different ways. The title bar of each window shows the table name and the type of recordset.

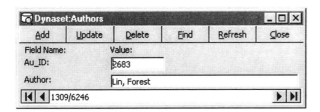

Figure 12.36   A record shown with a data control

Creating Databases

Visual Data Manager allows you to create a new database. We are going to create a new database and then open it as an existing database for further manipulation. These are the steps to create a database:

1. Choose File | New | Microsoft Access | Version 7.0 (or 2.0) MDB. (Version 2.0 is 16-bit and 7.0 is 32-bit.) A dialog box resembling the Open Project dialog box appears. Enter a name in the File-name box. You can also click an existing displayed name to open it; you'll be asked whether you want to replace it. A file with the MDB extension will be created after you click OK. If you select an existing file, its existing contents will be erased and the file will be used to store new data. So unless you mean to destroy an existing file, don't use it to create a new database.

NOTE   The odd thing is that Windows 95 identifies both as Microsoft Access 2.0 Database. Odder still is that an empty 2.0 file is 64 KB in size and the 7.0 counterpart is 40 KB. Using Visual Data Manager's File | Compact MDB | 7.0 MDB to compact a 2.0 file will reduce its size to 40 MB.

2. The title bar of VisData shows the new database name. Two windows now appear in the VisData window, namely Database Window and SQL Statement. The latter is empty (you can close this for now), and the former has only the Properties item. You can click the + sign to expand it to show all the default properties set for you. There is no table at this time. You need to create at least one table to store data.

3. Right-click the Database Window and choose New Table from the shortcut
    menu. The Table Structure dialog box appears (Figure 12.37); there is no
    entry at this time.

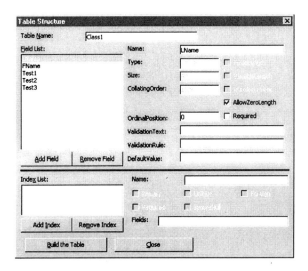

Figure 12.37   The Table Structure dialog box

4. Enter a table name in the Table Name text box at the top.

5. Click the Add Field button. The Add Field dialog box (Figure 12.38)
    appears.

6. Enter a field name, data type, size, etc. and then click OK to register the
    entry. The entry now appears in the Field List box in the Table Structure
    dialog box, and the Add Field dialog box is cleared for another entry.

7. Repeat step 6 to make more entries. Click Close when you are done. The
    Add Field dialog box disappears, and all the entries are in the Table Structure
    dialog box.

8. You can now click each item in the Table Structure's Field List to show the
    related items you have entered. If you want to remove an item, select it and
    click Remove Field. You can also add or remove an index.

9. Click Build the Table to save the table (click Close if you don't want to save the table). The Table Structure dialog box disappears, the new table appears in the Database Window.

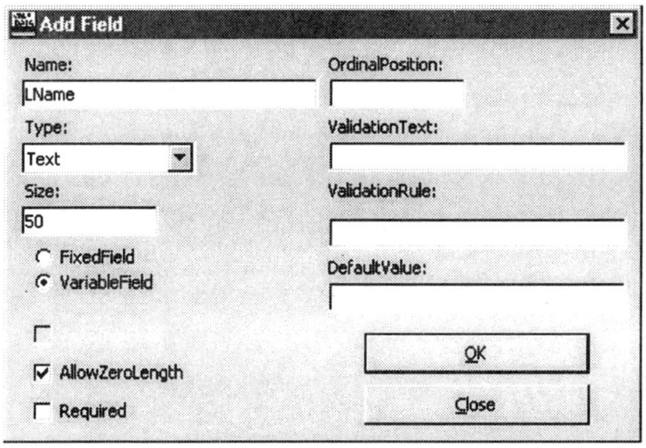

Figure 12.38   The Add Field dialog box

You can now do a number of things to this new table. If you right-click it, a list of options pops up. You can choose Rename to change its name or Delete to remove it. You can choose Design to open the Table Structure dialog box to change the design of the database. You can choose Open (or double-click the table) to show the data.

before open choose 1 button in first group and one in another.

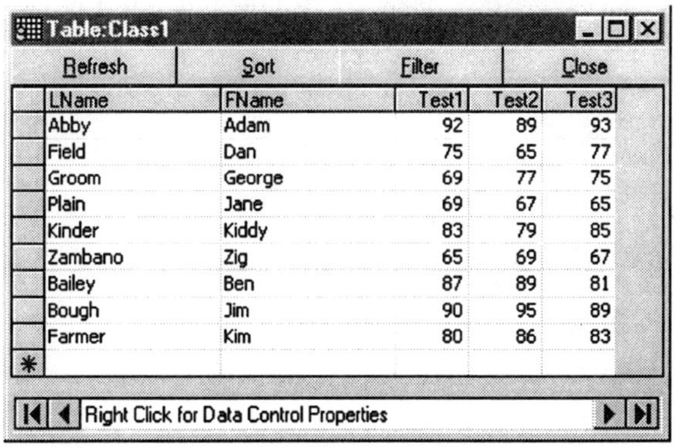

Figure 12.39   A completed table

Before you open the new table, you need to choose one button in the first group and another in the second group. The third button (Snapshot-type Recordset) in the first group doesn't allow you to add, update, or delete records. So before you want to open a new table to add data, you need to choose the first or the second button. An editable grid has an * sign marking the field for making the next entry. It also has the appropriate commands for certain actions.

The table in Figure 12.39 was created earlier and now filled with some records. This table is also opened after choosing the first button (Table) in the first group and the third button (DBGrid) in the second group of buttons. If you now make an entry and click another row, you'll be asked whether you want to commit the change. If you answer Yes, the change will be saved; otherwise, not saved. When you are done, just click Close to close the window.

Double-click on the table

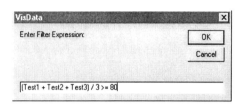

Figure 12.40   A formula for filtering records

You can use the Filter button to display only those records meeting the specified conditions. It leads to a dialog box (Figure 12.40). The example shows that we try to select records that have 80 or higher average of the three tests. After pressing Enter, all the other records will disappear. This operation does not affect the underlying records in the table.

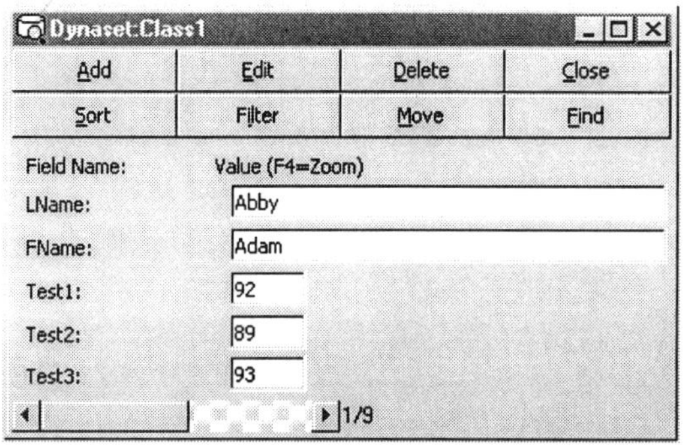

Figure 12.41   Showing one record at a time

If you want to show one record at a time, choose the first (Use Data Control) or the second (Don't Use Data Control) button in the second group on the toolbar before opening the table. The result (with Data Control) is shown in Figure 12.41. If you have also chosen Dynaset or Snapshot before opening the table, as we have done here, you can find or filter records.

Here you can use Add or Edit to change the data. Each will lead to a separate dialog box. You can use Filter the same way as explained earlier.

To find a record, click the Find button. Figure 12.42 appears. Here you click a field name, click an operator, and type a value. Clicking OK will lead to the first matching record being displayed. If you want to find the next matching record, click Find, check the Find Next check box, and click OK.

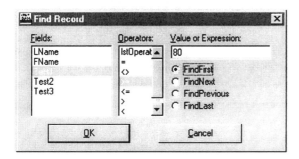

Figure 12.42   The Find Record dialog box

Designing Data Forms

You can use Visual Data Manager or **Data Form Wizard** to create a form based on an existing database. They will automatically add necessary controls and procedures. The form can then be used to add or edit records. The code will do most of the common tasks for you. You can alter the form or the code as necessary.

Both add-ins follow similar steps and will produce similar results. The following example uses VisData. Open or create the necessary tables inside Visual Data Manager. Then follow these steps:

1.   Choose Utilities | Data Form Designer. Figure 12.43 appears.

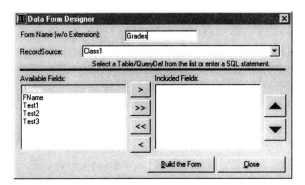

Figure 12.43   Data Form Designer

2. Type a name for the form to be created, *Grades* in our example. This string
    will become the default form file name, and *frm* will also be added at the
    beginning of the string to become the form's Name property.

3. In the RecordSource combo box, click the down arrow to show all the
    available tables. Select one by clicking it. All the available fields appear in
    the Available Fields list box.

4. Click the > > button to move all the field names from Available Fields to
    Included Fields. If you wish, you can click each field name and then click the
    > button to move it. If you want to remove them from the Included Fields,
    use < (removing one) or < < (removing all).

5. If you wish to change the fields' order, select one and click the ▲ or ▼
    buttons to move it up or down the list.

6. Click Build the Form button to start building the form (click Close if you
    don't want the form). Before you start this, you might want to observe the
    operation by moving Visual Data Manager to one side and exposing the
    Visual Basic IDE.

7. The Data Form Designer becomes empty after the form is built. You can
    build another form based on another table. Click Close when you are done.

The form designed by Data Form Designer is not affected by your choices on the
toolbar. Regardless of what you have chosen here, a data control is always
included in a form.

You can now run the form. If you started the current project with Form1 as the startup form, you need to change the startup form by using the Project | Project Properties | General tab. If you don't need Form1, you can remove it. If you now press F5 to run the program, the result is shown in Figure 12.44. It displays the first record of the 12GRADES2.MDB file in the default order of all the fields. You can now do a number of things to manipulate the records.

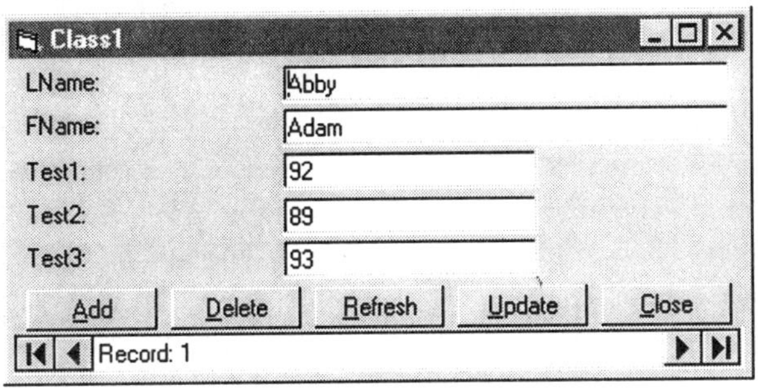

Figure 12.44   The form created by Data Form Designer

If you go to the Code window, you'll find several procedures, as shown below. They use many methods and intrinsic constants available to the data control and Data Access Objects (DAO; see another section below).

```
Private Sub cmdAdd_Click()
  Data1.Recordset.AddNew
End Sub

Private Sub cmdDelete_Click()
   'this may produce an error if you delete the last
   'record or the only record in the recordset
  Data1.Recordset.Delete
  Data1.Recordset.MoveNext
End Sub

Private Sub cmdRefresh_Click()
   'this is really only needed for multi user apps
  Data1.Refresh
End Sub

Private Sub cmdUpdate_Click()
  Data1.UpdateRecord
  Data1.Recordset.Bookmark = Data1.Recordset.LastModified
End Sub

Private Sub cmdClose_Click()
```

```
   Unload Me
End Sub

Private Sub Data1_Error(DataErr As Integer, Response As
Integer)
   'This is where you would put error handling code
   'If you want to ignore errors, comment out the next
line
   'If you want to trap them, add code here to handle them
   MsgBox "Data error event hit err:" & Error$(DataErr)
   Response = 0   'throw away the error
End Sub

Private Sub Data1_Reposition()
   Screen.MousePointer = vbDefault
   On Error Resume Next
   'This will display the current record position
   'for dynasets and snapshots
   Data1.Caption = "Record: " &
(Data1.Recordset.AbsolutePosition + 1)
   'for the table object you must set the index property
when
   'the recordset gets created and use the following line
   'Data1.Caption = "Record: " &
(Data1.Recordset.RecordCount *
(Data1.Recordset.PercentPosition * 0.01)) + 1
End Sub

Private Sub Data1_Validate(Action As Integer, Save As
Integer)
   'This is where you put validation code
   'This event gets called when the following actions
occur
   Select Case Action
      Case vbDataActionMoveFirst
      Case vbDataActionMovePrevious
      Case vbDataActionMoveNext
      Case vbDataActionMoveLast
      Case vbDataActionAddNew
      Case vbDataActionUpdate
      Case vbDataActionDelete
      Case vbDataActionFind
      Case vbDataActionBookmark
      Case vbDataActionClose
   End Select
   Screen.MousePointer = vbHourglass
End Sub
```

If you are curious, you can go to various objects' Properties windows and see
what has been done to the objects. Data1's DatabaseName and RecordSource
properties contain entries based on the data you supplied. There is a label control
array and a text box control array. Each text box's DataSource and DataField

properties are also set to proper values. These are the items you would normally set by yourself at design time, as we did earlier when you first used the data control.

All Visual Basic editions come with three custom controls, namely **databound list box**, **databound combo box**, and **databound grid control**. These have additional properties to better handle databases. There is also the **Report Designer** (**Crystal Reports**) that can be accessed from the Add-Ins menu. If you want to know more, there is plenty of pertinent online help.

SQL (Structured Query Language)

Most DBMS programs, including Access and Visual Basic, include a standard language known as **SQL**. You can use it to query (converse with) a database. This language is useful if you intend to look for specific records in a large database.

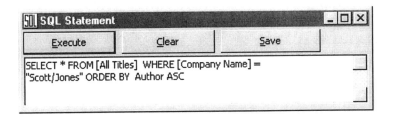

Figure 12.45   Entering an SQL statement

To test an SQL statement, open Visual Data Manager. Then choose File | Open Database and open the BIBLIO.MDB file. Type the statement shown in the SQL Statement dialog box (Figure 12.45) and click Execute.

Our SQL statement is this:

```
SELECT * FROM [All Titles] WHERE [Company Name] =
"Scott/Jones" ORDER BY Author ASC
```

The command keywords are commonly typed in uppercase; you can use any case you wish. Word wrap is automatic when you reach the end of a line. You can also insert a carriage return by pressing Ctrl+Enter.

In our statement, we want to select (show) all the fields (* means all) from the All Titles (enclose an entry in brackets when spaces are included) table where the

Company Name field contains the specified text string and display the result in ascending order based on the Author field.

When you click Execute or press Enter after typing the statement, you'll be asked whether this is a **SQL Passthrough Query**. Answer No unless you are querying a remote database.

If a query is successful, a window will appear, together with the specified fields and data, as shown in Figure 12.46. The output format is determined by the second group of three buttons on the toolbar. Figure 12.46 is the result of choosing third button (DBGrid) before executing the SQL statement.

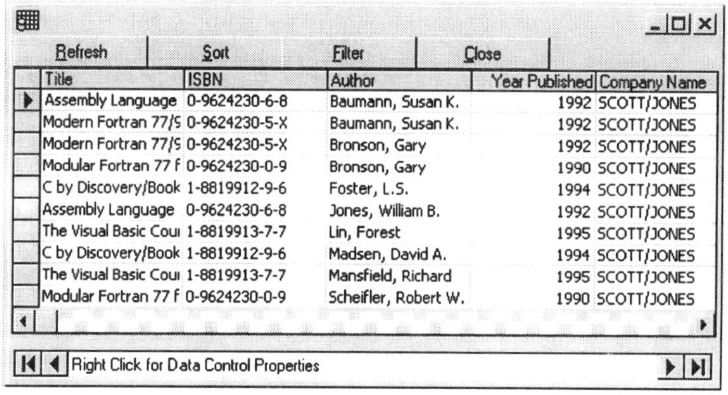

Title	ISBN	Author	Year Published	Company Name
Assembly Language	0-9624230-6-8	Baumann, Susan K.	1992	SCOTT/JONES
Modern Fortran 77/9	0-9624230-5-X	Baumann, Susan K.	1992	SCOTT/JONES
Modern Fortran 77/9	0-9624230-5-X	Bronson, Gary	1992	SCOTT/JONES
Modular Fortran 77 F	0-9624230-0-9	Bronson, Gary	1990	SCOTT/JONES
C by Discovery/Book	1-8819912-9-6	Foster, L.S.	1994	SCOTT/JONES
Assembly Language	0-9624230-6-8	Jones, William B.	1992	SCOTT/JONES
The Visual Basic Cour	1-8819913-7-7	Lin, Forest	1995	SCOTT/JONES
C by Discovery/Book	1-8819912-9-6	Madsen, David A.	1994	SCOTT/JONES
The Visual Basic Cour	1-8819913-7-7	Mansfield, Richard	1995	SCOTT/JONES
Modular Fortran 77 F	0-9624230-0-9	Scheifler, Robert W.	1990	SCOTT/JONES

Refresh   Sort   Filter   Close

Right Click for Data Control Properties

Figure 12.46   Records found by an SQL query

An SQL statement can be cleared by clicking the Clear button or saved with the Save button. You'll be asked to enter a name to save the query to the database file. This name will also appear in the Database Window as part of the database. A unique icon identifies it as a query and thus different from tables. To bring a statement back to the SQL window, right-click the query name in the Database Window and choose Design. The saved statement will reappear in the SQL window. If the window was closed, this action will open up the window.

You can also use Utility | **Query Builder** to build a query. A window similar to the Find dialog box (explained early) will appear. You specify the fields and conditions to select records. The name you specify here will also appear in the Database Window. When you select this name and then choose Design from the popup menu, a corresponding statement will enter the SQL Statement window. If you choose Open instead, the Query Builder dialog box will appear.

We can use code to read an SQL statement entered by the user in a text box. In Figure 12.47, we put an SQL statement in a text box. In the code below, the SQL command is used to query the database. The matching records are shown in the large text box.

(12DATASQL1.FRM)

```
Private Sub cmdQuery_Click()
    Dim Temp As String

    txtFound.Text = ""      'clear box for reuse
    Data1.RecordSource = txtSQL.Text
        'use SQL command in text box
    Data1.Refresh    'needed for re-search
    Do While Not Data1.Recordset.EOF     'entire database
        Temp = Data1.Recordset("fname") & vbTab
        Temp = Temp & Data1.Recordset("lname") & vbTab
        Temp = Temp & Data1.Recordset("test1") & vbTab
        Temp = Temp & Data1.Recordset("test2") & vbTab
        Temp = Temp & Data1.Recordset("test3") & vbCrLf
        txtFound.Text = txtFound.Text & Temp 'put in box
        Data1.Recordset.MoveNext    'goto next record
    Loop
End Sub
```

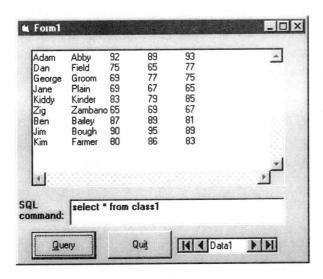

Figure 12.47   Using SQL and DAO objects

Our SQL command can be changed to one of the following:

```
SELECT * FROM Class1 WHERE Test1>=80
```

```
SELECT * FROM Class1 WHERE Test1>=80 AND Test2>=80 AND
Test3>=80

SELECT * FROM Class1 WHERE (Test1+Test2+Test3)/3>=80
```

In the first case, we want the records where Test1 $>=$ 80. In the second case, we want all three tests to be $>=$ 80. In the third case, we want the average.

In the above example, we enter a name in Data1's DatabaseName property and a table name in its RecordSource property. These steps establish the necessary connections to the database. Other than that, we have no use for Data1. If you wish, you can make it invisible by changing its Visible property to False. That will not affect our query, and the screen will become less cluttered at run time. The above arrangement lets the user control SQL statements and is thus quite flexible. If you want a fixed SQL command, you can enter it at design time into Data1's **RecordSource** field in the Properties window. Suppose you enter "SELECT * FROM Class1" at design time. In that case, you can delete the text box and the following line in the code, and the program will do the same thing. This arrangement does not allow the user to enter an SQL command.

```
Data1.RecordSource = txtSQL.Text
```

If you want to know more about SQL, search the online help for SQL. You'll find more than a dozen matching items. The SQL Subqueries topic provides quite a few examples.

DAO (Data Access Objects)

Instead of going through a data control to connect to a database file, we can use code to do that in the Professional Edition. To demonstrate how to do that, remove Data1 from Figure 12.47 and change the procedure to the following:

(12DATASQL2.FRM)
```
Private Sub cmdQuery_Click()
    Dim Temp As String
    Dim WS As Workspace          '3 DAO objects
    Dim DB As Database
    Dim RS As Recordset

    Set WS = Workspaces(0)
    On Error GoTo ErrTrap  'if fail to open
    Set DB = WS.OpenDatabase("12grades2.mdb")
        'open database
        'change drive/dir if necessary
    Set RS = DB.OpenRecordset(txtSQL.Text)
```

```
            'open table using SQL string
    txtFound.Text = ""        'clear box for reuse
    Do While Not RS.EOF      'entire table
        Temp = RS("fname") & vbTab
        Temp = Temp & RS("lname") & vbTab
        Temp = Temp & RS("test1") & vbTab
        Temp = Temp & RS("test2") & vbTab
        Temp = Temp & RS("test3") & vbCrLf
        txtFound.Text = txtFound.Text & Temp 'put in box
        RS.MoveNext
    Loop
    Exit Sub

ErrTrap:
    MsgBox Error
End Sub
```

If errors occur, there are two possibilities. First, Visual Basic may not recognize the three DAO objects declared at the beginning. In that case, you need to choose Project | References and check one of the available DAO libraries. Second, if the database cannot be found, you need to supply a path before the file name.

The connections to a database and its tables are now completely done by code. Here we use three commonly used objects—**Database, Workspace**, and **Recordset**—and their methods to maneuver an existing database. You can also create a database by using other objects and their methods.

Visual Basic uses many objects to manipulate databases. These are collectively called **DAO objects**. They are grouped in a library and installed in your system during installation. You can use the **Object Browser** to view this library. Just press F2 and select DAO from the Project/Library box. About 60 objects will appear in the Classes box. Some of these classes will give you numerous methods and properties. If you need help, click the ? button after selecting a desired object. For example, you can click the Workspace class, then the OpenDatabase method in the Members box, and then the ? button. The OpenDatabase Method topic will appear.

The Professional Edition includes DAO classes from which you can create DAO objects by using Dim and Set. These objects let you programmatically create new databases as well as manipulate existing ones. The Learning Edition doesn't allow creation of DAO objects. You can, however, create databases visually by using Visual Data Manager.

DAO can also serve as a key to **ODBC** (Open Database Connectivity) databases. There are many and incompatible database formats. To unify these disparate standards and make it easy for users to access remote databases, Microsoft has

Project
↓
References
↓
microsoft DAO 2.5/3.5 C.L.
└ Microsoft DAO 3.5 Object Library. ✓

successfully promoted the ODBC protocol, which is now commonly adopted. This
protocol allows an SQL server like Microsoft SQL Server to access most
databases. A Visual Basic application can use DAO objects and their methods and
properties to send SQL commands to an SQL server to maneuver remote
databases.

MULTIPLE-DOCUMENT INTERFACE

It was said earlier (Chapter 11) that a form is a super container because it can
contain other objects. By the same token, an **MDI (multiple- document interface)
form** is a super form because it can contain regular forms. An MDI form
becomes a parent form and other forms on it become child forms. An application
can have only one MDI parent form but as many child forms as you wish.

To add an MDI form, choose Project | Add MDI Form; this option becomes
dimmed (unavailable) after you have added an MDI form to the current project.
To remove the form, select it and then choose Remove MDIForm1 from the
Project menu (you can also right-click the form name in the Project window to
pop up this option). MDIForm1 is the default name as well as caption.

To convert a regular form to an MDI child form, change its **MDIChild** property's
default False value to True. At design time, you can add new forms and change
the MDIChild property to make them child forms. At run time, you can use code
to create multiple child forms on the fly. This will be demonstrated shortly.

Unlike a regular form, a child form is always modeless. As explained in Chapter
4, you can make a regular form modal in order to halt program execution and
require a user response. This cannot be done with a child form.

At run time, child forms stay within the parent form. You can move, close,
resize, maximize, or minimize these windows within the borders of the parent. If
you drag a child window beyond a border of the parent window, one or both
scroll bars will appear in the parent window. If you minimize a child window, its
reduced title bar appears at the bottom of the parent window. If you minimize the
parent, it completely appears. A regular form has the ShownInTaskbar property
whose True property can be changed to False. An MDI form has no such
property. The form always appears in the taskbar.

An MDI parent form has few properties. The list in its Properties window is
much shorter than the one for the regular form. With MDIForm1 selected, you
can press F1 to show the online help. From this screen you can show related

events, methods, and properties. Again, the lists are shorter than those for the regular form.

One unique property is **AutoShowChildren**. The default value is True. That means child forms, when created at run time, are automatically shown. You can use it at design time or run time to assign True or False value to show or hide child forms. If a new child form is not shown automatically, you can use the Show method to display it at a proper time.

An MDI form can contain only controls that have the **Align** property. Among the standard controls, only the data control and the picture box control possess that property. If you attempt to add anything else, a command button for example, you'll get an error message.

A picture box, as you learned in Chapter 11, can contain other controls. You can thus add a picture box to an MDI form and then add other controls in the picture box. When MDIForm1 is selected at design time, double-clicking the picture box tool in the Toolbox leads to a stretched picture box appearing at the top of the form. In this case, a picture box's Align property defaults to 1 - Align Top, instead of 0 - None as in the case of a regular form. You can change to any one of the four sides, but changing to 0 - None has no effect.

To create multiple child forms at run time, use the cloning techniques you learned in Chapter 9. Declare variables as Form1 (or another form name, or Form or Variant for a generic type), use Set and New to create new instances (clones) of Form1, and use Load or Show to display them. The procedures below produce the display in Figure 12.48.

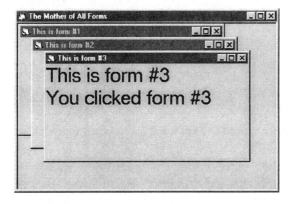

Figure 12.48   Multiple child windows created at run time

```
Private Sub MDIForm_Load ()     'from MDIForm1
    Dim I As Integer
    Dim Frm(1 To 3) As Form1   'declare array

    MDIForm1.Show
    MDIForm1.Caption = "The Mother of All Forms"
        '"MDIForm1." can be omitted
    For I = 1 To 3
        Set Frm(I) = New Form1
            'create clone form, assign to alias
        Frm(I).Caption = "This is form #" & I
            'show each child form's caption
        Load Frm(I) 'load and show each child form
                    'can also be: frm(i).Show
    Next I
    Arrange vbCascade      'or 0
End Sub

Private Sub Form_Click()        'from Form1
    Screen.ActiveForm.Cls      'clear previous text
    Me.FontSize = 20       'size for current form
    Print Me.Caption
      'print current form caption in current window
    Print "You clicked " & Right(Me.Caption, 7)
End Sub
```

This project requires two forms at design time, MDIForm1 and Form1. The latter's MDIChild property is changed to True at design time (this cannot be set at run time). We also changed the startup form (choose Project | Project1 Properties and open the Startup Object combo box) from the default Form1 to MDIForm1. If this is not done, the result will be somewhat different. When a child form is loaded, the parent form is automatically loaded; the reverse is not always true. If MDIForm1 is the startup form and the Show method is applied to it, it (the parent) will be loaded, but not Form1. If the Show method is not used here or Form1 is the startup form, both will be loaded.

The first procedure is attached to MDIForm1 and the second to Form1. If both are placed in MDIForm1, clicking a form will do nothing.

In the first procedure above, we use an array with three elements to represent three new instances of Form1, each of which inherits all the program code and properties of Form1. We use the Load statement to load and display each clone form; you can also use the Frm(i).Show method to do the same thing. At the end, we use the **Arrange** statement to arrange the forms in mode 0 (vbCascade). This statement is actually redundant because Cascade is the default mode. You can also use 1 (vbTileHorizontal), 2 (vbTileVertical), or 3 (vbArrangeIcons) to arrange the windows differently.

When the user clicks each child form, the Form_Click procedure in Form1 is executed. The **Me** and **ActiveForm** properties then show which form has been clicked. These two refer to the same form most of the time; they may, however, vary under some circumstances. Me refers to the form being executed; ActiveForm to the form that has the focus. A form may contain a timer being executed, but another form may have the focus. In this situation, Me and ActiveForm may refer to different forms. You can also use ActiveControl with ActiveForm to identify the control that has the focus; see the online help for details.

The Mother of All Forms - [This is form #3]

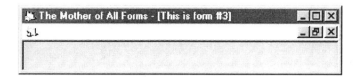

Figure 12.49 A child window's caption

Since the default values of Form1's BorderStyle and ControlBox have not been changed, we can move, close, resize, maximize, or minimize each displayed window. Maximizing a child window will cover up the parent window. The resulting caption (Figure 12.49) clearly identifies their relationship.

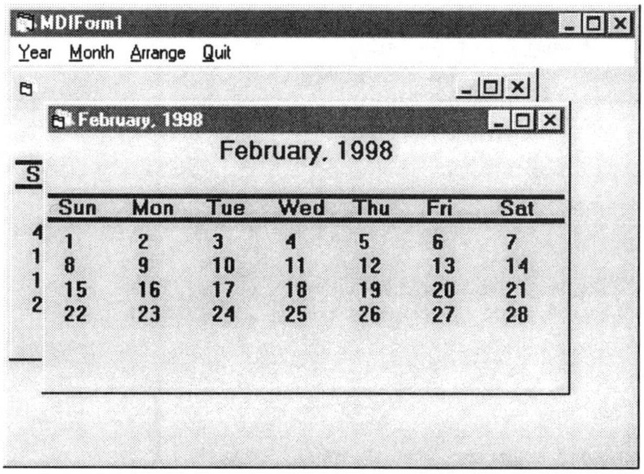

MDIForm1
Year Month Arrange Quit
February, 1998
February, 1998
Sun Mon Tue Wed Thu Fri Sat
1 2 3 4 5 6 7
8 9 10 11 12 13 14
15 16 17 18 19 20 21
22 23 24 25 26 27 28

Figure 12.50 Displaying multiple child forms

We are going to modify our calendar application at the end of Chapter 8 so that multiple months, each occupying a child form, can be displayed at the same time. The user interface is shown in Figure 12.50. As in the example we discussed earlier, we use two forms, MDIForm1 and Form1; the former is designated as the startup form and the latter's MDIChild property is set to True. Each new child form is created on the fly as the user selects a new month. We also have a module that contains two global variables; these variables need to be visible throughout the application and persistent during the program's execution.

The application offers four menus. Clicking the Year menu drops down a list of years ranging from 1997 to 2000. There is also the User option in this menu. It leads to an input box to prompt the user to enter a specific year. If nothing is set at the outset, 1997 is used. Once a year is chosen, it is assigned to a global variable named Yr and stays the same until another is selected.

The Month menu offers 12 monthly choices. Selecting a month leads to a new child form displaying the selected year/month. The Arrange menu lets you choose one of the three display modes.

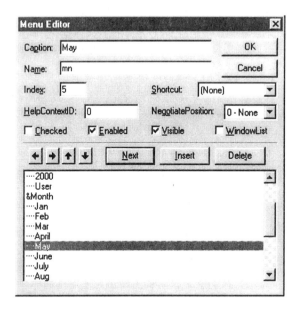

Figure 12.51   Creating a menu array

To simplify coding, each group of related menu options are put in a **menu array**. This way, we can easily find out what option the user has chosen. For example, if the user selects Jan (the first option) in the Month menu, the Index variable in the code returns 1. We can then use this number to create the calendar for that month.

To create a menu array, use the same name for the same group of related options but assign each option a different Index number. As shown in Figure 12.51, we use Mon for all the monthly options and give Jan the Index value of 1, Feb that of 2, and so on.

When the user selects an option from the Month menu, the mnuMon_Click procedure is executed. It loads another instance of Form1. This executes the Form_Load procedure with the selected year and month values. A new calendar is thus created. A Static variable is used to keep track of the number of child forms created.

The Arrange menu lets you choose one of three display modes. Choosing a different mode here can lead to trouble. The latest year and month values will be used to display all the child forms, resulting in one monthly calendar being displayed in different forms. One remedy for this is to set Form1's AutoRedraw property from the default False to True at design time; you can also do it with code at run time. In this setting, when child forms are rearranged (redrawn), the original contents will reappear.

The Form_Load procedure shown below is modified from the one shown near the end of Chapter 8. Compare them and you can see the changes. The comments in the code provide all the necessary explanations.

(12CALEND.VBP)

```
Public Yr As Integer, Mon As Integer    'year, month
       'from 12CALEND.BAS

Private Sub Form_Load()
    Dim Col(1 To 7) As Integer
    Dim Wk(1 To 7) As String
    Dim Mon_Yr As Date, WkDay As Integer
    Dim MaxDay As Integer, DayNum As Integer
    Dim RowNum As Integer, ColNum As Integer
    Dim ColDist As Single    'control column distance
    Dim I As Integer
    Dim Temp As Variant

    Wk(1) = "Sun"
    Wk(2) = "Mon"
    Wk(3) = "Tue"
    Wk(4) = "Wed"
    Wk(5) = "Thu"
    Wk(6) = "Fri"
```

```
Wk(7) = "Sat"

Mon_Yr = Mon & "/1/" & Yr   'get mm/dd/yy string
WkDay = WeekDay(Mon_Yr)
    'get weekday for 1st day of month

Select Case Mon        'what month?
Case 1, 3, 5, 7, 8, 10, 12
    MaxDay = 31
Case 4, 6, 9, 11
    MaxDay = 30
End Select

If Mon = 2 Then       'Feb, handle leap years
    If Yr Mod 4 = 0 Then
       If Yr Mod 100 = 0 And Yr Mod 400 <> 0 Then
          MaxDay = 28
              'if divisible by 100 but not by 400
       Else
          MaxDay = 29
       End If
    Else
       MaxDay = 28     'if not divisible by 4
    End If
End If

FontSize = 12
Temp = Format(Mon_Yr, "mmmm, yyyy")
    'get month, year, spelled out
Caption = Temp      'show Mon/Yr in form caption
CurrentX = (ScaleWidth - TextWidth(Temp)) / 2
Print Temp      'center Year/Month
Print
DrawWidth = 3          'thicker line
Line (0, CurrentY)-(ScaleWidth, CurrentY)
    'horizontal line
ColDist = ScaleWidth / 7    'spacing columns
Temp = -ColDist + 100    'start 100 twips from left
FontSize = 10

For I = 1 To 7
    Temp = Temp + ColDist
    Col(I) = Temp       'assign 7 column positions
    CurrentX = Temp
    Print Wk(I);        'print 2nd line
Next I

Print
Line (0, CurrentY)-(ScaleWidth, CurrentY)
CurrentY = CurrentY + 100    'down 100 twips

For RowNum = 1 To 6        'up to 6 rows
    For ColNum = WkDay To 7  '7 cols each row
        CurrentX = Col(ColNum)
```

```
                          'move to proper weekday
                  If ColNum = 7 Then WkDay = 1
                      'new line start with col 1
                  DayNum = DayNum + 1         'counter 1 to 31
                  If DayNum > MaxDay Then Exit Sub
                  Print DayNum;
                  Next ColNum
            Print
      Next RowNum
End Sub

Private Sub mnuYr_Click(Index As Integer)
      Static ExCheck As Integer
          'to remove previous check mark
      mnuYr(ExCheck).Checked = False
          'delete any previous check
      Yr = Index + 1997     'index=0 to 4
          '1997 if Index is 0 (first option)
      mnuYr(1).Checked = False
          'Option 1 was checked by default
          'uncheck it now
      mnuYr(Index).Checked = True
          'check the current selection
      If Yr >= 2001 Then    'if User is selected
          Yr = InputBox("Enter a year")
              'get year from user
      End If
      ExCheck = Index
          'save previous check's index
End Sub

Private Sub mnuMon_Click(Index As Integer)
      Static CalForm(1 To 12) As Form1
          'to clone Form1
      Static FNum As Integer    'form index
      FNum = FNum + 1
      Mon = Index           'get selected month
      If Yr = 0 Then Yr = 1998
          'if no yr, then 1998
      Set CalForm(FNum) = New Form1
          'produce a new duplicate
      Load CalForm(FNum)  'show duplicate
End Sub

Private Sub mnuArnge_Click(Index As Integer)
      Arrange Index
      '0 = cascade; 1 = hor. tile; 2 = ver. tile
End Sub

Private Sub mnuQuit_Click()
      End
End Sub
```

TIP: List of Open Windows

At run time, you can click an application's menu to display a list of open MDI child windows—similar to the way a list of open projects' names appears (near the bottom) when you click the Visual Basic File menu at design time. The current (top) form is also check-marked. You can click another form caption in the list to bring it to the top. You have to take extra steps to make your application behave this way.

Suppose that at run time you want to show the months the user has selected (created) in the current session. The list of selections (child windows' captions) appears at the bottom of the monthly options when the user clicks the Month menu at run time. To make this happen, follow these steps:

1. Go to the Menu Editor window, shown in Figure 12.51.

2. Highlight the &Month item in the menu outline at the bottom.

3. Click the WindowList box to enter a check mark.

4. Click OK to exit.

You can also do the same thing from the Properties window by changing a menu's WindowList property from False to True. Only one menu in the entire menu system can have its WindowList property set to True; if you try to do it to another menu, either an error will occur (Menu Editor window) or the previous selection will be deselected (Properties window).

DRILL

_9_ 21. A grid control's cell entries in the same row are separated from one another with Chr(__).

____ 22. A data control's _____ property value must be set to True if you don't allow the user to change a displayed record.

____ 23. A data control's _____ property is used to load a database.

____ 24. A data control's _____ property stores all the tables of a database.

_____ 25. A bound control has this/these unique properties:
   a. DataSource
   b. DataField
   c. RecordSource
   d. both a and b
   e. all of the above

Index

_____ 26. To create a menu array, you need to give one name to all the menu options in the same group but give each option a different _____ number.

Windowlist

_____ 27. If you check the _____ property in the Menu Editor window, opening the menu at run time will show a list of open MDI child forms.

_____ 28. This is used to find matching records in a database:
   a. DAO
   b. SQL
   c. MDI
   d. DDE
   e. API

Arrange

_____ 29. To arrange MDI child forms in Cascade mode, you need to use the _____ method.

Align

_____ 30. An MDI parent form can be a container for objects that have the _____ property.

PRACTICE

■ 25. Create a project which consists of a form and a single widened and empty text box. When the user types a string in the box at run time, it is automatically converted to uppercase. The displayed characters must retain the order of the original typed characters. (Use SendKeys.)

■ 26. How do a grid control's Row/Col and Rows/Cols differ?

■ 27. Modify Listing 2 so that when the space bar is pressed, the current cell's content will be displayed in Text1 and the cursor will go to Text1 for editing.

■ 28.   Modify the above so that the cursor will move to the end of the entry in Text1.

■ 29.   Modify the above so that when Enter is pressed (while the text box has the focus) the focus will return to the cell in the grid.

■ 30.   How is a database linked to an application?

■ 31.   What are bound controls? How are they linked to a database?

■ 32.   Use the Data Form Wizard to create a data form as shown in Figure 12.52. It should show the Titles table in the BIBLIO.MDB database.

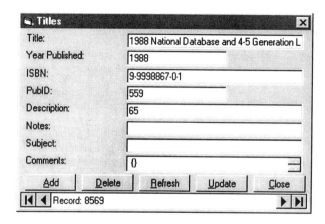

Figure 12.52   Displaying database records

■ 33.   Modify Figure 12.50 so that when the Year menu is clicked, the open child forms' captions will be displayed at the bottom of the menu.

CHAPTER PROJECT

A. (12HIDE.VBP)

Create an application that shows a MDI parent form and four child forms, together with four menus, as shown in Figure 12.53. The Form menu has the Hide and Show options. When Hide is selected, the current form disappears. When Show is selected, the form selected in the List menu is redisplayed. The

List menu displays all the available forms. The Arrange menu lets the user choose one of the three display modes.

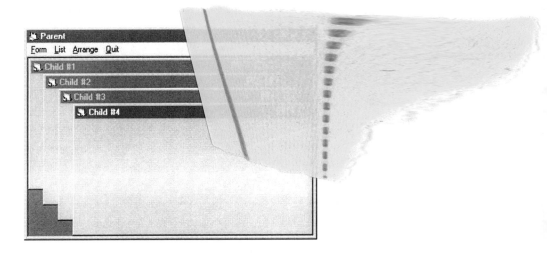

Figure 12.53   Manipulating MDI forms

B. (12GRID2.VBP)

This project creates a spreadsheet program shown in Figure 12.54. It has a grid control, a text box, and a menu. The program should behave as follows:

1. When you move the pointer to an empty cell and press a key, the corresponding character appears in the text box and the cursor goes to the text box for typing more characters. The typed characters appear in the cell as well as the text box. When you press Enter, the focus goes back to the original cell. If you type something and click another cell, the focus goes to that cell; the text is erased from the text box but retained in the original cell.

2. If the current cell has an entry, you can press the space bar to show the entry in the text box. The focus shifts to the text box and the cursor is located at the end of the text for editing.

3. The first row (row 1) and the first four columns (A to E) are entered by the user. The last two columns (E2 to F5) are entered when a proper menu option is selected.

4. The menu can be opened in three ways: clicking Menu, pressing Alt+M, and pressing the right mouse button (popup menu) when the pointer is on the grid or the form.

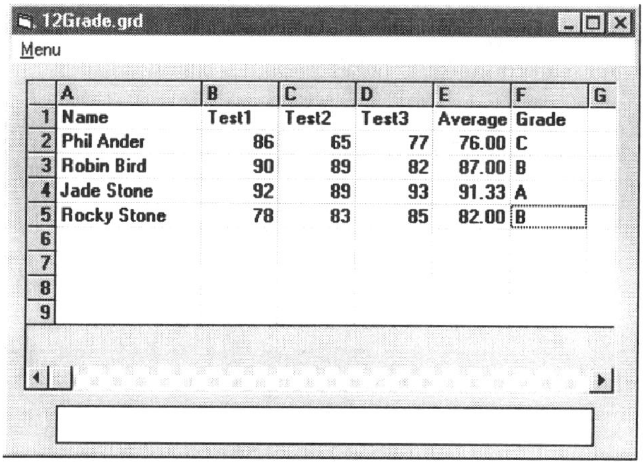

	A	B	C	D	E	F	G
1	Name	Test1	Test2	Test3	Average	Grade	
2	Phil Ander	86	65	77	76.00	C	
3	Robin Bird	90	89	82	87.00	B	
4	Jade Stone	92	89	93	91.33	A	
5	Rocky Stone	78	83	85	82.00	B	
6							
7							
8							
9							

Figure 12.54   A spreadsheet program

The menu contains six options: Open, Save, Print, Clear, Avg, Grade, and Quit. The menu can also be popped up when you right-click the grid control.

When Open is chosen, a common dialog appears and all the files matching *.GRD are shown. You can select one to open it. The companion disk has the 12GRADE.GRD file in the \PROJECT directory.

Save also uses a common dialog to let you save the current grid (selected cells) to disk. If no cell is selected, a message is given. If you supply a file name without the GRD extension, it is automatically added. If a matching disk file is found, you are given the Yes and No options to overwrite the file.

The Print option prints selected cells. If no cell is selected, a message is shown. A common dialog is not used.

When the Clear option is clicked, the current cell's entry, if any, is erased. If multiple entries are selected, their contents are erased.

When you move the pointer to column E and select Avg, the average of the three previous numbers is entered. If the pointer is somewhere else when Avg is selected, a beep is made and nothing else happens. Grade is entered in column F the same way.

C. (12CHILL.FRM)

This program lets you look up a table (Figure 12.55). Our example is a wind-chill index table. Open opens a data file (12CHILL.TXT in drive A's TEXTFILE directory) and puts the numbers in the top text box. (You can also type them and insert the required Tab by pressing the Ctrl+Tab key combination.) Moving the scroll bars at the bottom displays corresponding numbers for temperature (top row), wind speed (left column), and the wind chill index based on the two factors. The index is based on the column and row numbers in the scroll bars.

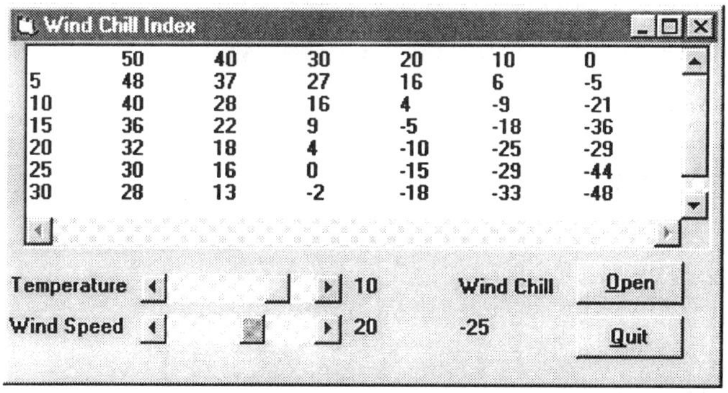

Figure 12.55   Looking up a table

D. (12POLL.FRM)

This project lets you tabulate poll data. Open opens a data file (12POLL.TXT in drive A's TEXTFILE directory) and displays it in the top text box. It also displays the tabulated result of the first column (Sex in our example). When you move the scroll box at the bottom left, the label above it shows which column and the tabulated result appears in the bottom text box. Figure 12.56 shows the result of moving the scroll bar to the President column.

Our simulated poll questionnaire consists of the following questions and options:

1. Sex: 1. Male, 2. Female
2. Age: 1. 18-25, 2. 26-35, 3. 36-55, 4. 55+
3. Race: 1. White, 2. Black, 3. Hispanic, 4. Other

4. Party: 1. Democrat, 2. GOP, 3. Independent
5. Ideology: 1. Very liberal, 2. Moderately liberal, 3. Moderately conservative, 4. Very conservative
6. Income: 1. -15K, 2. 16-25, 3. 26-45, 4. 46-100, 5. 100+
7. President: 1. Bush, 2. Clinton, 3. Perot, 4. Undecided

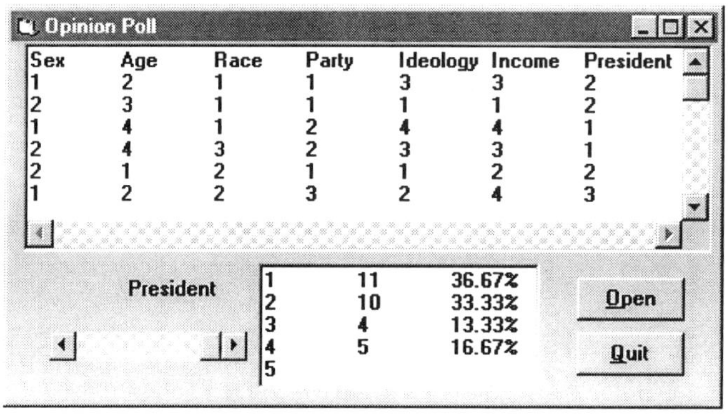

Figure 12.56   Tabulating poll data

E.   (12GRID3.VBP)

This project uses a grid control to manage poll data. The user interface consists of a grid control, two text boxes, and a menu.

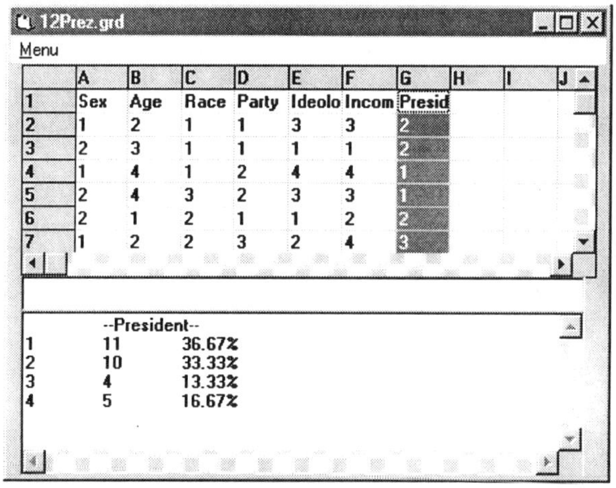

Figure 12.57   Tabulating a single column

When the program starts, an empty grid appears with a title row containing letters A to J and a title column consisting of numbers 1 to 100. The grid is ready for you to enter data or open a data file.

The grid and the middle text box are similar to those in project B. The only exception is that when you type something in the text box and press Enter, the focus shifts one cell to the right (use SendKeys) so that you can use the numeric keypad to quickly enter a row of data.

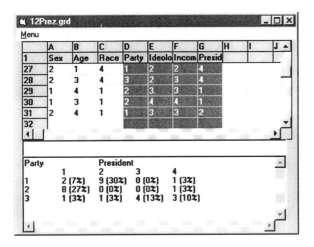

Figure 12.58   Freezing row 1 and showing Crosstab result

The popup menu consists of the following options:

    Open
    Save
    Print
            Data
            Output
    Tabulate
    Crosstab
    Clear
    Row Lock
    Quit

The Open, Save, Clear, and Quit options are the same as those in the preceding project. Print/Data prints selected cell data as before. Print/Output prints the output displayed in the bottom text box.

The Tabulate option is to count the current column and tabulate each number and its percentage. The result is shown in the bottom text box (Figure 12.57).

Before you choose the Crosstab option, you need to select two or more columns (click any cell in a specified column, hold down the Shift key, and click a cell in the ending column). The numbers in the first and the last columns are crosstabulated. Figure 12.58 shows the result after you select columns D-G and then choose Crosstab from the menu. (Use the run-time Col and SelCol properties in code to handle the two columns.)

The Lock Row option is to freeze row 1 (together with row 0) so that it will remain displayed as you scroll data upward, as shown in Figure 12.58. This option toggles between freezing and unfreezing row 1. (When a row is frozen, you cannot enter data in its cells; also, the data cannot be altered, saved, or printed.)

Our simulated poll questionnaire consists of the same questions and options as shown in the previous project. The companion disk contains the 12PREZ.GRD file in the \PROJECT directory.

FUN AND GAME

(The following programs' code lines are too long to be listed here. You can load them from the companion disk and examine them or print them out.)

A. (TICTACTOE.FRM)

This project provides a tic-tac-toe game (Figure 12.59). You can choose a one-player game or a two-player game. In a two-player game, the first player clicks a piece to enter an 0 and the second to enter an X.

In a one-player game, the player clicks a piece to enter an O and the program responds with an X. The player is not allowed to enter the middle piece in the first move; this is intended to make the game more evenly matched between the player and the computer.

When a winner is determined, the caption indicates that and one of the counter numbers changes; in a tie game, no counter number is changed. The board is frozen for further entries. Click New to start a new game and increase the Game # counter by 1.

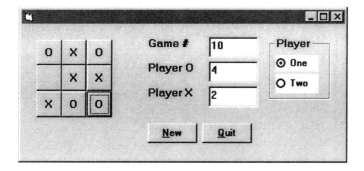

Figure 12.59   A tic-tac-toe game

B.   (MATCH.FRM)

This program tests your ability to remember displayed letters (Figure 12.60). There are two boards (picture boxes), each containing nine command buttons created at run time. At the beginning of run time, the command buttons are blank (without captions). You are to click one on the left to display a letter and then click one on the right to display its caption. If the two match, Score increments by 1 and the captions remain. If not, only Tries increments by 1 and the two displayed captions disappear after one second, which is controlled by a timer.

You have to take turns to click a blank piece between the left and the right board. Clicking a piece out of order leads to a beep and nothing else happens. The same thing happens when you click a piece whose caption is already shown.

The letters on the left are randomly generated. Each letter is unique. The letters on the right are the same as those on the left, except scrambled by using the Rnd function.

Clicking New starts the game anew, with a new set of random letters as well as a clear scorecard.

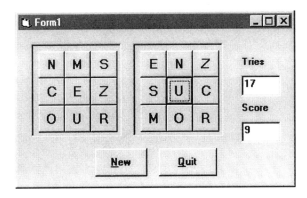

Figure 12.60   A matching game

Appendix A
Glossary

 A

Absolute/Relative coordinates   An absolute coordinate is a point in a graphics container measured from the top and left margins. A relative coordinate, in contrast, is a point measured from the current position.

Access key   A letter designated in an object's Caption property to let the user press Alt and that letter key to shift the focus to that object. At design time, you add an & before a letter to designate it as an access key. The letter will be underlined.

ActiveX   The new name for expanded OLE. ActiveX components are individual programs that follow Microsoft's COM (Common Object Model) standard. These components may be ActiveX controls that appear in Visual Basic's Toolbox, ActiveX servers that provide functions for other applications, or ActiveX documents that can be run by a Web browser. VB5 allows you to create all these.

API (Application Programming Interface)   The gateway to let a Windows application access dynamic-link libraries (DLLs) available in Windows and other packages. You can use the Declare keyword to call many external functions included in various Windows DLL files.

Application   A complete collection of visual elements and program code, which constitute a complete program; interchangeably used with *program* or *project*.

Argument   A value, variable, or expression supplied to a command to complete a specific instruction; also known as a parameter.

Array   A group of related variables that share the same name. The individual variables are known as elements. Each element is distinguished from another by an index number. An array may have one or more ranges of elements; each range is a subscript. Multiple subscript ranges make multidimensional arrays.

Array function   A function that lets you assign an arbitrary number of Variant-type elements to a Variant variable. The variable can then be maneuvered like an array. This function combines the DATA and READ commands available in most versions of Basic.

B

Bitmap   A picture containing a series of predetermined dots. If you stretch it, the dots become bigger and farther apart and the picture becomes coarse. A bitmap file has the BMP extension.

Boolean expression   A conditional expression that evaluates to true or false.

Bound controls   Controls that can bind (link) database records and fields to the screen. They include label, image, text box, check box, and picture box. Also known as data-aware controls, they are used to display data stored in a file.

Branching   A programming technique of directing program execution to another location without returning to the original point. If, Select Case, and sometimes GoTo are used for branching.

Break mode   The state when program execution is temporarily halted. You can use many ways to make Visual Basic go into break mode. A number of debugging tools are available in break mode.

Breakpoint   The point in the Code window to pause program execution and to shift to break mode for debugging. Press F9 or click the Margin Indicator Bar to set/unset a breakpoint.

Built-in function   A subprogram that comes with Visual Basic's programming language. Each built-in function usually requires one or more arguments and returns a value. There are numerous built-in functions. The Help system's Contents tab has the Programming Language book. Opening it leads to a long alphabetic list of books. Opening each book results in one or more functions starting with that letter. You can double-click each to display more details.

C

Calling   Diverting program execution to another procedure and, when the procedure is finished, returning to the original point.

Check box   A control that allows the user to check it to make a selection. Multiple selections can be made by the user.

Class   A program that provides the formal definition of an **object**. It determines how the included data can be manipulated by the included procedures. Users of a class (such as CommandButton or TextBox) can create copies (objects) and put them in their applications. Classes are the foundation of OOP (object-oriented programming).

Clipboard A memory area set aside by Windows for temporary storage of data. Any Windows-compliant program can use the Clipboard to send or receive data. Clipboard is recognized by Visual Basic as an object.

Code Or program code; instructions in a computer program telling the computer what to do.

Code window A window used to write and edit Basic code lines. You can use this window similar to the way you use Windows Notepad or the DOS Editor. The quickest way to go to this window is to press F7 or double-click an object on the form.

Collection An array-like object that can contain members of different data types. Visual Basic maintain many internal collections to handle objects. Users can create their own collections and manipulate them like arrays.

Combo box A control that combines a list (display) box at the bottom and a text (edit) box at the top. To select an item in the list, the user can type text in the edit box or click a displayed item.

Command button A control with a unique 3-D look. A Click procedure is usually attached to a command button. When the user clicks the button, the procedure is executed.

Comment A remark to document program lines. Add a remark after an apostrophe ('); this is usually placed at the end of a line. You can also use Rem placed at the beginning of a separate line. Anything after ' or Rem is ignored by Visual Basic.

Common dialog control A custom control that provides uniform dialog boxes for five common tasks: opening a file, saving a file, printing text, selecting a color, and selecting a font.

Constant A variable (symbol) with a predefined and unchanging value. Visual Basic comes with many system-defined constants known as **intrinsic constants**. So instead of using a number to assign a color, you can use vbRed, vbCyan, etc. You can use the **Const** keyword to create a user-defined constant known as a **symbolic constant**.

Control   A graphical object placed on a form. A control is fetched from the Toolbox to be put on a form. When an application is run, the user can click (or take some other actions to) a control to interact with the application.

Control array   An array of multiple controls of the same type. They all share one name but are distinguished by different index numbers.

Control structure   A block of statements that are executed if a condition is met. Such a block usually starts with If, Do, For, For Each, With, or Select Case. There are various ways to end each block.

CurrentX, CurrentY   Run-time properties for form, printer, and picture box; not available at design time. You can assign a twip value to CurrentX to move the print head to a horizontal position. Use CurrentY to move the print head vertically. You can also use these to read the current position of the print head.

Custom control   Also known as an OLE custom control or ActiveX control. It's stored in a separate file with the OCX extension. It can be added to the Toolbox and used like any other control. By adding custom controls to an application, you are using components (objects) created by others. The Learning Edition of Visual Basic comes with a few custom controls. The Professional and Enterprise Editions include many more. There are also numerous custom controls for sale by third-party vendors.

Custom menu   A menu you use the Menu Design window to design and attach to an application. The menu bar at the top of a form displays all the menu options. The user can select a menu option to do something. You need to write code to respond to such a selection.

D

DAO   Data access objects; a series of object classes defined in the Microsoft Jet database engine and included in Visual Basic. The objects derived from the classes can be used in code to programmatically maneuver databases.

Data control   A control that includes the database engine of Microsoft Access. It can be used to view the records of databases created by Access and other popular programs. A companion Visual Data Manager can be used to create a simple database, which can be viewed with a data control.

Data tip   Comparable to the tooltip feature available in most Windows programs. In break mode, when you move the mouse pointer over a variable name or when you select an expression, something may pop up to show the current value. This is a data tip.

Database   A collection of information on related items. A computer database conssists of one or more tables, each of which consists of multiple records, each of which contains multiple fields. A record can be compared to a row and a field to a column in a spreadsheet.

Debug   To identify and eliminate program errors. This word is also recognized as an object by Visual Basic. When you use code to output to the Debug object, the result will be shown in the Immediate window.

Declarations section   An area in the Code window where module-level variables are declared. When Full Module view is on, this is the topmost part of the Code window. When the cursor is in this area, the Object box shows (General).

Design time   The time when you design a program interface and write program code; different from run time and break time. The Visual Basic title bar shows [design] at design time.

Designer window   A window for designing a form or an ActiveX component. A form appears inside this window. You can then add existing objects to visually design a user interface.

Directory list box   A control that displays all the available directories. At run time, the user can double-click any directory to make it current.

Dockable window   A window that can be attached (docked) to one side of the IDE window. It can also be linked to another dockable window; multiple windows can be linked to become one unit.

Drive list box   A control that displays all the available disk drives. At run time, the user can click a displayed drive letter to change to that drive.

Dynamic array   An array with no fixed subscript range. When needed, the range can be specified dynamically, by the program or the user. This arrangement can make better use of memory.

E

Ellipsis button   A button with an ellipsis (also known as a Three-dot button) appearing in the Settings box of the Properties window, in place of the usual down arrow. Clicking this button can lead to a color palette or dialog box.

Enum   An enumeration (list) of constants that can share the same name and be tied together as a unit. In the Object Browser, enumerations are treated as classes and their variable (member) names and values are visible.

Event   An action which a Visual Basic object can recognize. When the user does something, such as clicking an object or pressing a key on the keyboard, the code attached to the object is executed, thus responding to the event.

Event procedure   A group of instructions placed in a procedure template (beginning with Sub and ending with End Sub). An Event procedure is attached to an object. When an event occurs, such as the user clicking the object, the code in the procedure is executed.

Event-driven programming   The technique of writing a computer program that will await a user response and react to an event initiated by the user or the system.

Expression   A statement fragment consisting of values, variables, and operators and returning a single value.

F

File list box   A control that displays a list of file names matching the attributes set in the Pattern property.

Focus   The state in which an object can interact with the user. An object has the focus when it is clicked or tabbed to. It will then respond to pressing keyboard keys or clicking a mouse button. Some objects cannot receive the focus.

Form   A container that holds other objects. A form looks like a peg board at design time and is transformed into a window at run time.

Form Layout window   A window in the IDE which you can use to specify a form's position at run time. You can drag a form inside this window or right-click a form here to pop up a list of options and choose one.

Form-level variable   A variable declared in the Declarations section of a form; it can be accessed by all the procedures in the form, but not outside.

Frame   A control to contain option buttons and other controls. Like a form, it serves as a container containing other objects.

Full Module View   All the procedures in the Code window are displayed in a continuum, normally with each separated from the next by a separator line.

Function procedure   A user-defined general procedure that returns a value. A function procedure can also be used like a sub procedure.

G

General procedure   A procedure defined by the user; it can be a sub procedure or a function procedure.

Global   The broadest variable (or procedure) scope. When a variable is declared with the **Global** or **Public** keyword in the Declarations section of a standard module, it is visible throughout the application. A public procedure is also global because it can be called by all the other procedures in the application. A private procedure can be called only from the same module.

Graphical controls   Four controls—label, line, shape, and image—that serve mostly decorative purposes, to make a user interface more attractive or informative. They cannot receive the focus (you cannot tab to them) and have few related methods, events, or properties.

Graphics container   A control that can contain graphics. They include form, image control, and picture box control.

Grid Control   A custom control that supplies columns and rows, and stores data in cells as in a spreadsheet program.

H

Horizontal/Vertical scroll bar   A control that lets the user move the scroll box inside to designate a value. The designated value is the scroll box's position between the minimum value (one end of the bar) and the maximum value (the other end of the bar).

I

Icon   A bitmap picture limited to 32 by 32 pixels. They are most commonly used to graphically represent an application in the Windows environment. An icon file has the ICO extension.

IDE   Integrated Development Environment. Visual Basic's IDE provides a complete set of tools and features for you to develop an application.

Immediate window   The window where you can enter a variable or expression to get an immediate result. This was previously known as the Debug window or the Immediate pane.

Input box   A type of window that pops up in the middle of the screen to prompt the user for an input. The user can be given quite a few options. Program execution is suspended until the user chooses an option.

IntelliSense   A feature to facilitate coding. When you type something in the Code window, a sample syntax or list box may pop up to help you complete a statement.

J

Jump   An underlined term appearing in an online help screen. Clicking a jump displays a new screen containing related information.

K

Keyword   A word reserved for Visual Basic's use. It has a special meaning to Visual Basic and should not be used for your purpose such as a variable name.

L

Label   A control that is most often used to show a text string on the screen, usually placed next to a text box or another object to guide the user.

Last Point Referenced (LPR)   A point in a graphics container where drawing last occurred. You can use CurrentX and CurrentY to move the print head to a specific point or tell you where the LPR is.

Line continuation character   It consists of a space followed by an underscore (_) placed at the end of a line in the Code window. Visual Basic will accept the line below as the continuation of the same line. This allows you to break one logical line into multiple physical lines.

Line control   A control that appears as a straight line inside a graphics container. It has coordinate properties that can be set at design time or run time to control the line's length and position. You can use various border styles to determine the line's appearance.

Line label   A text string ending with a colon and placed at the beginning of a line. A line label has to conform to the rules for a variable name. A line label (or a line number) marks a location for GoTo or GoSub to branch execution to.

List box   A control that displays at run time a list of items from which the user can make one or more selections.

Local   The narrowest variable scope. When a variable is local (declared or used only in a procedure), it does not exist outside the procedure.

Locals window   A window that will show in break mode all the available variables and their current values.

Logic error   An error related to programming logic, occurring only at run time. Errors in variables, procedures, and arrays can lead to wrong results or unintended program flow.

Looping   A programming technique of repeatedly executing a group of statements until a condition is met. For and Do are commonly used for looping. The For Each and With commands are also useful in maneuvering some items.

M

Margin Indicator Bar   A gray area on the left side of the Code window where different symbols will appear to indicate different states and activities.

MDI form   Multiple-document interface form, a super (parent) form that can contain other (child) forms. It allows an application to have multiple windows as in many Windows programs. The user can then open new windows or close and manipulate existing ones.

MDI and SDI   Multiple document interface and single document interface. The default IDE in VB5 is the MDI environment. The IDE is contained in an outer window. Forms are confined to designer windows and many individual windows can be docked to any of the four IDE borders. You can use Tools | Options | Advanced tab to check SDI Development Environment to switch to the SDI mode in the future. In SDI, the outer window is gone and forms stand by themselves.

Message box   A small window that appears in the middle of the screen to display a message. The user can be given a limited number of options. The user must choose an option before program execution will continue.

Metafile   A picture file with the WMF (Windows metafile) extension that stores graphics in vector format. Instead of predetermined dots, the algorithm for those dots is saved. When such a file is stretched, more dots will fill up the expanded space. The picture's integrity is thus preserved. This mechanism also makes metafiles larger.

Method　A statement (command) directed at one or several objects. Print, for example, is a method that can be applied to a form, printer, picture box, or the Immediate (Debug) window.

Modal (or modeless)　A type of window that requires a user action before the focus can shift to another object; program execution is suspended until an action is taken. An input box or message box is modal. A modeless window, like a regular form window, requires no such user action. You can use argument 0 (vbModeless) or 1 (vbModal) with the Show method to make a form modeless or modal.

Module　A container of program code. Each module is saved to a separate file. There are three types of modules: form module, standard module, and class module. A **form module** can contain code and visible objects. A **standard module** contains only declarations and procedures that can be used by the entire application. A **class module** contains declarations and procedures to create a class.

Module-level variable　A variable declared (without using the Global keyword) in the Declarations section of a module; it can be accessed by the procedures in the module, but not outside—unless it's a public variable.

N　**Named argument**　A feature that allows you to use names (like variables) in arguments for built-in functions as well as user-created general procedures. You can assign values to these names when you supply arguments to a function. If you use this arrangement, you can place arguments in any order rather than the required rigid order when names are not used.

Nesting　A programming technique of including a command or block of statements inside another command or control structure. After the nested command is finished, control returns to the nesting command.

O　**Object**　A program that combines code (methods) and data (properties). The code is used to maneuver the data. An object is derived from a **class** and inherits its code and data. A programmer can put together objects such as command buttons and text boxes to quickly create a useful application. This is like using prefab parts to build a house.

Object box　The little box under the title bar of the Properties window. It contains all the names of the objects in the current project. You can show the list by clicking the red down arrow next to the box. The left combo box in the Code window is also called the same name and will show the same items.

Object Browser   A tool that allows you to browse objects. Press F2 to open its dialog box. Use Project/Library (top left combo box) to select a project or application. Use Classes (left list box) to select an object. Use Members (right list box) to select a property or method (sub or function procedure). Click a member name to show its details in the bottom pane. You can use the Object Browser to show intrinsic constants, to copy a function to the Code window, to move the focus to a procedure in another module, or to browse the objects of another application, such as Excel.

OLE (object linking and embedding)   A technology created by Microsoft for computer users to create compound documents. Based on this technology, a word processing document may contain a spreadsheet or a graph created by other applications. Visual Basic provides many OLE tools. You can create an application that lets users access Word, Access, Excel, and so on. The availability of this technology is what makes Visual Basic a popular front-end programming tool.

Object variable   A variable that can be used to maneuver objects (forms and controls). It must be specifically declared with an appropriate command such as Dim, ReDim, Static, or Global. Use the Set command to assign an object to an object variable at run time.

Option Base   A statement in the Declarations section of a form or module specifying the base (lowest) number of an array's range.

Option button   A control that lets the user choose only one out of the available options. Option buttons in a container are mutually exclusive; only one can be chosen. However, you can use a frame control to provide another group of options.

Option Explicit   A statement in the Declarations section of a form or module specifying that all variables must be declared before they can be used.

P

Passing by reference   A programming technique of getting a procedure to pass (transfer) a variable's memory location to the called procedure. This allows the called procedure to alter the original value of the variable.

Passing by value   A programming technique of getting a procedure to pass (copy) a variable's value to the called procedure. The called procedure can maneuver the value but cannot alter the original copy.

Printer object   The name recognized by Visual Basic as a printer. You can specify this object with Print to print text. If Printer is not specified, output goes to the current window instead.

Procedural programming   The technique of writing a computer program that will, when it is run, execute from top to bottom one line at a time.

Procedure   A subroutine or subprogram that performs a specific task. A procedure is usually attached to an object in order to make the object respond to an event.

Procedure View   Each procedure in the Code window is displayed as a separate unit. Other procedures are not visible.

Procedure template   Or empty procedure; a procedure containing only the first and last statements. Visual Basic provides a procedure template, but you are required to fill in other statements in between.

Project   A collection of elements to complete an application. At design time, you work on a project. When the project is completed, it becomes an application, which is ready to run. Multiple projects can be combined into a project group.

Project Explorer window   Also called Project window; a window that lists all the elements of the current session, including one or more projects, each of which may include one or more forms and other items.

Property procedure   A user-defined general procedure. There are three types: Property Get, Property Let, and Property Set. You use these to define and call property procedures. Property procedures can sometimes replace sub or function procedures. But mostly they are used to add properties to a class.

Properties window   The window usually appearing on the right side of Visual Basic's IDE. You use this window at design time to set the properties (attributes) of objects. When no pertinent object is selected, this window is empty.

R   **Random-access file**   A file consisting of uniform records. All the records have the same length and number of fields. All the comparable fields have the same length and data type. Such a file allows manipulation of individual records—unlike an unstructured sequential file.

Recursion A programming technique of getting a procedure to call itself. There is a limit as to how many times this can happen.

Run time The time when your application is executed; opposite of design time. The Visual Basic title bar shows [run] at run time.

Run-time error An error that occurs at run time, when a program is executed. It can be caused by a faulty program or user action such as not supplying a disk when saving data. You can make your program trap such an error at run time and handle it accordingly.

S

Scope The extent to which a variable (or procedure) can be seen or accessed. A variable in one procedure is normally not visible to or accessible from another procedure. You can, however, broaden a variable's scope.

Sequential file Disk data that is saved and read in sequential order. Like a piece of music or movie saved to a cassette tape, a sequential file is saved to disk or read from it one byte after another in a prearranged order.

Settings box A little box in the Properties window; the right field in the properties list, next to a property name. The current value for the selected property appears here for you to edit. You can also click the down arrow next to it to display all the available options. If an ellipsis appears instead, click it to show a dialog box.

Single Stepping Executing code one statement at a time. Press F8 repeatedly to do that. Visual Basic gets into break mode. A number of tools are available for debugging your code.

Sizing handles The solid squares that surround a selected object. When the pointer moves to a sizing handle, it becomes a two-headed arrow. Drag this arrow to increase or decrease the object's size.

Shape control A control that can appear inside a graphics container as a rectangle or circle. You can choose different colors or hatch patterns to fill the inside.

Split bar A line that splits the Code window into two halves; a little rectangle at the top of the vertical scroll bar in the Code window, just above the upward arrow. Double-clicking it adds a dividing line in the middle of the

Code window; double-cling the dividing line clears it. You can also choose Window | Split to do the same thing.

SQL   Structured Query Language. A common and simple language used to query databases. Most remote databases are SQL databases. They follow the ODBC (Open Database Connectivity) standards which allow users to use SQL commands to maneuver their records.

Standard EXE   A project to create a standalone executable program. VB5 lets you create several other types of projects. But a novice is most likely to use only Standard EXE projects.

Standard Module   Or code module; a separate file with the BAS extension containing procedures and data declarations (but not forms or controls), which can be accessed by all the other elements in the same application.

Statement   A complete instruction to the computer to perform an act. A statement usually occupies one line. Multiple statements, however, can stay in the same line, each separated from another with a colon (:).

Static variable   A variable whose value remains (is not erased) between calls. It is visible in the area where it is declared. Declare a static variable with Static instead of the regular Dim.

Structure   See User-Defined Data Type.

Sub procedure   A user-defined procedure that does not return a value.

Syntax error   A programming error that occurs at design time. Incomplete or incorrect statements will trigger a syntax error. If Visual Basic's syntax checking feature is on (default), a brief error message appears, telling you what is wrong.

T

Template   A reusable base module containing common elements to create applications. You add to this module the elements you commonly need for an application. After the module is saved as a template, it can be used again and again. For example, you can create and save an About form as a template. You can then add it to any application you develop.

Text box   A control that can serve as an input or output field. You can edit an entry and use code to arithmetically maneuver entered numbers. Multiple lines can be entered or displayed, and scroll bars can also be provided to scroll the displayed text.

Three-dot button   An ellipsis appearing in the Settings box of the Properties window, in place of the usual down arrow. Clicking this button can lead to a color palette or dialog box.

Timer control   A control which will automatically execute a specific procedure at a preset interval. The interval, such as one second, can be set at design time or run time. At each interval, the Timer event will be triggered and the Timer procedure will be executed. You can use this mechanism to do something at a specific interval, such as displaying a digital clock. This arrangement does not interfere with your doing something with your PC.

Toolbar   A bar consisting of multiple buttons, each of which represents a menu option. These buttons can be used as shortcuts for menu options. VB5 includes several intrinsic toolbars. You can also create your own custom toolbars. The Standard toolbar contains the most common commands and is displayed by default.

Toolbox   A vertical window usually placed on the left side of Visual Basic's IDE. It contains all the tools available for you to add controls to the current form.

Twip   A unit of measurement for Visual Basic objects. A twip is 1/20 of a point, or 1/1440 of an inch.

U

User-Defined Data Type   A data type, also known as a structure, that can contain multiple elements of different data types. It must be created with Type...End Type in the Declarations section of a module. After a structure has been created, you can declare a variable to be that type. Combine the structure name and each individual element name with a period, and use this combination as you would an ordinary variable.

V

Value   Anything, such as a number or a string of characters, that you assign to a variable and is stored in the specified memory area. Statements, functions, or expressions also return values.

Variable   A name specified by you to designate a memory location to store a value. A variable can be assigned different values on different occasions.

Variant   The default Visual Basic data type. If you use a variable without declaring it, Visual Basic treats it as a Variant, which can hold any type of data.

W **Watch window**   A debugging window into which you can enter variables and expressions to observe their values in break mode. The expressions can be edited in break mode; their values will change accordingly.

Appendix B
Computer Math

A computer may appear intelligent, but at its basic level it can "understand" only whether power is on or off. To give it an instruction, we need to go by 1 (on) or 0 (off). The two digits of 1 and 0 then form the basis of binary (base 2) math.

The building block of binary math is the **bit**, which is a contraction of two words, namely **binary digit**. A bit can have the value of either 1 or 0, as shown in the following table.

Binary	Decimal	Calculation
1	1	1
10	2	2+0
11	3	2+1
100	4	4+0+0
101	5	4+0+1
110	6	4+2+0
111	7	4+2+1
1000	8	8+0+0+0
1001	9	8+0+0+1
1010	10	8+0+2+0

When you read binary numbers, read from right to left. When a digit goes beyond 1, the excess is carried to the next number on the left. The above table shows some examples of equivalent binary and decimal (base 10) numbers, and the methods for converting the former to the latter.

Each bit has the decimal value of 2 to a certain power. The first (rightmost) is 2 to the power of 0 (by definition, $2^0 = 1$), the second 1, the third 2, and so on. Binary and decimal numbers are related as shown below:

Decimal	128	64	32	16	8	4	2	1
2^n n =	7	6	5	4	3	2	1	0

Based on the above table, 2 to the power of 7 is 128.

Depending on whether a bit is on or off, the following binary number:

0 0 1 1 1 0 0 1

can be translated to its decimal equivalent this way:

0 + 0 + 32 + 16 + 8 + 0 + 0 + 1 = 77

By putting 8 bits together, as in the above example, you will get a byte and up to 256 variations (11111111 in binary equals 255 in decimal; that and 0 add up to 256 possible combinations). The 255 ASCII (and ANSI) values are based on this principle. The following table shows some examples of decimal, binary, and ASCII equivalents:

Decimal	Binary	ASCII Character
49	00110001	1
50	00110010	2
51	00110011	3
. . .		
65	01000001	A
66	01000010	B
67	01000011	C
. . .		
97	01100001	a
98	01100010	b
99	01100011	c

Bytes can go up to thousands, millions, billions, and more. For simplicity, programmers use KB (kilobyte), MB (megabyte), and GB (gigabyte). These numbers coincide with some unique numbers shown below:

Power of 2	Abbreviation	Decimal
2^10	KB	1024
2^20	MB	1048576
2^30	GB	1073741824

Thus, 1KB is 2 to the power of 10 (2 multiplied by itself 9 times or 2x2x2x2x2x2x2x2x2x2), 1MB the power of 20, and 1GB the power of 30.

Binary numbers are difficult to maneuver, so programmers use octal (base 8, 1 byte) and hexadecimal (base 16, 2 bytes). An octal digit can be 0 to 7, and a hex digit can be any of the following 16:

Hex	0 1 2 3 4 5 6 7 8 9 A B C D E F
Decimal	0 1 2 3 4 5 6 7 8 9 10 11 12 13 14 15

Hex numbers are marked with H or h at the beginning. To tell Visual Basic to go by a hex number, you also need to precede it with the & sign, such as:

```
Print &H3B8D2
```

The above statement will print 243922.

The following shows how this number can be converted to the equivalent decimal value:

Hex number	3	B	8	D	2
Calculation	$3x16^4 +$	$11x16^3 +$	$8x16^2 +$	$13x16^1 +$	$2x16^0$
Decimal	$196608 +$	$45056 +$	$2048 +$	$208 +$	$2 = 243922$

By default, Visual Basic outputs a numeric in the decimal format. You can use the Oct and Hex functions to convert it to a respective format; these are covered in Chapter 7. A program in Chapter 5 and a chapter project at the end of Chapter 8 can be used to convert between binary and decimal numbers.

Appendix C
Basic Commands

This appendix lists some of the commonly used Basic commands. You can get a quick reference of each command's purpose and syntax. They are grouped according to the order of their appearance in the book. For more details or concrete examples, check the specified chapter.

If you want a more exhaustive list, try the online help. Select Help and then Contents. The resulting screen has the Programming Language item. Clicking it displays a tall window on the right side of the screen. It contains several hundred items. You can click each to show more details.

The following conventions used here to show command syntax are the same as those used in Visual Basic's online help:

- Keywords are capitalized.
- Italics indicate user-supplied arguments.
- [ ] enclose optional additional arguments.
- | separates two options where only one is required.

Printing Text (Chapters 2, 3)

Use the **Print** command (method) to output text to four objects: a form, a picture box, the Debug window, or the Printer object. (You can combine it with # to output to a disk file; see the last section in this appendix.) If no object is specified, output goes to the current form by default.

You can use ? as a shortcut. The space after it can be omitted. The ending quotation mark is also unnecessary. Visual Basic will supply them after you move the cursor away from the current line.

The following list shows some examples:

```
Print varX      'variable value goes to current form
Print "xyz"     'output text string to form
Debug.Print varX 'variable value goes to Debug
Picture1.Print "xyz" 'goes to picture box
Printer.Print "xyz"  'goes to printer
```

User Interaction (Chapters 4)

Use an input box if a program needs an input from the user. The program code then handles the supplied input. It follows this syntax:

```
X = InputBox(prompt[, [title] [, [default] [,xpos,ypos]]])
```

If you want a program to pause and display a message, use a message box, which can be used as a statement or a function:

```
MsgBox msg[,type] [,title]]          'statement
X = MsgBox(msg[,type] [,title])      'function
```

The optional *type* argument can be one of the numbers in Table 6.1 (Chapter 6), each of which leads to a different set of options.

A value is returned if a message box is used as a function. Such a value is a number that reflects an option chosen by the user. Table 6.2 shows all the available numbers and what they mean.

Both input box and message box are **modal**. Program execution is halted. The user must choose an option from a displayed box for the program to continue. Many things about them, such as color, cannot be changed. You can, however, use a modal form, which gives you more ways to determine its appearance and behavior, to replace an input box or message box. Follow this syntax to make a form modal:

```
formname.Show 1
```

The 1 argument pauses program execution when the involved form is displayed. On the form you need to have some options for the user to choose the next step.

Conditional Statements (Chapter 6)

Use an If-Then control structure to determine whether one or more blocks of statements inside the structure should be executed. If-Then is useful if options are only a few. If options are more than a few, use Select Case instead of If-Then.

If-Then
```
If condition1 Then
    statements
[ElseIf condition2 Then
    statements
ElseIf condition3 Then
    statements
```

```
Else
    statements]
End If
```

Select Case . . . End Select

```
Select Case test_expression
    Case expression1
        statements
    Case expression2
        statements
        . . .
    [Case Else 'if all options not matching
        statements]
End Select
```

A test expression is usually a variable, whose value you want to match one of the Case expressions. If a match is found, the relevant block is executed; all the others are ignored. If there is a second match, it is also ignored. If no match is found, the optional Case Else clause is executed. If this clause does not exist, then the entire control structure is ignored. Each Case expression can include commas to separate a list of values or the To keyword to specify a range of values from lower to higher.

Looping (Chapter 6)

Use For-Next to execute the statements inside the loop a number of times, which is controlled by a counter and a step value. A For loop can nest one or more For loops to handle more complex tasks such as sorting an array or creating a multiplication table.

For-Next

```
For counter = start To end [Step increment]
    statements
    [Exit For]
    statements
Next [increment]
```

The **Step** argument is optional. If omitted, the default Step increment is by 1 after each iteration. The Step argument is required if you intend to increment the Step value by a higher/lower number or if you want to decrement it (decrease it after each iteration).

Use a For Each-Next loop to maneuver the elements in an array or collection of objects.

For Each-Next

```
For Each element In group
    statements
    Exit For
    statements
Next element
```

Use Do-Loop to execute the statements inside the structure until a condition is met. The condition can be placed at the beginning, in the middle, or at the end.

Do-Loop

```
Do
    statements
    If condition Then Exit Do
    statements
Loop

Do
    statements
Loop While | Until condition

Do While | Until condition
    statements
Loop

While condition
    statements
Wend
```

In an infinite loop, like the first example without the Exit clause, you can add **DoEvents** method or function to let the user activate a Windows event such as clicking a Quit button.

With-End With

Use a With-End With loop to maneuver objects and structures (user-defined types). In the following example, object names are omitted inside each With-End With loop.

```
Private Sub Command1_Click()
    With Text1      'object name
        .Height = .Height * 2 'omit "Text1"
        .Width = .Width * 2
        .ForeColor = vbRed
        With .Font
            .Size = 20   'omit ".Font"
            .Bold = True
        End With
        .Text = "Hello World"
    End With
End Sub
```

Formatting Numbers (Chapters 3 and 7)

Use the **Format** command to control how numbers are displayed. Here is an example:

```
Print Format(num, "$#,#.00")
```

Here *num* is a variable whose value you want to control. The output will include the $ sign at the beginning. Commas will appear in a large number. Decimal numbers are rounded to two decimal places. When a whole number is involved, two zeros appear after the decimal point.

In the following example, commas don't appear and a period appears at the end if a whole number is involved:

```
Print Format(num, "#.##")
```

Chapter 5 (near the end) supplies much more detail about shaping numeric displays.

Format can also be used to control how date and time numbers are displayed. Here are some examples:

```
Print Format(Now, "h:mm:ss a/p")
Print Format(Now, "m/d/yy h:mm:ss ampm")
Print Format(Now, "mmmm dd, yyyy, dddd")
```

They produce these results:

```
9:39:45 a
3/17/94 9:39:45 AM
March 17, 1994, Thursday
```

The last few sections of Chapter 7 supply a great deal more information.

Sub and Function (Chapter 8)

You can put related program lines in a subprogram and call it from other subprograms. Such a subprogram can be a **sub procedure** or **function procedure**. Both are general procedures, as contrasted from event procedures. A function procedure, like a built-in function, returns a value. A sub procedure, like an event procedure, does not.

To create a general procedure, go to the Code window first. Then select New Procedure from the View menu. Select Sub or Function and supply a name. The procedure template will appear for you to type code lines.

Sub or function follows this syntax:

```
[Static] [Private] Sub subname [(argumentlist)]
    [statements]
    [Exit Sub]
    [statements]
End Sub

[Static] [Private] Function functionname _
[(argumentlist)] [As type]
    [statements]
    [Exit Function]
    [statements]
End Function
```

Static is to retain local variables' values between calls. Private is to prevent other modules from accessing a general procedure.

To call a sub procedure, simply invoke its name or optionally add the **Call** keyword before the procedure name. To call a function procedure, use the procedure name (followed by a pair of parentheses) as part of an expression, similar to the way you use a built-in function. The following shows how to call a function procedure:

```
    Sub Form_Click ()
        Print randnum ()         'to call function
    End Sub


    Function randnum ()          'function name
        randnum = Rnd            'return to caller
    End Function
```

In calling a sub or function procedure, you can pass arguments to the procedure either by value or by reference (default). The latter lets the called procedure access the original value. To call by value, you must use the **ByVal** keyword. This sends a copy to the procedure and does not allow it to alter the original. You can alternatively use a pair of parentheses to call by value without using the ByVal keyword.

To pass an argument to a sub procedure, use one of these formats:

```
    subname argument
    Call subname (argument)
```

To pass an argument to a function procedure, use this format:

```
varX = funcname (argument)
```

To pass by value, add an extra pair of parentheses around the argument.

Trapping Run-Time Errors (Chapter 8)

Use one of the following statements to trap a run-time error:

```
On Error Goto line
On Error Resume option
```

Line is a line number or line label, which marks the location to branch execution to when an error occurs. In this location you need to set up an error-handling routine to tell the program what to do next. The entire structure may look like this:

```
Sub XXX ()
   . . .
   On Error GoTo ErrLine      'if error
   . . .
   Exit Sub         'if no error, skip below
ErrLine:            'line label
   MsgBox Error     'pause to show error message
End Sub
```

You can use **Resume,** followed by **0, Next,** or a line (number or label). 0 resumes execution with the line that caused the error; Next resumes with the next line.

Object Alias and Cloning (Chapter 9)

To create an additional copy of an existing form, use one of the following techniques:

```
(1)    Dim Frm As New Form1      'not Form
       Frm.Show
(2)    Dim Frm As Form1          'can be Form
       Set Frm = New Form1
       Frm.Show
```

In the first technique, you cannot use Form in lieu of Form1. In the second, you can use Form as well as Form1. If you use Form, you can use variable Frm to reference a regular form as well as an MDI form. The **New** command in both cases creates a new form. In the second technique, if New is not used, Frm becomes an alias of an existing form; no new form is created.

To create a copy of a control, change its Index to 0 at design time and use Load and Visible to clone it at run time:

```
Load Command1(1)       'create 1st clone
Command1(1).Visible = True 'show it
```

To use an alias name for a control, try the following technique:

```
Dim C As CommandButton     'declare object variable
Set C = Command1           'assign object to var
```

In the first line, you can use **Control** instead of a specific control type name. In that case, you can use variable C to reference any control.

Use **Count** and the following to maneuver forms and controls collections (internal arrays of cloned objects):

```
Forms(number)             'form array
formname(number)          'control array
formname.Controls(number) 'same as above
```

File Input and Output (Chapter 10)

Open a file with the following syntax:

```
Open file [For mode ][Access access ] As [#] filenumber
```

where the following parameters have various options:

file	A text-string argument signifying a file name. A new file will be created or an existing file overwritten if Output is the specified *access*.
mode	Can be Random, Binary, Input, Output, or Append; if not specified, Random is the default.
access	Can be Read, Write, or Read Write.

You can add Len to open a random-access file:

```
Open file [For mode ][Access access] _
As [#]filenumber [Len = reclen]
```

Len is 128 bytes if not specified.

You can open a file with the following minimum arguments:

```
Open "testfile" As #1
```

This is legal. Since you do not specify anything, the following default values kick in:

mode	Random is the default.
access	Read Write is the default.
reclen	Record length is 128 bytes.

Use the following statements to open a sequential file for output and save data in a text box:

```
A$ = "a:testfile"              'file name to open
Open A$ For Output As #1      'open for output
Print #1, Text1.Text     'send from text box to file
Close #1                        'close file
```

Use the following routine to pull in a sequential file and put it in an existing text box:

```
Open "filename" For Input As #1      'open for input
Do While Not EOF(1)            'not end of file
    Line Input #1, X$
        'pull from disk and assign each line to x$
    B$ = B$ & X$ & vbCrLf
        'add to B$ + line break
Loop
Close #1                         'close file
Text1.Text = B$                  'show in text box
```

Appendix $\mathcal{D}$

Answers

CHAPTER 1, A QUICK TOUR

1.Standard; 2.Toolbox; 3.Properties; 4.20; 5.Code; 6.T; 7.F; 8.b; 9.a; 10.d;
11.c; 12.c; 13.d; 14.c; 15.e; 16.b; 17.Procedure; 18.e; 19.e; 20.d; 21.a; 22.c;
23.d; 24.e; 25.b; 26.a; 27.a; 28.d; 29.c; 30.b

1. Choose File | New Project. If prompted, choose Yes or No to save changes.
    The New Project dialog box appears. Double-click Standard EXE. The form
    designer window appears with Form1 inside it. If the Properties window is
    open, it contains information about Form1. If the Project window is open,
    Project1 and Form1 appear inside this window.

2. Double Form1 to open the Code window. Click the X button at the top right
    corner to close each window. Choose View | Code to open the Code window
    and View | Object to open the designer.

3. Click the X button to close the window. Press Ctrl+R, choose View |
    Project Exlorer, or click the corresponding button on the Standard toolbar
    (fifth from the right) to open the Project window. Click the form name in this
    window and click the View Object or View Code button.

4. Click the X button to close it. Click the last button on the Standard toolbar or
    choose View | Toolbox.

5. Click the X button to close it. Press F4 to open it. You can also choose View
    | Properties or the fourth button from the right on the Standard toolbar.

6. Drag the designer's title bar to move it. Drag the designer's border lines to
    resize it. Use the designer's scroll bars to show different parts of the form.
    Use the right and bottom sizing handles of Form1 to change the form's size.

7. If the Form Layout window is not open, open it by choosing View | Form
    Layout Window. Right-click Form1 in the middle of this window, choose
    Startup Position | Center Screen (or Center Owner).

8. It lets you specify the run time position of a form. A form picture appears inside this window. You can drag it to a particular location and the form will appear there at run time. You can right-click this form picture and click Startup Position to select an option.

9. Right-click the window and check/uncheck Dockable.

10. It can be docked (attached) to any of the IDE borders; just drag the title bar to a side to dock it. It can be undocked by dragging the title bar to the middle of the IDE window. It can be linked to another dockable window; just drag the title bar and drop it on another dockable window's title bar. An undocked dockable window floats on top of an undockable window.

11. When an undockable window, like the Code window, is maximized, all the other undockable windows are also maximized and covered up. To bring one of them to the top, press Ctrl+Tab or Ctrl+F6 repeatedly to cycle through all the hidden windows. Dockable windows are not affected by these keys. They are either attached to a border or on top of an undockable window.

12. Right-click a toolbar or the menu bar and choose Customize. Open the Toolbars tab and choose New. Enter a name and click OK. Open the Commands tab and drag three commands to the new toolbar. Go to the Toolbars tab and choose Delete and OK.

13. Right-click the menu bar or any displayed toolbar and check one of the popup list. This list also appears when you choose View | Toolbars.

14. Click the title bar or the arrow (Pointer) icon and press F1.

15. Choose Help | Help Topics | Index. Type "textbox" in the top box. Double-click "TextBox Control."

16. Click the text box control in the Toolbox and then press F1.

17. After showing the topic, choose Options | Print Topic. The Print dialog box appears. Make necessary adjustments and click OK.

18. Change the two labels in Figure 1.25 to Mile and Kilometer. In Figure 1.24, change the formula to:

    txtOutput.Text = txtInput.Text * 1.609

19. Reverse the two labels. Change the formula to:

    txtOutput.Text = txtInput.Text / 1.609

20. Adjust the two labels and change the formula to:

    txtOutput.Text = txtInput.Text * 12

21. Select Print from the File menu. Select Current Module on the left side. Select Code on the right side. Click OK to print.

22. Select the form by clicking the form itself or the form name in the Project window. Then use File | Save Form. You can also right-click the form name in the Project window and choose Save Form.

23. Use File | Save Form to save a copy to a drive. Then use File | Save Form As to save the same file to another drive or a different file name on the same drive.

24. If you want to open a recent form file, open the File menu and click one of the names appearing the the bottom of the menu. Otherwise, choose File | Open Project (or click the Open Project button on the Standard toolbar). In the File-name box, type *.*frm* and press Enter to show only form file names; or in the Files-of-type box, open the box and select All Files. When the desired file is shown, double-click it to open.

25. Use File | Open Project to open a form file. If the Project window is not shown, open it with View | Project Explorer. Click the form name in this window and then click View Object or View Code.

26. It determines run time tab order. The object that has the 0 value gets the focus at the beginning of run time. When you press Tab repeatedly, the focus goes to the object with the value of 1, 2, and so on.

27. The first statement shifts the focus at run time to Text1; the user can then type text without having to tab to the text box. The second converts the entry in Text1 to a numeric and assigns it to a variable named varX.

CHAPTER 2, CODE, OUTPUT, AND DEBUG

1.d, 2.c, 3.a, 4.b, 5.d, 6.c, 7.e, 8.f, 9.c, 10.Split, 11.e, 12.a, 13.d, 14.b, 15.c, 16.e, 17.Rem, 18.b, 19.a, 20.d; 21.b, 22.F, 23.T, 24.Stop, 25.T, 26.T, 27.EndDoc, 28.F, 29.Input, 30.a

1.   Of the eight sizing handles that surround a form, only the three at the bottom right are enabled and all the others are disabled. You can change the form's size but not its position against the designer window.

2.   The default startup position is Windows Default. Each time you run the form, it appears in different locations, cascading from top left downward and rightward and then back again. If you change it to any other option in either the Properties window or the Form Layout window, the position becomes fixed.

3.   The first is the line number from the beginning of all the code and the second is the column position. These numbers disappear when the toolbar is docked. They show different things when the cursor is not in the Code window.

4.   It displays various icons indicating various states and activities. For example, you can add a bookmark on a line and quickly move to that line in the future. You can also set a breakpoint on a line to halt program execution for debugging.

5.   Click before a line to select that line. Double-click to select the current procedure. Hold down Ctrl and click this area (or press Ctrl+A) to select all the displayed code.

6.
One screen left	Ctrl+PgUp
One screen right	Ctrl+PgDn
Top of the current procedure	Ctrl+Home
Bottom of the current procedure	Ctrl+End
Previous procedure	Ctrl+↑
Next procedure	Ctrl+↓

7.   Procedure View (left) and Full Module View (right). In Full Module View (default), the Code window displays all procedures in a continuum, maybe separated by separator lines. In Procedure View, the Code window displays only one procedure at a time. Click each button to change to that view.

8   Double-click the Split bar at the top of the vertical scroll bar. Double-click the separator line to merge the two panes. You can also drag the line up or down to adjust the two panes.

9.   Add the following line between Select and End Select:
     Case "^"
          Sum = Val(txtOp1.Text) ^ Val(txtOp2.Text)

10.
```
Sub cmdClear_Click ( )
    txtOp1.Text = ""
    txtOptr.Text = ""
    txtOp2.Text = ""
    txtOut.Text = ""
End Sub
```

11. Add the following line at the end of the procedure:

    txtOp1.SetFocus

12.
```
Sub Form_Click ( )
    Dim I As Integer
    For I = 1 To 10
        Debug.Print I;
    Next i
End Sub
```

13. Each new group of numbers is printed in the same line, on the right side of the previous numbers. To put each new group in a new line, put Debug.Print at the beginning of the procedure. This will force printing in a new line.

14. Put the Stop command before the Next line. To resume, press F5.

15. Add the following line before the Next line:
        Print I;

16. Cls does not work in the Immediate window. You need to select text and press Del to delete the whole or part of the display.

17. You can do it at design time or in break mode when both windows are open. To copy, highlight text and press Ctrl+Ins (or Ctrl+C). To paste, go to the other window and press Shift+Ins (or Ctrl+V). You can also drag selected text from one window to another to move; to copy, hold down Ctrl as you drag and drop.

18. To force VB to pause program execution and go into break mode. To place a breakpoint on a line, move the cursor there and press F9 (press another time if you want to remove it); you can also click the Margin Indicator Bar to set/unset a breakpoint. When you press F5 to run the program, it pauses when a breakpoint is encountered. You can then press F8 to single-step through future lines and observe variables in the Locals window.

19. It displays all the variables in the current procedure and their current values in break mode.

20. To let you enter a variable or expression to produce an immediate result. You can also use the Debug keyword to output to this window.

21. It will end program execution, the same as clicking the End button on the Standard toolbar.

22. It opens a file named TESTFILE in the current directory in drive A to write data to it. If the file does not exist, a new one will be created. If one matching the specified name already exists, new data will be added to the end of the existing data.

23. To output information to four devices: form window (default), printer, Debug, and picture box. If the command is used alone, namely no object is connected to it, the output goes to the current window. To output to another device, connect it to Print with a period, such as Debug.Print Printer.Print, or Picture1.Print.

24. Select I*J and a data tip will appear.

25. 9. I goes through three passes, for each of which J goes through three passes. The net effect is that Num will have the value of 3 x 3 at the end.

CHAPTERS 3, FORMS AND OUTPUT FORMATTING

1.b, 2.e, 3.e, 4.c, 5.F, 6.d, 7.d, 8.a, 9.c, 10.b, 11.T, 12.d, 13.b, 14.e, 15.T, 16.T, 17.a, 18.b, 19.d, 20.d, 21.c, 22.d, 23.e, 24.$13, 25.$0013, 26.1234567.9, 27.1234.00, 28.a, 29.a, 30.d

1. They are the values of the Left, Top, Width, and Height properties. The numbers also appear in the form's Properties window. The numbers represent distances expressed in twips.

2. A twip is 1/20 of a point, which is 1/72 of an inch. An inch has 1440 twips (20 * 72). A twip is then 1/1440 of an inch.

3. An object, such as a text box, no longer automatically aligns to grid lines. If you place the border of an object between grid lines, the object stays where you place it and does not snap to an existing grid line. This gives you more control in designing a crowded interface.

4. The control box at the top left corner disappears at both design time and run time; all the buttons at the top right also disappear. You can no longer use any of these to end a program. Instead, choose End from the Run menu, or click the End icon on the Standard toolbar.

5. The form window fills the entire screen at run time. It no longer responds to any mouse action--even if you set ControlBox to True at design time. To end the program, press Ctrl+Break to switch to break mode. If the Immediate window appears, type End and press Enter. You can also use the menu bar or the Standard toolbar to end.

6. Double-click the from's control box or click the X button to close the window. To restore it, click the View Object button in the Project window, press Shift+F7, or choose View | Object.

7. Three things could happen. If typing is required, the cursor goes to the Settings box for you to type something. If there is a list of options, each double-click selects the next option. If there is a dialog box, it will appear.

8. Select the form by clicking it. Press F4 to open the Properties window. Double-click BackColor from the list; click Palette to make the color palette appear. Click one of the available color boxes.

9. Select the current form by clicking it. Choose Color Palette from the View menu. Click one of the color boxes. Click the X button if you want to close the color palette.

10. Choose Color Palette from the View menu; the Color Palette window appears. Click the Custom Colors button; another row of color boxes appear at the bottom. Click a box for which you want to define a color; the Define Colors button appears. Click the button and the Define Color window appears. Define a color and click the Add Color button; click Close instead if you want to abort.

11. Double-click the current form. When the Code window appears, click the down arrow in the Procedure box. Scroll up the list to show Click and click it. The Form_Click procedure template appears. Enter the following:

   Caption = "Form Demo"

   Press F5 to run the program. Click the window and the caption appears.

12. Put the following in the Form_Load procedure.

   WindowState = 1

The Form1 button appears in the taskbar--although no form is shown. Click the button to restore the form.

13. A method is a statement directed at an object. Print is an example. You can use Print alone or Form1.Print to print something to the Form1 window. An event is mostly an action taken by the user, such as clicking a mouse button. To respond to an event, you can write a procedure, which is then known as an event procedure.

14. The statements in the procedure are executed when a project's startup form is run. Initialization can be automatically done this way. To display screen output, you must use the Show method; otherwise, nothing will be shown.

15. Show is a method directed at a form. So Form2.Show will load as well as show (display) Form2. Load is a statement (a command not specifically tied to any object) that puts an object in memory without displaying it.

16. Hide is a method which is the opposite of Show. Form2.Hide hides Form2 without unloading it. Unload, like Load, is a statement. Unload.Form2 removes the form from memory.

17. Like Ctrl+Tab, it lets you cycle through all the undockable windows. You can use it to quickly switch from Form1 to Form2, Code, Project, Properties, etc. Clicking a window brings it to the top and makes it current. Pressing Ctrl+F6 once brings the most recently active window to the top.

18. It's a method directed at a form. If you use PrintForm alone in code, executing it will print the current form the way you see it. If you want to print another form, specify it, such as Form2.PrintForm. The result is the same as using the Print option from the File menu to print a form at design time.

19. The procedure for Form1's command button is:

```
Sub Command1_Click ( )
    Form1.Hide
    Form2.Show
End Sub
```

The procedure for Form2's command button is:

```
Sub Command1_Click ( )
    Form2.Hide
    Form1.Show
End Sub
```

20. Put these lines at the beginning of the first procedure:

    ```
    Caption = "Form 1 Demo"
    Form2.Caption = "Form 2 Demo"
    ```

21. Put the two assignment lines in Form1's Form_Load procedure.

22.
    ```
    Sub Show2_Click ( )
        Form2.Show
    End Sub

    Sub Hide2_Click ( )
        Hide
    End Sub
    ```

23. Add this line at the end:

    ```
    Form2.Top = Form1.Top + Form1.Height
    ```

24. Change the Case order as follows:
    ```
    Case 1
        Top = Top + Height
    Case 2
        Left = Left + Width
    Case 3
        Top = Top - Height
    Case 0
        Left = Left - Width
    ```

25. Semicolon does not move the print head after printing the last character. Comma moves the print head to the next print zone, which is 14 columns from the previous. If neither is present at the end of a Print statement, the print head moves to beginning of the next line.

26. Spc moves the print head X spaces to the right of the current print head. Tab moves the print head to column X in the same line. If X is less than the current column, then the print head moves to column X of the line below.

27. These are run-time properties that can control the print head's position. You can assign a twip value to CurrentX to move the print head horizontally. If you use CurrentX = 1000, you move the print head to 1000 twips from the left margin of the window. CurrentY controls the print head's vertical position, its distance from the top of the window.

28. 3CROSS.FRM

29. 3PRNDEM.FRM

30.
```
Sub Form_Click ( )
    Font.Name = Printer.Fonts(3)
    Font.Size = 15
    Print "This is font "; Font.Name; "; size "; Font.Size
    Font.Name = Printer.Fonts(4)
    Font.Size = 10
    Print "This is font "; Font.Name; "; size "; Font.Size
End Sub
```

31.
```
Sub Form_Click ( )
    CurrentX = 2000
    CurrentY = 1500
    Print CurrentX, CurrentY
End Sub
```

32. 3DIAMND.FRM

33. Add "Printer." before each Print, CurrentX, and CurrentY. Add Printer.EndDoc at the end.

CHAPTER 4, COMMON CONTROLS

1.d, 2.b, 3.c, 4.T, 5.Default, 6.Cancel, 7.a, 8.a, 9.b, 10.b, 11.F, 12.PasswordChar, 13.c, 14.1122, 15.33, 16.3366, 17.1122, 18.Value, 19.F, 20.T, 21.a, 22.b, 23.F, 24.T, 25.T, 26.b, 27.e, 28.c, 29.b, 30.c

1.
```
Sub Form_Load ( )
    Command2.Visible = False
End Sub

Sub Command1_Click ( )
    Command1.Visible = False
    Command2.Visible = True
End Sub

Sub Command2_Click ( )
```

```
   nand1.Visible = True
   nand2.Visible = False


   imand1_Click ( )
   nand2.Visible = Not Command2.Visible
```

attached to the object called (General). You can click this object when pull down the Object list from the Code window. After you select this ct, pull down the Procedure list and you will find the procedure there. If Module View is checked, the procedure is visible without additional steps.

4.
```
Sub Form_Load ( )
   Command1.Default = True
   Text1.Width = Text1.Width * 4
   Text1.TabIndex = 0
   Text1.Text = ""
End Sub

Sub Command1_Click ( )
   Print Text1.Text
   Text1.Text = ""
End Sub
```

5. Put Cls at the beginning of the Command1_Click procedure.

6.
```
Sub CB_Click ( )
   CB.Width = CB.Width * 2
   CB.Height = CB.Height * 2
   CB.Left = (Form1.Width - CB.Width) / 2
   CB.Top = (Form1.Height - CB.Height) / 2
   CB.Caption = CB.Height
End Sub
```

7.
```
Sub Form_Load ( )
   Label1.AutoSize = True
   Label1.Caption = "Click the window to change."
End Sub
```

```
Sub Form_Click ( )
    Label1.Caption = "This line can be visible or invisible."
    Label1.Visible = Not Label1.Visible
End Sub
```

8. Change the Top and Left values as shown below:
```
        Label1.Top = 1440
        Label1.Left = 2880
```

9. Change the first line below to the second line:
```
        Text2.Text = Text2.Text & NL & Text1.Text
        Text2.Text = Text1.Text & NL & Text2.Text
```

10. Add this line in the procedure:
```
        Text3.Text = Val(Text1.Text) ^ 3
```

11. 4TMPSCAL.FRM

12.
```
Sub HScroll2_Change ( )
    Dim C As Single, F As Single

    F = HScroll2.Value          'put HScroll1 val in F
    C = (F - 32) * 5 / 9        'conversion formula
    Label1.Caption = C          'show C value in Label1
    Label2.Caption = F          'show F value in Label2
    HScroll1.Value = C          'move HScroll1
End Sub
```

13.
```
Sub HScroll1_Change ( )  'set Max to 10
    Text1.Text = "Year # " & HScroll1.Value
    Text2.Text = Format(1000 * (1 + .065) ^ HScroll1, "#.00")
End Sub                      'display 2 decimal places
```

14.
```
Sub HScroll1_Change ( )
    Label1.Caption = "$" & HScroll1.Value
    Text2.Text = Text1.Text * HScroll1.Value & " Yen"
End Sub
```

15. Add a text box and two labels. Then add this procedure:

```
Sub Text1_Change ( )
    Dim varX, varY, Total
```

```
    varX = Text1.Text        'get entire number
    varY = Int(varX)         'get integer portion
    Total = varY * 60 + (varX - varY) * 100
            'hour portion * 60 + min portion * 100
    Label2.Caption = Total & " minutes"
End Sub
```

16.
```
Sub Text1_Change ( )
    Dim varX, varY, Total
    varX = Text1.Text        'get entire number
    varY = Int(varX)         'get integer portion
    Total = varY * 16 + (varX - varY) * 10
        'pound portion * 16 + ounce portion * 10
    Label2.Caption = Total & " ounces"
End Sub
```

17. A letter key that allows the user to press it in combination with Alt to shift the focus to a designated object. To create an access key, put an & before a designated letter in an object's caption. The letter will become underlined.

18. Use a label. The label's TabIndex property value should be 1 less than the text box's. Designate a letter in the label's caption as an access key. When the user presses the access key, the focus will shift to the text. Since a label cannot receive the focus, the next object gets the focus.

19. Change List1's Sorted property to True. Change Command1's Default property to True and add this procedure:

```
Sub Command1_Click ( )
    List1.AddItem Text1.Text
    Text1.Text = ""
    Text1.SetFocus
End Sub
```

When you type something in Text1 and press Enter, the above procedure will be executed.

20.
```
Sub List1_Click ( )
    Text1.Text = List1.Text
End Sub
```

21. Draw a frame and enlarge it. Click the desired tool in the Toolbox. Move the pointer inside the frame and start dragging. The object will appear and

become part of the frame. To move existing objects, select them and use cut and paste.

22. A frame is like a parent to the objects inside it, similar to the way a form is related to the objects inside it. When a frame moves, all the objects inside move also. If you delete the frame, all the objects inside will disappear. An object's Top and Left properties are related to the frame, not the form.

23. Put one group on a form and the other inside a frame. Or put each group inside a separate frame. This allows the user to choose an option from each group. Otherwise, only one option can be selected from all the options.

24. 4CNVTEMP.FRM

25. 4NUMBER1.FRM

26. 4NUMBER2.FRM

27.
```
Sub Command1_Click ( )
    Dim varX
    Static Sum              'static variable
    varX = InputBox("Enter a number", sum)
    varX = Val(varX)                'convert to value
    If varX = 0 Then End            'if 0 entered or Cancel clicked
    Sum = Sum + varX 'add up each entry
    Command1.Value = True           'execute procedure
End Sub
```

28.
```
Sub Command1_Click ( )
    Static Sum, Ctr, Ave
    Ctr = Ctr + 1           'counter, track number of entries
    varX = InputBox("Average " & ave, "Sum " & sum)
    varX = Val(varX)
    If varX = 0 Then End
    Sum = Sum + varX
    Ave = Sum / Ctr         'get average
    Command1.Value = True
End Sub
```

29.
```
    If varX = 0 Then
        varY = MsgBox("Are you sure?", 4)
        If varY = 6 Then End
```

End If

30. A function returns a value; a statement does not. An input box is always used as a function. The entry made by the user in the input box is the returned value. It can be assigned to a variable and maneuvered in many ways. When a message box is used as a statement, it merely displays a message and returns no value. If it is used as a function, a value, which is a number depending on the option chosen, is returned and can be maneuvered by code.

31. 4CARENT.FRM

CHAPTER 5, THE BASICS OF BASIC

1.e, 2.F, 3.T, 4.F, 5.a, 6.c, 7.d, 8.b, 9.a, 10.a, 11.c, 12.c, 13.b, 14.d, 15.d, 16.Explicit, 17.VarType, 18.F, 19.d, 20.1, 21.33, 22.1, 23.True, 24.False, 25.e, 26.200, 27.global, 28.standard, 29.static, 30.Public Const

1. 2748

```
10 * 16 ^ 2 = 2560
11 * 16 ^ 1 =  176
12 * 16 ^ 0 =   12
-------------------------------
              2748
```

2. 438

```
6 * 8 ^ 2 + 6 * 8 ^ 1 + 6 * 8 ^ 0 =
384       + 48        + 6   =   438
```

3. A restricted keyword by itself cannot be used as a variable name. An unrestricted keyword can be used as a variable if you declare it first; this should normally be avoided. A restricted keyword can be used as an object name if you place it inside a pair of straight brackets, such as [For].

4. The first increase's varX's original value by 1. The second assigns varX2's value to varX1. The third is illegal because an arithmetic operator is not permitted in a variable.

5. A period is used to connect an object and a property, such as Form1.Caption. The ! sign is used to connect a form and a control, such as Form1!Text1.- Text. You're now encouraged to use a dot to replace the !. The & sign is an operator used to concatenate strings and numerics. The _ character is used to

connect an object and a procedure. This last sign can be used in a variable name, but not the others.

6. A statement is a complete instruction like a sentence. An expression combines variables and/or constants. Consider the following:

Print varX + 1

This line is a statement because it's a complete instruction; the computer will do something after this line is executed. Print is a keyword with a special meaning to the computer. varX + 1 is an expression combining a + operator, a variable (varX), and a numeric constant (1). It is also an argument that supplies something to Print to complete a task.

7. A variable is a name you give to Visual Basic to specify an amount of memory for storing data. A value is the data you store in the variable. A variable can change its value (stored data) from one moment to another.

8. Variant. If you use a variable without declaring it first, Visual Basic treats it as a Variant. It has no fixed length and can expand up to 8 bytes to accommodate a large numeric and up to 64KB to store a text string.

9. A memory area with 8 bytes is set aside to store data up to that length. Even if nothing is assigned to the variable, it has the length of 8 bytes.

10. Dim varX as String * 10

If more is assigned, only 10 are retained. If fewer, the variable is padded with extra spaces to make up a total of 10 characters.

11. The variable has the initial length of 0. You can then assign a string that is up 2GB in length.

12. The overflow error will appear because the product exceeds an integer data type. Since both operands are integers, Visual Basic performs an integer multiplication. When the product exceeds the limit, Visual Basic cannot store the whole thing as an integer. The solution is to add a suffix (such as ! or @) to tell Visual Basic to go by a higher-precision data type.

13. The first will trigger the overflow error because Visual Basic treats both numbers as integers and performs an integer addition. Since the sum exceeds an integer's limit, the error results. In the second case, the & tells Visual Basic that this is a long integer. The sum is thus stored as a long integer, and no error occurs.

14. It prints "abc" to the screen. Variable Arr is a Variant to which three array elements are assigned. In the For loop, each element is concatenated to variable varX. The last line prints the concatenated text string.

15. Integer and Variant( ). Variable varA, being a Variant, can be assigned any data type. The first assigned value, 123, is an integer; so TypeName returns Integer. Then an array is assigned; so TypeName prints Variant( ).

16. The first performs a division and returns the result. Visual Basic treats the result as a Single or Double data type. In the second case, Visual Basic returns the whole number quotient and discards any remainder. The returned value is either an Integer or Long Integer data type.

17. \ extracts the whole number quotient. Mod returns the remainder. In both cases, the operands will be converted to integers if necessary and rounded off.

18. In the first case, \ has higher precedence over Mod. First 40 \ 3 evaluates to 13. Then 100 Mod 13 returns 9 (remainder). In the second case, 100 Mod 40 evaluates to 20. Then 20 \ 3 returns 6.

19. The first Boolean expression (varA $>$ = varB) evaluates to True (-1); read the statement as:

    If varA is greater than OR equal to varB, Then . . .

    The second statement has two conditional expressions. The first is true, but the second is false. The compound expression thus returns False (0).

20. It negates the Visible property of Text1. If Text1 is visible at design time, the statement will make it invisible. If Visible is set to False at design time, the statement will make it visible.

21. 3. The Mod operator has higher precedence than +. 11 Mod 3 returns the remainder of 2. 1 + 2 returns 3.

22. 246 and 5. When one operand is a numeric and the other is a number stored as text, + performs an addition. The second number indicates the data type to be Double (see Table 4.2).

23. 123123 and 8. Since both are text strings, Visual Basic performs a concatenation. The second number shows the result to be a String data type.

24. varX=3, varY=0. 01 Or 10 returns 11 in binary, which is 2+1=3 in decimal. 01 And 10 returns 0 in both binary and decimal.

25. Put a comment after an apostrophe (') or Rem. Rem must be placed at the beginning of a separate line. An apostrophe can be placed anywhere. Anything after Rem or ' is ignored during execution.

26. Yes. Separate one from another with a colon (:). It is, however, not a sound practice because such code is hard to read, debug, or document.

27. A separate file with the BAS file name extension. Like a Basic file of the old days, it contains code and declarations. However, it cannot contain objects as a form can. A module can be incorporated into multiple applications.

28. When a variable is declared (using Dim) in a procedure or used without declaration, it is a local variable. It exists and can normally hold a value when the procedure is executed. It ceases to exist when the procedure is finished.

29. A global variable exists whenever an application is run. It can be seen by all the components of the application, such as a procedure in a form or module. This can lead to side effects because its alteration in one area can affect its behavior in another area. A global variable is declared with the Global keyword in the Declarations section of a module, not a form.

30. The area of a form or module containing only variable declarations. In the Code window of a form or module, there is a (general) item in the Object box. After you click it, the Procedure box should show (declarations). You can now declare variables.

31. s a built-in variable name that has been assigned a constant value. You can use the online help to show many intrinsic constants. Some examples:

    vbRed
    vbBlue
    vbCrLf
    vbTab

    Consider this statement:

    Text1.Text = "line1" & vbCrLf & "line2"

    If Text1's MultiLine property is True, two lines will appear.

32. It is used to define a constant—declaring a variable and assigning a value to it. Once defined, the variable name can be used in place of the assigned value. However, you cannot assign another value during execution. That

distinguishes a constant from a variable. A constant can be defined in a procedure, at form level, module level, or global level.

33. The first will print "Joe" and the second nothing. The second Fname is a local variable and is different from the first. This happens even if you've declared Fname at the form level.

34. "Joe" is printed to the screen by both procedures. Command2 can now "see" this form-level variable.

CHAPTER 6, PROGRAM FLOW

1.b, 2.a, 3.c, 4.F, 5.T, 6.T, 7.F, 8.F, 9.T, 10.F, 11.F, 12.d, 13.b, 14.a, 15.F, 16.F, 17.F, 18.F, 19.T, 20.10, 21.9, 22.F, 23.T, 24.T, 25.F, 26.Until, 27.c, 28.e 29.F, 30.e

1. By default Visual Basic compares text strings in Binary mode. The two compared strings are equal if they match in spelling as well as case. If you add Option Compare Text in the Declarations section, then case is ignored. In that case, "Ace" and "ace" will be considered equal.

2. No. If varX is 100, the first will show "small" and the second nothing. To make the second identical to the first, change its second expression to:
    varX <= 100

3.
```
Sub Command1_Click ( )
    Dim Age As Integer

    Age = InputBox("Enter your age:")

    Select Case Age
    Case Is < 21
        Print "You're a minor."
    Case 21 To 65
        Print "You're an adult."
    Case Is > 65
        Print "You're a senior citizen."
    End Select
End Sub
```

4. This is a useless expression. It will match anything. If varX is neither, then both will be true. If varX is "yes", then the first is false but the second is

true. If varX is "no", then the reverse. So whatever the value of varX, this line will be executed.

5.
```
Sub Form_Click ( )
    Dim varX As Integer
    varX = InputBox("Enter a number:")
    Select Case varX
        Case Is < 100
            Print "small"
        Case 100 To 200
            Print "medium"
        Case Is > 200
            Print "big"
    End Select
End Sub
```

6.
```
Sub Form_Click ( )
    Dim varX As String
    varX = InputBox("Enter a character:")
    Select Case varX
        Case "A" To "Z", "a" To "z"
            Print "alphabet"
        Case "0" To "9"
            Print "digit"
        Case Else
            Print "invalid"
    End Select
End Sub
```

7. The first will match a test expression that returns any value, so it's a meaningless expression. The second expression will be executed only if varX has the value of 0. The Both expressions should thus be avoided.

8. Depending on the value of varX, the expression will return five possible remainders: 0, 1, 2, 3, and 4.

9. Divide any supplied name into three groups. Both uppercase and lowercase entries are included. In the last case, if only z and Z are used, then a name like Zimp will be excluded because it goes beyond a single Z.

10. It's a legal but meaningless expression. I will match nothing because the higher value is placed before To and the lower value after it. Reverse the order and it may match something.

11.
```
Sub Form_Click ( )
    Dim varX As Integer
    Dim I as Integer

    varX = InputBox("Enter ending number:")
    For I = 1 To varX
        Print I
    Next
End Sub
```

12.
```
Sub Form_Click ( )
    Dim varX As Integer, varY As Integer, I As Integer
    varX = InputBox("Enter beginning number:")
    varY = InputBox("Enter ending number:")
    For I = varX To varY
        Print I
    Next I
End Sub
```

13.
```
Sub Form_Click ( )
    Dim varX As Integer, varY As Integer
    Dim varZ As Integer, I As Integer

    varX = InputBox("Enter beginning number:")
    varY = InputBox("Enter ending number:")
    varZ = InputBox("Enter step number:")

    For I = varX To varY Step varZ
        Print I
    Next I
End Sub
```

14.
```
Sub Form_Click ( )
    Dim I As Integer
    For I = -20 To -10 Step 2
        Print I
    Next I
End Sub
```

15. 6 is shown. When I has 1, J goes from 1 to 3. varX is 3 at this point. Then I goes to 2 and J goes from 2 to 3; varX is 5. Then I goes to 3 and J goes from 3 to 3; varX is 6 at the end.

16. 4 and 0. I is 1 more than the ending value after the looping operation. varX starts out with no value. Multiplying 0 to each successive number produces 0.

17.
```
Sub Form_Click ( )
   Dim I As Integer, J As Integer
   For I = 0 To 4
      For J = 1 To 5
         Print I + J; 'same line
      Next J
   Print              'new line
   Next I
End Sub
```

18.
```
Sub Form_Click ( )
   Dim I As Integer, J As Integer
   For I = 4 To 0 Step -1
      For J = 5 To 1 Step -1
         Print I + J; 'same line
      Next J
   Print              'new line
   Next I
End Sub
```

19.
```
Sub Form_Click ( )
   Dim I As Integer
   Do While i < 10
      I = I + 1
      Print I
   Loop
End Sub
```

20.
```
Sub Form_Click ( )
   Dim I As Integer
   Do
      I = I + 1
      Print I
   Loop While I < 10
```

End Sub

21.
```
Sub Form_Click ( )
    Dim I As Integer
    Do
        I = I + 1
        Print I
    Loop Until I > = 10
End Sub
```

22.
```
    Do
        I = I + 1
        Print I
        If I = 10 Then Exit Do
    Loop
```

23.
```
Sub Form_Click ( )
    Dim I As Integer
    Do
        I = I + 1
        Print I
        If I = 10 Then GoTo out
    Loop
out:
End Sub
```

24. In the first, the loop is not entered if the condition is not met. In the second, the loop is entered at least once because the condition is placed after the statements.

25. It prompts the user to enter a number. If no number is entered, then execution branches to line 20, thus existing the procedure. If the supplied number is higher than 100, then it prints "It's too high." If the number is from 50 to 100, then it prints "It's OK." If the number is below 50, the it prints "It's too low." Then another prompt appears. If the user supplies "yes", execution branches to line 10 again; if not, the procedure ends.

26.
```
Sub Command1_Click ( )
    Dim varX
    Do
        varX = InputBox("What's the asking price?")
```

```
        If varX = "" Then Exit Sub
        If varX > 100 Then Print "It's too high."
        If varX <= 100 And varX >= 50 Then Print "OK."
        If varX < 50 Then Print "It's too low."
        varX = InputBox("Try again?")
    Loop While varX = "yes"
End Sub
```

27.
```
Sub Command1_Click ( )
    Dim varX
    Do
        varX = InputBox("What's the asking price?")
        If varX = "" Then Exit Sub
        If varX > 100 Then Print "It's too high."
        If varX <= 100 And varX >= 50 Then Print "OK."
        If varX < 50 Then Print "It's too low."
        varX = InputBox("Try again?")
    Loop Until varX = "no"
End Sub
```

28.
```
Sub Command1_Click ( )
    Dim varX
    Do
        varX = InputBox("What's the asking price?")
        If varX = "" Then Exit Sub
        If varX > 100 Then Print "It's too high."
        If varX <= 100 And varX >= 50 Then Print "OK."
        If varX < 50 Then Print "It's too low."

        Do
            varX = InputBox("Try again?")
            If varX = "yes" Or varX = "no" Then
                Exit Do
            Else
                MsgBox "You must enter yes or no"
            End If
        Loop
    Loop Until varX = "no"
End Sub
```

29.
```
Private Sub Command1_Click( )
    Dim I As Integer, J As Integer, K As Integer
```

```
    For I = 1 To 9
       For J = 1 To 9
          Print Chr(I + 64) & J;  'print on same line
          K = K + 8       'increment 8 tab stops
          Print Tab(K);   'move print head by 8
       Next J
       K = 0              'go back to new position
       Print             'a new line
    Next I
End Sub
```

30.
```
Private Sub Form_Click( )
    Dim Num1, Num2, arrNum1, arrNum2
    arrNum1 = Array("A", "B", "C", "D", "E", "F", "G", "H", "I")
    arrNum2 = Array(1, 2, 3, 4, 5, 6, 7, 8, 9)
    For Each Num1 In arrNum1
       For Each Num2 In arrNum2
          Print Num1 & Num2; Tab(Num2 * 8);
             'printer product, move print head by 5
       Next Num2
       Print          'a new line
    Next Num1
End Sub
```

31. 6TABULATE1.FRM

32.
```
Private Sub Form_Click( )
    Dim DecreaseRate As Single
    Dim Total As Single
    Dim I As Integer, YearNum As Integer

    Total = 3000
    YearNum = 5    'number of days
    For I = 1 To YearNum
       DecreaseRate = Total * 0.3    'rate of decrease
       Total = Total - DecreaseRate     'total
       Print "year " & I, Total
    Next I
End Sub
```

33. Add Label3 (change Caption to Name), Text3 (change Name to txtName and erase Text), and Command3 (change Name to cmdPrint and Caption to Print) to the left. Add the following code:

```
Sub cmdPrint_Click ( )
    Printer.Print txtName.Text
    Printer.Print txtInc.Text
    Printer.Print txtTax.Text
    Printer.EndDoc        'flush printer buffer
End Sub
```

34. There are two ways to do that. The first is to change its TabIndex to 0 at design time. The other way is to add this procedure:

```
Sub Form_Load ( )
    txtName.TabIndex = 0
End Sub
```

When the program is run, this procedure will automatically shift the focus to Text3.

35.
```
Select Case Income
    Case Is > 263750
        Tax = T4 + (Income - 263750) * 0.396
    Case Is > 147700
        Tax = T3 + (Income - 147700) * 0.36
    Case Is > 96900
        Tax = T2 + (Income - 96900) * 0.31
    Case Is > 40100
        Tax = T1 + (Income - 40100) * 0.28
    Case Else
        Tax = Income * 0.15
End Select
```

36.
```
Private Sub Form_Click()
    Dim intA As Integer
    Dim intB As Integer
    Dim I As Integer
    Dim Sum As Integer

    intA = 0          '1st number
    intB = 1          '2nd number
    Print intB;       'print 1st number
    For I = 2 To 10
        Sum = intA + intB   '2 previous numbers
        Print Sum;    'print
        intA = intB          'put 2nd value in 1st var
```

```
            intB = Sum        'put sum in 2nd var
        Next I
End Sub
```

37.
```
Private Sub Form_Click()
    Dim intA As Integer
    Dim intB As Integer
    Dim I As Integer
    Dim Sum As Integer

    intA = 0            '1st number
    intB = 1               '2nd number
    I = 1            '1st term
    Print intB;        'print 1st num
    Do While I < 10
        I = I + 1     'control looping
        Sum = intA + intB   '2 previous numbers
        Print Sum;  'print
        intA = intB        'put 2nd value in 1st var
        intB = Sum       'put sum in 2nd var
    Loop
End Sub
```

38.
```
Private Sub Form_Click()
    Dim intA As Integer
    Dim intB As Integer
    Dim I As Integer
    Dim Sum As Integer
    Dim varX As Variant

    intA = 0            '1st number
    intB = 1               '2nd number
    I = 1
    varX = Val(InputBox("Which term?"))
        'get user input, convert to numeric
    If varX < = 1 Then Exit Sub
        'if no entry or 1
    Do While varX > I
        I = I + 1    'track terms
        Sum = intA + intB   '2 previous numbers
        intA = intB        'put 2nd value in 1st var
        intB = Sum       'put sum in 2nd var
    Loop
```

```
        Print "Term"; varX; "= "; Sum
End Sub
```

39.

```
Private Sub Form_Click()
    Dim Divisor As Integer
    Dim I As Integer
    Dim Pi As Double

    Pi = 4  'initial value of pi
    Divisor = 1   'divisor
    Do While DoEvents()    'infinite loop, allow break
        I = I + 1   'control odd or even
        Divisor = Divisor + 2   '3, 5, 7...
        If I Mod 2 Then
            Pi = Pi - 4 / Divisor    'odd
        Else
            Pi = Pi + 4 / Divisor     'even
        End If
        Caption = I & " : " & Pi      'show caption
    Loop
End Sub
```

40.

```
Private Sub Form_Click()
    Dim varA As Integer, varB As Integer
    Dim Str1 As String, Str2 As String

    varA = 0: varB = -1
    Select Case varA        'determine varA's value
    Case Is > 0
        Str1 = "varA is positive"
        Select Case varB     'determine varB's value
        Case Is > 0
            Str2 = "varB is positive"
        Case Is < 0
            Str2 = "varB is negative"
        Case 0
            Str2 = "varB is zero"
        End Select
    Case Is < 0
        Str1 = "varA is negative"
        Select Case varB     'determine varB's value
        Case Is > 0
            Str2 = "varB is positive"
```

```
       Case Is < 0
           Str2 = "varB is negative"
       Case 0
           Str2 = "varB is zero"
       End Select
   Case 0
       Str1 = "varA is zero"
       Select Case varB    'determine varB's value
       Case Is > 0
           Str2 = "varB is positive"
       Case Is < 0
           Str2 = "varB is negative"
       Case 0
           Str2 = "varB is zero"
       End Select
   End Select
   Print Str1  'varA's value
   Print Str2  'varB's value
End Sub
```

CHAPTER 7, BUILT-IN FUNCTIONS

1.a, 2.d, 3.c, 4.d, 5.e, 6.a, 7.b, 8.F, 9.T, 10.c, 11.b, 12.b, 13.400, 14.300, 15.F, 16.Pmt, 17.a, 18.F, 19.e, 20.d, 21.c, 22.b, 23.a, 24.T, 25.1000, 26.Timer, 27.T, 28.T, 29.3/18/98, 30.Weekday

1. Fix chops off any decimal fraction. Int does the same thing except when an argument is a negative number with a decimal fraction. In that case the number is rounded down. So Int(-1.1) returns -2.

2. Print Fix(10 * Rnd) + 1

    Rnd can return 0 to 0.9999. Multiplying this number by 10 returns 9.999. Fix (or Int) chops off the decimal portion.

3. If the argument is >0, then a new random number is generated each time the program is run--even though the same positive number is used. If it is 0, it returns the previously generated number. If you supply the same negative number, the same random number will be returned again and again. If you supply a new negative number, a new random number will be generated.

4. Atn(4 / 3) returns 0.9273 radian as the angle's value. The following formula converts it to 53 degrees:

Atn(4 / 3) * 180 / (Atn(1) * 4)   'Atn(Y/X)*180/Pi

Either formula below will return the value of R as 5:

4 / Sin(Atn(4 / 3))   'R=Y/Sin
3 / Cos(Atn(4 / 3))   'R=X/Cos

5. SLN: 680
    DDB: 1560.00, 936.00, 561.60, 336.96, 5.44
    SYD: 1133.33, 906.69, 680.00, 453.33, 226.67

6. Double-click one of the option buttons to go to the Code window. The Click
    procedure template appears. Enter the statement shown below:

Sub Option1_Click (Index As Integer)
    cmdCalculate_Click 'call sub when clicked
End Sub

7. Nothing. Clicking it at this point does not trigger its Click procedure because
    its Value property has been set to True at design time. If you press Enter
    after typing the numbers, you will trigger this procedure. The same thing
    happens if you click another option button and then return to SLN. In order
    to make SLN respond to clicking for the first time, it should not be selected
    (Value set to True) at design time.

8. Nothing. Since no option button is selected, the code in Command1_Click
    procedure detects no option chosen and skips all the control structures. At the
    end, the variable D has nothing assigned to it. This is then shown in Text4.
    Thus nothing is shown.

9.
Sub cmdPrint_Click()
    Printer.Print txtCost.Text
    Printer.Print txtSalvage.Text
    Printer.Print txtLife.Text
    Printer.Print txtResult.Text
        'print 4 textbox text
    Printer.EndDoc 'flush printer buffer
End Sub

10.
Sub cmdPrint_Click()
    Printer.Print lblCost.Caption, txtCost.Text
    Printer.Print lblSalvage.Caption, txtSalvage.Text
    Printer.Print lblLife.Caption, txtLife.Text

```
      Printer.Print txtResult.Text
      Printer.EndDoc  'flush printer buffer
   End Sub
```

11. Pmt(.08 / 12, 10 * 12, 10000, 0, 0) = 121

12. Pmt(.08 / 12, 10 * 12, 0, 10000, 0) = 55

13. Change I = txtInt.Text / 12 to:

    I = txtInt.Text / 12 / 100

14. Change I = txtInt.Text / 12 to
        If I > 1 then I = txtInt.Text / 12 / 100

15. 7MORT3.FRM

16. Replace the Strn= line with:

    Strn = InputBox("Enter a string.")

17. The program has two of this line:
        For J = Asc("a") To Asc("z")
    Change it to:
        For J = Asc(" ") To Asc("~")
    Make sure there is a space inside the first pair of quotes.
    Also change the Dim declaration to:
        Dim Count(32 To 126) As Integer
    ANSI 32 is the space character and 126 is the ~ character. The characters in
    between are printable.

18. Add & before a letter in the label, such as &Enter. Set the TabIndex property
    to 0 for the label and 1 for the first text box. When the user presses Alt+E,
    focus goes to the object that has the TabIndex property next to the label.

19. Add & in the Caption property of each. You can now press either access key
    to change the result.

20.
```
Sub Text1_Change ( )
   If Text1.Text = "" Then
      Text2.Text = ""      'if nothing, erase
   Else                 'if something, show
      Text2.Text = Asc(Text1.Text)
   End If
```

End Sub

21. Reverse the two labels at the top. Change Asc(Text1.Text) to Chr(Text1.Text).

22. Set the Interval property to 1000 at design time. Write the following code and run the program.

```
Sub Timer1_Timer ( )
    Static staK As Integer
    staK = staK + 1
    Print staK, "second"
    If staK = 10 Then End
End Sub
```

23. Change the timer's Interval property to 60000 at design time and write the following procedure.

```
Sub Timer1_Timer ( )
    Static staK As Integer
    staK = staK + 1
    If staK = 50 Then
        Print "Warning, you've 10 minute left."
    End If
    If staK = 60 Then End
End Sub
```

24. Visual Basic uses a Double (8-byte) number to handle date-time data. The integer portion represents date and the decimal portion is used for time. A date number can be positive or negative. The dividing point for date is 12/30/1899 and the starting point for time is midnight. A negative integer represents a day before the dividing point and a positive integer a day after that. Each day is 1 apart. So 0.0 represents midnight 12/30/1899. -1.5 is noon the day before and 2.5 is noon two days after.

25. Add Timer1 and Text1 to the form. Change Timer1's Interval property to 1000. Add the following line to the Timer procedure.

    Text1.Text = Hour(Now) & ":" & Minute(Now) & ":" & Second(Now)

26. Add Timer1 and change its Interval to 1000 at design time. Add the following procedure.

```
Sub Timer1_Timer ( )
    Static staK As Integer
```

```
    Text1.Text = staK
    staK = staK + 1
    If staK = 60 Then End
End Sub
```

27. Add Timer1 and change its Interval to 1000 at design time. Declare variable varK at the form level. Add the following two procedures.

```
Sub Form_Load ( )
    varK = 60
End Sub
```

```
Sub Timer1_Timer ( )
    varK = varK - 1
    Text1.Text = varK
    If varK = 0 Then End
End Sub
```

28. Declare variable varX at the form level. Add the following two procedures.

```
Sub Form_Load ( )
    varX = Timer
End Sub
```

```
Sub Form_Click ( )
    Print CInt(Timer - varX)
End Sub
```

29. Add the following line to the end of the Form_Click procedure to call the procedure and assign the current Timer value to varX:

    Form_Load

30. 7TIMER2.FRM

31. 7TIMER3.FRM

32. 377 days.

```
    Print DateValue("4/1/97") - DateValue("3/20/96")
    Print DateDiff("d", "3/20/96", "4/1/97")
```

CHAPTER 8, MANAGING PROCEDURES, DEBUGGING, AND PROJECTS

1.d, 2.a, 3.c, 4.b, 5.T, 6.F, 7.F, 8.d, 9.e, 10.Property Get, 11.a, 12.syntax, 13.b, 14.d, 15.T, 16.F, 17.F, 18.d, 19.d, 20.b, 21.c, 22.c, 23.e, 24.Sub Main, 25.T, 26.F, 27.Environment, 28.T, 29.e, 30.a

1. A sub caller is a complete statement, but a function caller is an expression and cannot stand alone. A function caller must have a pair of parentheses at the end, but sub caller normally does not—unless Call is used or you mean to pass arguments by value. To return a value to the caller, the called function uses the function name to communicate with the caller. A sub procedure returns no value to a caller.

2. Normally, when you pass an argument to a procedure, you do it by reference. The procedure has access to the memory address and can alter its value. If you pass an argument to a procedure by value, you hand it a copy of the argument, not the original address. The original value cannot be changed by the procedure.

3. Put the ByVal keyword before a specific variable's name in the called sub or function procedure's header. You can also add an extra pair of parentheses to a specific variable of the caller. This method does not require the use of ByVal anywhere.

4.
```
Function Avg(ParamArray Nums())
    Dim I As Integer
    Dim Item As Variant
    Dim Total As Single

    For Each Item In Nums
        Total = Total + Item    'add up array elements
        I = I + 1
    Next Item
        Avg = Total / I      'return average
End Function
```

5.
```
Public Function Pay(Deduct, Hours, Rate)
    Dim Pay1 As Single
```

```
        If Hours < = 40 Then
            Pay1 = Hours * Rate    'regular
        Else
            Pay1 = Rate * 40 + Rate * 1.5 * (Hours - 40)
        End If          'overtime
        Pay = Pay1 * (1 - Deduct)   'return after deduction
    End Function
```

6.
```
Function Commission(Price, List, Sell)
    Dim ComRate As Single   'commission rate

    If List = False And Sell = False Then
        ComRate = 0         'if none
    End If
    If List = True Or Sell = True Then
        ComRate = 0.035     'if only one
    End If
    If List = True And Sell = True Then
        ComRate = 0.07      'if both
    End If
    Commission = ComRate * Price    'return call
End Function
```

7.
```
Sub Form_Click()
    Dim Num As Integer
    Dim RetVal As Long

    Num = 10
    RetVal = Fac(Num)
    Print RetVal
End Sub

Function Fac(Num)
    Dim I As Integer, Total As Long

    Total = 1
    For I = Num To 1 Step -1
        Total = Total * I       '10*9*8...
    Next I
    Fac = Total
End Function
```

8. No, change Dim to Static or make I a form-level variable. Dim sets I to 0 each time the procedure calls itself and so the If statement is never true.

9. The string will be printed to the screen three times. The procedure will call itself twice. When I reaches 3, the second Print is executed twice and 3 is printed each time because the procedure was called twice.

10. 5, 4, 3, 2, 1, 0 will be printed. The Test procedure is called and 5 is passed. The procedure continues to call itself when Arg greater than 0.

11.
```
Private Sub Command1_Click()
  Print "Sum "; Test(10)
End Sub

Function Test(Arg)
  Static Sum     'Static to keep value
  If Arg > 0 Then 'continue until 0
   Sum = Sum + Arg 'add each Arg to sum
   Test (Arg - 1)  'call self and pass 1 lower value
  End If
  Test = Sum     'return to call with sum
End Function
```

12.
```
Property Get MyName( )
  MyName = "John Smith"
End Property
```

13. In Command1_Click, the MyName line calls the Let procedure, which assigns the passed name to the form-level MeName variable. The NickName line calls the Get procedure, which assigns a string to MyName, which is assigned to NickName. The last line prints the MeName and NickName properties.

14. Add Text2 and change the calling procedure to this:

```
Private Sub cmdSet_Click( )   'Listing 2
  Set TxtDemo(Text2) = Text1  'arg1=text2, arg2=text1
  . . .
```

    Then change the property procedure's header to this (add another variable to the original):

Property Set TxtDemo(Wid, varX)
    . . .

Since Text2 is the first passed argument, it is assigned to variable Wid. The Property Set procedure then processes only Text2 and does nothing to variable varX, which contains Text1.

15. Change the calling statement to this:

Set TxtDemo(0, 0, Width, vbBlue, vbCyan, 20, "Demo") = Text1

Change the procedure header to the following. Also, replace all the values in the procedure body with the variables (A, B, C, etc.).

Property Set TxtDemo(A, B, C, D, E, F, G, W)

16.

```
Dim BkCo, FntSize, FrCo      'module-level vars

Private Sub Command1_Click()
   Form1.CusBox = False     'restore original values
End Sub

Private Sub Form_Click()
   With Text1
      BkCo = .BackColor    'store original values
      FntSize = .FontSize
      FrCo = .ForeColor
   End With
   Form1.CusBox = True      'call proc to change values
End Sub

Property Let CusBox(Prop As Boolean)
   If Prop Then  'if True
      With Text1
         .BackColor = vbCyan
         .FontSize = 12
         .ForeColor = vbBlue
      End With
   Else        'if False
      With Text1
         .BackColor = BkCo
         .FontSize = FntSize
         .ForeColor = FrCo
      End With
```

End If
End Property

17. A breakpoint is the line where Visual Basic goes into break mode. To set a breakpoint, move the cursor to the desired line and press F9; you can press F9 a second time to turn it off. You can also click the Margin Indicator Bar to set a breakpoint. When execution reaches this line, Visual Basic halts execution and goes into break mode. A number of ‹ ebugging tools become available.

18. The Stop statement is highlighted, and Visual Basic goes into break mode.. This is the same as setting breakpoint on the Stop line. Various debugging tools are now available.

19. Just move the pointer over a variable's name and its current value will pop up. If you want an expression's value, highlight it and its data tip will pop up.

20 Yes. Just choose Tools | Add Watch. If the cursor is on the desired variable or an expression has been highlighted, it enters the Expression box; if not, nothing appears here. Click OK after you make an entry in the Expression box. The expression will appear in the Watches window.

21. Right-click the desired line and choose Toggle from the popup menu. Then choose Bookmark from that list. Do the same thing to remove the bookmark.

22. Just select it and press Del from the keyboard. You can also right-click it to select it and pop up a shortcut menu. You can then choose Add Watch, Edit Watch, or Delete Watch.

23. Choose Call Stack (Ctrl+L) from the View menu or click the three-dot button at the top right of the Locals window to show the Call Stack dialog box. It shows existing procedures and how they are related. You can choose to show a related procedure.

24. The Erl and Error are functions that respectively return a line (if any) where error is located and the error message. Error can be given a numeric argument to return a particular error message. It can also be used as a statement to simulate an error occurrence. Err is an object with methods and properties. The default property is Number, so Err and Err.Number return the same value.

25. 2 and 1. The first Print line causes an error (division by zero). So execution is diverted to ErrTrap. Number 2 is then printed. The Resume Next line

directs execution back to the statement after the error line, which then prints 1.

26. (1) Form1 is removed, and the Project window shows nothing under Project1. At this point, the startup object (Project | Project Properties | General tab) is changed to Sub Main—since there is no form. (2) Form1 reappears and is added to the Project window. The startup object remains Sub Main. If you want to run the new Form1, you'll have to change the startup object from Sub Main to Form1.

27. A project file has the VBP extension, plus the name supplied by you. This is an ASCII file listing all the component files of the project. When you load this file, all the component files—if they can be found—are automatically loaded. This saves you the trouble of having to load them separately and manually. If a project consists of only a form file, you don't need a project file; you can load that form file by yourself without having to maintain a separate project file.

28. When you have multiple modules loaded, you can select a name in the Project window and choose View Code or View Form to go to a module. You can right-click a name in the Project window to pop up the shortcut menu and do a number of things to the file, such as saving, removing, or printing. You can also drag a file from My Computer or Explorer to the Project window to add a module to the current project.

29. Press F2 to show the Object Browser. Select a project from the Project/ Library box (top left). Click a module name in the Classes box. The Members box displays all the available options. Scroll to the desired option. Double-click it or click it and click View Definition (fourth button from the left). The cursor goes to the desired procedure.

30. Use Project | References to show all the applications with browsable objects. Check the desired one, Microsoft Excel for example, and click OK to close the dialog box. Press F2 to show the Object Browser. From the Project/Library box at the top, click the down arrow to show all the options. Click Excel to show its classes. Click a desired one to show its methods and properties. Click a method or property to show its details at the bottom panel.

31.
```
Function Rept(Char, Num)
    Dim I As Integer
    Dim Temp As String

    For I = 1 To Num
        Temp = Temp & Char
```

```
      Next
      Rept = Temp
   End Function
```

32.
```
Function Faht (Cent)
   Faht = (9 / 5) * Cent + 32
End Function
```

33.
```
Function Fibon(Num)
   Dim intA As Integer
   Dim intB As Integer
   Dim I As Integer
   Dim Sum As Integer

   intA = 0          '1st number
   intB = 1          '2nd number
   I = 1
   Do While Num > I
      I = I + 1     'track terms
      Sum = intA + intB   '2 previous numbers
      intA = intB        'put 2nd value in 1st var
      intB = Sum         'put sum in 2nd var
   Loop
   Fibon = Sum
End Function
```

34.
```
Function Reverse(Strn)
   Dim I As Integer
   Dim Temp As String

   For I = Len(Strn) To 1 Step -1 'from last to 1st
      Temp = Temp & Mid(Strn, I, 1)    'get each letter
   Next
   Reverse = Temp                'return
End Function
```

35.
```
Private Sub Command1_Click()
   Dim varA As Integer, varB As Integer
   Dim Str1 As String, Str2 As String

   varA = 0: varB = -1
```

```
    Select Case varA        'determine varA's value
    Case Is > 0
       Str1 = "A is positive"
       Str2 = Select2(varB)
    Case Is < 0
       Str1 = "A is negative"
       Str2 = Select2(varB)
    Case 0
       Str1 = "A is zero"
       Str2 = Select2(varB)
    End Select
    Print Str1  'A's value
    Print Str2  'B's value
End Sub

Function Select2(Num2)
    Select Case Num2    'determine B's value
    Case Is > 0
       Select2 = "B is positive"
    Case Is < 0
       Select2 = "B is negative"
    Case 0
       Select2 = "B is zero"
    End Select
End Function
```

CHAPTER 9, ARRAYS, CONTROL ARRAYS, AND COLLECTIONS

1.c, 2.F, 3.T, 4.Base, 5.42, 6.F, 7.T, 8.5, 9.T, 10.F, 11.F, 12.B, 13.T, 14.550, 15.2, 16.control array, 17.F, 18.F, 19.TypeOf, 20.b, 21.c, 22.d, 23.e, 24.a, 25.Nothing, 26.Me, 27.b, 28.c, 29.F, 30.1

1. A group of related variables sharing the same name. A one-dimensional array has one subscript range, which supplies index numbers to identify each of the elements in an array. A multidimensional array has multiple subscripts. An array can be declared with the Dim statement in the Declarations section or with the Dim, ReDim, or Static statement in a procedure.

2. It will print -10, -9 ... -1. The ReDim statement is legal. Negative numbers are allowed here, but the one before To must be lower than the one after it.

3. An array with no fixed subscript range. For a form-level array, declare an empty array in the Declarations section with the Dim keyword. Before an array is used in a procedure, supply a required subscript range with the ReDim keyword. The value can be determined by the program or by the user. For a local array, the empty declaration is not necessary.

4. Put the first line below at the beginning of the procedure. Replace the middle line of the procedure with the second line below.

```
K = 64
Num(Row, Col) = Chr(K)
```

5.
```
Sub Form_Click ( )
    Dim Col As Integer
    Dim Row As Integer
    Dim K As Integer
    Dim Num(1 To 3, 1 To 3) As Integer

    For Row = 1 To 3        'assign to array
        For Col = 1 To 3
            K = K + 1
            Num(Row, Col) = K
        Next Col
    Next Row
    For Row = 1 To 3        'print array
        For Col = 1 To 3
            Print Num(Col, Row),    'same row
        Next Col
        Print               'new line
    Next Row
End Sub
```

6.
```
Sub Form_Click ( )
    Dim Col As Integer
    Dim Row As Integer
    Dim K As Integer
    Dim Num(1 To 3, 1 To 3) As Integer

    For Row = 1 To 3        'assign to array
        For Col = 1 To 3
            K = K + 1
            Num(Row, Col) = K
        Next Col
```

```
        Next Row
        For Row = 3 To 1 Step -1     'print array
            For Col = 1 To 3
                Print Num(Row, Col),     'same row
            Next Col
            Print                 'new line
        Next Row
    End Sub
```

7.
```
Sub Form_Click ( )
    Dim I As Integer
    Dim Ele1 As Integer
    Dim Num As Integer

    Num = InputBox("How many elements?")
    ReDim Arr(Num) As Variant      'dynamic array
    For I = 1 To Num
        Arr(I) = InputBox("Enter next element:", "Element #" & I)
        If Arr(I) = "" Then Exit For
    Next I

    Ele1 = Arr(1)        'first element
    Print "Element  1 ", Ele1
    For I = 2 To Num
        Print "Element "; I, Arr(I) 'print each
        If Val(Arr(I)) < Val(Ele1) Then Ele1 = Arr(I) 'exchange
    Next I
    Print "The lowest element is : "; Ele1
End Sub
```

8.
```
Sub Form_Click ( )
    Dim I As Integer
    Dim J As Integer
    Dim Ele1 As Integer
    Dim Num As Integer

    Num = InputBox("How many elements?")
    ReDim Arr(Num) As Variant      'dynamic array
    For I = 1 To Num
        Arr(I) = InputBox("Enter next element:", "Element #" & I)
        If Arr(I) = "" Then Exit For
    Next I
```

```
      Ele1 = Arr(1)        'first element
      Print "Element  1 ", Ele1
      For J = 2 To I - 1
         Print "Element "; J, Arr(J) 'print each
         If Val(Arr(J)) > Val(Ele1) Then Ele1 = Arr(J) 'exchange
      Next J
      Print "The highest element is : "; Ele1
   End Sub
```

9.
```
Sub Form_Click ( )
   Dim I As Integer
   Dim J As Integer
   Dim Ele1 As Integer
   Dim Num As Integer
   Dim Num1 As Integer

   Num = InputBox("How many elements?")
   ReDim Arr(Num) As Variant      'dynamic array
   For I = 1 To Num
      Arr(I) = InputBox("Enter next element:", "Element #" & I)
      If Arr(I) = "" Then Exit For
   Next I

   Num1 = GetHigh(Arr())    'call func
   For J = 1 To I - 1
      Print "Element "; J, Arr(J) 'print each
   Next J
   Print "The highest element is : "; Num1
End Sub

Function GetHigh(Arr())
   Dim I As Integer
   Dim Num As Integer

   Num = Arr(1)        'first element
   For I = 2 To UBound(Arr)
      If Val(Arr(I)) > Val(Num) Then Num = Arr(I) 'exchange
   Next I
   GetHigh = Num     'return high
End Function
```

10.
```
Sub Form_Click ( )
   Dim I As Integer
```

```
    Dim J As Integer
    Dim Ele1 As Integer
    Dim Num As Integer
    Dim Num1 As Single

    Num = InputBox("How many elements?")
    ReDim Arr(Num) As Variant        'dynamic array
    For I = 1 To Num
        Arr(I) = InputBox("Enter next element:", "Element #" & I)
        If Arr(I) = "" Then Exit For
    Next I

    Num1 = GetAvg(Arr(), I - 1)
        'call func, pass array and num of elements
    For J = 1 To I - 1
        Print "Element "; J, Arr(J) 'print each
    Next J
    Print "The average is : "; Num1
End Sub

Function GetAvg(Arr(), EleNum As Integer)
    Dim I As Integer
    Dim Sum As Integer

    For I = 1 To EleNum
        Sum = Sum + Val(Arr(I))
    Next I
    GetAvg = Sum / (I - 1)
End Function
```

11. If a local array is involved, pass it to a sub procedure like this:

    Call SubName(ArrayName( ))

    Here Call is optional. If omitted, the outer pair of parentheses must be erased. If you want to pass another argument, use a comma to separate one from another. The called argument may look like this:

    Sub SubName (Arr( ))

    Here we use a different name for the array. The same name can be used as well. They both refer to the same array. Changing one will also change the other.

12. varX = Avg(Num( ))

```
Function Avg (Sum( ))
    Dim varY
    . . .
    Avg = varY
End Function
```

The Num( ) array is passed to the function named Avg, which stores the array in the array named Sum( ). The two are the same array, so you can use the same name here. The called function returns a value by assigning it to the function name.

13.

```
Sub Command1_Click ( )
    Dim I As Integer
    Dim  Sum As Single

    Dim Shoe As Sportshoes  'declare type
    Shoe.Kind(0) = "tennis"
    Shoe.Kind(1) = "baseball"
    Shoe.Kind(2) = "bowling"
    Shoe.Cost(0) = 20
    Shoe.Cost(1) = 23
    Shoe.Cost(2) = 35
    For I = 0 To 2
        Print Shoe.Kind(I), Shoe.Cost(I)
        Sum = Sum + Shoe.Cost(I)
    Next I
    Print "Total = "; Sum, "Average = "; Sum / I
End Sub
```

14.

```
Private Sub Form_Click()
    Dim Arr As Variant
    Dim I As Variant
    Dim J As Variant

    Arr = Array(1, 2, 3, 4, 5, 6, 7, 8, 9)
    For Each I In Arr
        For Each J In Arr
            CurrentX = J * 400 - TextWidth(I * J)
            Print I * J;
        Next J
        Print
    Next I
End Sub
```

15.
```
For I = 1 To 5
   For J = 1 To 3
      Print Arr(J)(I),
   Next J
   Print
Next I
```

16.
```
Private Function Max(All As Variant)
   Dim I As Integer
   Dim Hi As Variant

   Hi = All(0)   'put 1st element in hi
   For I = 1 To UBound(All)
      If Hi < All(I) Then Hi = All(I)
   Next I
   Max = Hi      'return hi val to caller
End Function
```

17.
```
Private Function Min(All As Variant)
   Dim I As Integer
   Dim Lo As Variant

   Lo = All(0)   'put 1st element in hi
   For I = 1 To UBound(All)
      If Lo > All(I) Then Lo = All(I)
   Next I
   Min = Lo      'return hi val to caller
End Function
```

18.
```
Private Sub Above(All As Variant)
   Dim I, A1, A2, Sum, Avg
   For I = 0 To UBound(All)
      Sum = Sum + All(I)
   Next I
   Avg = Sum / I

   For I = 0 To UBound(All)
      If All(I) > Avg Then
         A1 = A1 + 1
      Else
         A2 = A2 + 1
```

```
        End If
    Next I
    Print "average: "; Avg
    Print "above average: "; A1
    Print "below average: "; A2
End Sub
```

19.
- Copy a control to the Clipboard and then paste it on the same form. You'll be asked whether you want to create a control array.

- Give the same Name (not Caption) property to two or more controls of the same time. You'll also be asked.
- Set a control's Index property to an integer value. After that, when you change a control's Name to the same as the one with an Index value, Visual Basic will keep track of index numbers.

20. It's a variable to which you can assign an object. An object (control) can have its name changed at design time, but not at run time. However, you can use an alias (a substitute name) to maneuver the object. To do that, you need to use Dim (or another command) to declare a variable. Then use Set to assign an object's name to the variable. You can then use the variable to maneuver the object.

21. Declare a variable as type Form1 (or another name you have given to the existing form). Use Set to assign to the variable a New Form1; this creates a new copy. Use the Show method to display the new copy.

22. If you declare an object variable to be a specific object type, such as ListBox, TextBox, or CommandButton, you can use the variable to reference only the specific type of controls. If you declare it to be a Control, then you can use it to reference any type of controls.

23. 9METRIC.FRM

24. 9CLONE1.FRM

25. Set Text1's TabIndex to 0. Set Add button's Default to True. Then add this procedure:

```
Sub cmdAdd_Click ( )
    List1.AddItem Text1.Text
    Text1.Text = ""
    Text1.SetFocus
End Sub
```

26. 9SORTADD.FRM

27. 9SORTNUM.FRM

28. 9SORTFUNC.FRM

29. 9SORTBOX.FRM

30. 9CALC.FRM

31. 9PASCAL.FRM

32.
```
Sub Form_Click()
    Dim I As Integer
    Dim Num As Integer

    Num = 10
    ReDim Fib(Num)
    Fib(1) = 1: Print Fib(1);       '1st num
    Fib(2) = 1: Print Fib(2);       '2nd num
    For I = 3 To Num
        Fib(I) = Fib(I - 1) + Fib(I - 2)
        Print Fib(I);       'sum of 2 previous
        Fib(I - 2) = Fib(I - 1) 'assign 1st val. to 2nd elem.
    Next I
End Sub
```

33.
```
Function Fibon(Num)
    Dim I As Integer

    If Num < 1 Then
        MsgBox "You've passed an invalid value."
        Exit Function
    End If
    If Num = 1 Or Num = 2 Then
        Fibon = 1
        Exit Function
    End If

    ReDim Fib(Num)
    Fib(1) = 1: Fib(2) = 1
    For I = 3 To Num
        Fib(I) = Fib(I - 1) + Fib(I - 2)
```

```
        If I = Num Then Exit For   'exit with last num
        Fib(I - 2) = Fib(I - 1) 'assign 1st val. to 2nd elem.
    Next I
    Fibon = Fib(I - 1)
End Function
```

34. 9DICE1.FRM

35. 9DICE2.FRM

36. 9DICE3.FRM

CHAPTER 10, FILE AND DATA MANAGEMENT

1.d, 2.T, 3.ItemCheck. 4.Locked, 5.F, 6.b, 7.c, 8.b, 9.T, 10.T, 11.e, 12.T, 13.F, 14.ChDir, 15.Kill, 16.F, 17.e, 18.a, 19.e, 20.FileLen, 21.LOF, 22.FreeFile, 23.b, 24.Len, 25.Loc, 26.Seek, 27.a, 28.e, 29.b, 30.T

1. By default it is set to 0 - None; selecting a new item deselects a previously selected item. If you change it to 1 - Simple, you can select multiple items, but doing so only one at a time. If you change it to 2 - Extended, you can hold down Shift to select a block or Ctrl+Shift to select another block without deselecting previously selected blocks.

2. It adds "ace" to the existing items in the List1 list box and places in the second place (0 is first).

3. They are properties for a list box or combo box and available at both design time and run time. They are both arrays containing lists of items. List contains the items added to the List property at design time or using the AddItem method at run time. ItemData entries can be added at design time by entering via the Properties window or assigning values at run time. You can keep the two in sync and maneuver each corresponding pair as a unit.

4. Add List1 to a new form. Stretch it as shown. Add the following code:

```
Sub Form_Load ( )
    List1.AddItem "Honolulu"
    List1.AddItem "San Francisco"
    List1.AddItem "Los Angeles"
    List1.AddItem "Washington"
    List1.AddItem "Seattle"
```

```
    List1.AddItem "New York"
End Sub
```

5.
```
Sub List1_Click ( )
    List1.RemoveItem List1.ListIndex
End Sub
```

6. At design time, change the list box's Sorted property to True. Add the
    following line inside (anywhere) the Form_Load procedure:

    ```
    List1.AddItem "Vacation Destinations:", 0
    ```

7.
```
Sub List1_Click ( )
    Text1.Text = "You've chosen " & List1.Text & " City."
End Sub
```

8. Add this line at the beginning of the List1_Click procedure:

    ```
    If List1.Selected(0) Then Exit Sub
    ```

9. List1 is a list box's Name property. The ListIndex property indicates the
    index value of the selected item. List is a string array containing all the items
    in a list box. So List1.List(List1.ListIndex) returns the name of the selected
    item. It's the same as List1.Text or List1 for short.

10. Add Combo1 to the form. Choose style 0 or 1 (the figure shows style 1). Use
    Replace (from the Edit menu) to replace all List1 with Combo1. Erase the
    Selected line (to identify a selected item in a list box; not applicable in a
    combo box) and add the following line to anywhere inside the Form_Load
    procedure:

    ```
    Combo1.Text = "Vacation Destinations:"
    ```

11.
```
Sub Combo1_Click()
    Dim Cost As Integer
    Select Case Combo1.List(Combo1.ListIndex)
        Case "New York": Cost = 1200
        Case "Seattle": Cost = 500
        Case "San Francisco": Cost = 700
        Case "Los Angeles": Cost = 750
        Case "Washington": Cost = 900
        Case "Honolulu": Cost = 1500
```

```
   End Select
   Text1.Text = Combo1.Text & " costs $" & Cost & "."
End Sub
```

12.
```
Sub Form_Load()
   Combo1.AddItem "Honolulu"
   Combo1.ItemData(Combo1.NewIndex) = 1500
   Combo1.AddItem "San Francisco"
   Combo1.ItemData(Combo1.NewIndex) = 700
   Combo1.AddItem "Los Angeles"
   Combo1.ItemData(Combo1.NewIndex) = 750
   Combo1.AddItem "Washington"
   Combo1.ItemData(Combo1.NewIndex) = 900
   Combo1.AddItem "Seattle"
   Combo1.ItemData(Combo1.NewIndex) = 500
   Combo1.AddItem "New York"
   Combo1.ItemData(Combo1.NewIndex) = 1200
   Combo1.Text = "Vacation Destinations"
End Sub

Sub Combo1_Click()
   Text1.Text = Combo1.Text & " costs $" & _
   Combo1.ItemData(Combo1.ListIndex) & "."
End Sub
```

13. In a list box, there is no Text property in the Properties window. At run
    time, List1.Text returns the name of an item selected from the list box. In a
    combo box, you can change the Text property (Combo1 is the default) at
    design time or run time—if you choose style 0 or 1. Your text appears in the
    edit box (top) of the combo box and is not part of the items to be selected by
    the user. If the user chooses an item, then it goes to the edit box, replacing
    the original text; the Combo1.Text property is also assigned this value (the
    name of the selected item). If you choose style 2, you cannot assign a value
    to this property at design time or run time. You can only use Combo1.Text
    to read what the user has chosen.

14. Add the following lines to the end of List1_Click

```
   Dim varX As Single
   varX = Val(txtAve.Text)
   Select Case varX
      Case Is >= 90
         txtGrade.Text = "A"
      Case Is < 90 And varX >= 80
```

```
        txtGrade.Text = "B"
    Case Is < 80 And varX > = 70
        txtGrade.Text = "C"
    Case Is < 70 And varX > = 60
        txtGrade.Text = "D"
    Case Else
        txtGrade.Text = "F"
End Select
```

15. The current directory and its subdirectories are displayed. An open folder icon represents an open directory. A closed folder signifies a closed directory. A vertical scroll bar appears if there are undisplayed items.

16. The files in the current directory are displayed in the box. A vertical scroll bar appears if there are undisplayed items. To display hidden files, change the Hidden and System properties to True at design time or run time.

17. The default pattern is *.*, meaning every file. Change the Pattern property to "*.frm;*.mak". Don't forget the semicolon, but no quotes.

18. When used with the first three, it returns the index value of the selected item. For example, if the user selects the fifth item, ListIndex has the value of 4 (0 is first). When used with Dir1, ListIndex may return the following values:

    -1 Current directory
    -2 Parent directory
    -3 Parent of parent directory
    0   First subdirectory
    1   Second subdirectory
    2   Third subdirectory

19.
MkDir	Creates a new directory.
ChDir	Changes to another directory.
RmDir	Removes an existing directory.
ChDrive	Changes to another drive.
CurDir	Returns the current directory name.
Dir	Returns file or directory names matching a pattern.

20. REN can only change file names. Name, on the other hand, can change a file's name, move a file without changing its name, move it and change its name, and change a directory name.

21. The file is set to read-only (1), hidden (2), and system (4); $1 + 2 + 4 = 7$. The file is no longer visible and cannot be erased.

22.
```
Sub cmdReadOnly_Click ( )
   Dim varA As Integer
   varA = GetAttr(File1)
   If varA = 1 Then       'if read-only attribute present
      varA = 32                   'change to normal
   Else
      varA = 1
   End If
   SetAttr File1, varA     'set attribute
End Sub
```

23.
```
Sub cmdName_Click ( )
   Dim Msg as String, varX
   Msg = Dir1 & "\" & File1     'get path and file name
   varX = InputBox("Change this file to?", , Msg)
   Name Msg As varX                'change old to new name
   File1.Refresh           'refresh screen display in File1 box
End Sub
```

24.
```
Sub cmdKill_Click ( )
   Dim Msg as String, varX
   Msg = Dir1 & "\" & File1     'get dir path and file name
   varX = MsgBox(msg, 4, "Kill this file?")        'Yes/No
   If varX = 6 Then               'if Yes chosen
      Kill Msg           'kill dir path and file name
      File1.Refresh                'refresh File1 box
   End If
End Sub
```

25.
```
Sub cmdFont_Click ()
   CommonDialog1.Flags = 1
   CommonDialog1.Action = 4
   Text1.FontName = CommonDialog1.FontName
   Text1.FontSize = CommonDialog1.FontSize
End Sub
```

26. Add the following line to the end of the procedure:

```
If CommonDialog1.FontItalic Then Text1.FontItalic = True
```

27.
```
Sub cmdColor_Click ()
   Dim varX
   CommonDialog1.Action = 3
   varX = InputBox("1=Fore; 2=Back")
   If varX = 1 Then
      Text1.ForeColor = CommonDialog1.Color
   Else
      Text1.BackColor = CommonDialog1.Color
   End If
End Sub
```

28. These are used to save data to a sequential file. Print # works the same as
Print except outputting text to a disk file. Formatting characters and functions
such as comma, semicolon, Spc, and Tab work the same way. Quotes and
commas are not saved. Write # saves quotes and commas; formatting
characters have no effect.

29. These are used to read a sequential file. Line Input reads all the characters up
to but not including a carriage return. Input # reads up to but not including a
comma or carriage return; quotes are not read. Line Input is commonly used
to pull everything from disk. Input # is used to pull in records written with
Write #.

30. Change the first line in the procedure to the second line below:

```
FileName = "a:\testfile"       'old
FileName = Text2.Text          'new
```

31.
```
   If Text2.Text = "" Then
      MsgBox "You must enter a file name in Text2"
      Exit Sub
   End If
```

32
```
   Dim varX as String
   varX = Left(FileName, 1)       'get first char
   If varX < > "a" And varX < > "b" Then
      MsgBox "You must save to drive A or B"
      Exit Sub
   End If
```

33. The first pulls in one character from a sequential file #1 and assigns to a Variant variable. The second pulls in a record (up to a comma or carriage return) and assigns it to Variant variable varX.

34. The following default values are in effect:
    mode   Random is the default.
    access   Read Write is the default.
    reclen   Record length is 128 bytes.

35. Get (read) the next record from a file opened as #1 in Random mode and assign the record to a string variable called A$. Since the argument for record number is missing, the next record is the default.

CHAPTER 11, GRAPHICS AND ANIMATION

1.T, 2.F, 3.a, 4.F, 5.d, 6.d, 7.c, 8.label, 9.BackStyle, 10.c, 11.d, 12.e, 13.a, 14.b, 15.a, 16. LPR, 17.T, 18.c, 19.b, 20.BF, 21.a, 22.Picture, 23.b, 24.c, 25.a, 26.T, 27.AutoSize, 28.b, 29.Picture, 30.DrawMode

1. These have twip values representing the horizontal and vertical coordinates of a line control's position. One end of the line is represented by X1 (distance from the left margin) and Y1 (from the top margin) and the other end by X2 and Y2. These properties can be changed at design time or run time to move or stretch the line.

2. Enclosed two-dimensional shapes that can be oval or rectangular. You can make a shape completely round by choosing Circle from the Shape property options. If you choose Oval, you can also manually make it into a complete circle. In square or rectangle, you can choose to have the angles sharp or rounded.

3. RGB requires three arguments, each is a number from 0 to 255. The first argument is for red content, the second for green, and the third for blue. This can create 256^3 possible combinations. QBColor requires a single argument, which is a number from 0 to 15. You can thus set only 16 colors with this old function inherited from Quick Basic.

4. Add the following to the end of the GetColor procedure.

```
Text2.Text = R        'show Red scroll number in text box
Text2.BackColor = RGB(R, 0, 0)      'get red
Text2.ForeColor = RGB(255, 255, 255)        'white text
```

```
       Text3.Text = G
       Text3.BackColor = RGB(0, G, 0)
       Text3.ForeColor = RGB(255, 255, 255)
       Text4.Text = B
       Text4.BackColor = RGB(0, 0, B)
       Text4.ForeColor = RGB(255, 255, 255)
```

5.
```
Sub HScroll1_Change ( )
    Dim SV As Integer           'scroll value
    HScroll1.Min = 0            'set scroll min value
    HScroll1.Max = 15           'set scroll max value
    Text1.BackColor = QBColor(HScroll1.Value)
        'get backcolor
    SV = HScroll1.Value
    If SV = 15 Then SV = -1
        'to prevent going over 15
    Text1.ForeColor = QBColor(SV + 1)
        'get forecolor
    Text1.Text = "BColor: " & HScroll1.Value & "  FColor: " & SV + 1
        'show text and number
End Sub
```

6. At design time, change BackStyle to Opaque and FillStyle to Transparent. In the code, change FillColor to BackColor.

7. Top and Left are distances from the top and left of the screen, measured in twips. ScaleTop and ScaleLeft, both of which default to 0, are the topmost and leftmost position where you can write or draw things.

8. Width is how wide the form window is, including borders. ScaleWidth, about 100 twips less than Width, is the width of the area where you can write or draw things. ScaleWidth reflects the far right position measured in twips. Divide this value by 2, and you will get the midpoint. Height includes the title bar and is 420 twips greater than ScaleHeight, which reflects the bottom position of the form.

9.
```
    Line (ScaleLeft, ScaleTop)-(ScaleWidth, ScaleHeight)
    Line (ScaleLeft, ScaleHeight)-(ScaleWidth, ScaleTop)
```

10.
```
Sub Form_Click ( )
    Dim I As Long
    Dim X1 As Long
```

```
      Dim X2 As Long
      Dim Y1 As Long
      Dim Y2 As Long

      I = 1440   '1 inch
      X1 = ScaleLeft + I
      X2 = ScaleWidth - I
      Y1 = ScaleTop + I
      Y2 = ScaleHeight - I

      Line (X1, Y1)-(X2, Y1)    'top
      Line -(X2, Y2)      'right
      Line -(X1, Y2)      'bottom
      Line -(X1, Y1)      'left
   End Sub

11.
Sub Form_Click ( )
   Dim I As Long
   Dim X1 As Long
   Dim X2 As Long
   Dim Y1 As Long
   Dim Y2 As Long

      X1 = ScaleLeft      'far left
      X2 = ScaleWidth     'far right
      Y1 = ScaleTop       'top
      Y2 = ScaleHeight    'bottom

      For I = 100 To 2000 Step 100
         Line (X1 + I, Y1 + I)-(X2 - I, Y1 + I)
         Line -(X2 - I, Y2 - I)
         Line -(X1 + I, Y2 - I)
         Line -(X1 + I, Y1 + I)
      Next I
   End Sub

12.
Sub Form_Click ( )
   Dim I As Integer

      Scale (-20, 20)-(20, -20)
      For I = 0 To 20
         Line (0, 20 - I)-(20 - I, 0) 'top right
         Line -(0, I - 20)  'bottom right
```

```
        Line -(-20 + I, 0)   'bottom left
        Line -(0, 20 - I)  'top left
    Next I
End Sub
```

13. Change the second line to:

```
    X1 = ScaleWidth
```

14. 11QUAD.FRM

15. Draw a one-inch square box filled with diagonal-cross hatch lines. The box is located 100 twips from the top and left margins.

16.
```
Sub Form_Click ( )
    Dim HC As Long
    Dim VC As Long

    FillStyle = 7        'diagonal cross hatch
    HC = ScaleWidth / 2    'horizontal center
    VC = ScaleHeight / 2   'vertical center
    CurrentX = HC - 720    '1/2 inch left
    CurrentY = VC - 720    '1/2 inch up
    Line -Step(1440, 1440), , B
End Sub
```

17.
```
Sub Form_Click ( )
    Dim X1 As Long
    Dim X2 As Long
    Dim Y1 As Long
    Dim Y2 As Long

    FillStyle = 7        'diagonal cross hatch
    X1 = ScaleWidth - 1440 '1 inch from right
    Y1 = ScaleHeight - 1440 '1 inch from bottom
    X2 = ScaleWidth          'far right
    Y2 = ScaleHeight         'bottom
    Line (X1, Y1)-(X2, Y2), , B
End Sub
```

18.
```
Sub Form_Click ( )
    Dim X As Long
```

```
        Dim Y As Long

        FillStyle = 7        'diagonal cross hatch
        X = ScaleWidth         'far right
        Y = ScaleHeight        'bottom
        Line (0, 0)-(X, Y), , B
     End Sub
```

19. PSet (I, Sin(I))
    The line begins at the middle of the left margin and ends at the middle of the right margin.

20. The number of waves will double.

21. A higher number, such as 0.1, increases the distance between dots. A lower number does the opposite.

22. A smaller value leads to a smaller number of petals in the flower. A higher number does the opposite.

23. Line (0, 0)-(X, Y)
    Each dot is connected to the moving point (0, 0), thus creating a different pattern.

24. The pattern is changed. The radius, X axis, or Y axis values can all be changed and the results will be a variety of patterns.

25. 11SPIRAL.FRM

26.
```
Sub Form_Click()
    Dim R As Single
    Dim Pi As Single

    Width = ScaleHeight      'create perfect square
    Width = 2 * ScaleHeight - ScaleWidth
    Scale (-10, -10)-(10, 10)   'Cartesian scale
    Pi = 4 * Atn(1)
    R = 8          'radius
    FillStyle = 4   'hatch line
    Circle (1, -1), R, , -0.001, -Pi / 2 'explode
    FillStyle = 1   'transparent
    Circle (0, 0), R, , -Pi / 2, -Pi * 2
End Sub
```

27.
```
Sub Form_Click ( )
    Dim R As Single
    Dim Pi As Single

    Width = ScaleHeight      'create perfect square
    Width = 2 * ScaleHeight - ScaleWidth
    Scale (-10, -10)-(10, 10)
    Pi = 4 * Atn(1)
    R = 8          'radius
    FillStyle = 4   'hatch line
    Circle (-1, -1), R, , -Pi / 2, -Pi 'explode
    FillStyle = 1    'transparent
    Circle (0, 0), R, , -Pi, -Pi / 2
End Sub
```

28. The three option boxes are elements of a control array. Just double-click one of them and enter two lines in the procedure template:

```
Sub Option1_Click (Index As Integer)
    Call cmdClear_Click  'clear previous graph
    Call cmdDraw_Click   'draw new graph
End Sub
```

29. 11SPRING.FRM

30. 11SCALE.FRM

CHAPTER 12, ADVANCED TOOLS

1.d, 2.e, 3.6, 4.e, 5.b, 6.KeyPreview, 7.a, 8.T, 9.F, 10.Source As Control, 11.F, 12.F, 13.F, 14.SetText, 15.SelText, 16.GetData, 17.Public, 18.c, 19.InsertObjDlg, 20.d, 21.9, 22.ReadOnly, 23.DatabaseName, 24.RecordSource, 25.d, 26.Index, 27.WindowList, 28.b, 29.Arrange, 30.Align

1. Add the following to the beginning of the last If control structure:

    ```
    If K = 45 Or K = 46 Then Exit Sub
        ' "-" = 45, "." = 46
    ```

2. Add the following to the beginning of the last If structure:

    ```
    If K = 8 Then Exit Sub
    ```

3. Add the following line at the beginning of the procedure:

    If K = 27 Then End

4. Change the last If line to the following lines:

    C = Chr(K)
    If C < "0" Or C > "9" Then

5. They are keyboard events that occur when the user presses a keyboard key. KeyPress occurs when an ANSI key is pressed. Other keys, including functions keys, cursor keys, and editing keys, trigger KeyDown and KeyUp but not KeyPress. KeyDown occurs when a key is pressed, KeyUp when the pressed key is released.

6. When you press an extended (non-ANSI) key or key combination, KeyDown is triggered; releasing it triggers KeyUp. The ANSI key code value of the pressed key is assigned to the KeyCode variable. If another key is combined, its value is assigned to the Shift argument. This key can be Shift (1), Ctrl (2), or Alt (4). For example, if you press F1, KeyCode is 112 and Shift is 0. If you press F1 in combination with Shift+Ctrl+Alt Shift has the value of 7 (1+2+4).

7. Declare the following variables at the form level:

Dim A As Integer, B As Integer

Sub Form_Load ()
    A = Command1.Left   'assign original position
    B = Command1.Top
End Sub

Sub Form_MouseDown (B As Integer, S As Integer, X As Single, Y As Single)
    Command1.Move X, Y   'move to clicked location
End Sub

Sub Form_MouseUp (Button As Integer, Shift As Integer, X As Single, Y As Single)
    Command1.Move A, B   'restore original position
End Sub

8. Change the second line to:

    CurrentY = ScaleHeight / 2

9. Add the following lines to the beginning of the procedure:

   ```
   Static Num As Integer
   Num = Num + 1
   ```

   Add the following line to the end of the procedure:

   ```
   Print num
   ```

10. Add the following statement after the original Circle statement:

    ```
    Circle (X, Y), 30
    ```

11. Add FillStyle = 1 before the first Circle statement and FillStyle = 0 before the second Circle statement.

12. Change the Cls line to:

    ```
    If S = 2 And B = 2 Then Cls
    ```

13. Change the Source line to the following:

    ```
    Source.Text = ""
    ```

14. Add the following line:

    ```
    Caption = "R=" & x & "; G=" & Y & "; B=" & (X + Y) / 2
    ```

15. After you create a menu structure, all the menu names (Name properties) will appear in the Properties window. To display the properties related to a menu, press F4 to open the Properties window (if it is not open or visible). Click the red down arrow near the top. The Object box opens up. All the object names appear; these include menu names. Click a menu name and the Properties window contains only the items related to this menu.

16. Select Menu Design from the Window menu. In the ensuing Menu Design window, enter &Menu for the menu caption and Menu as its name. For each option, indent it to the next level and use the displayed items as its caption and "op" plus a number as its name. Use a hyphen for the caption of the separator bar. Exit the window and write four procedures resembling the following:

    ```
    Sub Op1_Click ()
        Caption = "Option 1"
    End Sub
    ```

17. Write the following procedure:

```
Sub Form_MouseDown (B As Integer, S As Integer, X As Single, Y As Single)
    If B = 2 Then PopupMenu menu
End Sub
```

18. Change the Button argument to 1, like this:

```
    If B = 1 Then PopupMenu menu
```

The menu pops up, but the first option is not highlighted as before. Clicking another point on the form also moves the menu there—instead of clearing it.

19. Change the statement to:

```
    If B = 1 And S = 2 Then PopupMenu menu
```

20. Add this procedure:

```
Sub Form_Load ()
    menu.Visible = False
End Sub
```

21. At design time, choose Menu from the Object box of the Properties window and change the Enabled property to False. The menu is dimmed right away. To disable it at run time, use this procedure:

```
Sub Form_Load ()
    menu.Enabled = False
End Sub
```

The menu is dimmed at run time. The popup menu still works.

22. From the Menu Design window, select the desired option and click the Checked box to enter an X. You can also do it in the Properties window by changing the Checked property value from False to True.

23. The first procedure below will designate Op1 as checked. The second procedure will allow the user to check and uncheck the option.

```
Sub Form_Load ()
    Op1.Checked = True
End Sub
```

```
Sub op1_Click ()
```

```
    Op1.Checked = Not Op1.Checked
End Sub
```

24. The following procedure will do the trick:

```
Sub Form_Load ()
    If Op1.Checked Then Caption = "Option 1"
End Sub
```

25.
```
Sub Text1_Change ()
    Text1.Text = UCase(Text1.Text)
        'convert each typed char to uppercase
    SendKeys "{end}"
        'cursor to end of string for more typing
End Sub
```

26. The former are available only at run time. They return the row and column coordinates of the current cell; they can also be used to move the cursor to the secified cell. The latter are available at both design time and run time. They specify the number of rows and columns for a grid.

27.
```
Sub MSFlexGrid1_KeyPress (K As Integer)
    If K = 32 Then
        Text1.Text = MSFlexGrid1.Text
        Text1.SetFocus
    End If
End Sub
```

28. Add the following line to before End If:

```
    SendKeys "{end}"
```

29.
```
Sub Text1_KeyPress (K As Integer)
    If K = 13 Then MSFlexGrid1.SetFocus
End Sub
```

30. Add Data1 to the form. Specify its DatabaseName property to load a database file. After that, the tables in the database appear in the RecordSource property list in the Properties window. Select a table to show the records in it. Then use bound controls to link to the records and fields.

31. They bind (link) database records to the screen so that the data can be viewed. They include: label, image, text box, check box, and picture box. They have the DataSource and DataField properties to link to a database's records and fields. After a database file is loaded and a table selected, you need to specify these two properties of a bound control to point to the right data.

32 If this wizard doesn't appear in the Add-Ins menu, choose Add-Ins | Add-In Manager, check VB Data Form Wizard and click OK. Choose Add-Ins | Data Form Wizard. Follow the instructions. Use Browse to open BIBLIO.MDB and select Single Record and Titles. This will create the frmTitles form. Use the Project Properties dialog box to designate the newly created form as the Startup Object. Press F5 to run the form.

33. Select MDIForm1. Display its Properties window. Click the down arrow in the Settings box. Select mnuYear to display its properties. Double-click WindowList to change the default False value to True.

Index